# The Politics of the Middle East

# The Politics of the Middle East

## SECOND EDITION

**MONTE PALMER**
Emeritus, Florida State University

THOMSON

WADSWORTH

Australia • Brazil • Canada • Mexico • Singapore
Spain • United Kingdom • United States

THOMSON
WADSWORTH

*The Politics of the Middle East, Second Edition*

*Monte Palmer*

Executive Editor: David Tatom
Assistant Editor: Anne Gittinger
Editorial Assistant: Eva Dickerson
Technology Project Manager: Michelle Vardeman
Marketing Manager: Janise Fry
Marketing Assistant: Teresa Jessen
Marketing Communications Manager: Nathaniel Bergson-Michelson
Project Manager, Editorial Production: Marti Paul
Creative Director: Rob Hugel
Art Director: Maria Epes

Print Buyer: Rebecca Cross
Permissions Editor: Roberta Broyer
Production Service: Matrix Productions Inc.
Copy Editor: Susanna Sturgis
Illustrator: George Barile
Cover Designer: Garry Harman
Cover Image: ©Martin Harvey/CORBIS
Cover Printer: Webcom
Compositor: Integra Software Services
Printer: Webcom

Library of Congress Control Number:
2005935194

ISBN-13: 978-0-495-00750-0
ISBN-10: 0-495-00750-1

**Thomson Higher Education**
**10 Davis Drive**
**Belmont, CA 94002-3098**
**USA**

For more information about our products, contact us at:
**Thomson Learning Academic Resource Center**
**1-800-423-0563**

For permission to use material from this text or product, submit a request online at
**http://www.thomsonrights.com.**
Any additional questions about permissions can be submitted by e-mail to
**thomsonrights@thomson.com.**

# Contents

# Preface

The four years since the publication of the first edition of *The Politics of the Middle East* have witnessed the September 11, 2001, attacks on the United States followed in turn by a war on terror. Iraq has been occupied and threats on Syria and Iran have followed apace. Many Muslims fear that it is Islam that is under attack. And yet, the war on terror remains a stalemate. Madrid and London have witnessed cataclysmic attacks and jihadist assaults on Saudi Arabia, the world's leading oil producer, have been relentless. In the Holy Land, four years of terror and counterterror have given way to the birth of a Palestinian state, albeit a state of minute and uncertain size.

Reflecting these and related events, the second edition of the book has been substantially revised. The chapter on Israel has been restructured to include a discussion of both Israeli and Palestinian politics, and a much-needed chapter on Turkey has been added. The Iraqi chapter has been largely rewritten and remains a work in progress. Palestine's evolution toward statehood also remains a work in progress. Semiannual updates on all of the chapters are provided at the book's companion website: http://politicalscience.wadsworth.com/palmer2e/.

The second edition of *The Politics of the Middle East* has been written with the student in mind. Every effort has been made to make this edition both readable and informative. Jargon has been reduced to a minimum as has esoteric detail of interest only to scholars.

Ted Peacock and Dick Welna inspired this book. Ted's retirement from the publishing business is a matter of great sorrow for all who knew him. Ted was very pleased by Wadsworth's acquisition of F. E. Peacock, Publishers, as am I. It has been a pleasure working with David Tatom and Anne Gittinger on the second edition of *The Politics of the Middle East*. I would also like to thank my copyeditor, Susanna Sturgis.

I would like to thank the instructors who reviewed *The Politics of the Middle East* for its second edition: Robert J. Bookmiller, Millersville University; Ahmed El-Afandi, Winona State University; and James M. Lutz, Indiana University–Purdue University at Fort Wayne.

As in the previous edition, circumstances make it difficult for me to thank the countless individuals who have guided my study of the Middle East over the past four decades. Most are residents of the region and many would prefer not to be mentioned by name. I thank them collectively and beg their understanding. I would, however, like to acknowledge the assistance of Dr. Sabri Ciftci in reviewing the Turkish chapter and Dr. Hilal Khashan in reviewing the Palestinian materials. Both sections were new to this edition, and their help was invaluable. Errors of fact and judgment remain my own.

# 1

# Introduction

## Continuity and Change in the Middle East

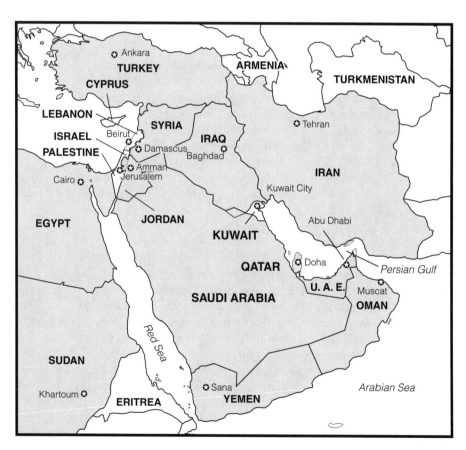

For more detailed views of these countries, please refer to the individual country map in each chapter.

Few regions of the world approach the Middle East for the richness of its past, the turmoil of its present, or the uncertainty of its future. The world stands in awe of the region's religious and historical shrines, but it is political tumult that has made the Middle East the focal point of international relations for more than half a century. This attention is not likely to diminish in the years to come.

In the pages that follow, we will trace the evolution of Middle Eastern politics in the modern era. We will also suggest the likely direction of the region's politics during the coming decade. Particular emphasis will be placed on the politics of Egypt, Israel, Palestine, Syria, Saudi Arabia, Iraq, Iran, and Turkey, the eight countries or near-countries most likely to shape the character of the Middle East during the coming decade. These countries also hold the key to resolving the region's most enduring problems, including the Arab–Israeli conflict, the continuing crises in Iran and Iraq, and the war on terror. In the process, we will also have much to say about the region's halting transitions from authoritarianism to democracy and from socialism to capitalism.

## WHAT IS THE MIDDLE EAST?

Before we embark on this journey, a few comments are in order regarding the geography, culture, demography, and economy of the Middle East. The Middle East is generally defined as the vast geographic area that embraces North Africa and much of western Asia. As indicated on the adjacent map, it is bordered on the south by the countries of sub-Saharan Africa, on the north by Greece and eastern Europe, and on the northeast by Afghanistan, Russia, and the newly independent states of Central Asia (Cressey 1960). The latter could reasonably be considered part of the Middle East, for most are Islamic in character and many have strong cultural and ethnic links to Turkey and Iran (Herzig 1995; Winrow 1995). Much the same could be said of Afghanistan.[1]

Three geographic features have had much to say about the character of the Middle East and its people. The first is the region's location at the crossroads between Europe, Asia, and Africa. Rare indeed was the empire on any one of the three continents that did not leave its stamp on the region. Modern empires have done the same. No sooner had the British and the French relinquished their grip on the Middle East than it became the primary battleground in the Cold War between the United States and the former Soviet Union. Most recently, the Middle East has become the focus of America's war on terror. The United States is not a colonial power, it just seems that way.

The second key geographic factor is the Middle East's abundant oil reserves. The region possesses some 68 percent of the world's oil, most of which is found in four countries: Saudi Arabia (25%), Iraq (11%), Kuwait (9%), and Iran (8.5%). These figures do not include vast reserves of natural gas. Oil has brought the

---

1 Eritrea, Djibouti, and Somalia, three partially Arabized countries in the Horn of Africa, are considered by the Arab League to be part of the Middle East.

region incredible wealth, but it has also made it the subject of conflict and international intrigue (Gillespie and Henry 1995), a topic that will be elaborated upon throughout the book.

The final geographic factor that has shaped the Middle East's unique character is the scarcity of its water. The Middle East contains 5 percent of the world's population, yet possesses less than 1 percent of its freshwater. Inevitably, access to freshwater has been a primary source of conflict in the region, a situation that can only get worse as water reserves continue to deteriorate (World Bank 1996; Zietoun 2005). In 1955 only three Middle Eastern countries were classified as "water-scarce," but in 1990 that category encompassed fourteen countries (Darwish 1994). It is expected to include virtually all of the Middle East by 2025. The region must allocate its use of freshwater on a rational basis if this very real potential for conflict is to be avoided (Allan 1999). It must also find more reasonable mechanisms for sharing the water resources that do exist (Allan 2001). Nowhere is the conflict over water potentially more lethal than in the efforts of Israel and Palestine to work out a formula for sharing water resources that are inadequate for either.

In addition to being a geographic region, the Middle East also constitutes a cultural region, the citizens of which share a broad array of social and cultural patterns that differ markedly from those of the inhabitants of sub-Saharan Africa, eastern Europe, and South Asia. Many of these cultural values reflect the pervasiveness of the Islamic religion and the region's tribal past, topics to be discussed shortly. They also reflect the influence of common historical trends and, for the Arabs, a common language. Cultural and social similarities have made the political boundaries of the Middle East extremely porous, and events in one area usually have ramifications throughout the whole region.

Although most people in the Middle East share a common culture, the region is also marked by profound ethnic, religious, and linguistic diversity (Barakat 1993). Ethnically, the Middle East might usefully be viewed as a large circle with the Arabs at its core and the non-Arabs at the periphery (Flory and Agate 1989). Prominent among the latter would be the Turks, Iranians, Israelis, Kurds, and Berbers. Both the Arabs and the non-Arabs are divided by religious and sectarian conflicts. The Muslims are divided between Sunni and Shi'a sects, the Jews range from reformist to ultraconservative, and the Christians are divided into a seemingly infinite variety of denominations, many of which trace their origins to the days of Jesus. Interspersed with the region's three major religions are an endless array of smaller religious minorities, including the Alawites, the Druze, the Yazidis, and the Zoroastrians.

The basic economic and demographic features of the Middle East are summarized in Table 1.1. It portrays a region of profound extremes. Kuwait and the United Arab Emirates rank among the wealthiest countries in the world, Egypt and Sudan among the poorest. The countries of the Middle East also vary dramatically in the size of their populations. Bahrain has less than a million citizens, while Egypt and Iran have more than 70 million. As we shall see throughout the book, both factors—wealth and demography—have played a major role in shaping the destiny of the region.

**TABLE 1.1** Demographic Characteristics of the Middle East

| Country | Population[1] | GDP/Capita (US $)[2] | % Below Poverty Line[3] | Literacy (%)[4] | % 14 or Younger[5] | Life Expectancy at Birth[6] | Birth Rate (%)[7] |
|---|---|---|---|---|---|---|---|
| Algeria | 32,531,853 | 6,600 | 23 | 70 | 29 | 73 | 1.22 |
| Bahrain | 688,345 | 19,200 | NA | 89 | 28 | 74 | 1.51 |
| Egypt | 77,505,750 | 4,200 | 17 | 58 | 33 | 71 | 1.78 |
| Gaza | 1,376,289 | 600 | 81 | NA | 49 | 72 | 3.77 |
| Iran | 68,017,860 | 7,700 | 40 ('02) | 79 | 40 | 70 | .86 |
| Iraq | 26,074,906 | 2,100 | NA | 40 | 27 | 69 | 2.70 |
| Israel | 6,276,883 | 20,800 | 18 ('01) | 95 | 35 | 79 | 1.20 |
| Jordan | 5,759,732 | 4,500 | 30 ('01) | 91 | 22 | 78 | 2.56 |
| Kuwait | 2,335,648 | 21,300 | NA | 84 | 27 | 77 | 3.44 |
| Lebanon | 3,826,018 | 5,000 | 28 ('99) | 87 | 27 | 73 | 1.26 |
| Libya | 5,765,563 | 6,700 | NA | 83 | 34 | 77 | 2.33 |
| Mauritania | 3,086,859 | 1,800 | 40 ('00) | 42 | 46 | 53 | 2.90 |
| Morocco | 32,725,847 | 4,200 | 19 ('00) | 52 | 32 | 71 | 1.57 |
| Oman | 3,001,583 | 13,100 | NA | NA | 43 | 73 | 3.32 |
| Qatar | 863,051 | 23,200 | NA | 83 | 24 | 74 | 2.61 |
| Saudi Arabia | 26,417,599 | 12,000 | NA | 79 | 38 | 76 | 2.31 |
| Sudan | 40,187,486 | 1,900 | 40 ('04) | 61 | 43 | 58 | 2.60 |
| Syria | 18,448,752 | 3,400 | 20 ('04) | 77 | 37 | 70 | 2.34 |
| Tunisia | 10,074,951 | 7,100 | 8 ('01) | 74 | 25 | 75 | .99 |

**TABLE 1.1** (Continued)

| Country | Population | GDP/Capita (US $) | % Below Poverty Line | Literacy (%) | % 14 or Younger | Life Expectancy at Birth | Birth Rate (%) |
|---|---|---|---|---|---|---|---|
| Turkey | 69,660,559 | 7,400 | 20 ('02) | 87 | 26 | 72 | 1.09 |
| UAE | 2,563,212 | 25,200 | NA | 78 | 25 | 75 | 1.54 |
| West Bank | 2,385,615 | 800 | 59 ('04) | NA | 43 | 73 | 3.13 |
| Yemen | 20,727,063 | 800 | 45 ('03) | 50 | 47 | 62 | 3.45 |
| Middle East | 460,301,424 | 8,678* | 33* | 73* | 34* | 72* | 2.20* |

1. July 2005 estimate.
2. Purchasing power parity, 2004 estimate.
3. 2000 estimate unless year is specified; rounded to nearest whole number.
4. Percentage of population 15 years or older who can read and write; rounded to nearest whole number.
5. Percentage of population under the age of 14; rounded to nearest whole number.
6. Age of life expectancy at birth.
7. Population birth rate.
*Average

SOURCE: www.cia.gov/cia/publication/factbook

## SOME COMMENTS ON POLITICS

Before discussing political issues, we accept Harold Laswell's dictum that politics is "who gets what, when and how" (Laswell 1958). A particular virtue of Laswell's definition is that it applies the world over, so it places Middle Eastern studies in a global framework. Politics is politics, wherever it occurs.

A second virtue of Laswell's definition is that it places Middle Eastern politics within the broader constellation of social science disciplines. Indeed, Laswell's definition of politics could serve equally well as a definition of economics, sociology, or culture. This broad applicability is important, for as we shall see shortly, the lines between politics, society, economics, and culture are often difficult to discern in the Middle East. Laswell's definition is also broad enough to incorporate international influences on the region's politics. This aspect is crucial, for few areas of the globe have been subject to greater international pressures than the Middle East.

A third virtue of Laswell's definition is that it encompasses both conflict and cooperation. The struggle for control of scarce resources is conflictive by nature, but victory in that struggle depends upon the marshaling of collective forces, be they families, tribes, religious groups, ethnic associations, political parties, or nation-states. One cannot understand the politics of the Middle East without understanding how the people of the region coalesce in the struggle to determine who gets what, when, and how.

And finally, Laswell's definition of politics is dynamic. This, too, is an important consideration, for the Middle East is an ever-changing region in which new complexities are constantly being added to the old. One must appreciate the influence of the past without becoming stuck in the belief that history must necessarily repeat itself. Rather, a constant and pervasive tension exists between the ways of the past and the demands of the present.

## SOME ORGANIZATIONAL COMMENTS

In the present chapter we will examine three cultural–historical factors that have helped to provide Middle Eastern politics with its unique character: tribalism, Islam, and colonialism. The chapter also provides a brief overview of the tortuous evolution of the region in the postcolonial era with a special emphasis on the war on terror and U.S. efforts to reshape the way the region does politics.

Each of these diverse factors has imprinted the inhabitants of this region with a view of society and politics that is characteristically Middle Eastern. Tribalism organized society on the basis of kinship ties. In the process, it fragmented the Middle East into a multitude of tribal communities, each representing a world unto itself and each in conflict with its neighbors. Islam brought to this tribal world a message of unity and faith and attempted to reorganize the region into a grand religious state (*umma*) according to the precepts of the Koran (Khadduri 1955). Islam became the faith of the vast majority of the region's people, yet tribalism and kinship remained the primary form of social organization. Western colonization of the Middle East began in the nineteenth century, challenging the ways of the East with Western visions of secularism and of societies organized as nation-states rather than as tribes or religious communities (Emerson 1960). The West viewed itself as "modern" and condemned the region's kinship and religious values as archaic. If the Middle East were to attain the power and prosperity of the West, according to the "modernists," the Middle East would have to reinvent itself along Western lines (Palmer 1997).

Turkey and Iran were not colonized but were introduced to Western values by a multitude of commercial and military contacts. Both attempted to resist the West by becoming Western. Saudi Arabia and Yemen (North) also escaped Western colonization but had little contact with the West in the years prior to World War II. They remain among the most traditional areas in the Middle East today.

The modern values instilled by Western imperialism and subsequent Western efforts to dominate the region have left an indelible mark on the Middle East, as have the efforts by leaders of Turkey, Egypt, Iraq, Iran, and many other countries to transform their countries into regional military–industrial powers. And yet, the region has not become modern in the Western sense of the word. Rather, aspects of modernity coexist in an uneasy tension with the values of Islam and tribalism, each attempting to assert its dominance. Religious extremism, ethnic conflicts, and political instability have been the result.

This mix of kinship, religion, and Westernization has produced a culture that differs substantially from that of the surrounding areas. It has also produced a cultural region of infinite complexity. Although most residents of the Middle East share at least some of the region's cultural characteristics, the influence of those characteristics varies dramatically from country to country and even from individual to individual. All Middle Easterners do not behave alike any more than all Americans or all Europeans behave alike, but as we shall see throughout the ensuing analysis, the existence of a shared culture does influence the politics of the region.

## THE IMPORTANCE OF KINSHIP

The study of Middle Eastern politics logically begins with a discussion of kinship. It could not be otherwise, for the most enduring social relationships in the Middle East have traditionally been those of blood (Barakat 1993). Small nuclear families were virtually indivisible from larger extended families consisting of grandparents and several layers of aunts, uncles, cousins, and grandchildren. Networks of extended families merged into clans (encompassing second, third, and sometimes fourth cousins) and eventually into tribes. All members of a tribe were presumed to have a common ancestor, the tie of blood, although this was not necessarily the case. Tribes reached their zenith in nomadic societies such as those of the Arabian Peninsula, while extended families and clans tended to remain the dominant form of social organization in settled areas (Barakat 1993; Gellner 1987; Hart 1998; Wittfogel 1957).

Tribes in fertile areas tended to become sedentary cultivators, while those of the Middle East's vast deserts adopted a nomadic lifestyle, moving from place to place in search of water and pasture. Even the most fertile areas of the Middle East, however, were limited in the number of people they could support, and the weaker of the sedentary tribes were forced into a nomadic existence (Cressey 1960). Most of the tribes in the Arab east, including the tribes of Israel, had their origins in the Arabian Peninsula. It is this common origin that explains the similarities in the Arabic and Hebrew languages, both of which belong to the Semitic language group. Iranians, by contrast, are believed to be descendants of the Aryan tribes that invaded the area in approximately 900 BCE; the name *Iran* reflects their Aryan ancestry. They would later adopt the Arabic script, but the Iranian (Farsi) language has little in common with its Semitic counterparts. Much the same is true of the Turks and Kurds, both of whom represent distinct ethnic configurations (Coon 1961).

The extended family, along with the clan and the tribe, nurtured individuals into adulthood, teaching them what to believe and how to behave. Paramount was the demand for total and unquestioned loyalty to the family. An individual's survival was inseparable from the survival of the family, and individuals who lacked the support of a strong family possessed neither status nor power. Loyalty to the family was followed by loyalty to the clan and in turn by loyalty to the tribe. There was little basis for loyalty beyond the tribe, for nation-states did not exist. Extended families competed for control of the clan; clans competed for control of the tribe (Gellner 1987; Gluckman 1965). Tribes, for the most part, existed in a state of uneasy conflict as they competed for pride, power, and pasture.

The emphasis on kinship solidarity is easy to understand, for kinship provided the best hope for security in a very uncertain world (El-Aref 1944). Some idea of the pervasive insecurity of life in traditional kinship societies is provided by Ayrout's description of governmental efforts to modernize an Egyptian village during the 1930s.

> The customs, life and manners of the peasant should be looked at attentively, patiently and sympathetically. Then we can account for the failure of many attempts to improve village housing.
>
> At (village) B, the windows are spacious and large, and thus exposed to cold, heat and burglars. The inhabitants therefore stop them up with bricks.
>
> At (village) D, the stairs are outside the house. Security has been over-looked. The result is that the fellahin (peasants) destroy the stairs and build up steps of mud from inside the house.
>
> At (village) E, the builders have decided, for the sake of health, to permit no mixing of people and animals; there is an outer cattle pen. But this does not offer enough security against robbery and disease. Therefore the peasants rebel and drive them into the bedroom (Ayrout 1962, 129).

The need for kinship solidarity encouraged marriages within the clan, that is, among first and second cousins. In some instances, marriage alliances were arranged shortly after birth. In others, a son was given the option of marrying a female cousin before other alliances were considered. Such marriages strengthened family cohesiveness and reduced the possibility of tensions arising from conflict over mate selection and the payment of dowries. When marriage occurred outside of the family, it was between members of parallel social strata. The marriage of kin continues to be common in many areas of the Middle East and is particularly common in Iraq (58%), Saudi Arabia (55%), Kuwait (54%), and Jordan (50%) (Zein 1996, 9).

Most other tribal customs also evolved to promote kinship solidarity; not the least of these was a profound respect for age. More than any other factor, seniority determined one's position within the family. Such respect for age finds expression in the Arabic proverb "One day older, one year wiser." In general, it was the eldest male who ruled the family. The eldest female supervised the affairs of the women. Allocating authority on the basis of age and gender had the benefit of minimizing conflict within the family. Unfortunately, it also added rigidity to the structure of Middle Eastern society by rewarding age and gender at the expense of merit.

Family solidarity was further strengthened by cultural and religious beliefs that glorified the virtues of resignation, acceptance, and fatalism. Such beliefs promoted the survival of the family and larger kinship groups by encouraging individuals to accept their fate as the natural order of things. One way or another, they learned that rebellion against the rigidities of patriarchal authority was both immoral and useless. The socialization process, moreover, was simple and direct. Daughters emulated their mothers, sons their fathers. Prevailing norms were sanctified by the religions of the day and reinforced by social pressures. One got along by going along. The acceptance of traditional customs was also facilitated by the physical and intellectual isolation of the traditional environment. Most individuals lived in isolated tribes and scattered villages. Even the residents of the preindustrial cities of the pre-Islamic era found communications hampered by status divisions and a pervasive sense of interpersonal distrust born of kinship antagonisms. What was to be gained by sharing information with potential enemies? Because the early residents of the Middle East seldom came in contact with new information, they had little cause to question their social beliefs. It was the way of their world.

Interviews conducted by Daniel Lerner in rural Turkey during the 1950s illustrate both the profound respect for age and the fatalistic outlook of early Middle Eastern societies.

> (In your community who is the one whose thoughts are most highly respected?) My uncle the Sheikh. He is tall, old and respectable. He sits on his pillow all day long in his own tent and people of the tribe come around for advice. (Why is he a leader?) He is the eldest in the family and the people in the tribe go for the advice of the eldest. (Why?) Our respect is according to age, for experience counts a lot with us (Lerner 1958, 323).

What remained of individual freedom was constricted by the all-compelling need to protect the family's honor. Families operated on the principle of collective responsibility, and errant behavior by one family member brought shame—and danger—to the family as a whole. As in the American legend of the feuding Hatfields and McCoys, incidents of theft, murder, and sexual license were avenged against the family rather than the individual. The burden of maintaining family honor fell disproportionately on females, for the slightest sexual indiscretion by a female cast shame on the whole family and often resulted in her death at the hands of a father or brother. In societies in which everyone was watching everyone else, it was far better to seclude women than to have the family's honor fall prey to the prying eyes of neighbors. In Egypt, Sudan, and much of Africa, the female genitalia were mutilated before puberty to reduce the potential for infidelity. This practice continues among the poorer classes today (*Cairo Times,* July 28, 2003). Honor killings are also common throughout the region.

Finally, the kinship cultures of the Middle East placed immense value on large families. The honored woman was the woman who produced an endless number of children; the good man was the man who could sire such a brood. Families of twelve or more children were commonplace, with the numbers even higher in polygamous families. Again, the logic of the kinship system demanded large families. The power of a family was often a function of its size, and male children were a vital economic asset. The need for children was made all the more urgent by the prevalence of tribal warfare and by unsanitary living conditions that killed a majority of children before the age of ten.

Beyond shaping the values and behavior of their members, the family and the tribe determined their occupations, selected their spouses, defined their recreational groups (mainly relatives), protected them from their enemies, cared for them in illness and in old age, and policed their behavior to minimize interfamily conflict. In so doing, the kinship unit provided the individual with his or her identity. One's station in life was essentially that of the family or tribe.

The same principles can be applied in the social and economic spheres, with all members of the same age and gender performing nearly identical or readily interchangeable tasks (Nash 1966). If one family herded sheep, most families herded sheep. With little specialization, production was low and most tribes eked out a meager existence with little margin for error. Droughts and other external disasters were devastating and further accentuated the uncertain nature of a traditional life described by Thomas Hobbes as being "solitary, poor, nasty, brutish and short" (Hobbes 1651). Power and authority within the Middle Eastern family were patriarchal: the dominant male, usually the eldest, exercised near-absolute authority over the members of the family. Decisions flowed from top to bottom and were seldom subject to dispute. The same pattern was followed within the clan and tribe, with the eldest male of the dominant family or clan serving as its sheikh. Other clan leaders formed a tribal council, with their influence corresponding to the power of their family or clan. In theory, tribal leadership was based upon merit and constituted a form of tribal democracy. In reality, power was often hereditary.

Once in power, tribal leaders consolidated their authority by assuring that much of the tribe's wealth found its way to supporters and allies. Favors were granted as an act of generosity by the tribal leader, thereby creating a bond of obligation between the chief and the supplicant. Even today, the king of Saudi Arabia holds a weekly session in which any citizen of the kingdom can petition the king for a special favor, be it an operation, a scholarship, or forgiveness for a transgression.

Beyond force and the distribution of economic rewards, the power of the chief was rooted in a tribal culture that stressed loyalty, passivity, respect for age, and conformity. The chief was the patriarch or father of his family, and his power, while often compassionate, was absolute.

As stronger tribes dominated their neighbors, patriarchal authority was transformed into patrimonial authority; the major difference was that the chief could no longer claim kinship to all members of his realm (Bill and Springborg 1997). Unable to count on the kinship loyalties of the conquered tribes, patrimonial leaders often aligned themselves with a charismatic religious leader in the hope of substituting religious ties for those of kinship (De Corancez 1995; Vassiliev 1998). This blend of tribal and religious authority, as we shall see in Chapter 5, remains the foundation of government in Saudi Arabia. It was also common for victorious leaders to take wives from conquered tribes, thereby creating a new basis for kinship alliances. By and large, however, conquered tribes were ruled by force. When its power waned, usually with the passing of the dominant chief, the dominant tribe would splinter and the process of conquest and decay would repeat itself.

## THE CONSEQUENCES OF TRIBALISM

The Middle East has undergone profound changes in the past century, but tribalism has left an indelible stamp on the political process of the region (Khoury and Kostiner 1990). Although rarely nomadic and bearing little resemblance to the swashbuckling bedouins of Western cinema, tribes remain the dominant form of social organization in the more traditional areas of the Middle East, including most of the Arabian Peninsula. Saudi Arabia and the sheikhdoms of the Persian Gulf, however modern they may appear, remain tribal monarchies. Tribal leaders also hold sway in large areas of Iraq and will be key actors in that country's search for political unity in the aftermath of the U.S. occupation. During the 1980s, a civil war between competing factions of South Yemen's Marxist government was transformed into a tribal war as each side turned to its tribal allies for support. Despite its Marxist appearance, South Yemen's government was tribal in content. It is important, accordingly, not to be swayed by labels or official ideologies, which may be superficial in nature and thus profoundly misleading.

Families and clans, moreover, persist as the dominant form of social organization in places whose tribal past is far behind them. Saddam Hussein's closest associates were drawn largely from his family, as were those of Hafiz al-Assad, the former president of Syria. Saudi Arabia and the Gulf sheikhdoms are family enterprises. Politics in Lebanon, perhaps the most modern of the Arab states, continue to be dominated by big families, a circumstance that is pervasive throughout the region.

Other influences of tribalism are more subtle, but no less important. Many observers find the kinship traditions of the Middle East to be inherently authoritarian, inegalitarian, and antidemocratic (Khashan 2000b). Loyalty to family continues to compete with loyalty to the state, and it is probably safe to assume that most people in the Middle East place the interests of the extended family far above the interests of the state. As a result, politics in the Middle East is inherently dependent upon family connections or *wasta*. In most countries of the region it is difficult to accomplish anything politically without a kinship contact of one form or another.

The emphasis on large families has also resulted in the Middle East's having one of the highest rates of population growth in the world. The population of Egypt, for example, has increased from approximately 20 million in 1960 to more than 70 million in 2006; Iran's population has grown at a similar rate. While both countries have made progress in economic and social development, their populations have increased more rapidly than the capacity of the state to meet their basic needs. Unemployment is high, education lagging, housing scarce, and services dismal. The potential for political instability has increased apace and can only get worse, because approximately half of the population of the Middle East is under twenty years of age.

The influence of kinship is waning, but family ties continue to provide a critical support network for individuals in a region marked by inefficient governments (Barakat 1993). As Sharabi notes, "one conducts oneself morally only within the primary structures (family-clan-sect); for the most part, one lives amorally 'in the jungle,' in the society at large" (Sharabi 1988, 35).

Although it is easy for Westerners to condemn the negative influence of kinship loyalties on the politics of the Middle East, they are likely to view with envy the sense of belonging, caring, and family solidarity that permeates Middle Eastern culture. It is also profoundly ethnocentric of the West to assume that it alone has found a key to social paradise. The depersonalization and psychological pressures of Western society suggest otherwise.

## RELIGION AND POLITICS
## IN THE MIDDLE EAST

Religion and politics are so intertwined in the affairs of the Middle East that it is often difficult to distinguish one from the other. Israel proclaims itself a Jewish state, yet lacks a formal constitution because of the inherent difficulty involved in defining precisely what constitutes a Jew. Iran is a theocracy, the senior leaders of which are Islamic clerics. Saudi Arabia, Pakistan, Iran, and Sudan proclaim the Koran to be their constitution, and an even larger number of countries have made Islam the official religion of the state and the Koran the ultimate source of law.

Many of the region's dominant political groups are also overtly religious in character. Turkey has been ruled by an Islamic political party for much of the current decade, Israel's religious parties have a profound influence on policy making in the Jewish state, and—much to the chagrin of the United States—religious parties have emerged as the dominant force in Iraq. Islamic fundamentalists pose a continuing challenge to the secular governments of the Middle East; in 1990 they launched a civil war in Algeria that has claimed more than 100,000 lives to date. Egypt has been spared a civil war, but Islamic fundamentalist groups remain a potent force in that country and throughout the region. Far more lethal are the jihadists, a small group of fundamentalist extremists who have vowed to impose religious rule by terror. Jihadists have been responsible for most of the carnage in Algeria; it was jihadists who launched the September 11, 2001, attacks on the United States. Saudi Arabia appears to be next on their list.

The mingling of religious and political values is equally pervasive among the people of the Middle East. A recent survey in Cairo, for example, found that some 71 percent of the respondents favored religious censorship of the mass media. More than 90 percent supported religious instruction in Cairo's schools (Palmer, Sullivan, and Safty 1996). The percentages in a comparable survey of Lebanese Muslims were similar (Khashan and Palmer 1998).

The Middle East's position as home of three major religions has also subjected the region to far greater intervention by the major powers than would otherwise have been the case. In 1917 Britain supported "the establishment in Palestine of a national home for the Jewish people," and the emergence of Israel as an independent state in 1948 owed much to the support of the United States and the Soviet Union. As we shall see in Chapter 3, the support of world Jewry continues to provide Israel with far greater influence on the international stage than its small population and minuscule size would otherwise justify.

Of the three major religions to emerge from the Middle East, Christianity and Judaism are well-known in the West and require little elaboration. This is far less true of Islam, the chosen faith of some 90 percent of the Middle East's population. According to United Nations figures, Islam claims nearly 2.1 billion adherents worldwide, the distribution of whom is estimated in Table 1.2. One simply cannot understand the politics of the Middle East without at least a rudimentary knowledge of the Islamic faith.

## Islamic History

Islam has much in common with both Judaism and Christianity, and a clear line of progression exists between the three religions (Busse 1997). The Torah, the holy book of Judaism, glorifies an all-powerful God—the one God—who created the universe and stands in judgment of its inhabitants. Jews, according to the Torah, are the "chosen people." They enjoy a special relationship with their God, but are minimally concerned with garnering new converts to the Jewish faith. The Christian Bible consists of two testaments: the Old Testament is the Jewish Torah, and the New Testament transforms Judaism into a mass religion centering on the figure of Christ, the Son of God. In contrast to the Jews, Christians are evangelical and are enjoined by God to convert all humankind to his glory. Christians, too, view themselves as a chosen people possessed of a special relationship with God.

**TABLE 1.2** Islam Today

| Region | Muslim Percentage of Population |
|---|---|
| The Arab World | 90–100 |
| Non-Arab Areas of the Middle East, Including Central Asia (excluding Israel and Armenia) | 90–100 |
| South Asia (India: 5–20%) | 90–100 |
| Remainder of Asia (Indonesia: 90–100%) | 0–50 |
| Sub-Saharan Africa Adjacent to the Arab World | 50–100 |
| Remainder of Africa | 0–50 |
| Europe (Russia, Albania, Serbia, Bosnia: 5–20) | 3–6 |
| North America | 3–6 |
| Latin America | 0–5 |
| Oceania | 0–5 |

SOURCE: These figures represent composites gleaned from multiple sources, including country figures from the *CIA Factbook*. Figures vary from source to source and are often dated and unreliable.

The God of the Jews and the Christians is also the God of the Muslims. Indeed, *Islam* means submission to the will of God. Members of the Islamic faith are referred to as Muslims, meaning "those who submit to God's will." Islam acknowledges the major prophets of the Jews, including Adam, Noah, Moses, and Abraham. Jesus is recognized as a major prophet, but not as the Son of God. Islam does accept the virgin birth of Jesus, and the Koran contains a separate chapter devoted to Mary. The Koran, the law of God as revealed to the Prophet Mohammed, refers to Christians and Jews as "People of the Book." From the Islamic perspective, Christians and Jews were converted to a belief in the one God by earlier prophets, but have refused to accept the teachings of the Prophet Mohammed, God's final prophet. As believers in the one God, they are to live in peace among Muslims in return for a compensatory tax. Muslims also view themselves as God's chosen people and, like the Christians, believe that it is their religious duty to convert all non-Muslims to the glory of God.

Much like the Torah and the Bible, the Koran provides Muslims with a guide to salvation. The Koran, however, far exceeds either the Torah or the Bible in instructing believers on the ordering of their political, economic, and social lives, a topic to be addressed shortly. The Prophet Mohammed (570–632 CE) proclaimed the birth of the Islamic faith in 610 CE, following his summons as the final prophet of God. Muslims refer to the period before this date as the *jahiliya,* or time of ignorance. The Prophet Mohammed was born in Mecca as a member of the Hashemite clan of the tribe of Quraysh. Mecca at that time was the center of a multitude of idolatrous religions, most of which focused on the Kaaba, an ancient temple believed to embody the divine presence (Peters 1994). Awed by the Kaaba and its pantheon of gods, the tribes of the region began making annual pilgrimages to Mecca, declaring the month of pilgrimage to be free of raiding and bloodshed (Armajani 1970). Mecca's holy status, as well as its location on the main caravan routes to Syria, Egypt, Palestine, and Iraq, transformed the city into a cosmopolitan trading center familiar with the basic tenets of both Judaism and Christianity. Elements of both would be incorporated into Islam.

Like most prophets, Mohammed was condemned as a heretic. In 622, he and his followers were forced to flee to the neighboring city of Yathrib, now called Medina. The *hijra,* the flight of the Prophet Mohammed and his followers, marks the beginning of the Islamic calendar. Political economists might note that much of the opposition to the Prophet Mohammed was based upon the fear that his monotheistic message would destroy the pilgrimage so important to the prosperity of Mecca (Brockelmann 1960). At the time, Yathrib was in a state of near civil war, and the Prophet Mohammed was welcomed as both its political and its spiritual leader. His political role added a practical dimension to his spiritual views, and unlike either Judaism or Christianity, Islam addressed political issues in great detail.

In 630 the Prophet Mohammed returned victorious to Mecca, whose inhabitants were duly converted to Islam. The new religion also incorporated the pilgrimage, thereby allaying the major economic concerns of Mecca's merchants. The remainder of the Arabian Peninsula would soon fall under the Prophet's sway as his legions, fired by religious zeal and the lure of booty, offered the vanquished a choice between salvation or death. As People of the Book, Jews and Christians were allowed to live in peace with their Muslim hosts.

The Prophet Mohammed's successors would extend the Islamic empire throughout the Middle East and incorporate large areas of Spain, most of eastern Europe, and the northern regions of the Indian subcontinent, including the current countries of Afghanistan, Pakistan, and Bangladesh. Muslims now constitute approximately 11 percent of India's one billion citizens. While much of the early empire was forged by the sword, merchants and missionaries would later extend the sway of Islam to regions as distant as Indonesia and Malaysia, most of whose current inhabitants are practicing Muslims. China and Thailand also have large Muslim minorities. Labor migrations in the post–World War II era would also establish large Muslim minorities in the countries of Europe and North America. In most places, they constitute the second largest faith after Christianity.

## The Basic Principles of Islam

Mohammed, it is important to note, is revered as a prophet of God rather than as an extension of God. He was a mortal being chosen by God to receive his message; he possessed no supernatural powers. Islam acknowledges both angels and the devil, who is a fallen angel. God also created the jinn, creatures who "are intermediate angels, the psychic forces that can lead man from the physical to the spiritual world through the labyrinth of the intermediate world or barzakh.

Others are malefic forces that have rebelled against God, in the same way that some men rebel against the Divinity" (Tabatabai, n.d., 236).

Muslims are expected to execute five obligations, often referred to as the pillars of Islam. First, they must witness that "There is no God but God and Mohammed is his Prophet." This, as Armajani writes, "is the most oft-repeated sentence in the world of Islam. It is whispered in the ear of the newborn child, it is repeated throughout his life, and it is the last sentence uttered when he is laid in the grave. It is used to call the faithful to prayer and it has served as the battle cry of Muslim soldiers in all the wars of Islam" (1970, 45). Second, Muslims are required to pray five times a day at specified intervals. The first prayers begin at dawn, and the last end late in the evening. In most Islamic countries radio and television programming is interrupted during the periods specified for prayer. Third, Muslims are expected to give generously of their wealth. This includes both *zakat,* a religious tax equal to 2.5 percent of an individual's income, and the broader practice of giving alms to the poor. Fourth, Muslims are expected to fast during the holy month of Ramadan. The fast is not obligatory for travelers or the ill, but must be executed when their circumstances have normalized. Finally, every Muslim is required to make at least one pilgrimage, or *hajj,* to Mecca if their circumstances allow. Most Muslim countries assist their poor in making the *hajj.* In addition to the pillars of Islam, Muslims are obliged to obey Koranic injunctions against drinking alcohol, gambling, eating pork, and committing usury, and are generally encouraged to be honest and decent citizens who serve the Islamic community by engaging in good works.

**Jihad**   Although this is not a formal pillar of Islam, Muslims are also expected to serve their faith by fighting in jihads, or holy wars. One of the clearest admonitions in this regard is the Koranic passage stating that "Warfare is ordained for you, though it is hateful to you; but it may happen that ye hate what is good for you" (Koran 2:216). Many fundamentalist groups, it should be noted, do consider jihad to be an obligatory pillar of Islam.

Muslims, however, are quick to note that the concept of jihad embraces the struggle against all forms of evil. This, as explained by Sheikh Atiyyah Saqr, an eminent Muslim scholar associated with Cairo's venerable Al-Azhar mosque, can mean many things.

> Among the types of jihad are struggling against one's desires, the accursed Satan, poverty, illiteracy, disease, and all evil forces in the world. . . . Jihad is also done to avert aggression on the home countries and on all that is held sacred, or in order to face those who try to hinder the march of the call of truth. In Islamic Shari'ah [law] Jihad in the Cause of Allah means fighting in order to make the Word of Allah most high and the means of doing so is taking up arms in addition to preparation, financing and planning strategies ("Fatwa: What Is Jihad in Islam?" 2002).

Jihad, then, possesses two faces. The first, jihad in the cause of Allah, stresses the protection and expansion of the faith. It is this jihad that confronts the West in its efforts to control the Middle East and stem jihadist terrorism. The second face of jihad, often referred to as "the great jihad," serves as a guide toward achieving moral purity and is perceived by many Muslims as a vital part of their culture. They resent the term *jihadist* being applied to violent Islamic radicals, suggesting that it perverts the true meaning of the concept.

We use *jihadist* to distinguish Islamic extremists who are wedded to violence in their quest for an Islamic state from the far larger body of fundamentalist groups who are willing to pursue their goals by peaceful means. This use of the term is also common in the Islamic media.

**The Law of Islam**    The foundation of Islamic law is the Koran, the word of God as revealed to the Prophet Mohammed. As the word of God, the Koran is absolute and unassailable, and it cannot be changed. Heated debates, however, continue to take place over the precise meaning of many passages. When early Muslims were faced with circumstances not fully addressed by the Koran, they sought guidance from both the sayings and the behavior of the Prophet Mohammed, a body of tradition collectively referred to as the Sunna (Dekmejian 1995). Islamic scholars have recorded the existence of some 600,000 Hadith (sayings of the Prophet) and, while many scholars distinguish between the behavior of the Prophet (Sunna) and the sayings of the Prophet (Hadith), most information on the Prophet Mohammed's behavior is provided by the sayings. The line between the Sunna and the Hadith, then, is fine indeed. Only those Hadith that date from the early years of Islam are considered to be authentic or "orthodox." The others, some of which originated centuries after the passing of the Prophet, are categorized as being either fair or weak in authenticity. Each Hadith begins with an acknowledgment of its source, along the lines of "So-and-so said to so-and-so that the Prophet handled this matter in a particular way." Only about 2,500 Hadith fall into the orthodox category, although there is no consensus on this figure.

As the realm of Islam expanded and the memory of the Prophet became more distant, Islamic law had recourse to *ijtihad,* a consensual interpretation reached by leading Islamic scholars or *ulema* (Schacht 1964). This practice continues today in the Shi'a branch of Islam, but was restricted several centuries ago by the Sunnis. As a result, Sunni doctrine is far more rigid and resistant to change than its Shi'a counterpart. While Shi'a doctrine continues to evolve, Sunni doctrine does not. Tensions between the two branches of Islam have increased accordingly, a topic that finds elaboration throughout the book.

Collectively, the Koran, the Sunna, the authentic Hadith, and to a lesser extent, the *ijtihad,* constitute the body of Islamic law referred to as the *Sharia.* This is the law that guides the lives of Muslims. As the modern world presents endless circumstances unanticipated by the Sharia, Islamic scholars also have recourse to the use of analogy (Levy 1962; Schacht 1964). A leading religious scholar, for example, was recently asked if artificial hearts were allowed by the Sharia. His response was to cite the Prophet's acceptance of artificial limbs for those wounded in battle, because they helped the body to function properly. He also noted that the Prophet had simultaneously distinguished between artificial limbs and cosmetic operations designed to beautify the body. The latter were forbidden. In this regard, the Sharia divides acts into five categories: obligatory, meritorious, permissible, reprehensible, and forbidden (*haram*) (Schacht 1964, 107).

## Formal Islam versus Informal Islam

Islamic law tended to be formalistic and impersonal. Many Muslims, accordingly, began to form religious groups of a less legalistic and austere nature that would enable them to pursue the mystical search for truth and achieve a personal union with God (Al-Shaibi 1991; Gilsenan 1978; Hamzeh and Dekmejian 1996). Although early theologians resisted the establishment of such groups, whose members were referred to as Sufis, they gradually gained acceptance and now constitute an important part of the Islamic community (Johansen 1996). Historically, the most famous of the Sufis were the Whirling Dervishes, a group renowned for incorporating whirling dances into their rituals.

Sufism, however, was only one form of popular or informal Islam. The advent of colonialism found Islam challenged by Europe's superior military and economic power as well as by its heady ideal of a society ordered on the principles of secularism and reason (Dekmejian 1985). Particularly offensive to devout Muslims were the Westerners' use of alcohol and lack of prudence in the dress of Western women. Far worse, from the Islamic perspective, was the speed with which educated and affluent Muslims began to adopt European practices.

The Islamic reaction to the challenge of Westernization was twofold. On one side, Muslim intellectuals such as Jamal al-Din Afghani (1838–1897) and Mohammed Abduh (1849–1905) attempted to strengthen Islam by interpreting Islamic doctrine in a manner that would accommodate the technological advances of the West (Dekmejian 1995). In their view, science was the gift of God and was fully compatible with Islamic law. On the other, a succession of preachers lashed out at the growing influence of Western values and called for a return to a society based on the fundamental principles of the Koran and the Sunna. Lacking a better term, scholars of the era referred to the Islamic reaction as *fundamentalism,* a term previously ascribed to Protestant extremists in the United States. In 1928, the popular reaction to Westernization took organizational form when Hasan al-Banna, a teacher of Arabic in Egypt, founded the Muslim Brotherhood under the rallying cry "God is the answer" (Mitchell 1969). The goal of the Brotherhood, as will be discussed at length in Chapter 2, was to restore Egypt to an Islamic form of government similar to that practiced by the Prophet Mohammed.

Since the founding of the Muslim Brotherhood, so many varieties of Islamic fundamentalism have emerged that they are difficult to classify. Indeed, Dekmejian documents the emergence of some 174 fundamentalist groups between 1970 and 1990 (Dekmejian 1995, 1998; Eickelman and Piscatori 1996). Some advise their followers to flee from the present era of corruption and ignorance by forming religious colonies in the mountains or deserts; others advocate reforming society from within. Of the latter, some fundamentalist groups focus on political action while others minister to the faithful by providing social services and guidance. Of those that focus on politics, some seek to destroy secular governments by force, others to capture them by legitimate means (Hamzeh 2000). Some groups focus on a single strategy; others combine a multitude of strategies. Some groups are very narrow (strict constructionist) in their interpretation of an Islamic state; others, especially the Shi'a, are more flexible. Some want to combine Islamic theology with the benefits of Western technology; others reject all vestiges of Westernization. Regardless of the vast differences within the fundamentalist movement, the ultimate goal remains the same: to return to a political and social order founded on basic Islamic principles.

Much of the non-Islamic world associates Islamic fundamentalism with the violent activities of jihadist groups in Algeria, Egypt, Iran, Iraq, and, above all, with the September 11 attacks on the United States. The focus on jihadist violence has diverted attention from a broader Islamic revival that has occurred throughout the Muslim world since the 1970s. The revival is reflected in increased attendance at mosques, electoral victories for Islamic parties, sporadic outbreaks of violence, and a growing support for Islamic issues in public opinion surveys (Bill 1984). The most visible evidence of the Islamic revival has been the resurgence of Islamic dress among the women of the Middle East, although a considerable debate exists over the exact meaning of the veiling phenomenon (Saleh 1990). To some, it is a sign of piety and possibly also a symbol of support for the Islamic revival. For others it is the result of family pressure or simply a way of repelling overtly aggressive males and avoiding the cost of fancy clothes. Other explanations suggest that it increases marriageability. In Europe, Islamic dress is rapidly evolving into a symbol of Islamic identity. The Europeans are not amused and have attempted to outlaw the wearing of head scarves and other forms of Islamic dress in schools.

Scholars have attempted to explain the Islamic revival in a variety of ways. Some see it as part of a clash of religions that has ebbed and flowed since the Crusades and beyond (Davis 1987; Shepard 1987). As Westernization has become more prevalent in the region, so has the Islamic reaction. Others see the Islamic revival as a defensive reaction to a flawed process of modernization. Westernization attempted to replace the traditional political institutions of the Middle East with those of Europe but succeeded only in creating political systems that were tyrannical, corrupt, and exploitative. Rather than solving the region's problems, Westernization merely added to its despair. As the coherence of Middle Eastern societies weakened, a growing number of individuals turned to popular religious groups to meet their material and psychological needs (Hinnebusch 1985; Mustafa 1995).

## The Political Consequences of Islam

The influence of Islam on the history and political evolution of the Middle East has been profound. The conversion of the Middle East to Islam created a political community that transcended the bonds of kinship. It thus paved the way for a dazzling Islamic civilization that could not have been achieved by the region's inward-looking tribes, each of which was a world unto itself. It also transformed the Middle East into a cultural configuration, most members of which shared a common religious identity, value structure, and history. As a result of this shared identity, political linkages in the Middle East tend to be far stronger and more prevalent than they are in other geographic regions such as Latin America, Africa, or Asia. Little happens in one area of the Middle East that does not have repercussions throughout the region as a whole: the spread of Islamic fundamentalism is a case in point. The Arabs form an even tighter cultural configuration, blending a common language and ethnic identity with intense pride in being the founders of Islam. Arab history was also Islamic history, and the glories of the Arab world were essentially those of the Prophet Mohammed and his Arab successors, the caliphs.

The highly political character of Islam also provided the Middle East with a philosophical orientation that found the unity of religion and politics to be both logical and desirable. If one believed in an all-powerful God, what was to be achieved by separating them? This is a very important consideration, for it helps to explain why many people in the Middle East do not share the Western aversion to religious rule.

The Islamic experience, moreover, provided the peoples of the Middle East with a profound sense of historical pride. As the next section will illustrate, the Islamic empires of the Middle Ages achieved a level of civilization unknown in Europe at that time. Unfortunately, the glories of the past stand in stark contrast to the impotence of the Islamic world today. Understandably, Muslims find themselves pondering the reasons for their fall from grace. Some blame their leaders. Others blame the West. Most blame both.

Perhaps because of this strong sense of historical presence, the most potent political symbols in the Middle East today tend to be Islamic symbols. King Abdullah II of Jordan is a direct descendant of the Prophet, while the official title of the king of Saudi Arabia is "His Majesty, the protector of the two holy shrines [Mecca and Medina]." Iran, of course, is an Islamic theocracy. Recent years have also seen religious currents dominate elections in Turkey, Iraq, Palestine, and Saudi Arabia. Similar results can be expected throughout the region as pressure for greater democracy continues to mount. Democracy is designed to reflect the popular will, and the popular will in the Middle East is heavily influenced by religion.

Political opposition in most countries of the Middle East has also taken religious form; Islamic fundamentalism has become the dominant avenue of resistance to the region's authoritarian regimes. Algeria has been reduced nearly to civil war, while Egypt was long the focus of protracted religious violence. It is the fundamentalists, moreover, who now provide the main opposition to peace with Israel.

**Islamic Influence on Economic Development**   The Islamic states generally rank lower on World Bank indices of economic development than most other areas of the Third World, with the exception of Africa. The oil states enjoy a higher standard of living than most countries of the world, but that wealth is based almost entirely on royalties from oil deposits that were developed by the West. Should the oil disappear, there would be little to sustain their economies.

Because economic and technological developments require a high level of innovation and creativity, some scholars have suggested that the region's slow pace of development can be attributed to the rigidity of Islamic law and Islam's emphasis on fatalism and passivity. The Koran and the Hadith, for example, stress God's control over all dimensions of human life, leaving little scope for human volition. Indeed, no phrase is more common in the Muslim world than *insha'Allah*, "if God wills." Other observers, however, note that great civilizations did flourish under Islamic rule. They also point out that the Prophet Mohammed was an innovator par excellence and cite the many passages in the Koran that inspire innovation and creativity. The slow pace of development in the Middle East, in their view, is attributable to the divisive legacy of tribal culture, an adverse colonial history, and the emergence of an international system that has found it expedient to fragment the Muslim world into a myriad of mini-states, none of which is strong enough to challenge the interests of the West.

**Islam and Democracy**   Similarly, a debate has emerged over the compatibility of Islam with democratic political systems. As with most complex religions, Islam contains both democratic and antidemocratic traditions. Those who argue that Islam is inherently democratic stress its emphasis on equality. Everyone is equal in the eyes of God, and all Muslims share the same rights and obligations. The emphasis on equality is reinforced by the fact that orthodox (Sunni) Islam does not have a priesthood or hierarchical authority structure. Rather, questions of import, including succession and religious leadership, have traditionally been decided by consultation. The Prophet Mohammed, it will be recalled, refused to name a successor, leaving that choice to his followers. Islam, moreover, stressed tolerance toward Christian and Jewish minorities ("People of the Book") living within the Islamic world. A wide variety of groups could and did prosper under Islamic rule.

In the view of those who stress Islam's democratic underpinnings, the Middle East's addiction to authoritarianism is a manifestation of its tribal past, the selfish nature of its elites, and the meddling influence of foreign powers, not its Islamic heritage. Much the same argument may be made about the subjugation of women. Islam embraced limited polygamy, but it also eliminated many of the worst abuses of gender discrimination common in the pre-Islamic era.

The arguments of those who contend that Islam is inherently antidemocratic, however, are also strong. Armajani (1970), for example, argues that consultation over succession and other issues of key importance have been limited to a very few individuals, and have had more to do with smoke-filled rooms than with current notions of popular sovereignty. He goes on to note that Greek law, the foundation of Western concepts of democracy, is based upon the reasoning power of man. Being relative rather than absolute, human law can keep pace with changing circumstances and lends itself to the art of compromise so critical to democratic practice. Islamic law, by contrast, is the revealed law of God and is not subject to change by human beings.

Constituting a moral imperative, it does not lend itself to compromise or change (Armajani 1970, 108).

## THE TRIBE VERSUS ISLAM: CONFLICT AND ACCOMMODATION

Islam created a political community that transcended the bonds of kinship, but clans and tribes remained the basic units of social organization for the vast majority of the region's people. An inherent tension thus developed between a religion that accorded absolute loyalty to the vicars of God and a tribal lifestyle that made personal survival dependent on kinship loyalty. During periods of civilization and refinement such as those characterized by Abbasid Baghdad or Fatimid Cairo, the Islamic state extended its dominance over the tribes, curbing internal warfare and stimulating commerce and agriculture. When centralized authority weakened, the tribes reasserted their own, pillaging caravans and attacking the agrarian villages on the fringe of the desert. Political relationships between the sacred and the profane, then, were much like the persistent tension between the desert and the sown: the fellahin, or peasants, extended their realms during times of plenty, and the desert reclaimed its own during periods of drought and famine.

This tension between Islam and the tribe existed in the social sphere as well. Like other religions, Islam could only find acceptance for its principles by accommodating the dominant customs of the day, however repugnant they may have been to its founder (Rubin 1995). The dominant principle in Islam was submission to the one God and the creation of an Islamic state or *umma*. To achieve this goal, Islam incorporated customs such as polygamy that were deeply entrenched in the local culture. The Prophet Mohammed himself remained monogamous throughout his marriage to his first wife, to whom he was devoted. After she died, Mohammed took wives from diverse tribes in order to consolidate the core of the Islamic movement with ties of blood as well as faith. The founder of modern Saudi Arabia would follow the same practice during the early decades of the twentieth century. Polygamy also served an important social function by facilitating the large families so important to the survival of the tribe and offering a support system for women and children left destitute by the ravages of tribal warfare. Having said this, we note that Islam greatly restricted the practice of polygamy by limiting a man to four wives and requiring that all wives be treated with total equality.

The most powerful movements in the precolonial history of the Middle East were those that combined religious and tribal authority. The Islamic invasions relied heavily on tribal armies, and the Prophet Mohammed himself decreed that four-fifths of the spoils of war against the infidels should go to the armies and one-fifth to the Islamic state. Tribal warfare thus continued to be a way of life, only with its focus transformed into a religious cause. This pattern continued well into the twentieth century in much of the Middle East, with the fusion of religious and tribal authority providing the foundation of Turkish, Moroccan, Saudi, and Libyan kingdoms.

# THE ISLAMIC CONQUEST

The Prophet Mohammed died on June 8, 632, having extended Islam throughout most of the Arabian Peninsula. His passing created a crisis of succession, for Mohammed, in keeping with his role as prophet, had declined to name a successor. Some of his followers believed that the successor should be a member of the Prophet's family, while others thought he should be drawn from the broader reaches of the Quraysh tribe or selected on the basis of piety and good works. Space limitations preclude recounting the succession process, but suffice it to say that the first four caliphs were both early supporters and relatives of the Prophet Mohammed. Abu Bakr, the first caliph, was a close friend and father-in-law of the Prophet Mohammed, as was Umar, the second caliph. Uthman, the third, was a son-in-law of the Prophet Mohammed and a member of the powerful Umayyad clan of the Quraysh tribe. Ali, number four, was both the Prophet's cousin and his son-in-law, making him the logical candidate for the caliphate in the eyes of those who believed that the caliph should be a direct descendant of the Prophet (Tabatabai, n.d.). The first four caliphs are referred to as the "orthodox caliphs."

Abu Bakr maintained Islam's domination of the Arabian Peninsula in the unsettled circumstances following the Prophet Mohammed's death. This was not an easy task, for many of the tribes, having been converted by force, rebelled against the Islamic government. Some even tried to extend their power by discovering their own prophets (Armajani 1970). Umar, fueled by Islamic zeal and the need to occupy the energies of his tribal warriors, extended the Islamic conquest to Egypt, the Fertile Crescent (Syria, Palestine, Lebanon, Iraq), and much of Iran. Expansion brought the Islamic empire much-needed wealth, for Muslims were not required to pay taxes other than the *zakat*. Conquests continued under Uthman, but the leadership of the Islamic state was losing much of its religious zeal as Uthman, now in his seventies, allowed his relatives to usurp most of the senior positions in his administration. Corruption was rampant, with Uthman reportedly selling governorships for cash or slave girls (Armajani 1970). His most lasting contribution to Islam was the formal canonization of the Koran.

## Sunni versus Shi'a

Ali succeeded Uthman in 656. He removed most of the latter's appointees and moved the seat of government to Kufa, an ancient city not far from the present city of Baghdad. Mu'awiya, the governor of Syria and a relative of Uthman, refused to recognize Ali as caliph, thereby precipitating a civil war between a Syrian branch of Islam heavily influenced by Byzantine culture and an Iraqi–Iranian branch heavily influenced by Persian culture. Ali prevailed, but Mu'awiya consolidated his position in Syria and in 660 CE had himself proclaimed caliph. Islam now had two caliphs, giving rise to a theological schism as fundamental as that separating Protestants and Catholics in post-Reformation Europe. As the cousin and son-in-law of the Prophet Mohammed, Ali was the only acceptable candidate for Muslims who believed that the caliphate should remain in the family of the Prophet. He was also a pious man and a brilliant intellect who earned the support of those who believed that the caliphate should be awarded on the basis of merit. Beyond the question of doctrine, the conflict between Mu'awiya and Ali was also one of geopolitics. The center of Mu'awiya's support was Damascus and Jerusalem, while Ali found strong support among the Persian officials who increasingly dominated the eastern regions of the empire. Was Islam to be ruled from the west or from the east?

After Ali's assassination in Kufa in 661, his supporters—referred to as the Shi'at Ali, or partisans of Ali—rallied around his two sons, Hasan and Husayn, both of whom were subsequently assassinated. The Shi'a believe that Hasan was murdered by Mu'awiya in 673 and that Husayn was murdered in 680 by Yazid, Mu'awiya's successor, in order to prevent him from establishing a rival caliphate in Iraq. Both would subsequently become holy martyrs of Shi'a Islam.

With the death of Hasan and Husayn, the Shi'a rejected the legitimacy of the Umayyad caliphs and created a branch of Islam that differed profoundly from the Sunni. As described by Yahya Armajani:

> Failing to establish their claim by politics or by war, the Shi'is separated permanently from the majority and founded a religion of their own, complete with theology, philosophy, government, and ethics. Religiously, Shi'ism has Zoroastrian, Nestorian, and other overtones, and has supplied Islam with mysteries, saints, intercessors, belief in atonement, and a spirit of high cult, all of which are repugnant to the majority of Sunnis. The Sunnis consider the Koran infallible, while the Shi'is place infallibility in a man, the Imam who is sinless and has been considered as a man-God (Armajani 1970, 101).

The Shi'a belief that the hidden imam would reappear and lead the Muslim community to salvation led to the evolution of religious leaders empowered to rule the Shi'a community until the imam's return. Such individuals, often referred to as ayatollahs, are imbued with mystical powers that transcend those of the temporal world.

In sharp contrast to the mysticism of the Shi'a, the Sunnis follow a more literal interpretation of the Sunna, or way of the Prophet. There are no hidden imams, nor are Sunni spiritual leaders imbued with supernatural powers. Aside from the caliphate, now vacant, the religious elites of Sunni Islam consist of learned scholars or ulema, the most senior of whom are the mufti (senior religious judge), the directors of *Waqfs* or religious endowments (charitable works), and the rectors of Islamic universities such as Al-Azhar University in Cairo. Aside from these positions, Sunni Islam lacks an overarching organizational structure, and each congregation more or less selects its own preachers and prayer leaders. In many instances, the selection is made by the government.

Mystical powers and a more complex organizational structure enable Shi'a leaders to mobilize their followers far more effectively than their Sunni counterparts (Halm 1997). As we shall see in Chapter 7, both played a crucial role in sustaining the Islamic revolution in Iran. Such differences also raise questions about the ability of fundamentalist leaders in Sunni countries such as Egypt, Saudi Arabia, and Algeria to sustain revolutions once they get started. The profound differences between Shi'a and Sunni Islam also cast doubt on the prospects for a unified

Islamic world should an increasing number of Middle Eastern countries fall under the sway of Islamic regimes. Revolutions are initially fueled by emotion, but they are sustained by discipline and organization. Perhaps in response to this problem, many Sunni fundamentalist groups have embraced such Shi'a concepts as the imam (renewer of the faith) and the emir (prince of the faithful) that provide a profound emotional link between the fundamentalist leaders and their followers.

## The Glories of the Empire

Following the death of Ali, the last of the four orthodox caliphs, power shifted from the Arabian Peninsula to the Umayyads in Damascus, and from there to the Abbasids in Baghdad, the Fatimids in Cairo, the Andalusians in Spain, and the Ottoman Turks in Istanbul. At one time or another, the Islamic empire encompassed large portions of Spain, eastern Europe, and India. The Ottoman Empire in the West was paralleled by the empire of Safavid Turks in Tehran (1502–1736). The Umayyads and the Ottomans were Sunni, while the Abbasids, the Fatimids, the Andalusians, and the Safavids were Shi'a. Egypt would later become Sunni.

The era of empire and expansion saw the Middle East emerge as the center of world civilization (Hourani 1997). The Islam that emerged from the era of empire and expansion, however, was a far more complex religion than that of the Prophet Mohammed and his immediate successors. The invasion of Syria and Palestine had brought the desert warriors of Arabia into contact with the splendors of Byzantium, while their conquests in Mesopotamia had introduced them to the rich civilization of Persia (Hitti 1956). The demands of empire also proved too taxing for the informal style of rule that had characterized the early years of the Islamic era and forced an ever greater reliance on professional administrators. The bedouin warriors who had spearheaded the Islamic invasion were poorly suited to the task of administration, and the job fell naturally to the more cultured Syrians and Persians, depending upon the location. In the process, the center of political power in the Islamic world shifted from the Arabian Peninsula to the new centers of imperial power. Indeed, with Mu'awiya's establishment of the Umayyad caliphate in Damascus, the Arabian Peninsula had ceased to be the political center of Islam (Brockelmann 1960).

Great empires brought commerce, culture, and science to the region, but the empires inevitably succumbed to fragmentation born of social and economic jealousies, rebellions, religious schisms, and corrupt administration.

The final thrust of empire was provided by the Ottoman Turks in the west and the Safavid Turks in the east. At its zenith, the Ottoman Empire stretched from North Africa to Vienna. Had Vienna fallen, the history of Europe might have been far different. As it is, the Turkish occupation of eastern Europe established a strong Islamic presence in the region, particularly in Bosnia and Albania.

The Safavids, also of Turkish origin, invaded Iran in 1500 and, under the leadership of Shah Abbas, extended their empire to include Afghanistan, Pakistan, northern India, and most of the Muslim areas of Central Asia. The Safavids soon embraced Persian language and culture and made Iran the center of their empire. In the process they also became zealous Shi'as, putting them at odds with the

Sunni Ottomans and condemning the two empires to centuries of conflict. Neither empire was able to overcome the other, and the schism between the two Islamic powers served only to weaken the Muslim world in the face of a resurgent West.

## The Empire in Decline

In spite of its earlier glories, the final centuries of the Islamic empire were ones of stagnation and decline as local leaders asserted their independence from central authority and the European powers began a relentless colonization of Muslim territories (Antonius 1965; Zeine 1958). This decline was as true of the Ottomans in the west as it was of the Safavids in the east. Indeed, it was only jealousy among the European powers that kept the Ottoman Empire, the "sick man of Europe," from collapsing more rapidly than it did (Marriott 1956).

Some authors have attributed the empire's decline to the fragmentation of Islam into diverse sects, while others blame the continuing influence of tribalism and kinship. Gifted leaders forged glorious empires, only to see their efforts squandered by squabbles among less-gifted heirs. There were, however, more practical reasons for the decline of the empire. Except for brief periods of enlightened leadership, the rulers of the empire were corrupt and despotic. Indeed, the Prophet Mohammed's efforts to forge an Islamic nation based upon trust between the rulers and the masses had long ago given way to fear and alienation. The more brutal governments became, the more individuals sought protection within the confines of their tribal, religious, and ethnic communities.

The Islamic empire, moreover, had little in common with the modern nation-state in which the citizens of a particular geographic region form a political community based upon common interests and shared identity. Rather, the Islamic empire had become a grand mosaic of tribal, religious, and ethnic groups, each with its own interests. The Turks explicitly acknowledged this situation by making the leader of each religious sect responsible for the well-being of its members: the patriarch of the Greek Orthodox Christians was responsible for his flock, and so forth. Each group was considered a *millet,* and was more or less self-governing as long as it remained quiescent and paid its allotted tribute to the sultan. By its very nature, the *millet* system fragmented the people of the Middle East and militated against the process of nation building.

In combination, the above factors kept the Islamic empire from keeping pace with the social, economic, political, and technological changes that were occurring in Europe. While the Islamic empire languished, the more advanced European colonial powers had evolved into industrial nation-states. Nationalism replaced kinship as the basis for social integration, while religious doctrine was challenged by philosophies based on science, reason, and individualism. Industrialism created wealth and commerce, and it stimulated advances in education and medicine. It also created advances in bureaucratic technology that enabled the state to control the affairs of its citizens in a manner unknown in the East.

Predictably, an industrialized Europe found the Middle East easy prey for its imperial ambitions. Indeed, the life of the average individual in the Middle East at the dawn of the nineteenth century was not markedly different from that of the average individual during the lifetime of the Prophet Mohammed. Most lived in tribes or other kinship groups, and education was largely restricted to memorization of the Koran. Disease and famine remained common.

Although the Islamic empire collapsed in the face of pressure from an industrialized West, it had already transformed Islam from an obscure desert religion into a global religion that now claims approximately one-fifth of the world's population as adherents. It also provided the Middle East with a cultural cohesion and identity that continues to define the region's character. Nevertheless, the empire was not able to eliminate the scourge of tribalism. This task was made even more difficult by a political culture of distrust and alienation born of centuries of despotic rule.

## THE ERA OF COLONIALISM

Although space limitations preclude a full accounting of the collapse of the Islamic empire, suffice it to say that the years between 1900 and the start of World War I in 1914 saw a steady erosion of Ottoman power in Europe as one after another of the Balkan regions either proclaimed its independence or was reclaimed by the Austro-Hungarian Empire (Marriott 1956). Turkey was also forced to allow Russia to intervene in Turkish affairs on behalf of the Orthodox Christians and France to serve as the protector of the empire's Roman Catholics. The picture was much the same in Iran, with the Safavids and their successors losing ever-larger swaths of land to the Russians.

Prior to the nineteenth century, Western penetration of the Middle East had been indirect, taking the form of commercial concessions and demands for extraterritorial rights. Sustained colonization of the region began with the French occupation of Algeria in 1830, and the establishment of a British protectorate in Egypt in 1882. Also during this period, the sheikhdoms of the Persian Gulf placed their foreign affairs in the hands of the British in exchange for an annual stipend and guaranteed territorial rights. With the dismemberment of the Ottoman Empire at the end of World War I, Syria and Lebanon became mandates of France, while Iraq and Palestine fell to the British. The French had already colonized much of North Africa, and the British were well ensconced in Egypt and the Persian Gulf. Under the mandate system, the European powers were expected to prepare the territories under their control for eventual independence and self-government. This responsibility, however, did not weigh heavily on the minds of either the French or the British.

### Political and Economic Consequences
### of the Colonial Experience

European motivations for colonization of the Middle East were both economic and strategic. From the economic perspective, the lands of the Middle East represented a rich market for European goods. It was also hoped that they would provide a cheap and reliable source of raw materials such as oil for the industries of Europe. From a strategic perspective, the European powers viewed the Middle East as a region of key geopolitical importance, control of which could tip the European balance of power in their favor. British interest in the region was particularly strong, for the Middle East provided the most direct route to India, the crown jewel of the British Empire. In the case of Italy's occupation of Libya, the ostensible motivation for colonization was national pride: Mussolini rallied his followers with promises of a new Roman Empire.

The most immediate result of Western colonialism was the further fragmentation of the Middle East into a multitude of small dependencies, all of which would eventually become independent countries. A few areas, notably Turkey, Iran, North Yemen, and the central parts of the Arabian Peninsula, were spared colonization, Turkey and Iran for political reasons involving the European balance of power and the Arabian Peninsula because of its inhospitable terrain.

The countries created, moreover, had more to do with the global interests of the colonial powers than with the background and interests of the peoples affected. Thus, Kuwait, a sparsely populated region smaller than the state of Rhode Island, was made an independent country while the homeland of the Kurds, which encompassed much of northern Iraq and adjacent areas in Turkey, Syria, and Iran, was not. As the Kurdish example illustrates, boundaries were drawn with little concern for the ethnic and religious composition of their inhabitants, paving the way for the ethnic and religious conflicts that have become endemic to the region. Colonial administrators, moreover, did little to ameliorate communal tensions in the colonies. Rather, most found it expedient to consolidate their control by playing one group against another, thereby exacerbating tensions that were already well developed.

Having staked their claim to the region, the colonial powers set about restructuring Middle Eastern society to make it compatible with their economic and strategic interests. This required that the economies of the colonial territories be integrated into the economy of the European power. Rather than developing their own industrial and technological base, the territories supplied the economies of Europe with raw materials and absorbed their excess industrial production. Thus, when they achieved independence, most states in the region were predominantly agricultural and continued to depend upon the mother country for financial and technological assistance. This relationship was particularly strong in France's North African colonies of Morocco, Algeria, and Tunisia and continues to be so today. Indeed, so many North Africans migrated to France in search of work that they now constitute some 6 percent of the French population.

Effective economic exploitation also required that the legal systems of the colonies be brought into line with those of the colonial power. This posed a variety of problems. Most laws pertaining to individual behavior, for example, were based on Koranic law and were often at odds with the secular legal codes of Britain and France. Confused legal systems emerged that were a mixture of both. In some cases, different laws applied to different groups, with Europeans abiding by one set of rules and natives by another. Laws in the rural areas tended to remain more traditional than those in the city. Such confusion continues in the Middle East today, with the current revival of Islamic values resulting in a re-Islamization of many of the region's legal systems.

Particularly problematic were laws pertaining to property. Much land in the Middle East was the collective property of the clan or tribe, and land rights were based upon custom rather than written deeds. In other cases, land was technically owned by the state but was controlled by a particular family or clan. Again, there were no written deeds. Colonial economic policies, however, required stringent definitions of ownership, and collective lands were subsequently deeded to their presumed owners, more often than not the tribal chief or other dignitaries who spoke in the name of the clan or tribe (Warriner 1957). Collective land thus became private land, with the prominent families becoming landlords and the less prominent becoming peasants or landless sharecroppers. Such feudal distinctions, minimal at first, became pronounced as later generations of the landed families moved to the urban areas, leaving the management of their farms to exploitative foremen with little interest in the welfare of the peasants. This process was particularly pronounced in Iraq but occurred in other areas as well.

The absence of deeds continues to be a serious problem in the Israeli-occupied West Bank. The Jordanian government was in the process of issuing deeds when the territory was seized by Israel in the June War of 1967. Because land without formal deeds was presumed to be the property of the Jordanian government, the Israelis claimed it as their own and began to distribute it to Jewish settlers.

The economic and strategic exploitation of the colonies also required an infrastructure of roads, railroads, canals, and telecommunications, few of which existed during precolonial times. Although designed to serve the Europeans, the new infrastructure stimulated communication among the peoples of the Middle East in a manner that had not been possible in the past. In so doing, it facilitated the spread of the nationalist and religious movements that would eventually spell the end of colonialism (Cole 1993).

Colonial exploitation also meant that the Middle East had to be made safe for Europeans. Key to this process was the institution of modern health practices and the control of diseases that had long been the scourge of the region. However laudable this may have been from a humanitarian perspective, it had the unintended effect of triggering a population explosion. As noted earlier, Middle Eastern culture had traditionally placed an intense emphasis on large families. With the introduction of modern health techniques, more children survived the rigors of childhood and more adults lived longer. Culture, however, responds slowly to such changes; often it takes several generations. High birth rates, accordingly, continued to be the norm, producing far more people than the meager agrarian economies of the region could sustain. Although population growth is easing, populous countries such as Egypt, Iran, and Algeria face crushing financial problems as they attempt to feed, clothe, care for, educate, house, and employ populations that have tripled or quadrupled in the six decades since the end of World War II.

The population crisis, in turn, created a crisis in urbanization as rural migrants flocked to the cities in search of work. Urbanization brought an ever larger share of the population into contact with Western lifestyles. Closer contact with the West led some migrants to adopt Western values. This was particularly common among those who worked for foreigners or who were able to get a Western education. Urbanization, however, also brought slums, grinding poverty, and a sense of hopelessness as the poor came to realize the extent of their misery. For many recent migrants, moreover, direct contact with foreigners served only to heighten their resentment of the foreign powers who had both humiliated them and desecrated their religious values. As will be discussed shortly in greater depth, it was this sense of outrage that fueled the nationalist movements of the colonial era. It continues to fuel Islamic fundamentalism today.

The efficient exploitation of a colonial territory required a class of cooperative natives to assist in controlling the indigenous population. This class generally consisted of police, soldiers, minor administrators, teachers, and commercial clerks. British administrators built on their experience in India, where they had sought "to form a class who may be interpreters between us and the millions whom we govern; a class of persons, Indian in blood and color, but English in taste, in opinions, in morals, and in intellect" (Mansingh 1986, 40). The French did much the same.

In order to create a class of "cooperative natives," the colonial powers often established rudimentary school systems and imposed their language as a second and frequently official language. The French, for example, "discouraged" the teaching of Arabic in its North African colonies, hoping to supplant it with the French language and culture. Algeria, an Arabic country, would thus attain independence with most of its citizens illiterate in their native language. The same was true to a lesser extent in Morocco and Tunisia. Nevertheless, education did provide access to the mass media and, eventually, made possible the emergence of indigenous newspapers, radio, and cinema.

The emerging Westernized elite was usually headed by the sons of tribal leaders, old aristocrats from the former regime, and native merchants, many of whom had been educated in the West. While this elite reaped the material advantages to be gained from association with the colonial power, the lower classes sank ever deeper into poverty and despair.

This Westernized elite played a profound role as an agent of social change. Its members served as role models or style setters for the youth of the colonies. They were living proof of the advantages that accompanied Westernization and of the superiority of Western lifestyles. They would also become the vanguard in the Middle East's struggle for independence. It was they who wanted power and it was they who fanned the flames of nationalism and independence. Some pressed for consultative assemblies and a gradual transition to independence. Others plotted revolution. As a general principle, the intensity of the response to the Western domination was in direct proportion to the scope of the Western presence. The more intrusive the presence of the West, the more violent the Middle Eastern response.

Finally, the "civilizing" activities of the colonial powers included limited experimentation with consultative assemblies. Such experiments usually occurred during the latter stages of colonial rule.

The impact of colonialism on the Middle East, then, was profound. It fragmented the area into a multitude of mini-states, each with its own set of elites and vested interests (Owen 1992). It was these elites who would eventually lead the drive to independence. Colonialism brought about a revolution in health care, but it also ignited a population explosion that has condemned much of the region to poverty. Colonialism enhanced the region's economic and communications infrastructure, but only to the degree that it served the economic and strategic interests of the mother country. Upon receiving their independence, most states in the region remained economically dependent on the West. Colonialism introduced Western education to the Middle East, albeit to a small class whose purpose was to serve the interests of the colonial powers. In so doing, it spread the heady philosophies of nationalism and socialism that became the hallmark of the region during the revolutionary upheavals of the 1950s and 1960s. Colonialism, however, also shook the confidence of a people that had been profoundly confident of the superiority of its culture and forced that people to reassess its prospects for the future (Smith 1957). While some in the region advocated increased Westernization, others argued that the solution to their problems lay in a return to Islam as it was practiced during the era of the Prophet and his immediate successors. Still others looked for ways to bridge the gap between the material superiority of the West and the moral superiority of Islamic culture.

For all of its impact, however, colonialism did not succeed in reshaping the region. Rather, it merely added one more layer of complexity to an already complex region. The Middle East, as Sharabi writes, has become "modernized" without becoming modern (Sharabi 1988, 23–24).

## POLITICS OF THE MIDDLE EAST SINCE WORLD WAR II

It was in this environment that the Middle East embarked upon the post–World War II era. Not only had the region been divided into a multitude of small countries, but each found itself fragmented by kinship, class, ethnicity, religion, ideology, and levels of modernity. Few had stable governments, and all were struggling to build political institutions that could meet the needs of their people. To make matters worse, the world itself was being divided into U.S. and Soviet power blocs. Countries in revolt against their colonial rulers inclined naturally toward the Soviet Union. Most had little interest in communism, but their immediate concerns were the possibility of an imperialist revival and the desire for rapid economic growth regardless of its short-term costs in freedom or economic sacrifice. In contrast, regimes that still clung to tradition inclined toward the United States and looked to the former colonial powers for protection against the revolutionaries. So it was not long before the region was divided into competing blocs: a progressive, socialist bloc headed by Egypt and Syria, and a pro-American conservative bloc centering on Saudi Arabia, Iran, Iraq, and Jordan. Iraq would fall from the ranks of the conservatives in 1958, igniting Western fears that the region's massive oil resources would soon fall into the hands of the Soviets. Washington spared no efforts to stem the "Red Menace."

The tortured history of the Middle East during the post–World War II era reflects this lethal blend of domestic fragmentation, institutional weakness, and international manipulation. In many instances, events happened with such rapidity that it is difficult to establish clear lines of cause and effect. Everything seemed to be happening at once. In other cases, events moved slowly, only to explode into cataclysmic events such as the June War of 1967, the stunning 1979 victory of the Islamic Revolution in Iran, or the Palestinian uprising of 2000.

The events of the post–World War II era fall into several historical periods, each with its own characteristics, constraints, and opportunities. The years between the end of World War II and the defeat of the Arab forces in June 1967 are referred to as the *era of revolution and optimism*. During this period the countries of the region shook off the remaining vestiges of colonialism and became fully independent. It was also a period of profound optimism in the Arab world as a new generation of modernizing leaders led by Gamal Abdel Nasser struggled to unite the Arab world under the banners of nationalism, socialism, and modernity. Industrialization and education were pursued with a vengeance, and the people of the region increasingly migrated from the rural areas to massive urban conglomerates such as Cairo and Baghdad. In addition to accelerating the process of social change, the populist revolutions added yet another layer of complexity to the political mosaic of the Middle East. Further complicating this complexity was the birth of Israel in 1948 and the still ongoing struggle to forge a lasting peace between the Jewish state and its regional neighbors.

Israel's crushing defeat of the Arab armies in the June War of 1967 shattered Nasser's vision of socialist modernity and led to an *era of disillusionment and reassessment*. The June War was far more than just another scrimmage between the Arabs and the Israelis. It reshaped the politics of a region. From a geopolitical perspective, Israel now controlled all of Palestine, including the more than one million Palestinians living in the Gaza Strip and the West Bank. From a psychological perspective, the June War humiliated the Arabs and created an atmosphere of profound self-doubt. This can only be understood in the context of the equally profound optimism that had preceded the war and the very real belief that more than two decades of military and industrial modernization had leveled the playing field between Israel and the Arabs.

The defeat also shattered faith in the secular promises of Arab nationalism. Prosperity would come, Nasser had promised, when Israel had been defeated and a unified Arab nation had claimed its rightful place in the world community. It was the Arabs, however, who had been defeated, and the Arab world, which had waited in vain for Arab nationalism to lift it from poverty, was now overwhelmed by an abiding sense of despair. By destroying faith in secular nationalism, moreover, the June War created a psychological vacuum. Faith and hope are essential elements of the human experience, and many people in the Arab world now sought salvation by returning to Islam, particularly the idealized vision of Islam preached by the Muslim Brotherhood. Yet another layer of complexity was added to the Middle Eastern equation.

By 1979, Islamic fundamentalism had emerged as the dominant political force in most areas of the Middle East, launching what we refer to as the *era of Islamic resurgence*. This period began with the Islamic victory in Iran, which was soon threatening to spawn Islamic revolutions in many countries that had formerly championed secularism, including Egypt and Algeria. The fundamentalists also turned on the tribal monarchies of the Gulf, accusing them of hypocrisy, immorality, and subservience to the United States, a topic discussed at length in Chapter 5. The peace treaty signed between Egypt and Israel in 1979 also contributed to the restructuring of politics in the Middle East and ended the myth of Arab solidarity.

By 1990, the world had again changed. The collapse of the Soviet Union in that year ushered in an era of American dominance that President George H. W. Bush would proclaim the *era of the new world order*. The new world would be one of peace and harmony in which the peace dividend, the monies saved from the end of the arms race, would be used to promote development, democracy, and stability. The Middle East would now have to adjust to U.S. control of the world's economic and political systems, its staunch support of Israel, its advocacy of capitalism, and its unbridled hostility to Iran and the threat of an Islamic revolution (do Ceu Pinto 1999; Tibi 1997).

Alas, it was not to be. No sooner had the era of the new world order begun than Saddam Hussein, the Iraqi dictator, challenged U.S. might by invading Kuwait. While the details of this venture must await Chapter 6, suffice it to say here that Iraq's much-vaunted army was crushed in approximately 100 hours. U.S. forces were within striking distance of Baghdad, but allowed Saddam Hussein to remain in power. Plans had been drawn for the occupation of Iraq, but cooler heads prevailed. Pandora's box would remain unopened for another decade. As it was, the U.S. presence in the Gulf had been strengthened. Iran was put on notice that it could be next, and Saddam Hussein's power was shackled by crippling sanctions and U.S.-imposed no-fly zones that covered the northern and southern regions of the country. The war was over, but U.S. planes would patrol Iraq for another decade. The no-fly zones proved costly, cumbersome, and bloody. The harsh economic sanctions punished the poor, but did little to cripple the power of Saddam Hussein. U.S. intelligence reports, now proven false, indicated that he was on the verge of developing weapons of mass destruction. The United States was vilified in the Islamic world for killing innocent Muslims.

The Islamic resurgence was also undergoing a transformation. Iran, its driving force, had been weakened by a long and deadly war with Iraq that spanned most of the 1980s. Iranian zeal was also sapped by the passing in 1989 of the Ayatollah Khomeini, the patron saint of the Islamic resurgence. This did not bring an end to the resurgence or to Iran's involvement in it. Rather, its center of gravity shifted to a loose and deadly network of Sunni jihadists forged by Hassan Turabi, the gifted Sudanese religious leader.

Turabi, the dominant Sunni religious intellectual of the era, dreamed of an unified Islamic movement that embraced Muslims in all of their diverse views, Sunni and Shi'a, moderates and radicals. Only a unified Islamic movement, Turabi argued, could drive the United States from the Middle East (al-Turabi 1997). Iran and Osama bin Laden were the two main pillars of Turabi's network. Bin Laden was viewed in Saudi Arabia and much of the Sunni world as the "hero of Afghanistan," a title he earned in the 1980s jihad against the Soviet occupation of Afghanistan. Bin Laden was credited with organizing the "Afghan Arabs," a broad group that included all Muslim volunteers fighting against the Soviets. He had also played a key role in channeling Saudi and Gulf money to the Taliban. The United States had supported bin Laden's anti-Soviet jihad via the Pakistani government intelligence service, ISI (Gunaratna 2002). This seemed logical at the time, for U.S. intelligence agencies had long supported Islamic fundamentalism as a means of blocking Soviet penetration into the region. Turabi needed bin Laden's organizational skills. He also needed Saudi money and bin Laden's ability to mobilize the Afghan Arabs, many of whom had returned to their native countries to foment revolution. Others constituted a free-floating pool of jihadist fighters anxious for the next war against the infidels. Iran provided Turabi with financing, revolutionary technology, and access to Iran's Hezbollah network. In return, Iran's religious revolutionaries gained access to the Sunni world. It also seems that Iran had planned to use Sudan as a hub for its revolutionary activities in the Arab east. An extensive network of roads and facilities were constructed, many built by bin Laden's construction company.

Turabi's network evolved between 1991 and 1993 and was immediately linked to a surge of terrorist activity throughout the region. Algeria dissolved into civil war in 1991; its most radical jihadist group, the GIA, was funded by Turabi's network (Boukra 2002). The network provided aid to the feuding warlords in the Somali civil war on the condition that they drive U.S. troops from the country. U.S. casualties were heavy and the United States departed in 1993. Bin Laden was on the ground. Iran remained in the background. Iran's hand was far more visible in Turabi's 1994 assistance to the Muslim forces in the Bosnian civil war. Bin Laden's Afghan Arabs were reportedly integrated into the Bosnian forces while Iran paid the bills and provided weapons. In 1995, the battle shifted to Saudi Arabia when jihadists attacked the Saudi National Guard barracks in Riyadh. Five Americans were killed, scores wounded. A few months later, the target was the Khobar Towers, a U.S. Marine facility in the Saudi city of Dhahran. Some 241 Americans were killed. The first attack was attributed to bin Laden; the second to a local group calling itself the Saudi Hezbollah. This seemed to suggest Iranian complicity, but this was conjecture. The bombing of U.S. embassies in Tanzania and Kenya followed in 1998. Iranian support for a Lebanese Hezbollah that was driving Israeli forces from the positions they occupied in southern Lebanon was not a matter of conjecture. Iran did not deny the charges, but did note that the Israeli occupation was a contravention of international law. In its view, Hezbollah was a national resistance organization, not a terrorist organization. The United States disagreed, and Iran made its way to the top of the U.S. list of countries supporting terror. Israel, defeated, withdrew from Lebanon in 2002.

Despite the successes of the Turabi network, Iran and bin Laden remained competing poles in the murky world of global terror. Neither was willing to submit to the dominance of the other. Tensions between the Sunni and Shi'a also loomed large. Turabi was willing to accept the Shi'a as brothers. Most Sunni jihadists were not. Iranian aid was welcome, but not Iranian leadership.

U.S. and Saudi pressure on the Sudanese president led to Turabi's arrest in 1996. Bin Laden was forced from Sudan in the same year and sought refuge in Afghanistan, where he was welcomed by the Taliban leadership. The Taliban were a group of fanatical religious students who had managed to seize power over most of Afghanistan in the chaotic years following the defeat of the Soviets (Rashid 2000).[2] Their views had much in common with the Wahhabi doctrine of Saudi Arabia. Women were veiled and denied education, and all traces of Westernization were obliterated. These included music and football. Even ancient Buddhist statues hewn on mountain cliffs were destroyed on the grounds that they were an affront to Islam. The Taliban did not control areas of Afghanistan that bordered Iran and were predominantly Shi'a. Iran intended to see that they stayed that way.

The relationship between bin Laden and Iran deteriorated. Bin Laden fought with the Taliban; Iran fought against them. The picture repeated itself in Pakistan. Pakistani groups—including ISI, the government intelligence service—supported bin Laden and the Taliban; Iran was fueling religious strife in Pakistan by funding Shi'a extremist groups. Iran was also plotting a Shi'a uprising against Saddam Hussein in Iraq, albeit without noticeable success. Saddam Hussein had attempted to forge an anti-American alliance with bin Laden, but was apparently rebuffed.

## ERA OF GLOBAL TERROR

The September 11 attacks were blamed on bin Laden and his al-Qaeda network, but al-Qaeda is but one of a multitude of jihadist groups that have vowed revenge on the United States and its allies for their domination of the Islamic world and their support for Israel. Their numbers continue to grow. All aspire toward the establishment of Islamic rule in the Middle East and throughout the Islamic world.

Terror, of course, was not new. Nor was it primarily Muslim. Numerous terrorist groups—the IRA, ETA, the Tamil Tigers, drug gangs, skinheads, the Red Guards, the Weathermen, and the contras, to mention but a few of the more prominent—had all been part of the political scene during the four-plus decades of the Cold War. Most, however, were localized groups with specific goals. The IRA, ETA, and the Tamil Tigers were movements of national liberation. The skinheads harked back to the Nazi era, but had little in the way of a coherent organization. The Weathermen and similar groups parroted leftist slogans, but collapsed for a lack of popular support. The drug lords were businessmen. They used violence to protect their turf, but had little interest in destroying the United States. It was, after all, their major market.

---

2 They belonged to the Deobandi school of Sunni Islam, whose primary base is Pakistan.

The terror heralded by September 11 was different. It was not the work of local groups but of a massive international jihadist network pieced together by bin Laden and associated groups during the Afghan war against the Soviets. By the advent of the new millennium, bin Laden's al-Qaeda network had established branches in at least sixty countries. It was well armed and technically sophisticated, and it had forged a financial network so complex that it continues to defy global efforts to stem the flow of money to jihadist groups. The al-Qaeda network also enjoyed significant support throughout the Islamic world and was supported directly or inadvertently by a number of governments and charitable organizations. These and other themes are discussed in the chapters that follow. They are also addressed at length in *At the Heart of Terror* (Palmer and Palmer 2004).

President George W. Bush proclaimed a war on terror. A flurry of UN resolutions condemned the attacks on the United States, and the world community pledged to fight the new terror with all the resources at its disposal. They had little choice. If the United States could be attacked with impunity, no country in the world was safe from the jihadists and their venom.

But how to prosecute the war? It was a new kind of war that pitted sophisticated military power against religious fervor. There were no massed armies, tank formations, or clearly demarcated fronts. The United States possessed the power to obliterate whole countries, but to what avail? The enemy struck from within and was indistinguishable from the overwhelming majority of the world's 1.2 billion Muslims who believed that terror was abhorrent to the teachings of Islam. They were also its primary victims and feared terror more than the Americans. In the fight against terror, the United States needed the assistance of the world's Muslims, not their animosity. To make matters worse, many jihadist groups and their sympathizers were protected from American reprisals by the civil liberties of the Western countries in which they resided. Britain was rapidly becoming their nerve center. France and Germany were not far behind.

Perhaps because of the strange and unfamiliar nature of this new war, the United States and the world's major powers soon found themselves at odds over the best way to defeat this new and most vicious of enemies. The European Union, Japan, and China preferred a strategy narrowly focused on eliminating al-Qaeda and other jihadist groups that threatened the West. This was basically a defensive approach that placed a premium on diplomacy and the coordination of global antiterrorist agencies. The war against terror was to be a collective effort that used force with the greatest of reluctance.

The United States, by contrast, viewed the war against terror as a carte blanche to rid the Islamic world of anti-American elements, Islamic and otherwise. Particularly high on the U.S. wish list was the destruction of rogue countries capable of developing weapons of mass destruction. President Bush proclaimed that the United States would not sit idly by while its enemies plotted their next move. Rather than responding to events, the United States would preempt them.

Most nations of the world embraced the bombing of Afghanistan. It could not have been otherwise. The Taliban, the extreme religious fanatics who ruled Afghanistan, had allied themselves with bin Laden and sheltered his base camps.

It was from Afghanistan that bin Laden managed his network, and it was from Afghanistan that he plotted his attacks on the United States and its allies.

The major divide between the United States and the rest of the world resulted from America's insistence that the war on terror be used as a pretext for toppling Saddam Hussein, the president of Iraq. The United States accused the Iraqi dictator of supporting terrorism and building weapons of mass destruction. Unspoken was the U.S. desire to reshape the Middle East in a manner that would stabilize the world's oil supply, humble hostile regimes in Iran and Syria, and strengthen the security of U.S. allies in the region. Foremost among the latter were Saudi Arabia and Israel. Democracy was added to the mix as an afterthought. Of the major powers, only Britain supported the American plan. When the invasion of Iraq was blocked in the United Nations, the United States and Britain ignored the UN and went it alone.

## How America's War on Terror Has Transformed Politics in the Middle East: Action and Reaction

American plans to eliminate terror by restructuring the Middle East were shaped by a dangerous blend of urgency, anger, crusader zeal, naïveté, flawed intelligence, and a profound misunderstanding of the region. Afghanistan was bombed; Iraq occupied, embargos imposed, governments intimidated, financial and religious institutions scrutinized, and suspects incarcerated. It was understood that mistakes would be made, but such was the price of war. Things would be sorted out with time.

First and foremost, the U.S.-led attacks on Afghanistan and Iraq placed the leaders of the Islamic world on notice that they faced preemptive strikes if they threatened U.S. or Israeli interests in the region. In a vague set of pronouncements termed the *Bush Doctrine,* the United States announced that it would strike its adversaries before they had a chance to strike the United States. What constituted a clear and present danger to U.S. interests? The United States has been making up the rules as it goes along, but Iran and Syria are high on the list of potential targets.

Simultaneously, friendly countries were placed under intense pressure to attack what the United States considered to be the causes and purveyors of Islamic extremism. Among other things, the United States demanded that Muslim governments alter the Islamic content of their education systems, bring private mosques under government control, impose strict accounting rules on Islamic charities and Islamic banks, and keep moderate extremist groups—those willing to pursue the goal of an Islamic state by peaceful means—under tight rein. Countries that drag their feet have found that their relations with the United States grow chilly, at best. The United States even turned on the Saudi monarchy, its longtime ally and guardian of the two holiest sites in Islam and 25 percent of the world's oil. Again, the U.S. is making up the rules as it goes along. Britain and other allies kibitz from the sidelines.

The United States has also dramatically increased its on-the-ground presence in the region. U.S. forces occupy Iraq, patrol Afghanistan, are firmly ensconced in the Gulf region, and have extended their position in the Horn of Africa. The United States also conducts joint military maneuvers and joint antiterrorist operations with a broad range of countries including Egypt, Israel, and Turkey. A legion of U.S. advisers has been dispatched to "upgrade" security services throughout the Islamic world. A few countries have allowed the United States free rein to pursue suspected terrorists on their territory.

In the current political climate, few decisions of import in the Middle East and broader Islamic world are made without adjustments for the war on terror. The United States may not be loved, but it is feared—all the more so because of the gunslinger image of the Bush administration in the world's media. No one is quite sure when the United States will strike next.

Does this means that the United States has been successful in achieving its goals of stamping out terror, eliminating weapons of mass destruction, guaranteeing a stable oil supply and generally reshaping the Middle East to make it more compatible with U.S. and Israeli interests?

Not at all. The war on terror has become, at best, a stalemate. Bin Laden remains at large, as do his al-Qaeda network and its various offshoots and clones. U.S. efforts to transform Islamic educational, charitable, and financial institutions have produced meager results. Both money and recruits continue to flow to the terrorists, and the Muslim world is firmly convinced that the United States has declared war on Islam. Muslim cooperation in the war on terror has decreased steadily. The jihadists may have found it more difficult to attack the United States, but they have found plenty of targets in Europe and the Middle East, including American technicians in Saudi Arabia and American troops in Iraq.

The picture is much the same on the broader Middle Eastern front. Afghanistan is reverting to a haven for jihadists, Iran continues to pursue a nuclear weapons program, and Israel and Saudi Arabia are less secure than ever.

The war in Iraq has been a particularly dismal experience. As originally conceived, the war was to be the centerpiece of U.S. efforts to reshape the Middle East. Saddam Hussein's support of terrorism would be terminated, his massive army disbanded, and his weapons of mass destruction destroyed. Israel, Kuwait, and Saudi Arabia would breathe easier. A grateful Iraqi population would welcome the United States as a liberator and Iraq would become a solid U.S. ally in the region. U.S. bases in Iraq would serve as a staging ground for attacks on Syria and Iran, the two remaining obstacles to U.S. control of the region. The United States would use its influence with its new Iraqi ally to lower oil prices by disrupting the OPEC oil cartel. Plans were even made to export Iraqi oil via Israel.

Alas, no terrorists and no weapons of mass destruction, no hero's welcome, no staging ground for attacks on Syria and Iran, no disruption of OPEC, no pipeline to Israel. Liberation gave way to occupation and the death and maiming of thousands of U.S. military personnel. Oil prices skyrocketed; the occupation of Iraq inflamed jihadist groups in Saudi Arabia, Kuwait, and Jordan; and the U.S.-engineered election increased Iranian influence in the governing of Iraq. How could such a wonderful plan have gone so wrong? See Chapter 6.

**What Comes Next?**   Each stage in the evolution of Middle Eastern politics was ushered in by a cataclysmic event that shook the region, and sometimes the world at large as well. The era of revolution and optimism was ushered in by the Second World War; the era of disillusion and reassessment by the Arab collapse in the June War of 1967; the era of Islamic resurgence by the victory of the Ayatollah Khomeini in Iran; the era of the new world order by the collapse of the USSR; and the era of international terror by the September 11, 2001, attacks on the United States.

And yet, each of these major transitions was preceded by a changing dynamic within the region itself. Nationalist movements had surged in the Middle East long before they erupted in the rebellions that launched the era of revolution and optimism. World War II was merely the catalyst. The era of disillusion and reassessment was similarly preceded by decades of Arab ineptitude, confusion, and disunity. The collapse of the Arab armies in the June War of 1967 was merely the coup de grace. The era of Islamic resurgence crowned a decade of escalating religious fervor that should have been visible to all. The same is true of the collapse of the Soviet Union that gave way to the era of the new world order. In retrospect, it is now clear that the Soviet Union had begun to collapse long before it splintered into some fifteen independent countries in 1990. This is equally true of the collapse of the new world order. In retrospect, the September 11 attacks on the United States should have been predictable. A jihadist attack on the World Trade Center had occurred in 1993; it was followed by attacks on U.S. military facilities in Saudi Arabia in 1995 and 1996 and attacks on the U.S. embassies in Kenya and Tanzania in 1998. The United States chose to interpret them as unique and isolated events. The result was the carnage and dismay that accompanied September 11.

And thus it is with the present. Signs of change are everywhere. The era of terror is too unstable to persist for an extended period. We might begin by recalling that tension between Islam and the West has historically increased in proportion to the Western presence in Islamic lands. History doesn't always repeat itself, but American attempts to reshape the Middle East have raised the U.S. presence in the region to unprecedented levels. Anti-Americanism has surged accordingly. Anti-Americanism does not necessarily lead to violence or support for terror, but it is a factor.

The underlying causes of violence abound in the region. These include feelings of frustration, fear, anxiety, and hopelessness as well as economic inequalities, unfulfilled expectations, and the agony that accompanies rapid social change. The majority of the people in the Middle East desperately want solutions to their problems. Added to this volatile mix are the religious and ethnic tensions that permeate the region and that we currently see being played out in Iraq.

Little is being done to address these violence-fueling fears and frustrations. The governments of the region are corrupt, incompetent, self-serving, and oppressive. Israel treats its Jewish citizens with care, but not the Palestinians. Global aid-granting agencies have also failed to address the situation. The vast majority of U.S. aid to the Middle East goes to Israel, a developed country, and Egypt, a key U.S. ally. Most of that assistance, moreover, is military aid designed to promote U.S. interests in the region. Simultaneously, the United States has attempted to suppress UN reports documenting that things are really as bad as they are (United Nations Development Programme 2005). Other aid-granting agencies aren't doing much better. Most bicker among themselves and use aid monies as a subsidy to facilitate their exports.

Particularly worrisome is the weakness of democracy in the region. Democracy, whatever its faults, provides the people of a country with the means of adjusting "who gets what, when and how" before passions erupt in violence. What passes for democracy in the Middle East is largely a farce. Elections are rigged, opponents intimidated, and unfavorable results canceled. The winners cling to power for dear life (literally and figuratively) and the losers plot their revenge. Frustration and violence increase apace. These and other problems of Middle Eastern democracy are discussed throughout the chapters that follow.

The inability of the United States and its allies to address the causes of terror and violence is all the more disturbing because of the growing availability of weapons of mass destruction. Iraq did not have nuclear weapons, but Israel and Pakistan do. Iran is rapidly developing the capacity to produce nuclear weapons, and it possesses rockets capable of striking Israel. Whether its nuclear program has evil intent is a matter of debate. Israel and the United States say yes. Russia and Iran say no. Europe is unsure. Egypt is rumored to be developing both rockets and nuclear weapons, and Russia has reportedly agreed to sell Syria "sophisticated weapons." In both cases, the details remain sketchy. Israel has threatened to launch a preemptive strike against Iran's nuclear facilities. The Iranians worry that the United States is encouraging Israel to do so. Whether or not this is the case, the United States admits that U.S. personnel are active in Iran.

Terrorist groups, for their part, have become sophisticated international organizations capable of purchasing and deploying weapons of mass destruction, including small-scale nuclear weapons. A black market for such weapons does exist, much of it fueled by the massive supply of nuclear material that vanished with the breakup of the Soviet Union. Pakistan and North Korea have also added to the supply. Al-Qaeda and its spinoffs have attempted to acquire nuclear weapons. There is a high probability that they will eventually do so.

Unfortunately, the nations of the world are in disarray over how to deal with the growing threat of violence. Mechanisms have been established for the sharing of data on terrorist-related matters, but cooperation has been hampered by bureaucratic red tape and national jealousies. The United States and the European Union disagree on what to do about Iran's nuclear program just as they disagreed about what to do with Saddam Hussein. They also disagree over the threat posed by the Muslim Brotherhood, Hezbollah, and Hamas. All are large Muslim organizations that advocate Islamic rule. All have been active in fighting Israel's occupation of the areas that it conquered in the June War of 1967. All also oppose the U.S. presence in the Middle East, including its occupation of Iraq. At the same time, all proclaim their willingness to seek their goals by peaceful means. The United States argues that these organizations represent a clear and present danger to world security. The European Union, China, Japan, and Russia disagree. The United Nations wrings its hands because it can do nothing without the cooperation of the major powers. More to the point, it can do nothing without the cooperation of the five countries that possess veto power in the Security Council: the United States, France, Britain, Russia, and China.

The United States lacks a clear plan for the Middle East. U.S. troops pour into Iraq at the same time that the United States and Britain are scurrying to find an exit strategy. President Bush renewed his threats to Iran and Syria in his 2005 State of the Union address. His secretary of state hurriedly informed world leaders that U.S. plans did not include a strike against Iran. The United States calls for democracy in the region, but recants when the leaders of Saudi Arabia and Egypt are offended. The United States crafted a road map for defusing the Israeli–Palestinian conflict, but did nothing when Israel ignored it. The European Union, for its part, is so divided that it cannot agree on a common foreign policy strategy.

American resolve to risk another prolonged war in the Middle East has also been shaken by its disastrous experience in Iraq. Both the Congress and the American public have lost their patience with a failed war that has produced little but casualties, astronomical budget deficits, and a sham democracy that favors the Iranians. The United States may bomb Iran, but no one seriously expects another U.S. effort to occupy a Muslim country. Britain, America's staunchest ally, has been equally humbled by the war in Iraq and is rethinking its uncritical support of U.S. foreign policy.

Added to other precursors of change is a heightened sense of urgency. The major powers are under intense pressure from their citizens and security officials to eliminate the twin scourges of terror and weapons of mass destruction before they lose the capacity to do so. Islamic leaders feel a similar pressure to counter the globalization of Western pop culture before it further erodes the religious and social traditions upon which their power depends. Political leaders in the Middle East are struggling to cope with the inequalities and frustrations resulting from the global transition to capitalism. Unemployment is mounting and the safety nets upon which the poor—the majority of the population—have long depended are being shattered. This may make economic sense in the long run, but in the short term it is increasing instability and violence.

And so it is that the Middle East is careening toward an uncertain future that will have much to do with the future of the United States and the world at large. Hopefully, the chapters that follow will provide a better understanding of the dynamics that drive the political process in the Middle East.

**What Is Terrorism?**   Because the war against terror has become such a pervasive part of life in the Middle East and the West, it may be useful to say a few words about the nature of terror. This is easier said than done, because there is little consensus on the topic. Neither scholars nor politicians have been able to hammer out a common definition of terror. Each country has its own definition of terror and the United States has several. Needless to say, this is a source of some confusion.

Many scholars define terrorism as politically motivated acts of violence committed by an individual or small groups of individuals. This is the definition employed in this book. Terrorist acts include assassination, kidnapping, hijacking, chemical attacks, suicide bombers, and bombs planted in cars, trains, ships, and aircraft, to mention only the most obvious. All are readily employed by small groups of individuals who strike with deadly precision and then fade undetected into the broad mass of society. The U.S. Army refers to such attacks as "low-intensity conflict." Small nuclear devices may soon come online.

The objective of the terrorists is not to occupy all or part of a country, but to terrorize political leaders into complying with their political objectives. Bin Laden's attacks on the United States were intended to force an American withdrawal from the Islamic world. Bin Laden may also have believed that the shock of the attacks would throw the United States into chaos and precipitate a civil war. The September 11 strikes did not achieve these objectives, but the war goes on. Particularly vulnerable are the Middle Eastern oil supplies upon which the economies of the world depend. Saudi Arabia alone possesses some 25 percent of the world's oil supplies and has now become the target of sustained jihadist terrorism.

Other popular definitions of terrorism blend acts of terror committed by individuals and small groups with guerrilla warfare. Guerrilla groups possess armed militias and are intent on seizing all or part of a country. They use terrorist tactics to achieve their objectives, but they also engage government troops in battle. The FARC in Colombia, for example, possesses some 10,000 armed troops; some estimates suggest the number may be as high as 20,000. In many cases, conflicts that begin with terrorism by small groups escalate into full-scale guerrilla wars. This was clearly the pattern followed in Iraq.

Still other definitions of terrorism stress that terror is not solely the preserve of fanatics and independence movements. Terror is also used by governments to achieve their policy objectives. The United States, for example, actively encouraged Muslim terrorists and guerrilla groups to attack Soviet targets in Afghanistan during the 1980s. The Soviet Union was the sworn enemy of the United States and Soviet control of Afghanistan threatened U.S. interests in the Middle East. After the Soviets were driven from Afghanistan, bin Laden and other terrorist groups nurtured by the United States turned upon their former patron. Russia uses terror to combat separatist groups in the breakaway province of Chechnya, and Israel uses terror to counter terrorist attacks by Palestinians demanding an end to Israeli occupation of the occupied territories. Authoritarian governments in Latin America have been renowned for using death squads to eliminate domestic opponents. Terrorist tactics employed by governments are referred to as "state terrorism." Most governments of the world resort to state terrorism in one guise or another, although they are reluctant to admit it.

## AN ORGANIZATIONAL NOTE

In the chapters that follow, we will examine the political process in those countries and quasi-countries most likely to shape the future of the Middle East during the coming decade. The discussion in each chapter is organized according to the historical periods reviewed above, with the greatest emphasis placed on the present day. As we shall see, Middle Eastern politics is the product of a wide variety of factors. The elites of the Middle East attempt to orchestrate who gets what, when and how, but often their best-laid plans go for naught because of the weakness of their political institutions. Middle Eastern leaders tend to be strong, but their political institutions are not. Elites and institutions, in turn, are constrained by the attitudes and behaviors of their citizens. Finally, the behavior of both states and elites is profoundly influenced by the regional and international environment. Most Western scholars stress domestic factors such as elites and groups in their analysis of Middle Eastern politics. Scholars from the Arabic and Islamic worlds, by contrast, attribute most of what happens in the region to the machinations of the major powers and particularly the United States. In their view, it is the major powers that determine who gets what, when and how. Both perspectives are vital to an understanding of how the people of the Middle East do politics; each adds important insights into what has become a very complex puzzle.

# 2

# Egypt

## The Tortuous Road to Democracy

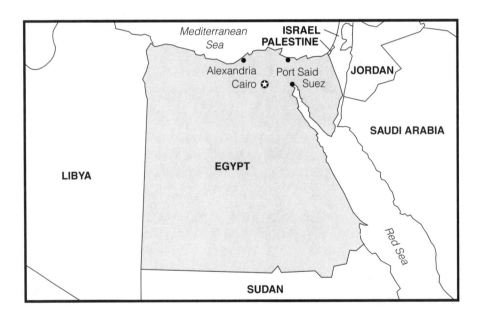

Egypt is the core state of the Arab world. Egypt possesses the Arab world's largest population, its dominant army, its most vibrant mass media, and its strongest industrial base. Egypt is also host to the Arab League, a regional organization designed to increase political, military, and economic cooperation among the Arab states. No other Arab state approaches Egypt's regional and international influence.

This dominant position is summed up by the Arabic expression *"umm al-Arab"*—mother of the Arabs. Little happens in Egypt that does not have a direct impact on its neighboring countries. During the 1950s and 1960s, Egypt was the focal point of an Arab resurgence that ignited anti-Western revolutions in Lebanon, Jordan, Iraq, Syria, Yemen, and Libya. Not all were successful, but the tide of Arab nationalism appeared irresistible. American interests in Saudi Arabia and other oil-producing states were placed in jeopardy, as was the security of Israel, a state that most Arabs believed to be a creation of Western imperialism.

Politics in the Middle East, however, are subject to abrupt and startling changes. The 1980s and 1990s found Egypt championing regional cooperation. Peace was made with Israel, and Egypt became the ally of the United States. Egyptian cooperation remains vital to maintaining order in the most volatile region in the world.

Understandably, the United States and its Western allies are struggling to ensure that Egypt remains a bastion of moderation and regional cooperation. Toward this end, the U.S. provides Egypt with some $2 billion in foreign assistance each year. The World Bank, the International Monetary Fund, and various other donors also provide Egypt with foreign aid. All in all, Egypt receives more foreign assistance than any other country of the Third World. In return for their aid, the United States and other international donors have pressured Egypt to increase the pace of its transition from a socialist dictatorship into a capitalist democracy. A democratic and capitalist Egypt, in their view, is essential to the stability of the Middle Eastern region (World Bank 1992).

Progress toward democracy and political moderation, unfortunately, is being undermined by Egypt's grinding poverty, by a widening gap between rich and poor, and by a population that grows more rapidly than the country's fragile economy can support. The Egyptian population is losing patience with its government, and not without cause. The most prominent characteristics of that government are stagnation, corruption, and ineptitude.

In this chapter, we will trace Egypt's tortuous path toward democracy and capitalism. Whether Egypt succeeds in these endeavors will have a great effect on the future of democracy and stability in the region.

## HISTORY AND CULTURE

The glories of pharaonic Egypt require little recounting. Egypt was the cradle of Western civilization; its pyramids and monuments stand in testimony to a people of dazzling creativity. The pharaonic period, however, came to an end several thousand years ago as Egypt succumbed to a seemingly endless succession of foreign invaders, including the Babylonians, Persians, Greeks, Romans, Arabs, Crusaders, Turks, French, and British. Indeed, Egypt did not reclaim full control of its own destiny until 1952. Modern Egyptians remain intensely proud of their pharaonic heritage. Egyptians are Arabs in language and culture, but they are also profoundly aware of their uniqueness as Egyptians.

Of the long procession of foreign invasions, none had a more lasting influence on Egyptian society than the Arab invasions of the seventh century. Fired by the zeal of the new Islamic religion, tribal armies from the Arabian Peninsula imposed their language, culture, and religion on a vast territory that ranged from

Spain in the west to India in the east. Arabic became the language of Egypt, and Islam the religion of more than 90 percent of its population. Of the non-Muslims, most were Coptic Christians (Carter 1986). The Coptic Church centered on the Patriarchate of Alexandria, one of the four major centers of early Christianity, the others being Rome, Constantinople, and Antioch. Egypt also possessed a substantial Jewish minority.

By the tenth century, Egypt had become the political center of the Islamic world, a position that it maintained for some two hundred years. The splendors of Cairo dazzled visitors of this era.

> There was a throne in one of them that took up the entire width of the room. Three of its sides were made of gold on which were hunting scenes depicting riders racing their horses and other subjects; there were also inscriptions written in beautiful characters. . . . A balustrade of golden latticework surrounded the throne, whose beauty defies all description. Behind the throne were steps of silver. I saw a tree that looked like an orange tree, whose branches, leaves, and fruits were made of sugar (Khusraw in Behrens-Abouseif 1990, 7).

It was during this era that the Al-Azhar mosque, the world's oldest and most famous center of Islamic learning, was established. Al-Azhar is both a mosque and a university, and its sheikh (rector) is one of the most influential political figures in modem Egypt.

The history of modern Egypt begins with the reign of Mohammed Ali, an Albanian adventurer sent to Egypt as part of a joint Turco–British military operation designed to end the French occupation of Egypt. Napoleon had invaded Egypt in 1798, hoping to add the North African state, an Ottoman possession, to the French empire. Ever fearful of French power, the British joined with the Turks to frustrate the venture. The French were evicted, and Mohammed Ali surfaced as the head of an Egyptian government nominally loyal to the Ottoman sultan. Mohammed Ali, however, felt little loyalty to the sultan or to any other power (Marsot 1984; Fahmy 1997). His dreams were of empire, with Egypt as its base. Egyptian fellahin (peasants), welded into the strongest army in the Middle East, soon conquered much of the territory that now constitutes Sudan, Israel, Jordan, and Saudi Arabia (Cuno 1992; Dodwell 1931; Goldschmidt 1988). On two occasions, they threatened to conquer Turkey itself, but both efforts were stymied by the British army (Lawson 1992). Turkey had become a pawn in Britain's efforts to establish a balance of power in Eastern Europe, and the British would not allow those efforts to be upset by an Albanian adventurer (Marriott 1956). Mohammed Ali was forced to abandon his dreams of empire but was recognized by the British as the hereditary monarch of Egypt. Egypt's royal family was born.

By and large, the political and economic structure of Egypt during this period was remarkably similar to the feudal system of medieval Europe. An aristocracy of large landowners provided financial support to the monarchy in exchange for the right to rule their fiefdoms as they saw fit. How they achieved these objectives was of little concern to the royal family (Lane 1954; Toledano 1990).

The profligate lifestyle of the royal family exhausted Egypt's meager financial resources and led to increasingly desperate efforts to extract ever more revenue from Egypt's fellahin. Alas, the fellahin had nothing more to give. (Cole 1993). The construction of the Suez Canal in 1869 provided the Egyptian government with royalties from canal traffic, but even this new source of revenue could not satisfy the appetites of the monarch. Short of cash, the khedive (king) sold Egypt's 40 percent share in the Suez Canal to British and French investors. Now they, supported by other private investors, owned the Suez Canal (Longgood 1957).

Once the canal funds had been squandered, the heirs of Mohammed Ali turned to deficit financing. Egypt had little in the way of new resources, so it was only a matter of time until it defaulted on its loans. Britain and France responded by seizing the Egyptian customhouses. Henceforth, customs revenues, Egypt's most reliable form of taxation, would reach the khedive only after Egypt's creditors had been paid (Henry 1996). The seizing of the customhouses sparked a brief rebellion in 1881, with the rebellion's leader, Ahmed Urabi, proclaiming: "By the name of Allah, beside whom there is no God, we shall no longer be inheritable and from this day on we shall not be enslaved" (Scholch 1981). The Urabi revolution led to the British occupation of Egypt, but it also marked the first outpouring of Egyptian nationalism. It would not be the last (Meyer 1988).

Egypt, however, did not become a British colony (Berque 1967). Rather, a protectorate was established in which the heirs of Mohammed Ali ruled with the active guidance of the British high commissioner. This arrangement provided Britain with a strong military presence in Egypt that would continue in one form or another until after the Second World War.

The British protectorate was unpopular from its inception. The palace chafed under the fiscal rules imposed by the British high commissioner, and much of Egypt's predominantly Muslim population was offended by the British disregard for Islamic culture. Westernized Egyptians, in particular, smarted from racist policies that excluded them from British-owned hotels and restaurants (Goldschmidt 1988). They were also deeply offended by the "capitulations," a legal system that allowed foreigners to be tried in special consular courts staffed by non-Egyptians (Berque 1967). Prosperous Egyptians exempted themselves from the vagaries of Egyptian law by purchasing a foreign passport, as did members of Egypt's large Greek and Jewish communities, the dominant forces in Egyptian commerce (Beinin 1998). Egyptians had become second-class citizens in their own country.

By the early 1920s, hostility to British occupation was finding expression in two political movements. The first was the Wafd Party, a broad coalition of nationalist groups dedicated to liberating Egypt from British rule (Berque 1967, 284). The second was the Muslim Brotherhood, a secret religious organization dedicated to the creation of an Islamic state in Egypt (Husaini 1956). There was considerable overlap between the two movements, as the Muslim Brotherhood was also fanatically opposed to the British presence in Egypt.

The British granted Egypt quasi-independent status in 1922 but retained the right to station troops on Egyptian soil. Egyptian politics throughout the interwar period was a three-way struggle between the British Embassy, the king, and the Wafd (Gershoni and Jankowski 1995; Youssef 1983). King Fu'ad, the monarch of the era, had little love for either democracy or the British. He was deposed by the British shortly before World War II for his pro-German leanings. Fu'ad was succeeded in office by his son, Farouk, a particularly corrupt and inept leader who shared the despotic inclinations of his father (Al-Fatah 1990). During the war Egypt was transformed into a staging ground for British forces in the Middle East.

The end of the war ushered in a period of profound political instability. The British sought to remain a key force in Egyptian politics while the king, more corrupt than ever, struggled to rule as an absolute monarch. The Wafd continued to press for greater democracy, but the party had lost much of its nationalist zeal and become the party of the wealthy (Berque 1967). The influence of the Muslim Brotherhood had been weakened by the assassination of its founder.

The turmoil of Egyptian politics was paralleled by growing violence between Jews and Arabs in the British mandate of Palestine, Egypt's neighbor to the northeast. Britain withdrew from Palestine in 1947, and the United Nations partitioned the area into Arab and Jewish sections as a prelude to establishing separate Jewish and Arab countries. War between the Palestinian Arabs and the Jews erupted immediately upon the British withdrawal, with most Arab states, including Egypt, entering the war on the side of the Palestinians.

King Farouk sent his army to Palestine in the misguided belief that the Jews couldn't fight. Once victory was achieved, he assumed, Jerusalem would be ruled from Cairo (Youssef 1983). Poorly led and poorly armed, the Egyptian forces succeeded in liberating only the Gaza Strip, a sparse coastal area adjacent to the Egyptian border.

Smarting from their defeat at the hands of the Jews and frustrated by the ineptness of their political leaders, a small group of junior army officers headed by Gamal Abdel Nasser formed the Free Officers, a secret military organization dedicated to the modernization of Egyptian society (Baker 1978). Most of the Free Officers were from lower-middle class backgrounds and had been profoundly influenced by the rhetoric of the Wafd and the Muslim Brotherhood. In general, their ideology was a blend of populism and nationalism. Egypt, according to the slogans of the young revolutionaries, was to be liberated from the British. It was also to be liberated from its parasitic aristocracy, and from the exploitative class of Greeks and Jews that dominated the Egyptian economy. The Free Officers were also motivated by a desire to avenge the humiliations of Egypt's colonial past. Servility to foreigners could no longer be tolerated.

Arab defeat in the Arab–Israeli war of 1948 had also undermined whatever domestic support the king may have enjoyed. Rioters swept through Cairo in January 1952, torching many of the "foreign-only" hotels and clubs that were so offensive to nationalists. The king made little effort to quell the turmoil. Approximately six months later, on July 22, 1952, the Free Officers ousted Farouk in a bloodless coup. The king sailed for Italy on his royal yacht while Nasser and the Free Officers set about the task of ruling Egypt.

This task would not be an easy one. The Egyptian population was mired in poverty and disease and was growing at an alarming rate that outpaced Egypt's meager resources. More people meant more starvation. Land remained concentrated in the hands of a small aristocracy hostile to the revolution, and British troops were stationed throughout Egyptian territory. Fears of a Western counter-coup were pervasive: it seemed unlikely that the Western powers would accept a challenge to their dominance of the region. Centuries of foreign domination and misgovernment, moreover, had created a chasm of distrust between the government and the people. Recoiling from oppressive rulers, Egyptians sought security within their families rather than from the state. For the Coptic minority, security was also found in religious solidarity. Egyptians, accordingly, were slow to develop the sense of political community or civic culture that had played such a crucial role in the political development of the West. Rather, Egypt became a society of families and clans, each competing with the others for scarce resources. Egyptians distrusted the government and they distrusted each other. As Nasser described this painful situation shortly after the Free Officers seized power in 1952:

> Every leader we came to wanted to assassinate his rival. Every idea we found aimed at the destruction of another. If we were to carry out all that we heard, then there would not be one leader left alive. Not one idea would remain intact. We would cease to have a mission save to remain among the smashed bodies and the broken debris lamenting our misfortune and reproaching our ill-fate. . . . If I were asked then what I required most my instant answer would be, "To hear but one Egyptian uttering one word of justice about another, to see but one Egyptian not devoting his time to criticize willfully the ideas of another, to feel that there was but one Egyptian ready to open his heart for forgiveness, indulgence and loving his brother Egyptian" (Nasser 1955).

## The Era of Revolution and Optimism

The revolution of 1952 ushered in a new era of optimism. The quasi-parliamentary institutions that had evolved under the monarchy were abolished and replaced by the Revolutionary Command Council (RCC), which was composed of Nasser and his most trusted associates among the Free Officers (El-Din 1992; Gordon 1992). Abolished, too, were the Wafd and other political parties. Efforts had been made to work with the Wafd and other political groups in order to place Egypt on the path to democracy, but to no avail. The military demanded unity and sacrifice while Egypt's civilian politicians sought little more than a continuation of the corrupt and divisive policies of the old regime. Egypt needed sacrifice and discipline, not chaos (Dekmejian 1975). Following a 1954 attempt to assassinate Nasser, the Muslim Brotherhood was also driven underground and remained dormant throughout much of the Nasser era.

Changes in the economic and social arena were equally dramatic (Beattie 1994; Wahba 1994). Egypt's largest farms were expropriated by the government and their lands redistributed among the peasants. This redistribution deprived the landed aristocracy of much of their power and provided the regime with a Robin Hood image among the poor. Schools and health clinics mushroomed as the government sought to eliminate the scourges of illiteracy and poverty. Graduates of the new schools and universities were guaranteed jobs with the government.

At first, Nasser and the Free Officers remained mostly in the background, allowing formal power to be exercised by General Neguib, a respected military leader of moderate political views. The appointment of a figurehead president was meant to reassure both the West and Egypt's established elite that the new regime did not pose a threat to their interests. Nasser and the Free Officers, moreover, needed time to figure out how best to modernize Egypt and its population. None of Egypt's new leaders possessed broad experience in government or economics. They would have to learn by trial and error (El-Gamassy 1993; Ginat 1997).

General Neguib chafed under the figurehead role assigned to him and challenged Nasser for leadership of the revolution (Neguib 1955). He was removed from office in 1954, some two years after the July revolution, and Nasser ascended to the presidency (Woodward 1992).

The Nasser who replaced General Neguib possessed a far clearer picture of Egypt and its future than had the young officer who deposed the hapless Farouk almost two years earlier. Nasser believed that Egypt's future prosperity would be secured through a program of rapid industrialization that would bring the country and its population up to par with the nations of the West. The West was invited to cooperate in Egypt's modernization, but only if they treated Egypt as a sovereign and independent nation. Foreign troops would no longer be welcome on Egyptian soil. Nasser was ambivalent toward Israel. He had little love for the Jewish state but placed the economic development of Egypt above foreign policy concerns. Israel could exist as long as it did not threaten Egypt's security.

The centerpiece of Nasser's modernization plan was the Aswan Dam, a towering structure that would span the narrows of the Nile River in a sparsely populated region not far from the Sudanese border. Electric power generated by the dam would fuel an economic miracle, providing jobs for Egypt's masses and transforming Egypt into a modern industrial state. The dam would also control the Nile's floods, providing a dramatic expansion of Egyptian agriculture. In addition, the Aswan Dam was to be a symbol of hope and progress: a symbol that would legitimize the revolutionary regime and generate popular support for its programs. Nasser also attempted to build trust between the government and the masses by forging a "social contract" in which a benevolent dictatorship would use the resources of the state to provide all of its citizens with an acceptable quality of life (Amin 1995). Economic democracy would take precedence over political democracy (Nasser, n.d.).

The West applauded Nasser's goal of economic development and his moderate stance toward Israel. Nasser seemed likely to emerge as a stabilizing force in this tumultuous region, and aid was promised for the construction of the Aswan Dam. The honeymoon between Nasser and the West, however, was short-lived. The United States pressured Nasser to join a proposed military alliance designed to encircle the Soviet Union. He refused, claiming that the new alliance, the Central Treaty Organization (the Baghdad Pact), was merely colonialism in a new guise. The purpose of his revolution had been to liberate Egypt from foreign domination, not to encourage it.

Turning his words into action, Nasser demanded the evacuation of British troops from Egyptian soil, a demand reluctantly accepted by a Britain still clinging to dreams of empire. Clashes between Palestinian fighters seeking shelter on Egyptian soil and the Israeli forces further complicated matters. They soon escalated into clashes between Israeli forces and the Egyptian army, with the latter suffering heavy loses. Nasser demanded Western arms to better resist Israeli incursions. The West refused, citing a desire to avoid an arms race in the region. Nasser responded by purchasing arms from the Soviet bloc. In one fell swoop, the West's monopoly of power in the Middle East was shattered. The Soviet Union had gained entrée into the Middle East and the Mediterranean basin, and the Western alliance (NATO) had been placed at risk. The United States demanded that Nasser rescind the arms deal with the Communists. He refused, and in 1956 the United States canceled its aid for the Aswan Dam (Gorst and Johnman 1997; Kingseed 1995; Kunz 1991). Nasser responded by nationalizing the Suez Canal, vowing to use its revenues to finance the Aswan Dam. It was Egypt's sovereign right to do so, as the canal was wholly within Egyptian territory.

Israel, fearful of Nasser's escalating popularity in the Arab world, conspired with Britain and France to bring down the Nasser regime. Israeli forces stormed the canal in October of 1956, while Britain and France demanded the right to occupy the Suez Canal under the pretext of protecting international shipping (McNamara 2003). The second Arab–Israeli war had begun. When Egypt refused to cede the canal, it was occupied by British and French forces. The three conspirators, however, had failed to consult with the Eisenhower administration, which was attempting to counter Soviet influence in the Third World by stressing America's history as a revolutionary, anticolonial power (Brands 1993; Holland 1996). Eisenhower sided with Egypt, forcing the French, British, and Israeli forces to withdraw from Egyptian territory. Nasser reigned victorious.

In just two years, then, Nasser had evicted British troops from Egyptian soil, broken the Western arms monopoly in the Middle East, nationalized the Suez Canal, and defeated, albeit politically, the combined forces of Israel, France, and Britain. In the eyes of Egypt and the entire Arab world, Nasser had become a hero of towering proportions; a leader who more than met Weber's description of a charismatic leader "endowed with supernatural, superhuman . . . powers" (Weber 1947).

The experience of the 1956 war changed the direction of Egyptian policy in three key ways. First, Nasser began to transform Egypt into a socialist economy, a process that began with the nationalization of British and French property shortly after the 1956 war. This process continued over the next few years until virtually all nonagrarian enterprises employing more than a handful of workers had been nationalized and placed under government control. Nasser, however, was not a communist. Rather, he went out of his way to base Egyptian socialism on Koranic principles (Al-Sharbasi, n.d.). His goal was to create an Egypt that was as equitable as it was prosperous. Socialism and military rule were merely the means to that end (Hosseinzedeh 1989, 71–72). Capitalism and party politics, in the view of Nasser and his colleagues, had brought Egypt little more than poverty, inequality, and conflict. Egypt's military leaders would use their authority to ensure that

Egypt's scarce resources were allocated in a just and productive manner. Once economic and social development had been achieved, Egypt would become a true democracy in which educated and prosperous Egyptians could make wise and judicious choices. Such, at least, was the theory.

Second, having abolished Egypt's traditional political parties, Nasser was finding it difficult to rule without a political organization of some type. An Egyptian population drugged by centuries of oppression and foreign domination had to be energized if the revolution were to achieve its goals. This task could only be carried out by a political party.

While Nasser needed a political organization to mobilize the Egyptian masses, he remained deeply opposed to the revival of a multiparty system. Nasser believed that interparty conflict would merely reinforce the schisms of an Egyptian society already fragmented by conflict and distrust. He also feared that a strong political party would challenge the authority of the military regime. Nasser wanted a political organization capable of defending the revolution and mobilizing the masses, but he did not want an independent political organization that would constrain his own authority.

Nasser, accordingly, began to experiment with the creation of a government-sponsored political organization that would perform the role of political parties without the tension and conflict created by excessive competition. Egyptians would learn democracy and civic responsibility within the confines of a single political party. With time and economic development, guided democracy would give way to pluralistic democracy.

The result of this experimentation was the Arab Socialist Union (ASU). The ASU would be open to all Egyptians who weren't enemies of the revolution, a category that included large landowners, communists, and the Muslim Brotherhood. The new party would penetrate all echelons of Egyptian society, from the remotest villages to the slums of Cairo (Baker 1978, 109–14). Its members would be the revolution's cadres. They would mobilize the Egyptian masses and guide their energies toward the achievement of revolutionary goals. They would also be the eyes and ears of the revolution, constantly vigilant to the machinations of its enemies. The new party would also serve as a forum for debate, a channel of communication, an agent of political socialization, and a conduit for recruiting the "best and the brightest" into the service of the revolution.

Finally, Nasser's near defeat in the Arab–Israeli war of 1956 convinced him that Egypt would never be free from external threat as long as his Arab neighbors remained subservient to the West. His resentment of foreign domination was shared by thousands of students, military officers, and intellectuals throughout the Arab world. Indeed, Arab nationalism was rapidly becoming the dominant political ideology of the region (Doran 1999). The message of Arab nationalism was both simple and powerful: The Arabs are one people united by a common history, a common culture, a common language, and, for the most part, a common religion. Once powerful, the Arabs were now fragmented into a multitude of petty countries manipulated by the Western imperialists and Israel. All that was required for a resurgence of Arab power was the reunification of the Arab people into a single state.

Despite its potent message, the Arab nationalist movement had historically lacked a dominant leader capable of marshaling its diverse and conflicting factions. Nasser provided that leadership. A union of Egypt and Syria was forged in 1958, and was followed in a few months by the overthrow of the pro-Western monarch of Iraq. Saudi Arabia, Lebanon, and Jordan all teetered on the brink of collapse. Once the Arab world was united, Nasser vowed, the humiliation of 1948 would be redressed. Israel would be returned to the Palestinians and Egypt would become the core of a reunified Arab state.

But the dreams of Arab unity and socialist prosperity proved elusive. The union with Syria was short-lived, and pro-Western regimes in Lebanon, Saudi Arabia, and Jordan were stabilized by the United States and Britain. The 1960s also found Egypt embroiled in the Yemeni civil war, a disastrous involvement that paralleled the U.S. experience in Vietnam. Egyptian forces controlled the major cities but could not subdue the tribes that dominated Yemen's impenetrable countryside (Al-Hadidi 1984). The morale of the Egyptian forces flagged as defeat became inevitable. The collapse of the Yemeni venture was followed in short order by the outbreak of the June War of 1967. This conflict, the third of the Arab–Israeli wars, would see Israel rout Egyptian forces in less than six days.

Results on the socialist front were equally depressing. Having abolished the private sector, the Egyptian government soon found itself saddled with a massive bureaucracy that produced little but consumed much. It oppressed the masses and refined corruption to an art form (Palmer, Leila, and Yassin 1988).

The political front was equally problematic because Nasser's state-sponsored political party, the ASU, failed to become the revolutionary instrument that he had hoped for (Baker 1978). Fearing any independent source of political authority, Nasser and his supporters kept the ASU under tight rein. The ASU also suffered from a shortage of cadres willing to dedicate their lives to the revolution and its objectives. While some Egyptians joined the ASU out of revolutionary fervor, most were motivated by expediency and opportunism. Membership in the ASU increased one's chances of securing a good position in the bureaucracy and provided connections, or *wasta*. It was also the avenue to power at local and regional levels. Opportunists, unfortunately, make poor cadres. They are dedicated to themselves, not to larger goals. The ASU would thus become a large self-serving political bureaucracy not unlike the Communist Party bureaucracy of the Soviet Union.

## The Era of Disillusion and Reassessment

Nasser's dreams of unity, socialism, and empire came tumbling down with Egypt's disastrous defeat in the June War of 1967, an event discussed at some length in the introductory chapter. The Israelis occupied the Sinai Peninsula, the Suez Canal was littered with sunken ships, the economy collapsed, and the Egyptian population was demoralized. The military, once viewed as the saviors of Egypt, was disgraced, its officers scorned (Hamid 1992). Arab nationalism and socialism were equally victims of the war. Both had proven to be false gods. Abdul Hakim, the commander of the Egyptian forces and longtime friend of Nasser, committed

suicide under somewhat clouded circumstances. Nasser resigned, but his resignation was rejected in the face of a mass outpouring of popular support. Nasser was
a tarnished hero, but a hero nonetheless.

Surveying the wreckage of the 1967 war, Nasser launched a scathing critique
of his own regime and called for the establishment of a democratic political system. As Abdel Magid Farid recounts Nasser's comments at the meetings of the
Revolutionary Command Council:

> What is important is that the leaders do not criticize and carp at each
> other because it is we, the high-ranking officials in the system, who have
> caused the system to crack. Each one of us is destroying what another
> one is doing. . . . Moreover, sensitivity among us has reached the point
> where we are afraid to criticize each other at meetings. I believe that the
> only solution is for us to create a real "challenge" in the true sense of the
> word, to hasten to correct the mistakes that have been committed (Farid
> 1994, 87–88).

**The War of Attrition**    In 1969, once his army had been rebuilt by the Soviet
Union, Nasser launched what he referred to as the "war of attrition." The
Egyptians could not force the Israelis from the Suez Canal, but artillery bombard-
ments and lightning raids could make them pay dearly for their occupation.
Nasser well understood that Israel was reluctant to accept heavy casualties and
viewed this as the major chink in the Israeli armor.

The Egyptian attacks achieved their goal, but rather than force an Israeli withdrawal from the Suez Canal, they prompted an Israeli effort to bomb Egypt into
submission. Israeli bombs destroyed military bases and industrial plants and reached
the very environs of Cairo itself. Nasser was again rescued from devastation by the
Soviets, who, in effect, took over Egypt's air defenses, including the piloting of
Egyptian aircraft. A truce was declared in 1970, and Nasser died shortly thereafter.
The dominant figure of modern Arab history had passed from the scene.

Nasser was succeeded in office by Anwar Sadat, his vice president and a charter member of the Free Officers. The situation facing Sadat was bleak. The disastrous June War had been compounded by the devastating war of attrition. The
Soviets had quelled the Israeli attack, but not without extending their control over
Egypt. Two decades after the revolution, the country remained dependent on
a foreign power. Indeed, when Sadat assumed power there were some 21,000
Soviet "advisers" in Egypt (Zahran 1987).

Anwar Sadat, moreover, possessed none of Nasser's charisma. Many Egyptians
viewed him as a weak individual who had been placed in office as a figurehead
president until more powerful forces could sort out the course of the revolution (Heikal 1983). The Soviet Union distrusted Sadat, preferring that the
Egyptian presidency go to an Egyptian military leader with communist leanings.
American officials didn't have much faith in Sadat either; they assumed that his
tenure in office would be brief (Heikal 1983).

It didn't help that Egypt's political institutions were in disarray. The facade of
guided democracy established by Nasser remained a farce, and the Egyptian

bureaucracy became more lethargic than ever. If the ASU had served Nasser poorly, it served Sadat not at all. The leaders of the ASU opposed Sadat's presidency in 1970 and subsequently used the ASU apparatus to undermine his authority.

Sadat, however, proved to be remarkably resilient. He crushed an attempted coup by leftist elements in the ASU in 1971 and moved rapidly to create a counterweight to the left by reviving the Muslim Brotherhood. The fundamentalist Brotherhood was not granted legal status, but it was allowed to establish branches in schools and universities and to perform welfare services for the poor of Egypt's teeming slums. From this base, it and its more extremist spinoffs gained control of the "street" and were soon engaged in pitched battles with the Egyptian left. The situation remained dicey.

Simultaneously, Sadat attempted to open negotiations with both Israel and the United States. He received encouragement from neither. In 1971, accordingly, Sadat signed a new fifteen-year treaty of cooperation and friendship with the USSR. The formal opening of the Aswan Dam was celebrated by the two countries the same year. Though dramatic in scope, the new treaty was little more than a stopgap measure for both sides. The USSR was reluctant to weaken its access to the Mediterranean and assumed that Sadat's reign would be short. Sadat, by contrast, viewed the USSR with profound distrust and doubted that the USSR would allow an armed crossing of the canal. This armed crossing was paramount, for unless Sadat could cross the canal, neither he nor Egypt would be able to emerge from the shadow of the past. Much was promised by both sides, but little was delivered. Indeed, barely a year later Sadat expelled the Soviets for "excessive caution" in regard to a future conflict with Israel. Rather than facilitating a new war with Israel, the Soviets had become an obstacle to Sadat's efforts to reclaim the Sinai Peninsula.

Sadat's eviction of the Soviets paved the way for a rapprochement with the United States, yet seemed to preclude any serious effort to force an Israeli withdrawal from the Suez Canal. How could Egypt attack Israeli positions without Soviet support? It was the Soviets, after all, who had built, trained, and armed the Egyptian military. Without a credible show of force, Israel had little cause to take the Egyptian leader seriously. Much the same was true of an Egyptian population who had watched Sadat's much-heralded "year of decision" pass without action. The domestic situation had continued to deteriorate, and so had Sadat's grip on power.

In retrospect, the unknown element in the equation appears to have been King Faisal of Saudi Arabia. Relieved at the passing of Nasser, the Saudi monarch found the moderation of Sadat much to his liking. He certainly had little desire to see the resurgence of a radical regime in Egypt. He also understood that the Arabs could not normalize relations with Israel from a position of weakness. A successful crossing of the canal by Egyptian forces, in Faisal's view, would shore up Sadat's tottering regime and establish the Arabs as a credible fighting force. For these reasons Saudi Arabia largely financed preparations for a limited Arab attack on Israeli positions along the Suez Canal and Syria's Golan Heights. One could also speculate that the Saudis were behind the expulsion of the Soviets as well.

Israeli intelligence monitored the Arab buildup but found it difficult to give credibility to an Egyptian army that it had humiliated only five years earlier. Israeli contempt for Arab military capability also made it difficult for them to imagine an Egyptian attack without Soviet support.

When the joint Egyptian–Syrian attack occurred on October 6, 1973, the Jewish holy day of Yom Kippur, Israel was caught unprepared. The Egyptian army displayed consummate skill in crossing the Suez Canal, and Israeli forces were forced to retreat with heavy losses. Egyptian forces had also benefited from Soviet support despite the strained relations between the two countries (Hermann, Hermann, and Anderson 1992). Without massive U.S. aid to Israel and the profound lack of coordination between the Egyptian and Syrian forces, the situation could have been far worse. Israeli forces eventually regrouped, and by the time the hostilities ceased, they had occupied still more Egyptian territory. The damage, however, had been done. The Egyptians had demonstrated their capacity to fight, and the myth of Israeli invincibility had been shattered. Saudi Arabia, Libya, and other oil-producing countries, though not engaging in the hostilities, slashed oil exports to the United States and its European allies. At long last, the Arabs had used their oil weapon. The economic structure of the industrial world was shaken, and world attention was focused on Sadat.

The United States arranged for a withdrawal of Israeli forces from the Suez Canal in January of 1974. The United States and Egypt reestablished diplomatic relations in June of the same year. Egypt had begun its slide into the American orbit. Over the next five years the process would accelerate dramatically.

Egypt's victory in the October War also freed Sadat from Nasser's shadow and transformed him into the "hero of Suez." His popularity soaring, Sadat crushed his opponents and proclaimed sweeping economic reforms designed to revive Egypt's moribund economy. Key to these was the *infitah* (new economic opening) that lifted Nasser's ban on capitalism (Gillespie 1984). Henceforth, Egypt would possess a mixed economy in which private-sector firms would be free to compete with the public sector. American aid and Western investment, Sadat promised, would make Egypt the economic hub of the Middle East. Egypt had traded guns for butter (Waterbury 1978). The "peace dividend" would allow Egypt to scale back its military expenditures and concentrate on economic development. Prosperity was assured. Also assured was a revival of Egypt's capitalist class as an additional counterweight to Sadat's leftist opponents (Imam 1987).

While Sadat was going from victory to victory on the international front, the domestic scene had started to unravel. Having assisted Sadat in crushing the left, the Muslim Brotherhood and its offshoots now represented the best-organized political force in Egypt other than the army. There was also growing evidence of fundamentalist influence in the latter. By the mid-1970s, the Islamic groups had sensed their growing power and had begun to press Sadat, who had been a member of the Muslim Brotherhood during the prerevolutionary era, to Islamize the Egyptian political system. Even more threatening were the embryonic jihadist extremists spawned by the Brotherhood. The former had renounced violence; the latter thrived upon it.

The *infitah,* for its part, had severely aggravated social tensions in Egypt. The new capitalist class acquired extraordinary wealth that it displayed with unabashed ostentation, while the lifestyle of the ordinary Egyptian continued to deteriorate. The gap between rich and poor was widening and becoming ever more visible. Class tensions came to a peak in 1977 when, upon the strong urging of the United States and the International Monetary Fund, Sadat cut government subsidies on bread and other vital commodities. Riots erupted throughout Egypt and were quelled only by the reinstatement of the subsidies (Gillespie 1984). Sadat had violated the social contract forged between Nasser and the Egyptian people.

Shaken by the riots, Sadat promised the Egyptians a return to democracy. Egypt, Sadat declared, would have three independent political parties: a party of the left that incorporated the Nasserites and the Communists, a party of the capitalist right, and a party of the center. There would be no religious parties. Claiming to stand above politics, Sadat would not belong to any of the three parties. Virtually all government officials, however, became members of the centrist party, it being well understood that this was the party of Sadat—an understanding that would be made official a few months later. The National Democratic Party had been born and Sadat was its president. The NDP took over the buildings and organizational network of the now-defunct ASU. The more things changed, the more they stayed the same. Egypt had become a multiparty state, but only one party mattered.

It was at this moment that Sadat stunned the Egyptian public by proclaiming his willingness to go "even unto" the Israeli parliament in his unrelenting search for peace. Menachem Begin, the Israeli prime minister, provided the requisite invitation and Sadat duly addressed the Israeli Knesset in November 1977. This address led to the Camp David Peace Accords sponsored by U.S. President Jimmy Carter. Entitled "A Framework for Peace in the Middle East," the accords would lead to the signing of a formal peace treaty between Israel and Egypt on March 26, 1979. Much of the Sinai had already been returned to Egypt, and the rest would be forthcoming in stages.

While the world applauded Sadat's dramatic peace initiatives—both he and Begin would receive the Nobel Peace Prize—conditions on the domestic front continued to worsen. Jihadist violence bordered on open warfare. In October 1981 Sadat was assassinated by the Islamic extremists that he had earlier nurtured. The Egypt of Anwar Sadat became the Egypt of Hosni Mubarak.

## Egypt under Mubarak: The Eras of Islamic Resurgence and the New World Order

The passing of Sadat found Egypt in a quandary. Dependence on the Soviet Union had given way to dependence on the United States. Peace had been made with Israel, but Egypt had been ostracized from the Arab world. Islamic extremists, having achieved victory in Iran, now viewed Egypt as their next target. The assassination of Sadat had merely been the opening salvo in what promised to be an enduring conflict.

Egypt's political institutions were in disarray and offered little support to the new president. As Mubarak summarized the situation a few years after taking office:

> We had before us [upon assuming office] the prospect of crumbling pub-lic services and utilities. The situation was the result of years of accumu-lated paralysis and neglect. . . . The flow of water was inadequate and irregular. Electric current fluctuated, and extended blackouts were com-mon. . . . The decay of the sewer system turned some streets and quarters into swamps. . . . Free education has lost much of its effectiveness and the expense of college education is oppressive to Egyptian families. Then there are the problems of housing shortages, rising prices, vanishing goods, and of houses collapsing on their inhabitants (Mubarak 1985).

In order to survive, the Mubarak regime would have to strengthen both Egypt's political system and its economy. The Egyptian population had wearied of slogans and symbolic gestures: either the government would meet the needs of its population or its survival would be in question. Neither political nor economic reform would be easy. Movement toward greater democracy threatened to empower the Muslim Brotherhood. Mubarak, moreover, had little faith in the Egyptian masses. As he would explain to the U.S. Congress:

> This country was under pressure for years and years, and when you open the gate for freedom, you will find many terrible things taking place. If you have a dam and keep the water until it begins to overflow, and then you open the gates, it will drown many people. We have to give a grad-ual dose so people can swallow it and understand it. The Egyptians are not Americans (Mubarak 1993, A3).

The economic situation was equally dicey (Harik 1997). The social contract introduced by Nasser had provided Egyptians with jobs and subsidies in return for their patience. In spite of the partial shift to capitalism, things had remained much the same under Sadat. Nothing short of drastic economic reform was likely to revive Egypt's moribund economy. Serious economic reform, however, required a cutback in the subsidies that now consumed some 30 percent of the Egyptian budget. It also required trimming the Egyptian bureaucracy and transforming Egypt's state-owned industries into viable enterprises. This, however, could be achieved only by closing the inefficient factories (which meant most of them) and trimming the workforce of the others. Such measures would swell the ranks of Egypt's unemployed, which already hovered around 25 percent. A reduction in subsidies, however, might provoke riots similar to the bread riots of 1977. A repeat performance could well throw the country into chaos.

This was the environment when Hosni Mubarak assumed the presidency of Egypt in October 1981. The transition was orderly, but the underlying tensions could not be disguised. Mubarak, like Sadat before him, continued to rule under the "emergency" provisions of the Egyptian constitution, but promised progress toward democracy as soon as the country had returned to normal. He also called upon Egyptians "to work harder and do more." The economic situation was grave, he said, adding that "Egypt's problems cannot be solved by the government alone." These were sobering words for an Egyptian population long accustomed to flamboyant promises and inflammatory rhetoric. In the meantime, Mubarak attempted to split the ranks of the fundamentalists by distinguishing between the Muslim Brotherhood and the jihadists. While the latter were prosecuted as the assassins of Sadat, the Muslim Brotherhood was allowed to organize on a quasi-legal basis.

Despite government efforts to control religious extremism, the ensuing years would witness a gradual upsurge in political violence, much of it centering on Islamic issues. Particularly serious was the 1986 riot by Egyptian security guards, a special low-level military unit used by the Ministry of the Interior to guard public buildings. Staffed by young recruits, the security guards went on a four-day rampage in which bars, tourist hotels, and other symbols of Westernization offensive to the fundamentalists were burned. Order was restored by the army, but the regime's authority was clearly shaken.

Also problematic was growing pressure from the United States and the international community to end Egypt's economic chaos by privatizing its economy. With the 1986 riots still fresh in his mind, however, Mubarak was reluctant to further inflame mass emotions by threatening the social safety net of a people already living on the brink of disaster. Large public-sector enterprises were put on the auction block, but this and other reforms were not applied with enthusiasm (Harik 1997). Western hopes for a wholesale restructuring of the Egyptian economy were disappointed. Nevertheless, the transition from socialism to capitalism was moving in the right direction according to the U.S. and its allies (Lofgren 1993).

Egypt's participation in the 1991 Gulf War as an ally of the United States also played poorly with Egyptian citizens and might have led to widespread rioting had the war not ended so quickly (Interviews, Cairo, 1991). The jihadists capitalized on this sentiment to press their attack on the government; they actually seized control of many smaller towns and villages. In some cases, the security forces looked the other way (Aoude 1994, 19).

By 1993, the Egyptian minister of the interior would openly declare, "We are at war. People will have to die on both sides" (*NYT,* Nov. 28, 1993, A8). Mubarak's response to the escalation in jihadist violence was brutal, but less than effective. Each claim of government victory was followed with a new round of assassinations and attacks on foreign tourists. The latter devastated the Egyptian economy as tourist revenues dropped by some 40 percent.

Mubarak was elected to a third term as president in 1993 in a process the *New York Times* described as "a strange, ungainly ballet where choreographed admirers are herded in from the wings to pay homage to a leading man with no rival" (*NYT,* Oct. 4, 1993). His primary goal was eradication of the jihadists. The attack on jihadist terrorism was as vicious as the terrorism itself, but by 1998 the level of violence had abated and Mubarak claimed victory over his adversaries. The jihadist threat had not vanished, but the jihadists had been forced to change tactics, a topic that will be elaborated shortly.

A fourth term of office would follow in 1999, with procedures not markedly different from those of 1993. The liberalization of the economy picked up steam, but little progress was made on the democratic front. Capitalism, in Mubarak's plan would come first. Democracy would follow once the promise of capitalist prosperity had been fulfilled. September of 1999 would witness another attempt on Mubarak's life, by a lone knife-wielding assailant. (An earlier attempt was made in 1995.) Mubarak survived with a small cut on his hand, and the event was written off as the work of a lunatic. Nevertheless, the assassination attempt raised serious questions about the ability of the Egyptian security services to protect the president, and heads rolled (Apiku 1999). It also raised serious questions about the fate of Egyptian politics after Mubarak. The Egyptian president had yet to name a vice president, and no heir apparent was in sight, although Mubarak's son was appointed to the governing board of the NDP in the spring of 2000.

In the fall of 2000 two events threatened the stability of the Mubarak regime. The first was the eruption of violence in the Israeli-occupied West Bank and Gaza Strip, portions of which were nominally under the control of the Palestinian Authority. The Israelis responded with an overwhelming display of force that left more than 504 Palestinians dead during the first eight months of the uprising, approximately one-third of them under the age of eighteen. Riots protesting the Israeli action erupted in Egyptian universities and were mirrored by massive protests following Friday prayers at Al-Azhar mosque. Mubarak, the strongest supporter of peace with Israel in the Arab world, withdrew the Egyptian ambassador from Tel Aviv in protest, a move taken over the strong objections of the United States. Diplomatic relations with Israel were not severed, but a key pillar of regional stability had threatened to collapse. In reality, Mubarak had little choice in the matter: as he well understood, protests of any variety could soon turn against the government.

The second event that threatened to alter the course of Egyptian politics was the 2000 parliamentary elections, the first round of which resulted in a humiliating defeat for the NDP. The party of Mubarak had captured only 27 percent of the seats in the People's Assembly; an absolute majority was required for victory. The independents, including seven members of the Muslim Brotherhood, swept a majority of the seats in the first round of the elections. The NDP was faced with the prospect of minority status in the parliament if the same trend continued in the second round, which would be conducted to fill seats for which no candidate had won a majority of the votes in the first round.

The situation, however, was not as dire as it appeared at first. No sooner had the results of the first stage of the election been announced than the vast majority of the independents elected to the Assembly "joined" the NDP. Some were true independents who shifted to the NDP for opportunistic reasons, but most were longtime NDP members whose flawed backgrounds were an embarrassment to a party suffering from accusations of corruption and influence peddling. A critical point, however, had been made. A majority of the Egyptian electorate had voted against the NDP. It was only the treachery of the pseudo-independents that had allowed the party to retain its dominance of the Assembly.

Fraud was blatant during the second stage of the elections, and the NDP retained its overwhelming majority in the People's Assembly. However, the

Muslim Brotherhood picked up more than enough seats to make it the leading opposition group. It would undoubtedly have won more seats if the security forces had not forcibly kept Brotherhood supporters away from the polling booths (Sal'eh 2000).

During this period, Jamal Mubarak, the president's son, staked his claim for leadership of the National Democratic Party and the country once his father stepped down. Proclaiming himself the spokesman of Egypt's youth, he had conducted a series of youth conferences for younger political leaders throughout Egypt in the four months leading up to the election, the last of which was entitled "Returning Hope to the National Democratic Party" (Jabar 2000a).

As the magnitude of the NDP's debacle became known, Jamal Mubarak seized the moment to condemn the party for having totally lost contact with the Egyptian population; he called for the immediate replacement of the discredited leadership with younger cadres, for whom he was the obvious spokesman (Jabar 2000a). He also complained that people were fed up with a party they viewed as corrupt and self-serving, further noting that the extension of the emergency laws did little to help its image. Given the nature of Egyptian politics, such a statement would have been unthinkable without the approval of his father.

### Egypt and the Era of Global Terror

President Hosni Mubarak rushed to condemn the September 11, 2001, attacks on the United States and pledged his country's full support to America's war on terror. Mubarak, after all, had been fighting the jihadist threat long before the United States entered the fray. The war on terror promised more money for Egyptian security services and a carte blanche for Mubarak's repression of the regime's opponents, Islamic and otherwise.

This, however, was before Mubarak fully understood how the war on terror was to be fought. Washington demanded that Egypt and its Arab neighbors reform Islamic schools and charities, eliciting cries that the United States had declared war on Islam. The U.S. responded that Islamic schools fueled anti-Americanism and that some charities were funding terrorist organizations. The protests began with university students but soon broadened to other segments of Egyptian society. Washington's demands were a blatant interference in Egypt's internal affairs, confronting Mubarak with the cruel choice of standing with the United States or standing with Islam. Mubarak dodged the issue, reaffirming his commitment to Islam while assuring Washington of his continued support.

But he could not dodge the U.S.-led war on Iraq. Anti-American riots erupted with such ferocity that the regime, stunned, let them run their course for several days. Mubarak had little choice but to openly condemn the war. The war on Iraq, he warned Washington, would lead to chaos in the Middle East. The Muslim Brotherhood smiled.

Sensing that the regime had been shaken by the intensity of the antiwar riots, its opponents intensified their calls for true democratic reform. As if by magic, a new political movement, "Enough" (of Mubarak), appeared from nowhere and captured the public imagination (*Daily Star* [Beirut], Feb. 25, 2004). The

United States did its part by calling for sweeping democratic reform in the region. It had little choice: democracy was rapidly becoming the main justification for a disastrous war in Iraq. In the face of Egyptian and Saudi objections, the United States backed down on its calls for democracy, but reform was in the air.

This was the environment in which Hosni Mubarak prepared for the 2005 presidential elections. The only real question was who would the lone candidate be, Mubarak or his son. Both remained coy while pictures of Jamal smiled down from billboards. Both spoke elegantly about the need for reform and greater openness in Egyptian politics, but Mubarak scoffed at the opposition's suggestion that there should be more than one candidate for the presidency. (Al-Jazeera, Jan. 30, 2005).

And then suddenly, apparently without warning to his own party, Mubarak announced that the constitution would be amended to allow for multiple candidates in the upcoming presidential election, then about eight months away (*Al-Ahram Weekly,* March 3–9, 2005). The parliament was ordered to enact the amendment.

But why? Speculation was rampant. Had Mubarak bequeathed democracy to Egypt as the crowning act of his twenty-five-year rule? Or was it merely a ploy to gain popular sympathy and taunt the United States? If the U.S. really wanted democracy in this most fragile of regions, let them have it. Some saw it as a great risk. Others noted that a ruling party that regularly produced 95 percent majorities was not in danger of being swept from power. Egypt's other parties were fragile, with little in the way of organizational structure. They made noise, but little more—with the exception of the illegal Muslim Brotherhood. The Supreme Guide of the Brotherhood made a cryptic statement saying that the organization was weighing running a candidate in the election. He also threw down the gauntlet to the United States, stating: "We have candidates who are capable of ruling the world and not just Egypt" (*Al-Ahram Weekly,* March 3–9, 2005). Not to be outdone, the United States announced that it was granting $1 million to nongovernmental organizations to facilitate their monitoring of the election (*Al-Ahram Weekly,* March 3–9, 2005, or following week). Presidential elections in Egypt had suddenly become interesting, and all the more so because of Egypt's dominant position in the Arab world.

What ensued was a wonderful circus. The leading opposition candidate campaigned from jail, and government judges, fearing blatant fraud, refused to monitor the elections. They later relented after prolonged negotiations with the regime. Opposition parties threatened to boycott the election, but some of them also relented. The Muslim Brotherhood remained on the sidelines, but urged people to vote. When the dust had settled, Mubarak had to make do with 88 percent of the vote. Only 23 percent of the Egyptian electorate had bothered to cast ballots.

Does this mean that the election was yet another exercise in futility? Not at all. The regime had been forced to allow opposition candidates to run for office. This was an important first and set a precedent for future elections. Indeed, many Egyptians viewed the 2005 election as a dry run for the next presidential election six years hence, when Hosni Mubarak will not be a candidate and the opposition will have had ample time to prepare. The election also demonstrated the indecision and confusion of the NDP, whose leaders were not informed of Mubarak's decision to allow open elections. Perhaps more embarrassing was the 23 percent voter turnout. This by itself showed just how much the regime had lost touch with the Egyptian population. It also indicated that the NDP was no longer able to get out the vote. Lest there be doubt on these issues, the 2005 parliamentary elections saw the Muslim Brotherhood gain some 88 seats in the People's Assembly. The figure would have been higher were it not for blatant fraud. Mubarak's National Democratic Party retained control of the People's Assembly, but the Brotherhood had made its point. Free elections could well result in a Brotherhood victory.

## EGYPTIAN POLITICS TODAY AND BEYOND

The eras of Nasser and Sadat were punctuated by dramatic events, each of which threatened to alter the course of Egyptian history. Mubarak's long tenure has seen few such events. It has been a cautious regime that has found decisive action difficult. Progress has been made in Egypt's transition from socialism to capitalism, but it has been slow and halting. Progress toward democracy has also been slow and halting. The government appears to be immobilized, bending to pressures when they become insurmountable but lacking a clear vision of Egypt's future.

In the remainder of this chapter, we will explore possible explanations for the profound caution of the Mubarak presidency. In the process we will have the opportunity to examine Egypt's political institutions, the actors that give life to those institutions, and the broader cultural, economic, and international pressures that shape Egyptian politics.

### Elites and Institutions

As all roads in Egypt lead to Hosni Mubarak, the logical place to seek clues to the plodding nature of the Mubarak regime is within the personality of Mubarak himself. Rather than being a visionary on the scale of Nasser or Sadat, Mubarak seems to view himself as a senior bureaucrat assigned the responsibility of guiding the ship of state through troubled waters. Far more cautious than his predecessors, he proceeds slowly, making narrow, step-by-step decisions based upon consultations with a wide variety of groups. He also tends to read reports in great detail and does not like surprises. For better or for worse, Mubarak's personality lends itself to incrementalism. It is not clear, however, that his incremental mode of decision making is conducive to solving Egypt's massive social and economic problems. Massive problems often require radical solutions.

Many observers also believe that the broader elite surrounding Mubarak has lost its zeal (Jabar 2000a). While the regime continues to rule in the name of Nasser's revolution, little of that revolution remains. Indeed, one gets the impression that Mubarak's supporters are more concerned with clinging to their privileged positions than they are with finding solutions to Egypt's daunting social and economic problems (Maisa 1993). This point is critical to understanding the immobility of Egyptian politics, for the secondary elite under Mubarak plays a greater role in the decision-making process than it did under either Nasser or Sadat. This is partly a function of Mubarak's personality, but it also reflects the greater complexity of Egyptian politics in the present era.

During the Mubarak regime, this secondary elite has included senior military officials, the inner circle of the ruling National Democratic Party, the Presidential Office, heads of key bureaucratic agencies, and senior members of the Islamic religious establishment. Collectively, they represent the pillars of the Mubarak government.

The Presidential Office, for example, is a special bureaucracy of several thousand members who assist the president in political and security matters (Gomaa 1991). It also includes a special intelligence service and a special presidential army, the Republican Guards. Its leaders serve as "gatekeepers," regulating access to the president and controlling the information the president receives on key issues.

The heads of Egypt's major bureaucratic agencies, in turn, advise the president on key policy issues. Collectively they form a cabinet headed by a prime minister whose major responsibility is guiding the president's program through a subservient parliament dominated by the semiofficial National Democratic Party. Prime ministers are changed at will, and the formation of a new "Government" is often used to signal a change in policy. If the new policies are successful, the president takes the credit. If the policies fail, the prime minister and cabinet take the blame and give way to a new "team."

The details of most economic policies are crafted by the prime minister in association with the various economics ministers. This group constitutes the core of the "economic club" (Bahgat 1991). The president sets the tone, while the prime minister and cabinet work out the details (Bahgat 1991). Much also depends on the ability of the ministers to force the president's policies through a moribund bureaucracy, a challenging task at best.

**The National Democratic Party**   The National Democratic Party is Mubarak's link to the civilian power structure at the national and local levels. Much like the Arab Socialist Union of the Nasser and Sadat eras, the National Democratic Party is a massive political bureaucracy. Village and neighborhood organizations form the base of the NDP's organizational pyramid, followed in turn by organizations at the district (*markaz*) and provincial (governorate) levels. This elaborate structure is capped by a national secretariat headed ultimately by President Mubarak and his son, Jamal.

The role of the NDP leadership is to provide Egypt's quasi-military regime with resounding majorities in the parliament. Possessing little in the way of a concrete ideology, Egyptians are attracted to the NDP by the lavish use of *wasta*. NDP members enjoy greater access to government jobs and receive preferential treatment in their dealings with Egypt's all-pervasive bureaucracy. Both concerns are of vital importance in a country in which little can be accomplished without "connections" of one kind or another. The NDP also ensures its dominance by providing landowners, businessmen, and other notables with privileged positions in the party apparatus. Jamal Mubarak complained that he had heard a provincial leader brag of bringing a drug dealer into the party because the dealer had a large following (Jabar 2000a). The notables reciprocate by using their considerable influence to "encourage" voting for the NDP. Election laws have also been manipulated in favor of the NDP.

The NDP's domination of the People's Assembly has enabled Hosni Mubarak to rule under the guise of parliamentary democracy without fear of serious opposition to his policies. Much like the other pillars of the Mubarak regime, the NDP is experiencing deep internal divisions. Personality conflicts abound, younger leaders are frustrated by the dominance of the party's old guard, liberal and conservative wings of the party spar over economic and social policy, and local leaders chafe under the centralized control of national leadership. Efforts to increase the membership base of the party have only increased these conflicts. Whether recent shakeups in the party's executive committee—including the addition of more Copts and women—can alleviate the tension remains to be seen (*Cairo Times,* Feb. 10, 2000). Finally, the party has suffered from the same lethargy and opportunism that beset the ASU. It is motivated by patronage rather than ideology. Indeed, it is difficult to pin down precisely what the party stands for, other than perpetuation of a status quo that is becoming increasingly untenable.

Jamal Mubarak has called for sweeping reforms, accusing the NDP of lethargy, stagnation, insensitivity, venality, and incompetence. In particular, he has complained that the party has been deluded by its "paper membership" into believing that it has the support of the masses. In reality, he noted, the party was dominated by discredited leaders who had lost touch with Egypt's changing circumstances. The party had failed to exercise care in the selection of its candidates and had lost its cadre of dedicated party workers. The NDP, he said, could not sustain its dominant position in Egyptian politics without a gigantic effort to build a new generation of younger cadres who were in touch with Egypt and its problems (Jabar 2000a, paraphrased by the author). Other reports have accused provincial leaders of selling places on the party's election list (El Ebraash and El Shathli 2000).

**The Islamic Establishment**    The Islamic establishment consists of the senior Islamic religious figures in Egypt, the foremost of whom are the minister of religious endowments, the grand mufti or judge, and the rector of Al-Azhar, Cairo's renowned Islamic university. These leaders are surrounded by a variety of senior religious scholars collectively referred to as the ulema. The government plays a dominant role in the appointment of senior religious officials, thereby assuring that the religious establishment is headed by individuals whose views are compatible with those of the president. Under Nasser, the Islamic establishment was headed by religious scholars who shared the regime's reformist views. Under Sadat and Mubarak, it has become more conservative. No matter what their perspective, all Egyptian governments have sought the blessing of the ulema for their policies.

Egypt's senior religious leaders are appointed by Mubarak and preach religious moderation. Their role is to persuade devout Muslims that working within their traditional Islamic institutions is a more effective strategy for achieving Islamic goals than adopting the violent tactics of the extremists. Understandably, the Mubarak regime goes out of its way to make the "government ulema (clergy)" appear effective in supporting Islamic morals. Mosques are built and maintained by the Ministry of Waqfs (religious endowments), Al-Azhar University has been expanded and glorified, Islamic programs abound on Egyptian television, and Egypt maintains a separate Koranic radio station. The Egyptian media also break for prayers five times a day, following Islamic tradition. Senior Islamic leaders have free access to Mubarak, and their influence has increased in response to the extremist threat. Inevitably, the subservience of the official Islamic elite to the Mubarak regime has diminished its moral authority. It is not an independent voice in Egyptian politics (Mullaney 1995, 233–34).

**The Military**    Of the five pillars of the Mubarak regime, the military is by far the most important. Egypt continues to be a predominantly military regime, despite its progress toward democracy. Most of Mubarak's senior advisers are drawn from the military, as are key figures in the Presidential Office, the bureaucracy, the NDP, and the local government apparatus. This is particularly true of governors and district officials. Military officers enjoy subsidized housing and every other perk that a poor society can bestow upon them.

In spite of its privileged position in Egyptian society, the Egyptian military is not necessarily of one mind. Many officers are loyal to Mubarak, but others incline toward the Nasserites, the Islamic fundamentalists, or various other groups. Indeed, the military leadership has long been cautious in its criticism of the fundamentalist movement. By and large, most operations against the jihadists have been carried out by special units such as the secretive Task Force 777 or security forces under the control of the minister of interior rather than by the army. Information concerning this and most other military questions, unfortunately, remains limited. Most recently, speculation has surfaced in the Arabic press on the attitude of the military toward the ascent of Jamal Mubarak (*Osbou al-Arabi,* July 26, 2004). Would the military accept a civilian president, even a son of Mubarak? Beyond doubt, it will have a major voice in the naming of Mubarak's successor when that time comes.

Suffice it to say that Mubarak works hard to assure the officer corps that its privileged and influential role in Egyptian politics will remain intact. He has also modernized the military. This is a source of pride among the military, but causes worry among the Israelis. Also of concern to Israel have been nuclear experiments that Egypt failed to report to the International Atomic Energy Agency (*Middle East Times,* Jan. 28, 2005).

**The Bureaucracy**    The incremental nature of Mubarak's decision making is also dictated by his inability to implement his policies in a timely fashion. For all of its talk of bureaucratic reform, the Mubarak regime continues to depend upon a bureaucracy widely described as self-serving, lazy, corrupt, rigid, lacking in creativity, insensitive to the public, and fearful of taking responsibility (Palmer, Leila, and Yassin 1988). Indeed, the Egyptian bureaucracy is now viewed as a major obstacle to the economic and social development of Egyptian society (Allam 2000).

Nevertheless, it continues to absorb massive resources and generally serve as a brake on Egypt's social and economic development. The aid-granting nations have called for a severe downsizing of the bureaucracy, but Mubarak has resisted. Most senior bureaucrats were appointed for political reasons and their removal would weaken an already nervous regime (Gomaa 1991). The government also fears that exacerbating the already severe unemployment situation will stimulate popular unrest.

**The Parliament**    On paper, the Egyptian parliament differs little from the parliaments of Europe on which it was patterned. The People's Assembly (*majlis ash-shaab*), or lower house, is popularly elected, while the Consultative Assembly (*majlis as-shoura*), or upper house, is largely appointed. The Egyptian Constitution stipulates that the People's Assembly must approve all legislation including the annual budget (Arab Republic of Egypt: www.parliament.gov.eg). As in the United States, the Assembly can override a presidential veto by a vote of two-thirds of its members. This, however, has yet to happen. Laws enacted by the president during periods of emergency rule must be submitted to the People's Assembly for ratification once the emergency period has ended. Both the prime minister and the members of his cabinet are responsible to the People's Assembly. Confidence may be withdrawn from the Government as a whole (prime minister and cabinet) or from an individual minister. In the latter instance, the minister in question is forced to resign but the Government remains in place. Members of the People's Assembly also possess the right to interrogate ministers and the senior members of ministerial staffs. Finally, the People's Assembly plays an important role in the nomination of the president. If a president dies, resigns, or is incapable of fulfilling presidential responsibilities, the president of the People's Assembly serves as the head of state until a new president is elected.

The constitutional powers of the People's Assembly, unfortunately, are largely theoretical. It is the leader of the National Democratic Party—President Mubarak—who has the final say on what legislation the assembly will pass. Somewhat fair legislative elections, moreover, have only become a feature of Egyptian politics in the last few years, and even these elections have been structured to ensure overwhelming victories by the semiofficial NDP. Voter turnout has traditionally been low, and opposition parties often choose to boycott elections as a means of protesting questionable electoral procedures. Only the ploys of the technically banned Muslim Brotherhood make things interesting. The Brotherhood is under no illusion that it will be allowed to dominate the assembly, but its role as the leading opposition party allows it to use the assembly as a national pulpit for airing its views, and also to keep track of anti-Islamic legislation. Many legislators go along, fearing to be branded opponents of Islam (Muslim Brotherhood home page, question and answer section: www.ummah.org/ikwan).

In addition to its weakness and general ineffectiveness, the People's Assembly has also been wracked by corruption scandals involving its members, ranging from narcotics trafficking to the securing of huge loans from government-owned banks without collateral, few of which were repaid. Many Assembly members, it seems, have also dodged their military service (*Al-Ahram Weekly,* Aug. 23, 2003).

The Consultative Assembly, or upper house of the parliament, is a less democratic body: one-half of its members are selected by the president. The

Consultative Assembly, as its name suggests, is an honorific debating society designed to air issues of public importance (Bianchi 1989). Cynics refer to it as a rest home for "burned-out" officials (Springborg 1989).

Does this mean that the Egyptian parliament is totally irrelevant? Not at all. The existence of a functioning parliament and the holding of parliamentary elections, however flawed, are important steps in the democratic process. The NDP always wins, but opposition parties have the opportunity to present their case and put members of the cabinet on the hot seat. This, too, has contributed to the immobility of the Mubarak regime, which wants to move toward greater democracy but is fearful of the results. The opposition parties, although poorly represented, have also benefited from the considerable disarray that exists within the ruling establishment. Egypt's social and economic problems are so massive that no one is quite sure how to solve them. While some of Mubarak's advisers advocate more capitalism, others demand a return to socialism. By and large, the regime appears to be stalled somewhere between the two (Ansari 1985). The same is true in virtually every area of debate. To some extent, the parliament serves as an important lightning rod in Egyptian politics. The Egyptian population is extremely frustrated, and the parliament provides a forum for the partial airing of those frustrations.

**The Courts**    The Egyptian Constitution provides for an independent judiciary as well as for a Constitutional Court. The Constitutional Court supervises the judicial system and possesses the right to declare laws and other acts of government unconstitutional. It also interprets laws judged to be ambiguous. The broader structure of the Egyptian legal system is based upon French (Napoleonic) canon law, with adjustments being made for the predominantly Islamic character of Egyptian society. Islamic law takes precedence in marriage, divorce, and similar areas referred to as personal statutes. The Islamic fundamentalists would like to see the Koran's role in Egyptian law greatly expanded, and the Mubarak regime seems to be moving, however grudgingly, in this direction.

The Egyptian courts operate with reasonable efficiency in dealing with routine matters and are generally free of political influence. Politically sensitive issues are more problematic. Indeed, a former judge recently created a minor stir by stating that executive interference in the courts threatened whatever independence they may have enjoyed (*Cairo Times,* Jan. 30, 2003). The Constitutional Court's power to review government decisions can be overridden by the president's emergency powers, and the president also has the option of sending issues of state security to military courts rather than to civilian courts. Jihadists are generally tried by military courts, thereby depriving them of procedural rights guaranteed by the constitution. The military has its own legal system and is not subject to civilian law.

These limitations aside, the Constitutional Court has played an important role in strengthening Egyptian democracy. Legislation, including unfair election laws, is often declared unconstitutional by the court. The court has also played a vigorous role in blocking government attempts to restrict the activities of political parties and has been accused of subverting the parliament by bringing its members to trial for grand fraud and trafficking in narcotics (Rizk 1999b). The judiciary plays some role in supervising Egypt's elections and recently created a storm by refusing to supervise the 2005 presidential election. They later agreed to serve after consultations with the president.

The Constitutional Court cannot rival the presidency as a source of political power, but it has at least developed some precedents for independent action (Maisa 1993). The president has also allowed unpopular policies to be overridden by the Constitutional Court as a means of saving face. Rather than appear to be backtracking in response to popular opposition, he can claim to be strengthening Egyptian democracy. Recently, for example, the court invalidated a controversial law prohibiting female students from wearing Islamic dress to school. The government capitulated in the name of democracy, thereby freeing itself from a policy that would have been difficult, if not dangerous, to enforce.

The institutional pattern outlined above contributes to the immobility of Egyptian politics in several ways. First, because all initiatives for action depend on President Mubarak, his personal tendency toward caution serves as a brake on the whole system. Second, the Presidential Office, the military, the NDP, the religious establishment, and the bureaucracy all attempt to "capture" Mubarak as a means of increasing their own power. Mubarak, like his predecessors, has attempted to avoid such manipulation by pitting one agency against another (Salwa Gomaa 1993, personal communication with the author). This grand balancing act provides the president with multiple sources of information, but it also creates confusion within the ranks of the government. Third, the quasi-democratic nature of Egypt's political institutions has made it increasingly difficult for the regime to silence the opposition. Elections, although not entirely "free," are held and opposition candidates do speak out. This, too, has led to Mubarak's increased caution. Finally, the bureaucracy can neither execute Mubarak's policies effectively nor meet the needs of the Egyptian population. Both failings reinforce Mubarak's ability to act with decisiveness.

## THE GROUP BASIS OF EGYPTIAN POLITICS

The concept of civil society centers on the belief that progress toward a more democratic society requires a strong framework of nongovernmental associations to stimulate public debate and to serve as a buffer between the rulers and the ruled (Kornhauser 1959; Norton 1994). The components of civil society in Egypt fall roughly into five categories: (1) political parties; (2) pressure groups; (3) private voluntary organizations (PVOs and NGOs); (4) sectoral interest groups that, while lacking a clear organizational structure, command the attention of the government; and (5) public opinion.

Egypt has witnessed the rapid growth of nongovernmental groups and associations and now possesses far more of them than any other Arab country. Most play a role in focusing public attention on the Mubarak regime and thus help to explain its caution. What is the role of Egyptian parties, groups, and associations in the democratic process? Two points are of particular interest. First, many of Egypt's most active nongovernmental agencies incline toward religious fundamentalism. Therefore, their commitment to creating a more open society is open to question, at least as "open society" is understood in the West. Second, many of Egypt's nongovernmental associations were created by the government in order to better control the Egyptian population. This applies to political parties, labor and professional unions, and benevolent associations.

Although it is convenient to break Egypt's civil society into its component parts for the purpose of discussion, it is vital to understand that each part builds upon the others. Nowhere is this interaction more evident than with the Islamic movement, the only serious opposition to the Mubarak regime. The fundamentalists operate at all levels of Egypt's civil society, and each level has become a battleground in the struggle to determine Egypt's future.

This being the case, it may be useful first to provide a survey of the main components of Egypt's civil society and then to focus specifically on the continuing struggle between the Mubarak regime and the fundamentalists for control of Egypt.

## Political Parties

The Mubarak era has witnessed a proliferation of political parties that would have been unthinkable during the administrations of his predecessors (Kassem 2000). Some have deep roots in Egyptian society, while others are little more than empty shells left over from the Sadat era. The picture is further complicated by the fluidity of Egyptian parties. Parties emerge only to merge with their competitors or to splinter as a result of personality conflicts or ideological differences. The runup to the 2005 presidential election witnessed the recognition of some fifteen legal opposition parties, not including the Muslim Brotherhood.

For all of its complexity, the Egyptian party system is dominated by four distinct tendencies: the socialist left, the center, the capitalist right, and the Islamic groups. The parties of the left, now dominated by the Nasserites and the Tagammu (communist, far left), advocate a return to socialism. For many Egyptians, the dynamism of the Nasser era stands in sharp contrast to the rudderless drift of the present regime. Leftist promises of full employment and free services also possess a strong appeal for the millions of Egyptians facing unemployment, escalating health and educational costs, and inadequate housing. The capitalist right is dominated by the New Wafd, a party that advocates a complete break with Egypt's socialist past. The religious right has largely taken over the Socialist Labor Party and wants to transform Egypt into an Islamic theocracy. In effect, the Socialist Labor Party is little more than a front for the Muslim Brotherhood. Spanning the middle of these disparate and seemingly irreconcilable tendencies is the ruling National Democratic Party. Its ideological position, such as it is, calls for a mix of socialism, capitalism, and religion. Of the above parties, only the NDP and the religious right possess more than a skeletal organizational structure. The New Wafd finds its major support within the business community, while the base of the Nasserites and other leftists is among students and intellectuals. The religious right has fairly broad-based support, but, as will be discussed shortly, it is centered in the lower and middle classes. All Egyptian parties are beset by deep internal divisions.

A rare survey conducted by the semiofficial Al-Ahram Center for Political and Strategic Studies indicates that 8.4 percent of the Egyptian population is associated with a formal political party. Figures for individual parties were not available, but it is safe to assume that the overwhelming majority of that 8.4 percent are affiliated with the National Democratic Party (Al-Ahram Survey 1998).

A leading Egyptian intellectual and former director of the Al-Ahram Center for Political and Strategic Studies attributes the weakness of opposition parties to the negative image of the opposition presented by the government media. This stigma, he suggests, "has made many citizens reluctant to stand behind the banners of the opposition parties for fear of being branded as an opponent of the regime (Sha'ib 1999, translated by M. Palmer). The head of ad hoc opposition parties' coordination committee, in turn, attributes the dismal showing of the legal opposition parties to the cozy relationship between the opposition and the powers-that-be (Salah Eissa, in Abdel-Latif 2000, 1).

The influence of Egypt's quasi-democratic parties is threefold. First, the existence of a broad range of political parties creates the appearance of democracy, a matter of great importance to the Mubarak regime. Second, the existence of multiple legal political parties has fragmented the opposition into so many diverse groups that coordinated opposition to the Mubarak regime has become virtually impossible. The opposition made a much-publicized effort to close ranks in the run-up to the 2005 presidential election, but produced little but wrangling. Third, the weakness of the legal party system has politicized Egypt's professional associations, labor unions, and other pressure groups, a topic to which we turn next (Sha'ib 1999).

On the plus side, the opposition parties do focus attention on the regime's obvious failings. They have also played a major role in demanding an alternative to Mubarak. Whether it was their influence that forced Mubark to open the 2005 presidential election to multiple candidates is a matter of debate. The United States was also pressuring Mubarak to move in that direction.

## Pressure Groups

During the later years of the monarchy a wide variety of labor unions, business organizations, professional associations, and other Western-type pressure groups emerged in Egypt. With the advent of revolutionary socialism in the 1950s, the business groups disbanded, while the labor, peasant, and professional associations were brought under government control (Bianchi 1989, 126–44; Posusney 1997). Egypt's professionals were also organized into a variety of government-sponsored syndicates in order to better control their activities and ensure their subservience to the regime. Of these, the most prominent were the syndicates of the journalists, lawyers, teachers, and engineers (Bianchi 1989).

Sadat's 1974 *infitah,* or new economic opening, witnessed a revival of business associations. The influence of these associations, however, has been weakened by their inability to agree on a common strategy for dealing with the Mubarak regime. Labor, peasant, and most professional associations remain under government supervision today, but that supervision has lessened as syndicate elections have become increasingly dominated by opposition parties, including the Muslim Brotherhood. Indeed, by the mid-1900s, the Muslim Brotherhood dominated most of Egypt's twenty-two main professional organizations, including medical, legal, and engineering associations, demonstrating that the appeal of fundamentalism was not limited to the lower classes.

Prompted by the Muslim Brotherhood's growing influence within Egypt's professional associations, recent legislation has tightened governmental control of all groups and associations, leading to renewed charges of dictatorship and oppression. Human Rights Watch has openly condemned the 1999 Associations Law, claiming that it unreasonably restricts freedom of association and assembly. The Engineers' Syndicate was "sequestered" for alleged financial irregularities committed by its Brotherhood-dominated leadership and placed under government control. The syndicate's attempts to hold a conference in 2004 were blocked by the government (March 18, 2004).

The government has also countered Brotherhood influence by encouraging other factions to become more active in the struggle for control of Egypt's professional associations. This effort has met with some success, with the Nasserites gaining control of the Bar Association in 2000. In the 2005 elections, the Brotherhood attempted to regain control of the Bar Association by including a broader range of political and religious views in its electoral slate. The Brotherhood even considered adding a Coptic Christian (Coptic Christians represent some 10,000 voting members of the Bar Association) and a jihadist to its slate (*Al-Ahram Weekly,* Feb. 24, 2005). The Nasserites also broadened the base of their membership. The Brotherhood lost the presidency, but did gain a majority of seats on the executive council of the Bar Association (*Middle East Times,* April 4, 2005). The NDP wasn't even close.

These examples suggest that democratic process is alive and well at the subnational level. Particularly positive has been the willingness of staunchly ideological groups such as the Muslim Brotherhood and the Nasserites to broaden their appeal for the sake of winning elections. Compromise is the essence of democracy. Curiously, neither saw fit to include a woman—women make up 30 percent of the Bar Association's membership—on their list (*Al-Ahram Weekly,* Feb. 24, 2005).

In contrast to the professional associations, labor unions have remained relatively docile. Government unions control workers in the state-owned factories and Egypt's expanding private sector has remained largely un-unionized (*Al-Ahram Weekly,* May 1, 2003, and June 16, 2005). High unemployment does not help matters. Workers are more concerned about keeping a job than about political activism. The government, for its part, has become business-friendly.

## Private Voluntary Organizations
## and Nongovernmental Organizations

Political parties and pressure groups are manifestly political in orientation. Private voluntary organizations (PVOs) and nongovernmental organizations (NGOs)—the terms are often used interchangeably—ostensibly exist to provide material and spiritual services to the population. By the year 2000, Egypt could boast some 15,000 registered NGOs, more than any other Arab country. The actual number is larger, for many of the smaller NGOs don't bother to register with the government. This does not mean that they are not political. NGOs led the charge for greater democracy in the period leading up to Egypt's 2005 presidential election. Indeed, a strong network of NGOs is critical to building a civil society. Not all NGOs, of course, are wedded to democracy. Extremist religious groups are also NGOs, as are the charities and educational groups that support them.

Egypt's treatment of its NGOs has been one of several sources of contention with the United States. The Egyptian government considers U.S. support for NGOs that advocate democracy to be interference in its internal affairs. (*Al-Ahram Weekly*, March 3–9, 2005). The United States, for its part, criticizes Egypt for not doing enough to regulate Islamic charities that wittingly or unwittingly support terrorism. Egypt does regulate Islamic charities, but some have traditionally been controlled by extremist groups on an "informal" basis. This is not a minor consideration, for some Islamic benevolent societies have more than a million members (Mustafa 1995).

## Informal Sectors

In addition to the parties and pressure groups surveyed above, Egyptian politics is also influenced by a variety of social sectors including the residents of Greater Cairo, students, the Copts, the various social classes, and women.

**Cairo as a Pressure Group**    The citizens of Cairo, although seldom thought of as a pressure group, represent a critical sector whose interests must be addressed (Weede 1986). Cairo is the seat of Egypt's government and its center of industry, commerce, banking, communications, mass media, education, religion, culture, health care, and tourism. Little of significance occurs in Egypt that is not controlled in one way or another from Cairo. The metropolitan area's more than 15 million residents constitute approximately a fifth of Egypt's population—more if some 3 million commuters are added to the total. A strike in Cairo can cripple the entire country. When one speaks of controlling "the streets," it is the Cairo streets that are meant. To lose control of Cairo is to lose the capacity to rule.

Not surprisingly, the citizens of Cairo receive favored treatment in terms of food distribution, services, education, and housing. Even this, however, has been inadequate to quell the frustrations that accompany living in one of the world's most crowded metropolises. Traffic is horrendous, water in short supply, sewage treatment and health facilities inadequate, smog unbearable, and the cost of housing beyond the reach of the average citizen. Many of Cairo's citizens cling to flats in buildings slated for demolition while others crowd into the city's some sixty-eight shantytowns ("random areas" in Egyptian parlance), few of which have adequate water, sewage disposal, or electricity (*Al-Ahram Weekly*: http://weekly.ahram.org.eg/2005/725/fe1.htm).

Life in many areas of Cairo is difficult, but nowhere near as difficult as in the countryside. In a cruel irony, the favored position of Cairo has led to the city's inordinate growth. A city whose population was 3 million in 1960 will become a city of 20 million in a few years. Cairo is where the action is.

Faced with this dilemma, the Egyptian government has embarked upon a program to develop magnet cities to stem the migration to Cairo. Unfortunately, this will reduce Cairo's share of the budget from 60 percent of the national budget, already inadequate, to 40 percent (*Al-Ahram Weekly:* http://weekly.ahram.org.eg/2005/725/fe1.htm). There have also been thoughts of moving the capital, although that is unlikely. How could Cairo not be the capital of Egypt?

**Students**    Students are the most idealistic, the most intellectually aware, and the most articulate segment of Egyptian society. Their awareness of injustice is unfailing. The politicization of Egyptian students is also catalyzed by a profound sense of insecurity and frustration. Many Egyptian students (some place the figure at 25 percent or higher) face the prospect of unemployment after graduation. Of those who do find jobs, many will find them in the lower rungs of the bureaucracy—a marginal existence at best.

Civic disturbances are generally initiated by university students and, if promising, are joined by disgruntled workers, high school students, and other dissidents. This was certainly the case of the massive demonstrations protesting the U. S. -led invasion of Iraq. It was also true of the "Enough" (of Mubarak) movement that mushroomed before the 2005 presidential election. Some student disturbances are spontaneous; most are inspired by external political groups such as the Nasserites or the Muslim Brotherhood.

The ruling NDP is attempting to strengthen its student wing, but it is the fundamentalists who are now the dominant force in student politics. The government's response has been to clamp down on student organizations and, failing that, to keep demonstrations bottled up within university compounds. Fundamentalist students are also arrested on a regular basis as a means of intimidation (Schemm 1999).

**The Copts**    Coptic Christians represent approximately 5–10 percent of the Egyptian population and constitute a far higher percentage of the population in the politically sensitive area of Greater Cairo. Egypt's Coptic community long predates the Muslim invasion: Alexandria was one of the original centers of the Christian church.

Copts are well represented at all levels of Egyptian society, and despite religious differences, they share a common culture with Muslim Egyptians. Historically, they have not formed a distinct political group (Farah 1987, 57). This picture, however, is rapidly changing. The dramatic rise of the Islamic fundamentalists and their demands for an Islamic state now threaten to destroy Egypt's long tradition of tolerance and religious harmony. Religious conflicts, commonplace since the later days of the Sadat regime, have intensified in recent years. President Mubarak has condemned the growing tension between Copts and Muslims and warned that it represents a threat to Egypt's political stability.

**Women as a Political Force**   The political role of women in Egypt is difficult to assess. By Middle Eastern standards, Egyptian women have made dramatic progress toward economic and political equality (Sullivan 1986). Females now constitute approximately 30 percent of the urban labor force. The picture is much the same in the field of education, with females now accounting for approximately one-third of the students attending Egyptian universities—a dramatic increase over the 7 percent of the prerevolutionary era. Progress in the areas of education and employment has been far greater in the urban areas than in the countryside, where the illiteracy rate among rural females is around 70 percent. Egyptian women will probably continue to make gains in the economic sphere, in as much as Egyptian economic realities increasingly require families to have two incomes. Indeed, a good job contributes markedly to a woman's marriageability. Women also possess the right to vote, and they are represented in the People's Assembly and to a lesser extent, in the cabinet.

By Western standards, Egyptian women remain an exploited underclass in a male-dominated society (Rugh 1986). However, progress has been made. A 1979 personal statutes law requires a man to notify his wife in writing that he has divorced her. The law also states that the wife has the right to divorce her husband if he chooses to take a second wife, a practice limited largely to the rural areas. In such an instance, the woman retains a legal right to the family's lodging until she remarries or until the children are no longer in her custody, at 12 years old for girls and 10 years for boys. A 2000 version of the Personal Statutes Law further broadened the ability of women to file for divorce. This is not a minor consideration, for it is estimated that some 7 million people are currently seeking legal separation (Hammond 2000; Sachs 2000). The growing desire for divorce is attributed to rising education levels, increased social acceptance of divorce, violence against women, and the larger role that women are playing in the Egyptian economy (*Middle East Times,* 2003–2//*Middle East Times,* 2003–32).

Less progress has been made in abolishing female genital mutilation (FGM), a traditional practice in many areas of Egypt, Sudan, and some twenty-eight other African countries. A 2003 conference on FGM highlighted the problem, but suggested that it could only be eradicated by a combination of legislation, education, and the empowerment of NGOs willing to tackle the problem (*Al-Ahram Weekly,* June 26, 2003).

Women's groups proliferate, but are divided between government sponsored women's groups and feminist NGOs (*Al-Ahram,* June 16, 2005). The former push for equality of opportunity and health and legal issues. The latter focus on political equality and marital violence. Both attack female genital mutilation. The surge of Islamic fundamentalism has produced a greater conservatism in Egyptian society, and even the economic gains of Egyptian women are being called into question.

**Survival Networks**   Underpinning the groups and interests discussed above is a vast array of networks that help the poor survive under very difficult economic circumstances. People trade *wasta* (connections) to get things done, local groups form to share resources and arbitrate disputes before they erupt into violence, and self-help groups aid those in greatest need (Singerman 1995). The survival networks have little formal structure, and they tend to form and dissolve as circumstances dictate. Many revolve around a local charismatic leader whom the locals respect and look to for guidance. This is particularly the case in the shantytowns that engulf Cairo and other large cities. Political activism is limited, though some shantytowns have forced the government to provide free water and electricity (Bayat 1997a). This does not mean that the survival networks have no political significance. Without them, the potential for violence would increase dramatically.

**Public Opinion**    Public opinion in Egypt finds expression in a variety of outlets ranging from the ubiquitous political joke to periodic riots. Other indicators of public opinion include commentary in the press, results of elections (such as they are), and even the dress code adopted by Egyptian citizens. Islamic dress is prominent among females, but commentators are not sure whether such dress is a political commentary, a fashion statement, or merely a convenience (Radwan 1982; Rugh 1986, 149).

As in so many other instances, Mubarak is attempting to strike a balance between freedom of expression on one hand and the regime's security on the other. Assessing public opinion in Egypt remains difficult. The government does not allow the free use of opinion polls, for adverse results could serve as an invitation to revolution if they showed majority support for the Muslim Brotherhood or for jihadists. A unique exception to this rule was a 1997–1998 public opinion poll conducted by the Al-Ahram Center for Strategic and Political Studies. Among other things, the results indicated that the citizens of Cairo vote at a lower rate than citizens in the rural areas and are less inclined to join political parties than their rural counterparts. Egyptian youth have also shown less interest in joining formal political parties than their elders. If one reads between the lines, these figures suggest that the NDP is losing its grip in Cairo and must rely on the influence of local notables allied with the NDP to score large majorities in the rural areas. It is also interesting to note that the public sector is more involved in electoral politics than the private sector: the former is under the direct control of the NDP. The higher and better-educated classes are more politically aware than the lower classes but choose to work through pressure groups rather than political parties (Al-Ahram Survey 1998).

The survey also found that the citizens of Cairo were cynical, while those of the countryside were more willing to give the government the benefit of the doubt. The sincerity of rural responses to the questionnaire, however, remains open to doubt, for the rural areas have little familiarity with such things and many respondents may have been inclined to disguise their views (Palmer, Sullivan, and Safty 1996).

For the first time since 1952, the Egyptian press is now playing an important if guarded role in criticizing government policies. Mubarak's policies are openly criticized by the opposition press, something that would not have happened while Nasser and Sadat were in power. Mubarak prides himself on not having confiscated a single publication during his tenure in office. Egypt's leading literary figures were asked to testify to this fact during the tenth anniversary of Mubarak's rule, with Naguib Mahfouz, Egypt's Nobel Prize–winning author, acknowledging that

Egypt enjoyed extensive freedom of the press "within the limits of our traditions" (*Al-Ahram,* Oct. 10, 1991). This does not refer to the growing role of religious authorities in censoring materials they believe to be morally objectionable. At the very least, journalists criticizing the regime are no longer threatened with imprisonment for expressing their opinions (*Daily Star,* March 6, 2004).

Egyptian public opinion has traditionally found expression in the sarcastic political humor that fuels conversation in Cairo's ubiquitous coffee shops. While much of Egypt's political humor loses its bite in translation, suffice it to say that Nasser himself found it to be a subversive force and attempted to suppress it (Hamouda 1990). Much of the current Egyptian humor portrays Mubarak as a plodding and indecisive bureaucrat.

While difficult to assess, public opinion is taken very seriously by the Mubarak regime. The information section of the Presidential Office is charged with both monitoring and shaping public opinion, as are the Ministry of Information and the National Democratic Party. Riots and demonstrations get the most attention, but election results are also studied with great care (Schemm 1999). The results of the 2000 and 2005 parliamentary elections caught the attention of all of the above agencies, as did the 23 percent voter turnout for the 2005 presidential election. As might be expected, the opinions of Cairo's residents are of far more importance to Egypt's leaders than the opinions of Egypt's provincial citizens. Cairo is the pulse of Egypt.

## Islam and Civil Society in Egypt

Egyptian intellectuals point to Egypt's burgeoning civil society as a dramatic force in the country's evolution toward a more democratic political system. As suggested earlier, however, the dominant force in Egypt's civil society consists of Islamic activists of diverse persuasions. They are less concerned with creating a democratic Egypt than with establishing an Islamic Egypt.

Viewed in this light, Egypt's parties, associations, and other components of civil society have become the arena for a three-way struggle between a government attempting to perpetuate the status quo, political reformers attempting to push Egypt toward greater democracy, and Islamic activists attempting to create a more Islamic society. The two main forces in this struggle are the government and the Islamic activists. The conflict between these two opposing forces has become the stuff of Egyptian politics.

The terms *Islamic fundamentalists* and *Islamic movement* encompass a broad spectrum of citizens who support a more Islamic society (Shukri 1990). Islamic activists range from individuals who support a greater role for religion in Egypt's political life to the jihadists intent on seizing power by force. Occupying the middle ground is the Muslim Brotherhood. The Brotherhood advocates the attainment of an Islamic state by peaceful means, if possible.

The number of Egyptians preferring a more Islamic state in one form or another is large indeed. An informal survey of American University of Cairo students, for example, found that almost 55 percent of the respondents were sympathetic to the Islamic revival while 45 percent were not. Needless to say, the Copts predominated in the latter category (Palmer, Sullivan, and Safty 1996). The same survey also illustrated the profound influence of religion on Egyptian society, with more than 90 percent of the population supporting religion in schools and 70 percent supporting religious censorship. Support for these figures may be found in Egypt's overflowing mosques; the survey results leave little doubt that Islam should provide the moral underpinning of Egyptian society.

Islamic activists of one kind or another have penetrated all the levels of Egyptian civil society (Mustafa 1992, 1995). While united in the goal of achieving a more Islamic state, members of the Islamic community do not agree on what an Islamic state is to look like, how it is to be achieved, or how it is to be governed. Indeed, the main weakness of the Islamic revival has been the dissension within its ranks.

**The Muslim Brotherhood**   The Muslim Brotherhood is the oldest, largest, and most visible element of the Islamic right. It is also the mother lode from which the jihadists have splintered. Created in the 1920s by Hasan al-Banna, the Brotherhood preached a message that was both simple and poignant. Egypt's plight, in the view of the Brotherhood, was caused by the decadence of the ruling elite and by the foreign influences that sustained that elite. God's word, as revealed by the Prophet Mohammed, was both clear and unequivocal. To follow the word of God was to achieve eternal salvation; to ignore it was to court damnation. It was the duty of Muslims to crush foreign decadence and forge a government based on Islamic principles. The strategy of the Brotherhood was threefold: teaching and preaching, providing welfare services for the poor, and political activism (Husain 1956, 103–105). Given the oppressive nature of Egypt's regimes, that activism inclined toward violence. Nevertheless, the Brotherhood's strategy was based upon the belief that it was possible to reform Egyptian society from within. Nasser drove the Brotherhood into hiding following a failed assassination attempt in 1954, but its organizational roots remained intact. When it was revived by Sadat in 1971, it soon gained control of the street and became a critical element in Sadat's effort to crush the left. Sadat's reliance upon the Brotherhood provided the organization with quasi-legal status, and it was officially viewed as a "reformist" organization seeking to fulfill its religious objectives within the framework of Egypt's "constitutional" political system (Hinnebusch 1988). The Brotherhood's leadership had also aged: the firebrands of the prewar era had become the elder statesmen of the 1970s.

The tacit acceptance of the Brotherhood as a quasi-legitimate political organization provided it with increased scope for political activity. Election alliances were forged with the New Wafd and other parties of the capitalist right. More recently, the Brotherhood has simply incorporated the Socialist Labor Party and the much smaller Liberal Party. The Brotherhood has also made repeated attempts to inspire an Islamic political party similar to that which has ruled Turkey throughout much of the past decade. The most recent attempt came during the prelude to the 2005 presidential election and was summarily denied (Al-Jazeera, March 23, 2005). Mubarak was not worried about a serious challenge from Egypt's largely symbolic opposition parties, but he was definitely worried about an Islamic challenge, however moderate its facade.

Government efforts to tame the Brotherhood have been a dismal failure. The Brotherhood contests elections under surrogate labels and dominates Egypt's most important student and professional unions. It also controls the street. Rare are the demonstrations that do not bear the stamp of Brotherhood influence. Underpinning its political activities is a vast network of Islamic schools and clinics. Most surpass government schools and clinics in the quality of services that they offer (S. E. Ibrahim 1996, 60–61). In many ways, the Brotherhood has created a social infrastructure parallel to that of the state. It also runs or controls thousands of mosques.

Is the Muslim Brotherhood a violent organization? "No," say its leaders. "We are not a violent organization." Does the Brotherhood support jihads in Palestine and elsewhere. "With pride." Does the Brotherhood believe in democracy? "That depends on your definition of democracy. If democracy means that people select who leads them, then the Ikwan (Brotherhood) accepts them. If it means that people can change the laws of Allah and follow what they wish to follow, then that is not acceptable (Muslim Brotherhood home page, question and answer section, 2005: www.ummah.org/ikwan; some punctuation modified).

**The Violent Extremists (Jihadists)**   Not all Muslim Brothers, however, accepted al-Banna's assumption that it was possible to reform Egyptian society from within. Shocked by Nasser's rush to modernity, Sayyid Qutb, one of the Brotherhood's leading intellectuals, argued that the secular society being forged by Nasser differed little from the *jahiliya,* the time of ignorance that prevailed in pre-Islamic Arabia. Mohammed had created an Islamic society by destroying the heathen society of his day. It was now the obligation of modern Muslims to do the same. There was no room for compromise between the sacred and the profane (Moussalli 1999).

Sayyid Qutb was put to death by Nasser, but his writings would provide the philosophical foundation for the jihadist movement that emerged in the 1970s. Like him, they rejected the idea that Egyptian society could be reformed from within. The jihadists gained notoriety in 1974 when an organization known as the "military group" provoked a direct confrontation with the Sadat regime by occupying a military barracks. Whether inspired by naïveté, idealism, or both, the attempted coup (if such it was) was crushed by Sadat, and many of its leaders paid with their lives. The movement later resurfaced as Jihad, the group that assassinated Sadat on October 6, 1981.

Unlike the Muslim Brothers, the jihadists constitute a minute segment of Egyptian society. They do, however, have a following. At various times, there have been as many as ninety different fundamentalist groups active in Egypt; their size and policies vary dramatically (Mustafa 1992, 1995; Shukri 1990). Some attempted to destabilize the government by assassinating key officials or foreign visitors, including the 1981 assassination of Sadat and the 1997 slaughter of some sixty-seven tourists at Luxor. Others have sought to isolate themselves from Egypt's corrupting environment by building religious communities in the desert. Biding their time, they wait for the moment of return. Some of Egypt's more prominent jihadist groups associated with Osama bin Laden's al-Qaeda movement and were instrumental in planning the September 11, 2001, attacks on the United States (Gunaratna 2002; Thompson 2004). Indeed, the jihadist movement in Egypt laid the groundwork for the jihadist movement that now threatens much of the world (Palmer and Palmer 2004).

Jihadist leaders during the 1970s and 1980s tended to be young and well educated individuals of rural origin who were frustrated by the decadence and inequities of Egyptian society (Ansari 1986; Ayubi 1980; Ibrahim 1980). More recently, there is evidence that the extremist leadership is being drawn from the lower classes (S. E. Ibrahim 1996, 74). During their initial years, the jihadists were well funded and enjoyed a broad base of support throughout Egyptian society, including the military, the police, and the educational system. In the fall of 1994, for example, the government began a purge of pro-Islamic teachers from Egypt's 25,000 schools, a venture that would seem doomed to failure before it began (*NYT,* Oct. 4, 1994, A4).

Faced with a jihadist challenge that bordered on open revolution, Mubarak intensified his antiterrorist campaign on all fronts. Jihadist groups were attacked with a new savagery and their leaders forced to flee. Suspects were arrested and tried by military courts, thereby avoiding the niceties of civilian law. Some were put to death; others received long prison terms. The security around tourist sites was increased, and border patrols were strengthened.

The above moves were matched by efforts to reassert government control over domestic mosques and Islamic benevolent associations. As the policy was described by the minister of waqfs: "We do not order preachers to discuss specific subjects and we do not send them written sermons. . . . Individuals who undertake to give sermons or religious lessons in a mosque must obtain prior permission . . . from one of the 27 regional offices of the Ministry" (Zaqzuq 1999). He further noted that the target date for nationalizing Egypt's 27,000 private mosques was 2002. The goal was not met and some 20,000 remained "unnationalized" well after that date with no change in sight. Past efforts to rein in the domestic (nongovernmental) mosques have failed for lack of certified preachers, and the questionable reliability of those who have been certified.

More subtly, the Mubarak regime has attempted to deny the terrorists the glory of martyrdom by referring to them as common criminals. Constant reference is also made to the virtual civil war launched by the jihadists in Algeria, a conflict that has claimed some 100,000 lives over the course of the past decade. Few Egyptians welcome the prospect of similar carnage on the Nile.

The government has also attempted to shore up its Islamic credentials. Censorship of books judged inappropriate by Al-Azhar has increased, as has funding for mosques and other overtly Islamic projects. The American University of Cairo was forced to remove two books from its curriculum: Maxime Rodinson's *Muhammat* and Alifa Rifaat's *Distant View of a Minaret.* The latter had been part of the university's core curriculum for the previous five years (Shoreh 1998). Al-Azhar has subsequently been given the right to search and seize materials that it finds immoral (*Al-Ahram Weekly,* June 17, 2004).

On the international front, Egypt and the United States pressured Kuwait and other Gulf states to curtail the donations of their citizens to fundamentalist organizations working in Egypt. Kuwaiti fundamentalists, in particular, were accused of supporting their Egyptian brethren (Saadeq 1999b). More often than not, this meant suspending contributions to Islamic NGOs with suspected links to the jihadists. Egypt also put pressure on the United States and the countries of Western Europe to stop sheltering known jihadist supporters, an effort marked by Egypt's hosting of an antiterrorist summit in 1996. U.S. cooperation increased precipitously in the wake of the 1997 bombings of the U.S. embassies in Nairobi and Dar es Salaam.

By the end of 1990s, government antiterrorist measures had taken their toll and the imprisoned leaders of Egypt's main two jihadist groups, the Islamic Group and the Jihad, declared a truce and called for an end to "military operations" (Barakat and Sadiq 1998). The new initiative was duly announced by the "Islamic Lawyers," a shadowy group that serves as intermediary between the imprisoned members of Jihad and the Islamic Group) and the outside world (Al-Zaiyat 2002).

It wasn't government antiterror measures alone, however, that forced the truce. As the Islamic lawyers conceded, the jihadists contributed to their own decline. The intensity of jihadist violence had proven repulsive to many Egyptians who were otherwise supportive of the Islamic revival. The violence seemed to have become an end in itself. The extremists had lost touch with the values of the broader Islamic community and had inadvertently pushed people toward the government's position. In much the same manner, violence against tourists caused severe economic hardship among the vast number of Egyptians who depended upon the tourist industry for their survival. The tactics of the extremists thus ran counter to the economic interests of many of their potential supporters. The leadership of the jihadists was also becoming increasingly divided. Diverse groups found it difficult to coordinate their activities, and growing tension existed between the leadership in prison, a group now in its fifties, and the younger activists who were managing the day-to-day operations of the movement. Tension also existed between the leadership in Egypt and the leadership in exile, in part because the former were bearing the brunt of the government crackdown.

Other problems abounded. The jihadist leadership had lacked a realistic assessment of the government's antiterrorist capacity. As a result, casualties were high. The jihadists also lacked concrete solutions to the problems confronting Egyptian society. The slogan "God is the solution" was not enough for an increasingly sophisticated population searching for tangible solutions to practical problems. Finally, the critiques of the jihadist movement focused on its parochialism and its failure to learn from the experience of extremist movements in Iran, Malaysia, Algeria, Pakistan, and Afghanistan, countries in which the jihadists had scored major successes.

Whatever the case, the Mubarak regime responded to the truce by releasing about a thousand jihadists from prison. Mubarak claimed that this was an act of compassion. The jihadists interpreted it as his keeping his part of the bargain. The United States was not amused.

If the strategies of the Mubarak regime have been successful in stemming the tide of violence, they have neither crushed the jihadist movement nor altered its goals. Rather, they have forced the jihadists to adjust their strategies to reflect declining popular support and the growing effectiveness of the government's antiterrorist campaign (Al-Zaiyat 2002).

This new strategy, while still a matter for debate, involves bringing the jihadist movement back in line with its support base and portraying the jihadists in a positive rather than a negative light. The more the jihadists can capture the high ground, the more the Mubarak regime will be forced to bear the burden of its ineptitude, secularism, repression, and corruption. In the meantime, the jihadists will have time to rebuild and train new cadres and to improve their organizational effectiveness.

There is no clear indication that the jihadists have forsworn the use of violence. Jihadist violence abated after the assassination of Sadat in 1981, only to reassert itself with a vengeance a few years later (S. E. Ibrahim 1996). Those jihadist leaders forced to flee abroad have likened their flight to the Prophet's flight from Mecca to Medina (Saadeq 1999b). Once the heat is off, they will return. Indeed, in 2004 Egyptian-based jihadists blew up an Egyptian hotel on the Egyptian–Israeli border, killing approximately 39 people and wounding 159. The Egyptian government responded by arresting some 2,400 suspects. Driving the jihadists out of Egypt has also had the unintended effect of forcing them to shift their field of operations to Saudi Arabia, Iraq, Palestine, and other areas of the world (Saadeq 1999b; Palmer and Palmer, 2004). The jihadist attacks, although sporadic, continue.

Although Mubarak's anti-jihadist strategy was successful in forcing a lull in jihadist terror, it did little to allay many of the basic causes of the jihadist movement. The economic position of the poor continues to be desperate, a sharp contrast to the brash ostentation of the rich. There are few signs that the government has enhanced its capacity to meet the needs of the poor. Opportunities for non-Islamic political expression, moreover, have decreased. By emasculating the legitimate political parties, the government has left its opponents little choice but to incline toward the more extremist groups.

## THE CONTEXT OF EGYPTIAN POLITICS

In addition to its institutions and actors, Egypt's politics are profoundly influenced by the cultural, economic, and international environments. All have contributed to the immobility of the Mubarak regime, some by impeding change and others by forcing a more rapid pace of change than the system can bear.

### Political Culture

Three aspects of Egypt's political culture are particularly important to understanding Egyptian politics and, in particular, the immobility of the Mubarak regime. The first and most obvious of these is Islam, which has already been discussed at length. Suffice it to say that Islamic values must be weighed in all policy decisions.

Second, occasional riots notwithstanding, Egyptian political culture is seemingly docile. Islamic militancy continues to cast a shadow over Egypt's uncertain march toward democracy, if such it is, but the much-feared jihadist uprising has yet to materialize. Egyptian passivity is often attributed to the centuries of foreign domination that taught the Egyptian people that revolt was futile. Over time, this sense of hopelessness became part of the Egyptian cultural map that was passed on from generation to generation. Whether or not this explanation is valid, the apparent docility of the Egyptian population has been a clear plus for the Mubarak regime (Al-Manoufi 1979).

Third, centuries of foreign domination created a chasm of distrust between the government and the people. Recoiling from oppressive rulers, Egyptians sought security in the solidarity of their families rather than in the protection of the state. In the case of the Coptic minority, security was also to be found in religious solidarity. Egyptians, accordingly, were slow to develop the sense of political community or civil society that loomed so large in the political development of the West. Rather, Egypt became a society of families and clans, each competing with the others for scarce resources. Egyptians distrusted the government, and they distrusted each other. This sense of distrust and political alienation continues to haunt a Mubarak regime that is trying desperately to mobilize the Egyptian masses behind his programs. Rare is the Mubarak speech that does not call upon Egyptians to work harder for the good of their country. Unfortunately, the corruption and mismanagement that pervade Egyptian government offer little in the way of inspiration. Survival remains the primary concern of most Egyptians.

## Political Economy

While there can be little doubt about the influence of culture on Egyptian politics, the influence of economics is equally pervasive ( Richards 1991; Richards and Waterbury 1990; Waterbury 1983). Nasser's revolution, in the view of many political economists, was a revolt of the middle classes against an exploitative aristocratic class. Nasser's "social contract" with the Egyptian public was essentially an economic contract that traded political acquiescence for economic security. The quality of services was rudimentary, but few Egyptians starved.

The socialism of the Nasser era proved unequal to the task of economic development, and Sadat inherited a country that was falling ever deeper into debt as it attempted to maintain a welfare system that promised Egypt's citizens jobs, housing, education, medical care, and subsidized food. Viewed from the political economic perspective, the economic realities of the 1970s left Sadat little option but to experiment with capitalism and scale back the economic burden of Nasser's welfare society.

The economic dislocations created by Sadat's *infitah* helped to fuel the Islamic revival that was to become the dominant political force in Egypt. Most of the leaders of the fundamentalist movement came from economic classes that were excluded from power by the Sadat regime (Habib 1989).

As one might expect, Mubarak's rush to capitalism has not been without its problems (Sullivan 1990). Egypt's social contract has become increasingly tattered, and the gap between rich and poor is ever more glaring. While Egypt's per capita income in 1998 was $1,294, its minimum wage was "$20 a month for a six-day, 48-hour work week" (U.S. Government 1998). Efforts to extend privatization to the countryside have led to threats of violence (El-Gawhary 2004). Egyptian unemployment figures continue to hover between 10 and 13 percent, although informal estimates place the number at closer to 30 percent. As a leading Egyptian economist noted in a 1999 interview, no one is quite sure of the government's standard of employment (interviews 1999). Is it a steady, full-time job, or does it include part-time or seasonal employment? All seem to be included in the government figures, which thus disguise severe underemployment. Particularly worrisome, from the government's perspective, are mass fears that future privatization, including that of Egypt's unprofitable heavy industries, will result in layoffs and reduced benefits. These fears are not without basis, for some 185,000 public sector employees have taken early retirement since 1992 (*Middle East Times,* 2004–2005). Investors, for their part, complain of the lack of transparency in Egyptian companies, and the business community complains of bureaucratic strangulation (*Al-Ahram Weekly,* Dec. 18, 2003).

Despite the problems, Egypt's transition from socialism to capitalism is now in midstream, and the international financial community is pushing Mubarak to complete the process with all due haste. Growing disparities in wealth, they argue, invariably accompany the transition from socialism to capitalism. Such is the nature of capitalism. If investors are to create jobs and wealth, they must be rewarded for their risks. Over time, the industries that they create will provide the jobs and skills necessary to lift Egypt from its poverty. In the meantime, the United States and the International Monetary Fund are urging Mubarak to bite the bullet and to stay the course.

Out of realism or caution, the Mubarak regime has been disinclined to rush the pace of economic reform (*Middle East Times,* 2004–2005). Rather, the regime has attempted to walk a fine line between providing enough reform to stimulate the Egyptian economy while simultaneously keeping mass tensions in check by maintaining what is left of the social contract. Economic reforms may be essential for future development, but they cannot be allowed to threaten the stability of the regime. Rarely does a day go by in which *Al-Ahram,* Egypt's semiofficial newspaper, does not reassure Egypt's masses that the poor will not be forgotten. Mubarak has also promised not to privatize either the utilities or strategic military industries, both of which employ a high percentage of the Egyptian workforce. Key consumer goods continue to receive government subsidies, and reform of an obstructionist bureaucracy has remained as elusive as ever.

Vacillation sustains the Mubarak regime from year to year, but it does not solve Egypt's underlying social and economic problems. Indeed, the longer the regime delays taking decisive action, the more severe its economic problems become. Each year a million new Egyptians come of age and require education, housing, and health care. Each year a new wave of graduates from Egypt's high schools and universities compete for jobs that do not exist. For the present, Egypt's deficits are being covered by oil revenues and foreign assistance from the United States and other aid donors including the European Union, Japan, and the World Bank.

This hasn't placed Egypt on the path to self-sufficiency. Foreign aid must inevitably end, and dependence on oil revenues leaves Egypt vulnerable to sharp fluctuations in the world oil market. Oil prices have skyrocketed during the Iraq War, but they probably won't stay high forever.

### Egypt and the West: Dependence or Interdependence?

International and regional pressures have also contributed to the immobility of the Mubarak regime. The United States provides Egypt with $2 billion in foreign assistance per year. The price of that aid has been quite explicit. The United States and other donor nations are placing enormous pressure on Egypt to complete its transition from socialism to capitalism, a transition that is currently in process, with the most difficult stages of privatization yet to be implemented. The United States has also called upon Egypt to promote democracy, but has been reluctant to push reforms that might empower the Muslim Brotherhood or more violent extremist groups. It backed down from its 2004 democratic initiative in the face of Egyptian and Saudi Arabian complaints. The United States has left unspoken its expectations that Egypt will honor its peace treaty with Israel, protect Saudi Arabia and the Gulf sheikhdoms, and stand as a U.S. ally against Iraq and Iran. To American dismay, Egypt refused to participate in the 2003 U.S.-led invasion of Iraq and has condemned the U.S. occupation that followed. It has, however, honored its peace treaty with Israel and shows little interest in another devastating war with its Jewish neighbor. For the moment, the United States is satisfied. U.S. pressure is profoundly unpopular in Egypt, and bold headlines in Egypt's semiofficial *Al-Ahram* newspaper routinely proclaim that Egypt is an "equal partner" of the United States. Alas, the U.S. presence in Egypt is so massive that it is difficult to ignore. To make matters worse, the $3 billion in U.S. aid to Israel is simply transferred to the Israeli treasury, while the $2 billion granted to Egypt is minutely controlled by a massive U.S. Agency for International Development (USAID) bureaucracy in Cairo, the organizational chart for which is ten pages long. The Egyptians find this differential treatment demeaning and drag their feet on projects of primary interest to the United States. Indeed, virtually all of the projects and subprojects funded by USAID have to be approved by both the United States and Egypt, a laborious process that pits the U.S. bureaucracy against the Egyptian. Again, the result has been vacillation and indecision as the Mubarak regime struggles to convince the United States that it is a valuable ally while simultaneously trying to prove to its own people that it is not a U.S. puppet. The U.S. occupation of Iraq has made this a very difficult task.

## LOOKING TOWARD THE FUTURE

The Egypt of today bears little resemblance to that of the Nasser era. The Revolutionary Command Council has given way to a constitutional structure not dissimilar to that of France. Executive power is divided between a strong president and a weak prime minister selected by the president. Legislative authority resides in a parliament elected in somewhat fair elections, and the Constitutional Court possesses the power to declare acts of the government unconstitutional. It has done so on several occasions. The single-party apparatus of the Nasser era has been replaced by a multiparty system, albeit a multiparty system in which the government's party always wins. The Egyptian press is freer than at any time since the revolution of 1952, and the rigid socialism of the earlier era has been challenged by a growing private sector.

Nevertheless, the Egypt of today is very much the product of the Nasser years. The president of the Egyptian republic is still a military officer, as are his major advisers. The parliament and the courts, though vigorous in the execution of their responsibilities, pose little challenge to the president. In spite of some progress toward privatization and economic reform, the Egyptian economy continues to be hamstrung by a massive bureaucracy. Decentralization has been much discussed by government leaders, but few effective measures have been taken in that direction. Egypt continues to be an intensely centralized state.

The Egypt of today has also inherited the problems of the past (McDermott 1988). The population explosion continues. The 20 million Egyptians of the revolutionary era have now become 70 million. That figure is expected to reach 125 million by the year 2020. Poverty continues, although few Egyptians are threatened with starvation. Housing shortages are critical, as are unemployment and underemployment.

The capitalist reforms of the Sadat and Mubarak eras have also created new problems. Much of the new wealth that has been produced by the *infitah* has gone to a relatively narrow stratum of Egyptian society. While a minority of the Egyptian population enjoys unparalleled prosperity, most Egyptians find life increasingly difficult. Many Egyptian intellectuals believe that Egypt is in danger of becoming dependent upon the United States. Whether or not their fears are justified, the $2 billion in foreign aid that the United States provides to Egypt annually does assure that American views will receive a careful hearing in Cairo. The growing strength of the Islamic revival, moreover, poses a clear and present danger to the Mubarak regime should it venture toward real democracy.

Also on Egyptian minds is the advanced age of President Mubarak. Now in his fifth term of office and approaching eighty years of age, he is unlikely to run for a sixth term. Who will take over when he goes? His son Jamal? A democratically elected president? A general beholden to the United States (there are several)? The Muslim Brotherhood? The jihadists? Stay tuned. Updates can be found at http://politicalscience.wadsworth.com/palmer2e/.

# 3

# Israel and Palestine

## One Land, Two Claimants

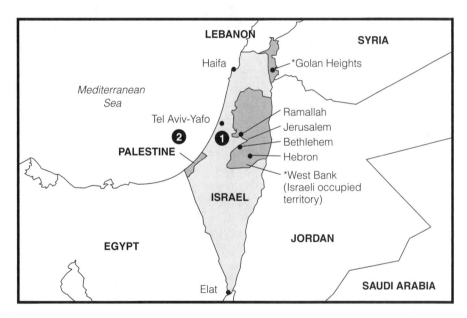

1. Israel has made Jerusalem its capital. This move has not been recognized by the U.S. and most other countries around the world.
2. Palestine refers to the area under the control of the Palestinian Authority. Formal statehood has yet to be recognized by the U.S. and most other countries around the world.

The Arab–Israeli conflict has shaped the politics of the Middle East since Britain decreed in 1917 that Palestine would be a home for the Jews. Since that date, both Jews and Arabs have revolted against British rule, four

Arab–Israeli wars have been fought, two intifadas (uprisings) have pitted the Palestinian masses against the Israeli occupation, Israel has been subjected to an unrelenting wave of terror, and thousands of Palestinians have been killed as a result of Israeli reprisals. Innocent civilians have suffered the most. The Arab–Israeli conflict has also cast a long shadow over America's war on terror. The United States fears that the festering conflict between the Israelis and the Palestinians is fueling anti-Americanism in the Islamic world and building support for al-Qaeda and other jihadist movements. All of this turmoil for control of a piece of land about the size of New Jersey!

Ah, but this is not an ordinary piece of land. It is the focal point of three major religions: Judaism, Christianity, and Islam. For Jews, the survival of Israel is linked to the survival of the Jewish faith. For Muslims, Palestine symbolizes Western efforts to crush Islam and its glories. For Christians, Palestine is the land of the Messiah and the holiest shrines in Christendom. All things considered, Israel and Palestine garner more press coverage per square inch of territory than any other land on earth.

For the moment, cooler heads have prevailed and hesitant steps are being taken toward a lasting resolution of this most enduring of conflicts. A Palestinian state has emerged in the Gaza Strip and the Palestinian terror has abated. And yet, optimism may be premature. None of the basic issues separating the Israelis and the Palestinians have been resolved. Both demand control of the West Bank and both claim Jerusalem as their capital. Israel demands security guarantees against future terrorist attacks, and presumably the right of hot pursuit should those attacks occur. Such guarantees would violate Palestinian sovereignty. The Palestinians demand the right of Palestinian refugees to return to Israel if they wish to do so. This is summarily rejected by the Israelis. Scarce water resources are vital to both communities, yet may be inadequate for either.

Complicating the mix are fears that the peace process cannot be sustained. Hamas and other groups responsible for terrorist attacks in Israel have become major actors in Palestinian politics. There can be little peace without their consent. Israel, for its part, continues to expropriate Arab land and colonize the West Bank—hardly a recipe for lasting peace. The United States, the European Union, Russia, and the United Nations have designed a grand "road map" for peace in the Holy Land, but lack the will to enforce its provisions. The Israelis and the Palestinians ignore it when it suits them. But there is cause for hope. A majority of both populations do want peace. No secure future is possible without it.

The following pages will discuss these issues more fully and provide a guide to the way that the Israelis and the Palestinians do politics. We begin with an historical review and then move on to a discussion of the Israeli and Palestinian political systems. Then we return to the future of the Arab–Israeli conflict.

## HISTORY AND CULTURE

The lands of geographic Palestine, like most of the Middle East, stretch deep into the reaches of history (Sharkansky 1991). Semitic tribes from the Syrian and Arabian deserts began to settle in the region around 5000 BCE, with the Hebrews arriving in approximately 1300 BCE. The term *Semitic* refers to a linguistic grouping that includes both the Hebrew and Arabic languages (Orlinsky 1961, 145).

From the Israeli perspective, the history of Israel begins when Moses, the leader of a nomadic Hebrew tribe, was guided by God to lead his people into Palestine (or Canaan, as it was then known). As recounted in the Bible:

> And the Lord said unto Moses in the plains of Moab by the Jordan at Jericho, "Say to the people of Israel, when you pass over the Jordan into the land of Canaan, then you shall drive out all the inhabitants of the land before you, and destroy all their figured stones, and destroy all their molten images, and demolish all their high places, and you shall take possession of the land and settle in it, for I have given the land to you to possess it" (Numbers 33: 50–55). And I will give to you and to your descendants after you, the land of your sojournings, all the land of Canaan, for an everlasting possession (Genesis 17: 8).

The Israelites were successful in conquering much of Canaan—the name *Israel* was first used during this period—but subsequently succumbed to invasions by the Philistines, Egyptians, Babylonians, Persians, Greeks, and Romans (Orlinsky 1961). The invasion of the Philistines forced the Hebrew tribes to unite under Saul in 1020 BCE, which marks the creation of the first Israeli kingdom (Roth 1963). The reigns of David and Solomon, which soon followed, represented the "golden age" of ancient Israel. During David's rule Jerusalem was conquered and made the capital of the Hebrew state. David also designed the temple that was to become a central focus of the Jewish faith (Orlinsky 1961, 64).

Space does not allow a recounting of the history of ancient Israel; for our purposes, it is enough to say that internal conflicts led to the fragmentation of the Jewish state and its subjugation by a variety of foreign invaders, including the Assyrians, the Babylonians, and the Romans. It was the Romans who expelled the Jews from the Holy Land in 135 BCE, giving rise to the Diaspora—the dispersion of Jews throughout Europe and the Middle East.

Aside from serving as a source of national pride, the ancient history of most countries has little relevance to their modern politics. This is not the case with Israel. Israel bases its claim to Palestine on the Jewish kingdoms of ancient Israel. Indeed, some Israelis argue that the modern state of Israel should incorporate all of the lands of ancient Israel, an area that would include portions of Lebanon, Jordan, and Syria (Gilbert 1979, 1). For many Jews, moreover, the lands of Israel are more than an artifact of history; they are the "Promised Land." The Temple of David is a holy site of profound political and religious significance, as is Hebron, the capital of the Jewish state prior to the conquest of Jerusalem (Sharkansky 1997b). Israelis often talk of "collapsed time," as if the period of some two thousand years that passed between the expulsion of the Jews from Jerusalem and the creation of the Jewish state of Israel in 1948 was little more than a momentary interruption in the course of Jewish history. The Jews have merely returned to their promised land.

The dispersion of the Jews opened the path to new invasions from the Arabian Peninsula. Of these, the most enduring was the invasion triggered by the spread of Islam. More than 7,000 Arab tribesmen laid siege to Jerusalem's Roman fortresses. Many brought their wives and children and remained in the new land, which was infinitely more hospitable than the sands of Arabia (Levy 1957). The garrison at Jerusalem fell toward the end of 636. The rest of Palestine followed. Unlike earlier invaders, the Arabian Muslims retained their ties with Mecca, and Palestine was integrated into the Islamic empire. Except for certain intervals during the Crusades, it would remain so until it was occupied by the British during World War I. Although most Palestinians adopted Islam, a sizable Christian population remained, as did a substantial number of Jews.

Expelled from the lands of Israel, the Jews migrated throughout Europe and the Middle East, either assimilating with the dominant Christian or Muslim populations or living in minority enclaves. They had little choice, for both European and Middle Eastern societies at the time were organized along religious lines. One either joined the majority population or lived apart from it. Persecution was frequent, but less so among Muslims than among Christians, who blamed Jews for the death of Christ. Political leaders often found it expedient to divert mass hostility from their own regimes by focusing it on the Jews. This tactic was particularly brutal in nineteenth-century Russia, where tsars openly encouraged mobs to rush Jewish quarters and slaughter defenseless Jews (Rodinson 1969; Sachar 2005). Pogroms, as the massacres of Jews were called, were condemned by the world's democracies, but not much was done to stop them.

## Zionism

As the situation in Eastern Europe became increasingly untenable, a growing number of Jews looked to the lands of their ancestry as a potential refuge. This interest was stimulated by the publication of Theodor Herzl's *A Jewish State* in 1896. Herzl's book gave birth to the Zionist movement, whose first congress was held in 1897. Herzl argued that Jews would never be fully assimilated in Europe. Continued persecution was inevitable and unavoidable. The only solution, he argued, was the creation of a Jewish home in which Jews would be able to live without persecution and practice their religion as they wished. Argentina and Uganda were both suggested as possible sites for the new home, but the suggestions were rejected for lack of emotional appeal. Only the promise of return to the ancient lands of Zion (Israel) would suffice to rally the entire Jewish community behind the Zionist project (Rodinson 1969, 13). The first Zionist Congress was followed by the establishment of what would become the World Zionist Organization, which was charged with creating a Jewish state in Palestine.

Zionism, as preached by Herzl, was preeminently an expression of Jewish nationalism. The Jews would have their own country, much as the French and British had theirs. Religious Jews could practice their faith as they saw fit, but Israel would be a home for all Jews, secular as well as religious. Judaism is a culture as well as a religion, and even fully assimilated Jews such as Herzl possessed a strong emotional attachment to Jewish traditions (Orr 1994). The wave of anti-Semitism sweeping Europe, moreover, did not distinguish between religious and nonreligious Jews. Both groups were persecuted equally.

The emergence of the Zionist movement was paralleled by embryonic stirrings of Arab nationalism. The stage was thus set for an inevitable clash between two rival ideologies: Judaism and Zionism on one side, Islam and Arab nationalism on the other. Zionism and Arab nationalism were secular ideologies, but both drew heavily upon religious symbolism. The former was based on ancient history and religion; the latter on almost 1,500 years of continuous residence in the Holy Land, perhaps more depending on one's interpretation of history. To make matters even more complex, al-Aqsa mosque, the third holiest shrine in Islam, had been erected on the foundation of the Temple of David, the holiest shrine of the Jews. Christian shrines also abounded, rendering Jerusalem and the surrounding territories an area of intense emotional concern for members of all three faiths.

The Ottoman authorities had eased the ban on Jewish immigration to Palestine in 1880, and in a steady trickle Jews began to join the approximately 24,000 who resided in Palestine at the time. These new settlers, between 20,000 and 30,000 in number, are referred to as the first aliyah, or wave of immigration, a Hebrew word suggesting "going up" (Arian 1997, 403). Jews, however, represented only about 10 percent of the population, and thoughts of a Jewish state were remote at best (Pappe 2004; Rodinson 1969). A second aliyah arrived in the years between 1905 and the outbreak of World War I. Most of these immigrants were Russian socialists fleeing from the failed Russian revolution of 1905. It was this group that would subsequently set the ideological tenor for the Israeli state and provide much of its early leadership. Nevertheless, numbers remained small, and by the end of World War I, Jews constituted no more than 12 percent of the Palestinian population, or 85,000 out of a total population of 739,000 (Rodinson 1969, 20).

Although immigration to Palestine was slow in the years prior to World War I, the Zionist Organization actively sought the support of Western governments for its project. Their efforts came to fruition during World War I as a British government anxious to gain the support of American and Russian Jews for the war effort assented to their demands. The issue was contentious, but shortly before the end of the war Lord Balfour issued a vaguely worded statement declaring Britain's support for the Zionist cause. A parallel statement would later be issued by the League of Nations.

> His Majesty's Government view with favour the establishment in Palestine of a national home for the Jewish people, and will use their best endeavours to facilitate the achievement of this object, it being clearly understood that nothing shall be done which may prejudice the civil and religious rights of existing non-Jewish communities in Palestine, or the rights and political status enjoyed by Jews in any other country (Fraser 1980, 18).

Upon the defeat of the Ottoman Empire in World War I, Britain was assigned the mandate for Palestine, and the Jewish Agency, the executive body of the Zionist Organization, accelerated its settlement of Jews in Palestine. The Balfour Declaration, however, was shrouded in conflict from the date of its announcement. The British had earlier implied that control of Palestine would go to the Arab leader of Mecca in return for his willingness to lead a revolt against the Turks, although this matter, too, remained ambiguous (see Chapter 5).

Also problematic was the vague wording of the Balfour Declaration itself. What precisely was meant by the phrase "national home for the Jews"? Did this mean that Jews were free to settle in Palestine or, as interpreted by the Zionists, did it call for the establishment of a Jewish state? If one accepted the latter interpretation, how was this state to be established without prejudicing the "civil and religious rights of existing non-Jewish communities"? Matters were further confused by the nature of the mandate system established by the League of Nations. Mandates were not colonies. Rather, the mandatory powers were entrusted with leading the former Axis colonies toward self-government. At least on the surface, this implied a government that represented all of the residents of the territory.

The Zionists, however, acknowledged no ambiguity. The Jewish Agency began to buy land in Palestine and to provide financial assistance for Jewish immigrants. The initial waves of immigration were disappointing, but the numbers increased rapidly with the rise of Hitler and his threatened extermination of the Jewish people. By 1936, Jews constituted 30 percent of the Palestinian population, compared to less than 12 percent in 1922.

As immigration increased, the Jewish community began to develop its own political institutions, or Yishuv. These included an elected assembly with the power to levy taxes and an all-encompassing labor union called the Histadrut. In addition to its role as a labor union, the Histadrut also served as an investment company, landowner, insurance company, and social security agency. Eventually, the Yishuv would add a military wing, the Haganah. The Yishuv thus functioned as a state in itself and was far better organized than the Palestinian community, which was fragmented by family and personality conflicts.

Invariably, the rapidly increasing number of Jewish immigrants threatened the Arab population in Palestine, many of whom found themselves marginalized by the growing economic dominance of the Jews. Much of the land purchased by the Jewish Agency had been sold by absentee Arab landlords, many of whom lived in Beirut. As land purchases increased, the number of displaced Palestinians increased along with it.

Fearing that they would soon become a minority in their own land, the Palestinians revolted against the British authorities in 1936. The British responded with force, but the rebellion raged for three years before it was fully suppressed. The intensity of the Palestinian revolt, together with mounting anti-British sentiment throughout the region, forced the British to rethink their Palestinian strategy. World War II was rapidly approaching, and the British had become increasingly apprehensive over pro-Axis sentiments among the Arabs. The Middle East lay astride the route to India, the Jewel of the British Empire, and by the mid-1930s Britain's military and industrial establishments were becoming increasingly dependent upon Middle Eastern oil. German domination of the Middle East would jeopardize Britain's access to both India and oil.

Faced with these new realities, the British began to vacillate in their support for the Zionists. In 1939, the British government issued a white paper that sharply reduced the level of Jewish immigration to Palestine and severely restricted the sale of Arab land to Jews. Palestine was also promised eventual independence as a bi-religious state in which the Arabs would constitute a two-thirds majority. From the

Zionist perspective, the timing of the white paper could hardly have been worse. Anti-Semitism in Germany and other areas of Europe was approaching its peak, and Palestine was viewed as the main refuge for Europe's beleaguered Jews.

Now it was the Jews who revolted against the British: terrorist organizations such as the Irgun and the Stern Gang launched violent attacks against British targets (Bauer 1970; Rodinson 1973). A truce was called during World War II, but the Jewish revolt resumed in 1944. In 1945, the Haganah, the military wing of the Yishuv, joined the fray. Two future Israeli prime ministers, Menachem Begin and Yitzhak Shamir, played leading roles in the terrorist struggle against the British (Begin 1951).

The Jewish revolt raged until 1947, when the British government announced that it would withdraw from Palestine within a few months. The issue was turned over to the United Nations, which subsequently announced that Palestine would be divided into two independent entities, one Jewish and the other Arab. The arrangement satisfied neither side, and upon the withdrawal of the British forces on May 14, 1948, David Ben-Gurion proclaimed the rebirth of the Israeli state. War flared as Arab armies surged into Palestine to reclaim Palestine for the Arab world. They succeeded only in retaining two patches of the original Palestine mandate: the Gaza Strip, a narrow coastal plain adjacent to Egypt, and a far larger segment of land on the west bank of the Jordan River. A majority of the Palestinians fled the country under circumstances that continue to be debated. The Israelis claim that the Palestinians were urged to flee by Arab leaders, while the Palestinians point to the systematic terror employed by Israeli forces against Arab villagers. The most vicious instance of this was the massacre of all 254 inhabitants of the Palestinian village of Deir Yassin, the news of which was used to set the residents of neighboring villages to flight (Polk, Stamler, and Asfour 1957).

Arab bitterness against Israel was intense. Arab nationalists viewed the Jewish state as an extension of Western imperialism in the heart of the Arab world. Theodor Herzl, the founder of the Zionist Organization, had indeed proclaimed that "[w]e should there form a portion of the rampart of Europe against Asia, an outpost of civilization as opposed to barbarism" (Herzl 1896, 29). Muslim leaders similarly railed at the fall of Muslim lands to the Jews, and Egypt's Muslim Brotherhood sent volunteers to fight in Palestine. Underlying the hostility toward Israel was a profound sense of Arab humiliation. Even today, Arabs refer to the 1948 war as the *nakba,* or catastrophe.

## The Era of Revolution and Optimism

Israel entered the era of independence with profound optimism. The revolt against the British had been successful, the Arabs had been defeated, and Israel had been reborn. The regional environment was hostile, but the new state enjoyed strong support from Western powers as well as world Jewry. Even the Soviet Union had hastened to recognize the Jewish state.

The problems, however, were many. Israel was desperately poor and depended upon foreign support for its survival. Defense expenditures were enormous, and the influx of new settlers strained the meager resources of the new state to the breaking point. Many of the new arrivals were survivors of the Holocaust who had earlier been denied entry to Palestine by the British. Even more problematic were the Jewish refugees from Arab countries who now flooded into Israel to escape retribution for the Arab defeat in the 1948 war. The culture of the Middle Eastern (Sephardic) Jews was far more conservative than that of their European counterparts, and their integration into Israeli society would prove difficult.

Few problems, however, were greater than that of the Palestinians. While the birth of Israel had brought an end to one diaspora, it had created another. It was now the Palestinians who were homeless. If the Jews viewed the future with optimism, the Palestinians, many of whom were relegated to squalid refugee camps, viewed it with despair. All that remained of Palestine was the Gaza Strip and the West Bank. Jerusalem was divided, with the Old City remaining in Jordanian hands. Egypt administered the Gaza Strip in the name of the Palestinians, while King Abdullah of Jordan incorporated the West Bank into his realm in 1950. Palestinians living in the West Bank became Jordanian citizens. In one fell swoop, the population of the new kingdom of Jordan would become 70 percent Palestinian. The coronation of the self-proclaimed Jordanian king was celebrated in 1950. He was assassinated by Palestinians in 1951. Palestinians wanted the return of their land, not incorporation into a tribal kingdom.

Disorganized and distraught, some 800,000 of Palestine's 1.3 million Arab residents became refugees. Of these, many sought shelter in makeshift camps on the West Bank and in Jordan, Syria, Lebanon, and Egypt (UNRWA, www.un.org/unrwa/refugees/whois.htm; accessed 9/2/2005). By 2003, the number of refugees would have swelled to 4,255,120, of whom 1,259, 810 lived in camps. The increase was due to births as well as new waves of refugees created by the 1967 Arab–Israeli war. From centers of despair, the camps would evolve into centers of militancy. Palestinians with marketable skills found jobs in Saudi Arabia and the largely tribal areas of the Gulf. Jordan granted citizenship to Palestinians who had been residents of the West Bank when it was incorporated into the kingdom of Jordan in 1950. About 200,000 Palestinians were granted citizenship by Saudi Arabia. Others migrated to the West. Jobs, however, were scarce. Western Europe was awash with refugees from the Second World War, and Palestine's neighbors were struggling to find jobs for their own people. Competition from the Palestinians was not welcome. Some 160,000 Palestinian Arabs would remain within Israel and would subsequently be referred to as Israeli Arabs. Israel vowed that there would be no return of the refugees.

The Palestinian resistance began in the early 1950s as sporadic attempts by dispossessed farmers to reclaim farms and harvests, resulting in skirmishes with Israeli border guards. Coordination was elusive, for the Palestinian community prior to the war had been fragmented by clan politics and was not prepared to act in concert. Nationalist sentiments, though loud, were largely expressed by students and intellectuals living in Egypt and Lebanon. It was they who formed resistance groups to counter the Israeli occupation. Some of these, such as the Popular Front for the Liberation of Palestine, were heavily ideological and blended communism with Arab nationalism. Others, such as Yasir Arafat's al-Fatah movement, were pragmatic and avoided ideological issues for the sake of building unity and cohesion.

The resistance, which was overwhelmingly secular in nature, advocated the creation of a secular Palestinian state in which all religions would be free to worship as they pleased. The Muslim Brotherhood, the dominant fundamentalist group of the era, was active in the 1948 war, but was subsequently driven into remission by Nasser.

Resistance groups launched raids into Israel and, though doing minimal damage, added to the general unease of the Israeli population, which was still uncertain of its survival. Israel responded with reprisals against neighboring countries. These, in turn, prompted the Arabs, led by Egypt, to create the Palestine Liberation Organization to keep the Palestinians under control. The Palestinian resistance groups, called fedayeen (freedom fighters), were excluded from the organization. The PLO was proclaimed by an Arab summit meeting in 1964, and a charter was eventually issued that called for a united Palestine under Arab control. Only Jews who were living in Palestine prior to 1948 would be allowed to remain. The Palestinian Liberation Army was formed, consisting of Palestinian units within the various Arab armies, but it had little freedom of action and posed little threat to the Israelis. The PLO was largely controlled by Nasser's Egypt, but this did not stop other Arab countries from interfering in its internal affairs. The Palestinians became pawns in an unrelenting cold war for supremacy of the Arab world (Kerr 1971). Most Palestinians, for their part, viewed Nasser and the Arab nationalists as their best hope for liberating their homeland.

Israel might make peace with its neighboring countries, but how could it make peace with a people that held claim to the same land? This was all the more problematic because Israel was a Jewish state. The incorporation of a Palestinian population the size of the Israeli population would destroy the Jewish character of the state and pose inordinate security problems. Indeed, the estimated 160,000 Palestinians remaining in Israel at the time of independence, although formally Israeli citizens, were considered security risks and placed under military control. Travel of any distance required a military permit and, because it was often difficult to tell a Jew from a Palestinian, the latter were required to carry special identity cards. Palestinians were also not allowed to serve in the military (Rodinson 1969, 51). The Israelis did not want to integrate the Palestinians into the new Jewish state. They had conquered Palestinian land but were unsure what to do about the Palestinians.

Equally pressing for the new state was the problem of land. Approximately 80 percent of Palestinian land had been vacated during the war and was now being used by the Israeli government to settle Jews. How could it be returned to its Palestinian owners? (Rodinson 1969, 51). If anything, Israel needed more land for Jewish settlers.

Israel's first government was headed by David Ben-Gurion, the leader of the Mapai (Labor) Party. Ben-Gurion was a committed Zionist and an equally committed socialist. Israel was to be not only a Jewish state but a state that stressed social equality. Ben-Gurion would become the towering figure of modern Israeli history, and it was his hand, more than any other's, that set the course of Israel's history. Despite Ben-Gurion's stature, he lacked a majority in the Knesset and was forced to piece together a coalition government from parties representing Israel's many ideological currents.

Political debate in Israel revolved around five primary concerns: security, Jewishness, land, peace, and nation building. Security came first, for unless the survival of the state could be assured, everything else was moot. Security issues focused on defense, but they also involved the economic viability of the new state. Israel was a small country with few natural resources, and its survival depended on its capacity to supply the needs of its population. Israel was also to be a Jewish state: a place where Jews could live without prejudice, and a haven for a people still reeling from the horrors of the Holocaust. To survive, Israel required the support of the Jewish community worldwide, and its foreign policy had to reflect the concerns of that community. The issue of land was equally problematic. In addition to historic considerations, additional land would be required to settle more Jews. Land, moreover, was vital to the defense of Israel. At its narrowest point, Israel was only ten miles wide, and its communications could easily be severed by an enemy attack. The small size of the state also dictated the need for buffer zones. Israel could defend itself, but little would be gained if the country were destroyed in the process.

Ultimately the security of Israel would require a lasting peace with its Arab neighbors. But at what price was peace to be achieved? Acceptance of the prevailing UN peace plan would require a return to Israel's pre-1948 boundaries and the repatriation of a large Palestinian population. This prospect was anathema to many Israelis and posed a security nightmare. A return of the Palestinians might also limit further Jewish immigration. Israelis wanted peace, but it would have to be a peace that addressed Israel's overriding concerns for security and the Jewish character of the state.

Adding to the political debate was Israel's need to galvanize itself into an effective nation. Israel's political institutions, while largely inherited from the Yishuv, had to be strengthened and extended. Masses of new immigrants, many from Middle Eastern backgrounds, also had to be integrated into the social, economic, and political life of the nation. The new immigrants had to become something more than Jews; they had to become "modern" Israelis. Little could be achieved without the rapid development of the Israeli economy. Aid from the world Jewish community was generous, but the state's economic survival required more than handouts. Israel had to become economically viable in its own right.

Debates over the handling of the Arabs were particularly intense. While Ben-Gurion advocated an iron fist toward the Arabs, Moshe Sharett, his foreign minister, pushed for accommodation, arguing that Israel's long-term survival depended upon peace with its neighbors (Sheffer 1996). Sharett believed that the use of excessive force would create more problems than it solved (Brecher 1974). So vital was foreign policy to Israel's security that virtually all cabinet meetings began with a debate on this topic.

The question of religion was so contentious that it prevented the establishment of a formal constitution. The price for the participation of the religious parties in the ruling coalition, moreover, had been control of the rabbinical courts by the Orthodox rabbis as well as large subsidies to synagogues and religious schools and the suspension of public transport on the Sabbath. Many of these "blue laws" were supported by American Jews, leading one secular Israeli Jew to note with bitterness, "The salvation of the American Jews is conveniently assured by the strict religious observance imposed on Israeli Jews, while their consciences are assuaged and their supposed duty as Zionists fulfilled at the price of certain financial sacrifices" (Rodinson 1969, 49).

Unable to agree on a constitution, Israeli leaders established guidelines for the country's ongoing institutional development through a variety of basic laws passed by the Knesset during the ensuing years. The first of these, the basic law defining the procedures of the Knesset itself, was not passed until 1958. Others included laws dealing with land under Israeli control (1960), the president (1964), the government (cabinet) (1968), the state economy (taxes and the budget) (1975), the army (1976), and the Jerusalem law, which formally established Jerusalem as the capital (1980) (Rabinovich and Reinharz 1984, 41). The Law of Return was passed in 1950 and is generally treated as a basic law. The Law of Return states that every Jew has the right to come to Israel as an immigrant. A 1952 law extended the Law of Return by allowing all Jews the right to Israeli nationality even if they chose to retain their original nationality.

Israel's political situation was far less chaotic than the circumstances might suggest, for the Israelis, much like the British, possessed an unwritten constitution. The basic rules of Israeli politics were developed during the mandate era and were broadly accepted by the Israeli population. Stability was also provided by the dominant position of the Mapai Party, now the Labor Party, and the profound respect accorded David Ben-Gurion. Being encircled by hostile neighbors also left little scope for internal dissension. Israelis could either work together or perish. Ben-Gurion's policies sometimes stretched the limits of Israeli democracy, but the tensions of the period left little time for debate.

In 1952, Ben-Gurion strained his popularity by proposing that Israel accept war reparations from West Germany. The thought that the Germans could atone for the Holocaust was repugnant to a broad spectrum of Jews and sparked severe rioting in Jerusalem. Money, however, was of the essence. Defense expenditures consumed between 30 and 40 percent of the budget, and the costs of settling Jewish immigrants was enormous (Rodinson 1969, 45).

In 1953, a second crisis erupted over Ben-Gurion's hardline policy toward the Arabs. In October of that year, a woman and two children were killed in a Palestinian raid on an Israeli village. The Israeli army responded with a brutal attack against a Jordanian village, blowing up some forty houses and killing fifty-three villagers (Rodinson 1969, 69). The raid symbolized Israel's iron-fist policy toward terrorism and served notice to Arab leaders that they would be held responsible for Palestinian attacks originating from their territory. A strong show of force, in Ben-Gurion's view, was also needed to calm an Israeli population increasingly anxious about the capacity of the Jewish state to defend itself. There had been a net outflow of Jews from Israel in 1953. Security had come to mean far more than the defense of Israel's boundaries. In order to survive, the Jewish state had to provide a secure domestic environment for its citizens. The Palestinian raids could not defeat the Israeli army, but they could raise the cost of living in Israel to unacceptable levels. Ben-Gurion accepted responsibility for ordering the reprisal raid, and resigned a few months later. He was replaced as prime minister by Moshe Sharett.

Crisis followed crisis, and in 1955 Ben-Gurion, then minister of defense, ordered a raid on Egyptian troops in the Gaza Strip, reportedly to punish the Egyptian authorities for allowing Palestinians to launch raids into Israel from the Gaza region. Forty Egyptian troops were killed, and many more were wounded. In reality, there had been little Palestinian "infiltration" into Israel during this period, and the Israeli press speculated that the Israeli attack had been designed as a preemptive measure to teach the Egyptians a lesson and to reassure a nervous Israeli public (Yaari in Rabinovich and Reinharz 1984).

Infuriated by the Israeli assault, Nasser demanded more arms from the United States. Washington equivocated, indicating that it would provide arms only if Egypt joined the newly formed Baghdad Pact. As discussed in Chapter 2, Nasser chose instead to purchase arms from the Soviet bloc, thereby breaking the West's arms monopoly in the Middle East. The United States canceled its aid for Nasser's Aswan Dam, and Nasser retaliated by nationalizing the Suez Canal.

Israel was becoming ever more frightened by Nasser's aggressiveness and his growing popularity within the Arab world. Arab nationalism, which had long been simmering without a leader, was rapidly solidifying behind the profoundly charismatic Nasser. Following the attack on Gaza, moreover, Nasser had organized the heretofore irregular bands of Palestinian fighters into fedayeen, an organized guerrilla force trained and supplied by the Egyptian army. Their effectiveness increased apace and could not be ignored by the Israelis.

Israel was not the only country that feared Nasser's growing power. Britain and France had been stung by Nasser's nationalization of the Suez Canal, and France was increasingly apprehensive about Nasser's support for an Algerian revolution that was threatening to engulf France itself. Negotiations between Britain, France, and Israel led to a plan to seize the canal. Israeli forces were to march to the canal while the British and French intervened as neutral parties to assure that the canal would remain safe for international shipping.

The plan was executed to perfection, its only real flaw being the exclusion of the United States. The U.S. was involved in an increasingly bitter struggle with the Soviet Union for the hearts and minds of the Third World and was determined to counter Soviet propaganda by presenting itself to the countries of Asia and Africa as the world's "first new nation" (Holland 1996). Like the Third World countries, the United States had revolted against colonial oppression and therefore understood the needs and aspirations of emerging nations. To support the tripartite attack on Egypt would have placed the United States in the imperialist camp and left the Soviets free to expand their influence in areas that were seething with revolution.

With its global strategy at risk, the United States pressured Israel and its allies to withdraw from Egyptian territory. Nasser emerged the victor and, as recounted in the preceding chapter, launched his campaign to unify the Arab world, perhaps the greatest nightmare of the Israeli leadership. All, however, was not lost. Israel had again demonstrated its military prowess and now actively began to perpetuate the myth of its military invincibility. Israelis believed that the more the Arabs believed in the invincibility of the Israel Defense Forces (IDF), the less likely they would be to initiate aggressive adventures and the more easily their troops would become demoralized. UN troops were also stationed on the Egyptian–Israeli border, thereby offering Israel protection from Egyptian attack. This, however, was not an unmixed blessing, for it provided Nasser with time to develop his army and bring the Arab world under his sway.

The 1956 war had a profound impact on Israeli foreign policy. By choosing to ignore the United States, Israel had been denied the fruits of a dazzling military victory. The United States was too powerful and too important to Israel's survival to allow this to happen again. The interests of the United States would have to be accommodated. Even more important, the United States would have to be convinced that a strong Israel was in its national interest. This would require the redoubled efforts of the American Jewish community, the largest in the world outside of Israel itself.

The presence of UN observers in the Sinai Peninsula increased Israel's sense of security, as did the growing support of the United States. Domestic tensions, however, remained. Israel's citizens come from a broad variety of social and ideological backgrounds. Many of Israel's earliest settlers came from eastern and central Europe and were very Western in outlook. It was they, often referred to as the Ashkenazi or western Jews, who fought the war for independence—the Arab–Israeli War of 1948—and who established Israel's political institutions. Independence brought a massive influx of Middle Eastern or Sephardic Jews to Israel. The Sephardic or eastern Jews knew little of Western ways, possessed few technical skills, and generally reflected the traditional attitudes of the countries from which they had migrated. By and large, they formed a lower class in Israeli society, with considerably less power and wealth than their Ashkenazi counterparts; the vestiges of this gap still exist (Smooha 1998).

Also problematic was the growing debate over the role of religion in Israeli society. This issue came to the fore in 1962 with the case of Brother Daniel. Brother Daniel, a Jew who had converted to Christianity to avoid persecution during World War II and who had played a major role in assisting other Jews to avoid persecution, now demanded Israeli citizenship under the Law of Return. His request was rejected, and the case was taken to the Israeli Supreme Court for resolution. Among other points, Brother Daniel argued "that the concept 'nationality' is not identical with the concept 'religion' and that a Jew by nationality need not be a Jew by religion" (quoted in Rabinovich and Reinharz 1984, 152). The case was decided in favor of Brother Daniel.

On May 23, 1967, Nasser increased the stakes in his dangerous game of political brinkmanship by closing the Straits of Tiran to Israeli shipping. The straits controlled access to the port of Elat, the main point of entry for most of Israel's oil imports. The major powers, according to Nasser's strategy, were expected to save the situation much as they had in 1956, but they did not. The Israeli military launched a "preemptive" strike with devastating force, and the war was over almost before it began. Israel now controlled a vast expanse of Arab land stretching from the Suez Canal to the Golan Heights and including all of Palestine. The number of refugees mushroomed, and so did their despair.

## The Era of Disillusion and Reassessment

Israel's dazzling victory in the June War of 1967 dramatically transformed the political equation in the Middle East. Talk of driving Israel into the sea now appeared ludicrous, and the heady slogans of Arab nationalism had given way to a profound sense of mass disillusionment. The 1948 war was called the catastrophe, *nakba,* by Arab historians; the 1967 war was dubbed "the setback," or *naksa.*

The Palestinians' despair deepened with the realization that the Arabs and Nasser would not be able to liberate Palestine. Indeed, it was doubtful that Egypt, Syria, and Jordan would be able to liberate their own lands. If Palestine were to be liberated, it would have to be the Palestinians who led the charge.

The PLO was restructured in 1968. Most of the diverse resistance groups joined it, and its charter, renamed the Palestinian National Charter, stressed the existence of a unique Palestinian identity and the leading role of the PLO in the liberation of Palestine. Yasir Arafat, as the leader of the dominant al-Fatah movement, was elected the president of the PLO. He would dominate it as well as al-Fatah. The PLO's member groups remained largely autonomous. Arafat orchestrated the operations of al-Fatah and controlled the growing PLO bureaucracy, but he could not control the operations of its more radical groups. Arab governments continued to meddle in the affairs of the PLO, which was also plagued by ideological and personality conflicts among and within member groups. Saudi Arabia would become the patron of al-Fatah while Syria and Iraq supported the radical groups. As described by the PLO website:

> The Popular Democratic Liberation Front of Palestine (PDFLP) evolved after a split within the PFLP, following a similar split in late 1968 which had led to the creation of the PFLP-General Command. The Arab leadership of the Al-Baath party in Iraq formed the Arab Liberation Front, which was preceded by the establishment of Al-Sa''ika (thunderbolt) by the Al-Baath party in Syria. Finally, the Front for Popular Struggle opted out of Fateh (www.palestine-un.org/plo/intro.html).

Because of the fractious nature of the Palestinian resistance, the Palestinian National Charter pointedly warned that "the conflicts among the Palestinian national forces are secondary, and should be ended for the sake of the basic conflict . . ."(Charter 1968). www.palestinecenter.org/cpap/documents/charter.html

A new wave of refugees, probably numbering about 250,000, fled the occupied territories in the wake of the 1967 war; most went to Jordan. The PLO fled with them, and soon established a state within a state on the east bank of the Jordan River. Simultaneously, a strong Palestinian presence was established in southern Lebanon. The choices were inevitable. Both Jordan and Lebanon possessed an abundance of Palestinian refugee camps and both provided easy access to Israel. Both also possessed weak governments that were unable to prevent Palestinian attacks on the Jewish state. Jordan, with its easy access to the West Bank and established resistance networks, was the preferred choice.

All, however, was not well. Tensions between the Palestinians and their Jordanian hosts increased as Palestinian attacks on Israeli targets brought Israeli reprisals against Jordanian targets. Within the PLO disagreements over strategy mounted. Arafat preferred a war of attrition based on limited raids against Israeli targets in the occupied territories, if not Israel itself. With time, so the argument went, the Israelis would tire of the attacks and evacuate the occupied territories. In the meantime, the PLO would be establishing a strong base of operations in Jordan. The Popular Front for the Liberation of Palestine, by contrast, argued that the Arabs, Palestinian or otherwise, would never defeat an Israel supported by the United States. The only option, in its view, was to make the United States and its allies reconsider its support for Israel. The West had created the Palestinian crisis; now they would have to solve it. How was pressure to be brought on the West? By terror and the hijacking of Western aircraft. Between September 6 and 9, 1970, the PFLP hijacked three international airliners and forced them to land at remote Jordanian airfields. The PFLP was part of the PLO and the PLO was blamed. King Hussein's power itself was called into question. Civil war erupted and during "Black September" the Jordanian army crushed the Palestinian resistance. Syria had threatened to side with the Palestinians, but was dissuaded by Israeli aircraft. With little option, the PLO fled to Lebanon, where it effectively seized control of southern Lebanon.

While the Arab world entered an era of disillusionment and reassessment, the mood in Israel was one of guarded euphoria. The Jewish nation was more secure than it had been at any point in its short history, and the lands of ancient Israel had been restored. In addition to their religious significance, the occupied lands provided a buffer between Israel and its adversaries and were available for settlement by Israel's ever increasing Jewish population. Or perhaps these territories could be traded for peace, thereby bringing to an end two decades of bitter confrontation.

The very magnitude of the Israeli success brought new challenges. Israel had reclaimed the lands of ancient Israel, but approximately one million Palestinians were living on those lands. The Palestinian population, moreover, was expanding rapidly. How was Israel to enjoy the fruits of its victory when the lands of ancient Israel remained occupied by Palestinians? The lands could be incorporated into Israel, but the absorption of a large Palestinian population represented an unacceptable security risk and threatened the Jewish character of the state. How could a Palestinian population approximately one-third that of Israel's Jewish population be allowed to vote in Israeli elections? Israel, moreover, offered its citizens cradle-to-grave health and welfare programs that already consumed a lion's share of the country's budget. The addition of a million largely destitute Palestinians to the rolls would bankrupt the system. In the view of many Israelis, Israel's goal should be to keep the land but not its residents.

Israel also faced conflict with the United States and the Soviet Union over the disposition of the occupied territories. American policy dictated trading land for peace in the hope of ending a crisis that had helped the Soviets extend their influence in the Arab world. The Soviets, for their part, were under intense pressure from their Arab allies to rebuild their shattered armies and counter U.S. support for

Israel. Although the Soviets had little faith in the Arab capacity to fight, they could not deny Arab demands without losing credibility among their regional allies. The Soviets, too, were ready to trade land for peace.

The process of exchanging land for peace was fraught with difficulty. A lethal blend of religiosity, nationalism, and fear had combined to threaten any Israeli government that advocated withdrawal from the occupied territories. In addition, the occupied territories varied in their significance. The Sinai Peninsula did not constitute part of ancient Israel and, with proper guarantees for Israeli security, could conceivably be traded for peace. Jerusalem, by contrast, was the focal point of the Jewish faith and was nonnegotiable. As the site of the ancient kingdoms of Judea and Samaria, the West Bank also had considerable religious significance, while the Gaza Strip and the Golan Heights had less. While Israel could return some land, it was politically infeasible to return it all.

These problems were exacerbated by a transformation in Israeli society. Sephardic Jews had become a majority in the country and were beginning to assert their influence, as were a growing number of Sabras, or native-born Israelis. In general, the Sephardic Jews and the Sabras were more religious and nationalistic than the Ashkenazi Jews and strongly opposed trading land for peace. They also had begun to question the socialist underpinnings of the Israeli state and were demanding a greater role for the private sector in Israel's economic affairs. The euphoria of the 1967 victory, by easing Israel's profound sense of insecurity, had allowed the previously muted ideological divisions inherent within Israeli society to come to the fore.

As the government vacillated, external events began to dictate the course of Israeli politics. In November of 1967, the United Nations passed UN Resolution 242 calling for Israel to withdraw from occupied territories in return for peace and secure boundaries. Israel signed the agreement, presumably under pressure from the United States, but soon lost interest in the project.

The debate was rendered moot as Egypt used its massive artillery, which had been rebuilt by the Soviets, to pound Israeli troops near the Suez Canal (Smith 1992, 216). Egyptian forces were not strong enough to drive the Israelis out of the area, but they were clearly in a position to increase the cost of occupation (Muhammad Hassanain Haykal 1969 in Laqueur and Rubin 1984, 414–427). In so doing, Nasser played upon the main weakness in Israel's security: its reluctance to accept a large number of casualties. In part, this is a function of Israel's small population. The IDF simply cannot afford to engage in conflicts that result in massive casualties. The aversion to casualties, however, is also rooted in a deep cultural reverence for life. News in Israel travels quickly, and when a soldier is killed or wounded, everyone seems to know someone who knew the victim. As a result, losses are taken personally, adding to the insecurity of an already skittish population.

Israel, however, maintained its air of superiority over the Egyptians and relied on the saturation bombing of Egyptian positions to stem the assault (Shlaim and Tanter 1978). Not only would Egypt be forced to accept Israeli terms, according to Israeli strategists, but Egyptian leaders would be taught an important psychological lesson.

This strategy, however, assumed that the Soviets would remain passive. They did not. Rather, they joined the fray on the side of the Egyptians, manning anti-aircraft missile sites and piloting Egyptian aircraft. Israeli losses began to mount, and Israeli leaders found themselves under increasing pressure from the United States to end the conflict. The last thing that the United States wanted was to transform Egypt into a Soviet satellite. Israel reluctantly accepted a U.S.-sponsored cease-fire on August 7, 1970. Once again, Israel had overplayed its hand and found itself in confrontation with the United States (Shlaim and Tanter 1978).

The war of attrition ground to a halt in 1970 and was followed by international efforts to reopen the Suez Canal, which required a partial Israeli withdrawal from the Sinai Peninsula. The Israeli cabinet divided on the issue, and negotiations broke down. Egypt had earlier accepted the international plan, and Israel's refusal to do so convinced Anwar Sadat, now the leader of Egypt, that there could be no serious negotiations with Israel until the Arabs had reestablished their credibility on the battlefield. Until this happened, Israel would have little incentive to return any of the territory occupied in the 1967 war. In retrospect, Israeli scholars faulted the Israeli government for not having a coherent policy. What appeared to the Arabs as intransigence, they believed, was merely the incapacity of a deeply divided government to make a decision (Shlaim and Yaniv 1980, 244).

Arab preparations for the 1973 October (Yom Kippur) War were discussed in the preceding chapter and require little elaboration at this point. Israeli intelligence had monitored the Arab buildup, and the Israeli military had begun to mobilize for war, albeit in an unobtrusive manner designed to allay Western concerns (Bartov 1981, quoted in Rabinovich and Reinharz 1984, 240–46). Israeli analysts pointed out that another lightning-swift victory would not be without its advantages. Israel would gain a breathing space of several years while the Arabs struggled to rebuild their armies. Israel's aura of invincibility would also be reinforced and would continue to take its toll on the Arabs and their Soviet supporters. Having been the victim of another Arab attack, moreover, Israel would be under little pressure to return the occupied territories.

Israeli authorities differed on the urgency of the Arab threat. How could one give credence to Arab armies that had been humiliated just five years earlier in the June War of 1967, or to an Egyptian army that had been further humiliated in the "war of attrition"? Military victories were not Israel's problem. The difficulty, or so it seemed, would be in winning the political battles that followed. Sadat, moreover, had expelled the Soviets a year earlier, and it was extremely difficult to envision a sustained Egyptian attack without massive Soviet support. Sadat's domestic position had also become increasingly precarious, and his menacing gestures were easily written off as bravado designed for home consumption.

As a result of this vacillation, Israel was caught unprepared when Egyptian and Syrian troops launched a joint attack on October 6, 1973, the Jewish holy day of Yom Kippur. The Egyptian army displayed consummate skill in crossing the Suez Canal, and Israeli forces were forced to retreat with heavy losses. Without massive U.S. aid and profound confusion in the relationship between Egypt and Syria, the situation could have been far worse. Israel's forces eventually regrouped and by the cessation of hostilities they had occupied even more territory. The damage, however, had been done. Israel's defense perimeter had been penetrated, and the myth of Israeli invincibility had been shattered. It was no longer certain that future wars would go as well as wars past.

It was at this point that the United States intervened, in the person of Henry Kissinger, the U.S. secretary of state. Kissinger was of Jewish origin and sympathetic to Israel, but he was also intensely frustrated by the paralysis of Israeli politics. Israeli security, in his view, demanded peace with Egypt and the normalization of relations with the Arab world. Toward this end, and not without considerable resistance from the Israeli leadership, he used his diplomatic skills and the full weight of the U.S. government to forge a 1974 agreement between Egypt and Israel, leading to the disengagement of their armies in the Suez Canal zone. Under the terms of the agreement, Egypt would normalize relations with Israel while the latter would begin a gradual withdrawal from the Suez Canal and the Sinai Peninsula. The United States would provide security guarantees and a UN peacekeeping force would patrol the demilitarized area. The Israeli government could not achieve sufficient consensus to either resist Kissinger or take effective action on any other issue (Shlaim and Yaniv 1980, 251).

Following Egypt's lead, the PLO softened its strategy of confrontation and placed its major emphasis on gaining international recognition for the PLO and the Palestinian cause. International diplomatic pressure, according to the Palestinian strategists, could do more than hijacking to force an Israeli retreat. Sadat, now embraced by Kissinger as an international statesman, urged this shift, as did King Hussein of Jordan and the Saudi monarchy. The October War, in their view, had made its point. Now was the time for diplomacy. The Arabs did not want another war with Israel.

The results of Yasir Arafat's diplomatic initiative were spectacular. In October of 1974, an Arab summit conference recognized the PLO as the sole representative of the Palestinian people. It also recognized the right of the Palestinian people to establish an independent national authority under the command of the PLO. All liberated land—including the West Bank and Gaza Strip, once they were liberated—would be under the authority of the PLO. Jordan would relinquish its claim to the West Bank. A month later, Arafat addressed the General Assembly of the United Nations and the PLO was shortly accorded "observer status" at the UN. The PLO couldn't vote, but it had received international recognition. It became a full member of the Arab League in 1976, and by 1977 had been granted various forms of diplomatic recognition by some 100 countries. There were, of course, dissenting Arab voices. Syria feared a sellout that would leave the occupied Golan Heights under Israeli control. Syrian-sponsored groups within the PLO followed suit. Even many of the mainline groups within the PLO had their doubts. International plaudits were wonderful, but nothing was happening on the ground.

Israel's humiliation in the October/Yom Kippur War had weakened the Labor Party's grip on power; in one way or another, the party had been in control since the earliest days of the republic. It was already immobilized by internal bickering and corruption scandals. The Likud, a coalition of right-wing parties that had emerged a few years earlier, came to power in 1977 under the leadership of Menachem Begin, a former leader of the Irgun militia in the struggle against the British. Perhaps reacting to a pervasive sense of malaise, the Israeli electorate turned again to a strong and decisive leader, albeit a leader of the far right that Ben-Gurion had earlier suspected of antidemocratic tendencies.

Begin, an ultranationalist, vowed that not an inch of ancient Israel would be returned to the Arabs. The immobility of Israeli politics had come to an abrupt end. Perhaps because of his hardline credentials, Begin was able to pursue negotiations with Egypt that involved trading the Sinai Peninsula for peace. The Sinai Peninsula was not part of ancient Israel and possessed none of the religious associations of Jerusalem and the West Bank. If Egypt could be neutralized, Begin argued, the main Arab army would be removed from the fray and Israel would have a free hand in dealing with its smaller Arab neighbors. His logic was impeccable.

The Camp David Accords between Egypt and Israel were duly signed on September 17, 1978, with the active participation of the United States. A formal treaty of peace between the two countries followed in March of 1979. Middle Eastern politics had undergone yet another transformation.

## The Era of Islamic Resurgence

In the 1979 peace treaty, Israel traded the Sinai Peninsula for peace with its most powerful neighbor. The land would be returned in stages, thereby assuring that Egypt remained faithful to its commitment. The peace accords also stated that Israel would give the Palestinians autonomy on the West Bank and the Gaza Strip within five years. In this blueprint, land would be traded for peace and the Arab-Israeli conflict would come to an end.

There were, of course, complications. Egypt was the only Arab signatory to the agreement, and Sadat had taken it upon himself to speak not only for Egypt but for both the Palestinians and the Arab world as a whole. The Arab states rejected the agreement and severed their relations with Egypt. But the damage had been done. With Egypt removed from the military equation, the remaining Arab states were at Israel's mercy. This vulnerability was increased by the "special relationship" between Israel and the United States. Never, President Reagan would boast upon assuming the presidency in 1980, had Israel had a better friend in the White House.

No sooner had the peace treaty with Egypt been signed than Begin ignored his promise of Palestinian autonomy and called for the immediate settlement of the West Bank and Gaza by Jews. Begin acknowledged that the accords did speak of Palestinian autonomy, but "clarified" that the autonomy provisions of the accords applied only to the people, not the land. The Palestinians could move toward self-rule if they wished, but the land belonged to Israel. Only Jewish settlement of the occupied territories, in Begin's view, could preclude a future Israeli government from trading the land for peace. Jewish settlements would create "new realities" to which the world, including his Labor opponents, would have to adjust. Perhaps encouraged by Begin's policies, radical elements among the settlers unleashed a wave of terrorism against the Palestinians. Begin seemed reluctant to control the violence, and in June of 1980, the UN condemned Israel for its settlement policy. The Palestinian Liberation Organization (PLO), for its part, had begun a long slide into civil war.

The following month, the Knesset passed a law unifying Jerusalem and making it the official capital of Israel. Begin underscored the point by moving the prime minister's office to Arab East Jerusalem. The move violated UN Resolution 242 and signaled Israel's refusal to acknowledge the status of Jerusalem as a divided city. The world's dominant powers, including the United States, also refused to recognize the change in Jerusalem's status. Simultaneously, Begin attempted to build popular support for his aggressive Arab policy with a borrow-and-spend economic policy that gave Israelis a false sense of economic prosperity. It also placed them deeper in debt and led to a mutiny within Begin's own ranks. Begin narrowly survived two votes of no confidence in 1980, and a Likud victory in the 1981 elections seemed unlikely.

Begin, however, remained defiant, and three weeks before the elections ordered the bombing of an Iraqi nuclear reactor. Jews, he vowed, would never again be the victims of mass destruction. The Israeli left denounced the attack as an election ploy, and the bombing was duly condemned by the United Nations.

The Likud emerged from the 1981 elections with forty-eight seats in the Knesset, one more than Labor's forty-seven. Begin, as the leader of the largest party in the Knesset, was asked to form a new coalition government. He did so with the inclusion of the religious parties, beginning his second term as prime minister with a shaky one-vote majority in the Knesset. The defection of a single vote could topple his government.

Undeterred by the narrowness of his victory, Begin ordered the bombing of Beirut by Israeli aircraft. The PLO may have established itself in a Lebanon devastated by civil war, he preached, but it would not be allowed to find shelter for its activities in civilian districts (*NYT,* July 18, 1981). The bombing of Beirut was followed in December of 1981 by the formal annexation of the Golan Heights. A war of words erupted between Begin and U.S. President Ronald Reagan, and Israel was again condemned in the United Nations. Begin was also challenged by a vote of no confidence in the Knesset, but the result was a draw and Begin remained Israel's prime minister.

On June 6, 1982, Begin ordered the invasion of Lebanon, proclaiming his intention to establish a twenty-five-mile security zone in southern Lebanon. After that goal was accomplished, Israeli troops pushed toward Beirut, bombing the city for eleven hours on August 12 before invading its western suburbs on August 14. Reagan phoned Begin to protest, but the invasion continued. Israel's immediate concern was the curtailment of terrorist activity, but its longer-range goals were the destruction of the PLO and the transformation of Lebanon into an Israeli client state capable of securing Israel's northern border. Christians constituted approximately 50 percent of the Lebanese population at this time, and talks had occurred between some Christian leaders and the Israelis.

Israel's desire to destroy the PLO was motivated by a variety of considerations. Israel's northern border could never be secure as long as the PLO remained the dominant force in southern Lebanon. It would also be impossible for Israel to establish a Christian-based client state in Lebanon as long as the PLO controlled the southern half of the country. A Christian state in Lebanon, the Israelis reasoned, could only sustain itself against its Muslim adversaries by making peace with Israel. The two states would also share a mutual interest in crushing the PLO.

In the broader scheme of things, Israel was distressed by the increasing acceptance of the PLO in international circles. Indeed, Begin feared that the PLO's diplomatic successes might succeed where its terrorist tactics had failed and force a return of the occupied territories. These fears mounted in June of 1980 when a meeting of Western European governments openly called for Israel to open direct negotiations with the PLO. Begin bitterly rejected the suggestion, comparing the European position to the West's capitulation to Hitler at Munich. If Europe capitulated, could the United States be far behind? Would Israel once again win the military war only to lose the political peace?

Israel's supporters justified the invasion of Lebanon in order to achieve the objectives outlined above, but few were prepared for the horrors of the ensuing massacres of an estimated eight hundred Palestinian civilians by Israel's Christian allies in September of 1982. Ariel Sharon, Begin's minister of defense, admitted that Israel had helped to plan the attack. Later investigation also revealed that Israel had facilitated the entry of the Christian militias to the Sabra and Shatila refugee camps (*Time*, Oct. 4, 1982). The official commission established to investigate the massacres said of Sharon, "We know that the consideration (of possible bloodshed) did not concern him in the least. . . . The Defense Minister made a grave mistake" (*Time*, Feb. 21, 1983). Of Begin, the commission wrote: "For two days . . . he showed absolutely no interest in the camps. . . . His lack of involvement casts on him a certain degree of responsibility" (*Time*, Feb. 21, 1983). Several generals were also censured. Sharon would eventually be forced to resign as minister of defense, though he remained in the cabinet. Begin, while later offering to resign as a result of the massacres, was retained as prime minister. Also tarnished was Israel's image as a nation desiring peace with its neighbors.

Two days following the massacres, Reagan vowed on national television to get the Israelis out of Lebanon and announced that he was sending U.S. Marines to Beirut as part of an international peacekeeping force. Begin responded by saying that "Jews do not kneel but to God" (*Time*, Aug. 16, 1982). Begin resigned from office late in 1983 and was replaced as prime minister by Yitzhak Shamir, also a former resistance fighter against the British. Policy changed little, and relations between Israel and the United States remained strained.

In spite of the turmoil of the preceding years, 1984 found Israel on the verge of achieving all the goals of its Lebanese campaign. The PLO had agreed to evacuate Lebanon, and a friendly Christian government had been installed in Beirut. The Christian regime, moreover, had agreed to a long-term "security agreement" with Israel, thereby further isolating Syria, or so it seemed at the time. The approach of U.S. presidential elections also had a calming effect on President Reagan: he now seemed more concerned with reviving his sagging support among the American Jewish community than with pursuing a Middle East policy that had brought him little but grief (*NYT*, Jan. 2, 1984). Toward this end, the

Reagan administration announced the signing of a new military pact between the United States and Israel and seemed unmindful of Israel's accelerated settlement of the West Bank (*NYT*, Jan. 15, 1984; *NYT*, Feb. 12, 1984).

Israeli successes, however, proved more illusive than real. Lebanon had become a quagmire reminiscent of the U.S. experience in Vietnam and the Soviet debacle in Afghanistan. Between the start of the invasion and the end of 1984, 604 Israeli soldiers were killed and nine times that many wounded. An additional 141 Israeli soldiers were sent to prison for refusing to fight in Lebanon. These are devastating figures for a small state, and their impact was amplified by Israel's intense aversion to the loss of Jewish life. The Palestinians had been defeated, but Israel now found itself fighting an unanticipated war with Shi'a militias. A partial Israeli withdrawal from south Lebanon, moreover, had allowed the Syrians to reassert their influence in Beirut. Their first act was to force Lebanon's Christian government to cancel its security agreement with Israel.

Small and fleeting gains, then, had been made at great cost. To make matters worse, Israel's domestic situation was in disarray. The occupation of Lebanon was costing over a million dollars a day, inflation was approaching 1,000 percent per year, and Israel's foreign debt had passed the $24 billion mark, giving Israeli citizens the highest debt per capita in the world. Worries over Jewish emigration from Israel were also increasing, and the intense settlement of the occupied territories had unleashed more violence by both Jewish settlers and the Palestinians.

Israeli dismay was reflected in the 1984 elections, which returned Labor to power with a narrow plurality of forty-four seats in the Knesset to the Likud's forty-one. Thirteen other parties shared the remaining thirty-five seats. The Likud had been repudiated, but Labor, with hardly more than a third of the seats in the Knesset, could hardly claim a popular mandate. Shimon Peres, the leader of the Labor Party, sought a way out of the impasse by proposing a "national government" in which Labor and Likud would share power. Peres would serve as prime minister for the first twenty-five months and then relinquish power to Shamir.

Peres's tenure as prime minister was painful. December 1984 found him asking the United States for an economic bailout of $4.85 billion, much of it in the form of grants (*NYT*, Dec. 20, 1984). This request was followed in January 1985 by attempts to orchestrate a joint Israeli–Syrian withdrawal from Lebanon. When that effort failed, Israel announced its unilateral withdrawal from Lebanon with the exception of a four- to ten-kilometer security zone along the Israeli–Lebanese border. The security zone would be patrolled by the Christian-led South Lebanon Army with strong support from Israel. This objective was largely accomplished by the summer of 1985 (*NYT*, June 11, 1985).

That summer the United States increased its aid to Israel to $3 billion a year. The added financial assistance, however, was accompanied by American demands that Israel reform its economic system, something that all previous Israeli governments had been reluctant to do for fear of losing popular support. Tensions with the United States increased further in the fall of that year when the United States accused Jonathan Pollard, an American Jew employed by U.S. Naval Intelligence, of spying for Israel. Peres subsequently apologized for the incident (*NYT*, Dec. 2, 1985). Far more embarrassing was an October 1986 article in the *Sunday Times* (London) charging that Israel had been producing nuclear weapons for twenty years and possessed more than a hundred atomic bombs ( *JP,* Feb. 3, 2000). The nuclear technician who leaked the information was subsequently arrested by Israeli police and charged with espionage. In the meantime, relations with Syria remained tense, although neither side seemed anxious for renewed conflict (*NYT,* May 19, 1986).

For its part, the PLO was also in disarray. Its expulsion from Lebanon had precipitated a civil war within the organization, and Arafat and his supporters were forced to shift their operations to Tunis. Sadat had regained the Sinai Peninsula, but had done nothing for the Palestinians. Indeed, the Egyptians seemed to have grown tired of the Palestinians, as had the Arab world in general. An alternate Palestinian leadership consisting of mayors and local councils had also emerged on the West Bank, but proved ineffective (Sahliyeh 1988). The Israelis encouraged the new Palestinian leadership, but didn't give it sufficient authority to be effective. Exiled or not, the PLO remained the sole representative of the Palestinian people (Belqaziz 2004).

Such was the environment in mid-1987 when the West Bank and Gaza Strip erupted in violence. Called the intifada (ground rumbling), it pitted Palestinian youth wielding stones and Molotov cocktails against fully armed Israeli soldiers. There was no question of the Palestinians defeating the Israeli army, but neither was an increasingly demoralized Israeli army able to crush the uprising. The brutality of Israel's repression captured the attention of the world press. International pressure for a settlement of the Palestinian problem grew apace.

Israel's political disarray continued in the 1988 elections, in which the Likud gaining a one-seat plurality over Labor. Both parties had lost ground, with the Likud capturing forty seats in the Knesset to Labor's thirty-nine. Another national unity government was formed with Shamir as prime minister, but the government remained immobilized and existing policies remained in force. As the popularity of the major parties decreased, the influence of the smaller parties increased accordingly, with the religious parties the major beneficiaries. Israel was becoming a largely secular state, but its social life continued to be guided by the dictates of Orthodox rabbis.

The process of political decay intensified following the 1990 elections. Efforts to piece together a new government brought out the worst in Israeli politics.

> But almost everything that took place between March and June of 1990 had happened before: coalition horse trading, political blackmail and extortion by small extremist parties; shamelessly open political bribery; blatant and obsessive partisanship by the nation's top policymakers; complete disregard for matters of national interest . . . (Sprinzak and Diamond 1993).

"What was special about the 1990 spring crisis," noted one commentator, "was that it happened on a larger and more intense scale" (Brichta 1998, 8 InfoTrac).

## The Era of the New World Order

The disintegration of the USSR in 1990 was heralded as a new dawn for Israel. Approximately 3 million Jews in the Soviet Union, long captive in their own country, would now be free to emigrate to Israel or other countries of their own choosing. The collapse of the Soviet Union had also weakened the military and diplomatic position of Israel's main adversaries. This was particularly true of Syria, Iraq, Libya, and the PLO, all of whom had received the strong backing of the Soviet Union in their continuing conflict with Israel. As Abba Eban, a former Israeli foreign minister, wrote later, "Israeli security was strengthened a hundred-fold by the Soviet Union going from the 'anti' column to the 'pro' column. After all, it was the Soviet Union and not the Arabs that posed an existential threat to Israel in terms of life or death, to live or perish" (Abba Eban, cited in the *Orlando Sentinel,* Jan. 23, 1994).

The joy caused by the collapse of the Soviet Union was dampened by a deteriorating domestic situation. Debate raged over settlements, electoral reform, and the dominant role of Orthodox rabbis in Israel's religious life. These paled in comparison to debates over Lebanon and the intifada. The former had become Israel's Vietnam while the latter had contributed to the rise of the Hamas and threatened to transform the Palestinian–Israeli conflict into a war of religions.

In January of 1991, with the outbreak of the Gulf War, Iraqi Scud missiles rained down on Tel Aviv and other Israeli cities. The missiles, 39 in all, did not contain chemical agents, and the damage was limited to 1 direct death, 12 indirect deaths, 200 injuries, and damage to some 4,000 buildings (*JP,* March 9, 1991). Reports that focused on physical damage, however, totally missed the point. Israel's security perimeter had been breached, calling into question the government's ability to guarantee the security of the Israeli population. Earlier wars, moreover, had been fought by the large but poorly disciplined armies of Israel's neighbors, armies vulnerable to the technical and organizational superiority of the IDF. The Iraqi attack, by contrast, signaled Israeli vulnerability to missiles launched by countries far from its borders. Israel vowed to retaliate but was restrained by U.S. President George Bush, who feared that Israeli involvement in the Gulf War would inflame the region. There can be little doubt that he was correct.

The Iraqi attack rekindled a flagging intifada and unleashed a crescendo of Palestinian emotions throughout the region. After four decades of oppression and humiliation, the day of judgment seemed to be at hand. Palestinians throughout the region cheered Saddam Hussein and called for a mass revolution to rid the Middle East of America and its puppets, a veiled threat to the monarchies of Saudi Arabia, Kuwait, and Jordan.

In retrospect, it is clear that this was a tragic mistake. Saudi Arabia and Kuwait, fearing for their security, expelled Palestinian communities that had served them well for decades. They also questioned the effectiveness of the PLO in controlling Palestinian activism and curtailed their financial support accordingly. Popular sympathy for the Palestinians in the West evaporated, as did Palestinian hopes for liberation. Once again, optimism gave way to bitterness and despair.

At the same time, the intensity and spontaneity of Palestinian support for Saddam Hussein revived U.S. fears of regional chaos if the Palestinian conflict remained unresolved. The United States had cause for concern. Outpourings of popular support for Saddam Hussein had also shaken Egypt and Jordan, calling in question the survival of key U.S. allies in the region. King Hussein of Jordan, the staunchest of U.S. allies, openly supported the Iraqi dictator. The United States said nothing, well understanding that Palestinians constituted about 70 percent of the Jordanian population.

By midsummer 1991, Israeli Prime Minister Yitzhak Shamir, under intense pressure from the Bush administration, had agreed in principle to participate in peace talks with the Palestinians, which were to be held in Madrid. As always, the major focus of the American plan was land for peace. Simultaneously, Shamir had assured his Likud supporters that Israel would survive this new U.S. initiative much as it had survived those of the past. He also blasted the United States for tilting toward the Arabs, and Israel's right-wing press warned of a slow sellout by the United States (*JP,* Sept. 28, 1991). Progress in the Madrid negotiations was slow at best.

Also weighing heavily on the Shamir government was the cost of settling the influx of Soviet Jews arriving in Israel after the collapse of the Soviet Union, most of whom required housing and a broad range of social services. Estimates placed the cost of settling the Soviet Jews at $26.5 billion, an astronomical figure for an already strained budget. Israel approached the United States in search of $10 billion in loan guarantees for new housing projects, many of which would presumably be built in the occupied territories (UP, Feb. 1, 1992). President Bush agreed to the request in principle, but angered the Israeli government by making U.S. support conditional upon a moratorium on new settlements in the occupied territories and progress on the peace front. Both conditions were anathema to Shamir, who was intent on realizing the right wing's vision of a Greater Israel.

It was in this environment that Israelis went to the polls in the summer of 1992. Labor scored a narrow victory, and Yitzhak Rabin was now the prime minister. With Labor's return to power came hopes of a peaceful settlement of the Palestinian issue. Both the United States and Israel's Arab neighbors breathed a sigh of relief. Tensions between Tel Aviv and Washington eased, and the Madrid negotiations gained new momentum. The building of new Jewish settlements in the occupied territories was suspended.

The Madrid negotiations dragged on into 1993 but came to an abrupt end with the stunning news that Rabin and Arafat had been conducting secret negotiations in Oslo, Norway. Israel and the PLO signed a formal agreement for resolving their longstanding conflict on September 13, 1993, with Israel promising a negotiated withdrawal from large areas of the West Bank and Gaza in return for peace and Palestinian recognition of Israel (Wittes 2005). Critical details remained to be worked out, but the principle of exchanging land for peace had been accepted by both parties.

The new peace accords were greeted by an upsurge in violence as extremists on both sides attempted to scuttle the agreement. Violence on the Israeli side was spearheaded by the settlers and the parties of the extreme right. Palestinian violence was led by Jihad and Hamas, the leading Islamic fundamentalist groups in the occupied territories. In the wake of massacres and cries for vengeance, the optimism of Oslo gave way to renewed pessimism.

Nevertheless, at the end of 1993 Israel took the first steps toward transferring control of Gaza and Jericho and other minor areas of the occupied territories to the Palestinian Authority (PA), the quasi-governmental body established by the Oslo accords. The gradual transfer of territories to the PA continued throughout 1994 and 1995, as did the accompanying violence.

Rabin announced his intention to seek reelection in 1996, vowing to pursue the peace process to its logical conclusion. By contrast, Binyamin Netanyahu, the new leader of the Likud, promised a return to the policies of Begin and Shamir. Amid mounting political rhetoric over the future of the occupied territories, Rabin was assassinated by a young and unrepentant Jewish extremist. Israel was stunned. An emotional outpouring saw Israeli public opinion surge in favor of the peace process that Rabin had been so instrumental in starting. That support, however, soon waned in the face of suicide bombings by Arab terrorists, and Netanyahu won a narrow victory in the June 1996 elections. Fear had won out over the desire for peace.

Netanyahu revived the policies of Begin and Shamir with a vengeance, demanding that the Oslo accords be renegotiated and launching a frenzied building program in the occupied territories. The position of the Orthodox Jews was also strengthened, and the Israeli army was told to prepare for war with Syria (UP, Jan. 11, 1997). Violence surged, and once again a cloud settled over U.S.–Israeli relations. The United States demanded a freeze on settlements; Netanyahu responded by expanding them. By the fall of 1997, President Clinton, Israel's new best friend, had begun to snub the Israeli prime minister. As Netanyahu would quip, "He treats me like Saddam Hussein" (*IHT,* Nov. 20, 1997, 23).

Within two years of his election, Netanyahu had faced an indictment for cronyism, narrowly survived several votes of no confidence, and seen his majority in the Knesset shrink to a single vote. Even that vote was shaky. Rather than face losing a vote of confidence, Netanyahu acquiesced in the dissolution of the Knesset (*JP,* Jan. 5, 1999). He had been in office approximately two and a half years, considerably less than his four-year term.

The Knesset voted to dissolve itself on January 5, 1999, and new elections were scheduled for May 17 of the same year. Five candidates contended for prime minister, while thirty-one political parties vied for seats in the Knesset. A runoff election between the two leading candidates for the prime ministership seemed all but inevitable. In last-minute maneuvering, however, all candidates withdrew from the race except Netanyahu and Ehud Barak, the Labor/One Israel Candidate. One or the other would become the next prime minister of Israel. The campaign was bitter, even by Israeli standards. Netanyahu questioned the courage of Barak, a former commander in chief of the Israel Defense Forces and Israel's most decorated general (*IHT,* Jan. 11, 1999). Barak's supporters portrayed Netanyahu as "a man for whom use of lies and deception is an instinctive response to ordinary pressures" (*Ha'aretz,* May 16, 1999).

For all of the campaign's bitterness, differences between the two candidates were not as great as their rhetoric suggested. Barak promised to have Israeli troops out of Lebanon within a year, while Netanyahu promised to withdraw from Lebanon without specifying a date. Both accepted the principle that some land would have to be returned to the Palestinians, but remained vague on what and how much. Both were firm on the need to keep Jerusalem Israeli, crush terrorism, stimulate the economy, and protect the interests of the settlers. Netanyahu advocated new settlements, while Barak was content to expand those that already existed.

The political right applauded Netanyahu's passionate "no concession" policy, but the majority of Israeli voters did not. Barak swept to a dazzling victory with some 56 percent of the popular vote. By all accounts, the critical element in the election had been the shift in the vote of the Russian Jews from a pro-Netanyahu position in the 1996 elections to a pro-Barak position in the 1999 elections. Both candidates had heavily courted the Russian vote, with Netanyahu making several trips to the former Soviet Union.

The reign of Ehud Barak began with optimism that the peace process would move to a swift conclusion. Peace negotiations were immediately initiated with the Palestinians and the Syrians, and the Israeli withdrawal from Lebanon began shortly thereafter. It was completed in 2000. The PLO, for its part, had revised its charter to eliminate clauses offensive to Israel and the peace process. Everything was on track, or so it seemed.

Unfortunately, the optimism following the elections was misplaced. Peace was not achieved with Lebanon, Syria, or the Palestinians. Indeed, Israel's relations with Egypt and other "friendly" Arab states deteriorated, as did its relations with France and Russia. The stress of the negotiations, in turn, exacerbated the fragmentation of Israeli society, and Barak's popular mandate gave way to partisan wrangling.

The PLO was having its own difficulties, the foremost of which was transforming itself from a revolutionary organization into a Palestinian government capable of maintaining order and meeting the needs of the populations under its control. Already a huge bureaucracy that had lost its revolutionary zeal, the PLO/Palestinian Authority began to act like the other Arab governments. Arafat differed little from other Arab dictators, and a corrupt PLO bureaucracy served itself while providing few services to its subjects (Belqaziz 2004). Inevitably, it became distant from its population.

While Arafat attempted to secure a Palestinian state though negotiations, Hezbollah's defeat of the Israelis in Lebanon had bolstered Hamas and other Palestinian resistance groups by demonstrating that Arab land could be liberated by guerrilla warfare and terrorism. The PLO might have recognized Israel's right to exist, but Hamas and Islamic Jihad had not. Both condemned the Palestinian Authority for its corruption and subservience to the United States. The PLO, in their view, had sacrificed the Palestinian cause for its own survival (Belqaziz 2004). This view was shared by a growing number of Palestinians who waited in vain for the fruits of Oslo. If tangible results were not forthcoming, it would likely be Hamas that seized control of the Palestinian struggle.

Arafat pursued a complex strategy designed to consolidate his own power while holding both the Israelis and Hamas at bay. He preached peace and moderation to the world while simultaneously ignoring the role of the Al-Aqsa Brigades, the military wing of al-Fatah, in the armed struggle against Israeli occupation. How else could he counter Hamas's charges that he was soft on Israel? It is not at all clear that he even retained the ability to rein in the Al-Aqsa Brigades.

He certainly was not in a position to rein in Hamas and the Islamic Jihad. Always a master at making the best of a bad situation, he turned weakness to his advantage by pressing the United States to push for more Israeli concessions. How else could he keep the peace process on track? he asked.

The Israeli withdrawal from Lebanon was completed in the late spring of 2000, but retained the Sheba Farms, an area of about 264 square kilometers famous for the quality of its wine production. The UN sided with Israel, saying that the farms had been under the control of the Syrian army when Israel occupied them and thus they were not covered in the UN resolution calling for the Israeli withdrawal from Lebanon. The return of the farms would have to await peace between Israel and Syria.

Peace negotiations between Israel and Syria had foundered over Syria's demand that all Syrian territory occupied by the Israelis during the 1967 war be returned as a condition for peace with Israel. The Israelis, meanwhile, insisted on retaining a narrow strip of land on the Syrian side of Lake Kinneret (the Sea of Galilee), a key element in Israel's dwindling water supply (*JP,* Dec. 5, 2000). Israel's water supply, the Israelis argued, could not be held hostage to the whims of the Syrian regime.

Hezbollah, the Shi'a fundamentalist organization that had been the main force in driving Israel from southern Lebanon, used the Israeli occupation of the Sheba Farms to continue its high-profile struggle against Israel. It was also Hezbollah rather than the Lebanese army that patrolled the joint border between Israel and Lebanon, the Lebanese government having refused to take control of the border areas until the Sheba Farms were returned. In retrospect, it might have been wiser for the Israelis to return the farms to Lebanon, since there was no doubt that they would eventually be returned to either Lebanon or Syria. This move would have cut the wind from Hezbollah's sails and further isolated Syria in its negotiations with Israel. This action, however, did not take place and Hezbollah captured four Israeli soldiers, causing further embarrassment to the Barak government. In the meantime Hezbollah rockets were moving within range of Haifa and other major population areas. Israel had withdrawn from Lebanon, but it had not extricated itself from the Lebanese quagmire.

In the meantime, Ariel Sharon, the author of the Lebanese occupation and the Sabra and Shatila massacres, had taken over the temporary leadership of the Likud Party. Sharply critical of Barak's negotiations with the Palestinians, Sharon led a delegation of Israeli legislators and the accompanying contingent of security forces on a dramatic visit to the Temple Mount, the site of al-Aqsa mosque, the third holiest site in Islam and the historical site of the First and Second Temples that play such a central role in the Jewish faith (*NYT,* Sept. 29, 2000). Sharon's visit was a widely publicized gesture to reclaim Israeli sovereignty over the bitterly contested Mount and thereby to derail Barak's negotiations with the Palestinians.

Sharon's visit unleashed a cycle of violence and counterviolence. As the violence escalated, the Israeli army deployed tanks and helicopter gunships in an effort to crush the al-Aqsa intifada, as the uprising was now called, before it expanded into one similar to the intifada that had rocked the occupied territories between

1987 and 1990. The first intifada had led to the Madrid and Oslo agreements and the emergence of the Palestinian Authority. Who knew where a second intafada would lead?

The Oslo accords, however, had only sketched the broad outlines of an agreement, with all of the difficult issues to be resolved by negotiations, not the least of which was the status of Jerusalem and the building of settlements on Palestinian territory. Progress was made, but not enough. While many Israelis believed that Barak was making overly generous concessions in his offers to trade land for peace, the Palestinians despaired of ever receiving independence from Israeli occupation. This fear was made even more poignant by the continued construction of new Israeli settlements on lands claimed by the Palestinians. Sharon's visit to the Temple Mount triggered the al-Aqsa intifada, but its causes were the growing despair of a Palestinian population. Oslo had not worked.

In reality, both sides were struggling to bridge a gap that was unbridgeable within the political context of their respective communities. Arafat, rapidly losing control of the Palestinian community, pleaded that he had nothing more to give. Israel had placed some areas of the occupied territories under the control of the Palestinian Authority, but these areas were surrounded by armed settlements and, from the Palestinian point of view, amounted to little more than reservations similar to Indian reservations in the United States. The Israelis, moreover, had remained adamant in their demand that Jerusalem be united under Israeli control. The Palestinians might have partial control over the Arab sections of the Old City, but it would not be the independent capital of a sovereign Palestinian state. Indeed, the very nature of the proposed Palestinian state was open to debate. It was not to be a state that could pose a threat to Israel by maintaining a large army or harboring terrorist groups. By weakening Arafat, moreover, the Israelis were threatened with the prospect that the al-Aqsa intifada would become totally dominated by Hamas and other fundamentalist groups. Arafat, for his part, attempted to strengthen his grip on the Palestinian community by toting a machine gun and encouraging greater violence.

The final months of 2000 found Barak without a majority in the Knesset, condemned abroad for his brutal suppression of the Palestinians, and condemned at home for being too "restrained" in his treatment of the "emergency," as the al-Aqsa intifada was called in the Israeli press. Efforts to forge a government of national unity with Sharon and the Likud foundered on Sharon's demand that he be given veto power over any agreement with the Palestinians. Even the United States seemed to be deserting the ship, with the *Jerusalem Post* complaining about the "new evenhandedness of the Clinton administration" (*JP*, Nov. 24, 2000). This was the situation when a beleaguered Barak agreed to opposition demands for new elections to be held in May 2001. Public opinion polls at the time found Netanyahu to be the candidate of choice for most Israelis.

In the meantime, the al-Aqsa intifada had spread to Israel proper, with bomb blasts rocking Jewish cities and sowing consternation among an already skittish population. Nervousness reached crisis proportions among settlers in the occupied territories as stone throwing gave way to open battles between the settlers and the Palestinians. Perhaps even more threatening to the settlers were calls to dismantle some settlements in the name of peace. Indeed, the leader of the Meretz Party, a key element of Barak's coalition, declared, "We think the settlement program is the most foolish thing ever carried out by the Zionist enterprise" (*NYT,* Nov. 15, 2000).

On the international front, Israel found itself confronted with demands that its treatment of the al-Aqsa intifada be investigated by an international commission, a demand vigorously opposed by Israel but ultimately supported by the United States (UP, Dec. 12, 2000). It was now the Israelis who were being portrayed by the world press as the aggressors and the Palestinians as their victims. Even worse was the growing European support for an international force to separate the Israelis and the Palestinians, similar to the international force imposed upon Yugoslavia a year or so earlier (BBC, Dec. 8, 2000). Israel vehemently rejected the presence of an international force but reluctantly accepted an international fact-finding mission headed by former Senator George Mitchell of the United States (UP, Dec. 6, 2000; *Ha'aretz*, Nov. 14, 2000). Also disconcerting was the growing transformation of the Arab–Israeli conflict into a Jewish–Muslim conflict and the upsurge of attacks on Jewish targets throughout the world. Indeed, the Simon Wiesenthal Center reported that more than two hundred attacks on international Jewish targets had occurred during the first month of the al-Aqsa intifada, noting that the sixty attacks on synagogues represented "the largest number of attacks on synagogues since 1938, and the world has been silent" (UP, Oct. 20, 2000).

Arafat and Barak vowed their continued support of the peace process, with Barak declaring that the Palestinian question could only be solved politically (CNN, Dec. 8, 2000). An editorial in *Ha'aretz* echoed this view, commenting, "The policy of flexing muscles, which was shown to be a mistake in the past, may prove to be a mistake again" (*Ha'aretz,* Nov. 10, 2000). Arafat, too, was well aware of the dangers of prolonging a confrontation that had brought death and suffering to the Palestinian community, destroyed the Palestinian economy, and called into question both his authority and that of the Palestinian Authority (UP, Oct. 23, 2000). In a strange irony, the survival of both Barak and Arafat was linked to making the peace process work.

Barak's blend of compromise and repression played poorly among an Israeli population distraught by the violence of the intifada and dubious about the wisdom of Barak's concessions. On February 6, 2001, Ariel Sharon swept to a 63 to 37 percent victory over the embattled Barak. This time the Israeli electorate had placed security before peace.

## Entering the Sharon Era

Sharon's campaign had focused almost entirely on a pledge to crush the al-Aqsa intifada. Returned to power, he accelerated the assassination of Palestinian resistance leaders, the torture of Palestinians, and the collective punishment of Palestinian communities. The latter included curtailment of vital food and medical supplies. These measures were duly condemned in the U.S. State Department's annual report on human rights violations (*Ha'aretz,* May 30, 2001, March 13, 2001, and Feb. 22, 2001). The efficacy of Sharon's measures was openly debated in the Israeli press. The right wing criticized Sharon's restraint while the moderate press decried the influence of Sharon's iron-fist policies on world opinion. Peres, now foreign minister in the Sharon "national unity" government, candidly stated, "The most important lesson we have learned is that you can't put out a fire with fire" (*JP*, March 7, 2001). Sharon countered by asserting that he would not negotiate with the Palestinians until the violence had stopped. The Palestinians vowed that the violence would not stop until they had received their independence and the expansion of the settlements had ended.

Peres's assessment proved to be prophetic. Israeli tactics served only to inflame the conflict. Confrontations between Palestinian teenagers and Israeli troops escalated to mortar attacks on Jewish settlements and a growing number of suicide bombings within Israel itself, all clearly designed to play upon Israeli insecurities. In one rally alone, Hamas reportedly recruited 250 suicide bombers to serve in the struggle against Israeli occupation (UP, May 20, 2001). It was the ground war that captured the world's attention, but the psychological war was equally intense.

Perhaps in desperation, Sharon launched military strikes into Palestinian-controlled areas and attacked the camps and other strongholds of the resistance with helicopter gunships. When these measures didn't suffice, the camps were attacked by F-16s provided to Israel by the United States on the condition that they would only be used for defensive purposes. The United States condemned the attack, with U.S. Vice President Dick Cheney saying, "Yeah, I think they should stop; both sides should stop and think about where they are headed" (*Ha'aretz*, May 21, 2001).

Israel justified its actions in the name of national security; Foreign Minister Peres stated that Israel was engaged in a "battle for its existence" (*Ha'aretz*, May 16, 2001). Whether or not this was the case, the Jewish settlements in the occupied territories were clearly at risk, as was the ability of Israel to control the nature of a future Palestinian state.

The harshness of Israeli tactics led to an outpouring of world sympathy for the Palestinians and brought severe condemnations of Israel from European leaders. Particularly upsetting to the Israelis was the Danish foreign minister's call for sanctions against Israel (*Ha'aretz*, May 20, 2001; *JP*, March 28, 2001). The president of the International Red Cross added fuel to the fire by stating that Israeli settlements were "war crimes," an assertion that brought a sharp reproach from both the United States and Israel (UP, May 20, 2001). Washington was muted in its criticism of Israel, but endorsed the Mitchell Report as a basis for peace between the two sides (Mitchell Report, BBC, November 29, 2001). The Mitchell Report rejected Palestinian demands for a multilateral force to separate the combatants but otherwise apportioned the blame for the violence equally between the two sides, a position that placed the Palestinians on an equal footing with the Israelis in the negotiation process. Both sides were urged to stop the violence, and the Israelis were called upon to freeze the building and expansion of settlements.

Faced with a public relations disaster, the Israeli cabinet hired an American public relations firm to handle the damage control (*JP*, March 9, 2001). Guidelines were also sent to Israeli embassies on how best to parry the settlement issue

(UP, May 22, 2001). If Israel lost the media war, international pressures to impose an unacceptable solution on Israel could well prove insurmountable.

The Palestinians accepted the Mitchell Report. Sharon responded by approving more settlements, arguing that a freeze on settlements would be "tantamount to rewarding Palestinian violence" (*Ha'aretz,* May 10, 2001). Violence continued to mount on both sides but eased as Sharon, under intense pressure from Washington, declared a unilateral cease-fire. He also agreed to a temporary freeze on building new settlements. He did so, however, on the condition that all other terms of the report be implemented (*IHT,* May 30, 2001; *Ha'aretz,* June 6, 2001). Palestinian violations, in Sharon's view, would give him carte blanche to renew settlement building. Arafat called for an end to attacks within Israel proper, but Hamas showed little inclination to obey Arafat's orders (UP, June 6, 2001). Indeed, it was far from clear that Arafat had the capacity to control the violence, a topic hotly debated in the Israeli press. While Sharon blamed Arafat for the violence, high military intelligence officers openly voiced the opinion that Arafat had lost control of the situation and warned that Israel was "not far removed from full-scale war" (*Ha'aretz,* May 31, 2001).

Sharon countered by threatening to build a "Great Wall of China" around Israel and the Israeli settlements, an idea that was first floated by Netanyahu and later revived by Barak (UP, June 5, 2001). The Palestinians could have what was left. Netanyahu, sensing that the Sharon government would be making an early exit, positioned himself for a comeback by chiding Sharon for being soft on the Palestinians and placing the security of Israel at risk (*Ha'aretz,* May 31, 2001).

## The Era of Terror

The September 11 attacks on the United States confronted the Bush administration with an urgent need for a coherent antiterrorist strategy. Israel was reputed to be the world's leader in fighting terror and the United States adopted the Israeli strategy more or less in toto. Bush also found much to like in Sharon's hardline approach to dealing with suspected terrorists (*JP,* April 23, 2003). A strong bond of mutual respect soon linked the two men. Along the way, Israel's struggle against the Palestinian resistance melded with America's war on terror.

The al-Aqsa intifada had begun with stone throwing by Palestinian youth but soon escalated into a pattern of Palestinian attacks and Israeli reprisals, each more vicious than its predecessor. The spring of 2002 brought a full-scale military assault on refugee camps in the Palestinian city of Jenin followed by the bulldozing of houses. The Palestinians claimed that more than five hundred people had been killed and called for an international investigation of the massacre. They also renewed calls for an international force to protect the occupied territories from Israeli aggression. Sharon rejected both demands, claiming that Palestinian deaths only numbered in the dozens. He reluctantly agreed to an investigation of the Jenin affair only after President Bush joined the chorus of international leaders demanding that the Red Cross and the UN be allowed access to the site (*Guardian,* April 20, 2002.) The UN concluded that the Israeli attacks had not constituted a massacre, as the Palestinians had claimed, but acknowledged that they were horrible. U.S.-provided aircraft continued to blast housing blocks sus-pected of harboring terrorists. The aircraft were to be used for defensive pur-poses, and in Sharon's mind, fighting the terrorists was defensive. If the Palestinian community supported the terrorists, they would have to pay the price. Arafat was blamed for the terror and placed under virtual house arrest. President Bush called Sharon a man of peace (*WP*, April 19, 2002, A1). Both Israel and the Palestinians found the American position confusing.

Despite its brutality, Sharon's effort to crush the terror by force was a failure. Violence begot violence and the terror increased. It also penetrated Israel itself. Security officials claimed to have prevented 80 percent of the terrorist attacks, noting that there were only 3,838 attacks in 2003 as opposed to 5, 301 in 2002 (Harel 2004). Ben-Eliezer, then the minister of defense, acknowledged that force alone could not crush the terror. He also warned the Knesset's Foreign Affairs and Defense Committee: "Whoever thinks the IDF can stop terrorism is mistaken. Terrorism cannot be stopped with military maneuvers. The operations are in-tended merely to disrupt the terrorism and stop as many attacks as possible" (*JP*, April 2, 2002).

Nevertheless, in 2003 Sharon was elected for a second term in office on the pledge that he would crush terror once and for all. Both sides, the Israelis and the Palestinians, now believed that they were in a fight for their very survival. It was not a time for the faint of heart.

The terror, however, was not the only danger threatening the Jewish state. When Saddam Hussein boasted of having weapons of mass destruction, his claims were taken very seriously by a country that had suffered through his Scud missile attacks. During the Gulf War their warheads had not contained weapons of mass destruction, but who knew what would come next? Sharon urged a U.S. attack on Iraq, intimating a willingness to go it alone if Washington dithered. Bush's advisers had long advocated taking out the Iraqi dictator as a key move in stabi-lizing the region, a topic elaborated in Chapter 6.

Ironically, in preparing for an attack on Iraq, the United States was forced to concede that Israeli occupation policies were a major cause of the anti-Americanism sweeping the region. Washington wanted the support of Muslim leaders in the war against Iraq, and that required a toning-down of Sharon's iron-fist policies in dealing with the Palestinians. Indeed, Saudi, Turkish, Jordanian, and Egyptian leaders all warned President Bush that Israeli policies in Palestine had so inflamed emotions throughout the Middle East that it would be virtually impossible for them to support an American strike on Iraq. If Israel wanted safety from Saddam Hussein, it would have to bend on the Palestinian front.

Washington's solution to the Palestinian problem was a "road map" worked out in consultation with its European allies. President Bush launched the road map concept in a speech on June 24, 2002; he called for a two-state solution (land for peace) based on the emergence of new Palestinian leadership and the end to terrorist attacks against Israel (Freedman 2005). A road map, yet to be worked out, would guide the peace process to its final conclusion. The Palestinians believed their goal of an independent state was at hand.

During the ensuing months, the road map was drafted by the United States, the European Union, Russia, and the United Nations, later referred to as the Quartet. It was completed by the end of 2002, but Sharon persuaded Bush to delay its presentation until after the 2003 Israeli elections.

Sharon was returned to a second term in office as the head of a shaky coalition government and was duly presented with the final draft of the road map. The Palestinians, for their part, met Bush's call for new leadership by adding the position of prime minister to balance Arafat's power. The pressure for change, however, was not coming from Washington alone. The Palestinian legislature was also pushing Arafat for reform. After much resistance, he named Mahmoud Abbas, a moderate and outspoken advocate of the peace process, as Palestine's first prime minister.

According to the text of the road map:

> "A two-state solution to the Israeli–Palestinian conflict will only be achieved through an end to violence and terrorism, when the Palestinian people have a leadership acting decisively against terror and willing and able to build a practicing democracy based on tolerance and liberty, and through Israel's readiness to do what is necessary for a democratic Palestinian state to be established, and a clear, unambiguous acceptance by both parties of the goal of a negotiated settlement." The text of the road map went on to specify that negotiations between the two parties will end the occupation that began in 1967 based on the principle of land for peace embodied in United Nations Security Council resolutions 242, 338 and 1397. In short, the lands occupied by Israel in 1967, including all of the West Bank and old Jerusalem, would be returned to the Palestinian control. The two states would recognize the right of the other to exist and live in peace (*JP,* May 26, 2003).

The Palestinians accepted the road map; the Israelis cringed. Yet another naïve American initiative designed to empower the Palestinians and deny Israel its rightful heritage. Every U.S. president, or so it seemed, had at least one. Israel responded to the road map as it had responded to the prior initiatives, by "saying yes while meaning no" (*JP,* May 26, 2003). Faced with the need to keep a strong relationship with the United States, Israel demanded some 100 "corrections," a call echoed by American Jewish leaders and Israel's many supporters in Congress (www.haaretz.com, May 1, 2003).

The situation was difficult, but not urgent. The road map would not come into play until the terror had stopped and the Palestinians developed a viable democracy. Sharon pledged to see to it that the Palestinians fully executed their obligations under the road map (*JP,* Aug. 1, 2003). Arafat played his role by issuing belligerent communiques from his besieged headquarters, much of which had been reduced to rubble. The brutality continued on both sides, and Israeli settlements on the West Bank mushroomed. Indeed, statistics from Israel's Interior Ministry indicate that the number of settlers increased from 203,000 in 2000 to 231,443 by 2003. The number of settlers in 1982 was 21,700.

Despite its fierce reprisals, Israel found it impossible to stem the violence or crush the intifada. The reasons for its failure can only be outlined at this point, but are discussed at length in *At the Heart of Terror* (Palmer and Palmer 2004). The core of the violence, as the Israeli minister of defense acknowledged with great candor, was Palestinian despair (*Daily Star* [Beirut], June 22, 2002). In part, Palestinian despair was born of poverty and unemployment. It was also exacerbated by the relentless expansion of Jewish settlements and the corresponding expropriation of Palestinian land. Where else were the Palestinians to go? The neighboring Arab states didn't want them and were anxious to be rid of the camps they already had. This was particularly the case of Lebanon.

Desperation, in turn, led to radicalism. With few results to show for Arafat's negotiation strategy, the leadership of the Palestinian movement was shifting to Hamas and other radical groups. The struggle for independence was now being fueled by religious fervor. The severity of Israeli antiterrorist measures was also proving counterproductive. Indeed, it could be persuasively argued that the Israelis were creating more terrorists than they were eliminating (*Ha'aretz*, May 20, 2003). The Israeli press referred to "lost children," many of whom languishing in prisons that had become breeding grounds for terrorism (*Observer* [London], Feb. 9, 2003). The Israeli security forces also complained of declining morale among soldiers who were required to kill civilians. Indeed, a group of reservists issued a highly publicized public statement proclaiming: "We will not continue to fight beyond the Green Line in order to rule, to expel, to destroy, to blockade, to assassinate, to starve, and to humiliate an entire people" (Lazaroff 2002). This was followed in September 2003 by a petition signed by twenty-seven reserve pilots refusing to participate in "illegal and immoral" strikes in Palestinian areas (Myre 2003). The Israeli population itself was deeply divided over what to do about the terrorism. Most just wanted it to end. The IDF, for its part, complained of inadequate funds and equipment. And all of this was taking place in a fishbowl, where it could be dissected in grueling detail by the world press. By this time, the occupation of Iraq was going poorly, so President Bush, dismayed by the paucity of international support, was placing intense pressure on Israel for positive signs on the Palestinian front.

Faced with the reality that the terror could not be crushed by force and pressed by the United States to come up with a solution, Sharon became convinced that there would have to be some form of Palestinian state on some portion of the occupied territories. A majority of Israelis supported this position, as did a majority of American Jews. His strategy, accordingly, was to retain Israeli control over most of the West Bank by letting go of the Gaza Strip and, perhaps, a small strip of the West Bank. Peripheral areas would be sacrificed for the sake of keeping the biblical lands of Judea and Samaria. This would get Washington off his back and place the onus for peace on the Palestinians and justify Israeli reprisals against terrorist attacks.

Sharon made his announcement on New Year's Eve 2004. Blaming the Palestinians for the lack of progress, he took the high ground and proclaimed that Israel would make a strategic disengagement from the occupied territories. The White House was pleased, but Sharon's former allies in the Likud and other parties of the Israeli right charged that he had capitulated to the terrorists and provided them with a secure base of operations in the Gaza Strip. Rather than being a solution, they argued, it was the beginning of a capitulation that would see all of the occupied territories returned to the Palestinians. And after that, what? Hamas was gaining the upper hand in the intifada and Palestinian radicals were returning to Gaza from Beirut.

Clearly, Sharon's move was a gamble. Israeli fears were eased by the accelerated construction of Israel's massive security fence. Once completed, the infiltration of terrorists into Israel would be reduced but not eliminated (*Ha'aretz*, Sept. 1, 2005). The fence also served as a pretext for annexing more Palestinian land. This was matched with a massive buildup of settlements on the West Bank. Some were new; others were expansions of old settlements.

And yet, the fence seemed to contradict Sharon's strategy for retaining the West Bank. Was not the very construction of the fence an admission that the West Bank was not part of Israel? Apologists suggested that the fence was a temporary security expedient, but the settlers were nervous. With Gaza gone, could the West Bank be far behind? Thanks to the fence, Israel was subjected to yet more rounds of international criticism. Some adjustments in its route were duly made to satisfy the United States; other adjustments were obvious land grabs. The latter, but not the fence itself, would subsequently be declared unconstitutional by the Israeli Supreme Court.

Yasir Arafat died in November 2004, having outlived virtually every other leader of his generation. He was condemned as a terrorist and honored as a Nobel laureate, along with Yitzhak Rabin, for his role in negotiating the Oslo accords. Above all, he was the father and enduring symbol of the Palestinian movement. There could be no replacement for Arafat as long as he remained alive. The Israelis had threatened to assassinate him, but relented under international pressure. Rumors continue to swirl concerning the cause of his death in a French hospital.

The death of Arafat cleared the way for reform and the emergence of a new and more moderate leadership. Both were much needed if the Palestinian Authority were to emerge from the long shadow of corruption and regain the confidence of the Palestinian people.

Arafat's stature precluded the existence of a second in command, and Arafat, like most Arab leaders, had little interest in naming one. Mahmoud Abbas, a moderate, was elected president of the Palestinian Authority in January 2005 and called for an end to the terror. He also pressed for the implementation of the road map and urged that Sharon's promised evacuation of Gaza take place with all due haste. Local elections followed, with the results showing a deep and abiding split between the PLO and Hamas. Legislative elections had been scheduled for July 2005, but were delayed until January 2006 by Hamas's unexpected support in the local elections. Hamas had not fielded a candidate in the presidential elections, but now seemed poised to emerge as one of the strongest groups in the parliament. Indeed, it was possible that Hamas and its fundamentalist allies could control parliament. This was unacceptable to both Israel and the United States. How could they accept control of the Palestinian state by a terrorist organization that had vowed to liberate all of Palestine? The electoral strength of Hamas also sent shudders through a deeply entrenched PLO/al-Fatah apparatus that had gone unchallenged for almost four decades.

Hurried efforts were made to restructure the PLO into an instrument of national unity in which all major groups would be represented, Hamas among them. Hamas was open to membership in the PLO, but only if it would be an equal partner with the PLO, and only if it could keep its militia. Both demands were unacceptable to the PLO.

Arafat's passing also created problems for Israel. The man Sharon had blamed for the terror was gone. George W. Bush rushed to invite Mahmoud Abbas to the White House in a dramatic show of America's support for the "new" Palestine. Bush's enthusiasm was easy to understand. By now, the U.S.-led occupation of Iraq had gone terribly wrong, and the United States was desperate for progress on the Palestinian front. Bush certainly didn't want to face the prospect of a Hamas victory in Palestine. Abbas did his part by arranging a truce in attacks against Israel, the thirteenth since the beginning of the al-Aqsa intifada (al-Jazeera, Sept. 9, 2005). Whatever the case, the pressure was now on Sharon.

The Gaza Strip was duly evacuated in the late summer of 2005. It was a bitter pill for Sharon, who watched as the IDF evicted settlers from the Gaza Strip and a northern fringe of the West Bank. The process went smoothly, with minimal violence from either side. The Palestinian Authority had both land and a population under its control, but lacked sovereignty. That, according to the U.S. plan, would come with time and an end to the violence. No firm date for statehood has been set by either the United States or Israel (*Al-Quds,* Oct. 21, 2005). At any time, violence against Israel could bring renewed occupation.

Disengagement divided the Israelis as never before. Netanyahu was gaining control of Sharon's Likud Party and called for party elections to confirm his position as its new leader (*Ha'aretz,* Sept. 1, 2005). Sharon, finding himself in the unaccustomed position of moderate, appealed for the support of Labor and the Israeli left. Bush rushed to Sharon's aid, saying that the Palestinians would have to accept the "new realities" and urging America's allies not to put too much pressure on Israel's beleaguered leader (*NYT,* Sept. 4, 2005). In reality, the issue was a matter of months rather than years. New elections were scheduled for 2006. Bush urged Sharon to run in the coming elections, noting that "people want strong leaders. That's how I won the last elections . . ." (*Ha'aretz,* Sept. 15, 2005). Sharon would indeed run, but the path would not be easy. Dissension within the Labor Party had made the Likud-Labor coalition unworkable and the elections were moved ahead to March of 2006. Sharon added to the excitement by declaring that "life in Likud had become unbearable" (*Ha'aretz,* Nov. 22, 2005). He subsequently announced the formation of a new party, temporarily called National Responsibility, with polls predicting that he would sweep to victory with 30 percent of the seats in the Knesset, far more than either the Likud or Labor (*Ha'aretz,* Nov. 22, 2005). This became less certain as Sharon suffered a mild stroke in December of 2005. For further updates, see the website that accompanies this book: http://politicalscience.wadsworth.com/palmer2e/.

The al-Aqsa intifada wound down and with it the wave of terror and counterterror that had shaken both Israelis and Palestinians to their roots. The figures were awesome. Some 3,839 Palestinians had been killed and more than 36,000 wounded. The corresponding figures for Israel were 979 and 6,297 (BBC, Oct. 22, 2004). Most on both sides were innocent civilians. Many were children.

The numbers on both sides will increase when a final accounting is made. The Palestinians claim that there have been more than 52,500 Palestinians wounded, not to mention some 28,000 arrested. Both figures are disputed by the Israelis. Keeping body counts is not an exact science. Whatever the numbers, they describe unspeakable horror and loss. Comparable figures for the United States, based on population, would be fifty times larger. Losses of property were equally devastating, with Israel having destroyed 1,620 Palestinian homes in the occupied territories by early 2002 (UNRWA/*Ha'aretz,* March 12, 2002). The social and psychological trauma on both populations has been incalculable.

What comes next? The hard part. The Palestinians have to make their minuscule state work. This includes developing viable political institutions that can meet the needs of the Palestinian population and prevent terrorist attacks on Israel and Israeli targets on the West Bank. Judging from Washington's rhetoric, it also means accepting less than a return to Israel's 1967 borders and accepting a large number of Jewish settlers within their territory. The details remain vague. At least in Israel's mind, the road map and its demand for a return to Israel's 1967 border is dead. This is not the view of either the Palestinians or the Europeans, who see it as the basis for a final settlement. The envoy of the Quartet has also complained that "Israel is acting as if disengagement never happened" (Hass 2005).

Israel, for its part will have to do everything within its power to make Palestine's new government viable. This includes restraining itself in the face of the random terrorist attacks that remain inevitable until a Palestinian state is up and running. That could take years. It also means ceding more land to the Palestinian Authority and working out economic arrangements that will sus--tain a Palestinian economy dependent on foreign aid and employment in the Jewish state. Both sides will have to moderate their stands on Jerusalem, water, and the right to return issues guaranteed by UN documents of an earlier era. No one seriously expects Israel to accept an influx of some five million refugees, but the issues have to be dealt with, presumably within the broader context of land for peace.

What then, is the probability that the governments of Israel and Palestine can convince their respective populations to compromise on these most vital of issues? In attempting to shed light on this question we shall examine Israeli and Palestinian political institutions, the actors that give life to those institutions, and the broader economic, cultural, and international environments that influence the Israeli political process, which is among the most complex in the world.

## ISRAELI POLITICS TODAY AND BEYOND

An examination of Israeli politics over the past half century suggests three clear conclusions. First, Israel has succeeded admirably in the task of building a state that is both strong and democratic. Not only have Israeli political institutions stood the test of time, but they have enabled Israel to effectively dominate its regional environment. Second, the Israeli political process has shifted from the firm leadership of the Ben-Gurion era to a pattern of immobilization alternating with dramatic swings of policy. Rabin made peace, Netanyahu stalled the peace process, Barak reinitiated the peace process, Sharon shattered it only to preside over the creation of a probable Palestinian state in the Gaza Strip. Third, the Israeli polity has increasingly divided into two opposing camps. One camp is largely secular in nature and is willing to trade land for peace. The other is religious in character and prefers a policy that will impose peace upon the Arabs without the concession of land.

## Political Institutions

The structure of the Israeli political system consists of a set of "basic laws" that passes for a constitution, the Knesset (parliament), a prime minister elected by the members of the Knesset (MKs), a symbolic (but not necessarily passive) president also elected by the Knesset, a Supreme Court, and a large and powerful bureaucracy. The basic laws are expected to evolve into a formal constitution, and a committee of experts is working on the issue. If and when they complete their work, the proposed constitution will be sent to the Knesset for ratification (*Ha'aretz*, Oct. 6, 2004). That will not take place until consensus is achieved on the question of Jewishness and other critical issues.

The heart of the Israeli political system is the Knesset, a unicameral parliament of 120 members elected directly by the Israeli population on the basis of proportional representation. The term *Knesset* was adopted from the Haknesset Hagedola, the historic assembly of the fifth century BCE, and thus symbolizes the link between modern and ancient Israel (*JP*, Israeli Elections Primer, 1999).

As is typical of parliamentary systems, the ruling party or coalition of parties (the Government) possesses the power to pass any legislation it wishes as long as it possesses a majority (61 votes) in the Knesset. This includes the power to trade land for peace. There are no minority rights, and committees lack the power to alter the will of the majority. The only exception to this rule is the stipulation that the basic laws can be changed only by an extraordinary majority in the Knesset.

The winner-take-all nature of the Knesset contributes to the dramatic swings in policy that have characterized Israeli politics since the mid-1970s. The winners do as they please while the losers attempt to destabilize the ruling coalition and otherwise embarrass the Government in parliamentary debates and during the question period. Votes of no confidence are common, but generally fail (Brichta 1998). When the going gets tough, coalitions are adjusted or new elections are held. In large part, this stability results from the reluctance of party leaders to risk their power in new elections. As long as a party leader stands firm, the party's MKs will follow suit. This sense of party discipline has had the effect of shifting power from the Knesset itself to the Government in power. It is not the Knesset that makes policy, but the leaders of the parties that constitute the ruling coalition.

The vulnerability of the Knesset to these policy swings is aggravated by an electoral system that allocates seats in the Knesset on the basis of proportional representation. Any party that receives at least 1.5 percent of the vote receives seats in the Knesset in proportion with its percentage of the popular vote. This is not a severe problem in homogeneous societies, but Israel is not a homogeneous society (Schwartz 1994). A daunting number of parties fielded candidates in the 2003 elections, with 13 receiving seats in the Knesset. Sharon's Likud Party gained a plurality of 29.4 percent of the vote (38 seats), followed in turn by Labor, 14.5 percent (19 seats); Shinui, 12.3 percent (15 seats); Shas, 8.2 percent (11 seats), and so forth down the line.

This fragmentation, in turn, leads to a frantic process of coalition building. Coalitions require the reconciliation of a broad range of interests and have little choice but to pursue polices that offend the fewest coalition members. This need to reconcile diverse interests was particularly evident in the "national unity government" that saw Labor and the Likud share power between 1984 and 1990, and again following the 1999 and 2003 elections. This does not mean that the prime minister consults with his coalition partners. Labor shared the blame for Sharon's 2002 bloody attack on Jenin, but was not consulted on the issue (*JP,* March 6, 2002, and April 2, 2002). It would also be a mistake to equate immobilization with a lack of policy. Rather, immobilization leads to a continuation of policies that are already in place. In the Israeli experience this has meant a continuation of settlement building and delays in formulating a coherent plan for peace.

Israel's proportional representation electoral system, then, does little to force compromise among Israel's diverse factions (Sharkansky 1997b). Israel constitutes one large voting district with each notch on the political spectrum confident that it will receive at least a few seats in the Knesset. Parties have more to gain by "horse trading" after the election rather than they do by coming together before the election.

## Elites

Israel's paradoxical position as a strong democratic state increasingly beset by periods of immobilization interspersed with dramatic swings of policy is also explained by the nature of its elites (Barzilai 1999; Zalmanovitch 1998) Israel's leaders are deeply committed to the democratic process, and this is a source of strength for Israeli democracy. Losers have accepted defeat with relative grace, and the winners have not used their power to destroy their opponents—which is rare in the Middle East. If the leaders of a country are democratic, the masses generally follow suit. This is particularly the case in Israel, a country in which leaders often attract a passionate following.

Immobilization, by contrast, results from the deep ideological and personal divisions within Israeli elites. While Israel's elite pyramid is headed by the prime minister and senior members of the cabinet, no single leader can speak for more than a minority of Israel's citizens. Even Ben-Gurion, the charismatic "father of the country," was forced to rule with coalition Governments.

The Israeli elite is not limited to the leaders of political parties and related groups. Senior military officers exercise far more authority in Israel than would be the case in most Western democracies, a fact largely attributable to the state of tension that has long existed between Israel and its neighbors (Ben-Meir 1996). War heroes have been plentiful, and many have found their way into politics, not the least of whom are Barak and Sharon. Senior bureaucrats also have considerable latitude in shaping how government policies will be executed. It is they, in the final analysis, who determine how effectively political decisions will be carried out. They also control the expenditure of vast sums of money (Galnoor, Rosenbloom, and Yaroni 1998). Senior rabbis, including some located in New York, exercise profound influence over the social affairs of the country, just as Israeli business leaders also have much to say about the direction of the economy. Labor leaders, long key players in Israeli politics, remain influential but have seen their power decline in recent years.

Pluralism facilitates democracy by assuring that a multitude of voices are heard. It also keeps a single leader from becoming too dominant. Israeli democracy benefits from both. Too many voices, unfortunately, cause immobilization.

## Land for Peace: Differing Perspectives

However fragmented the Israeli elite may be, the dominant voice in the policy-making process is that of the prime minister. Nowhere has this fact been more evident than in the differing attitudes of Israeli prime ministers toward the occupied territories (Shlaim 1995). Rabin and Barak were willing to trade land for peace; Netanyahu and Sharon were not. Sharon eventually bowed to the twin forces of international pressure—mainly American—and terrorism to sacrifice a minuscule piece of land in hopes of gaining a lasting peace. Whether he has paved the way for peace remains to be seen. At the very least, he succeeded in stalling the al-Aqsa intifada and deflecting the American road map.

# THE GROUP BASIS OF ISRAELI POLITICS

In many ways, elites and groups are opposing sides of the same coin: the latter provide the power base for the former. Israel's pattern of immobility followed by dramatic policy change involves the nature of Israel's political parties, pressure groups, and mass behavior.

## Political Parties

It is not easy to classify Israel's political parties on the left–right continuum common in the West. Part of the problem lies in defining what is meant by the terms *left* and *right* in Israeli politics. In Israel, the left generally refers to parties advocating socialist economic policies, generous social programs, and a centralized state. The left also represents a secular vision of Israeli society, stressing the cultural rather than the religious dimension of the Jewish state. More recently, the left has been associated with a willingness to trade land for peace and the curtailment of settlements in the occupied territories. Labor/One Israel, the main "all-Israel" coalition of the left, reflects all of the above concerns, but garnered only about 18 percent of the popular vote in the 2003 elections. Labor/One Israel finds its center of gravity among the western (Ashkenazi) Jews and, following its defeat in the 1996 elections, was criticized by one of its MKs, who described it "as a party built around a yuppie, superior, Ashkenazi elite which doesn't grasp the sensitivities of Israeli society" (Shlomo Ben-Ami, cited in *JP,* June 22, 1996, 8).

Defining the Israeli right is far more problematic. The political right, at least as the term is used in Israeli parlance, refers to three more or less distinct themes: (1) parties advocating free-market capitalism supported by low regulation, low taxes, and low expenditure on welfare programs; (2) parties advocating ultranationalism; and (3) parties advocating a religiously oriented government. This configuration of ideological concerns has led the political right to place particular stress on maintaining Israel's control over the occupied territories. The right has also taken a hard-line stand on security issues. The Likud embodies all of the themes but tempers them with a desire to appeal to a broad spectrum of the voters on the center right, a base it requires to qualify as one of Israel's two "all-Israel" parties: parties capable of forming a Government.

The other parties of the right are more concerned with issues than with broad-based popularity and stress one of the three dimensions more than the others. The religious parties, for example, demand that Israel remain a Jewish state in deed as well as name. This requires that religious law supersede secular law and that Orthodox religious organizations receive favored treatment from the government. In the negotiations leading up to the formation of the Israeli state, a very secular Ben-Gurion signed a "religious status quo" agreement with the religious parties that stipulated that "the Sabbath and Kashrut (Jewish dietary law) were to be officially observed in the state, issues of marriage and divorce would be left in religious hands, and haredi circles would be allowed to maintain an independent educational system" (JP Israeli Elections Primer, 1999; Political Blocs and Parties).

### Pressure Groups

Most of Israel's major interest groups, like its political parties, evolved during the pre-independence era (Yishai 1998a, 3 InfoTrac). Among the most powerful are the settlers who have played a dominant role in blocking land-for-peace initiatives. Although constituting less then 4 percent of the population, they control several seats in the Knesset and often a cabinet seat as well. They have also had the strong backing of the Sharon government, the Israeli withdrawal from the Gaza Strip notwithstanding. Indeed, the withdrawal from Gaza was balanced by the accelerated settlement of the West Bank. Settler violence is also on the rise, and it is estimated that settlers possess more than 10,000 weapons (*Ha'aretz,* April 1, 2003). Even more powerful are Israel's rabbis and the several political parties that they lead. They play a key role in most coalition governments and keep Israel's blue laws intact. Most rabbis are also reluctant to see the historic lands of Judea and Samaria ceded to the Palestinians. This said, the rabbis are a much divided group. While the moderates have reluctantly accepted the evacuation of Gaza, the extremists called for civil disobedience and openly worried over the threat of a civil war (*Ha'aretz,* Jan. 14, 2005).

Smaller groups concentrate on influencing the votes of individual MKs. Because Israel has some 3,000 registered pressure groups, this is not an issue of minor importance. Yael Yishai quotes one frustrated MK as complaining, "We have lost the intimacy of the Knesset; there are corridors that you cannot cross in less than half an hour, because they catch you on your way. You cannot have lunch without somebody hovering over your head, you cannot sit in your room as somebody will enter without first knocking on the door . . ." (Yishai 1998a, 5 InfoTrac).

Some groups are stronger than others. Peace Now and B'Tselem are outspoken advocates of land for peace and make sure that Israeli human rights abuses receive global attention. Histadrut, the large labor federation, exercised profound influence on Israeli politics during the early days of the republic, but has seen its power wane with the emergence of competing unions and the growing strength of business organizations (Yishai 1998a). Much the same is true of the kibbutzim, the agricultural settlements that gave birth to many of Israel's early leaders, including Ben-Gurion. The military, as noted in earlier discussion, exercises inordinate influence on the policy-making process, with some wags suggesting that Israel is not a state with an army as much as it is an army financed by a state (Sharkansky 1997b). Nevertheless, the army's once unshakable position is being challenged by mothers' groups distraught over the loss of sons in Lebanon and the occupied territories. Women, while less powerful than the other groups discussed above, are represented by four major organizations and a dozen more are concerned with issues of gender-related violence. Environmental groups have also proliferated, as have ethnic and religious associations. Of the ethnic associations, those representing the approximately one million Jews who have immigrated to Israel since the collapse of the Soviet Union are particularly noticeable and have had a significant effect on the electoral process, swinging first to one side and then the other (*Ha'aretz,* May 9, 2000).

The weakest of Israel's major groups is the Israeli Arab community, about a million strong, which constitutes approximately 20 percent of the Israeli population. This represents a dramatic increase from the some 160,000 Palestinian Arabs who became Israeli citizens at the end of the 1948 war. Israeli Arabs have generally focused their efforts on the attainment of equal political and economic status within the Israeli political system, but have also displayed strong support for the al-Aqsa intifada and the formation of a Palestinian state. Although they are treated as second-class citizens, most Israeli Arabs have a higher standard of living than do most of the Palestinian Arabs living in the occupied territories. The goal of full equality, however, remains far from attainment because of a variety of factors including the Jewish nature of the state, low skill levels, anti-Arab prejudice among the Israeli Jewish population, and lack of effective organization within the Israeli Arab community (Khalife 2001). Rather than a single Israeli Arab party, there are several.

The sheer number of competing groups has contributed to both the democratization and the immobilization of Israeli politics. Israel is becoming more democratic in the broader sense of the word because more voices are influencing the policy-making process. The sheer number of those voices, however, has made the policy-making process increasingly complex. It has also dimmed hopes for a dramatic breakthrough in the peace process.

## THE CONTEXT OF ISRAELI POLITICS

Israeli ambivalence toward exchanging land for peace and most other issues has its roots within Israel's culture, political economy, and international environment. Indeed, each tends to counter, exacerbate, and generally interact with the others.

### Political Culture

Israeli political culture offers many clues to both the cohesiveness of Israeli society and its growing fragmentation. Whatever their differences, most Israelis share a strongly felt Jewish identity and a sense of mutual dependence (Aronoff 1989). This helps to explain the strength of Israeli political institutions as well as the phenomenal support that Israel receives from the world Jewish community. The survival of Israel is of vital concern to Jews throughout the world, even those who do not like Israeli policy. The same sense of common identity and common destiny would seem to explain the Israeli reluctance to suffer casualties and the extreme lengths to which Israeli leaders will go in efforts to free Israeli prisoners. Jewish suffering, wherever it occurs, becomes intensely personalized. Some writers refer to a Holocaust complex, suggesting that the past suffering of the Jews has resulted in an inordinate concern for security (Cohen 1994b).

The cohesive influence of Jewish identity and mutual dependence, while still a clear force in Israeli politics, is increasingly offset by deep conflicts over the key issues of land, peace, Jewishness, and security discussed throughout this chapter (Alpher 1995; Barzilai 1999; Ribak 1997). Israeli society is bitterly divided on these issues, and that division is unlikely to be healed in the near future. Indeed, Israel's political divisions seem to be growing as conservatives cling to their religious and nationalistic vision of Israel, while liberals increasingly define themselves as post-Zionists. Post-Zionism is described by Leon Hadar as follows:

> In essence, post-Zionism is a vision of those who want Israel to become "normal," to move beyond the century-long Zionist revolution and resolve some of the contradictions that Zionism and the term "Jewish state" have introduced. . . . Central to the post-Zionist perspective is the goal of separating synagogue from state in order to provide Israeli Jews with the same civic and religious rights their co-religionists enjoy in North America and Western Europe—to get married or be buried in civil ceremonies and to wed non-Jews, for example. . . . Finally, a main post-Zionist objective is a reconciliation between Israeli Jews and Palestinian Arabs, to be accomplished by recognizing the national rights of the two peoples, as well as by transforming Israel into a truly democratic state in which all of its citizens are equal under the law (Hadar 1999).

Judging from recent election results, post-Zionism has yet to become the dominant force in Israeli politics. Its emergence, however, does illustrate the growing cultural gap that confronts Israeli leaders in their efforts to deal with virtually all issues that confront Israeli society, not the least of which is the question of land for peace.

## Political Economy

While not denying the influence of culture on Israeli politics, political economists are inclined to find economic factors behind both the strength of Israel's political institutions and the growing fragmentation of Israeli society. The strength of Israel's political institutions, from an economic perspective, reflects Israel's success in providing for the basic economic and social needs of its citizens. The per capita income of Israel now hovers around $18,100 a year, which puts it on par with many states of western Europe. Political legitimacy has clearly been reinforced by economic legitimacy.

In this view, the changing tenor of Israeli politics mirrors Israel's transition from a largely socialist economy to an increasingly capitalistic one. Not only has this transformation strengthened the influence of capitalist groups in policy-making circles, but it has reinforced the class divisions within Israeli society. This fact has not gone unnoticed by opposition politicians (*Ha'aretz*, Sept. 23, 2004; Smooha 1998). As things currently stand, about 19 percent of Israeli families live below the poverty line (*Ha'aretz*, Nov. 23, 2004).

The sharp swings in policy that have characterized Israeli politics in recent decades have also been facilitated by economic factors. More often than not, changes of government have occurred during periods of economic decline, although security concerns have also been a factor (*JP*, Nov. 26, 2000; *Ha'aretz*, May 26, 1999). It would also be naïve to believe that the peace process does not have a strong economic component. Investors like stability, and both the Israeli economy and foreign investment declined during the years of the al-Aqsa intifada (*JP*, March 1, 2002). Peace would make Israel the financial and high-tech center of the region. Only the Palestinian issue stands in its way. Israelis are also well aware that economic deprivation is a key component in the activism of Palestinians on both sides of the border.

## Foreign Influences on Israeli Policy

It is doubtful that any country in the world can rival Israel in the degree to which its politics are influenced by external factors. These pervasive external pressures, which have figured heavily in much of the preceding discussion, are too complex to be easily summarized. However, several points will go a long way toward explaining the paradox of strong political institutions accompanied by chaotic policy making and an increasingly divided population. They also have much to say about Israeli attitudes toward the peace process.

The first point is that Israel was born in war and continues to live in a condition of "no war, no peace" with key countries of the region, including Syria and Iran. Barzilai (1999) argues that this situation has stimulated an intense sense of Israeli nationalism. It has also resulted in a profound sense of insecurity, even a garrison mentality. Distrust of foreign countries is high and is not limited to those of the Middle East. It is very hard for Israeli leaders to take security risks, including the return of the occupied territories. Negotiations, accordingly, tend to be protracted and characterized by vacillation.

Second, Israel cannot avoid external influences on its policy making. In part, external influence flows from the massive financial support that Israel receives from the United States and other international donors. The United States grants Israel more than $3 billion in foreign aid on an annual basis, which represents approximately one-third of the U.S. foreign aid budget. This figure does not include special military allocations that are channeled through the budget of the U.S. Department of Defense. Also "off budget" are special allocations designed to stimulate the Arab–Israeli peace process. The Israeli pullout from Lebanon was estimated to have cost "at least several hundred million dollars, much of which was provided by the United States" (UP, May 9, 2000). Over $3 billion has been requested to cover the costs of the withdrawal from Gaza. Plans are now in place to reduce U.S. nonmilitary aid to Israel over ten years, but that may depend on the pace of the peace process. Foreign influence on Israeli policy also results from Israeli dependence on the U.S. security umbrella. Israeli history might have been very different if it had not been for the pervasive and unflinching support of the United States. This does not mean that Israel and the U.S. see eye to eye on all issues, nor that Israel always bends to U.S. pressure. It does, however, listen carefully to Washington's views and tries not to embarrass its foremost ally. Israel's settlement policy has been a constant source of tension between the two countries. As Sharon would admonish his cabinet on the eve of the Gaza evacuation: "We can't expect an explicit U.S. okay to build freely in the settlements" (*Ha'aretz,* March 28, 2005). Whatever the crisis, maintaining strong ties with the United States is a cardinal principle of Israeli foreign policy.

A third form of external pressure on Israeli politics is found in the intimate links between the U.S. Jewish community and the Jewish community of Israel. Many Jews hold dual citizenship. New York, as Sharkansky notes, "competes with Jerusalem and Tel Aviv as the center of Jewish culture, religion, and politics" (Sharkansky 1997a). Some 600,000 Israeli citizens reside outside of Israel, and more than half of them vote in Israeli elections (*JP,* Feb. 8, 1998). For the 1999 elections, some 6,000 U.S. Jews flew to Israel to vote, and experts anticipated that U.S. Jews would contribute between $6 million and $8 million to the campaign coffers of Israeli candidates (*WP,* reprinted in *Daily Star* [Beirut], May 10, 1999, 5).

In addition, Jewish organizations in the United States play a significant role in Israeli affairs. Senior U.S. rabbis often maintain a large following in Israel's Orthodox community, and a U.S. Orthodox rabbi once unleashed a furor by declaring that Reform and Conservative Jews were not Jews at all but members of some other religion (*IHT,* April 2, 1977, 2).

American rabbis have also entered the fray in the land-for-peace debate, with more than a hundred U.S. rabbis declaring that there was no religious reason to require exclusive Jewish sovereignty over the Temple Mount, the massive stone plateau in Jerusalem that is considered holy by both Jews and Muslims (*NYT,* Dec. 7, 2000). There is little that happens in the United States Jewish community that does not have an impact on Israel. World Zionist leaders, too, seem fond of second-guessing the policies of Israel's leaders. The Jewish Agency, for example, continues to pursue its support of the settlers in the occupied territories with little regard for Israeli policy. Indeed, the World

Zionist Organization and the Jewish Agency often seem to be in competition with Israel's official settlement agencies.

Israelis often complain of being manipulated by larger foreign powers, but the reality of the situation is that Israel gives as well as it gets. Rather than being a dependency of the United States, Israel has been remarkably successful in shaping the policies of its major ally (Spiegel 1985). All recent U.S. presidents have openly proclaimed their friendship for Israel. The American–Israeli Political Action Committee (AIPAC) is among the strongest lobbies in Washington, and most U.S. senators and representatives find it easier to support the Israeli cause than to oppose it (*CSM,* April 19, 2002). As one representative quipped, "Voting against Israel has become like voting against lumber in Washington State. Except AIPAC does it all over the country" (*CSM,* June 28, 1991, 3). Also worth noting is the fact that Israel is a nuclear power—as yet, the only nuclear power in the Middle East—as well as the world's fifth largest arms exporter (*JP,* Feb. 2, 2000).

Thus, Israel's relationship with the world is one of profound interdependence. Israeli policy making is shaped by external factors, but Israel is not a passive partner in this process. In the final analysis, it will be Israel that determines its relationship with the Palestinians and the broader Arab world.

## THE POLITICAL SYSTEM OF PALESTINE

From 1968 to 1993, the Palestinian Liberation Organization was the political system of the Palestinian people. Other groups existed, but most were members of the PLO. The PLO was officially recognized as the sole legitimate representative of the Palestinian people by the Arab League in 1974. Most countries of the world eventually followed suit. Despite the PLO's tortuous history, no other organization possessed the authority or popular support required to challenge the PLO (Belqaziz 2004).

The PLO had two main objectives: unifying the Palestinian people and liberating the Palestinian territories occupied by Israel in 1948 and 1967. The two goals were indivisible. The liberation of Palestine could only be achieved through the unified action of the Palestinian people. It was not a democratic organization, but many voices were heard. As a practical matter, al-Fatah, the largest group in the PLO, dominated the organization, and Arafat dominated al-Fatah.

The goals of liberation and unity were to be achieved through an organization that comprised the Palestinian National Council, a smaller Central Council, and an even smaller Executive Committee. The Palestinian National Council was designed to assure the broad representation of the Palestinian population; it was gradually expanded from some 155 members in 1971 to 451 in 1987, on the eve of the first intifada (palestine-un.org/plo/intro.html, accessed Sept. 2, 2005). Direct elections were impossible because the PLO was illegal in the occupied territories. Theoretically, the Palestinian National Council was the ultimate source of authority in the PLO. In reality it was the weakest.

The Central Council reinforced the unifying role of the PLO by providing direct representation for member groups and diverse associations. These included farmers, economists, doctors, artists, writers, women, teachers, workers, jurists, youth, and engineers. More important, the Central Council gave direct representation to diverse Palestinian parties and resistance movements, the majority of which possessed their own militias. These included al-Fatah (6 representatives) and two from each of the following groups: Popular Front for the Liberation of Palestine, Democratic Front for the Liberation of Palestine, Arab Liberation Front, Palestine Liberation Front, Popular Struggle Front, Democratic Union, People Party, Popular Front–General Command, Al-Sai'qa, Islamic Jihad, and the Palestinian Arab Liberation Front (palestine-un.org/plo/intro.html, accessed Sept. 2, 2005). Heads of various committees—not the least of which was the military council—were also represented on the Central Council. Missing from the list was Hamas. Also missing were ultraviolent groups such as Abu Nidal's Black September, which had been responsible for vicious terrorist attacks against Jewish targets in Europe.

Leadership in the struggle for liberation was provided by the Executive Committee and its president, Yasir Arafat. Debates were bitter and resulted in a near civil war in 1983. Arafat stacked the PLO apparatus with his supporters, but found it difficult to rein in diverse militias intent on pursuing a strategy of violence. He had no control over Hamas. He spoke for the Palestinians and was blamed for Palestinian violence.

The Oslo accords (1993) were ratified by the Central Council and effectively transformed the PLO into the Palestinian Authority. A Palestinian organization created to liberate Palestine had agreed to Israel's right to exist in exchange for the promise that land would be exchanged for peace. On July 1, 1994, Yasir Arafat returned to Palestine after twenty-seven years in exile. On July 5, he took the oath of office as president of the Palestinian Authority and swore in twelve members of his first cabinet. He was in control of Jericho and Gaza city. Hebron and other areas were later added. In 1996, formal elections were held for the presidency and an eighty-member Palestinian Legislative Council (PLC) (Brown 2003). Arafat was confirmed as president of the Palestinian Authority and remained in that office until his death in 2004. PLC members were elected for three-year terms, but they remained in office until the legislative elections of 2006. It wasn't much, but it was a start. The rest of the occupied territories remained under Israeli control or were jointly administered by the two sides. Good behavior by the Palestinian Authority would be rewarded by a negotiated expansion of the Palestinian-controlled areas. Presumably, this would eventually lead to Palestinian control over most of the occupied territories and the evolution of a sovereign Palestinian state. All of this, however, remained fuzzy. As we have seen in the earlier discussion, optimism soon led to despair and the eruption of the al-Aqsa intifada in 2000.

The peace process began anew in 2003 with the road map proposed by the U.S. and its allies. A truce was declared, and the passing of Arafat in 2004 paved the way for a democratically elected Palestinian leadership at all levels. Mahmoud Abbas faced minimal opposition for the presidency. Marwan Barghouti, his far more radical rival, had vowed to run from his Israeli prison cell, but withdrew in the name of national unity. Israeli authorities had seized Barghouti, the secretary of the Fatah Higher Committee in the West Bank, on grounds that he was the power behind the Al-Aqsa Brigades. Hamas had rejected the Oslo accords and boycotted the election to protest the PLO's recognition of Israel. This created the illusion that Abbas spoke for a united Palestine. This was far from the case. While Hamas threatened from without, Barghouti, the leader of younger and dynamic elements within the al-Fatah movement, lurked from within. While not opposed to peace, both Hamas and Barghouti demanded internal reform and a stronger stance in negotiations with Israel.

Hamas showed surprising strength in the local elections and vowed to contest the legislative elections scheduled for July 2005. Consternation reigned in the Fatah camp and the legislative elections were hurriedly delayed until January 2006. Abbas pleaded for more time and, following intense discussions, prepared a new election law that increased the size of the Palestinian Legislative Council from 88 to132. Half of the members are to be elected in single-member districts, the other half by proportional representation of Palestinians in Gaza and the West Bank (*Al-Quds,* June 19, 2005). Single-member districts favor al-Fatah; proportional representation favors Hamas and the Islamic fundamentalist currents. The Legislative Council, though elected in Gaza and the occupied territories (the West Bank and Jerusalem), theoretically represents all the Palestinians.

But how were the January 2006 elections to take place when both the United States and Israel said that Hamas could not participate until they renounced terror? The U.S. vacillated under Arab pressure, but Sharon vowed to block the elections by withdrawing Israeli assistance, a clear signal that the Palestinians would have a difficult time conducting elections in the occupied territories (*NYT,* Sept. 17, 2005). He, too, softened his opposition to Hamas's participation in the elections while simultaneously escalating his assassination of the Hamas leadership (*Middle East Times,* Oct. 29, 2005). Hamas further muddied the waters by announcing that it might recognize Israel's right to exist within its 1967 borders, including old Jerusalem (*Ha'aretz,* Jan. 21, 2005; Sept. 22, 2005). It was also busy creating catchy election tunes that praised armed resistance and condemned the corruption and cronyism of the PLO (*Daily Star,* Sept. 13, 2005). Revenge attacks for the assassinations of its leaders also escalated, throwing the truce into question.

The PLO continues to exist, but its role remains clouded. Presumably, it offers a link to the broader Palestinian community (*Al-Quds,* July 1, 2005). Al-Fatah, now the ruling organization of the Palestinian state, merely notes that one of its goals is to repair the PLO (*Al-Quds,* July 5, 2005).

## Elites, Groups, and the Future of Palestine

The dominant political elites in Palestine are the leaders of the Palestinian Authority, most of whom are also leaders of the PLO and its core group, al-Fatah. The president of the PA is a member of al-Fatah as are its prime minister, most of the cabinet members, and a majority of the Legislative Council. The leaders of the al-Aqsa Martyrs' Brigades, al-Fatah's military wing, also fall in the elite category, as do the leaders of the PA's security services. They, too, are largely of al-Fatah origin, but not necessarily of one mind with the al-Aqsa Brigades.

Tensions within the al-Fatah leadership are manifest, but none more so than the rift between the historic leadership represented by Abbas and the younger leadership headed by Marwan Barghouti. At least for the moment, tensions are eased by personal and client networks as well as by the distribution of patronage. The leaders of Hamas also figure prominently in the Palestinian elite structure, as do the traditional big families of the West Bank (Schulz 2002). Of lesser status are the leaders of Palestine's diverse resistance groups, most of whom have retained their militias.

The ongoing wave of elections will force a substantial restructuring of Palestine's traditional political class. Hamas has challenged al-Fatah's control in the local elections and will have a sizable representation in the Legislative Council, as will Barghouti's core of al-Fatah radicals. Unless Abbas and the "historic leadership" can solve the PA's massive problems, it will be Barghouti and Hamas who move to the fore.

And massive problems there are, among them stopping terrorist attacks on Israel and providing security in the areas under PA control (*Al-Quds,* March 25, 2005). Security in the areas under PA control verges on chaos, facilitating attacks on Israel (*Daily Star,* July 27, 2005). These problems are not likely to be solved without providing jobs and cleaning up the corruption that has become the hallmark of the PLO and the PA (Denoeux 2005). Mahmoud Abbas, for his part, has vowed reform and a reorganization of the security services, but acknowledges that it is not within his capacity to force the militias to disarm. Efforts to do so, he laments, would result in civil war. His task will not be made easier by the growing fragmentation of the Palestinian elite class, and particularly the growing prominence of Hamas.

While space does not allow a review of all of the major parties and groups that will shape the future of Palestinian politics, two are of overwhelming importance: Hamas and al-Fatah. We would also be remiss if we failed to acknowledge that Palestine's cultural, economic, and international environments will also play a crucial role in shaping Palestinian politics.

## Fatah

Fatah's emergence as the dominant group within the Palestinian resistance movement was due largely to Arafat's singular focus on liberation and national unity. While most of his competitors within the PLO had Marxist leanings or were linked to a particular Arab government, Arafat placed action before ideology. The liberation of Palestine was Fatah's ideology (Belqaziz 2004). Everything else was secondary. When Palestine was liberated, it would have a secular democratic government that provided for the basic needs of its people. The same pragmatism characterized al-Fatah's strategy of liberation. Armed resistance was tried, as was terror. When opportunities for a negotiated settlement presented themselves, al-Fatah was willing to negotiate, although without renouncing its goal of a Palestinian state.

This approach allowed al-Fatah to recruit from the full spectrum of the Palestinian community, the one common goal of which was liberation. It also made al-Fatah the primary recipient of Saudi funding. While the Israelis demonized Arafat, the Saudis found him to be the pillar of moderation. The last thing they wanted was a new Nasser who would throw the region into turmoil. Arafat's critics suggested that he had been bought by the Saudis.

Competitors within the PLO possessed neither the size nor the wealth of al-Fatah, nor could their leaders match Arafat's stature. It was he alone who spoke for the Palestinian people. Competing groups, while constituting a majority on the PLO central committee, were too beset by ideological and personality conflicts to pose any real challenge to al-Fatah's dominance. By and large, they found it more advantageous to work within the PLO framework than to go it alone.

The organization of al-Fatah followed the classic revolutionary pattern. A patriarchal leader was supported by an executive committee that represented key agencies and groups within the organization. Among these were the Al-Aqsa Brigades, the military wing of al-Fatah. Periodic but infrequent party congresses were held, the sixth of which was scheduled for July 2005 but was delayed until after the legislative elections that had been rescheduled for January 2006. The fifth congress was held in Tunis in the late 1980s.

Reluctance to hold the sixth congress was due to the deep internal strains within al-Fatah itself. Arafat's dominance had suffocated the organization and transformed it into a self-serving and corrupt bureaucracy resistant to change. What remained of al-Fatah's revolutionary zeal was zapped by its transformation from a revolutionary organization into the "ruling party" in the aftermath of the Oslo accords (al-Zaatar 2004a). Mobilizing Palestinians in the struggle against Israel was relatively easy and straightforward. Governing Palestine, by contrast, required that al-Fatah stop terror, maintain security, and provide for the desperate needs of the Palestinian people. The organization was ill equipped to do so. Abbas himself called the situation in al-Fatah "disastrous" (UPI News Track, Aug. 26, 2004, InfoTrac).

With the passing of Arafat, younger leaders led by Marwan Barghouti demanded greater democracy and accountability from a leadership whose idea of openness was issuing terse press reports acknowledging that critical issues had been discussed. The "historic leadership," they suggested, was losing touch with reality. The executive committee, which met infrequently, was also accused of monopolizing power and not consulting with members of the council (*Al-Quds*, March 5, 2005). The Executive Committee leveled the same charge at Abbas. Members of key management committees resigned in protest and warned that al-Fatah's position in the street had declined precipitously and could no longer be taken for granted (*Al-Quds*, Jan. 4, 2005). The Al-Aqsa Brigades refused Abbas's call to give up their weapons and be integrated into the Palestinian security services. They also applauded Hamas's refusal to do so (*Ha'aretz*, Aug. 15, 2005). Making matters worse was the diffuse nature of the Al-Aqsa Brigades themselves. According to the Israelis, "dozens" of armed militias operate in the name of the Al-Aqsa Martyrs' Brigades (*Ha'aretz*, Sept. 14, 2005). Cadres (party activists) complained that they were unsure of their role in a revolutionary organization that is no longer revolutionary (*Al-Quds*,

March 5, 2005). Party leaders, in turn, complained of a lack of discipline among cadres and urged greater sacrifice (*Al-Quds,* Feb. 7, 2005).

## Hamas

Hamas, the dominant Islamic fundamentalist group in Palestine and the occupied territories, began as an offshoot of the Palestinian branch of the Muslim Brotherhood. The Brotherhood had established roots in the major Palestinian cities by 1946, two years before the proclamation of the Jewish state. The Muslim Brotherhood spread rapidly to Jordan after the annexation of the West Bank and became one of the main pillars of support for the young King Hussein, then in his late teens. Both the Brotherhood and King Hussein had conservative political views, and both feared Nasser's revolution. The fit was a natural one. With the rise of the PLO in the aftermath of the 1967 war, both the Muslim Brotherhood and King Hussein found another common adversary in Arafat. It could not have been otherwise. The PLO's control of the Jordan valley threatened the monarchy and its secular doctrine threatened the Brotherhood's vision of an Islamic state.

The Muslim Brotherhood prospered, but it lacked a military wing. This became a pressing issue with the outbreak of the first Palestinian intifada in 1987. The PLO/al-Fatah was armed and could filter fighters and weapons into the territories. If they were victorious, it would be they who ruled. To fill this void, Hamas was established in 1987 as the military wing of the Jordanian–Palestinian branch of the Muslim Brotherhood. *Hamas* is the Arabic acronym for Islamic Resistance Movement. It also corresponds to the Arabic word for "zeal." This, of course, didn't happen overnight. The nucleus of Hamas had emerged much earlier and was simply referred to as the Brotherhood's military wing (interviews, Jordan, 2000). The early members of Hamas were simultaneously members of the Brotherhood, but this is no longer the case. Hamas has developed its own identity. However, the 1988 Covenant of the Islamic Resistance Movement refers to the organization as one of the wings of the Muslim Brotherhood in Palestine. It also calls for the liberation of all Palestinian territory (www.mideastweb.org/hamas.htm, accessed May 6, 2002).

In common with the Muslim Brotherhood from which it evolved, Hamas utilizes three simultaneous strategies to achieve its objectives of liberating Palestine and achieving a more Islamic state: teaching and preaching, welfare, and politics. Teaching and preaching are carried out by Hamas's mosques and schools, while its welfare services are managed by the Islamic Association. These include a vast network of clinics, orphanages, and training centers, all of which are vital to the survival of a population suffering from high unemployment and extreme poverty. Particular emphasis is placed on caring for the families of martyrs who die in the struggle against Israel. It is vital, from the psychological perspective, that the fighters know that if they die their loved ones will be cared for. Hamas's political agenda long stressed terrorist strikes against Israeli targets, but has now expanded to include electoral participation. The two are coordinated, but are carried out by different branches of the organization. If elections can lead to liberation, so much the better. Israel and the United States categorically condemn

Hamas as a terrorist organization. The European Union accepts Hamas as a resistance and religious organization, but condemns its terrorist wing. Israel maintains that the one can't be separated from the other and is attempting to change EU policy.

The organizational structure of Hamas is much like that of most Islamic extremist groups discussed in Chapter 1, and like the organizational structures of the more extreme Islamic groups such as the Islamic Jihad. These are far smaller than Hamas, but possess sufficient "military" strength to disrupt Palestine's relations with Israel (Hatina 2001). Relations between Hamas and the Islamic Jihad are ambivalent. Cooperation is frequent, but so is competition for recruits and resources.

## Al-Fatah and Hamas: Which Is Dominant?

Al-Fatah and Hamas have polarized Palestinian society. But which is dominant? Al-Fatah controls the Palestinian Authority, represents national unity, possesses a venerable reputation as the head of the PLO, and enjoys the support of the international community (providing it stops terror). It also has the ability to move freely and its leaders are well known. Hamas, by contrast, possesses the zeal, organizational capacity, and discipline that al-Fatah has squandered. It also enjoys a reputation for honesty, sacrifice, and compassion, the latter because of its welfare services. Indeed, an internal al-Fatah document begrudgingly refers to Hamas's welfare organizations as the "secret of their success" (*Ha'aretz,* Feb. 20, 2005). Finances don't appear to be a problem as Hamas possesses the strong support of the Islamic fundamentalist movement, including the Muslim Brotherhood and Hezbollah. Al-Fatah, moreover, must now prove that it can rule under near-impossible circumstances (Rabbani and Toensing 2005). Hamas, by contrast, has the luxury of criticizing from the sidelines while things go from bad to worse on both the domestic and Israeli fronts.

Hamas, however, also has its problems. Its extreme religious position makes it unlikely that it will ever become an all-Palestinian party (Belqaziz 2004). Although Hamas did well in recent local elections, it is safe to assume that some of those votes were protests against the ineptitude of al-Fatah rather than support for a religious government in Palestine. Nor do votes for Hamas necessarily mean a rejection of peace with Israel. Hamas is flexible but vague on both issues. It supports democracy with Islamic values and calls for a just peace with Israel. That means a return to Israel's 1967 borders.

Other problems abound. Israeli assassinations have eliminated many of Hamas's more visible leaders and made campaigning in Israeli-controlled areas virtually impossible (Blanch 2003). Attacks by the PA security forces, which are controlled by al-Fatah, are also a constant threat (Bin Jadw 2004). Indeed, the Israelis claim that the PA is stopping as many terrorist attacks as Israel (*Ha'aretz,* March 23, 2005). This, while perhaps an exaggeration, suggests a very aggressive al-Fatah posture toward Hamas and other Islamic groups.

How does the Palestinian public feel? A June 2005 poll by the Palestinian Center for Surveys and Political Polls suggests that al-Fatah would have captured

44 percent of the vote and Hamas 33 percent had the legislative elections been held in July 2005 as originally scheduled (UPI News Track, June 15, 2005). The same poll addressed the main concerns of Palestinians. They were (1) improving the economy, (2) fighting corruption, (3) establishing a just peace with Israel, (4) establishing security and the rule of law, and (5) protecting national unity (*Al-Quds,* June 15, 2005). Opinion polls in the Middle East are less precise than those in the West, but al-Fatah would probably have eked out a narrow plurality had the legislative elections been held as scheduled (Tessler, Palmer, Farah, and Ibrahim 1987). At the same time, there can be little doubt that Hamas would have been in a strong position to influence government policies. The postponement of the legislative elections will give al-Fatah the opportunity to reform itself and improve its performance. Whether it can do so remains to be seen. It clearly has to make strong progress in the areas of providing security and ending corruption. Both challenges are of epidemic proportions (*Al-Quds,* May 13 and 18, 2005). (For updates, see this book's website.)

The military posture of Hamas will also exert a strong influence on the future of Palestinian politics. Hamas has accepted the truce with Israel, but retains the capacity to resume attacks against Israeli targets at any time. The Israeli minister of defense has warned that he will not stand idly by while Hamas builds an armed popular army under the nose of the Palestinian Authority (*Al-Quds,* May 17, 2005). President Abbas had frankly admitted that efforts to disarm Hamas would result in a civil war. He has refused to do so.

## THE CONTEXT OF PALESTINIAN POLITICS: CULTURE, ECONOMICS, AND THE EXTERNAL ARENA

### Culture

Palestinian culture in 1948 was similar to that of its neighboring Arab countries. Society was kinship-centered and characterized by an intense attachment to the land. For most Palestinians at the time, land was their livelihood, their security, and their identity. Powerful families contended for rule of the cities, while the rural areas remained under the influence of clan or tribal leaders. The urban population had attained a high level of education and tended to blend traditional and modern attitudes. In the rural areas, people remained largely traditional in outlook. There was minimal national awareness other than a widely shared concern over Jewish encroachment on Arab land. It was this concern that fueled the Arab revolt of 1936–39.

The 1948 Arab–Israeli war transformed a majority of the Palestinian population into refugees. Some languished in camps. Others migrated to the Gulf or the West. Traditional kinship alliances were shattered and a society wedded to the soil was left landless (Shemesh 2004). It was they, and especially the residents of the camps, who bore the burden of Palestinian despair. Images of a fertile and abundant land, now lost, were passed from generation to generation; a return to that land became the focus of Palestinian aspiration. One day, God willing, Palestinians would reclaim their patrimony and all would be well. The right of return remains a highly emotional issue and should not be discounted. The situation on the West Bank was less cataclysmic, and pre-1948 cultural patterns changed little until the Israeli occupation of 1967. The surge of settlement building under Begin and his successors unleashed a cycle of resistance and repression that culminated in the two intifadas. Israeli Arabs, for their part, found themselves second-class citizens in what was once their own land.

Palestinian efforts to cope with the twin scourges of defeat and colonization bred two distinct cultural responses. The first was survival and accommodation. One had to get along in a hostile environment with little effective Palestinian leadership. This was particularly the case during the 1980s. The second cultural response was the forging of a new Palestinian identity based on the concept of struggle and liberation. It was this concept that was the centerpiece of the PLO ideology (Schulz 2002). For a while, Israel attempted to foster accommodation by developing a new Palestinian leadership at the local level. These results weren't particularly successful and gave way to aggressive efforts to expand Jewish settlements. Invariably, this accelerated expropriation of Palestinian land eventually threatened to reduce Palestinian areas to "reservations" separated by blocks of fortified settlements. The importance of struggle to Palestinian identity increased accordingly. It was also strengthened by the growing hostility of Arab states to the Palestinians living in their midst. One way or another, a common identity was forced upon the Palestinians by a common plight from which there was no exit other than struggle.

Religion, needless to say, is also a key component of Palestinian politics. A review of religious attitudes analyzed by Grant and Tessler, found that some 37 percent of the population surveyed considered themselves very religious with another 23 percent considering themselves religious. Attitudes toward "political Islam" were roughly similar (Grant and Tessler 2002, 8; 18 InfoTrac). These figures correspond to the estimated 30 to 40 percent of the vote that Hamas and other Islamic parties received in the 2005 local elections. It also suggests that their appeal will probably not lessen in the near future. It is unlikely that Palestine could be transformed into a fanatical Islamic state, but a moderate Islamic government is not beyond the realm of possibility. The possibility will increase if al-Fatah should falter in its efforts to end corruption and otherwise meet the needs of the Palestinian population.

Finally, it should be noted that the Palestinians living in the occupied territories have observed Israeli democracy firsthand. They have been very impressed by what they have seen. This will make it very difficult for Palestine's leaders, most of whom possessed little direct contact with democracy, to resist demands for greater openness in their efforts to forge a Palestinian state.

## Political Economy

The influence of economic factors on the future of Palestinian politics is easy to summarize. It is an axiom of political science that unfilled economic expectations fuel violence. Economic expectations in Palestine are both increasing and unfilled. As earlier discussion indicated, economic issues top the concerns of Palestine's voters.

A corollary axiom is that economic prosperity builds support for the party in power. The converse is equally true. Al-Fatah may soon find its already shaky popularity in free fall unless it can find solutions to Palestine's massive economic problems.

Accordingly, both moderation and stability in the fledgling Palestinian state will be overwhelmingly linked to its economic viability (Diwan and Walton 1994; Garg and el-Khouri 1994). As things currently stand, the Palestinian economy is not viable. According to the World Bank, 50 percent of the Palestinian population lives below the poverty line and 16 percent cannot afford basic necessities. About one-fourth of the Palestinian workforce is unemployed (*Ha'aretz,* Nov. 23, 2004). Some of Palestine's woes are attributable to the intifada, but the fact remains that the Palestinian state, as presently constituted, lacks the economic base to support its population. The World Bank also warns that Israel's disengagement from Gaza won't help a Palestinian economy that it variously describes as being in "deep crisis," "dangerous," and "unsustainable" (*Ha'aretz,* Nov. 4, 2004). Massive foreign aid will keep things afloat, but the Palestinian economy is so integrated with that of Israel that it is unlikely to survive without access to employment within the Jewish state. That by itself gives Israel tremendous leverage over Palestinian affairs.

Economics influences politics, but the opposite is equally true. Can a Palestinian Authority renowned for its corruption and mismanagement effectively exploit the new nation's economic resources, meager as they may be? Also of concern is the PA's ability to spend what it receives in foreign aid on much-needed infrastructure development projects rather than squandering it on subsidies and corruption. Past performance is not a source of optimism.

## Palestine and External Affairs

The influence of external affairs on Palestinian politics has been discussed at length throughout this chapter and requires little elaboration. Suffice it to say that the fate of Palestine remains largely in the hands of Israel. It is Israel that will decide the ultimate size of the Palestinian state as well as its economic viability. It is also Israel that will decide how many settlements will be built on the West Bank, and it is Israel that will attempt to prevent the development of armed militias in Palestine. If the Palestinian Authority cannot protect Israel from terrorist attack, the Israelis will conduct raids into Palestine and reoccupy Palestinian territories as they see fit. It is also Israel that will decide on criteria for intervention. If history is any guide, the West will wring its hands in despair while the Arab League goes through its ritual of passing meaningless resolutions that it has no intention of implementing. Most will probably be cleared with the United States in advance.

## LOOKING TOWARD THE FUTURE

Two essential conclusions emerge from the history of the Palestinian–Israeli conflict. First, the fate of the two communities is inextricably linked. Neither is likely to enjoy a secure existence without the support of the other. Thus peace can only come with a solution that meets the minimum demands of both parties. Fortunately, a majority of Palestinians and Israelis do want peace. The core issue for the Israelis is the ability of the Jewish state to live a normal life in a secure environment. The core issue for a majority of Palestinians is a viable Palestinian state that embraces all of the occupied territories, give or take minor adjustments. Land for peace is the only formula for a peaceful solution to the crisis.

Dissenters on both sides are numerous and powerful. There is no longer any doubt about the ability of Palestinian extremist groups to inflict horrendous damage and loss of life on Israel. Many vow to do so unless their demands are met. Nor is there doubt about Israel's willingness to unleash the full weight of its military power on Palestinian targets, terrorist and otherwise. Israeli extremists speak of "transfer" of the Palestinians to Jordan, a polite word for ethnic cleansing.

If the extremists prevail, the carnage will continue for the foreseeable future. Terrorist acts will provoke ever more vicious reprisals, which will in turn inspire even more horrendous terrorist acts. Fences can be built, but they are of limited use against advances in terrorist technology that range from suicide bombers to missiles that can evade the Israeli security fence with ease. Israel is rushing to improve its antirocket technology, but it will only take a few rockets armed with biological or other weapons of mass destruction to wreck havoc in the densely populated Jewish state.

The second conclusion is that peace is unlikely to be achieved without the strenuous and sustained participation of the United States and other members of the world community. The U.S. has produced an endless series of solutions and road maps in an effort to quell the unrest in the region. All have succumbed to the U.S. government's reluctance to offend an American Jewish community that is, by and large, anxious to achieve a lasting peace in the region. Their condition is the requirement that the security of Israel be assured. If cooler heads prevail, there is hope.

# 4

# Syria

## The Politics of Minority Rule

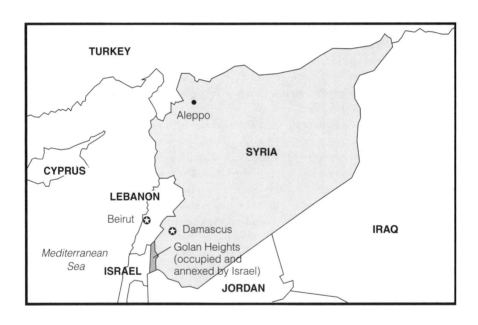

In the three decades between 1970 and 2000, Syria was transformed from a country plagued by coups and instability into one of the most politically stable countries in the Middle East. In the process, it became a major player in the affairs of the region. Syria cast a long shadow over the politics of Lebanon, was a key ally of Iran, and supported Hezbollah, Hamas, and other groups condemned as terrorists by the United States. Syria also held the key to a final settlement of the Arab–Israeli conflict and had much to say about the stability of Iraq and the

Persian Gulf. Indeed, Syria's role in the Middle East was often summed up by the adage "no war without Egypt; no peace without Syria."

Syria's transformation from a fragmented and divided country into a regional power was largely the work of a single individual: Hafiz al-Assad. This was a remarkable feat, for Syria possessed a relatively small population (18,200,000) and few natural resources. It was also threatened by the military sophistication of Israel, the domineering power of Turkey, and the massive armies of Iraq, all of which shared a contentious border with the Syrian state (see map).

Hafiz al-Assad died in 2000, bequeathing the Syrian presidency to his son, Bashar al-Assad. In the ensuing years, the famed stability of Hafiz al-Assad's Syria has given way to growing doubts over the ability of the son to survive in an increasingly hostile international and domestic environment. Of these, the greatest immediate threat to Bashar's survival is U.S. hostility toward Syria and its young leader. Syria and Iran are the only two countries in the Middle East that remain openly hostile to American dominance of the region.

The Syrian government's domestic woes stem largely from the country's retarded political and economic development as well as from a population that is fragmented into a multitude of religious sects, none of which care much for the others. Although Syria is a predominantly Arab (90 percent) and Sunni (70 percent) country, it has been ruled for the more than three decades by members of an Alawite minority that constitutes between 10 and 15 percent of the population, probably closer to the former.[1] The Alawites, although Arab, adhere to a branch of Shi'a Islam that accords Ali, the fourth caliph and son-in-law of Mohammed, a religious status nearly equal to that of Mohammed himself. The term *Alawite* means "follower of Ali"; a minority of the Alawites believe that the Angel Gabriel mistakenly revealed the Koran to Mohammed rather than Ali. Sunni Muslims often condemn the Alawites as heretics, and even other Shi'a treat them with suspicion.

The Druze, another quasi-Shi'a sect, constitute approximately 3 percent of the population. As with the Alawites, the exact nature of their religious views remains a closely guarded secret. Eleven different Christian sects, many tracing their origins to the earliest days of Christianity, constitute approximately 10 percent of the population. Added to the mix is an increasingly active community of ethnic Kurds (9 percent) as well as 110,000 Palestinian refugees, about 25 percent of whom live in camps. All of the above population figures are rough estimates and vary markedly from one source to another.

Latent distrust between its diverse religious sects is a fact of life in Syrian politics. Syria's leaders have traditionally filled key positions in the government with family members and members of the same sect, a practice that is very much in evidence today. Alawites formed the core of Hafiz al-Assad's inner circle and dominated the command structure of the Syrian security apparatus (military, police, and intelligence organizations). Of these individuals, the most influential tended to be the president's kin. Such practices, while necessary for the survival of the regime, served only to perpetuate the cycle of sectarian conflict. This policy has

---

1 The *CIA Factbook* (1999) lists the Alawites and the Druze as 16 percent of the population but does not distinguish between the two groups.

not changed during the presidency of Bashar al-Assad, Hafiz al-Assad's son. How could it? It is Alawite control of the security apparatus that keeps him in power.

Alawite domination has been facilitated by the fragmentation of the Sunni Arabs along class, family, and regional lines. The big families of Damascus have traditionally contended for power with the dominant families of Aleppo; the interests of wealthy Sunni merchants are often at odds with those of the poorer Sunni peasants; Westernized Sunni urbanites have found their domination of the Sunni community challenged by the zeal of the Sunni fundamentalists. The Arab Sunnites may be a majority of the Syrian population, but it is not a cohesive majority.

Social fragmentation has also been reinforced by geographic isolation. Syria's Alawite community was traditionally concentrated in the areas surrounding the coastal city of Latakia, the Druze in the mountainous areas near the Lebanese–Israeli border (the Jebel Druze), and the Kurds near the border with Iraqi Kurdistan. The Sunni Arabs were scattered throughout the country, but dominated the larger urban areas.

Finally, group divisions have been reinforced by economic conflict. Syria is a poor country in which every group must compete with every other group for its share of the country's resources. Historically, the Sunnis have been the winners in this struggle, and the Sunni merchant class controlled much of Syria's land and wealth. The minorities survived as best they could, but neither they nor the poorer Sunni peasants felt any warmth toward their landed masters.

Our focus in this chapter will be on the mechanisms of minority rule. We will explore the mechanisms that kept Hafiz al-Assad in power for thirty years and that will now determine the fate of his son, Bashar al-Assad. We will also examine the inherent contradictions between one-man rule and the development of sustainable political institutions.

## HISTORY AND CULTURE

Historically, the region referred to as Greater Syria stretched along the Mediterranean Sea from Egypt to southern Turkey (Hitti 1959; Pipes 1990). Thus it encompassed the present countries of Israel, Lebanon, and Syria, much of Jordan, and a small section of Turkey adjacent to the Syrian border. Like most of the Middle East, Greater Syria fell under the sway of a dizzying array of ancient civilizations, including those of the Aramaeans, Assyrians, Babylonians, Chaldeans, Persians, Greeks, Romans, Nabateans, and Byzantines. Although each civilization left its imprint on Syrian culture, the most enduring legacy of this era was the conversion of most of Greater Syria to Christianity. Antioch, together with Rome, Constantinople, and Alexandria, was one of the four Patriarchates of the Christian Church. Even today, some of Syria's smaller Christian sects continue to use the biblical languages of Aramaic and Syriac in their religious services.

The Muslim Arabs conquered Syria in 636 CE, and most of Syria's population eventually converted to Islam. The Syrians were far more urbanized and sophisticated than Arabia's bedouin warriors: Damascus and Aleppo, which trace their origins to approximately 2500 BCE, soon dominated the empire's bureaucratic apparatus.

Reflecting Syrian dominance, the seat of the Islamic caliphate shifted to Damascus in 661. During this period the Umayyad caliphs extended the Islamic empire from northern India in the east to Spain in the west. Damascus's days of glory, however, were limited, and control of the Islamic empire shifted to Iraq in 750, leaving Syria to be ruled by one or another of the contending Islamic powers until it became part of the Ottoman Empire in 1516.

Ottoman rule lasted until the Arab Revolt of World War I, and was characterized by a pattern of governance that allowed each of Syria's diverse religious communities to be self-governing as long as taxes were paid and revolts were few. This policy, often referred to as the *millet* system, perpetuated the fragmentation of Syrian society and delayed the emergence of nationalistic feelings among the Syrian population (Gelvin 1998).

## The Colonial Era

The outbreak of World War I found the Ottoman Empire allied with Germany and at war with Britain and France. The British, concerned with the threat of an Ottoman attack on the Suez Canal, inspired Sharif Hussein, the Arab governor of Mecca and a direct descendant of the Prophet Mohammed, to lead an Arab revolt against the Turks. Hussein's reward would be an Arab kingdom that encompassed much of what is now Saudi Arabia as well as virtually all of Greater Syria, although the details of the negotiations between the British and Hussein remain a matter of debate. British negotiations with the Arabs reflected a degree of perfidy, and in 1916 they compromised their implicit arrangement with the Arabs by agreeing with France to divide the region between themselves. The British would control Palestine and the area that is now Jordan and Iraq. The French would control the remainder of Greater Syria, including the present Syria and Lebanon. This agreement was followed in 1917 by the Balfour Declaration, a unilateral pledge by the British to make Palestine a national home for the Jews.

The Arab Revolt, the details of which were recounted in the introductory chapter and glorified in film and fiction, led to the triumphant entrance of Prince Faisal, the son of Sharif Hussein, into Damascus in 1918 (Gelvin 1998). The triumph, however, was short-lived as Arab forces were defeated by the French in 1920. Perhaps hoping to honor something of their earlier agreements, the British made Faisal the king of Iraq while Prince Abdullah, the second son of Sharif Hussein, was subsequently named emir (prince) of Transjordan, the precursor to the present state of Jordan. Both princes received their royal assignments on the condition that they would rule in cooperation with the British.

**Consequences of the Colonial Era**   The French authorities continued their dismemberment of Greater Syria by transforming Lebanon, a predominantly mountainous region inhabited largely by Christians, into an independent country. The Christians of Lebanon had long looked to France for protection from their Muslim neighbors and were far more receptive to French rule than Syria's Muslims. To give the new mini-state greater stature, the surrounding Muslim and Druze areas were added to Lebanon's Christian core. The French thus ensured that the new mini-state would inherit the communal turmoil of its larger neighbor.

France continued its divide-and-rule policy by fragmenting Syria into more or less self-governing provinces, each dominated by a different religious group: Latakia to the Alawites; Damascus and Aleppo to the Sunnis; the Jebel Druze to the Druze; and Alexandretta to the Turks. Real power, of course, resided with the French (Khoury 1997). Alexandretta would eventually be ceded to Turkey in a move to bolster Franco–Turkish relations, a decision that continues to rankle with Syria's leaders. The French also declared the Alawite Mountains to be a separate country, but later rescinded the declaration.

The harshness of French rule and a declining economy fueled a variety of nationalist movements, but most came to naught as a result of religious, class, and personality conflicts. Some early nationalists were supporters of Faisal and his vision of a united Arab kingdom; others sought the formation of an Arab republic that would incorporate much of the Arab east (Khoury 1997, 441–42).

The greatest stimulus of Arab nationalism, however, was not economic but cultural: the exposure of Syrian students to French culture and the seductive ideologies of nationalism, human rights, and Marxism (Dawn 1962). Those who studied at the Sorbonne or other universities dominated by French leftists were profoundly influenced by Marxist doctrine. As a result, both socialist and communist parties made their appearance in Syria during the colonial era.

However, the main ideological doctrine to emerge from the era of French rule was not Marxism but Ba'athism. Founded by Michel Aflaq and Salah Bitar, two Syrian students studying at the Sorbonne, the Ba'ath Party represented a fusion of Marxist social and economic principles with Arab nationalism. Aflaq was an Orthodox Christian; Bitar a Sunni Muslim. The goal of Ba'athists was the creation of a unified Arab state free of imperial domination (Aflaq 1963). It would be a socialist state in which a wise government assured both economic development and the equitable distribution of the resources. The new state would also be a secular one, in which ethnic and communal loyalties gave way to an overriding commitment to the Arab nation (Jabar 1966). The exact date of the party's origin remains a matter of debate, but its founding congress was held in 1947 (Batatu 1999).

With its banner of "unity, freedom, and socialism," the new party soon attracted a broad base of recruits among Syria's students and junior military officers. The egalitarian and secular orientation of the party made it particularly appealing to Syrian minorities who had long resented Sunni domination. The Ba'ath Party also found strong support among Sunni fellahin (peasants), many of whom subsisted in conditions of near servitude. Various socialist parties merged with the Ba'ath Party shortly after independence, giving the party its formal name of the Arab Socialist Resurrection (Renaissance) Party.[2]

The French could not block the emergence of Arab nationalism in Syria, but they slowed its progress by playing each group against the other. In the process, they deepened the fragmentation of Syrian society and assured that

---

2 The original party formed by Aflaq and Bitar was the Arab Resurrection Party. It merged with Akram al-Hawrani's Arab Socialist Party in 1953 to form the Ba'ath Party. The Ba'ath Party also incorporated other intellectual currents and was influenced by the philosophical writings of Zaki Arsuzi, an Alawite.

an independent Syria would find the task of nation building to be an arduous one (Zeine 1960; Ziadeh 1957).

## The Era of Revolution and Optimism

France, in the throes of World War II, agreed to Syrian independence in 1941. Elections were held in 1943, with the leaders of the National Party, an organization controlled largely by wealthy Sunnis and upper-class Christians, emerging victorious. Full independence, however, did not come until 1946 when the last of the French troops left the country under pressure from the British and Americans.

Syria's new leaders faced the challenge of forging a cohesive political community where none had existed before. They were also anxious to develop the Syrian economy, albeit in a manner that strengthened the power of Syria's landed and commercial classes. Both tasks would prove difficult (World Bank 1955). Syria's new leaders had few resources to draw upon, and none of its leaders possessed the charisma of Nasser or Ben-Gurion. The country's political institutions were untested and evinced few signs of legitimacy among the Syrian population. The Syrian military, the ultimate guarantor of the regime, was beset by the same factionalism that divided the country as a whole and showed ominous signs of being controlled by the Alawites and other minorities. Ba'athist and Communist influences within the military were also mounting. Factionalism within the military increased in the years following independence as both the Ba'athists and the Communists encouraged their younger supporters, most of whom belonged to various minorities, to enter the military college. Wealthier Sunnis, by contrast, found military service to be beneath their dignity and concentrated on commerce. The military thus served as the primary avenue of social mobility among the minorities and the poor. The Alawites took particular advantage of it.

The early years of independence were beset by religious tensions as well as by increasing conflict between the peasants and the large landowners. Only about one-third of Syria's peasants owned land; the remainder were sharecroppers who depended upon the goodwill of the landlord for their survival (Batatu 1999). The leaders of the National Party, immobilized by internecine bickering and personality conflicts, were unable to meet Syria's social and economic problems with a firm hand. The defeat of the Syrian army in the 1948 war with Israel further undermined popular support for the National Party and turned the army against a government that had sent it into battle ill equipped to win.

Such feelings were probably justified, for Syria had little in the way of an army at the time of independence. The National Party had entered the war buoyed by the euphoria of independence and the assumption that the Jews could not fight. The victory, they thought, would be an easy one, perhaps allowing Syria to reclaim territories severed by the British and French in the aftermath of World War I. What better way for the regime to shore up its sagging popularity?

The optimism that marked the beginning of the war merely added to the bitterness of defeat. A military coup d'état toppled the National Party in March 1949, bringing to a close Syria's first experiment in democracy (Carleton 1950). The first coup gave way to a second in August, followed by another in December of the same year. The pageant of coup and countercoup continued until 1954 when Syria embarked on yet another experiment in democracy. The Syrian political spectrum now ran the gamut from the old conservatives on the right to the Ba'athists and Communists on the left. They were soon joined by the supporters of Nasser, whose charismatic leadership had captured the imagination of the Arab world. The Nasserites espoused essentially the same goals as the Ba'ath Party (unity, socialism, and freedom), but found a broader appeal among Sunni Muslims. The Ba'athists and the Communists, by contrast, continued to find disproportionate support among minority groups. All three groups had supporters in the army. Growing Ba'athist influence in the military increased the party's political clout but also laid the foundation for a confrontation between the party's civilian and military wings. The civilian leadership possessed the titles and visibility; the military officers possessed the power.

The Ba'ath Party, which had entered the cabinet for the first time in 1949, showed clear signs of becoming a dominant force in Syrian politics. The parties of the center and right were poorly organized affairs that had little mass support. Most revolved around key figures or families and found it difficult to work with other parties in a productive manner.

The Communists, however, had also made considerable progress. Khaled Bakdash, the head of the Syrian Communist Party, was elected to the National Assembly in 1954. He was the first Communist member of parliament in the Arab world. Far more ominous, from the Ba'athist perspective, was the 1957 appointment of a Communist general as chief of staff of the armed forces. Nasserite power had also surged with Nasser's political victory over the Israelis, British, and French in the 1956 war. The Ba'athist leadership was thus threatened by the possibility of a Communist coup on one side and the juggernaut of Nasser's popularity on the other. Adding to the party's woes was the growing inability of its various factions to resolve their differences. Party documents of the era spoke of "chaos," and a "breakdown of discipline" (Batatu 1999, 143).

Faced with a dilemma from which there appeared to be no exit, the Ba'ath Party proposed a merger of Egypt and Syria. Nasser was originally reluctant, but accepted the proposal on the condition that all political parties would be banned with the exception of his newly created Arab Socialist Union (Heikal 1962). The Ba'athist leadership accepted Nasser's conditions, probably believing that they would be free to rule Syria as they wished while Nasser contented himself with Egypt. The Syrians also believed that they were more clever than the Egyptians and that the Ba'athist organizational structure would prove superior to that of Egypt's untested Arab Socialist Union (Palmer 1960). They turned out to be wrong on both counts.

The Syrian Ba'ath Party dissolved itself in compliance with Nasser's wishes, although many members of the party thought the dissolution premature.[3]

Ba'athist leaders became senior officials in the government of the new United Arab Republic (UAR); many of them moved from Damascus to Cairo. The euphoria of the moment spawned pro-unity uprisings throughout the Arab east, which were crowned by the overthrow of the Iraqi monarchy in July 1958.

---

3 Branches of the party remained in Iraq, Jordan, and Lebanon.

The new Iraqi leaders vowed their loyalty to the UAR, proclaiming that full unity of the three countries was merely a matter of time.

Euphoria, however, soon turned to despair as the Ba'athists found that their role in governing the UAR was largely illusory. In effect, most had been exiled to Cairo to keep them out of trouble. This was particularly true of the military leaders, for Nasser was well aware of Syria's history of instability and had no intention of risking a coup d'état. With their party disbanded and their leaders in exile, the Ba'athists watched from the sidelines as Egyptians ruled Syria with the support of Syrian Nasserites.

The more disenchanted Syrians became with the UAR, the more Egyptians asserted their authority in a futile effort to make the union work. More often than not, these efforts were clumsy and heavy-handed and served only to alienate ever larger segments of the Syrian population. Many Syrians found it ironic that an Egyptian bureaucracy that was losing the struggle to develop its own country would judge itself capable of ruling another. The final year of the union saw a misguided attempt to impose Egypt's socialist policies on Syria, a move that cost Nasser the support of the Sunni business community, which had once welcomed him as a counterweight to the radical policies of the Ba'athists and the Communists.

Not all of the union's troubles, however, were of its own making. The West plotted against the union at every turn, fearing that its success would destroy Western control of the Middle East and bring the region's massive oil reserves under the sway of Nasser and his Soviet allies. The revolutionaries in Iraq also shied away from joining the UAR, a topic discussed at greater length in Chapter 6. Even nature, it seemed, had turned against the union as Syria's largely agrarian economy suffered three successive years of drought.

The coup that brought the UAR to an end was carried out by Sunni officers on September 28, 1961. The Ba'athists and others, not wanting the coup to be interpreted as a minority putsch against a Sunni government, stood by in silent complicity. Michel Aflaq, the head of the Ba'ath Party, officially endorsed the coup after the fact.

The collapse of the UAR was welcomed by most of Syria's politicians, who, now free of Nasser, returned Syria to its earlier path of confusion and instability. The Ba'athists, Nasserites, and Communists were in disarray and unable to form a government. The leaders of the People's Party, which was associated with the business community in Aleppo, formed a government but enjoyed little support from either the populace or their political adversaries.

Although the Ba'ath Party had formally dissolved itself in 1958, a small cadre of the Syrian officers posted in Cairo had formed a "military committee" to save what they could of the party's military wing (Seale 1988). The former civilian leaders of the party, most of whom were now held in contempt by the military, were not informed of the committee's activities. Hafiz al-Assad, then a captain, was a junior member of the original plotters. With the breakup of the UAR, it was the military committee of the Ba'ath that reconstituted the Ba'ath Party. The old civilian leadership still claimed control of the "National (All-Arab) Command" but had little influence in Syria itself.

The confusion of the secessionist regime was evident in its foreign policy, the centerpiece of which was a call for reunification with Egypt, albeit on grounds more equitable to Syria. Nasser launched a vitriolic propaganda attack on the secessionist government, branding Syria's leaders as traitors to the Arab cause and lackeys of the West. Predictions of an imminent coup were so pervasive that they were openly discussed in the press.

In March 1963, a coalition of Ba'athists and Syrian Nasserites overthrew the secessionist government and immediately called for unity talks with Egypt. The preceding month had seen a parallel coalition of Ba'athists and Nasserites seize power in Iraq, and they too joined the unity negotiations. The unity discussions were short-lived; Nasser and his allies from Syria and Iraq used the occasion to ridicule the Ba'ath Party and condemn it for the breakup of the UAR (Kerr 1971).

Hardly had the dust settled on the unity discussions when the Syrian Nasserites attempted to overthrow their Ba'athist colleagues and reestablish the union with Egypt. The attempted coup was crushed by the military wing of the Ba'ath Party, leaving the party in total control of the country. All, however, was not well. The Syrian government was nominally headed by Aflaq and the civilian wing of the Ba'ath Party, while real power lay with the party's military wing, particularly the "military committee" that had rebuilt the party in the years following the breakup of the UAR (Seale 1988). The more Aflaq attempted to assert his authority, the higher rose the tensions between the two wings of the party.

While the Arabs quarreled among themselves, Israel chose the moment to divert water from the Jordan River and to extend its position in the demilitarized zone separating Israel and Syria. Syria responded to the Israeli incursions by shelling Israeli border settlements, a policy born more out of frustration than any hope of victory. Israel retaliated with air strikes, humiliating a shaky Ba'athist regime.

With few other options at its disposal, Syria played the Palestinian card. As early as 1964, Palestinian raids on Israel had been restricted by Nasser and other Arab leaders who feared that fedayeen (guerrilla) activities would provoke an Arab–Israel conflict that they were ill prepared to fight (Seale 1988). The Syrians thus formed their own Palestinian organization, Saiqa, and allowed it to attack Israeli border positions. While the Palestinians tied up the Israelis, so the plan went, the Ba'athists would have time to build a military organization capable of challenging Israel directly. Israel, however, had little interest in seeing the Arabs regroup under the benevolent guidance of the Soviet Union, the main foreign backer of the Ba'athist regime. Guerrilla attacks were met with air strikes against Syria, further demoralizing a Ba'athist leadership that was rapidly losing its grip on power.

An internal coup within the Ba'ath Party ousted the party's civilian wing in 1966, placing the military wing of the party in control of Syria's affairs. More concerned with fears of a countercoup than with the possibility of an Israeli attack, Syria's military leaders purged the military of some four hundred officers suspected of supporting the civilian leadership of the party (Seale 1988, 113). When this figure is added to the Nasserite officers purged in 1964 and the conservative officers purged in 1963, not much remained of the Syrian officer corps. It was certainly not in a position to fight a major war. In this state of internal turmoil, Syria entered the 1967 war with Israel. Predictably, Syrian forces were again humiliated and Israel seized the Golan Heights.

The dominant characteristics of Syrian politics over the course of the two decades between independence and defeat in the Six-Day War, then, were turmoil and political instability. Fleeting attempts at democracy gave way to a succession of coups and they to an abortive union with Egypt. The collapse of the union was followed by additional coups and eventual defeat at the hands of Israel in the Six-Day War. The crowning humiliation was the loss of the Golan Heights to Israel.

## The Era of Disillusion and Reassessment

Syrian politics during the years immediately following the June War of 1967 were dominated by power struggles within the military wing of the Ba'ath Party, with each leader blaming the others for the catastrophe. The struggle ended in November of 1970 when Hafiz al-Assad, then minister of defense, crushed his rivals and seized control of the government. He was named president in February 1971. This arrogation of power rankled Sunni Arabs, for until then, the formal title of president had always been reserved for them.

Al-Assad's goals upon seizing power reflected the complexity of his background. His most immediate goal was to consolidate his power, a challenging task given the tumultuous history of Syrian politics. Al-Assad also believed in Ba'athist ideology, albeit a Ba'athist ideology tempered with pragmatism and a strong dose of Syrian nationalism. If Arab unity were to be achieved, Syria would be at its core. The wounds of the war also had to be healed, especially the loss of the Golan Heights. All of these goals required a buildup of the Syrian military. They also demanded urgent measures to revive Syria's moribund economy.

The assets available to al-Assad for achieving his goals were limited at best. As an Alawite, al-Assad enjoyed little support among Syria's predominantly Sunni population. The Arab defeat in the 1967 war had also discredited the military and had seen nationalist fervor give way to a zealous Islamic fundamentalism. Al-Assad, moreover, was an austere individual with few charismatic qualities. He was a gray eminence who excelled in manipulating events from behind the scenes.

Al-Assad's main bastion of support was the military. This was not an unmixed blessing. The military was highly politicized, and even the military wing of the Ba'ath Party was divided within itself. The strongest guarantee of al-Assad's rule was not the military as a whole, but the Alawite core within the military.

Once in office, al-Assad moved rapidly to broaden the base of his regime by extending his hand to the Sunni merchant class and normalizing relations with his Arab neighbors (Dekmejian 1991). He also raised hopes for a return to democracy by reinstating the parliament and calling for the direct election of the president. Alas, there was only one candidate for the presidency and the National Assembly, now called the People's Assembly, was totally dominated by the Ba'ath Party, now an instrument of al-Assad's personal rule.

Assad's new constitution did little to quell Sunni hostility to his regime. Fundamentalist (Muslim Brotherhood) riots rocked Syria in 1973. The Sunni fundamentalists also invoked a provision of the Syrian constitution stipulating that the president of Syria was required to be a Muslim. This was a tricky proposition, for most Sunni and many Shi'a viewed the Alawites as heretics and thus as non-Muslims. Al-Assad skirted the issue by having the dominant Shi'ite leader in the Levant, the Imam Musa Sadr of Lebanon, issue a formal writ (fatwa) declaring that the Alawites were Muslims.

On the plus side, from al-Assad's perspective, the October War of 1973 had seen Syrian forces acquit themselves well before being forced back by the Israelis. Much as in Egypt, the war was considered a huge success by the Syrian population and added immeasurably to al-Assad's prestige. Syrian success in the initial stages of the October War also propelled al-Assad into the limelight of Middle Eastern politics, where he would prove to be a strategist of consummate skill.

The euphoria of Syria's near victory over Israel was short-lived. Egypt was moving rapidly into the American camp and showed ominous signs of willingness to sign a separate peace accord with Israel. Without the counterweight of the Egyptian army, Syria would be totally vulnerable to Israeli attack and able to do little to force a return of the Golan Heights. Increasingly in need of foreign protection, Syria moved closer to the Soviet Union. The alliance was a natural one. Syria received economic and military aid from the Soviet Union; the Soviets, having been expelled from their bases in Egypt prior to the 1973 war, maintained a strong presence in the Mediterranean basin.

The Soviets could protect al-Assad from his external enemies, but they could do little to quell the growing tension between al-Assad and the Syrian branch of the Muslim Brotherhood. Al-Assad's 1976 decision to aid the Christian forces in Lebanon's civil war fueled rumors that he planned to merge the Christian areas of Lebanon with the Alawite regions of Syria, thereby further fragmenting the historical Syria (El Khazen 2000; Seale 1988, 91). Although there was no foundation for such rumors, the Muslim Brotherhood proclaimed a jihad against the al-Assad regime.

Al-Assad's problems continued to mount throughout the rest of the decade as Egypt and Israel moved toward peace and attacks on the regime by the Muslim Brotherhood became increasingly violent. Fifty military cadets, most from Alawite backgrounds, were assassinated in Aleppo in June 1979, giving rise to speculation that the end of the al-Assad era was at hand. Merchant strikes erupted throughout the north of Syria in August of the same year, as did incidents of guerrilla warfare.

Al-Assad responded to the peace agreement between Egypt and Israel by joining Iraq in forging a unified Arab front against Egypt. Ideally, Anwar Sadat would be forced to rescind his agreement with Israel. At the very least, Egypt would be punished for breaking ranks with its sister states and a message would be sent to Israel that the Arabs remained united. By April 1979, even Saudi Arabia and Kuwait had severed their ties with Egypt, thereby depriving the latter of much-needed economic assistance.

Al-Assad apparently had little faith in Arab solidarity, for in October 1980, he publicly announced his support for Iran in the Iran–Iraq War that had erupted a few days earlier. Iraq and Syria severed diplomatic relations, while Syria's relationships with Jordan, Saudi Arabia, and Kuwait, the main supports of the Iraqi attack on Iran, turned cold. Al-Assad signed a treaty of friendship with the Soviet Union during the same month, thereby moving Syria firmly into the Soviet camp (Ramet 1990). The Soviet Union, not the Arab world, would protect Syria from Israeli attack.

On the domestic front, al-Assad responded to the attacks of the Muslim Brotherhood with a blend of force and accommodation. He increased welfare and patronage for Sunni supporters of the regime while crushing direct challenges to his rule with maximum force. Among instances of the latter was al-Assad's response to the continuing buildup of Brotherhood militias in the largely Sunni city of Hama. By early 1982, the Muslim Brotherhood had largely taken control of Hama and had begun to expand their influence throughout the region. His regime in jeopardy, al-Assad destroyed large sections of the city, killing as many as 20,000 people, innocent civilians as well as Muslim Brothers. Many sources place the figure at half that number, but by any reckoning, the loss of life was staggering.

The Hama massacre largely ended the fundamentalist threat in Syria. Its support base destroyed, the fragmented Muslim Brotherhood leadership fled to Iraq, Jordan, or Germany. Their mistake had been to shift from the hit-and-run tactics that had weakened al-Assad's government over the preceding decade to a strategy of direct confrontation with the army. Perhaps they believed that the military would revolt and join their revolution, but this did not happen. Al-Assad, always a master tactician, had selected the troops used to crush the uprising with care. They were Alawites. The Hama massacre also introduced a new level of brutality into Syrian politics, which would force al-Assad's adversaries to think twice before challenging him.

Hardly had the dust settled on the Hama massacre when Israeli troops launched a massive invasion of Lebanon, entering Beirut in September of 1982. As noted in Chapter 3, Israel now considered Syria to be the most direct threat to its security; it had viewed Syrian control of Lebanon with concern. Israel had also become increasingly apprehensive over the alliance between Syria and the Islamic Republic of Iran, an alliance that found pro-Iranian Hezbollah guerrillas attacking Israel from bases in Lebanon. Syria made a futile attempt to resist the Israeli invasion of Lebanon, losing much of its air force in the process.

Once again, it looked as though al-Assad was on the ropes. The Soviets, however, could not accept the loss of their main ally in the Mediterranean basin. By 1983 the Soviets had rearmed the Syrian military with advanced weapons, including air defense systems capable of challenging Israel's air superiority. The strong show of Soviet support for al-Assad blunted the Israel–U.S. effort to drive Syria from Lebanon. It also fueled speculation that Lebanon might soon be divided between its two more powerful neighbors. This did not take place, but Israeli forces continued to maintain a large security zone in southern Lebanon. Al-Assad had displayed an uncanny ability to surmount crisis after crisis, but the strain on his health had become manifest. In late 1983, he became seriously ill; rumors circulated that he had suffered a heart attack. Al-Assad's illness unleashed a power struggle among his major lieutenants, with each moving troops into Damascus in a bid to seize power. Dominant among these was al-Assad's younger brother Rifat, the commander of the infamous "Defense Companies" that had become the main prop of the regime. The Defense Companies were an army within an army, boasting more than 55,000 troops and their "own armour, artillery, air defense, and a fleet of troop-carrying helicopters" (Seale 1988).

The showdown between the president and his brother, described here by Patrick Seale, is particularly poignant as it illustrates the role of traditional family relationships in Syrian politics: "At Rifat's house in Mezze the brothers came at last face to face. 'You want to overthrow the regime?' Asad asked. 'Here I am. I am the regime.' For an hour they stormed at each other but, in his role of elder brother and with his mother in the house, Asad could not fail to win the contest" (Seale 1988, 432–33).

Although Hafiz al-Assad recovered from what proved to be severe exhaustion and purged those involved in the attempted putsch, the event demonstrated just how little institutional development had occurred in Syria during the seventeen years of al-Assad's rule (Dekmejian 1991, 206). Power resided with him alone, and no realistic provisions had been made for a smooth transition upon his passing. The power struggle, it is interesting to note, took place wholly within the ruling elite. If any other opposition to the regime existed, it remained on the sidelines.

Syria's domestic politics stabilized with al-Assad's return to power, buoyed in part by the discovery of high-quality, though limited, oil deposits. Although these were not comparable to those of Saudi Arabia and the Gulf states, development of the oil fields pumped much-needed money into the Syrian economy and eased al-Assad's financial dependence on his oil-rich neighbors. The latter were hostile to al-Assad, but they also feared his army and were not above buying his friendship. Al-Assad also took this opportunity to embark upon a gradual liberalization of the Syrian economy. Much as in Egypt, it was hoped that a revitalized capitalist sector would stimulate economic growth (Lawson 1996).

Tensions within Lebanon also continued to preoccupy the Syrian leader but moved toward resolution in 1989 when a Saudi-brokered peace recognized the existence of a special relationship between Syria and Lebanon. The civil war began to wind down, but only at the price of Syrian dominance. Lebanon would stabilize and revive, but the Lebanese–Israeli border remained a war zone in which Hezbollah guerrillas, supported by Iran and Syria, launched a devastating war of attrition against Israeli occupation forces. Israel would lose this indirect war, withdrawing its forces from southern Lebanon in the summer of 2000.

The more things seemed to improve, however, the more they fell apart. Iraq had gained the upper hand in the Iran–Iraq War and vowed retribution for al-Assad's support of Iran. Far more worrisome to al-Assad was the rise of Mikhail Gorbachev in the Soviet Union, an event that would see Syria's protector embark on a path of reconciliation with the United States and Israel. The army and the Ba'ath Party had sustained the regime internally, but it was the support of the Soviet Union that had enabled al-Assad to keep Israel at bay.

Once again it was an external event, the Iraqi invasion of Kuwait in 1990, that enabled al-Assad to rebound from almost certain disaster. The success of U.S. efforts to forge an alliance against Iraq depended upon participation by a broad coalition of Arab countries. Barring this support, a largely U.S. attack on Iraq would be perceived as American aggression against an Arab and Islamic country. This would inflame both nationalistic and religious emotions, hindering American military operations in the region and placing client governments at risk. Al-Assad's Syria, the historical center of Arab nationalism and resistance to the West, rushed to the aid of the United States, condemning Saddam Hussein as a traitor to Arab nationalism and joining the United Nations coalition against Iraq. A rogue state accused of fostering international terrorism thus became an ally of the United States. Tensions between the two countries remained, but al-Assad had gained a new lease on power by demonstrating his ability to promote U.S. interests in the region.

Having parried the external threat to his regime, al-Assad also moved decisively to strengthen his position at home. The core of his domestic program was the promulgation of Investment Law No. 10 of 1991. According to the Investment Law and related legislation, private-sector firms capable of easing Syria's unemployment crisis by creating new jobs were exempted from taxation for five years. They were also allowed to import equipment duty-free and to deposit their profits in Western banks, where they would be safe from the capricious hand of the Syrian government. Similar benefits were extended to private-sector firms that either increased exports or reduced imports (Lawson 1996, 13).

The new investment law opened the door to private-sector investment in Syria and resulted in the rapid expansion of private-sector enterprises. GDP increased by more than 7 percent over the next two years, creating a sense of optimism for the future (Melhem 1997, 3). Efforts were also made to clamp down on corruption, but most of these seem to have been largely symbolic. A regime that ruled by a combination of repression and corruption could hardly be expected to eliminate one of the main pillars of its authority. As Melhem noted, "Even within the still-limited private sector, 'the game is often fixed, with licenses doled out as favors to friends of the regime' " (Melhem 1997, 3).

Economic reforms were paralleled by continuing efforts to groom Basil al-Assad, Hafiz al-Assad's eldest son, for succession to the presidency. Basil, a career military officer renowned for his equestrian skills, was nicknamed "the golden knight" and reportedly enjoyed close ties with Syria's intelligence community (*The Middle East*, Dec. 1992, no. 217, 18–20). Rifat al-Assad, the president's brother, was allowed to return to Syria in 1992, but his bases of support, including the Defense Companies, had long since been disbanded (*The Middle East*, March 1994, no. 232, 12). At the same time, Hafiz al-Assad began to rein in the "regime barons," as Syria's powerful security chiefs were referred to. It would also see Basil begin to take charge of his father's personal security (*The Middle East*, March 1994, no. 232, 12). Hafiz al-Assad, it seemed, had named his successor.

By 1994, clouds again appeared on the horizon. In January of that year Basil al-Assad was killed in an automobile accident, rekindling speculation about who would succeed his father. Maneuvering increased apace. Syria's large public-sector firms were also resisting economic reform, and the more radical members of the Ba'ath Party decried al-Assad's shift to "guided capitalism" as a violation of the party's socialist principles. Both feared that further cutbacks in the public sector would result in a loss of jobs and increased unemployment. Such fears were not unfounded, for Syria's government enterprises had been deliberately overstaffed in order to provide employment to as many people as possible. Social welfare, not efficiency, had been their credo.

Al-Assad resolved the issue by continuing to relax restrictions on the private sector while simultaneously using the country's scarce resources to prop up a moribund public sector. Both masters had to be served: economic growth and political patronage. The compromise made no sense to Western economists who viewed capitalism as the solution to all of the world's ills, but it made a great deal of sense within the fragile mosaic of Syrian politics (Hamadi 1998, 20–21; Lawson 1996).

Having made a change of course on the economic level, al-Assad now found himself under intense pressure to do the same with foreign policy. The Oslo accords of 1993 had resulted in a tenuous peace between Israel and the Palestinians, and by 1994 the United States was increasing its pressure on al-Assad to follow suit. In typical al-Assad fashion, he bent to U.S. pressure by joining the peace process while simultaneously supporting terrorist groups opposed to peace, including Hezbollah and the Palestinian Hamas. If Israel wanted peace, it would have to pay al-Assad's price (Rabil 2003). In the meantime, al-Assad continued to maintain a military establishment roughly equivalent to that of Israel in terms of tanks, armored personnel carriers, aircraft, artillery, and warships. This was a largely defensive force, for the technical capacity of the Israeli military was far superior to that of Syria and there could be no thought of a Syrian attack on Israel without Egyptian support. Nevertheless, the Syrian military possessed more than enough weaponry to inflict unacceptable losses on an invading Israeli army. The military situation between the two countries thus remained a standoff.

In 1999, al-Assad was elected without opposition to a fifth term in office, but nature was now poised to achieve what his adversaries could not. Advanced in years and in ill health, al-Assad positioned his second son, Bashar, to succeed him as president of Syria. The grooming of Bashar for the presidency was precisely choreographed. Bashar's promotion to the rank of major in the Republican Guards was followed in short order by his promotion to colonel. He was also placed in charge of guiding events in Lebanon, and he followed in the footsteps of his older brother by leading the charge against corruption and smuggling in Syria (*Al-Waton al-Arabi,* June 10, 1999). Bashar's promotion to colonel was followed by key diplomatic assignments, including a long tête-à-tête with President Jacques Chirac of France. Rumors also circulated that Bashar would soon be elevated to the position of vice president (*Al-Waton al-Arabi,* June 10, 1999).

All, however, was not well. The summer of 1999 brought rumors of a failed coup organized by the regime barons and Hafiz al-Assad's brother Rifat. Both had recently been purged by al-Assad as one of several steps designed to assure Bashar's succession to the presidency. Adding to the intrigue were rumors that al-Assad had been alerted to the coup attempt by the United States, to ensure that al-Assad would remain in office during forthcoming peace negotiations with Israel. Al-Assad was a tough negotiator, but at least he was willing to negotiate (Mauran and Eddin 1999, 4–7).

The failed Sunni-sponsored coup was followed within weeks by an assault on Rifat's compound by Syrian security forces. As the events were reported in *Al-Waton al-Arabi,* a leading Arabic-language news journal, Rifat's compound in

Latakia had been under surveillance since January 1999, albeit without confrontation. On October 17 of that year, however, Rifat's compound, including his private port, was surrounded by army tanks and an ultimatum for his surrender issued by the commander. When Rifat ignored the summons, the tanks opened fire, with extensive loss of life. The Syrian press denied these allegations, claiming that the sole purpose of the attack had been to close Rifat's illegal port. The war between the brothers continued, as did the battle for succession.

During the spring of 2000 al-Assad replaced the prime minister and several members of the cabinet, shifting supporters of Bashar into key positions and otherwise breathing new life into a stagnant political apparatus whose prime virtue had been its loyalty to al-Assad (*Al-Hawadeth,* March 24, 2000, 30). New blood was entering the political system, but it was entering slowly.

Hafiz al-Assad, however, had yet to announce that Bashar would be his successor, a step that would require a constitutional amendment reducing the minimum age of presidential candidates from thirty-five to thirty-four. Bashar was thirty-four at the time. Plans were also made to have Bashar named a vice president of the Ba'ath Party and, presumably, to enhance his military credentials. Steps to achieve these goals were accelerated in the late spring of 2000 as al-Assad was reported to have suffered a major stroke, but had yet to be put in place when he died of a heart attack on June 10, 2000.

Speculation about Syria's fate following the death of Hafiz al-Assad ranged from imminent threats of civil war fueled by sectarian conflict and power struggles among the regime barons to a peaceful transfer of power dictated by the self-interest of the same barons, all of whom would suffer if the regime collapsed. In this scenario, Bashar al-Assad would be a figurehead president while the barons ruled from behind the scenes. Between those two extremes were predictions of a lull before the storm as the major players jockeyed for position as well as suggestions that Bashar would use the transition period to continue the process of building his own power base, a process initiated during his father's presidency. The longer the son remained in power, in this version, the greater would be his chances for survival.

The only one of the four hypotheses to be disproved during the initial year of Bashar's rule was the one that Syria would dissolve into political chaos, if not open civil war. There was no civil war, and observers of all persuasions were dazzled by the smoothness of the transition. Indeed, the Syrian political process hardly skipped a beat between Hafiz al-Assad's death on June 10 and Bashar al-Assad's assumption of the reins of power on July 17. With clockwork precision, the People's Assembly amended the Syrian constitution to allow Bashar to become president of the republic at age thirty-four, while the Ba'ath Party duly elected him as its president, the latter being a precondition of the former. This election was preceded by Bashar's promotion to the rank of lieutenant general and his appointment as the commander in chief of the armed forces. These appointments were made by a powerless interim president. The transition process was crowned by a plebiscite in which the Syrian population acclaimed Bashar as their president.

The smoothness of the transition process suggested a high level of agreement among the regime barons and other key actors less visible to the outside world, but it left open the question of who ruled Syria. At least for the moment, the lieu-tenants of Hafiz al-Assad had kept the regime intact by orchestrating Bashar's elevation to the presidency. The period of sorting out, including Bashar's efforts to consolidate his power, could now begin.

The first step in this sorting-out process was image building. The Syrian public had to be convinced that Bashar had the courage and resolve to stay the course, an issue of some doubt given his age and lack of political experience. The only pictures of the new president that were released by the regime, accordingly, were those of a stern and unsmiling Bashar, a pose that made him look older than thirty-four (*Al-Mushahid,* July 23, 2000, 18–19). Show trials of some of Syria's most corrupt offi-cials strengthened this image, as did widespread purges of the Ba'athist apparatus. Not only did Bashar seem to be demonstrating the power and resolve to "renew" the party leadership throughout the country, but the new generation of party leaders were, presumably, his people. The purges were also intensely popular; as one of Syria's more outspoken skeptics wrote, "The age of unthinking dinosaurs, who have been roaming the country for 40 years, is at an end" (Moubayed 2001, 6). Also contribut-ing to this image of power and resolve was Bashar's firm support for the al-Aqsa intifada and his uncompromising demands for a just peace with Israel that included the complete return of the Golan Heights. In more heated moments, Bashar con-demned Israel for perpetrating a "new Nazism" (*Ha'aretz,* Nov. 14, 2000). Relations with Iraq were also normalized in a move that demonstrated Bashar's courage in the face of U.S. pressure.

Balancing this effort to demonstrate strength and decisiveness was a dramatic move to build a strong base of popular support by easing the severity of his father's rule. Without criticizing his father directly, Bashar promised a new era of economic and political modernization that would bring Syria into the twenty-first century. In the economic realm, economic reform and other measures to stimulate foreign investment in Syria were accelerated, albeit in a gradual and prudent manner that reassured workers in the public sector that their jobs would be secure. Indeed, these workers received a 25 percent salary increase, in a thinly veiled move to reaffirm Bashar's ties with Syria's large public-sector workforce.

Moves in the political arena were particularly dramatic. Some six hundred political prisoners were released from prison and political debating societies were allowed to form in Syria's major cities (Hamid 2001; Moubayed 2005d). Leftist parties allied with the Ba'ath also received permission to publish party newspa-pers and to expand their political activities on the condition that they remained free of foreign connections and kept their activities visible to the government. Syria would move in the direction of democracy, Bashar proclaimed, but not nec-essarily the democracy of the West: "It is necessary that we have our own special democracy that will enable us to build a strong foundation capable of withstand-ing shocks, whatever their difficulty and intensity. In this regard it is necessary to broaden the experiment of the National Patriotic Front and strengthen it (*Al-Hawadeth,* Aug. 21, 2000, 12; translation by M. Palmer).

Efforts were also made to humanize the presidency. Bashar made a point of praying alone in Damascus's mosques and allowing the press to discuss his private life, including his marriage to the British-educated daughter of a prominent Sunni businessman. He was also portrayed as the champion of new information technologies and education reform, issues of intense popularity among Syria's youth. All in all, then, Bashar's strategy was one of controlled economic and political liberalization blended with political stability. There would be no power vacuum or a return to the chaos of the 1950s and 1960s. Things would change, but they would change gradually within the confines of Syria's social and political traditions (Hasba'ni 2000).

The strategy was well conceived and well executed, leaving observers with the eerie feeling that things had gone too smoothly and that problems lurked unseen behind a surreal facade. Indeed, no one was quite sure who was making decisions or what the balance of power was within the ruling circle (*Al-Waton al-Arabi,* Dec. 8, 2000, 28–30). Rumors of internal power struggles abounded. Some focused on conflicts within the ruling Alawite community. Others questioned Bashar's ability to gain acceptance among Syria's predominantly Sunnite population.

To the surprise of many, Bashar al-Assad has survived. He has survived because those who had ruled Syria for the previous thirty years had a vested interest in ensuring his survival. This list included the Alawite generals and intelligence officers, their loyal Sunni counterparts, the Ba'ath Party, a deeply entrenched bureaucratic establishment, and the core of Sunni merchants who had grown increasingly prosperous under the rule of Hafiz al-Assad. If the regime fell, they would fall. The prospect of certain retribution for thirty years of oppression and torture struck fear in the hearts of the most hardened generals and intelligence officers. A wave of terror against the Alawites would not be out of the question. Internal power struggles would be sorted out in time. For the moment it was better that Bashar serve as a symbol of continuity and hope. Syria needed both.

It also appears that Bashar has been more skillful in manipulating the byzantine intrigues of Syrian politics than his adversaries imagined possible (Moubayed 2005d). A silent power struggle was clearly taking place as Bashar and his key supporters attempted to ease the old guard out of positions of power, but its outcome was difficult to predict. Bashar appeared to be winning, but palace intrigues are by nature murky; solid information is hard to come by. In any case, two very dark clouds loomed on the horizon.

The first concerned the ability of Bashar al-Assad to transform the archaic political and economic systems inherited from his father into viable instruments of rule. The second concerned his relationships with the United States and Israel. Bashar was willing to accept peace with Israel, but it had to be a peace that included the return of the Golan Heights. Return of the Golan Heights would be a tremendous victory for the young president. He would have accomplished something that his father had been unable to do. Peace without the Golan Heights, by contrast, would be a defeat. Israel, for its part, was willing to return most but not all of the Golan Heights. If the United States used its pressure to force Israel to go all the way, it would be more than a victory for Bashar. It would be a clear signal to both friends and enemies that the Bashar al-Assad regime had the support of the U.S. government.

Alas, there were problems on both fronts. In the view of many, the Ba'athist regime was beyond reform. The problem, said a prominent Syrian journalist, was not Bashar or simplistic notions of the old guard versus the new guard; the problem was the system. By "the system," he meant a massive government bureaucracy and, by implication, the bureaucracy of the ruling Ba'ath Party. Both are characterized by corruption, incompetence, resistance to change, and fear of taking a decision that might offend a senior official. It was not a matter of Bashar being in charge, but of his inability to implement the economic, social, and legal changes that Syria so desperately needs. Bashar, he noted, is full of good intentions, but wishing does not make it so (Shaeebi 2005). This journalist is a friend of the regime who now feels comfortable criticizing the system while sparing the president.

Other critics, especially those living abroad, have been less generous. They argue that Syria is ruled by a narrow-based political party that clings desperately to power. It well knows that serious political reform will result in its collapse. As a result, it flirts with economic reform in the hopes that it will ease Syria's economic crisis. Real change, in the view of these critics, can only be brought about with democracy. That, they advise the U.S. government, will not happen as long as the Ba'ath Party remains in power, regardless of who is in charge (al-Haroub 2005). Whatever the case, real progress toward political and economic reform will inevitably lead to political instability. The only question is how long an oppressive security apparatus can keep the lid on.

## Syrian Politics in the Era of Terror: 2001 and Beyond

This brings us to Syrian politics in the aftermath of the 2001 attacks on the United States and the U.S.'s subsequent war on terror. On the international front, the years immediately following the September 11 attacks found the U.S. seeking Syria as an ally in its war on terror: Bashar al-Assad seemed sincerely interested in reform and Syria's contacts with Hezbollah, Hamas, and other groups accused of terrorism could provide useful information to U.S. intelligence agencies. Syria's long-standing hostility toward Saddam Hussein also suggested the possibility of Syrian support in America's looming war with Iraq. Indeed, as late as the fall of 2002, the Bush administration opposed a congressional bill placing sanctions on Syria. Syrian cooperation against al-Qaeda, the administration noted, had been substantial (*Ha'aretz,* Sept. 19, 2002). This said, tension between the two countries continued to grow over Hezbollah activities on the Israeli border and elsewhere.

The final breaking point came with the U.S.-led war against Iraq. Not only did it not join the U.S. coalition against Iraq, Syria became a vocal opponent of the war (Zisser 2005). Syria's mufti (high religious judge) even called on Muslims to take arms against the United States. It was unthinkable that such a statement could have been made without the support of high officials in Bashar al-Assad's regime.

If the Bush administration had been following the adage "no peace without Syria" before the Iraq war, it now turned that adage on its head. In Washington's view, there could be no peace in the Middle East *with* Syria. The logic was compelling. Syria was a key supporter of Iran, Hezbollah, Hamas, and the Iraqi resistance. With the Ba'athist regime gone, all would find the going rougher. Indeed, with the Ba'athist regime gone in Syria, Iran would be the only country standing in the way of U.S. domination of the region.

The war drums began to beat. The script had already been refined in the run-up to the Iraq war. Syria was accused of sponsoring terror, aspiring for weapons of mass destruction, and aiding the insurgency in Iraq. Congress duly imposed sanctions on Syria, and the administration's rhetoric contained not-so-subtle hints that Syria might be next on Washington's hit list. Like Iraq under Saddam Hussein, Syria was ruled by a minority regime that was despised by the majority. Few Syrians would mourn its passing. That, at least, was the message of the Syrian opposition (Al-Haroub 2005; Al-Miraazi 2003).

Bashar got the message and did his best to seal the Syrian–Iraq border. He also ordered Hezbollah to cool its activities on the Israeli border (Leverett 2005). Overtures of peace with Israel were also renewed. Washington was not listening. It appeared that Washington was looking for a pretext to destroy the Ba'athist regime—a task that would not be easy for an administration sinking ever deeper in the Iraq abyss. By 2004 its thoughts were focused on getting out of Iraq, not on venturing into another disastrous occupation. Cooler heads also pondered what a post-Ba'athist Syria would look like. Would democracy flourish or would the Muslim Brotherhood seize power much as Shi'a religious groups were doing in Iraq? Would the Arab "street" erupt, toppling pro-American regimes in Egypt, Jordan, and Saudi Arabia?

Similar questions weighed on the minds of Syria's policy makers as they plotted their survival strategy. Was the United States serious about overthrowing the regime or was it merely posturing? How much room did they have for maneuvering in the face of U.S. threats? What would it take to appease the United States without losing face in front of an increasingly critical population? Could they count on Arab or European support? Would Russia, once a key ally, come to their aid? Bashar traveled to Moscow in January 2005 and returned with a pledge for advanced weapons. Russia, Syria's major creditor, also wrote off 73 percent of Syria's debt. Were the Russians serious in their commitment to Bashar, or were they merely tweaking the U.S.? Whatever the case, the Russian deal boosted Syrian morale. Iran also reaffirmed its commitment to Syria. The Arabs offered platitudes.

Curiously, it was Syrian miscues in Lebanon that offered Washington the pretext it needed to increase its pressure on an uncertain Bashar regime. Lebanon, for all intents and purposes, had been a Syrian colony since 1976, when Syrian troops entered this most beautiful of countries in order to contain an out-of-control civil war. The Syrian occupation had been made with the tacit agreement of Israel and the United States in an effort to bring order out of the chaos. The end of the civil war in 1989 was based on an agreement that Syrian troops would conduct a phased withdrawal as the Lebanese situation stabilized. Alas, the Syrians didn't withdraw. Syria continued to maintain a large military and intelligence (secret police) presence in Lebanon. The Lebanese conducted democratic elections, but the winners of key positions had to be approved by the Syrians. The constitutionally prescribed term of the pro-Syria president of Lebanon ended in 2004, paving the way for a new presidential election. It was assumed that business would proceed as usual, but it didn't. Rather, anti-Syrian forces made ominous signs of running a pro-independence candidate for the presidency. Damascus responded by announcing that Lebanon's sitting president would serve another term (Harris 2005). Amending the Lebanese constitution would be a minor formality.

The Syrians, however, had miscalculated. Rafiq Hariri, the Lebanese prime minister and the man most responsible for rebuilding Lebanon in the aftermath of the civil war, resigned in protest. He also called for the end of the Syrian occupation and made ominous noises about running for the presidency. Because he was the most powerful man in Lebanon it is likely that he would have succeeded.[4]

That was, until his motorcade dissolved in the flames produced by a massive bomb planted under the pavement in the heart of Beirut.

The United States, already placing intense pressure on the Syrian regime to withdraw from Lebanon, blamed Damascus for the assassination. The French and the UN Security Council followed suit. Syria withdrew its troops in the spring of 2005. The loss of Lebanon was a severe blow to Damascus. The al-Assad regime had been forced to back down in the face of American pressure. Its ability to play the Lebanese card in negotiations with Israel had diminished, as had its control over Hezbollah. They remained allies, but Hezbollah's leaders clearly understood that future Syrian support could be iffy. The economic loss of Lebanon was staggering. Many Syrians—the estimates ranged between 500,000 and over a million—worked in Lebanon, and most of them sent money to their families in Syria. No one really knew for sure how much this amounted to. Also lucrative were the bribes extorted from Lebanese businesses by Syrian military and intelligence personnel. Some estimates place the loss of Lebanon to the Syrian economy at almost $3 billion, some $750 million of which represented bribes and extortions (*Daily Star*, March 22, 2005).

On the domestic front, the unseen battle between Bashar and the old guard moved toward a showdown in the months leading up to the Ba'ath Party congress scheduled for June 2005. Optimists hoped that Bashar would use the occasion to implement the democratic and economic reforms that he had promised upon assuming office. Many still had confidence in Bashar and hoped that U.S. pressure would encourage him to break the grip of the regime barons and launch a new era of democracy and economic growth. Pessimists remained skeptical. The last of the political debating societies had been closed down in 2005 and economic reforms remained timid. Syrians were encouraged to invest, but there had been little movement toward privatizing Syria's moribund public-sector industries. For all intents and purposes, Syria remained a police state run by a corrupt and lethargic bureaucracy (Abdulhamid 2005).

---

4 Lebanon has three presidents: the president of the country, a Christian; the president of the Government (prime minister), a Sunni; and the president of the Assembly, a Shi'a. Hariri not only challenged the Syrians, he also challenged the distribution of religious and ethnic power in Lebanon.

When the congress of the Ba'ath Party finally convened, the results were a mixed bag. In the biggest shake-up in Syrian politics since Hafiz al-Assad seized power in 1970, the old regime barons who had served the father so well for so long were replaced by younger Ba'ath loyalists (Moubayed 2005d). Bashar could no longer blame the lack of reform on the regime barons (Moubayed 2005c). The congress also promised that free and independent political parties would be allowed to form and implied that the security establishment would henceforth be less intrusive in the lives of Syria's citizens. The mechanisms for change had been put in place. And yet, it was not clear that anything had really changed. The Ba'ath remained the official party of Syria and all of the key positions in the country remained in the hands of Ba'athists.

# THE COMPONENTS OF SYRIAN POLITICS: INSTITUTIONS AND ACTORS

The pressing question, of course, is whether Bashar al-Assad can continue to survive the lethal mix of palace intrigues, stalled development, and American and Israeli pressure that threaten his existence (Perthes 2004). Before attempting to speculate on this question, we must take a closer look at Syria's political institutions and the actors who guide those institutions. We shall also examine the broader cultural, economic, and international factors that shape the way that Syrians do politics.

## Elites and Power in Syria

Hafiz al-Assad was the elite in Syria. It was he who made all of the key decisions, and he who appointed candidates to the key positions in the security services, military, government, and the Ba'ath Party (Abdou 1999; Batatu 1999).

Al-Assad's emphasis on loyalty above all else stunted the development of Syria's political institutions. A massive army existed to resist Israel, yet the effectiveness of that army was limited by the need to assure that it did not revolt. The Israelis do not worry about the potential for a military coup, but al-Assad did. Much the same applies to the Ba'ath Party, the bureaucracy, and the National Assembly. Al-Assad wanted political institutions capable of carrying out his nationalistic ambitions, but he was reluctant to give them the power to do so. Not surprisingly, the most effective institutions in Syria during his rule were the security services.

The tension between maintaining strong institutions and ensuring that those institutions would not threaten the president's position resulted in a political system that blended modern organizational structures with the traditional patrimonial networks of the Middle East (Hinnebusch 1990). By totally dominating the power structure, Hafiz al-Assad reduced his subordinates to little more than ciphers (Abdou 1999, 28–29). Now that he has passed from the scene, however, it is his son Bashar who must cope with a legacy of personal rule. The preeminent question in this regard concerns Bashar's personality. Does he possess the strength of character to dominate a political system forged by the iron will of his father? Bashar was trained as an ophthalmologist and speaks both French and English fluently. In 1994, upon the death of his brother, he was called back to Syria from London; at his father's urging, he entered the Syrian military college. He subsequently passed through the ranks, but without the trials by fire that had enabled his father to hone his political skills. Observers in Damascus quipped that Bashar was far too decent to rule Syria.

The ultimate trial by fire is now at hand. The Bush administration has increasingly moved toward the position that the Ba'athists must go, and the opponents of the regime are positioning themselves to pick up the pieces. Some are attempting to curry favor with Washington. Others, such as the Muslim Brotherhood, are keeping their own counsel. The Brotherhood has yet to regain its former strength in Syria, but Islamic sentiments are definitely on the rise.

## The Political Institutions of Syria: Form without Power

On paper, the organizational chart of the Syrian political system is relatively straightforward. Bashar al-Assad, as president of the republic, rules through six basic institutions: the Presidential Security Forces, the military, the Ba'ath Party, the cabinet, the parliament, and the bureaucracy. It is the leaders of these institutions, and particularly the leaders of the security services, the military, and the Ba'ath Party, who, after Bashar al-Assad, constitute the upper echelons of Syria's political elite.

**The Security Forces and the Military**    The Presidential Security Forces consist of at least four separate intelligence organizations, including Political Security, General Intelligence, Military Intelligence, and Air Force Intelligence (Batatu 1999). These are followed in order of importance by the Republican Guard, an elite military force some 10,000 strong. The Republican Guard is supported by the Special Forces and other elite units in the military, albeit with a command structure that precludes any one unit from dominating the others. These military units, in turn, are kept in check by party militias and intelligence organizations (Perthes 1997). Everyone is watching everyone else. They are also watching the Syrian population.

The pervasiveness of Syrian intelligence is illustrated by the story of a Syrian entrepreneur who, upon acquiring substantial wealth working in the Gulf, returned home to open a shoe factory. Rather than welcoming his investment, government agencies at all levels—including two intelligence agencies—became suspicious of his activities.

Why such concern with a man opening a simple shoe factory in a country suffering from staggering unemployment? What could they possibly want to know? The answer was "everything." How much money did he have? Was he a fundamentalist? Did he have ties to the United States or intelligence agencies in the Gulf? Whom did he plan to hire? What was their background? Economics is important, but not as important as politics.

Command of the Presidential Security Forces rests firmly in the hands of the Alawites, most of whom have been drawn from al-Assad's clan. It is they, often referred to as "regime barons," who constituted the inner core of the al-Assad regime. Of the thirty-one highest-ranking officers in Syria at the time of Hafiz al-Assad's death, nineteen were Alawites, and of these, twelve were related to al-Assad by either blood or marriage (Batatu 1999). Also part of the inner circle were two Sunni officers, Mustafa Talass and Farouk Shara'a, who served as the minister of defense and minister of foreign affairs, respectively. Both possessed a record of loyalty to Hafiz al-Assad dating back to the origins of the Ba'ath Party. The presence of these Sunni officers at the top of the elite structure softened the image of Alawite dominance and strengthened alliances with the Sunni community.

It was the most powerful regime barons who paved the way for Bashar al-Assad to assume the presidency in the uncertain days following his father's death. It was not a matter of convenience, nor of loyalty. Too much was at stake to risk a civil war that would, in all probability, have seen the Alawite barons overwhelmed by the Sunni majority. It was also a business decision. As Perthes notes, the regime barons had much in common with the Mafia.

> There is no doubt that the security apparatus accounts for much petty and grand corruption and other illegal business in the country. Most of the military and security bosses have become patrons of and partners in private business, or have taken commissions on contracts between the state and international suppliers. Smuggling has, to a large extent, been in the hands of the military, and has been enormously facilitated by the presence of the Syrian army in Lebanon. . . . (Perthes 1997, 149–50).

The result was that Bashar could reign while the barons sorted things out behind the scenes. The stage was thus set for a struggle between regime barons attempting to strengthen and expand their personal fiefdoms—often at each other's expense—and a young and inexperienced Bashar al-Assad attempting to consolidate his power by placing his own people in power. One of Bashar's first moves, for example, was to replace the minister of interior, the head of the state intelligence services, with a relative more to his liking. The new appointee, in turn, fell by the wayside in the purges of 2005. Cabinet reshuffles have been frequent, as have shifts in key provincial positions.

Needless to say, the members of the security forces are well cared for. Their salaries, housing, automobiles, and medical services all surpass those available to the average government employee. Opportunities for corruption abound. People entering Syria from Lebanon, for example, routinely tuck a bribe into their passport or identity papers when presenting them to customs officials. Those too naïve to do so find themselves waiting in line for several hours. Little gets done in Syria without a bribe of some sort.

Next in the hierarchy of power comes the Syrian military itself, a formidable force that, with the inclusion of the various security services, has some 400,000 members. This figure, according to Perthes, constitutes 15 percent of the Syrian workforce and approximately 40 percent of all government employees (Perthes 1997).

Military training is obligatory in secondary schools and universities, and the Ba'ath Party also maintains several militias. Alawites dominate the command structure, having headed seven of Syria's nine regular army divisions during the 1990s (Batatu 1999). Sunnis, as Drysdale and Hinnebusch note, are also well represented in the officer corps, albeit in less sensitive positions. Most are longtime Ba'athists and their presence gives at least part of the Sunni community a stake in the regime.

**The Ba'ath Party**    The Ba'ath Party probably ranks third in the power hierarchy, although this is a matter of some debate. As noted earlier in this chapter, the Ba'ath Party emerged in the post–World War II era as an amalgam of diverse Marxist and Arab nationalist currents. Today the Ba'ath Party consists of two separate organizations: the Regional (Syrian) Command and the National (Arab) Command. The National Command represents the Ba'ath Party's aspirations to be an "all-Arab" party, but it enjoys little real power.

The Regional (Syrian) Command, by contrast, is the center of political power in Syria; it is headed by Bashar al-Assad and includes senior members of the cabinet and the military. The Regional Command is followed in the Syrian hierarchy by the Central Committee, which brings together the heads of the nineteen branches of the party. It is they who manage local affairs in Syria. The military wing of the party is also well represented on the Central Committee.

The members of the Ba'ath Party's Regional Command are powerful individuals who are very much part of Syria's ruling elite. Indeed, there is a high degree of overlap between the president's inner circle and the Regional Command. Lower-level Ba'athist officials also control a great deal of patronage and clearly stand on the second rung of the elite hierarchy. Most are also Alawites (van Dam 1996, 123).

Ba'athist ideology provides the foundation of the regime's claim to legitimacy. Hafiz al-Assad justified his policies in terms of Ba'athist doctrine and cloaked himself in Ba'athist symbols of nationalism and socialism. His son is now doing the same, although socialist slogans now compete with talk of "balanced capitalism." The former reassure the poor that the regime has not deserted them, while the latter offers hope to a burgeoning capitalist class. How this plays out in the hearts and minds of the Syrian people is difficult to assess. Everyone applauds, but rumblings suggest that party diehards are not pleased with the shift to capitalism, muted though it has been.

The Ba'ath Party also serves as the regime's link with the Syrian population and particularly with its traditional base of support among the minorities, peasants, workers, bureaucrats, and soldiers. To strengthen this connection, the party maintains cells and branches in all villages, urban residential quarters, and factories. Labor unions, student groups, and professional associations are also tied to the party, as are youth and feminist organizations. Syrian children between the ages of six and eleven are required to join the Ba'ath Party's Vanguard Organization, while children between twelve and eighteen years of age have the option of joining the Union of Revolutionary Youth. Membership in the Union of Revolutionary Youth is not compulsory but it does bring certain privileges. Student unions at Syria's universities are also under party control, and faculty appointments must be cleared by party officials. Very little happens in Syria that is not controlled by the Ba'ath Party.

Most members of the party originally came from the ranks of minorities and lower-class Sunnis, and it is they, many of whom are now members of a middle class consisting largely of bureaucrats, who provide most of the regime's popular support. Members of the Ba'ath Party enjoy secure jobs and ample opportunities for corruption, but they have not been noted for their ideological zeal. Rather, the rank and file of the Ba'ath Party displays the same opportunism and lack of enthusiasm that characterizes the government bureaucracy.

Party documents reviewed by van Dam attribute the lack of ideological zeal among party cadres to two basic causes. First, the rush to rebuild the mass base of the party in the hectic days following the breakup of the union with Egypt resulted in the recruitment of individuals motivated more by self-interest than by commitment to party principles. Second, each faction within the party attempted to strengthen its position by recruiting as many relatives and co-religionists as possible. Opportunism led to corruption, and family and religious networking to nepotism and fragmentation. There is little evidence that these problems have diminished (Quilliam 1999).

Adding to the lack of ideological zeal was Hafiz al-Assad's transformation of the Ba'ath Party from a narrow-based party that stressed the commitment of its cadres to a mass-based party whose membership grew from approximately 65,000 in 1971 to more than a million twenty years later. The later figure, as Batatu notes, "constituted no less than 14.5 percent of all Syrians aged 14 and above" (Batatu 1999, 177). Of these, approximately one-fourth were females.

Whatever their shortcomings, the members of the Ba'ath Party are effusive in their support of Bashar al-Assad. Meetings of the Ba'ath Party are routinely televised, and at each mention of Bashar's name a cheering section jumps to its feet and chants, "Assad, Assad, Assad." A lack of enthusiasm can be dangerous in the macabre world of Syrian politics. What would happen if people said what they really felt?

Far more important in the grand scheme of things is the party's role within the regime's pervasive security apparatus. The Ba'ath Party maintains its own militias, and its local branches extend the regime's presence to the far reaches of the country. The party also scrutinizes applications for all government jobs of any importance, including military officers, bureaucrats, teachers, journalists, and diplomats. It is difficult to find a responsible official in Syria who is not a member of the party.

Finally, the various Ba'athist organizations are charged with indoctrinating new generations of Syrians in Ba'athist ideology. Ba'athism is preached at youth meetings and in the schools, and it is standard fare on Syrian television. Party censors also ensure that both the educational system and the mass media remain free of adverse influences. As in most areas of the Middle East, the advent of satellites and the Internet has made censorship more difficult. Bashar himself has nevertheless championed the Internet in an effort to boost Syrian productivity. But the opportunistic and survival-oriented nature of the Ba'ath Party makes it a profound obstacle to political reform. Indeed, fair elections would destroy the party as it is presently constituted.

**The People's Assembly and the Cabinet**    Below the Ba'ath Party in the power hierarchy lie the formal institutions of the Syrian state: the parliament or People's Assembly, the cabinet, and the bureaucracy. The Assembly is an elected body of 250 members dominated by the Ba'ath Party, which approves in advance all candidates for election.

Members of the Assembly belong to one of three groups: the Ba'ath Party, other members of the Progressive National Front, or independents. The Progressive National Front (PNF) was created by the Ba'ath in 1972 and consists of the Ba'ath Party and several other leftist parties including the Syrian Communist Party, the Arab Socialist Union (the remnant of the Nasserites), and several socialist groups that had splintered from the Ba'ath. The purpose of the PNF is to reduce opposition to the regime by providing other "progressive" parties with a piece of the action. Much like the members of labor unions and professional organizations, PNF members have traded their political independence for access to patronage. The government views groups outside the PNF with suspicion, much of which is probably justified.

While making no pretense at being democratic, the People's Assembly does provide key groups in Syrian society with access to government patronage. It also has played an increasingly important role in resolving conflict among competing social factions. These conflicts include both traditional communal rivalries and tensions between the public and private sectors.

As in most parliamentary arrangements, the People's Assembly is headed by a prime minister and cabinet who manage the day-to-day affairs of the government. The Government, meaning the prime minister and the cabinet, is dominated by the Ba'ath Party, and its senior members belong to the political elite. It is the president, not the prime minister, who hand-picks the ministers. This was the procedure under Hafiz al-Assad and continues to be the case under Bashar al-Assad. Bashar has given a greater role in the cabinet to the technocrats (people with technical training) than his father did, but the regime barons remain very much in evidence.

The cabinet also manages a sprawling bureaucracy that has traditionally been used to provide the regime's supporters with jobs and opportunities for corruption. Efficiency has thus been sacrificed to politics, and the bureaucracy does little to either promote economic development or build confidence in the government. The shift to capitalism has led to some restrictions on the bureaucracy, but it continues to be used as a dumping ground for the regime's supporters. This alone makes it impervious to serious reform. Overregulation and corruption, needless to say, have slowed Syria's halting transition to capitalism. The two go together, for bribes are required to circumvent regulations.

**Clientelism and Politics in Syria**    Political power in Syria, then, is wielded through a two-stage process. Patriarchal ties (kinship, religious/ethnic loyalties, and friendship) are used to control the institutions of the state, and the political institutions of the state are used to control the population. The key link in this process is the patron–client relationship. Hafiz al-Assad was the supreme patron, and all of the major actors in the Syrian political system were his clients. They all depended upon him for their positions, and their survival was linked to his survival. This does not mean that al-Assad's supporters lacked talent. Many were extremely skilled. Loyalty to al-Assad, however, took precedence over merit. Skill is reasonably abundant in Syria; loyalty is not. It was this network that orchestrated Bashar's meteoric rise to the presidency of Syria, and it is its members who are being retired as Bashar consolidates his own network of clients.

Each leader's clients, in turn, serve as patron for their own network of supporters based upon kinship, religious/ethnic, and friendship ties, a process that replicates itself throughout the diverse levels of the governmental, military, and party apparatuses.

The networks are solidified by *wasta* (influence or connections) and corruption. Corruption is the glue that holds the regime together by giving all of the regime's disparate parts a payoff for playing along. Force alone cannot achieve this objective.

It is possible to move up within the Syrian political hierarchy on the basis of merit, but the higher the place in the hierarchy, the greater becomes the need for the support of a powerful patron. Talent is important, but it is difficult for one to go far on the basis of merit alone. This blend of patrimonial and institutional authority provided Hafiz al-Assad with a monopoly of coercive force. Corruption and clientelism were the keynotes of the al-Assad regime for thirty years, but force was its ultimate guarantor. The situation remains so under the presidency of Bashar al-Assad, despite weak efforts to liberalize the regime.

**Civil Society in Syria**    The Syrian way of doing politics leaves little room for the independent expression of political views. There are no truly independent political parties in Syria. The press is stifled and public rallies that lack prior clearance are crushed by the police. All professional and social groups, including labor unions, student organizations, and professional associations, are controlled by the party. All are given an economic stake in the system in return for their political docility. Peasants are provided with cheap loans and assistance in marketing their products (at government regulated prices), workers receive a guaranteed wage (in government factories), professional associations set their standards in cooperation with the government, students are promised jobs in the bureaucracy. All have councils that allow them to discuss their special needs with the political leadership. Although social and professional groups do express their views to the political leadership, it is the latter that does most of the talking. The diverse social and economic councils help the regime keep in touch with the pulse of Syrian society. They are also expected to maintain control of their members.

Efforts to reach an accommodation with Syria's business elite has been more tricky. Capitalism was resurrected during the 1980s in an effort to resuscitate the Syrian economy, which was on the verge of bankruptcy. Capitalism, however, required a greater freedom of movement and communication than the government was willing to grant. It also meant that groups hostile to socialism would acquire inordinate wealth as well as the power to control their workers (Robinson 1998). The solution was twofold. First, capitalists willing to support the regime were allowed to prosper—if they made kickbacks to key officials (Quilliam 1999). Both sides, the political elite and the capitalists, prospered. Secondly, the political leadership began to slip quietly into the capitalist class. Political leaders invested in capitalist firms and used their influence to overrule bureaucratic obstructionism and assure that those firms prospered. Marriage alliances between the political elite and the capitalist class also became frequent. Arranged marriages are common in the Middle East and have traditionally been used to cement power and economic relationships. Bashar al-Assad, it will be recalled, married the daughter of a wealthy Sunni merchant.

The Damascus Spring, as Bashar's early reforms were referred to, promised a vibrant civil society in Syria (Cahen 2002). Hope continues, but Syria remains an authoritarian state. Whether that will change with growing domestic and international pressure remains to be seen. Western accusations that Syria killed Lebanese prime minister Rafiq Hariri have brought promises of greater political freedom, but the results have been meager.

**The Opposition**    The most visible opposition to the al-Assad regime, past and present, comes from the Muslim Brotherhood. The Brotherhood was not destroyed by the Hama massacre of 1982, but its leaders were forced to flee and the organization was driven underground. The leaders of the moderate faction fled—one faction to Germany and Jordan, while the leaders of the radical faction fled to Baghdad. In spite of its suppression, the Brotherhood maintains a network of secret cells in the predominantly Sunni areas of the country.

The Jordanian branch of the Syrian Brotherhood attempted to patch up its differences with Hafiz al-Assad's regime, proposing to become a member of the National Patriotic Front in return for the opportunity to retain a legal presence in Syria (Al-Qaisi 1999). Hafiz al-Assad was not interested, but said that he would consider the issue if the Brotherhood accepted the blame for the 1982 massacre (Al-Baiya'nooni 2001). The Brotherhood refused. The Brotherhood has again tested the waters by proposing that Bashar al-Assad call a "national conference" of all political groups in Syria (Al-Jazeera, April 3, 2005).

Bashar, like his father, has expressed little enthusiasm for rapprochement with the Brotherhood, but leaders of the moderate branch of the Syrian Brotherhood have been allowed to return to the country (Moubayed 2005d). Bashar, also like his father, cannot ignore the growing signs of an Islamic revival in Syria. These signs appeared in the later days of his father's rule and have mushroomed with the U.S.-led occupation of Iraq—so much so that the United States accused Syria of being a staging ground for the Sunni insurgents. Efforts are being made to close Syria's long and porous border with Iraq, but that is not an easy task. Saudi Arabia and Jordan are also attempting to prevent radical Islamic groups from infiltrating men and weapons into Syria. The Syrian Brotherhood says that it has renounced violence and merely wants to build a strong and united Syria that is capable of withstanding U.S. pressure. Whether or not this is the case, the Muslim Brotherhood is not the only fundamentalist group with an interest in Syrian politics. Jihadist groups sympathetic to al-Qaeda have emerged in Syria to support the jihad in Iraq.

Other traditional opponents of the Ba'ath Party have been "bought off" by the corruption and clientelism discussed earlier. This list would certainly include both the leftists and a large segment of the Sunni business elite. Appearances of tranquillity, however, are often deceiving. The Sunni remain restive under Alawite rule, and the National Patriotic Front is a marriage of convenience that could fall apart at the first sign of weakness. The alliance between the regime and Syria's business elite also remains tenuous. While working with the regime has its advantages, many capitalists believe that they could do much better in a free-market environment. Even the Alawites are divided among themselves. All groups, including various factions within the military and the security services, have been jockeying for position should the Ba'athist regime crumble under U.S. pressure. An apparent tranquillity born of fear and accommodation could well be the calm that precedes the storm.

Syria's external opposition groups, long of little importance, have gained new relevance as U.S. pressure on Syria mounts. Many, such as the umbrella Syrian Democratic Opposition Alliance, are headquartered in Washington (Al-Miraazi, 2003). Others are located in London or Paris. Cooperation among the opposition groups is minimal, but most have expressed a strong interest in being funded by the United States. Whether they have a base of support in Syria remains an open question (Al-Miraazi 2003). Syria's some two million Kurds have demanded greater freedoms, and tensions have erupted in demonstrations in the Kurdish areas adjoining the Kurdish areas of Iraq. Attempts to form a Kurdish party brought severe warnings from the regime (Al-Jazeera, June 27, 2004). The Kurds are not in a position to challenge the regime, but they do pose one more problem for an overburdened president.

## THE CONTEXT OF SYRIAN POLITICS

The keys to both Hafiz al-Assad's longevity and Bashar's future are to be found within the broader cultural, economic, and international context of Syrian society. The father was remarkably successful in manipulating each to his own ends; to survive, the son must do likewise.

### Political Culture

Cultural considerations permeate all dimensions of the Syrian political process. Of these, the most pressing dimension of Syrian political culture is the revival of long-suppressed Islamic fervor. The Muslim Brotherhood may be under wraps, but Syria is experiencing a fundamentalist revival. Why? Three explanations are widely cited. First, nationalism and socialism as preached by the Ba'ath are bankrupt. Despair is the norm, and for many Syrians, God is the answer. A closely related explanation is that the Islamic movement in its various aspects represents the only viable opposition to a corrupt and oppressive Ba'athist regime. At the very least, Islamic dress and related symbols allow Syrians to express their alienation from the regime. The third answer is that the Ba'athist regime has attempted to encourage a moderate form of Islamic expression as a counterweight to extremist groups. This by itself is an admission that efforts to transform Syria into a secular society have failed (Hamidi 2005). The process began in earnest during the 1990s, and Syria now boasts over 80,000 new mosques, not to mention the Assad Institute for Memorizing the Koran and some twenty-two Islamic institutions of higher learning. This does not mean that Syria's citizens are in a rush to join extremist Islamic groups, but the potential for a politicized Islam is in place if the government fails to improve the lot of the Syrian populace.

The influence of culture on Syrian politics is also to be seen in the strength of the kinship and sectarian ties that provided the foundation of al-Assad's patrimonial rule. Syria continues to resemble a mosaic of confessional and kinship groups more than it does an integrated political community. Each group is jealous of the others, and distrust between groups is pervasive. This profound sense of distrust and fear has been heightened by the regime's skill at playing one group against another (Nehme 2003). It has been further heightened by uncertainties surrounding the future of the Ba'athist regime.

Fear and distrust are also pervasive among individuals. The effectiveness of the regime's security services has made discretion a virtue and no one is quite sure of whom he or she can trust, a principle that applies to members of the security services as well. One should not equate Syria with the totalitarianism of Stalinist Russia, but few Syrians have been willing to express opposition to the regime in public. This has begun to change in the Bashar era, but when Syrians discuss the security services, they do so in hushed tones.

Fear and distrust, in turn, have reinforced well-established tendencies to classify others as "we" or "they." People are not neutral. They are either potential friends or potential enemies (Abdou 1999). In addition to further fragmenting Syrian society, this trend also strengthens the influence of the patron–client networks discussed earlier.

Weeden (1998) elaborates on this theme, suggesting that regimented pressures to sing the leader's praises creates an aura of complicity. How can you trust individuals who have openly praised the regime in an effort to feather their own nest or deflect the attention of the *mukhabarat* (secret services)?

Beyond fear and distrust, perhaps the dominant characteristics of Syrian political culture have been apathy and opportunism. Revolt has become futile and, aside from the Muslim Brotherhood, one sees few overt signs of opposition to the regime. At the same time, one also sees few signs of psychological commitment to the regime. Rather, most people bend to its carrot-and-stick policies, accepting the corruption and patronage offered, but giving little in return. The most important goal is survival. As American threats have called the future of the regime into question, some Syrians are taking sides, but most are reluctant to place their bets until the picture has clarified. All are watching the situation in Iraq very closely.

## Political Economy

Political economists, as one might suspect, find Syrian politics to be a function of economics. Their argument begins with the observation that the Ba'ath Party was supported by Syria's disadvantaged classes, notably minorities and the Sunni poor. With the Ba'ath Party's assumption of power, a socialist economic system shifted wealth and power from Syria's landed and commercial classes and redistributed it to the workers and peasants. It was they who supported the regime.

Interestingly enough, the greatest beneficiaries of Ba'athist rule were Syria's landed peasants, not the sharecroppers who lived on the margins of subsistence. It was the more prosperous peasants who became a new administrative middle class of bureaucrats, military officers, and party officials, all of whom depended upon the largesse of the state and the accompanying opportunities for corruption. It was also they who had a vested economic interest in keeping the regime in power. Batatu (1999) attributes this to the greater access of this class to educational opportunities, an advantage denied to the poorer Syrian peasants. All peasants, however, have benefited from Ba'athist rule, with illiteracy being reduced to some 12 percent of the male population and some 39 percent of the female. The life of the poor remains very difficult (George 2003).

Socialism has proved to be profoundly inefficient. Workers in Syria's large public corporations display a profound lethargy. Wages are low, incentives few, and promotions a function of longevity—hardly a formula for a bustling economy. An average Syrian bureaucrat, for example, earns about $106 per month (*Daily Star,* May 25, 2001). Commentators speak openly of the "sickness of time" that besets the Syrian public sector and the need to liberate it from bureaucratic rigidities. Hafiz al-Assad himself spoke of the need for Syrians at all levels to get more involved in their country and shoulder their share of responsibility (*Al-Hawadeth,* March 23, 2000, 30). It was this lack of drive among public-sector workers that forced the regime to experiment with capitalist reforms. Unemployment is now estimated to be in the 20–25 percent range and is presumably higher since the Syrian withdrawal from Lebanon (U.S. Department of State 2004).

The lethargy of the Syrian public sector does more than repress economic growth. As Lawson (1996) notes, periods of economic downturn in Syria have been accompanied by social unrest. If Bashar al-Assad's regime is to survive, it has little choice but to revamp the Syrian economy. But how? Socialism is enshrined in Ba'athist ideology, and the growing influence of the capitalist sector poses a threat to the entrenched positions of both the state and party bureaucracies. The regime also understands that dismantling its large public-sector industries will result in spiraling unemployment and more civil unrest.

As a result, the Bashar regime continues to pursue capitalist reforms in a steady but haphazard manner. Syria's capitalists have prospered to the extent that some observers believe that the capitalists have surpassed the Ba'athists in Syria's elite hierarchy (Robinson 1998). This transition is evidenced by the tendency of the sons of Ba'athist leaders to become capitalist businessmen rather than military officers. The United States is not impressed and notes with derision that "privatization is not even on the distant horizon" (U.S. Department of State 2004, 7). Even Syria's deputy prime minister noted that the country's private sector was more interested in establishing monopolies than in promoting free trade (*Daily Star,* Oct. 19, 2005).

Also from a political economic perspective, it is interesting to note that a strong tie has traditionally existed between the smaller Sunni merchants and the Muslim Brotherhood, a connection that exists throughout the Middle East. In the years leading up to the 1982 Hama massacre, much of the financing for the Brotherhood presumably came from the middle class, and Brotherhood violence was supported by merchant strikes throughout the north of Syria. Had the Damascene merchants joined the uprising rather than remaining passive, its results might well have been different. They did not. Syria's capitalists, like most other groups in Syria, find it difficult to speak with a single voice. Smaller merchants have benefited far less from the regime's shift to capitalism than have the larger capitalists. The small merchants also face increased competition from the large capitalists and fear that the globalization of the Syrian economy will work to their disadvantage. They want economic freedom, but not competition.

## Domestic Politics and the International Environment

If Syrian politics is the product of the cultural and economic factors discussed above, it also reflects Syria's tumultuous international environment. The evolution of Syrian politics outlined earlier in the chapter was largely a chronicle of Syria's conflict with its regional neighbors, both sister Arab states and Israel. Regional issues, in turn, were largely inseparable from the larger issues of the Cold War and, upon the demise of the Soviet Union, the advent of American hegemony. In many ways, it was these international pressures that forced Hafiz al-Assad to pursue the policies that he did. The conflict with Israel, in particular, forced Syria to spend its limited resources on defense rather than economic development. While the military developed, the Syrian economy did not. Then a changing world environment forced al-Assad to enter peace negotiations with Israel under conditions that favored the latter, just as it forced liberalization of the Syrian economy.

These same international factors help to explain al-Assad's longevity in office. Al-Assad's defiance of Israel added a measure of popular support to a regime otherwise lacking in charismatic qualities. The Soviet Union provided al-Assad with both economic and military support until its collapse in 1991 (Karsh 1991). It also protected him from Israeli attack. No sooner had the Cold War ended, moreover, than Syria reaped a $3 billion windfall by siding with the United Nations in the Gulf War of 1991; much of this aid came from Saudi Arabia and the Gulf countries (Robinson 1998).

The world, however, has changed. In the United States, the Bush administration rejects the proposition that there can be no peace without Syria and appears to be plotting the overthrow of the Ba'athist regime (de la Gorce 2004; Derhally 2005). The Israelis are encouraging such a move much as they encouraged the overthrow of Saddam Hussein. Russia has retained its ties with Syria, but is no longer in a position to challenge a determined U.S. administration. The European Union frets, but is too divided to block U.S. intervention in the region; this is even more true of the Arab states. Iran and Syria have rushed to sign a mutual defense pact, but to what avail? (*Guardian,* Feb. 17, 2005). Iran has its own problems with the United States. The best it could do would be to "encourage" Hezbollah to join the resistance against a U.S. invasion in the hopes of creating a replay of Iraq. Indeed, the best hope Bashar al-Assad's regime has of dodging U.S. pressure may well be the inability of the United States to extract itself from its disastrous occupation of Iraq. The deeper the U.S. sinks in the Iraqi swamp, so the logic goes, the less likely it is to embark on a Syrian adventure. The Iraqi situation should also give the U.S. pause to reflect on who will rule Syria if Bashar falters. It could well be the Brotherhood or worse.

## LOOKING TOWARD THE FUTURE

All things considered, the future of Bashar al-Assad's regime seems to hinge on several key issues. First, can Bashar assert his authority over the regime barons that played such an instrumental role in placing him in power? He seems to be making progress, but the jury is still out. Second, can Bashar pursue economic and democratic reforms with sufficient dispatch to meet the demands of an expanding and increasingly restless population? If not, domestic opposition groups, and the Muslim Brotherhood in particular, will increase their base of popular support. Both concerns will be moot if the United States decides to overthrow the al-Assad regime by one means or another.

# Saudi Arabia
## Modernizing a Tribal Monarchy

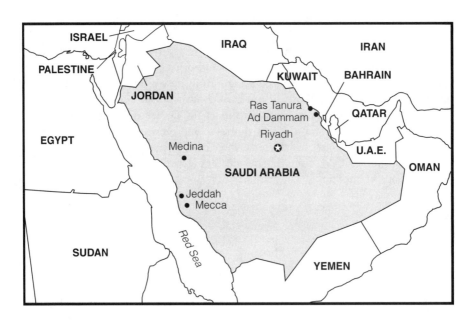

S audi Arabia, like so many of its neighbors, is a nation of paradoxes. Great wealth has brought the veneer of modernity, yet the country remains a tribal monarchy that bears the name of its ruling family. Saudi citizens are among the most pampered in the world, yet they enjoy few political rights. The Saudi monarchy prides itself on being the protector of the Islamic faith, yet it has become a prime target of the jihadist terror that is shaking the region. Saudi Arabia has built a dazzling network of universities to train its population, yet most of what gets done in Saudi Arabia is done by foreigners. Indeed, more than one-fourth of the Saudi population consists of foreigners. Saudi Arabia spends more on arms than any other state in the region, yet must rely on the United States for protection from its enemies.

These paradoxes suggest that Saudi Arabia may be less secure than its placid exterior suggests. The United States and its First World allies are worried. It could not be otherwise, for Saudi Arabia is the world's leading producer of crude oil and possesses approximately 25 percent of the world's proven oil reserves. Deposits of natural gas are almost as large. Saudi Arabia, moreover, is the dominant member of the Organization of Petroleum Exporting Countries (OPEC), a cartel designed to ensure that its members receive the highest possible price for their oil. What happens in Saudi Arabia does matter to the rest of the world.

By and large, "the kingdom," as Saudi Arabia is referred to in the Middle East, has used its phenomenal oil wealth to promote stability and moderation in the region. These conditions would not prevail if the kingdom's vast oil and financial resources were to fall under the sway of a less friendly regime. Indeed, even minor threats to the Saudi regime destabilize world oil markets.

The objectives of the present chapter are to examine the evolution of Saudi politics since World War II and to assess the challenges that face the Saudi regime in the coming decade. Toward this end, we will focus on four critical elements of the Saudi political equation: kinship/tribalism, religion, oil, and the royal family's special relationship with the United States. These four factors have been the pillars of Saudi stability since the end of World War II, yet each is showing signs of strain. As always, it's best to begin at the beginning.

## HISTORY AND CULTURE

The defining historical event in the history of the Arabian Peninsula was the birth of Islam in AD 610. Prior to the advent of Islam, the history of the Arabian Peninsula was largely that of the bedouin tribes that roamed its barren terrain in search of pasture and water. The struggle for survival pitted tribe against tribe, and raiding was the norm (Smith 1903; Vassiliev 1998). Nevertheless, Arabic culture flourished, and a few weeks each year were set aside for contests of horsemanship and poetry reading. The poets recorded historic feats of love and conquest, and spared no effort to extol the tribal virtues of independence, loyalty, courage, and personal honor. When the Saudis speak of tribal virtues, it is to these characteristics to which they refer.

In the days of antiquity a large meteor had fallen in the area that is now Mecca; the tribes of the region attributed the event to divine intervention. The meteor was eventually enshrined in a cube-shaped temple, the Kaaba, and became the focal point of annual religious pilgrimages, safe passage to which was guaranteed by custom (Armajani 1970). Over time, the tribe of Quraysh gained control of the region and its leaders assumed responsibility for providing food, water, and shelter to the pilgrims. They also constructed the city of Mecca around the Kaaba and transformed it into a major trading center linking the caravan routes from the Red Sea, Iraq, Syria, and Yemen.

The Prophet Mohammed was born into the Hashemite clan of the tribe of Quraysh. The birth of Islam further enhanced the importance of the Kaaba by requiring all Muslims to make a pilgrimage to the holy shrine. The Saudi monarchy, as the shrine's latest guardian, continues to provide for the needs of the pilgrims, a mammoth feat that involves caring for some two million pilgrims during the annual *hajj*.

The Quraysh, as the tribe of the Prophet Mohammed and the protector of the holy shrines, enjoyed a special position in the eyes of Muslims. This was especially the case for the Hashemite clan, the members of which could claim direct lineage to the Prophet. With the passing of the Prophet Mohammed and the orthodox caliphs, the Arabian Peninsula fell under the sway of successive Islamic dynasties, beginning with the Umayyads (Syrians) and ending with the Ottomans. Aside from maintaining a presence in Mecca, few caliphs had an interest in the barren and hostile wastelands of the Arabian Peninsula, and the region reverted to its old ways of tribal conflict. Islamic practice also became lax, and Hadith (sayings of the Prophet) were manufactured to justify the needs of the moment.

From the Saudi perspective, the next major event in the history of the Arabian Peninsula was the consolidation of Saudi control over Ad-Diriyah, an oasis town near the present city of Riyadh, in the early 1700s. While most tribes of the era were nomadic, some had settled around the region's oases and had become sedentary farmers (Vassiliev 1998).

The Saudis were oasis-dwellers; Saud ibn Mohammed, the founder of the Saudi dynasty, seized control of the oasis of Ad-Diriyah in 1710 (Vassiliev 1998). The Saudis soon conquered the neighboring tribes and became the dominant power within the Najd, the east-central region of the Arabian Peninsula. If they had remained only a tribal power, this probably would have been the extent of the Saudi empire. In 1714, however, Saud added a religious component to his tribal authority by forging an alliance with Mohammed ibn Abd al-Wahhab, a charismatic religious leader with a broad following throughout the region.

Abd al-Wahhab's teachings condemned the mystical beliefs that had infiltrated Islamic theology, not the least of which were those of the Shi'a. The practice of Islam, Abd al-Wahhab preached, must be based on the Koran and the Sunna, and nothing more (De Corancez 1995). In modern parlance, Abd al-Wahhab was a "strict constructionist," whose emphasis on the "fundamentals" of Islam make him a forerunner of the fundamentalist movement that is now shaking the Middle East (Al-Freih 1995).

Much as in Mohammed's time, tribal armies fired by the spirit of Islam and the lure of booty conquered much of modern Saudi Arabia, including the holy cities of Mecca and Medina, a feat that was accomplished in 1803 (De Corancez 1995). Alas, it was not to last. Family conflicts and the corruption of power sapped the strength of the Saudis and they were put to flight by the Shammar tribe in 1891 (Anscombe 1997). Granted asylum by the sheikh of Kuwait, the once-proud rulers of the Najd became refugees dependent upon the largesse of their hosts. The Turks had also sided with the Shammar in an effort to reassert their suzerainty over the Najd.

The story of modern Saudi Arabia begins in 1901 when Prince Abd al-Aziz al-Saud (a direct descendant of the founder of the Saudi dynasty), generally referred to as Abd al-Aziz or ibn Saud, rallied a handful of supporters (the number ranges from thirty to a hundred, depending upon the source), and descended by night upon the fort guarding Riyadh. The governor was killed and the population, rebelling from the oppression of the Shammar tribe, rose in support of the Saudis. By 1902, ibn Saud was master of Riyadh and the surrounding area. Upon the resignation of his father, he was proclaimed king. By 1904 the Saudis were again in control of all of the Najd, and by 1913 they had extended their authority to the neighboring province of al-Hasa, now the Eastern Province of Saudi Arabia. Abd al-Aziz's conquests again featured an alliance with Abd al-Wahhab's successors and followers, a group referred to as the Wahhabis, the tribal forces of the former being inspired by the religious zeal of the latter.

The real prize for both the Saudis and the Wahhabis, however, remained the Hijaz and its holy cities of Mecca and Medina. For the Saudis, the conquest of the Hijaz promised unchallenged control of the Arabian Peninsula and the prestige and power that accrued to the protector of Islam's holiest shrines. For the Wahhabis, control of the holy cities offered the opportunity to extend their puritanical doctrine far beyond the sandy wastes of the Najd and to bring an end to the moral laxity of the Hijaz, which they attributed to the Hashemites, the traditional custodians of the shrine.

Attacking the Hijaz, however, would not be easy. The outbreak of World War I had seen the British induce Sharif Hussein, the Hashemite governor of Mecca and a direct descendant of the Prophet, to revolt against the Turks with promises of an Arab kingdom that included most of Greater Syria. The tribal armies of Abd al-Aziz would be no match for those of a unified Hashemite kingdom supported by the British.

The Ottomans were defeated, but the promised Arab kingdom did not materialize. Far worse, in 1916 the British had signed a treaty with Abd al-Aziz recognizing his control of the Najd and al-Hasa (Al-Angari 1997). Though they did not become a British protectorate, the Saudis received a small stipend from London and agreed to respect British interests in the Persian Gulf. In the early 1920s Britain patched up its relations with Sharif Hussein by installing one of his sons as the king of Iraq and another as the emir of Transjordan, a newly created ministate designed to serve as a buffer between the British mandate of Palestine, recently proclaimed a "national home for the Jews," and its Arab neighbors. The new mini-state had the additional advantage of keeping the disputed region out of the hands of the French.

Abd al-Aziz had reclaimed the Saudi kingdom of old, but it was a poor kingdom with little room for expansion. Rebellions were frequent, and perpetual raiding among tribes threatened to splinter the kingdom into warring factions. Also of concern to the young king was the Ikhwan (brotherhood) movement, which was born in 1912. The Ikhwan began as a group of religious zealots dedicated to reasserting the austere Wahhabi doctrine among the tribes of the Najd, whose remote and migratory nature made religious conformity difficult. As Robert Lacy describes these Wahhabi zealots:

> The Prophet condemned personal ostentation, so the Ikhwan shunned silk, gold, jewelry and ornaments, including the gold thread traditionally woven round the dark bhisht or mishlah, the outer robe—and they also cut their robes short above the ankles. This was because the Prophet had declared clothes that brushed the ground to be an affectation, and the same went for luxuriant moustaches. So the Ikhwan clipped the hair on their upper lip to a mere shadow of stubbiness—while adopting a different rule for hair on the chin. In this case, they argued, it would be affectation to trim and shape, so beards must be left to grow as long and to straggle as far as God might will them (Lacy 1981, 142–43).

In order to better convert the bedouin to Wahhabi doctrine, the Ikhwan began to preach the virtues of agriculture and urged their followers to settle on desert oases where they would be under the direct control of Wahhabi preachers. The first settlement was established in 1912 and soon contained more than 10,000 residents. Religious indoctrination was intense, and the warrior spirit was shifted from raiding to the glorification of Islam.

Rather than resisting the Ikhwan movement, Abd al-Aziz embraced it as a vehicle for settling the tribes and organizing their members, now fired with religious zeal, into a more or less standing army. As Holden and Johns write: "In 1916 he ordered that all the bedouin tribes owing allegiance to him must also give up herding and join the Ikhwan, and their sheikhs were brought to Riyadh in relays for special religious instruction. They were to receive subsidies from the treasury and, in return, respect the King as their Imam and swear to uphold Wahhabist orthodoxy" (1981, 69). By 1917, according to Lacy, "there were over 200 such settlements dotted all over Najd, none of them more than a day's march from another, an extraordinary military network" (1981, 146). Although all had sworn allegiance to ibn Saud, that allegiance was secondary to their faith. Any conflict between the Wahhabi leaders and the king risked pushing the Ikhwan to the side of the Wahhabis. Particularly troublesome was the Ikhwan's opposition to the king's growing friendship with the British, whom the Ikhwan viewed as infidels. Then as now, the fundamentalists viewed the Arabian Peninsula as sacred territory not to be desecrated by non-Muslims (Holden and Johns 1981, 71).

Sporadic scrimmages between the forces of Sharif Hussein and ibn Saud's Ikhwan erupted into full-scale warfare in 1919, with victory going to the latter. The British attempted to strengthen Hussein's forces but hedged their bets by increasing ibn Saud's subsidy. One of the king's sons was also taken on a tour of England, marking the first time that any member of the Saudi royal family had ventured beyond the confines of the Arabian Peninsula. In 1922, the British worked out an amicable demarcation for much of the border between ibn Saud's kingdom and the recently created Hashemite Kingdom of Iraq. The boundaries of Kuwait, a British protectorate, were also delineated to the advantage of ibn Saud, who was now of growing interest to the British. In the same year the British received a concession for the exploration of oil in Arabia's Eastern

Province. In exchange for the concession, the king received an annual stipend of some $7,000 per year. Alas, the British failed to discover oil and allowed their concession to lapse.

Although Abd al-Aziz restrained the Ikhwan from attacks on the Hijaz, he made little secret of either his desire to conquer Mecca or his growing fear of attack by the Hashemite rulers of Iraq and Transjordan (Kostiner 1993). The Ikhwan, for their part, were incensed by Sharif Hussein's lax enforcement of Islamic law. The final insult came in 1924 when the Sharif of Mecca proclaimed himself the caliph, or successor to Mohammed. The position had been left vacant by the collapse of the Ottoman Empire.

The Ikhwan attacked, and by 1926 all of the Hijaz, including the holy cities of Mecca and Medina, was under the control of the Saudi forces. Abd al-Aziz ibn Saud was duly proclaimed the king of the Hijaz and swore to protect the holy places and provide for the pilgrims, the most profitable enterprise in the Arabian Peninsula at the time. Understanding that the residents of the Hijaz were more urban than his Wahhabi Ikhwan, ibn Saud promised to provide the region with a consultative council and a constitution. The council met for a period, but the constitution was never promulgated. Nevertheless, the residents of the Hijaz were spared the full wrath of the Ikhwan, much to the consternation of the latter.

Relations between the king and the Ikhwan became increasingly tense over the ensuing years and ibn Saud, fearing for his throne, recruited a new army drawn from townsfolk and loyal tribes to counter the Ikhwan. The confrontation came in 1929 when a rebellion by the Ikhwan was crushed by the king's forces. The king's authority was now absolute, but tensions between the tribal authority of the Saudis and the religious authority of the Wahhabis would remain an underlying theme of Saudi politics.

In 1932, ibn Saud unified his vast realm and named it the Kingdom of Saudi Arabia. With the Ikhwan destroyed and a new army in place, the king's rule was now secure. Indeed, the only conflict of major significance prior to the outbreak of World War II was a brief war with Yemen in 1934. The Yemenis were easily defeated, and ibn Saud added a large section of Yemeni territory to his new kingdom.

That kingdom, however, remained desperately poor, its major sources of income being the *hajj* and the meager subsidy provided by the British. This would change dramatically with the discovery of oil by a consortium of American companies in 1938 (Twitchell 1958). Profits were not immediate, but both the Arabian American Oil Company (Aramco) and the American government saw the wisdom of providing loans to a Saudi monarch perpetually in need of cash. Indeed, as early as 1943, President Roosevelt had declared that Saudi Arabia was vital to America's defense, thereby paving the way for U.S. aid to flow to the desert kingdom (Hart 1998; Holden and Johns 1981, 128). The relationship between the two countries was cemented in 1945 when President Roosevelt hosted ibn Saud aboard an American cruiser on a return trip from the Yalta conference of wartime leaders. The United States had become the defender of Saudi Arabia and its oil (Eddy 1954).

## The Era of Revolution and Optimism

Other than the ascendance of the House of Saud, the most significant aspect of Saudi history in the century preceding World War II was the success of the desert kingdom in avoiding colonization by the West. Although all of its neighbors, with the exception of Yemen (North), had been exposed to varying degrees of Westernization, the Saudis had not. As a result, the Kingdom of Saudi Arabia that entered the post–World War II era differed little from the first Saudi kingdom established in the mid eighteenth century. Ibn Saud was an absolute patriarch who ruled his kingdom as a tribal sheikh ruled his tribe. There were no political institutions to speak of, and the king's primary means of communicating with his subjects was the weekly *majlis* (council) at which he would meet with tribal leaders bound to him by oaths of personal loyalty. In grand patriarchal fashion, he would also hear petitions from citizens who had grievances or were in need of the king's help. This help was presented as a personal favor bestowed by a compassionate king. The *majlis* is a tribal institution that dates to antiquity and continues to be held by the king and the major princes as a symbol of "tribal democracy." A council of ministers or cabinet was not established until 1953. Decisions were made by the king and carried out by his sons and a few trusted advisers. Religious matters, including education and morality, remained in the hands of the ulema.

Oil revenues were viewed as the personal property of a king perpetually in debt, and the kingdom's financial resources were rapidly exhausted by the voracious appetites of the royal family. Little wealth trickled down to the kingdom's inhabitants, who numbered between one million and three million. The overwhelming majority of them were illiterate. Many also remained nomadic, and even those in the cities or agricultural settlements remained fiercely loyal to their tribes, far more so than to the Saudis. This sentiment was particularly strong in the Hijaz.

This was the political system that would guide Saudi Arabia into the era of optimism and revolution. The primary goal of the monarchy was to consolidate its hold over its vast domain. Tribal rebellions remained a threat, as did the prospect of an uprising by Hijazis chafing under the puritanical yoke of the less-sophisticated Saudis. Far more threatening were the Hashemite monarchs of Jordan and Iraq, both of whom viewed the Hijaz as their patrimony.

The king, moreover, had ruled for almost fifty years and was in ill health. It would not be the tribal warrior who guided Saudi Arabia into the postwar era, but his sons (Van der Mulen 1957). Succession was a matter of grave concern to the ailing monarch, for the Saudi kingdoms of yore had been weakened by quarrels over succession and thus fallen prey to their foes.

The king set the stage for an orderly succession by demanding that the contending princes, most of whom had different mothers, swear allegiance to Saud, his oldest son. Abd al-Aziz had also groomed Saud for the kingship by naming him crown prince; Saud used this position to place his own supporters in positions of authority. A council of ministers (cabinet) had been created just days before the king's death, and was also placed under the control of the crown prince. Saud now reigned supreme.

The situation, however, remained tricky. Faisal, second in line for succession, possessed far greater intelligence and organizational skills than his elder half brother. He had also served as minister of foreign affairs since the 1930s and possessed far broader knowledge of the revolutionary pressures shaking the Middle East than Saud, a man who had traveled little and could speak only a few words of English.

With the passing of Abd al-Aziz in 1953, the inner circle of the royal family was forced to choose between Saud and Faisal. It was a choice between internal cohesion on one hand and competence on the other. It was also a choice between the continuation of informal rule based on the inclinations of a single individual and efforts to provide Saudi Arabia with a formal political system capable of meeting the challenges of the future.

The crisis was settled, albeit temporarily, when Faisal embraced his brother and hailed him as king. Cohesion had carried the day. This was probably the best choice at the time, for it was doubtful that the kingdom could have survived a bitter succession struggle between Saud and Faisal, both of whom had strong allies within the royal family. Also weighing heavily on Saudi minds was the overthrow of Egypt's King Farouk in 1952, and his prophetic quip that the world was destined to have but five kings: the king of England and the four kings in a deck of cards. The kingdom, moreover, had suffered its first labor uprising only months earlier when most of the Aramco workforce walked off the job in a quest for higher pay and better housing and benefits (Holden and Johns 1981). For the first time in Saudi history, its tribal leaders had come face to face with the consequences of modern production techniques. However rudimentary it may have been, Saudi Arabia was developing a working class susceptible to political manipulation. The golden goose had produced more than wealth.

Cohesion, however, came at high cost. Saud had gone a long way toward consolidating his authority and resisted the constraints urged upon him by Faisal and his other brothers. Saudi oil revenues, now in the range of $235 million per year, continued to be treated as the king's personal income. Bribery and corruption were the order of the day, while bills went unpaid for months (Holden and Johns 1981, 180). Millions of dollars in military equipment were purchased from the United States. Much of it was too sophisticated for the Saudi army to operate, so it remained in its crates (Holden and Johns 1981, 168, 183). Even more money was spent on palaces and yachts as well as lavish government buildings that conveyed an image of progress. In the meantime, the kingdom sank deeper into debt. Stories of corruption and mismanagement during Saud's reign are too voluminous and too bizarre for easy recounting; they portray a chaotic political system unprepared to cope with either its sudden wealth or the tumultuous political environment of the Middle East. Suffice it to say that Saud's most lasting accomplishment was siring more than fifty legitimate sons and roughly the same number of daughters (Holden and Johns 1981, 177). None would rise to prominence upon their father's passing.

In the foreign policy sphere, Saud formed an alliance with Nasser, offering the latter lavish financial support for his Arab revolution in return for Egyptian support in Saudi Arabia's cold war with the Hashemite kingdoms of Iraq and

Jordan. There can be little doubt that the alliance was also a ploy to deflect Nasser's wrath from a regime that he had earlier ridiculed for being a lapdog of the West. With the explosion of Nasser's popularity following his political victory in the Arab–Israeli War of 1956, Saudi aid for the Egyptian leader became little more than tribute. Particularly dangerous was Saudi Arabia's heavy reliance on Egyptian and Palestinian workers. Most teachers and bureaucrats in the kingdom were either Egyptians or Palestinians, as were most oil workers. Most were fired by Nasser's rhetoric and formed a Nasserite fifth column within the kingdom.

Discontent with Saud's rule was not long in surfacing. A minor military coup was put down in 1954, and in 1955 a major prince openly suggested that Saud be replaced by the austere Faisal. The suggestion was premature, but by 1957, the internal situation had become so unstable that pressure from within the royal family forced Saud to grant Faisal executive powers. A resentful Saud remained king, but Faisal was in charge. Faisal moved rapidly to constrain the profligate Saud and generally put the Saudi financial house in order.

The struggle between Faisal and Saud, however, had only begun. Saud had been lavish in his gifts to the tribal chiefs, a group that would increasingly form the basis of his power. The king was also much beloved by a merchant class that had enriched itself by pandering to the needs of the royal family as well by a legion of petty princes who survived on his generosity. All resented Faisal's austerity measures.

At this point, three distinct wings were beginning to emerge within the royal family. The first centered on Saud and seemed to have few concerns beyond immediate gratification. Much like Louis XV, their motto seemed to be "après moi, le déluge." A second and much smaller group of princes was caught up in the wave of Arab nationalism sweeping the Middle East. They, variously referred to as the "free" or "red" princes, urged that Saudi Arabia transform itself into something approaching a constitutional monarchy. Falling between these two extremes was the inner core of the royal family whose primary concern was the survival of the family and its kingdom. They were contemptuous of both Saud and the free princes: The greed of the former had placed the kingdom on the path to ruin, while the misplaced idealism of the latter threatened it with extinction. The survival of the kingdom, in their view, demanded order and discipline. That order and discipline could only be imposed by Faisal.

The struggle between Faisal and Saud was tortuous. Saud remained king in name and lost no opportunity to undercut Faisal's authority. The United States also harbored dreams of using Saud as a counterweight to Nasser, much as the British had rallied the Arabs around Sharif Hussein in the Arab Revolt of 1916. As Eisenhower (1965) would note in his memoirs, "He [Saud] at least professed anti-Communism, and he enjoyed, on religious grounds, a high standing among all Arab nations." If anything, this policy was even more quixotic than Saud's support of Nasser and indicated just how little the United States understood either Saudi Arabia or the Middle East.

Perhaps to curry greater U.S. support, Saud cut his ties with Nasser and endorsed the Eisenhower Doctrine, a new U.S. program designed to stymie the Soviet Union and its agents in the Middle East, a direct reference to Nasser. Saud also settled his differences with the Hashemite kings of Jordan and Iraq. Solidarity made sense: if one monarch fell, the others could not be far behind. The United States, for its part, modernized the Saudi armed forces and pledged to come to the aid of the Saudi government if so requested. Yet another link had been added to the special relationship between Saudi Arabia and the United States.

The announcement of unity between Egypt and Syria in February 1958 sent shock waves through a royal family that had begun to fear popular rebellion more than foreign attack. Consternation turned to terror a few months later when the king regent of Iraq was ousted by a military coup and his body dismembered by an Iraqi mob demanding unity with the United Arab Republic.

Further adding to the tension within the royal family were efforts by an ill and unstable Saud to move his sons into positions of power. If Saud had his way, it would be they rather than Faisal who claimed the throne upon their father's death. The remainder of the royal family would be relegated to second-ary status.

A brief alliance had also been formed between Saud and the free princes, because the latter viewed Faisal as a greater obstacle to constitutional reform than the erratic Saud. Their logic was impeccable, for a few more years of Saud's rule would have all but guaranteed the end of the monarchy. The free princes pre-sented a draft constitution to Saud in 1960, hoping that the precariousness of his position would force him to bend to their will. Saud received the draft constitu-tion graciously, using it as a ploy to build support among the more liberal ele-ments of Saudi society. He then sent it to the kingdom's ultraconservative ulema for evaluation and certain rejection. He was not disappointed. The ulema promptly responded that the Koran was the constitution of Saudi Arabia and could not be constrained by a secular document (Holden and Johns 1981, 209–14).

During the next four years, the power struggle between Saud and Faisal intensified; Saud again granted Faisal executive powers, only to reassert his authority and undercut the latter's reforms. Saud also increased his payments to the tribal sheikhs, hoping that they would be able to turn the tide in his inevitable showdown with Faisal. The free princes weighed in by publicly free-ing their slaves and concubines, a move that gained worldwide publicity and raised serious questions about the type of regime that the United States and its allies were supporting (Holden and Johns 1981, 221).

The high drama of palace intrigues, moreover, was being played out in an increasingly tense regional environment. The union between Egypt and Syria, which had lasted only three years, had fired the imagination of the Arab world and placed the Saudi monarchy in danger of attack by both Nasser and the revo-lutionary regime in Iraq. Fear of Iraq was justified in 1961 when the Iraqi gov-ernment laid claim to both Kuwait and a large section of Saudi territory. The British stabilized the situation by sending troops to Kuwait, as did the Egyptians and the Saudis.

No sooner had the Iraqi crisis abated than the imam of Yemen, who exercised both religious and political authority—the title *imam* implied both—was over-thrown in September 1962 by a poorly organized military coup, whose leaders turned to Egypt for support. The Saudis had little love for the imam but feared the prospect of an Egyptian client state on their southern border. In desperation, they offered refuge to the deposed imam and began providing arms and money to the loyalist tribes. This was not a new process, for Saudi leaders had tradition-ally influenced Yemeni policy by bribing Yemen's tribal sheikhs, most of whom were in more or less constant revolt against the government.

The war in Yemen dragged on for the next five years with neither side able to claim victory. Egypt's heavily mechanized army was of little use in Yemen's impenetrable mountains, and Nasser had to content himself with control of the coastal plain and Yemen's few cities. The loyalist tribes, for their part, were no match for the heavy armor of the Egyptians and seldom ventured far from their mountain strongholds. Truces were declared but seldom held for more than a few days. The Egyptians bombed Saudi border towns, generating fears that an increas-ingly frustrated Egyptian army would soon invade Saudi Arabia.

Facing disaster on both the domestic and regional fronts, the royal family forced the abdication of Saud in 1964. They had no other choice. The process was a delicate one, as procedures for succession had not yet been established. Jealousies within the family were also intense, with each matrilineal brood fearing for its future. Faisal was to be the new king, but who would follow him?

Abdication procedures began in the early months of 1964 with a procession of tribal sheikhs and senior ulema declaring their support for Faisal. Key ulema then issued a fatwa (religious judgment) declaring Saud unfit to rule. Faisal was thus released from his earlier vow to accept Saud as king. This accomplished, some sixty senior princes formally announced their acceptance of the fatwa deposing Saud and indicated their support for Faisal. Only on November 2, 1964, after all of the key holders of power in Saudi Arabia—the tribal sheikhs, the ulema, and the royal family—had been brought in line, did Faisal swear on the Koran to rule Saudi Arabia according to the principles of Islam. It would be another several months before Khalid, the seventh son of Abd al-Aziz, was named crown prince. Saud, now in disgrace, would be forced to make do with an annual stipend of $43 million (Holden and Johns 1981, 239).

Faisal moved rapidly to put the Saudi financial house in order, a process aided by the ever-increasing inflow of oil revenues. Planning proceeded apace, as did efforts to rationalize the political structure. The war in Yemen remained the major preoccupation of Faisal's early years, but faded with Israel's devastating defeat of Egyptian forces in the June War of 1967. Faisal showed his support by declaring a jihad (holy war) against Israel, but Saudi forces did not engage in a war that was over almost as soon as it had begun.

All in all, the dominant characteristics of Saudi politics during the era of revolution and optimism were confusion and internecine conflict as a tribal monarchy attempted to cope with the dual challenges of sudden wealth and modernity. Both challenges were handled poorly. Much of the country's oil wealth was squandered, and little if any progress was made in developing effective political institutions that would reach beyond the inner circle of the royal family. The Saudi regime's major achievement during the era was surviving the onslaught of the nationalist revolutions that were sweeping the region.

## The Era of Reassessment

Although the nationalist tide collapsed with the Arab defeat in the June War of 1967, the fate of the Saudi regime was far from certain. The process of institution building was still in its embryonic stages. Corruption was rampant, expenses outstripped revenues, and the Saudi military posed more of a threat to the monarchy than did the country's external opponents. Difficult questions also remained concerning the royal family's role in the Arab struggle against Israel. How could the regime retain its ties with the United States, many Saudis wondered, when Israel had just conquered Jerusalem, the third holiest city in Islam, with U.S. support?

By 1970, Faisal had curbed the appetites of the royal family and the budget was in balance. The same year saw the death of Nasser and also marked the beginning of an upward spiral in oil revenues. Faisal could breathe a sigh of relief on both counts. Corruption and mismanagement continued to plague the system, but the country would soon have more money than its economy could absorb. During the Arab boycott imposed during the October (Yom Kippur) War of 1973, oil prices increased from $2.83 per barrel at the beginning of the boycott to $10.41 by 1974. Tensions between the United States and Saudi Arabia resulting from the boycott were a source of profound discomfort for both. The boycott also underscored the profound interdependence of the two countries. The United States needed Saudi support in maintaining world oil prices at levels it considered reasonable, and the Saudi royal family was more dependent than ever on the U.S. for its survival.

This mutual interdependence, heretofore based on a multitude of ad hoc arrangements and understandings, was formalized by a series of agreements between the two countries signed in 1974 and 1975. Among other things, the United States agreed to modernize the Saudi National Guard and the Saudi navy. Modern planes were also delivered. U.S. arms sales during the period jumped from approximately $500 million at the end of the 1973–74 fiscal year to almost four times that figure a year later (Holden and Johns 1981, 359). Also implicit in the deal was America's continued willingness to ignore Saudi Arabia's human rights violations. In return, Saudi Arabia stabilized world oil markets by producing more oil than her economic needs dictated. The kingdom was now awash in money.

By 1975, the firm hand of Faisal had guided the affairs of the kingdom for eleven years. Domestic stability had been restored and Saudi Arabia's special relationship with the United States had shielded the desert kingdom from its regional adversaries. In large part, domestic stability was a function of a social contract that substituted economic security for political rights. In lieu of political rights, Saudis were encouraged to "enrich yourselves." This process had begun modestly, but by the mid-1970s the kingdom had allocated some $141 billion on a vast array of projects ranging from port expansion to housing loans (seldom repaid) and everything in between. The austere desert kingdom of ibn Saud was now being transformed into a welfare state in which the Saudi population wanted for little.

Four main techniques were used to distribute the kingdom's vast oil wealth to the Saudi people: welfare, bureaucracy, the private sector, and corruption. Health care, education, and almost anything else that Saudis needed was free for the asking, as was a well-paying and minimally demanding job with the government. Those with an entrepreneurial bent were encouraged to start their own businesses, most of which prospered by contracting with the government. Anyone in a position of authority had ample opportunities for corruption. The higher one ascended on the elite pyramid, the more abundant the opportunities became. Contracts with the Saudi government required the *wasta* of a highly placed official, often a prince, and rare was the contract with a foreign company that did not provide a "commission" of 15 percent or more. In some cases, development proposals were designed solely in order to gain a commission. Development experts thus began to distinguish between "good" corruption and "bad" corruption: the former comprised "commissions" that facilitated the implementation of programs that the country needed, while the latter wasted money on useless projects created merely for the sake of acquiring bribes.

There were, of course, problems. Planning was made difficult by uncertain population estimates. Earlier estimates (1962) had placed the Saudi population at 3.3 million but were suppressed for being too small. Among other things, the royal family feared that low population estimates might encourage attacks by their poorer neighbors. It also seemed inadvisable to advertise the fact that foreign workers, most of them from other Arab countries, constituted a very large share of the Saudi population. By 1973, government estimates placed the population at 5.9 million Saudis and some 700,000 foreigners. A year later, however, a British estimate placed the population at 4.3 million Saudis and 1.5 million foreigners (Holden and Johns 1981, 393).

In addition to not knowing how many people to plan for, the early Saudi development plans were loose affairs that amounted to little more than wish lists compiled by various government agencies. With so much money available, spending was easier than planning. Accountability, moreover, had never been a strong point of the Saudi political system.

Faisal was assassinated in March 1975 by a deranged prince, and Khalid, his half brother, was proclaimed king. Henceforth, the hand on the tiller would be less firm. Khalid had minimal interest in the affairs of state, and Fahd, now proclaimed crown prince, would emerge as the power behind the throne (Holden and Johns 1981, 387). Fahd was pro-American in outlook and was anxious to strengthen the kingdom's special relationship with the United States. He was also more liberal than the royal family as a whole and far more liberal than the ulema. Also problematic was the fact that Fahd, who was vice chairman of the Council of Ministers (second deputy prime minister) as well as crown prince, was a member of the Sudairi clan, as was Sultan, the minister of defense. The only obstacle to a Sudairi sweep was Abdullah, the commander of the now modernized National Guard. In command of his own army, Abdullah would prove to be a powerful adversary to the Sudairis. Saudi policy continued along the course set by Faisal, but the change of leadership would have telling effects as corruption increased and discipline, never a strong point of the Saudi regime, declined.

Becoming more pronounced was the royal family's domination of the private sector. This was a relatively new development, for ibn Saud had issued a stern warning against mixing business with politics. Harmony demanded that each be supreme in its own realm. This separation was largely honored during the Faisal era, but collapsed under his successors as many of the country's dominant firms now began to acquire royal partners.

The 1970s, then, were an era of profound change for Saudi Arabia. Faisal reined in the worst excesses of the royal family and laid the foundation for a modern bureaucratic state. Once limited to a few key ministries, the Council of Ministers would expand to include a vast array of administrative agencies, most of which were dedicated to infrastructure development and social services. By necessity, Saudi commoners began to play a larger role in the day-to-day management of their country, although key positions remained in the hands of the royal family (al-Gosaibi 1998). The regime's claim to legitimacy, long based upon tribal and religious values, was now strengthened by the evolving social contract that offered Saudi citizens economic abundance in exchange for political compliance.

## The Era of Disillusionment

If the benign international environment of the 1970s had enabled the Saudi regime to consolidate its authority, the advent of the 1980s would test the resolve of the Saudi regime to a degree unknown since the Nasser era. Anwar Sadat's peace treaty with Israel had left the other Arab states exposed to Israeli attack, and Begin had thrown down the gauntlet by asserting Israel's claim to Jerusalem and the occupied territories. Saudi Arabia, the protector of Islam, was left to respond as best it might. The United States was an ally of Saudi Arabia, but it was also an ally of Israel. Far more devastating to the Saudi regime was the Ayatollah Khomeini's overthrow of the shah of Iran in 1979, which unleashed a wave of religious zeal that threatened to sweep all before it. Khomeini vowed to liberate the birthplace of Islam from a regime that he accused of moral laxity, cowardice, and submission to the infidels. Having long championed Islam against attacks from the left, the royal family now found its Islamic credentials challenged by an Islamic theocracy that undermined the very foundations of Saudi legitimacy. The Saudis did not have long to wait before the shock waves of the ayatollah's revolution reached the kingdom. In 1979, only months after the ayatollah proclaimed an Islamic republic in Iran, Muslim zealots seized the Great Mosque in Mecca and demanded the creation of an Islamic republic in Saudi Arabia. Perhaps more damaging to the credibility of the royal family was its inability to dislodge the fundamentalists without the assistance of foreign security forces. The fall of the shah also raised serious questions about the effectiveness of U.S. security guarantees. If the United States had been unable to save the shah, perhaps its most important ally in the region, would it be able to save the Saudi monarchy?

The 1979 seizure of the Great Mosque in Mecca was followed in 1980 by a confrontation between police and religious fanatics in the kingdom's Eastern Province. The Eastern Province is home to Saudi Arabia's Shi'a minority, estimated to number between 300,000 and 500,000, many of whom were suspected of harboring pro-Khomeini sympathies. This fear was made all the more plausible by a long history of Sunni oppression of the Shi'a, who were viewed as heretics by the puritanical Wahhabis (Chabry and Chabry 1987; Dumas 1995).

Tensions in the Eastern Province were even more ominous when viewed in the broader context of Khomeini's call for a Shi'a rebellion in Iraq (Abir 1993). If such a rebellion had transpired (and many observers at the time thought that it would), the Islamic revolution would have reached the Saudi border and could well have triggered Shi'a uprisings in the heart of the Saudi oil region. Kuwait, which also possessed a large Shi'a population, would have been threatened by internal turmoil as well.

Despite the danger, King Khalid seemed unsure how to respond. Clearly, it would be awkward for a Saudi regime that based its legitimacy on the protection of Islam to openly oppose an Islamic government that, in the view of many Muslims, had liberated Iran from decades of U.S. domination.

The Saudis made halfhearted gestures to accommodate Khomeini, but both sides realized that accommodation could only be temporary, at best. As always, the regime attempted to bolster its popular support with lavish outlays of money. The kingdom's third five-year development plan (1980–1985) called for spending $235 billion on infrastructure development and social services, a figure that did not include defense expenditures. This represented an increase of almost $100 billion over the expenditures of the second five-year plan, which had terminated the preceding year. Saudis had everything that money could buy with the exception of political freedom.

Not surprisingly, given their fear of Khomeini, the Saudis greeted Iraq's 1980 invasion of Iran with enthusiasm. Indeed, one of the intriguing mysteries of the era remains the role of Saudi Arabia in precipitating the war. Did the Saudis actively encourage Iraq to attack Iran by promising support, or did they merely rush to support Saddam Hussein once the war had begun (confidential interviews in Saudi Arabia, 1983)?

The outbreak of the Iran–Iraq War in 1980 also served as the catalyst for the formation of the Gulf Cooperation Council to promote security and trade among the oil monarchies of the region, long a major goal of Saudi foreign policy. In reality, the GCC could offer little in the way of its own defense beyond the military capacity of Saudi Arabia, and that capacity remained largely symbolic (An-Nafisi 1982).

The monarchy's problems, however, had only begun. Oil prices began to plummet in 1981, and by 1982 the kingdom was forced to draw upon its financial reserves to meet the expenditures promised in the new five-year plan. Saudi Arabia was also becoming Iraq's paymaster in its war with Iran, a role that further aggravated what the Saudis would refer to as a cash-flow problem.

Adding to the woes of the royal family was a lack of firm leadership. The years since Faisal's assassination in 1975 had seen a lethargic King Khalid increasingly recede into the background as Fahd became the effective ruler of the kingdom. Fahd possessed long experience in government but lacked both the shrewdness and the moral authority of the austere Faisal. In addition, his reputation for excess was offensive to the religious community, as was his desire to strengthen Saudi Arabia's special relationship with the United States.

Khalid's death in 1982 provoked neither a crisis of succession nor a discernible break in policy, as Fahd had been the effective head of state for some time. Abdullah, the commander of the National Guard, was duly sworn in as crown prince and first deputy prime minister, pitting the conservative Abdullah against the more moderate Sudairi clan. Not only did he have his own army, Abdullah also enjoyed stronger support in the religious community than the Sudairis.

In 1984, Saudi Arabia moved to stabilize oil prices by agreeing to become OPEC's "swing producer." If oil prices dropped, Saudi Arabia would produce less oil; if they increased, it would produce more. This would assure ample revenues for all concerned as long as all OPEC members adhered to their assigned quotas and did not cheat. The plan was a sound one, but the pressures of the Iran–Iraq War led to massive cheating and the price of oil continued to decline, reaching a low of less than $10 a barrel in 1986.

A revenue shortfall that had been an annoyance in 1982 had now become a full-blown crisis that threatened to exhaust the kingdom's financial reserves. Urged into action by the severity of the crisis, King Fahd threatened to slash expenditures in the forthcoming 1985–1990 development plan and called upon the Saudi population to work harder. The king's statements came as a shock to a Saudi population long accustomed to governmental largesse, but the blow was cushioned by promises to create a National Consultative Assembly, some members of which would be drawn from partially elected provincial councils (Abir 1993). Neither the threatened austerity measures nor the consultative assembly materialized. The government continued to pamper its citizens, albeit less lavishly than they were used to, and the plans for the assembly passed into oblivion.

Simultaneously, the king moved to strengthen his religious credentials by increasing the power of the ulema and the morality police, both of whom had seen their authority eroded during the preceding decade. In much the same vein, 1986 would see the king change his title from a simple "His Majesty" to "His Majesty, the Protector of the Two Holy Shrines." Irate at the king's move, Khomeini responded to Fahd's arrogation of religious authority by provoking anti-Saudi riots at the 1987 *hajj*. More than four hundred people were killed in the melee. Ruling Saudi Arabia was not as easy as it once had been.

The Iran–Iraq War ground to a halt in 1987, but the psychological war between the Saudi royal family and Iran's ayatollah continued. In 1988, Iran boycotted the *hajj* in an attempt to embarrass the monarchy, and in 1989 two bombs rocked Mecca on the anniversary of the 1987 riots. To make matters worse, the threat of a physical attack by Iran had merely been replaced by the threat of a battle-tested Iraqi army that was now the largest in the Arab world. Would Saudi Arabia be able to control the monster that it had helped to create?

The 1980s, then, found Saudi Arabia in a holding pattern. The decline in oil revenues had forced a reduction in spending, but the regime avoided severe economic disruptions by drawing on its massive financial reserves. By the end of the era, however, these reserves were nearing exhaustion. Far more difficult to parry was the tide of religious zeal inspired by Khomeini's Islamic revolution. The government responded by imposing even greater demands for piety upon the Saudi population, but made no concessions in the areas of popular representation. The 1980s, however, did not pass without change. The educational level of the Saudi population continued to increase, and thousands of students returned from the West with hopes of playing a more active role in shaping the affairs of their country. Many also found the forced piety of the kingdom to be an oppressive burden.

## The Era of the New World Order

The advent of the 1990s promised the Saudi regime a reprieve from the woes of the preceding decade. The Americans now dominated the region, and the Iran–Iraq War had crippled both of the kingdom's main adversaries. Khomeini had also passed from the scene, depriving the Islamic revolution of its charismatic leader.

All, however, was not well. The thrust of Khomeini's Islamic revolution had been blunted, but the balance of power in the Arab world was shifting to the fundamentalists. They were scoring clear gains in Jordan, Lebanon, Egypt, Algeria, and Sudan, and fundamentalist groups in Lebanon and the occupied territories had begun to dominate the struggle against Israel. Saddam Hussein still had a massive army and was less than subtle in demanding that the Gulf states assist in rebuilding his shattered country. Iraq, Saddam Hussein proclaimed, had saved the Gulf from the scourge of Khomeini. Now the oil kingdoms could meet their moral and financial obligations or face the consequences—which were as yet unspecified.

The main threat to the Saudi regime, however, was internal rather than external. Apart from an occasional border scrimmage, the kingdom had been spared foreign attack thanks to its alliance with the United States. But could the United States protect the monarchy from the enemy within? This was a difficult question to answer. The regime was being increasingly challenged by two conflicting forces: a Westernized middle class demanding greater participation in the affairs of the country and a fundamentalist movement intent on imposing a Khomeini-type theocracy on the kingdom. The struggle between the House of Saud and the Ikhwan of old had resurfaced.

Also worrisome to the royal family was the growing U.S. military presence in the kingdom (Lippman 2004). How much Western intrusion would a restive religious community tolerate? Potential threats from Iraq and Iran required a Western presence in the kingdom, yet that very presence threatened to inflame religious emotions.

No sooner had the new world order begun than Saddam Hussein challenged U.S. hegemony by asserting Iraqi sovereignty over Kuwait. The drama was closely watched by all countries in the region, for it promised to set the tone of regional politics for decades to come. The United States responded to Saddam's initiative with ambivalence, if not confusion. Saudi Arabia, for its part, downplayed the Iraqi threat and resisted a massive buildup of U.S. forces in the kingdom.

Denial changed to ambivalence with the Iraqi invasion of Kuwait on the morning of August 2, 1990. Iraqi troops overran Kuwait in a matter of hours and immediately established fortified positions on the Saudi border. Saudi Arabia's initial reaction had been to "open negotiations with Iraq about its intentions" via a hastily constructed "hot-line" (*NYT,* Oct. 4, 1990, A9). The Saudis also rejected an American request to close an Iraqi pipeline traversing Saudi territory for fear that the Iraqis might construe the closure as an act of war. These concerns were justified, for Saudi sources estimated that Iraqi forces could overrun the oil-rich Eastern Province in less than twelve hours and the entire country within three days; even less time would be required if Saudi air power proved ineffective (*NYT,* Oct. 4, 1990, A9). Indeed, the Saudi regime was so ambivalent about the proper response to the Iraqi threat that its armed forces remained only partially mobilized at the time of the invasion (*NYT,* Oct. 4, 1990, A9).

Despite Saddam Hussein's assurances that he had no intention of invading Saudi Arabia, Iraqi forces made several temporary incursions into Saudi territory. Growing tensions between the two countries proved increasingly difficult to resolve despite the hotline. It was only at this point, according to press reports, that the king made a request for U.S. assistance (*NYT,* Oct. 4, 1990, A9). Prince Sultan, the minister of defense, explicitly stressed that the American forces were there purely for defensive purposes and that the kingdom would not be used as a staging ground for an attack on Iraq (*NYT,* Sept. 2, 1990, 7).

Within a month, some 150,000 U.S. troops were in Saudi Arabia. About 10 percent of them were women (*NYT,* Sept. 24, 1990, 1). A conflict ensued between the rights of female GIs and a Saudi regime that imposed strict restrictions on female behavior, including prohibitions on driving. These restrictions, as well as the veiling of Saudi women and the practice of polygamy, unleashed a hailstorm of criticism against the Saudi regime in the international press. Why, Western feminists asked aloud, was the United States supporting such a regime? Compromises were worked out, with female GIs driving on military installations but refraining from doing so in civilian areas. Female soldiers were also required to wear long sleeves and otherwise do as little as possible to upset Saudi sensibilities. Neither side found the arrangement satisfactory. Presumably there were also Jewish soldiers among the U.S. forces, but neither the Americans nor the Saudis seemed interested in discussing the matter. When European troops and those from other Arab countries were added to the picture, the size of the foreign presence in the kingdom was enormous. Unlike the earlier U.S. presence, moreover, the Western buildup could not be confined to segregated compounds. War is a messy business.

Beyond offending religious sensibilities, the war demonstrated just how vulnerable the Saudi regime had become to outside attack. Despite its sophisticed equipment and occasional flashes of brilliance, the Saudi military performed poorly. There could no longer be any pretense about the kingdom's ability to protect itself from its powerful neighbors, which included Iraq, Iran, Syria, and Israel. The mutual defense provisions of the Gulf Cooperation Agreement had also been discredited. None of its signatories had come to the aid of Kuwait. More disconcerting was Yemeni, Jordanian, and Palestinian support for Saddam Hussein. In this regard, the

*New York Times* quoted a senior Saudi official as saying, "What has been proven is that handouts of money do not make friends. We gave tens of millions of dollars to King Hussein and to Arafat and they turned against us" (*NYT,* March 2, 1994). The same source indicated that the kingdom had "given away" some $100 billion since the early 1970s in a continuing effort to buy friends and mollify enemies. Also called into question was the loyalty of the millions of Yemenis and Palestinians working in Saudi Arabia, many of whom cheered Saddam Hussein as a liberator. Saudi dependence on foreign labor had become a threat to the kingdom's security.

Problematic, too, was the apparent confusion within the royal family over the handling of the crisis. King Fahd remained in Jeddah throughout the crisis, addressing the nation only to announce the arrival of the Americans. Apparently the war was managed by Sultan, the minister of defense and aviation, and his son, Khalid ibn Sultan al-Saud, who had taken command of the forces sent to Saudi Arabia by friendly Muslim countries.

The war drained Saudi Arabia of $55 billion, according to IMF estimates, and in spite of increased oil production, it further depleted Saudi financial reserves (Gause 1994). Indeed, the end of the war would see Western banks question the creditworthiness of the kingdom (Gause 1994).

The end of the war brought a rush of damage control. As early as November 1990, the king promised the establishment of a consultative council, although the details of the plan remained sketchy. U.S. troops were urged to depart with consummate haste.

The domestic repercussions of the war were not long in coming. No sooner had UN troops arrived in the kingdom than a group of Saudi feminists presented the governor of Riyadh with a petition requesting the right to drive. In addition to coming as a shock to an already beleaguered regime, the action spoke volumes about the context of Saudi politics. The petition read as follows:

> Your Highness, we have known you as an understanding person, you have the spirit of giving to cope with this modern world, believe in the role of working women according to the Islamic teaching, thus, we appeal to you, and on behalf of the ambitious Saudi woman, who strives to serve her country under the guidance of the Custodian of the Holy Cities and his wise government, to open your fatherly heart for us and take care of our human request and that is "Driving a Car" inside Riyadh City, and this request has many justifications; the most paramount of them are as follows:
>
> 1. The existence of a foreign man in the house and the necessity of being with him in the car.
> 2. The financial costs that most families bear as a result of his existence.
> 3. The occurrence of many immoral matters within the houses as a result of the existence of the servant or a driver.
> 4. Our belief in the replacement of men by women in the time of crisis like the one our country is experiencing these days, as a result of the

threat from those who harbored evil thoughts against us; these circumstances ask from men to be in the battle fronts, and from women
to secure the home front.

5. Give the woman more confidence in her ability to bear the responsibilities to share in building the nation and contributing in all
aspects (private document; copy in author's possession).

The petition was rejected, and probably ignored, and a few days later some
forty-five women drove their cars in a prominent area of the capital city.
According to the police report: "They were driving themselves, they were
unveiled, many people gathered around this movement which was led by three
women, repeating slogans like "Driving," "Liberty" (private document).

The males responsible for the offending females (fathers, husbands, brothers)
were duly chastised, but the incident served notice to the regime that Western
troops meant Western reporters. War correspondents had a field day with the
repressive policies of the Saudi monarchy, and domestic dissidents now played to
a world audience.

No sooner had the war ended, moreover, than both liberal and religious
groups in 1991 presented petitions to the king demanding an end to the rampant corruption that had become the hallmark of the royal family. The liberals'
petition stressed the need for greater representation in the affairs of government—democracy is too strong a word to use—while the petition of the ulema
demanded an end to the moral laxity that had crept into Saudi society. Public
petitions are rare events in Saudi Arabia, and each represented a challenge to the
authority of the regime. The petition signed by the ulema was particularly damning, for the kingdom was now more dependent than ever upon the support of
its religious leaders. It had also become increasingly clear that the main opposition was now coming from the religious right (Gause 1994).

In January 1992, the king responded to the petitions with a call for moderation
that included a thinly veiled threat of violence against those who lacked the good
judgment to comply (Gause 1994). A few months later, he issued three decrees outlining the "Basic System of Government" of Saudi Arabia. The Basic System could
not be labeled a constitution, for that would imply the superiority of secular law to
the Koran. Lest there be confusion on this matter, the Basic System specified that the
Koran was the source of authority in the kingdom. The king was referred to as the
ultimate executive authority. A Consultative Council was established, but it possessed
no legislative authority. The judiciary was recognized as an independent branch of
government, but the king appointed all judges. All Saudis were equal before the law
in conformity with Islamic practice, and both homes and private property were protected by the due process of law. Of particular interest was a provision giving the king
the right to name the crown prince. This was a dramatic departure from the existing
practice of consultation among the major princes in matters of succession. The very
provision of a written document outlining the distribution of authority was a new
step in what had been the most informal of political systems.

The king's announcements did not quell the concerns of the ulema. The same
year would see some one hundred members of the ulema sign a "Memorandum

of Advice," criticizing corruption, the laxity of government services, and the arbitrariness of law enforcement and financial procedures (Gause 1994, 35). This was heady stuff for a country in which criticism of the king was tantamount to treason. The ulema petition of 1991 also implicitly demanded religious participation in the areas of foreign policy and economics. If granted, it would come perilously close to giving the ulema powers equal to those of the royal family (Gause 1994).

The Council of High Ulema, the core of the religious establishment in Saudi Arabia, condemned the petition, but not without dissenting voices. Those who signed the petition had acted independently, but clearly had support throughout the religious establishment. The dissenters would subsequently resign for reasons of health (Gause 1994).

The 1992 Memoradum of Advice was followed by the formation of the Committee to Defend Legitimate Rights. This committee was founded by religious radicals, all of whom had had their activities restricted by the government. Several fled to London, where they served as the major voice of the Saudi opposition.

The aggressiveness of the ulema made a large American presence in Saudi Arabia all the more problematic for the regime. That presence, however, would be difficult to avoid. Saddam Hussein remained in power and was poised to strike as soon as the opportunity presented itself. The United States, moreover, seemed intent on using the kingdom as its main base of operation in the Gulf region. Were U.S. troops the guests of the regime, or had they become its masters?

The Consultative Council met for the first time in 1993, and the king announced a major reshuffle of the cabinet that was designed to make government operations more efficient. The king also attempted to appease the religious community by appointing a new grand mufti and creating a new Ministry of Islamic Affairs to strengthen religious teaching and proselytization (Gause 1994).

The situation worsened in 1995 as complaints by mainstream ulema gave way to jihadist terrorism. A bomb exploded at a National Guard base in November of that year, killing five U.S. military personnel and calling the stability of the regime into question. To make matters worse, King Fahd had become severely ill toward the end of 1995 and was forced to temporarily cede power to Crown Prince Abdullah at the beginning of 1996. Power would shift between the two men during much of that year, with lines of authority becoming blurred. A second terrorist bomb exploded at a U.S. base in November 1996, killing nineteen U.S. military personnel and injuring scores of others. The United States accused the Saudis of lax security, and would subsequently complain that the Saudi authorities were failing to cooperate with the United States in the joint investigation of the affair. Saudi Arabia was becoming more uneasy over the U.S. boycott of Iraq as well as the continuing U.S. support of Israel. The tensions, however, were manageable. Neither side saw much benefit in airing their differences in public.

## Saudi Arabia in the Era of Terror

After September 11, 2001, all that changed. The attacks on the United States unleashed a series of shocks that shook the Saudi kingdom to its core. Of these, the first was the revelation that bin Laden's attacks on the U.S. were largely a Saudi affair. Bin Laden, the leader of the al-Qaeda network, was a Saudi, and so were fifteen members of the attack group. Further investigation indicated that Saudi citizens had played a key role in the financing of al-Qaeda and other terrorist organizations. Fingers were also pointed at the Saudi educational and religious establishments for propagating a particularly virulent interpretation of Islam that spawned extremism and anti-Americanism. American televangelists joined the fray, calling for a crusade against Islam. President George W. Bush spoke of a crusade against terror. A 2002 Pentagon advisory committee called the Saudis the enemy and proclaimed: "The Saudis are active at every level of the terror chain, from planners to financiers, from cadre to foot-soldier, from ideologist to cheerleader" (*WP*, Aug. 6, 2002). President Bush rushed to assure the Saudis that the report was provided by an independent consulting group and did not reflect American policy.

The Saudis bristled, accusing the United States of giving in to hysteria generated by the Christian right and Zionist groups intent on destabilizing the kingdom because of its aid to the Palestinian uprising. Saudi clerics were more pointed, suggesting that the U.S. had declared war on Islam.

In a curious irony, both sides, the Saudis and the Americans, had played a key role in creating bin Laden and his al-Qaeda network. The story is too long for easy recounting, but suffice it to say that both the U.S. and Saudi Arabia had supported the Islamic uprising against the Soviet occupation of Afghanistan. Saudi Arabia had championed bin Laden as an Islamic hero. He was feted by the royal family, and his picture adorned mosques throughout the kingdom. The United States had channeled its aid to al-Qaeda through the Pakistani intelligence services (ISI). It all made sense. A shaky Saudi regime had bolstered its Islamic credentials by launching a jihad against the Communists. The U.S. had cleverly played the jihadist card in its unending struggle against Communism. The Soviets had been forced out of Afghanistan, but bin Laden and the surging jihadist movement did not go away. They turned on the United States. The Americans were nervous.

That, however, was history. The challenge facing the Saudi regime was to balance the competing demands of two key pillars of its rule: its commitment to protect Islam and its special relationship with the United States. Failure in either area could prove fatal to the monarchy.

The Saudis chose a dangerous middle course. Islamic charitable groups, previously operating without government supervision, were brought under nominal government control. It was also acknowledged that some materials used by the Saudi religious and educational establishments, about 5 percent, were inflammatory. The Saudi ambassador to the United States, a key member of the royal family, even acknowledged that some of the charitable giving by his family might have been naïve. All of these problems, Washington was assured, would be rectified. A media blitz also assured the U.S. public that Saudi Arabia was a staunch ally of the U.S. in the war on terror.

Balancing Saudi capitulation to American pressure was the dramatic announcement that the monarchy had ordered U.S. troops out of the kingdom. Some 500,000 U.S. troops had inundated Saudi Arabia during the Gulf War (*NYT,* Sept. 22, 2003). Most left after the war, but a sizable contingent remained for "defensive purposes." Rumors of secret U.S. bases abounded. More than any other single factor, the American presence had inflamed the Saudi religious establishment, not to mention a large portion of the Saudi population.

The United States also found itself in a quandary. U.S. policy makers were preparing for a new war against Iraq. How could the U.S. attack Iraq without Saudi support? Saudi bases were the center of the U.S. military presence in the Gulf region. Also looming was the question of Saudi stability. What would happen to Saudi Arabia and all of its oil if the monarchy fell? Did the U.S. really want to push this most fragile of kingdoms over the brink? What would come next?

In reality, both the U.S. and Saudi positions were created with smoke and mirrors; neither was pressing the other as hard as their bitter public exchanges suggested (Gresh 2003). Events were also overwhelmed by the buildup to the second war with Iraq. The Saudis condemned the proposed war and announced that no strikes on Iraq could be launched from Saudi Arabia—while secretly assuring the U.S. of their support. The United States, for its part, eased its criticism of the Saudi record on terrorism, and the crown prince was invited to President Bush's Texas ranch for a friendly visit. The U.S. secretary of state was particularly conciliatory, saying that terrorist concerns should not lead to a "rupture of relations with a country that has been a good friend" (*Guardian,* Nov. 28, 2002).

Both sides rushed to minimize the damage produced by the war. The Saudis avoided a direct confrontation with the U.S. by allowing American forces to launch air strikes from Saudi territory. This fact was not publicized in the kingdom. The U.S. reciprocated by promising to withdraw its troops from Saudi Arabia following the end of the war. It did so in September 2003, easing the main source of tension between the monarchy and the ulema. The regime also eased domestic tensions by promising local elections, a first in Saudi history.

Unfortunately, the dazzling defeat of Iraqi forces was followed by a disastrous occupation. The U.S. had planned for the war, but not for its aftermath, a situation discussed at greater length in Chapter 6. For the moment, suffice it to say that anti-Americanism soared. Radical preachers proclaimed a jihad to liberate Iraq from American occupation. These calls were buttressed by gruesome pictures of U.S. forces desecrating mosques and maiming innocent Muslims, many of them women and children. Outside observers placed the Iraqi death toll at over 20,000. How, the radical preachers asked, could there be any doubt that the U.S. had declared war on Islam? The radicals were not the only ones asking this question. Saudi jihadists joined the fray, many returning home from Iraq to fire a smoldering rebellion against the monarchy. A stream of terror against foreigners in the kingdom that had begun in the 1990s now focused on the monarchy. Jihadist control of Saudi Arabia would place its oil and holy places in the hands of the jihadists. What better way to defeat the Americans?

But it wasn't just the terror. The United States, so powerful in war, was proving vulnerable in occupation. American deaths were portrayed as victories for the jihadists. Spirits rose and recruits increased. Particularly disconcerting to the Saudis was the election of an Iraqi prime minister with strong ties to Iran, a charter member of President Bush's "axis of evil." An Iraq sympathetic to Iran would destabilize the Gulf region and inflame Shi'a emotions in Saudi Arabia's oil-rich Eastern Province. How, the Saudis wondered, could the Americans have allowed this to happen? Perhaps the United States wasn't able to support its friends in the region.

The longer the U.S. occupation in Iraq persists, the more difficult the Saudi position becomes. Indeed, the monarchy now finds gloom wherever it turns. It is assaulted by the jihadists for serving the great Satan, condemned by the clerics for reforms that undermine the kingdom's traditions, mocked by the liberals for the tepid nature of those reforms, overwhelmed by corruption, and chastised by the U.S. for being weak on terror.

There is, however, one bright spot on the Saudi horizon. Oil prices have skyrocketed in the wake of the U.S.-led war on Iraq. The $50-per-barrel ceiling has long since been broken. Some fear that oil prices may reach $100 per barrel. The kingdom is awash in money. More than ever, the U.S. needs the Saudis to keep oil prices in check. The third of the four pillars of Saudi rule, then, is solid. But is that enough? Can the kingdom bribe and pamper its way out of its deepening crisis at home and abroad?

## SAUDI POLITICS TODAY AND BEYOND

Before approaching this most vital of questions, it is necessary to take a closer look at the way the Saudis do politics. As in earlier chapters, we begin by examining the elites and institutions that guide Saudi politics, and then move to a discussion of the group, cultural, economic, and international factors that influence the Saudi political process.

### Elites and Power in Saudi Arabia: The Royal Family and Religious Leaders

The inner core of the political elite in Saudi Arabia, those individuals with a major voice in the decision-making process, are the surviving sons and grandsons of ibn Saud. It is they who run the country.

The core of the Saudi elite possesses six key characteristics: It is closed, old, sick, divided, nervous, and cohesive. The closed nature of the elite requires little elaboration. Entrance to the inner circle of the Saudi elite is limited to the sons of ibn Saud. Invariably, that makes them old. Age and lifestyles have resulted in a high incidence of illness. King Fahd, born in 1921, died in 2005, while Abdullah (1923), the new king, has passed his eightieth birthday and suffers from heart disease (Simons 1998). Sultan, the new crown prince, is approximately the same age.

Both age and illness dictate that there will be frequent changes of monarch in the coming decades. Periods of succession create a great deal of tension within the royal family and make sustained initiatives difficult.

Intensifying the caution—nay, immobilization—of the royal family are the deep internal divisions within it. Most are half brothers, so the major princes represent multiple matrilineal groupings. Of these, the Sudairis possess overwhelming dominance in terms of numbers. The prospect of Sudairi dominance is very real and threatens the power of the remaining clans. A major showdown within the family was averted when Abdullah was named crown prince following the death of Khalid, thereby assuring that a non-Sudairi would succeed Fahd. Yet another crisis was averted when Abdullah, now king, proclaimed Sultan, a Sudairi, the crown prince. The Basic System gave him the option of bypassing Sultan, a longtime rival, but the realities of family politics left him little choice in the matter. But what comes next?

Kinship rivalries are intensified by sharp debates over the pace of change within the kingdom. While some princes stress the need to bring Saudi Arabia in line with the dramatic changes occurring beyond its borders, others see change as a threat to both the regime and its Islamic faith (Doran 2004). Interestingly enough, this debate tends to pit the Sudairis, who incline toward more rapid change, against many of their half brothers, and particularly King Abdullah, who do not. Further conflict centers on issues of foreign policy, with the Sudairis favoring closer cooperation with the United States while Abdullah and many other princes want to ease Saudi dependence on the United States and pursue a more nationalistic "Arab" policy.

The Saudi elite is also exceedingly preoccupied with security. This nervousness is not difficult to understand, for the regime has become the more frequent target of both foreign aggression and internal subversion. Adding to Saudi worries has been the dramatic increase in fundamentalist fervor. Whatever its origins, this pervasive sense of insecurity has made the Saudi elite reluctant to embark upon new initiatives that might upset either a major group within Saudi society or its regional neighbors. The insecurity of the Saudi elite also goes a long way toward explaining the repressiveness of the regime and its reluctance to allow reforms that would curtail its authority.

The cohesiveness of the royal family is, by and large, a function of their mutual insecurity. Either they stand together or they fall together. At the same time, this need for cohesiveness often conflicts with the tendency of individual princes, all of whom are powerful individuals in their own right, to go it alone on key issues. Sons of the major princes, grandsons of ibn Saud, are rapidly consolidating their position as the elite in waiting, and now occupy key positions in the military and administration.

Cohesion within the royal family is enforced by a mixture of negotiations, group pressure, and economic payoffs. These tactics, however, do not always work. The "red" or "free" princes of the 1950s supported Nasser's Arab nationalist crusade and offered the world a vivid picture of the corruption and disarray within the royal family. In 2003, the royal family kidnapped a major Saudi prince from his Swiss palace when negotiations, bribes, and group pressure failed to stem his public exposés of the regime's corruption and decay. The operation was botched when the prince almost died. The crown prince blamed the minister of defense, who returned the favor. The affair was detailed by the Movement for Islamic Reform in Arabia (MIRA), an opposition group located in London, and publicized by the BBC and other news sources.

Less important positions are occupied by the some 6,000 princes—detractors suggest a figure of 30,000—who constitute the base of the royal family. Most are "cadet" members of the family, indicating that they are not in line to the throne. Many hold sensitive positions and are referred to as "His Highness" but not as "His Royal Highness" (Saudi Royals, Online Bios, 1999–2000).

The size of the royal family adds four critical dimensions to Saudi politics. First, the family is able to occupy key positions at all levels of government in Saudi Arabia, including the bureaucracy, the military, and the local governments. Very little escapes the purview of the royal family. Second, most princes of standing hold weekly sessions in which they address the problems of supplicants and grant favors. In the best of feudal traditions, this practice enables the royal family to build personal links with its subjects. It is not the state that provides, but a generous and compassionate monarchy. Third, the vast size of the royal family places it in competition with an emerging middle class for government positions and economic opportunities. It is an unequal competition that leads to considerable frustration among the Saudi middle class. Finally, a large share of the Saudi budget goes to finance the royal family and their royal lifestyle, with some 10,000 princes and princesses receiving generous monthly stipends from the national treasury (Viorst 1996, 6).

The major princes are followed in order of importance by the senior ulema, a category that would include the grand mufti, the ministers of *waqfs* and justice, senior officials in the ministries of Education and Higher Education, and the members of the Council of High Ulema. They may also include the members of the Supreme Council for Islamic Affairs, a new body created in 1994 to promote the influence of younger Islamic scholars whose views are more likely to parallel those of the regime than are those of the older religious elite (Joseph 1998). Adding to the power of the senior ulema is their control of Saudi Arabia's numerous religious universities as well as several government agencies, including the agencies for Religious Research, Legal Opinion, Propaganda and Guidance, and the Committee on Public Morality (the religious police) (Joseph 1998). It is the profound conservatism of these institutions that has led to U.S. charges that the Saudi religious elite promotes Islamic extremism and anti-Americanism. Indeed, the 2005 local elections were matched by the quiet appointment of an ultraconservative cleric as the minister of interior.

The royal family cannot risk a break with the religious establishment. It is they who certify the religious credentials of the royal family, one of the key pillars of its authority. It is doubtful that the regime could survive a widespread rebellion in the ranks of the senior ulema (Abir 1993).

Despite their interdependence, relations between the royal family and the religious establishment have not been free from tension. In part, this tension has centered on conflicts over the pace of modernization. The monarchy is conservative, but it is far less conservative than the ulema. The monarchy has shown some willingness to bend to the forces of change. The ulema, by and large, have not. Indeed, key elements in the ulema would like to turn back the clock, a position that would make them ideological allies of the jihadists.

This tension between the two elites represents a basic struggle for supremacy. This struggle has existed from the founding of the Saudi dynasty, when Abd al-Wahhab proclaiming himself the kingdom's supreme religious authority, or supreme sheikh, and ibn Saud adopting the title of General of the Wahhabis (De Corancez 1995, 8). The battle was revived in 1926, when relations between ibn Saud and the Ikhwan began to disintegrate; the Ikhwan were not fully defeated until 1929. It has resurfaced in the present era as the religious reformers—not to be confused with liberal political reformers—demand an ever more religious state and the jihadists pursue a war of terror against the monarchy. The religious reformers are demanding an end to corruption and the religious purification of Saudi society, not greater Westernization.

Secondary elites in Saudi Arabia fall roughly into two categories. First are the leaders of the modernizing middle class. Although commoners, they fill the senior positions in the bureaucracy, military, and the private sector that have not been preempted by the royal family. Most are well educated; many have advanced degrees from universities in the West. This modernizing elite is offset by the more conservative leaders of the middle and lower class, most of whom view modernization as a threat to Islamic values. They too occupy important positions in the religious, bureaucratic, military, and business communities. Even here, the picture is complex, for in general the modernizers are not antireligious. Rather, they advocate a more flexible program of modernization within an Islamic context. The inherent tension between the two secondary elites adds to the caution of the royal family, as does their shared concern over the family's excesses. Important tribal chiefs also constitute a secondary elite, but their influence has waned in recent years.

The power of the secondary elites rests on their role as managers and administrators rather than on their capacity to make major decision (Al-Gosaibi 1998). The senior princes make the decisions. Those in the secondary elites decide how those decisions will be implemented. This gives the secondary elites tremendous scope for determining what will and will not succeed in Saudi Arabia. It also gives them extraordinary opportunity for corruption. Saudis complain that every new regulation brings new demands for bribes (Al-Gosaibi 1998, 200).

## The Political Institutions of Saudi Arabia:
## Formal and Informal Roles

The two basic political institutions of Saudi Arabia are the Koran and the kinship ties that bind the royal family. Both exert a profoundly conservative influence on Saudi politics. By acknowledging the Koran as the constitution of Saudi Arabia, the royal family finds it difficult to expand beyond a system of politics that evolved in a far simpler time. The basic principles are valid, but the practice of politics in an era of globalization involves adaptations unforeseen by the Koran. Particularly knotty is the Koranic prohibition against payment of interest, an issue that has resulted in a strangely contorted banking system that issues depositors a share of the bank's profits rather than interest. Profits are allowed by the Koran; interest is not. The position of the Koran as the constitution of Saudi Arabia also increases the power of the senior ulema, for they are its interpreters.

The royal family is the locus of all secular authority in Saudi Arabia. Lest there be any doubt on the matter, the Basic System unabashedly stipulates that "the dynasty right shall be confined to the sons of the Founder, King Abd al-Aziz bin Abdul Rahman al Saud (ibn Saud), and the sons of the sons." The most eligible among them shall be invited, through the process of *bai'ah* (swearing allegiance) to "rule in accordance with the Book of God and the Prophet's Sunna" (Article 5b, Saudi Arabian Information Resource). A citizen shall pledge allegiance to the king on the basis of the Book of God and the Prophet's Sunna, as well as on the principle of "hearing is obeying," both in prosperity and diversity, in situations pleasant and unpleasant (Article 6). Aside from the obligation to "rule in accordance with the Book of God and the Prophet's Sunna," there are no formal constraints on the authority of the king and the royal family.

As sovereignty resides with the royal family, Saudi political institutions have no formal legitimacy or source of power other than what the royal family grants them. For all practical purposes, the royal family is the state. The king serves as the prime minister of Saudi Arabia; the crown prince as the deputy prime minister. The cabinet is named by the king and serves at the pleasure of the king, as do members of the Consultative Council, military officers, and all other senior officials in the kingdom. All ministries considered key to the security of the regime are headed by senior princes, foremost among which are the ministries of Defense and Interior (police) and the National Guard. Less sensitive ministries are headed by technocrats, with the exception of the Ministry for Islamic Affairs, Endowments (*Waqfs*), Dawa, and Guidance and the Ministry of Justice, which are controlled by the ulema. The ulema also play a major role in the ministries of Education and Higher Education.

The monarchy exercises its authority through a variety of formal institutions, the most important of which are the Council of Ministers, the massive bureaucracy that it guides, the military/security apparatus, the Council of High Ulema, and the Consultative Council.

**The Council of Ministers**  The Council of Ministers possesses both formal and informal functions. Its formal functions are to execute the decisions of the ruling princes and otherwise manage the kingdom's substantial bureaucracy. The latent function of the Council of Ministers is to forge a link between the monarchy and the secondary elites, most of whose members are drawn from the middle classes. Cabinet ministers supervise the spending of vast sums of money and thus have vast amounts of patronage at their disposal. This patronage is filtered through kinship and patron–client networks, ensuring that key segments of the population— including the tribes, the clergy, the business community, and the bureaucrats— have a stake in the system.

**The Bureaucracy**    In addition to executing the decisions of the senior princes and the Council of Ministers, the bureaucracy is responsible for providing the Saudi population with a reasonable level of services. The difficulty is that Saudi bureaucrats view their positions as a right rather than as an obligation. This is not hard to understand. Positions in the Saudi bureaucracy were designed to provide the Saudi middle class, now increasingly well educated, with their share of the nation's wealth. In the past, salaries were high, demands few, and performance minimal. Much of the work that got done was carried out by foreigners. This posed minimal problems during the boom years of the 1980s, but confronted the kingdom with a cash-flow problem during the lean years of the 1990s. Indeed, the past two decades have seen more than $330 billion sent out of Saudi Arabia by foreign workers. In 2003, remittances by foreign workers were approximately equal to 20 percent of the kingdom's gross national product (*Gulf News,* May 2, 2004). The monarchy now demands that Saudi officials pull their weight and has called for the "Saudization" of the bureaucracy and economy. All positions except those for which no Saudis are available will be filled by Saudis. Companies that fail to comply will not be awarded government contracts (*Arab News,* Feb. 10, 2005). The number of visas for foreign workers has also been reduced.

On the surface, the Saudization of the bureaucracy does not seem to be a daunting task. Unofficial estimates place the Saudi unemployment rate at 30 percent (*Arab News,* Feb. 10, 2005). Life, however, is not that simple. Many of the unemployed are graduates of religious universities and lack technical skills. Others are poorly trained yet refuse to accept menial positions. Women are excluded from many positions by cultural considerations.

The problem also lies within the Saudi bureaucracy itself. Saudi officials view their jobs as a right and have developed a distaste for hard work. If the government carries through with its pledge to reduce its dependence on foreigners, the quality of services will decline dramatically. If it attempts to reform the bureaucracy by reducing excess staff, it may politicize a middle class that it has bribed to be docile. Either way it loses. The same is true of government promises to impose harsh new penalties for negligence, waste of public funds, and corruption in all its diverse forms (*Arab News,* April 1, 2005). Corruption is part of the regime's income distribution system. The informal influence of the bureaucracy, then, is essentially negative. It consumes vast resources, provides an obstacle to effective government, and thrives on corruption. Reform is often promised, but implementation efforts have been largely symbolic. How does one reform a bureaucracy built on patronage without threatening the regime that created it? Adding to the confusion have been government threats to discipline any administrative official who criticizes any government programs or policies (*Financial Times,* Sept. 16, 2004, 12). Fear leads to paralysis, not productivity.

For their part, Saudis tend to blame the poor performance of their bureaucracy on the presence of too many foreigners, most of whom are supposedly only concerned with "ripping off" the Saudis. Needless to say, these differing explanations of Saudi Arabia's bureaucratic problems have led to tension between Saudi officials and the expatriates they supervise.

**The Security Services**     The same duality between formal and informal functions permeates the security services, which include the regular military, the National Guard, and various intelligence services, the details of which remain sketchy (Cordesman and Obaid 2005). The formal function of the security services is to protect the regime from its enemies, foreign and domestic. Its informal function, like that of the bureaucracy, is to provide jobs and patronage for the regime's supporters. Patronage, however, cannot guarantee the loyalty of the military or the kingdom's various other intelligence services. In 2004, a captured jihadist militant charged with beheading an American engineer claimed that his group had been aided by the police and security forces (CNN, June 21, 2004). Saudi authorities denied the allegations, but doubts remain. It is difficult to divorce the security services from a cultural and educational environment that places inordinate emphasis on an extremist version of Islam increasingly hostile to both the monarchy and the United States. Anti-regime violence has increased dramatically, and the royal family is ever alert to the possibility of a military coup.

Saudi efforts to preclude a military coup take a variety of forms. Sensitive leadership positions remain in the hands of the royal family, and the military is closely watched by various intelligence services. The Saudi military is also minute by regional standards: a small military is easier to control than a large one. The army and the National Guard each have about 75,000 troops, the air force less than a third of that number (*Economist* 2005). The army and the National Guard are each under the control of a different branch of the royal family, the intelligence services under a third. Everyone watches everyone. This is great for internal security, but poor for coordination.

The monarchy has compensated for the small size of its military establishment by stressing hardware rather than manpower. Saudi Arabia is one of the largest importers of arms in the Third World. Fancy hardware has its uses off the battlefield. Generals like sophisticated weapons even if they are beyond the technical capacity of their troops. Sophisticated hardware also plays well in parades, inspires the confidence of the masses, and serves as a warning to adversaries, of which the Saudis have many. Members of the National Guard are recruited from Saudis with bedouin backgrounds, thereby increasing the likelihood that they will share the regime's conservative tribal and religious values. Finally, the regular military and the National Guard are pampered with high salaries, cars, excellent housing, and superior health care. The perks of the National Guard are the best of the best (Dahy 1988).

The price of this elaborate system of control has been high. The military consumes an inordinate share of the national budget, but does little to deter the kingdom's external enemies. In the months preceding the 1991 Gulf War, it was estimated that Iraqi forces could have overrun the kingdom in three days. Distrust of its own military contributes to the caution of the regime and has increased its dependence on U.S. protection, albeit from a distance. Saudi Arabia also maintains a lose military alliance with the neighboring Gulf sheikhdoms via the Gulf Cooperation Council, but they, like Saudi Arabia, are too weak to resist an attack from their stronger neighbors (Anthony 2004). Saudi Arabia is also rumored to be considering the acquisition of weapons in an effort to counter Iran's nuclear program and to break its military dependence on the United States—a sobering thought indeed (*Guardian,* Sept. 18, 2003). Should the monarchy fall, who would control those weapons? Hopefully, it will remain no more than a rumor.

**The Consultative Council**    The formation of the Consultative Council was proclaimed in the tense days following the Gulf War, and its first session was held in 1993. The establishment of such a council had been promised during several earlier crises but none had materialized. As presently constituted, the Consultative Council consists of 150 members selected by the king. The council is charged with advising the king on a wide range of policy issues and may propose legislation; however, it possesses no legislative authority. Indeed, the Basic System goes out of its way to stipulate that the council is an expression of administrative rather than legislative authority. By and large, the members of the Consultative Council are both well educated and politically colorless, a combination of attributes that fits well in the Saudi political milieu (Dekmejian 1998, 11).

Although exercising no real power, the Consultative Council plays four roles of importance to the monarchy. First, it provides a link between the royal family and important segments of the Saudi population including both the "Islamic traditionalists and liberal modernizers" (Dekmejian 1998, 211). Recent expansion of the council has also provided representation for tribes and regions. Second, the council is part of the kingdom's patronage–income distribution system. Contacts (*wasta*) are required to get things done in this most personalized of political systems, and the council provides yet another avenue for making those contacts. Third, the Consultative Council has been particularly effective in suggesting adjustments to the kingdom's archaic commercial and legal procedures. Such adjustments are much needed, yet pose no threat to the monarchy. Finally, the Consultative Council helps to counter criticism of the Saudi system in the West by serving as a symbol of democratic reform. Thoughts of a partially elected council, however, remain premature.

The danger of the Consultative Council to the monarchy, of course, is that it does represent an embryonic legislature, statements to the contrary notwithstanding. Kuwait and Iran both have established meaningful legislatures, and pressure is mounting on Saudi Arabia to do the same.

**The Council of High Ulema**    The ulema are headed by the Council of High Ulema, a body created by the king to certify that the royal family rules "in accordance with the Book of God and the Prophet's Sunna." As such, the Council of High Ulema is the monarchy's first line of defense against its religious critics. The Basic System goes out of its way to justify the monarchy's role as the protector of religion, with Article 23 stipulating that "the State shall protect the Islamic Creed and shall cater to the application of Sharia. The State shall enjoin good and forbid evil, and shall undertake the duties of the call to Islam." In return for its support, the Council of High Ulema has been given management of Saudi Arabia's religious institutions and is allowed to censor the content of educational and cultural materials, including the mass media. It also guides the judicial process and keeps the lower ranks of the ulema in line.

The strict application of Sharia (Islamic) law by the Wahhabi religious establishment includes amputations for theft and public execution for murder, drug trafficking, and rape. All have prompted severe criticism of the Saudi regime by human rights groups such as Amnesty International. Such charges are summarily rejected by the Saudi Minister of Justice, Abdullah al-Sheikh: "Those who raise doubts that sharia law does not guarantee human rights are the enemies of God, religion and humanity and their hearts are full of hatred." He went on to note that the critics "have misled many people with lies and fallacies which they spread through the media" (AP, May 10, 2000, cited in Movement for Islamic Reform in Arabia, May 1–14, 2000).

The power of the ulema also finds expression in the presence of *mutawwatin* (Committees for Vice and Virtue), or religious police, as well as in the large number of religious universities, the graduates of which have difficulty finding jobs outside of an already overstaffed religious sector. It is largely they who fill the ranks of the religious police.

The king appoints the members of the Council of High Ulema, who are employees of the state, as are all members of the ulema. This gives the palace a high degree of control over the religious establishment, but that control is far from absolute. The monarchy is facing increased pressure from large segments of the ulema, often referred to as the religious reformers, to slow the pace of modernization in the kingdom.

In sum, Saudi political institutions influence the Saudi political process in four fundamental ways. First, they give representation to important groups in Saudi society. That representation is not democratic in nature, but it does give key groups access to the monarchy. Second, the Saudi political institutions are a key mechanism for the distribution of wealth. In part, that distribution takes the form of salaries and benefits; in part it takes the form of officially sanctioned corruption. By whatever route, the wealth of the kingdom does trickle down to a broad segment of the Saudi population. Third, the weakness of Saudi political institutions taxes both the budget and the patience of the Saudi population. It also limits the capacity of the monarchy to implement its projects and perpetuates Saudi dependence on foreign labor. Fourth, Saudi political institutions represent a potential threat to the regime. The security services possess a monopoly of coercive force and must be kept under constant surveillance. The Council of High Ulema embodies the tension that has always existed between the monarchy and the ulema. The Consultative Council must ultimately give way to demands for a more representative parliament.

Aside from the problems outlined above, perhaps the most glaring defect of the Saudi institutional structure is that it does not provide avenues for peaceful change. There are no formal mechanisms for the resolution of conflict, nor are there formal mechanisms for the Saudi population to express discontent with their rulers. Local elections were held in 2005, but the monarchy and its policies were not an issue. Most were swept by conservative religious candidates and local notables. This was a step in the right direction, but a very small one.

## The Group Basis of Saudi Society:
## Politics in the Absence of Civil Society

Saudi Arabia does not possess a civil society as the term is normally used in the West. There are no elections beyond the local level; political parties, student associations, labor unions, or other organized political groups are not allowed to organize. Even random gatherings are broken up by the security apparatus. Newspapers abound but do not criticize the royal family or its policies. They have become a bit bolder in discussing social problems in the wake of two Gulf wars. Satellite dishes are forbidden, but nevertheless exist in great profusion. The people have spoken.

Those groups that do exist are either business groups or Islamic benevolent associations. By 1998, for example, the government acknowledged the existence of some 142 charitable organizations in the kingdom (Saudi Arabian Government 1998). These came under intense scrutiny by the United States following the September 11 attacks. Many were accused of knowingly or unknowingly supporting jihadist organizations. Saudi officials acknowledge that state supervision of Islamic charities had been lax and that they weren't entirely sure of how many charities existed. The U.S. has been assured that the situation is being remedied. The issue, however, is touchy. Charity is one of the cardinal principles of Islam, and the royal family must take great care not to inflame the religious sentiments on which its legitimacy is based.

Business associations such as the Saudi Chamber of Commerce and Industry come the closest to resembling American style pressure groups and provide a link between the regime and the modernizing middle class. This is all the more the case because a majority of its governing board are appointed by the government (*Al-Nashura,* Sept. 8, 1986). Professional congresses exist for professors, engineers, doctors, pharmacists, chemists, and others, but they are sponsored by the government and have little scope for independent action (Abir 1993, 115).

Saudi efforts to slow the evolution of civil society are easy to understand. Most political activity is group activity, and the suppression of civil society is designed to prevent opposition groups from becoming organized. Political organizations, however innocent, generate demands for greater representation and association elections often serve as surrogates for national elections. That is precisely the role that professional associations play in Egypt and various other Middle Eastern countries. Political parties, if allowed, would propose alternate candidates for the leadership of the country. It is also likely that the emergence of political parties would fragment a society struggling desperately to create a sense of national identity and national purpose. Modernizers would contend with conservatives, religious moderates with religious extremists, Hijazis with Najdis. A free mass media, in turn, would risk offending deeply entrenched religious sentiments. It is not clear that the fabric of Saudi Arabia could withstand such strains.

The suppression of civil society, however, is not without its costs. Parties, associations, public opinion polls, and a free press provide political leaders with important feedback about the public mood. As a result, problems can be solved before they become serious. The Saudi regime, however, must operate without a barometer of public sentiment: its only feedback is that provided by the secret police and periodic outbreaks of violence (Champion 1999). Lacking clear feedback on popular sentiments, the regime tends to become increasingly cautious and diffident. Problems are not dealt with until they reach crisis proportions; Saudi hesitancy prior to the first Gulf War is a case in point.

The absence of a civil society in Saudi Arabia does not mean an absence of group pressures in the Saudi political process (Fandy 2004). As noted earlier, the ulema are a powerful group skilled at pursuing their interests. So, too, are the military, the bureaucracy, the business community, the tribes, and the broader reaches of the royal family. Each has a paramount interest in preserving its special position in Saudi society. The modernizers and the conservatives constitute less well defined groups, yet each represents a central current in the Saudi ideological debate (Dekmejian 1998). The debate takes place within the royal/religious framework of Saudi politics, with each side arguing how this best of all possible worlds could be made even better by greater or lesser degrees of modernization (Al-Rasheed 1996a, 1996b; Nehme 1994). The same debate permeates the military, bureaucracy, the royal family, and even the ulema. Modernization should not be equated with a decline in religiosity. Rather, the debate involves the expression of religion in Saudi society (Nehme 1995).

A large middle class has developed in Saudi Arabia, much of it educated in the West. While the middle class generally inclines toward the modernizing camp, many of its members remain conservative in outlook. The middle class also divides along regional lines. The more urban Hijazis, once the backbone of the Saudi Arabian bureaucratic and technocratic class, have now seen their position in these areas challenged by an increasingly well educated Najdi middle class (Abir 1993). However fragmented, the Saudi middle class is vitally concerned about its economic and political positions. Members of the middle class want greater participation in the political system, although this does not necessarily mean Western-style elections. They also want to see the economic perks of the boom years maintained, and most are frustrated by the "royal ceiling." This frustration has become all the more evident since the era of rapid economic development has peaked. Young Saudis no longer return with Western doctorates to become deans and directors. Indeed, Saudi Arabia is now facing an unemployment problem that is particularly severe among women and graduates of its Islamic universities. As Yamani writes:

> Today, there are more girls at schools and universities in Saudi Arabia than boys, and their results are academically getting better than their male counterparts (from below 10 percent at the beginning of this century, the national literacy rate stands today at an average in excess of 65 percent, with 80 percent male and 50 percent female). The biggest challenge in the future will be finding appropriate employment for these educated women in a balanced formula that both adheres to Islamic principles and meets the heightened expectations of this important portion of the population (Yamani 1998, 28).

**Islamic Opposition Groups**   The most immediate threat to the Saudi monarchy is provided by Islamic opposition groups. These come in two broad varieties. Most visible are the jihadists who have declared an unrelenting war of violence against the Saudi regime. Saudi jihadists, like their counterparts throughout the Islamic world, believe that a pure Islamic state can only be imposed by force. In their view, nothing is to be gained by cooperating with a corrupt monarchy that has sold its soul to the enemies of Islam. To the contrary, the very existence of the monarchy corrupts new generations of Saudi youth, squanders the kingdom's phenomenal oil wealth, and facilitates the U.S. crusade against Islam. To spare the monarchy, they believe, is to cooperate with the devil.

At present, the most prominent of the jihadists groups in Saudi Arabia is al-Qaeda Arabian Peninsula (QAP). The name suggests strong ties with bin Laden's al-Qaeda network, but this does not mean that it is under bin Laden's control. The generation of Saudi jihadists that was responsible for the 1995–1996 bombings of U.S. facilities in Riyadh and Dammam had different names and acted as independent contractors for bin Laden's al-Qaeda organization (Habib, n.d.). This said, there can be no doubt that bin Laden has a special interest in Saudi Arabia and that he views the defeat of the monarchy as the key to driving the U.S. from the region. A detailed discussion of the organization, operation, and vulnerabilities of jihadist groups is beyond the scope of this book, but can be found in the author's *At the Heart of Terror* (Palmer and Palmer 2004).

Less visible, but no less threatening to the monarchy, are the Islamic reformers. The two dominant reform groups are the Committee for the Defense of Legitimate Rights (CDLR) and the Movement for Islamic Reform in Arabia (MIRA). The leaders of both organizations were Muslim intellectuals who had signed the petitions and the "Memorandum of Advice" of the early 1990s. Indeed, Saad al-Faqih, the leader of MIRA, was a professor of surgery at King Saud University until 1994. Both fled to London to escape prosecution. Both organizations are small and rely heavily on the Internet and satellite to spread their message (Abedin 2005). Islamic reformists within Saudi Arabia have been arrested and subjected to persecution. This was probably a mistake, for flawed show trials have served only to popularize the Islamic reformists and further discredit the monarchy.

Much like the Muslim Brotherhood, with whom they have much in common, the Islamic reformers advocate the achievement of an Islamic state by peaceful and democratic means. The Muslim Brotherhood, while illegal in the kingdom, does have a strong following throughout Saudi Arabia and the Gulf region. On several occasions it has negotiated directly with the monarchy to resolve issues of mutual importance such as regional conflicts (Nada 2002a; Nada 2002b).

Which is the most threatening to the monarchy, the jihadists or the Islamic reformers? The answer is both. The jihadists hammer the regime with violence while the Islamic reformers seek an Islamic state through seduction and promises of democracy. The monarchy has attempted to crush both with a mix of repression, negotiations, bribes, jammed satellite transmissions, and promises of amnesty. The monarchy claims victory, but to no avail. Neither the jihadists nor the Islamic reformers will go away. Indeed, Saudi jihadists have returned from Iraq and Sudan with renewed zeal and skills (*WP,* July 11, 2004). More appear to be on their way (*Daily Star,* June 1, 2005). For the moment, the contest between the regime and its adversaries is a stand-off. The *Economist* Intelligence Unit gives Saudi Arabia a "D" in political stability (*Economist* 2005).

## THE CONTEXT OF SAUDI POLITICS

Having examined the basic elements of the Saudi political system, we turn now to the broader cultural, economic, and international contexts that shape Saudi politics. These influences on Saudi politics are not a minor consideration, for all four pillars of the Saudi regime—tribalism/kinship, Islam, oil wealth, and the special relationship with the United States—belong to this category.

### Political Culture

The political culture of Saudi Arabia has several aspects, all of which directly influence the behavior of the Saudi regime. Most help to explain its conservatism and extreme caution. The first point is that kinship ties continue to provide the foundation of Saudi society, a fact amply demonstrated by the power of the royal family (Long 1997, 2005). Saudis are intensely close to their families, and most find their clans and tribes to be a vital support group. A survey of student attitudes during the early 1980s, by way of illustration, found that Saudi students would choose a moderate-paying job close to their families over a higher-paying job in a different city (Al-Nimir and Palmer 1982). It is also interesting to note that a recent study sponsored by the Saudi government found that 56 percent of all marriages in Saudi Arabia are "between first and second cousins or more distant relatives" (*WP,* Jan. 16, 2000, A10).

The regime goes out of its way to strengthen traditional family values, with the Basic System stating that "the family is the nucleus of Saudi society. Its members shall be brought up imbued with the Islamic creed which calls for obedience to God" (Article 9), and "the State shall take great pains to strengthen the bonds which hold the family together and to preserve Arab Islamic values" (Article 10). This is not idle verbiage, for as noted earlier, the National Guard goes out of its way to recruit individuals from tribal backgrounds because of their greater attachment to the kinship and religious values upon which the regime bases its legitimacy.

The regime's stress on kinship also has its drawbacks. Ties to the tribe are probably stronger than ties to the nation, and the regime is particularly anxious to recruit members of "friendly" tribes for the security services. Efforts are also made to maintain a balance between tribes, thereby preventing any one tribe from becoming predominant. As might be expected given this policy, tensions between tribes occasionally erupt into violence (*Gulf News,* March 1, 2005). Unlike religious issues, such tensions do not pose a threat to the regime. The conservative nature of tribal values also reinforces the conservativism of Saudi religious views. A senior Saudi cleric recently stressed this point, saying, "Here in Saudi Arabia we have as many as 500 tribes and we live by certain norms. Preserving those norms is important" (*Arab News,* Oct. 20, 2004).

There can be little doubt that most Saudis take pride in Saudi Arabia's position as the heartland of Islam. Arabs, in general, believe that they occupy a special place in Islam, a view that is particularly strong among the residents of the Arabian Peninsula. Such views have been reinforced by the country's oil wealth, which many Saudis believe to be a sign of God's blessing. The regime is actively pursuing efforts to strengthen this sense of Saudi identity, but like so much in Saudi Arabia, data on the topic is scant (Nehme 1994).

Religion pervades all dimensions of Saudi life and is indivisible from politics. Islamic topics constitute about one-third of the curriculum of elementary schools, and approximately the same proportion of Saudi university students major in Islamic studies (Joseph 1998, 2). The monarchy presumably gains legitimacy from its role as the protector and propagator of Islam, but it is also constrained by the very intensity with which its citizens adhere to their religious values (Joseph 1998).

Saudi political culture is also characterized by profound apathy, a phenomenon that could be attributed to a variety of causes. Some observers see the Saudi population as having been bought off by a social contract that trades wealth for political docility, while others find the docility of the Saudi population to be a realistic response to a security apparatus that is as brutal as it is pervasive. A variation on this theme suggests that many Saudis possess a profound respect for power and will obey any regime that has the strength to impose its will. The regime's greatest mistake, from this Hobbesian perspective, would be to show signs of weakness, including bowing to demands for greater democracy. Yet another explanation for the docility of the Saudi population is the heavy dose of fatalism contained in some Islamic texts. God is omnipotent, and the will of individuals counts for little. If God wanted change, there would be change. Islam also stresses innovation and creativity, but these dimensions of Islam have received minimal attention by the religious establishment. There is insufficient data to sort out the above explanations of political docility in Saudi Arabia, but each would seem to explain part of the riddle.

Two other aspects of Saudi culture, both of them rooted in economics, pose a problem for the regime. First, Saudi Arabia has become a consumer society par excellence (Krimly 1999; Yamani 1998). Saudis have developed a taste for the finest in luxury goods, all of which must be imported from abroad. This posed little problem during the boom years but has eased with the escalation of oil prices precipitated by the Iraq War (Krimly 1999; Yamani 1998). Government calls for moderation have gone unheeded, by the royal family among many others. Extravagance and waste continue unabated (*Arab View,* 2003).

More problematic has been the reluctance of Saudis to engage in mundane labor. In part, the aloofness of Saudi citizens from greater involvement in their own economy reflects traditional tribal disdain for menial labor. It has also been the product of sudden wealth and government efforts to build political support by pampering the population. Attitudes toward work are changing, but they are changing very slowly (Dahy 1988). Yamani leaves little doubt that this lack of interest in work continues to be the case today: "In present Saudi life, we remark that the new generations are much less motivated than is necessary for our future success as a society that wishes to prosper and develop. They have very high expectations and they have been spoiled in having all their wishes met without effort or delay" (Yamani 1998, 135). Others fear that Saudis are becoming a nation of clerks. Few join the private sector and many avoid jobs that are technical and require long hours, proficiency in English, or manual labor (*Arab News,* July 9, 2004). Saudis want more, but are not willing to work harder. They are becoming educated without becoming motivated. Many are also falling prey to the seductions of the Internet and satellite TV. Indeed, Western channels are twice as popular as Arab channels (*Arab View* 2003). Clerics also worry about the prevalence of foreign pornography websites on the morals of the nation's youth. Cheating is also on the rise (*Arab View* 2003). Saudi youth, for their part, complain that the regime has failed to connect with them. That, at least, was the message of the low turnout by Saudi youth in the recent local elections (*Arab News,* Feb. 11, 2005).

## Political Economy

The guiding principle of political economy is that economics drives politics. Prosperity brings political stability; declining prosperity brings instability. On the surface, this would seem to be the case in Saudi Arabia (Aarts and Nonneman 2005). The legitimacy and stability of the Saudi monarchy have long been linked to an implicit social contract that trades the nation's fabulous wealth for docility. The state provides, and the population consumes. There are no direct taxes other than the 2.5 percent religious tax, *zakat,* imposed by the Koran. This tax is collected by the government (Yamani 1998).

What is unique about the Saudi Arabian case is that its prosperity is derived almost entirely from the export of a single product, oil. Indeed, Saudi Arabia is often described as a rentier state: a country that lives off the proceeds or "rents" of its natural resources. The oil was discovered, developed, refined, and marketed by U.S. firms (Aburish 1994; Alnasrawi 1991). Aramco, the U.S. operating consortium, was nationalized in the period between 1974 and 1980, but U.S. operatives continue to play dominant roles in all stages of the production and marketing process. Saudi Arabia now possesses a vigorous industry based upon the production and marketing of oil-based products, but these industries are largely staffed by foreign technicians. Saudis, by and large, have little involvement in their own economy, including the production of their most vital resource. As noted in the discussion of culture, they have become consumers rather than producers. This is an important consideration, for it burdens Saudi Arabia with the salaries of a massive number of foreign technicians performing tasks that could be performed by Saudi nationals, many of whom are already on the payroll.

What this means, from the political economic perspective, is that the stability of the Saudi monarchy is likely to rise and fall with the gyrations of the oil market. At current rates of production, a drop of $1 per barrel in the price of oil costs the Saudi government approximately $2.5 billion per year (U.S. Energy Information Administration, Jan. 1999). During the boom years of the 1970s and early 1980s, few Saudis seemed inclined to jeopardize a system that had made them among the most pampered people on earth. The precipitous decline in the price of oil during the 1980s and 1990s frayed the Saudi social contract that traded wealth for docility. It could not be otherwise, for the regime's revenues dropped from $101 billion in 1981 to $13.5 billion in 1986, and remained depressed until the turn of the century (U.S. Energy Information Administration, Jan. 1999). Saudi per capita income fell from some $15,000 in 1981 to approximately $7,000 by the year 2000. Calls for political reform from all segments of Saudi society increased apace, not the least of which were petitions from the clerics. All of this was new to Saudi politics.

The September 11 attacks on the United States and the subsequent war on Iraq triggered a surge in oil prices and the beleaguered monarchy is once again awash in oil. Indeed, in 2004 Saudi Arabia earned $106 billion from its oil exports, the largest annual income in its history (*Daily Star,* Jan. 18, 2005). This surge in oil prices shows few signs of stopping (*The Economist,* Survey of Oil, April 30, 2005). Saudi Arabia currently pumps 10 million barrels of oil per day (BPD). The U.S. government estimates that Saudi oil exports must reach 13.5 million BPD by 2010 and 20 million BPD by 2020 if they are to keep pace with world demand (*Daily Star,* June 10, 2004).

According to the logic of the political economist argument, the phenomenal surge in oil revenues should correspond to an increase in the stability of the Saudi regime. It has not. The monarchy is facing greater internal instability than at any previous time in its history. Why is this the case?

Some of the answers to this question are economic. Many are not. On the economic side are complaints that the non-oil sector of the Saudi economy remains under government control and is minimally productive. Rather than creating wealth, public-sector firms, the dominant force in the Saudi economy, tend to consume wealth. As if to underscore the inefficiency of its public sector, the Saudi government has now allowed foreign firms to prospect for oil in the kingdom, a practice that had earlier been discontinued by the state. Government jobs are part of the social contract and are viewed by Saudis as a right rather than a privilege. This problem is further aggravated by the fact that the private sector employs few Saudi nationals—less than 10 percent by some estimates (*GulfWire,* Nov. 13, 2000, 13). As a result, unemployment remains between 10 to 28 percent; the government admits to the former and the Saudi American Bank suggests the latter (*NYT,* Dec. 17, 2002). The oil sector, the source of more than 80 percent of Saudi Arabia's foreign exchange, employs only 1.5 percent of the population (Cordesman 2004).

Other economic problems abound. The management of the Saudi economy remains corrupt and lacks transparency. Foreign contracts invariably include a large commission for the official who helps arrange them, often 15 percent or more. Such practices originated as a means of distributing the nation's oil wealth to key individuals, but soon became so blatant that the government passed a law making it illegal for the same individual to serve as an intermediary for more than one contract. Whatever their merits as a strategy of distributing income, such exorbitant commissions raise the cost of doing business in Saudi Arabia and place a further strain on the Saudi budget. The monarchy vows to eliminate corruption, but it is not clear how this is to be achieved when members of the royal family are among the worst offenders. Adding insult to injury, much of Saudi wealth remains abroad. Wealthier Saudis, as the Movement for Islamic Reform in Saudi Arabia notes, have between $450 billion and $750 billion in foreign banks and securities, "enough to pay off Britain's entire national debt" (MIRA, Jan. 5, 2000, 12). Much of Saudi Arabia's physical infrastructure was built during the 1970s and early 1980s and is now in need of repair, an expensive proposition by any esti-mate. Problems of an eroding infrastructure have been further aggravated by ever increasing demands for housing, education, and employment. About half of Saudi Arabian citizens are younger than twenty-five, and the population is growing at a rate of 3.5 percent per year (MIRA, Jan. 5, 2000). Unemployment is already a problem in Saudi Arabia, and the government may have little choice but to con-tinue its expensive policy of finding jobs for new graduates in an already bloated bureaucracy.

The stability problem, however, is not merely economic. It is also cultural. The movement against the regime is being led by conservative religious elements who place their demands for a more religious state above economic concerns. While some of the jihadists and less violent extremists may be, or at least feel, econom-ically deprived, this could hardly have been the case of bin Laden. His family was among the wealthiest in the kingdom. The same is true of many other extremist leaders. At the same time, wealthy Saudis have long been suspected of supporting extremist movements throughout the Islamic world (*Daily Star,* July 15, 2005). Moderate Saudis have not resorted to violence, but they too are exerting grow-ing pressure for democratic and social reform. They want greater freedom of expression and are weary of the police surveillance, religious and otherwise. Cultural factors have similarly depressed the economy by making Saudis reluctant to accept low-status jobs. The problem is not a lack of jobs, but the unwillingness of Saudis to accept the jobs that are available. The cultural restrictions on women similarly deprive the kingdom of a highly skilled segment of the workforce. The case is worse than it seems, for men waste valuable work time by escorting their wives and daughters on routine errands that the women could accomplish them-selves if they were allowed to drive.

Violence in Saudi Arabia is also a function of an unstable regional environ-ment. The war in Iraq has stimulated terrorism in Iraq, and many Saudis who went to Iraq to fight the U.S. invasion are now returning home to take up the struggle against the monarchy. While most of the jihadist attacks have been directed at foreigners and government officials, at the end of May 2004 Saudi Arabia's oil facilities were a target. Should this trend continue, the one bright spot on the monarchy's horizon could become clouded. Needless to say, Saudi oil facilities are heavily guarded (BBC, June 3, 2004).

## The International Context of Saudi Politics

The influence of external events on Saudi politics can be discussed in terms of three general categories: external threats, external pressures for change, and the need for external protection. Covetous neighbors ranging from Nasser to the Ayatollah Khomeini to Saddam Hussein have all threatened to overthrow the monarchy by force. Bin Laden's al-Qaeda network shares this goal. Such attacks are easy to understand. The kingdom is both rich and weak. To control Saudi Arabia is to acquire the kingdom's phenomenal oil wealth. It is also to control the holiest places in Islam. Nor are the threats likely to recede. Iran appears on the verge of acquiring nuclear weapons and the current turmoil in Iraq threatens to bring a pro-Iranian regime to power in that country. This is not what the U.S. had in mind when it toppled Saddam Hussein in 2003, but Iran is the overwhelmingly dominant power in the region. It is also a power hostile to a Saudi monarchy that bankrolled Iraq's long war against Iran during the 1980s. Indeed, some believe that Iran is attempting to forge a Shi'a crescent that would encompass Iran, Iraq, Syria, Lebanon, and the oil-rich Eastern Province of Saudi Arabia. This is discussed further in Chapter 7. If the Saudi monarchy is nervous, it is not without cause.

External threats, in turn, have triggered intense pressures for change within Saudi Arabia. Two Gulf wars saw the kingdom inundated with U.S. troops. The continuing U.S. occupation of Iraq fans anti-U.S. hostility in the kingdom and has fueled terrorism within Saudi Arabia. America's war on terror has targeted the kingdom's religious, educational, and charitable organizations, all of which are key elements in the way the monarchy rules. The U.S. has also discovered that Saudi Arabia is not democratic and that it suppresses human rights. Changes have been demanded that, if implemented, would erode the monarchy's capacity to rule. The monarchy has allowed local elections and made other symbolic changes, but little more. Absolute monarchy is incompatible with democracy. That is all the more the case for a monarchy based on tribalism and religious extremism.

More subtle are the pressures for change from the Gulf states. Kuwait, Qatar, and other sheikhdoms are experimenting with democracy, and some allow a greater role for women in public life, including the right to vote. If the sheikhdoms can bend to the changing realities of the twenty-first century, some Saudis ask, why can't Saudi Arabia? These states all have similar political, social and economic systems. Added to the mix is the globalization of mass media, especially significant among which is the Al-Jazeera television network, the overwhelmingly most popular Arab satellite network in the region. Al-Jazeera is a profound force for change and democracy. The U.S. complains that Al-Jazeera is anti-American, but that is simply because Al-Jazeera opposes U.S. policy in the region. The U.S. is particularly sensitive to gory TV pictures of U.S. carnage in Iraq. Al-Jazeera's attacks on the United States are mild compared with its attacks on Saudi Arabia.

This, then, brings us to the kingdom's need for American protection. The ability of the U.S. to provide that protection may be in doubt. Anti-American sentiments within the kingdom were sufficient to force the withdrawal of U.S. troops in 2003. They remain offshore, and offer protection against an Iranian attack. That is necessary but not sufficient. The main enemy facing the kingdom is the enemy within. The U.S. bolsters Saudi internal security agencies, but the terror continues.

## LOOKING TOWARD THE FUTURE

Saudi Arabia at the dawn of the twenty-first century bears little resemblance to the desert monarchy forged by ibn Saud a hundred years ago. Poverty has given way to dazzling wealth, caravan trails to superhighways, nomadic bedouins to burgeoning cities, illiteracy to state-of-the-art schools and universities, illness to world-class hospitals, and tribal warriors to one of the most technologically sophisticated armies in the world. One way or another, everything is changing in Saudi Arabia—everything, that is, except its political system. How long it can stand against the tide of change remains to be seen (International Crisis Group 2004). The answer to this question will depend upon the ability of the monarchy to meet challenges in three key areas.

Of these, the most visible is the pervasive threat of terrorism. The monarchy has repeatedly claimed victory over the jihadists, but this is largely wishful thinking. There has been a persistent increase in jihadist terrorism over the past decade, and there is little reason to believe that it will subside in the near future (Teitelbaum 2005).

Less visible but equally potentially harmful is the challenge of political reform. The Saudi political system is based on tribalistic absolutism, oppression, corruption, its guardianship of Islam, its lavish outlays of oil revenues, and its dependency on the United States. Saudis are tiring of all this. Particularly upsetting to the religious community has been the monarchy's subservience to the U.S. Escalating oil revenues may give the monarchy breathing room, but they have not solved the problems of unemployment and declining income for a growing number of Saudis. The monarchy has taken timid steps toward political reform, but remains divided on the direction and extensiveness of that reform. This hesitancy is understandable. True reform, including reasonably fair elections, would probably lead to the end of the monarchy. Whether it would lead to an Islamic government remains to be seen. The hesitancy of the royal family is further heightened by the prospect of internal conflict as one aging leader gives way to another in rapid succession.

Adding to the kingdom's challenges is an increasingly volatile regional environment. A Shi'a-dominated Iraq aligned with Iran could prove to be as hostile to the kingdom as Saddam Hussein. Whatever the eventual outcome, the turmoil generated by the U.S. occupation of Iraq continues to fuel terrorism in the kingdom and to fan hostility toward a monarchy beholden to the U.S. for its survival. Ironically, one of the major shocks to the monarchy has been the confusion in American policy toward the kingdom in the aftermath of September 11, 2001. A strong mutual interest remains, but the once solid relationship has been frayed by persistent U.S. charges that Saudi Arabia is soft on terrorism and equally persistent perceptions that the U.S. has declared war on Islam. Indeed, of the four major pillars of Saudi rule—tribalism, Islam, U.S. support, and oil—only oil remains firm, and even oil may be shakier than it seems. Oil money is pouring in, but its distribution remains problematic. The average Saudi income is lower today than it was two decades ago.

# 6

# Iraq

## Chaos and Democracy in the Land of Milk and Honey

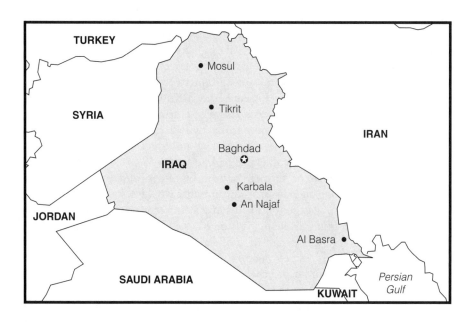

Iraq, the Mesopotamia of old, was a land of milk and honey. Its glorious rivers flowed through fertile plains and nurtured ancient civilizations that rivaled those of the Nile Valley. The hanging gardens of Babylon, one of the seven wonders of the ancient world, spoke to the genius of its people. With the Arab invasion in 633, Islam became the religion of most Iraqis. The Islam of Iraq, however, was tempered by a Persian culture rich in mysticism and was far less severe than the austere Islam of the Arabian Peninsula. Iraq, as discussed in Chapter 1, became the center of Shi'a Islam. By the ninth century, the land between the two rivers—which is what the name *Mesopotamia* means—had again emerged as the center of world civilization. Baghdad, the newly constructed capital of the Abbasid caliphs, dazzled the world with its science and philosophy. The *Arabian Nights* recounted its splendors and enchanted generations with its court intrigues. That, however, was long ago. The Mongol invasion of 1258 destroyed Baghdad, and with it the glories of the past. Mesopotamia was eventually absorbed by the Ottoman Empire and remained under Ottoman rule until it was occupied by the British during World War I (Polk 2005). Modern Iraq was cobbled together from three Turkish provinces in the aftermath of that war. It was an ungainly affair dictated by the interests of British colonial policy with scant regard for the background of its people. The oil-rich north was largely Kurdish. The south, a key element in British control of the Persian Gulf, was Shi'a. Sandwiched between the two was the "Sunni Triangle." Iraq was not one, country, but three.

Independence and massive oil reserves brought hope that Iraq would once again become the jewel of the Middle East. It was not to be. Stirrings of democracy were suffocated by tribal, ethnic, religious, and ideological conflicts. Brutal dictatorships oppressed the nation's people and pillaged its wealth. Of these, the latest was that of Saddam Hussein, a megalomaniac who crushed internal revolts by gassing Kurds and assassinating Shi'a religious leaders. This was of little concern to the United States as long as the Iraqi dictator was engaged in an eight-year war with the Islamic Republic of Iran. Who else was there to stop the Ayatollah Khomeini and the Islamic revolution that was sweeping the Middle East? It was only when Saddam Hussein invaded Kuwait in 1990 that the U.S. discovered the dark side of their erstwhile ally. During the following year the U.S. and its allies decimated Saddam's armies within hours, but not before the Iraqi dictator had launched missiles at Israel. The missiles did little damage, but he had made his point. Israel was vulnerable to Iraqi attack.

There were thoughts of occupying Baghdad, but wiser heads prevailed. Rather than suffer through a long and costly occupation that would destabilize the region, the United States left a chastised Saddam Hussein to serve as a counterweight to war-ravaged Iran. Far from repentant, Saddam Hussein boasted of having weapons of mass destruction and threatened to annihilate Israel, Saudi Arabia, and almost everyone else. Considered in retrospect, this was probably a mistake. His empty threats alarmed the U.S. and paved the way for the U.S.-led invasion in 2003.

More on this shortly. For the moment, suffice it to say that each change of regime in Iraq's modern history has brought death, destruction, and recrimination. And so it is today. The carnage, of the past pales before the devastation wrought by the destruction of the Saddam regime and the subsequent occupation of Iraq. The United States may boast of forging a new and democratic Iraq, but the Iraqis remain skeptical.

In the pages that follow we trace the tortured history of modern Iraq and examine its prospects for democracy and prosperity as it emerges from American occupation. The prospects are not bright, but the Iraqis are a talented and resilient people. Perhaps they can put the conflicts of the past behind them. Perhaps the world community will allow them to do so.

## HISTORY AND CULTURE

The ancient history of Iraq is beyond the scope of this chapter, and its early Islamic history was recounted in Chapter 1. Most problems confronting today's Iraq have their origins in the legacy of Ottoman rule. Iraq became part of the Ottoman Empire in the sixteenth century and remained under Turkish control until it was occupied by the British during World War I.[1] Several aspects of Ottoman rule shaped the political character of its former province. Under the *millet* system of administration, the Ottomans allowed the members of each religious sect to manage their own affairs as long as they paid their taxes and accepted the suzerainty of the sultan. Little effort was made to integrate the Shi'a, Kurdish, and Sunni communities into a whole; each remained a world unto itself. This tolerance toward minorities didn't mean that the Turks were impartial. On the contrary, the country was largely administered by Sunni Arabs, the co-religionists of the Ottomans. The Sunni also had better access to education than the Shi'a, and only Sunni were allowed to become officers in the Ottoman military (Batatu 1978). Indeed, a large segment of the Iraqi elite under the monarchy consisted of former officers of the Turkish army.

Also of relevance to the future of Iraqi politics was the Ottoman Land Code of 1858 (Haj 1997; Warriner 1957). Seeking to bring order to a system based on communal ownership of land, the new code registered tribal lands in the name of the tribal sheikh, thereby transforming them into his personal property. This process was extended under the Iraqi monarchy by a 1933 law outlining the rights and duties of peasants. As Warriner sums up the situation, "The sheikhs have now become legal owners of the dirah [tribal lands], the sirkals [foremen] have become the managers and agents; and the tribesmen have become share-cropping fellahin, with no rights or status" (Warriner 1957, 136). The situation was less severe in the Sunni and Kurdish north where the land was less fertile and did not lend itself as easily to plantation agriculture. The burden of the new feudalism, accordingly, fell largely on the Shi'a.

Britain had developed strong commercial and strategic interests in Iraq and the Arab Persian Gulf in the decades prior to World War I. Most had to do with oil and the region's strategic location along the route to India, the crown jewel of the British Empire. Eventually the British turned most of the Gulf's sheikhdoms into British protectorates, but Turkey had been a traditional ally of Britain and so the British saw little need for direct intervention in Iraq. This laissez-faire attitude would change in 1908 after control of the Ottoman Empire was seized by the Young Turks, a group of reform-minded officers with strong leanings toward

---

1 By 1914 the Ottomans had divided Iraq into three *vilayets* (provinces): Basra, Baghdad, and Mosul, with Baghdad being paramount (Dann 1969, 7).

imperial Germany. Plans for the construction of a Berlin-to-Baghdad railroad threatened Britain's communications with India, and the British responded by occupying the three Turkish provinces that now constitute Iraq, a task that took most of World War I (Elliot 1996). At the war's end, the final boundaries of Iraq were determined by a series of international conferences in which the victors in World War I divided up the colonial territories of the Axis powers. The San Remo Conference of 1920 awarded Britain control of Palestine, Jordan, and Iraq, while France was given control of Syria and Lebanon. In a British-staged plebiscite, a majority of the Iraqis voting approved Iraq's status as a British mandate. The Shi'a resisted British occupation as an affront to Islam, and the British, following the path of least resistance, relied on the Sunni elite that was already in place to conduct the affairs of state. The Shi'a majority remained among Iraq's dispossessed.

A provisional council was established to select a "constitutional monarch" for Iraq who would be acceptable to both the British and the Iraqis. The logical choice was Faisal ibn Hussein, the son of the Sharif of Mecca and, for several months, the king of Syria before he was expelled by the French. Although not an Iraqi, Faisal possessed strong Arab nationalist credentials and was a direct descendant of the Prophet Mohammed. This, it was presumed, made him acceptable to a majority of the Iraqis. The British, in turn, were reasonably confident of Faisal's pro-British leanings and were happy to ease their relations with his father, Sharif Hussein. Unable to rule Iraq directly, the British would rule it indirectly. Most of Iraq's upper-level civil servants were British, and Britain "advised" Iraq on matters of finance and foreign policy (Elliot 1996; Longrigg 1953).

The period of British rule, although brief, condemned Iraq to a future of violence by piecing together a country composed of three mutually hostile communities: the Sunni, the Shi'a, and the Kurds (Luldtz 1995). Whatever hope there might have been for unity was destroyed by British empowerment of the Sunni elite and by a divide-and-rule policy that played one group against another (Mufti 1996; Nakash 1994). Rather than laying a foundation for national unity, the British helped to destroy it.

Iraq was granted its formal independence in 1932 and was duly admitted to the League of Nations. The British, however, retained their military bases in Iraq and both trained and equipped the Iraqi army. The monarchy was also pro-British, as was General Nuri as-Said, the emerging strongman of Iraqi politics. King Faisal died unexpectedly in 1933 and was replaced by his son Ghazi, an inexperienced youth of twenty-one who lacked the ability to impose his will on Iraq's scheming politicians. Ghazi was killed in an automobile accident in 1939, and power shifted to Abd al-Ilah, the crown prince, who ruled in the name of Ghazi's infant son, Faisal II.

Abd al-Ilah's subservience to Britain was resented by a broad cross-section of Iraqi society, and by the mid-1930s, a variety of opposition parties had begun to emerge among Iraq's students, intellectuals, and army officers. Some were Iraqi nationalists, while others (particularly those of Sunni origin) called for the creation of a unified Arab state that would include Iraq, Syria, and Palestine. The precursors to the Iraqi Communist Party also emerged during this era, and soon developed a broad base of support among the urban Shi'a community. Growing political dissent erupted in periodic riots, with at least six coups and attempted coups occurring between 1936 and 1941 (Khadduri 1960). In 1941, nationalist army officers with strong ties to Nazi Germany seized power for a brief period before being crushed by British troops. The monarchy was restored, but Iraq remained under virtual British occupation for the remainder of the Second World War (Silverfarb 1994).

## The Era of Revolution and Optimism

The years following the end of World War II found Iraq to be an island of tranquillity in a region beset by turmoil and revolution. Abd al-Ilah, the regent, continued to rule in the name of the young king, but the real power resided with Nuri as-Said, Iraq's perennial prime minister and power behind the throne.

Iraq's tranquillity, however, was more apparent than real. Both the monarchy and Nuri as-Said were throwbacks to an earlier era in which Iraqi politics was the preserve of former Ottoman officers, tribal sheikhs, and feudal landowners, the sheikhs and the landowners often being one and the same. The former officers had also used their influence to acquire large landholdings and resisted efforts for land reform. All effective power remained in the hands of the Sunnis, but Shi'a sheikhs and landowners were allowed to prosper in return for supporting the regime. So repressive was the Iraqi monarchy that in 1943 the British ambassador complained that it was rapidly losing touch with reality (Cornwallis, cited in Elliot 1996).

In all, 61 percent of Iraq's arable land was in the hands of its large landowners, with another 15 percent or so in the hands of those with midsize holdings. Landed peasants, most of whom were located in the less fertile regions of the country, owned the remainder. The sharecroppers on the large plantations lived in ignorance and disease and were considered by the courts—most of which were controlled by the landowning families—to be little more than chattel.

While the regime clung to the past, radical political parties flourished, the most prominent of which were the Arab nationalists, the Communists, and the Ba'athists. The Arab nationalists enjoyed strong support in the army and had orchestrated the attempted coups of 1936 and 1941. The Iraqi Communist Party was founded in 1934 and by 1944 controlled twelve of sixteen Iraqi labor unions; 1944 was the first year that trade unions were recognized in Iraq. The Ba'ath Party was officially recognized in 1952. The Communists found their greatest support among the Kurds in the north and the Shi'a in the slums of Baghdad. The Ba'ath Party found support among both Shi'a and Sunni intellectuals. More important, it was able to establish a strong presence within the predominantly Sunni officer corps. Other parties existed, but these were largely symbolic entities that revolved around dominant figures such as Nuri as-Said. The Shi'a clergy, for their part, were growing restive with the secular direction of Iraqi politics.

The opposition demanded land reform, democracy, and the severance of Iraq's ties with the West. Nuri as-Said responded with repression and strengthened his ties with the feudal landowners. He also led Iraq into the U.S.-sponsored Baghdad Pact, an alliance of Western and Middle Eastern nations designed to contain Soviet expansionism and stabilize the pro-Western regimes of the region. Iraq was the only Arab country to join the organization; Nasser's opposition to the pact scared off such staunch supporters of the West as Jordan and Saudi Arabia. Opponents of the regime were brutally suppressed, and the regime's economic policies ground the poor ever deeper into despair.

The British ambassador pleaded for reform, but there was little that the West could do to salvage the monarchy (Gallman 1964). Egypt's political victory in the 1956 war electrified the Arab world, and the merger of Egypt and Syria in 1958 created a wave of nationalistic emotion that threatened to sweep all before it. Iraq and Jordan, the two Hashemite kingdoms, attempted to parry the nationalist threat by creating a federation of their two countries. Iraq mobilized two military divisions for service in Jordan. Both were fully armed and provided with ammunition, a rarity in Iraq (Gallman 1964, 203).

Seen in retrospect, this was a mistake. The units scheduled for service in Jordan overthrew the Iraqi monarchy on July 14,1958, and mobs dragged the bodies of Abd al-Ilah and Nuri as-Said through the streets of Baghdad (Fernea and Louis 1991). Ironically, Nuri as-Said had earlier assured the U.S. ambassador that there was little risk in sending Iraqi troops to Jordan, saying that "potential troublemakers were limited to a few hundred students and lawyers," and that "these could be kept under surveillance." When the U.S. ambassador inquired about the loyalty of the army, he was assured "that the army could be relied upon to support the Crown and the government" (Gallman 1964, 201).

The coup had been carried out by a tightly knit Free Officers, many of whom were ardent Arab nationalists. For the nationalists, the purpose of the coup was to add Iraq to the United Arab Republic. If Iraq joined the UAR, the three power centers of the Arab world would be unified and the dream of an Arab world stretching from the Persian Gulf to the Atlantic would be that much closer to realization.

Other members of the Free Officers were skeptical of unification with Egypt and Syria (Kienle 1990). Abdul Karim Qasim, the leader of the coup, seemed inclined toward a loose, federation in keeping with Iraq's multicultural traditions. Perhaps he also feared that his own power would be eclipsed by that of Nasser. Other officers, while nationalist in sentiment, worried about the socialist complexion of Nasser's domestic policies. Being an Arab nationalist did not necessarily make one a socialist. The Kurds and the Shi'a both feared that Iraq's incorporation in the UAR would render them small minorities in a Sunni Arab universe (Wiley 1992). The Communists, too, were wary of Nasser. No sooner had Egypt and Syria merged than Nasser put the Syrian Communists to flight.

It was Communist support among the Shi'a and the Kurds that provided the Communist Party with its best chance of seizing power in Iraq. The Kurds, although largely tribal, had established strong ties with Moscow and were primed for revolt against Baghdad. Communist support among the Shi'a, in turn, was heavily concentrated in Baghdad's squalid slums. This was a matter of vital importance, for Baghdad was the nerve center of Iraqi politics. To control the capital was to control the government. The Communist Party could now claim some 25,000 members, including a broad following among students, teachers, lawyers, and other intellectuals. These, in turn, were supported by legions of sympathizers attracted by the party's "Shi'a Program" and promises of land grants and social welfare (Dann 1969, 118; F. Ibrahim 1996). Both loyalists and sympathizers were organized into the Popular Resistance Forces, an armed militia that provided the Communist Party with a counterweight to the military. The party also mobilized its sympathizers in a variety of mass organizations such as the Partisans of Peace, the Federation of Democratic Youth, and the League for the Defense of Women's Rights.

An attempt by the Arab nationalists to overthrow Qasim and his Communist supporters was easily crushed, and vengeance became the order of the day. A reign of terror was unleashed against the Arab nationalists, much of it led by the Popular Resistance Forces and other Communist organizations. Arab nationalists, most of whom were Sunni Arabs, were hunted as spies and purged from both the military and the government. Many died, and thousands more were imprisoned. Brutality, much fueled by religious and ethnic hatred, became the norm.

Fearful of the growing strength of the Communists, Qasim attempted to boost his popular support by launching a bold program of social and economic reform. Land was promised to the peasants and a new personal statutes law banned polygamy, bolstered female inheritance rights, and offered women at least some protection against arbitrary divorce (Dann 1969, 246). Given the conservative nature of Iraqi society, Qasim's social reforms did more to undermine the regime than to support it (F. Ibrahim 1996).

The Kurds revolted in the spring of 1961, further sapping the power of a regime that was now adrift. In desperation, Qasim sought to regain the initiative by asserting Iraqi jurisdiction over Kuwait in June 1961; the oil-rich mini-state had just been granted independence by the British. Both Nasser and the British rushed to the aid of Kuwait, leaving Qasim with little choice but to back down.

Now devoid of support, Qasim was overthrown on February 8, 1963, by a coalition of Nasserite and Ba'athist officers. The Nasserites were soon purged, and the Ba'athists reigned supreme. All, however, was not well. The Iraqi Ba'ath Party was a house divided. The military section of the Ba'ath Party was dominated by Sunni officers who had joined the party to counter Qasim's shift to the Communists. The party's civilian wing, by contrast, continued to be dominated by Shi'a (F. Ibrahim 1996). The gap between the two factions was unbridgeable. Still smarting from the earlier purges of Sunni officers, the military wing of the Ba'ath Party launched a reign of terror against suspected Communists in the government. Between February and November of 1963, an estimated 10,000 Communists were arrested, most from Shi'a backgrounds. Hundreds, perhaps thousands, were killed (F. Ibrahim 1996).

Perhaps mercifully, Abd as-Salam Arif and a coalition of Arab nationalist officers seized power on November 18, 1963. The first Iraqi experiment in Ba'athist rule had lasted only nine months and had been, by any standard, a total disaster. Arif consolidated his position by placing Arab nationalist officers, many from his own tribe, in key positions. The latter were particularly influential in the intelligence services and secret police. Virtually all were Sunni. Now in control of Iraq, Arif proposed immediate unification with Egypt. Unity, however, was not to be achieved. Like its predecessors, the nationalist regime became paralyzed by internal dissension. Arif died in an accident in 1966 and was replaced in office by his brother Mohammed, a compromise candidate, but to no avail. The Arab nationalist regime was beyond salvation.

The most pronounced image conveyed by Iraqi politics during the era of optimism and revolution, then, was that of a country so divided within itself that effective government was impossible. Not only had the country suffered through two decades of coups and countercoups, but each had attempted to undo the policies of its predecessors. As a result, Iraqi politics was constantly being turned on its head. Each new elite, moreover, was wedded to an extremist position that alienated most of Iraq's already fragmented society. This was certainly true of Nuri as-Said, the Nasserites, and the Ba'athists. Qasim's flirtation with the Communists sent fear through the Ba'athist and nationalist communities, not to mention the Shi'a clergy, which was vying with the Communists for control of the Shi'a masses. Indeed, the Shi'a religious leaders went so far as to excommunicate Shi'a members of the Communist party (F. Ibrahim 1996). Each new regime, in turn, attempted to batten down the hatches by crushing the opposition. When the dam finally broke, the retribution was awesome.

Under these circumstances, institution building was impossible. Iraqi constitutions (each regime issued its own) were meaningless, for all effective power rested with the military. Even the army was divided against itself, and both the Communists and the Ba'athists developed party militias as a counterweight to the military, which didn't exactly inspire confidence in the latter.

Much the same was true in administrative development: each new regime purged the bureaucracy of its opponents, replacing them with its own supporters. Those not purged became immobilized with fear, for even the simplest decision might be interpreted as treason following the next coup. This danger was particularly acute if one attempted to enforce the law against the relative of a future dignitary yet unknown.

## The Era of Disillusion and Reassessment

By 1967, the Nasserite regime that had been in place in Iraq since 1963 was so beset by internal conflict that it had begun to crumble under its own weight. The humiliating Arab defeat in the June (Six-Day) War merely hastened its collapse. Sensing the inevitable, the Nasserites offered to form a coalition government with the Ba'ath Party. The latter, however, now sensed victory and bided its time.

The Ba'athist coup took place in July 1968. It was the tenth coup or attempted coup in a decade (Khalil 1989). Following the customary pattern, a communique was broadcast over Iraqi radio announcing that the army had seized power in the name of the people and that a new Revolutionary Command Council (RCC) had been formed (Kienle 1990). The customary purges took place within the army and the bureaucracy. Given Iraq's history of political turmoil, it was logical to assume that the Ba'athist coup would soon go the way of its predecessors and that Iraq's game of political musical chairs would continue well into the future. This, however, did not happen. There would be no more successful coups in Iraq prior to the U.S. invasion of 2003.

The new Revolutionary Command Council was headed by Ahmad Hasan al-Bakr, a Sunni Arab officer who had been active in the coup of 1963. He was supported by Saddam Hussein, his protégé and relative. Saddam Hussein was an important member of the civilian wing of the Ba'ath Party who would soon be elevated to membership in the RCC and become its vice chairman (Karsh and Rautsi 1991). Both Bakr and Hussein were from the region of Tikrit, as were several other officers in the RCC. During the early years of the monarchy, a senior officer from Tikrit had helped the region's more ambitious youth to gain entry into the military college, and this group now controlled both the RCC and the civilian apparatus of the Ba'ath Party. Although people in the Tikrit region did not constitute a tribe per se, many of them were interrelated in one way or another by marriage. This situation was not unusual, for marriage among first cousins is a common practice in Iraq.

The preeminent goal of the new regime was to consolidate its power by eliminating the mistakes made by the Ba'ath Party in its first encounter with power in 1963. One of the party's biggest problems in 1963, according to its own documents, had been competition between its rival blocs, a topic discussed above. To avoid a repeat of this scenario, power was concentrated in the hands of a small leadership council. Debate was encouraged, but once decisions had been taken, they were binding on all members of the party. Dissidents were purged. Many met with unfortunate accidents.

The party also acknowledged that its reign of terror in 1963 had kept it from establishing a strong base of support among the masses. Toward that end it created an array of women's, youth, peasant, labor, and other mass-based organizations. Membership in these organizations was voluntary, but membership had its privileges. The party vowed to reach an accommodation with the Kurds by acknowledging them as co-partners in a unified Iraqi state. An olive branch was also tendered to the Shi'a religious establishment, but to no avail. The long-established distrust that separated the two sides could not be bridged (F. Ibrahim 1996). The regime responded with violence but succeeded only in politicizing a growing number of Shi'a clergy. With the Communists in retreat, it would be these religious leaders who organized Shi'a resistance to the Ba'athist regime.

The Ba'ath government launched its social revolution in 1969 with the promulgation of a new agrarian reform law. The agrarian reforms, like those initiated by the Qasim regime, were designed to destroy the remaining power of the old landowning class, members of which continued to enjoy support among the military. Landowners were no longer entitled to compensation for lands confiscated, and much of the land was distributed free to the peasants. In the process, Iraq was transformed into a country of small and medium landowners, most of whom, the Ba'ath Party hoped, would be supportive of their benefactors.

In 1972, the Ba'athist regime gained broad popular approval by nationalizing the Iraqi Oil Company (IOC). Foreign ownership of Iraq's oil resources had been the last vestige of colonial domination, and the nationalization of the IOC enabled the regime to pose as the champion of Iraqi nationalism. It also provided the regime with countless new opportunities for patronage and payoffs.

In the same year Iraq signed a fifteen-year treaty of friendship with the Soviet Union. The USSR became Iraq's main supplier of arms and credit, and Iraq was sheltered from U.S. pressure by the Soviet security umbrella (Shemesh 1992). The Soviet Union also pledged to stop supporting the Kurds, with whom it had enjoyed a warm relationship. It would now be easier for the Ba'athist regime to rein in one of the remaining challenges to its authority.

In the meantime, the outbreak of war between the Arabs and Israel in October 1973 quadrupled the price of crude oil and transformed Iraq into one of the richest countries in the world. The Ba'athist government now had an economic carrot to add to the military stick that had kept it in power since 1968. Those who chose to join the party or participate in its affiliated organizations found easy access to lucrative positions in the rapidly expanding public sector.

Iraq's newfound oil wealth would also transform the country's physical infrastructure: roads, bridges, dams, airports and other public works projects mushroomed. It also created a huge "petrol" middle class, most members of which owed their good fortune to the Ba'ath Party. Shi'a increasingly joined the Ba'ath Party and its affiliate organizations, for this was the best route to a government job. Even before the oil boom, however, the party's egalitarian ideology had provided it with a reasonable following among Iraqi Shi'a. A major rift thus developed within the Shi'a community between those who supported the regime for economic or ideological reasons and those who opposed it for reasons of religious oppression (F. Ibrahim 1996).

Lavish outlays of oil wealth, however, were not able to quell growing agitation among the Kurds. By 1974, the government was convinced that the Kurds were transforming northern Iraq, the center of much of Iraq's oil, into a state within a state. The government sought a negotiated solution, but the gap between the two sides was too wide. With the collapse of negotiations, the government unleashed a full-scale military assault against the Kurds in the hope of beating them into submission. Iran, then a U.S. ally, seized the opportunity to furnish the Kurds with "artillery, sophisticated anti-tank weapons, and ammunition" (Ahmad 1984, 208). Covert aid was also provided to the Kurds by the U.S. and Israel.

Thanks to Iranian aid, the Iraqi army was unable to crush the Kurdish rebellion, and by 1975 the two sides had fought to a standstill. Two points, however, had become patently clear. First, the Ba'ath Party could not control Iraq without suppressing the Kurds. Second, the Ba'ath Party could not suppress the Kurds without the cooperation of Iran.

These realities set the stage for the Algiers Agreement of March 1975. Placing domestic considerations over foreign policy, Iraq agreed to give Iran equal rights to the Shatt al-Arab waterway in return for Iran's agreement to stop arming the Kurds (Biger 1989; Mostyn 1991).

With the Kurds cut off from Iran and Russia, their two main bases of support, the Ba'athist government moved rapidly to create a Kurd-free security zone along its borders with Iran and Turkey. While the numbers are vague, it is broadly acknowledged that tens of thousands of Kurds were forcibly resettled and their villages destroyed (Ismael and Ismael 1991, 182). Exhausted by the war and the flight of their main leaders, the Kurds could offer little resistance to the Iraqi army.

The Kurds, however, were not the only challenge to the Ba'athist regime. In February 1977, the Shi'a south erupted in violence, heralding what radical Shi'a would later describe as "the first Islamic revolution" (Baram 1989, 454). While this is an overstatement, there can be little doubt that the Shi'a religious establishment had become increasingly politicized as a result of Ba'athist repression.

The regime responded with its customary carrot-and-stick tactics, repressing the religious opposition while simultaneously providing the Shi'a with representation on the RCC, the highest political body in the land. The revolution, if such it was, fizzled as a result of conflicts within the Shi'a religious establishment. The senior Shi'a religious leaders remained apolitical, choosing to confront the Iraqi regime with piety and prayer, a policy that made it difficult for the radical clerics to develop a broad base of mass support.

The Ayatollah Khomeini, then guiding the Iranian revolution from his base in Iraq's holy city of Najaf, remained aloof from events in Iraq. This did not mean that he approved of the Ba'athist regime or its policies, but merely that he was unwilling to allow events in Iraq to distract him from the revolution in Iran. There would be ample time to deal with Saddam Hussein once the shah had been disposed of.

The end of the era of disillusion and reassessment, then, found the Ba'athists firmly in control of Iraq and Saddam Hussein firmly in control of the Ba'ath Party. All pretense of collective leadership was gone, and political influence was based upon personal contacts with Saddam Hussein and his relatives. Portraits of Saddam Hussein became ubiquitous, and his praises were offered in song and verse. While it was doubtful that Saddam Hussein believed that he was so beloved, the impression of omnipotence was an important tool in deterring popular unrest. There could be no doubt in the popular mind—and those of his enemies—that Hussein was in charge.

## The Era of Islamic Resurgence

The 1979 victory of Iran's Islamic revolution posed a serious challenge to the Ba'athist regime in Iraq. The two countries shared a common border and a majority of the Iraqi population were Shi'a. The Shi'a uprising of 1977 had been crushed, but it left little doubt that the fundamentalists had become a major political force in the Shi'a community.

On the plus side, from Saddam Hussein's perspective, Khomeini's Islamic revolution had pushed Saudi Arabia and the Gulf states into the Iraqi camp. For better or worse, Saddam Hussein, long viewed by the Gulf Arabs with suspicion, was now their first line of defense against the onslaught of the ayatollah. The United States was coming to hold the same view.

The threat from Iran was both military and political. The military threat was of minimal concern, for the once-vaunted Iranian army was in disarray following the collapse of the shah and the purging of its officer corps. Indeed, much of the Iranian army had simply melted away as recruits returned to their villages.

The threat of political subversion, however, was very real. The 1977 Shi'a uprising had been orchestrated by clerics sympathetic to Iran, and religious emotions among the Iraqi Shi'a had increased dramatically in the wake of Khomeini's victory. The loyalty of Iraq's Shi'a population, accordingly, remained an open question. Would feelings of Arabism and Iraqi nationalism bind them to the Ba'athist regime, or would the bonds of religion lead to a surge of support for Iran? This question remained unanswered, but there could be little doubt that at least part of Iraq's Shi'a community was sympathetic to the newly proclaimed Islamic republic. For the Kurds there was no ambivalence. Revolt would be imminent as soon as the Iraqi government showed signs of weakness.

In an effort to neutralize the Iranian threat, Saddam Hussein made a number of gestures to Iraq's Shi'a community, including the generous allocation of funds for mosques and Shi'a religious shrines. He also visited even the remotest Shi'a areas "where he made lavish promises of development, such as running water, electricity, the construction of roads and free allocations of television sets and refrigerators" (*Middle East Contemporary Survey*, 1978–79, 571). Similar promises were made to the residents of Baghdad's slums. Hussein also made overtures to the Ayatollah Khomeini suggesting that there was no reason the two countries could not live in peace as long as each respected the other's sovereignty. Iraq would not attempt to undermine Iran's Islamic government if the ayatollah agreed not to foment revolution among Iraqi Shi'a.

The ayatollah brushed aside Hussein's overtures, calling upon all Iraqi citizens to rise up against the Ba'athist regime. There was only one nation, the ayatollah proclaimed, and that was the nation of believers. Supporters of his revolution were not supporters of Iran, but supporters of God. This was a clever ploy, for it countered Saddam's efforts to brand Shi'a activists as agents of Iran.

Shi'a religious activists launched an uprising toward the end of 1979; Saddam Hussein countered with waves of arrests and executions. The members of the Dawa Party, the leading secret fundamentalist organization, were sentenced to death as a group. Most fled to Iran, as did members of various other fundamentalist organizations.

Relations between the two countries continued to deteriorate over the ensuing months, and in April 1980, Iraq and Iran placed their respective armies on full alert. In September of the same year, Saddam Hussein taunted the ayatollah by unilaterally abrogating the 1975 Algiers Agreement, which had given Iran equal control of the Shatt-al-Arab. Five days later, Iraqi forces launched a full-scale invasion of Iran, initiating a war that would drag on for eight years.

It is probable that the Saudis and Kuwaitis encouraged the Iraqi invasion of Iran with promises of financial support (Nonneman 1986). The Saudis were still reeling from the 1979 seizure of the Great Mosque in Mecca by Islamic groups and could only guess at the ayatollah's next move. Kuwait, for its part, possessed a large Shi'a population and, along with Iraq, was a logical candidate for the extension of the ayatollah's revolution. While the exact role of the oil kingdoms in the initiation of the war is difficult to sort out with certainty, there can be no doubt that both provided massive financial support to the Iraqi war effort. The United States, now smarting from Iran's seizure of American hostages, would also bolster the Iraqi war effort.

The Iraqi invasion was also prompted by the assumption that victory over Iran would be swift and certain. If this assumption were flawed, the results could be disastrous for both Iraq and, the Gulf states that had rushed to its side. It might be the Islamic revolution, not Saddam Hussein, who dominated the oil-rich Gulf.

Whatever Saddam Hussein's motivations, the war went poorly from the beginning. Iraqi forces penetrated deeply into the oil-rich province of Khuzestan, but soon found that their advance had outstripped their supply lines. They had also expected the largely Arabic-speaking residents of Khuzestan to rally to their cause, but the Iranians had foreseen this possibility and forcibly evacuated many of the province's Arab residents. Also contrary to expectations was the unexpectedly stiff resistance of Iran's military units, many of which were staffed by religious zealots welded into hastily mobilized revolutionary militias. Hopes of Arab solidarity also faded as Syria announced its support for Iran shortly after the outbreak of hostilities.

The situation worsened in 1982 as a Kurdish revolt forced Saddam Hussein to shift troops from the Iranian front to northern Iraq. Iranian forces had become increasingly well organized and by the end of 1982 had largely driven Iraqi troops from Iranian territory. Bowing to reality, Saddam Hussein made overtures of peace to the ayatollah. The latter, believing that Iraq was on the verge of defeat, rejected the peace offer out of hand. With Iraq conquered, his Islamic revolution would be unstoppable. The ayatollah was troubled by the fact that the Iraqi Shi'a had not revolted, but believed that they would surely do so once the Ba'athist regime had begun to crumble.

The onset of 1983, then, witnessed a reversal of roles. Now Saddam Hussein was on the defensive. Hundreds of thousands of civilians, Shi'a as well as Sunni, were forced to join the people's militia and sent to the front. Hussein's elite units remained in the rear and were ordered to shoot anyone who attempted to retreat. Some Iraqi Shi'a troops defected to Iran and fought against, their former comrades, but their numbers does not appear to have been large. A cease-fire was also signed with the Kurds in 1983, but it did not hold. Saddam Hussein responded by gassing the Kurds into submission. Before the war was over, a former Iraqi minister claimed that some 50,000 Kurds had been killed by poison gas while tens of thousands of others fled to Turkey and Iran (Ismael and Ismael 1991,183). Although such figures may be inflated, the number of Kurdish casualties was staggering. The regime also continued to target Shi'a activists, some six hundred of whom were reported by diplomatic sources to have been killed during the first three years of the war (*NYT,* April 3, 1984).

The ongoing rapprochement between the United States and Iraq was formalized by a renewal of diplomatic relations in 1984. The United States was now firmly committed to preventing an Iranian victory in the Iran–Iraq War. Iraq continued to receive some support from the Soviets, although the latter also went out of their way to maintain good relations with Iran.

Over the ensuing years Iranian forces attempted to overrun Iraqi positions in the largely Shi'a south. The Iraqis countered with high-altitude aerial bombings of Iranian oil facilities, cities, and military bases. The Iranians responded in kind, unleashing a "war of the cities," but they were less well equipped to carry out aerial bombardment than the Iraqis. The United States had also facilitated the Iraqi strategy by providing satellite data on the effectiveness of their air strikes (Karsh and Rautsi 1991). Still unable to stop the Iranians, the Iraqis resorted to the use of poison gas.

Iran launched a final assault on Iraq's Fao Peninsula in the spring of 1988; the sounds of battle could be heard in neighboring Kuwait. Much to the relief of the United States, the offensive collapsed and both sides accepted a UN-sponsored cease-fire that went into effect on July 19, 1988. Both sides had been devastated, leading to speculation by both Arabs and Iranians that the war had been an American plot all along.

The costs of the war for Iraq were enormous. Having once boasted a surplus of some $30 billion, Iraq left the war with an international debt of well over $60 billion; some estimates place the figure as high as $80 billion. Whether or not the debt would be repaid was a matter of conjecture, for much of the money had been provided by Kuwait and Saudi Arabia. In total, the war cost Iraq some $90 billion, not to mention the incalculable loss of life and property. If the latter are added to the equation, the total figure for Iraqi losses could reach as high as $452.6 billion. The corresponding figure for Iran would be in the vicinity of $644.5 billion (Alnasrawi 1994). Rare was the family that had not suffered the loss or maiming of a loved one.

## The Era of the New World Order

The collapse of the Soviet Union and the advent of U.S. dominance in the Middle East were not matters of undue concern for Saddam Hussein. A strong relationship had evolved between Hussein and Washington during Iraq's war with Iran and, for better or for worse, he remained Washington's best hope of checking Iranian dominance of the Gulf (Smolansky and Smolansky 1991). The passing of Khomeini had also deprived the Islamic revolution of its spiritual guide and Iran had been so devastated by the war that it would not pose a serious military threat to Iraq for some time.

Saddam Hussein opened the era of the new world order by warning Israel that if it launched a nuclear attack on Iraq, Iraq would reciprocate with gas attacks. The threat was soon followed up by the construction of missile launchers aimed at Tel Aviv (*NYT,* March 30, 1990). Western concerns were allayed by Iraqi assurances that its weapons development program was purely defensive. Saddam Hussein's rhetoric played well in an Arab world long frustrated by Israel's regional monopoly on nuclear weapons and was supported by a May 1990 meeting of Arab foreign ministers that affirmed the right of Iraq and all Arab states to develop weapons of mass destruction for defensive purposes. The U.S. managed to soften the language of the resulting communique, but the statement was a propaganda victory for Saddam Hussein, who continued to pursue his claim to Arab leadership (*NYT,* May 28, 1990).

Aside from Hussein's bluster against Israel, Iraq's lone discordant note was its verbal harassment of Kuwait, which Iraqi leaders had traditionally claimed as Iraq's nineteenth province. Iraqi harassment of Kuwait dated back to the early days of the Iraqi monarchy and was easily explained away by apologists who wanted to believe that Saddam Hussein was on the side of the angels: among other things, Kuwait had stationed troops in a disputed border region and appeared to be pumping oil from the Iraqi side of the border. Kuwait had also demanded repayment of the massive loans that it had made to Iraq during the Iran–Iraq War, loans that Iraq considered to be little more than Kuwait's contribution to keeping the ayatollah at bay (Baram and Rubin 1993; Musallam 1996).

In retrospect, it seems that the United States could have prevented the Gulf War by sending troops to Kuwait in July of 1990. The U.S., however, was intent on seeking an accommodation with Iraq, a strategy bolstered by assurances from both Egypt and Saudi Arabia that Saddam Hussein would not attack Kuwait. Saudi Arabia and the Gulf states were also adamant in their desire to keep U.S. troops out of the region (NYT, Sept. 23, 1990, 12). April Glaspie, the U.S. ambassador to Iraq, met with Saddam Hussein on July 25 and reiterated the official line that the U.S. wanted improved relations with Iraq. While the contents of the discussion remain a matter of dispute, Ambassador Glaspie is quoted in the New York Times as having said, "We have no opinion of the Arab–Arab conflicts, like your border disagreement with Kuwait" (NYT, Sept. 23, 1990, 12, 13).

Whatever the case, Iraqi forces did invade Kuwait on August 1, 1990, unleashing a wave of destruction on the affluent sheikhdom. A variety of factors undoubtedly contributed to Hussein's decision to invade, not the least of which was a compelling desire to erase the blot of his war with Iran. In addition to providing the victory that had eluded him in Iran, control of Kuwait would propel Saddam Hussein into regional leadership, bolster his popularity in an army reputedly primed for revolt, and provide the money needed to rebuild his war-shattered nation. It also appears that Saddam Hussein felt that he was being squeezed by the United States. The U.S., for example, had suddenly begun to criticize Iraq for the use of poison gas and other human rights abuses—actions that it had conveniently overlooked during the Iran–Iraq War. Iran had been crippled, and it was now Iraq and its massive army that posed the greatest threat to U.S. interests in the region. If a showdown with the U.S. were to come, Saddam Hussein may have reasoned, Iraq's bargaining position would be strengthened by its control of Kuwaiti oil fields, not to mention the proximity of Iraqi troops to the major oil fields of Saudi Arabia. Would the U.S. really risk a war under these circumstances?

Faced with the Iraqi occupation of Kuwait, the West responded with every means in its power short of all-out war. An economic boycott deprived Iraq of its oil income and an international armada was assembled to intimidate its leader into submission. Only a madman, so the logic went, would attempt to resist the combined forces of the world community The Kurds and the Shi'a were also encouraged to revolt, and Iraq was systematically cut off from all of its neighbors with the exception of Jordan. Saddam Hussein, however, stood pat.

In spite of the escalating tension, neither side seemed anxious to fight. General Colin Powell, the commander of U.S. forces, also doubted that the U.S. public would be willing to sustain massive U.S. casualties for the sake of propping up a desert sheikhdom (Gordon and Trainor 1994). Indeed, news reports at the time suggested that a war with Iraq could result in as many as 30,000 U.S. casualties.

The coalition attack finally materialized on January 17, 1991, almost six months after the Iraqi invasion of Kuwait. The war had two basic objectives: first, to liberate Kuwait, and second, to destroy the Iraqi army and with it Saddam Hussein's capacity to threaten Israel and his oil-rich neighbors. Aside from these objectives, not much thought was given to what would come next. This lack of foresight was unfortunate, for the ground war lasted only 100 hours, a figure that U.S. policy makers thought had a nice ring to it (Gordon and Trainor 1994; McCausland 1993).

In retrospect, it appears that Saddam Hussein did not expect a war. Allied bombers found Baghdad and its airport fully illuminated, hardly likely for a country expecting to be attacked. Iraq's elite troops also seemed to have had little intention of fighting the UN forces. Rather, they avoided destruction by retreating to Baghdad. The CIA estimated that 365 of the Republican Guard's 786 most advanced tanks remained in position to crush a potential popular uprising (Gordon and Trainor 1994).

With the war at an end, the coalition forces found themselves in a quandary. How was the United States to get rid of Saddam Hussein without occupying the country or allowing its dismemberment? Occupation would probably mean a long, costly, bloody, and unpopular police action for which U.S. troops were ill-equipped. Their mission was to fight wars, not kill civilians. U.S. President George Bush was also well aware of the problems that had plagued Israeli efforts to pacify the West Bank and Gaza Strip. The Israelis had tried every tactic in the book, but to no avail (Palmer and Palmer 2004). The dismemberment of Iraq might well destabilize the region and cause southern Iraq to slide into the hands of Iran. Did the United States, which had supported Saddam in his war against Khomeini's Islamic republic, want to see Iran on the borders of Kuwait and Saudi Arabia? Absolutely not!

The de facto strategy that emerged was to starve Iraq into compliance with UN demands. No oil would be exported, and no goods, with the possible exception of medicine, could be imported. Ideally, from the U.S. perspective, these new realities would force the Ba'athist regime to sacrifice Saddam Hussein and his weapons of mass destruction for the sake of remaining in power. The threat to Israel and Iraq's Arab neighbors would be gone, but Iraq would retain sufficient power to keep the Shi'a and the Iranians in check (Cockburn and Cockburn 1999). The United States would retain a deterrent force in Kuwait and other friendly states, including Saudi Arabia, thereby leaving no ambiguity about America's resolve to maintain its dominance in the region.

As might have been expected given its internal contradictions, the U.S. plan was doomed from the start. No sooner had the war ended than both the Shi'a and the Kurds erupted in rebellion. Unwilling to either occupy Iraq or accept its dismemberment, the U.S.-led forces stood by while Saddam Hussein's Republican Guards crushed both rebellions. Only when the carnage reached epic proportions did an embarrassed U.S. create a safe haven in Iraq's predominantly Kurdish and Shi'a areas to prevent Iraqi aircraft from strafing Shi'a and Kurdish villages.

The United States attempted to regain lost ground by welding the Iraqi opposition into an anti-Hussein alliance. This task, however, proved to be a daunting one. The opposition, in addition to being skeptical of American resolve, was frag-mented into some ninety groups by religious, ethnic, ideological, and personality conflicts. Once Hussein was gone, or so the scenario went, the alliance would pro-vide the basis for a pluralistic but unified Iraq.

The United States was also facing world condemnation for contributing to the starvation of innocent Iraqis. Nearly every day brought more news stories about the horrors of starvation in Iraq and Kurdistan. Couldn't food and medi-cine be allowed for humanitarian reasons? Such questions were particularly press-ing in the Middle East. In 1996, the U.S. relented and allowed Iraq to sell limited amounts of oil for humanitarian purposes. The oil-for-food program would be monitored by the UN to ensure that its proceeds went to the poor rather than to Saddam's troops. It seemed like a great idea, but about one-half of the foreign contractors, including many from the West, undermined the boycott by making secret kickbacks to Saddam Hussein (*NYT,* Aug. 10, 2005).

Perhaps more urgent were leaks in the boycott. Turkey, Iraq's largest trading partner, was experiencing severe economic hardships as a result of the blockade and was far less concerned about Iraq's weapons of mass destruction than it was about the evolution of a de facto Kurdish state in northern Iraq. Japan and Western Europe were also in the midst of economic recession, and trade with Iraq offered a much-needed economic stimulus. Few of America's allies, moreover, had any confidence that the U.S. boycott would attain its objectives.

Saddam Hussein was also having his troubles, most of them related to con-flict within his family. The Iran–Iraq War had seen Saddam Hussein concentrate power in the hands of a narrow group of relatives from his hometown of Tikrit, at least three of whom were viewed as his possible successors. As time passed, however, a power struggle emerged between Saddam's presumed heirs and his two sons Uday and Qusai, both of whom had begun to move into positions of power. Uday, an inveterate playboy with a reputation for drunken orgies and abducting women, had bludgeoned his father's food taster to death in 1988. When a young woman protested her abduction, he reportedly had her dipped in honey and thrown to a pack of hungry dogs (*IHT,* Feb. 11, 1997, 1). In 1992 he engaged in a public fistfight with Kamel Hassan, the head of the Republican Guards, and a few years later he shot his uncle, also a key member of the elite, seven times in the leg (*IHT,* Feb. 11, 1997, 1). Despite these diversions, Uday established a media empire and took over the country's (smuggled) oil sales, previously the preserve of Kamel Hassan. Qusai, of a more serious nature, had assumed control of the security services and was now responsible for Saddam Hussein's personal safety, replacing a Saddam son-in-law who was also the brother of Kamel Hassan. Qusai and Uday, it seemed, had now become their father's numbers two and three, respectively.

A newly inaugurated Clinton administration continued the cat-and-mouse game with Saddam Hussein, but there were few changes in U.S. policy. Saddam Hussein obstructed the activities of UNSCOM, the United Nations Special Committee responsible for assuring that Iraq did not possess nuclear weapons, only to back down when reprisals seemed imminent (Butler 2000a and 2000b; Graham-Brown 1999). Hussein's attempts to restrict the activities of UNSCOM suggest that the organization was at least partially effective in blocking Iraqi efforts to develop weapons of mass destruction (WMD).

The standoff continued through the turn of the century and beyond as the U.S. attempted to overthrow Saddam Hussein with a combination of air strikes, boycotts, futile efforts to stimulate a military coup from within the ranks of Saddam's generals, and equally futile efforts to weld Iraq's opposition into a cohesive force. The Arabic-language news journals reported at least two attempted coups during the era, but neither was successful (*Al-Kaisi,* Aug. 6, 1999). Meanwhile Saddam Hussein developed a doomsday defense against an anticipated invasion by the United States.

## Iraq in the Era of Terror

The Bush administration that took office in 2000 inherited the Iraqi problem that had been simmering for more than a decade. The no-fly zones had proven excessively costly and had taken their toll on U.S. personnel and equipment. The blockade had taken a horrendous toll on Iraqi citizens but hadn't weakened Saddam's grasp on power or his apparent ability to build weapons of, mass destruction. Both the blockade and the air strikes by planes patrolling the no-fly zones spawned accusations that the U.S. had declared war on Islam and fueled virulent anti-Americanism in the region. Added to this was a mounting body of intelligence indicating that Saddam Hussein was on the verge of realizing his quest for nuclear weapons. The intelligence was flawed, but that was not known at the time. In retrospect, it appears that Saddam Hussein may have fueled rumors of nuclear weapons to keep Iran, and perhaps Israel, at bay. Whatever the truth, the stalemate between the two countries could not continue.

The president's main advisers, the so-called neoconservatives, had long argued that a strike against Iraq was imperative (Schwartz 2005). In their view, the United States had a historic mission to free the world from evil and make it safe for democracy and capitalism. Saddam Hussein was evil incarnate, and Israel and other American allies were at risk. The destruction of the Iraqi dictator, they argued, would also put Iran, Syria, North Korea, and other pariah states on notice that the U.S. meant business: they could comply with U.S. policies or suffer the consequences. This by itself would reduce the anti-U.S. terror of the preceding decade. To underscore the point, Iraq would be transformed into an American ally—read military base—capable of maintaining the stability of the Gulf and its oil. American influence on Iraqi oil supplies would also break the grip of OPEC, the global oil cartel. Iraq, for its part, would be transformed into a prosperous capitalist democracy much as Japan and Germany had been transformed into democracies in the aftermath of World War II (Jennings 2003).

By their own admission, the neoconservatives had found it difficult to convince the president of their position (Wolfowitz 2003). An attack on Iraq was opposed by Secretary of State Colin Powell, who, as head of the Joint Chiefs of Staff, had guided the 1991 war against Iraq. He well understood the dangers posed by Saddam Hussein, but he also understood global politics and the dangers of getting bogged down in the Middle East.

The balance between Powell and the "neo-cons" changed after September 11, 2001. The United States needed an antiterrorist strategy, and it needed it now. President Bush embraced the neo-con argument. He also found much to like in the antiterrorist policies of Ariel Sharon, the Israeli prime minister. The Israelis had long advocated preemptive strikes against countries supporting terrorism as well as collective punishment against Palestinian communities that sheltered terrorists. They welcomed international cooperation in the fight against terrorism but would go it alone if need be. International condemnation of Israel's antiterrorist methods was unfortunate, Sharon lamented, but was not a matter of grave concern. Nor did Israel get bogged down in legalities that protected the rights of terrorists. Israel understood its interests and struck first. If mistakes were made, they got sorted out later on. Sharon, too, encouraged an attack on Iraq and supported his arguments with data supplied by Israeli intelligence. It, too, was flawed.

The ensuing months saw the emergence of a "Bush Doctrine" that was a curious blend of neo-con concerns about weapons of mass destruction and Israeli antiterrorist strategy. The United States, the president said, would not sit back and wait for the terrorists to strike again. It would also strike at countries that supported terrorism. With Afghanistan's Taliban leaders in flight, Iraq was next on the list. Based on its record of supporting terrorism, Iran should have been next. Not to worry, Iraq would serve as a staging ground for an attack on Iran, a much tougher nut to crack. It would also have been difficult to engage in a prolonged war with Iran while Saddam Hussein remained poised to strike from the sideline. Iraq, moreover, would be a particularly easy target. The Iraqi people were seething with hostility toward Saddam Hussein and would welcome the U.S. as liberators. Saturation bombing would destroy Iraqi military positions and U.S. casualties would be light. The U.S. knew the terrain from the earlier war.

All of this had a nice ring in theory, and doubters found themselves outside the decision-making loop. Of these, the most prominent was Secretary of State Powell. And yet there appeared to be good cause for doubt. Assumptions that the world would support a war on Iraq would indeed prove unfounded. Of the major powers, only Britain supported the U.S. Much the same was true of the assumption that America's Middle Eastern allies would fall in line. All warned of chaos and a surge of anti-Americanism that had already reached alarming proportions. The Arabs, with few exceptions, remained on the sideline. Saudi Arabia and Egypt, America's key allies in the region, led the opposition to the war. Saudi Arabia eventually allowed the use of Saudi bases for air strikes but pretended that it hadn't. Turkey, a longtime U.S. ally, also opposed the war and refused to allow U.S. troops to launch assaults from Turkish territory. All of this was unfortunate, but the U.S. was prepared to go it alone. Israel rushed to offer troops, and rumors abounded that Israel had dispatched commando units to Iraq. The U.S. declined the offer and pressured Israel to avoid acts of provocation that would exacerbate an already difficult situation.

Defeating Saddam Hussein, however, was not the problem. Advanced technology and the bravery of the American-led forces easily bested the Iraqi army, although the contest lasted longer than the 100 hours of the 1991 war. The naysayers had been proven wrong, and President Bush proclaimed that the

United States and the Iraqi people would work together to build a democratic and prosperous Iraq. It was his finest hour.

The months and years that followed were considerably less fine. Some two and a half years after the occupation had begun, more than 2,000 American military personnel had been killed. The number of U.S. wounded appeared to be a state secret. Estimates of the Iraqi dead hovered around the 25,000 mark (*Guardian,* July 19, 2005). The flow of Iraqi oil destined to offset the cost of the U.S. occupation had been slowed to a trickle by saboteurs. Basra and Mosul, Iraq's second and third largest cities, were effectively under control of rebel militias. Much the same was true of Baghdad's large slum areas.

Adding to the administration's misery was its growing realization that the goals of the invasion were slipping from its grasp (Diamond 2005; Phillips 2005). Rather than using Iraq as a staging ground for an attack on Iran, the occupation of Iraq drained the U.S. capacity to attack Iran. An emboldened Iran pronounced the U.S. defeated and accelerated its nuclear program. Rather than joining the fight against terrorism, Iraq became its breeding ground. Rather than transforming Iraq into an ally of the United States, Iraq's newly elected government was becoming an ally of Iran. Rather than increasing the security of Israel and other U.S. allies in the region, the war had placed them in greater jeopardy. Rather than coming down, oil prices skyrocketed.

When the war had gone so right, how could the occupation have gone so wrong? The answer to this question has two basic components. The first focuses on the realities of Iraqi and Middle Eastern politics. The second focuses on the policies of the United States.

The U.S. was correct in assuming that the overwhelming majority of Iraqis shared America's desire to be rid of Saddam Hussein. Most Iraqis also found thoughts of democracy appealing, although there was little agreement on what that democracy would look like or who should be in control. This, unfortunately, was where the congruence of U.S. and Iraqi views ended. Liberation was fine, occupation was not. Neither was the transformation of Iraq into a staging ground for U.S. military forces in the region. Once it had become obvious that the U.S. was going to destroy Saddam Hussein and the Ba'athist regime, Iraq's major groups began focusing on life after the U.S. occupation. All understood that there would be a brutal struggle for power. The Kurds would push for an independent country, while the Shi'a vowed that they would never again be oppressed by a Sunni minority. The Sunni, not without reason, feared that they would be the victims of a bloodbath similar to those that followed all earlier changes of power in Iraq's modern history. Each group was also divided within itself. All groups and factions attempted to exploit the U.S. occupation for their own benefit.

The Kurds had developed a virtual state within a state under the protection of the U.S. no-fly zone and hoped to consolidate their position under the U.S. occupation. They also saw the U.S. occupation as an opportunity to recapture and extend Kurdish control in the oil-rich Kirkuk region. With the Iraqi army in disarray, they possessed enough military strength to do so. Not so with the Turkish troops massed on the border. The Kurds needed the U.S. to keep the Turks at bay. Deep divisions existed within the Kurdish community, but they were papered over for the sake of providing a united front to the U.S. and the Arabs.

The Shi'a were divided between secular and fundamentalist groups, and the latter between competing clerics. All shared the common goal of establishing an Islamic government in Iraq, but differed vehemently over who would control that government and what links it would have to Iran. Iranian-backed clerics offered passive cooperation with U.S. authorities while they bided their time and waited for the U.S. to elect them to power. They were originally challenged by Muqtada as-Sadr, the son of an assassinated Iraqi religious leader, who challenged the U.S. in an effort to establish his own religious credentials. He was successful, but patched up his differences with the Iranian-supported leadership for the sake of controlling the elections. Things would be sorted out once the U.S. left. In the meantime, it was his militias who controlled the Baghdad slums. Battles ensued when the U.S. challenged his power, but the U.S. eventually backed off (*Azzaman,* July 21, 2005). It couldn't fight all of the Iraqis at once. Iran had also begun to bolster other Shi'a militias. The Shi'a cooperated with the Kurds in calling for elections, but both knew that a struggle over the issues of Kurdish autonomy and control of Iraq's oil resources loomed on the horizon.

This left the Sunnis, Iraq's traditional rulers, the odd group out. The Shi'a and the Kurds allowed elections that worked to their advantage to proceed. Sunni groups, by contrast, attempted to derail efforts to form a stable government, attacked occupation forces, assassinated military and police recruits, sabotaged oil and other economic facilities, and attempted to precipitate civil war by attacking Shi'a and Kurdish groups. Some of the Sunni groups were remnants of Saddam Hussein's elite forces, others were secular nationalists, while still others were Islamic extremists intent on building a Sunni religious government and equally intent on blocking Shi'a rule. Even the moderate Sunni boycotted elections that looked likely to place the Shi'a and the Kurds in power. For many Sunni the logic of resistance was simple: vengeance was a certainty if they lost, so their only hope for a sustainable future was to prevent the Shi'a from seizing power and to force the U.S. to guarantee them an equal share in the governing of Iraq. Barring this, the best option would be to force a civil war. Saddam's former armies could revive much faster than parallel militias among the Shi'a.

Added to the mix were Iraq's neighbors. Syria and Iran both had a vested interest in seeing the U.S. occupation fail. Both possessed long and porous borders with Iraq, making the infiltration of men and arms virtually unstoppable. Indeed, a decade of U.S.-imposed boycotts had refined smuggling to an art form. Saudi Arabia and Kuwait feared an extension of Shi'a influence, and volunteers from both countries joined the Sunni resistance. It is also safe to assume that large sums of private Saudi money found its way to the Islamic resistance. The Turks menaced the embryonic Kurdish state by massing troops on the Iraqi border. They also launched raids into Iraqi Kurdistan. All of Iraq's Arab neighbors favored moderate Sunni rule in Iraq, as did the Turks. The Kurds demanded U.S. protection and threatened to shoot Turks if they crossed the border. In the meantime, they were cleansing Arabs and ethnic Turks (Turkomen) from Kirkuk and other Kurdish areas. The U.S. government was torn between its two allies and remained immobilized. Al-Qaeda seized the opportunity to forge a new jihad and joined the fray. Iraq had not sponsored jihadist terror, but now became its center.

All of this caught the Bush administration by surprise. It shouldn't have. It was the stuff of Iraqi politics and was well known by both government and academic experts. Indeed, this was the very scenario that had dissuaded the U.S. from occupying Iraq in 1991. The U.S. administration subsequently admitted that it had had no plans for Iraq after Saddam Hussein was defeated (*WP*, Dec. 25, 2004, A01). Occupation was one of the things to be sorted out once the war was over. Perhaps they assumed that the intuitive logic that had been so successful in dealing with American politics would be applicable in Iraq. This assumption was as naïve as the assumption that Iraqis would welcome the U.S. occupation of their country.

Unrealistic assumptions were also fueled by Iraqi opposition groups living off Washington's largesse and buoyed by hopes that the U.S. would make them the next rulers of Iraq. The CIA and the Defense Department each had its own groups. None survived the first round of elections. Similar turf wars have been pervasive throughout the occupation.

Adding to the administration's woes was its estrangement from the international community. The U.S. and Britain had defied the United Nations and ignored the advice of their allies, who were now snipping from the sidelines. Animosities were compounded when the U.S. decreed that France, Germany, and other allies would be blocked from lucrative rebuilding contracts. To the victors go the spoils.

The administration further added to its problems by demonstrating a profound insensitivity to Iraqi emotions and traditions. Christian missionaries were employed in the administration of U.S. aid programs, and there were suggestions that Iraqi oil would be exported via Israel (*JP*, Aug. 24, 2003). Muslims railed at American efforts to spread the Christian gospel and recoiled at the prospect of an American imposed peace with Israel. They also objected when plans were announced to transform Iraq into a permanent military base. All of this was colonialism revisited. All of it played into the hands of the extremists. None of it had anything to do with building democracy in Iraq.

A growing reliance on Israeli antiterrorist tactics also served the U.S. poorly (Palmer and Palmer 2004). Israeli tactics were those of a small country threatened with destruction and clinging desperately to the lands that it had occupied some thirty-five years earlier. The U.S. was a superpower attempting to win the hearts and minds of the Iraqi people and hoping to turn the country over to a pro-U.S. government as soon as possible. Suspects were rounded up by the thousands, air strikes obliterated the innocent as well as the guilty, and cities were destroyed in efforts to uproot the terrorists. By 2005, some 25,000 Iraqis had been killed. The economy was shattered and unemployment soared. The costs of the destruction are probably incalculable. U.S. occupation tactics made sense from the perspective of a superb military attempting to occupy an enemy country, but killing Iraqis is a strange way of attempting to win friends and influence people. Terror increased in Iraq much as it had in Israel. Washington attributed each surge in American casualties to the desperation of the terrorists. Victory was at hand. The military attributed growing American losses to insufficient personnel, faulty equipment, and the growing sophistication of terrorist weapons and terrorist strategy (*NYT,* Aug. 14, 2005; May 19, 2005; and Oct. 6, 2004). Clearly, the military and the administration were not on the same page. This was all the more evident when Colin Powell left the administration.

The United States proved unable to provide either services or security, and it soon became obvious to most Iraqis that the U.S. was losing. With new U.S. elections looming, leading Republicans began to question the war. The administration was not only in a race against time with the terrorists, it was also in a race against time with the American public. Talk of exit strategies and troop reductions mounted, as did U.S. casualties. Amid the assurances that things were going well were frank admissions by the military that Iraqi security forces were not prepared to take control of the country (*NYT,* July 21, 2005). Iraqis began placing their bets accordingly. No one wanted to be on the losing side. Hoping to bolster his deteriorating position, the president again linked Iraq to the war on terror and vowed to see the struggle to its end (*Agence France Press*/Yahoo, Aug. 13, 2005; *WP,* Aug. 23, 2005, A10).

## FORGING A NEW IRAQ

Given this combination of Iraqi realities and U.S. confusion, there was no way that the occupation could have gone right. Unfortunately, it is this same mix of Iraqi realities and U.S. confusion that is shaping whatever political system Iraq is to have in the future. In the remainder of the chapter we examine the tortuous process of building institutions capable of welding Iraq into a unified country. This includes a deeper examination of the institution-building process, the actors driving that process, and the cultural, economic, and international factors that will shape its ultimate outcome.

### Institution Building in the New Iraq

Political institutions—the governmental apparatus—are essentially a set of rules and organizational charts designed to allocate power and apply the laws of the land. Some institutions are more logical than others, but in the final analysis, their effectiveness depends on the interests of the people that guide them and the level of their acceptance by the public. Elites can abide by the rules, or they can subvert them into instruments of personal dominance and oppression. This has been the norm in the Middle East, but never more so than during the reign of Saddam Hussein. The Iraq public had no voice in the governing of their country and resisted Saddam's rule with varying degrees of apathy, deceit, and rebellion. This was not sufficient to topple the Iraqi dictator, but the level of popular hostility to Saddam's regime did encourage the U.S. to believe that occupying Iraq would be a relatively easy process.

Upon formalizing his power in 1979, Saddam Hussein reshaped the existing Ba'athist institutions to his liking, changed them at will, and filled them with his people. By and large, they resembled the political institutions of Syria as discussed in Chapter 4. Indeed, the parallels between the two regimes are striking and provide a useful lesson in minority rule. Much as in Syria, the Ba'athist regime in Iraq was able to consolidate its authority and bring an end to three decades of profound instability. Both Ba'athist regimes were brought to power by military coups. Both were dominated by members of a minority group that had gained social and economic mobility by entering the officer corps: the Alawites in Syria and the Sunni Arabs in Iraq. Both drew most of their inner circle from a narrow geographic region: the Latakia hinterland in the case of the Syrians, the region of Tikrit in the case of the Iraqis.

The leaders of both regimes, Hafiz al-Assad in Syria and Saddam Hussein in Iraq, would increasingly place relatives in key security positions, and both would adopt a carrot-and-stick policy toward their country's major ethnic and religious groups, rewarding factions that chose to cooperate and brutally suppressing those that did not. Both leaders were increasingly consumed with ambition and suspicion. Both created "cults of personality" in an effort to convince their subjects of their invincibility. The two regimes established virtually identical political structures, including the "National Command" of the Ba'ath Party that paid tribute to the fiction of party unity. Both established symbolic parliaments to sing their praises and give their regimes an aura of legitimacy. The security of both rested on a vast network of secret service organizations, Ba'athist militias, and elite military units headed by relatives and staffed with members of their own minority sect. Both established socialist economic systems and became allies of the Soviet Union. Both sought closer ties with the United States in the mid-1980s and began, however hesitantly, to liberalize their economies. Both groomed their sons to follow them in office. Perhaps the major difference between the two regimes was Saddam Hussein's ability to establish the dominance of the civilian wing of the Ba'ath Party, while Syria remained under the control of the Ba'ath Party's military wing.

Saddam's institutions were demolished with the war and members of the Ba'ath banned from participating in the new Iraq. This had the advantage of wiping the slate clean and building confidence in the new government. It had the disadvantage of eliminating most people who knew how to run the bureaucracy and security services. In the rebuilding of Japan and Germany, it might be noted, a core of officials from the defeated governments had been allowed to shape the new government under the watchful eyes of the Allied powers.

The void left by the destruction of Saddam Hussein and his Ba'athist apparatus meant that the institution-building process had to start from scratch. In reality, it was worse than starting from scratch, for the new institutions had to overcome mass alienation born of generations of oppressive rule.

At minimum, there had to be a constitution, an executive of some sort, a parliament, and a judicial system. The bureaucracy also had to be rebuilt. Until this was accomplished, the laws passed by the new government could not be implemented and the needs of the people for basic services could not be met. Essential to the success of Iraq's emerging political, administrative, and economic institutions was the development of an effective security apparatus. Neither the government nor the economy could function effectively in a chaotic environment. The U.S. stated that it could not end its liberation of Iraq until the country was secure.

Not only did the organizational structure of Iraq's new institutions have to meet the unique circumstances of the country, but they also had to be guided by individuals who would abide by the rules. The new institutions were to enshrine the principle of law over whim and guarantee that megalomaniac dictators would be a thing of the past. Finally, they had to garner the support of the Iraqi population. To succeed in Iraq, democracy would require a vibrant civil society that forced its leaders rule in a responsible manner. In this regard, it is important to bear in mind that political institutions are never neutral. There are always winners and losers (Palmer 2006). The trick, in the Iraqi case, would be to assure that Iraq's new institutions gave the vast majority of Iraqis a stake in the new political system. All of Iraq's key groups had to buy into the system.

The United States began the process of rebuilding Iraq's political institutions during the early years of the occupation with a curious mix of urgency, idealism, prudence, vengeance, and self-interest. Urgency dictated that some form of administrative and security apparatus be set up to stem the chaos and meet the basic needs of the Iraqi people. This sense of urgency increased as U.S. losses mounted. Idealism dictated that Iraq would have a democratic government, as did assertions by Washington that democracy had been one of its main goals in attacking Iraq. Prudence and vengeance dictated that the Ba'athists be removed from government positions and be replaced by the opponents of Saddam Hussein. Self-interest and realpolitik dictated that the new institutions favor the United States and its plans for transforming Iraq into a key U.S. ally. Iraq was to be led by secular Shi'a opposition leaders who had worked with the U.S. in its efforts to overthrow Saddam Hussein. They claimed to have a broad base of popular support, and the U.S. found it convenient to believe them.

The results were not encouraging. Elections for a constitutional assembly were held and were dominated by the Shi'a clerics with strong ties to Iran. U.S. efforts to create an Iraqi security force capable of containing the militants also went poorly. Recruits flocked to apply for the jobs, but those hired lacked the discipline and dedication the U.S. authorities had hoped for. Many fled in the face of sustained resistance. Others deserted to the resistance. Whatever the case, the U.S. military frankly admitted that it would be a long time before Iraqi forces were in a position to secure their country. Some suggested that it might be 2009 or beyond. The U.S. might have done well to consider why Iraqis had rushed to apply for security positions in these most dangerous of circumstances. Some came in search of jobs in a country without jobs. Others were sent to smuggle arms to their various militias and to provide a "presence" in the security services that would serve their group well in years to come. Indeed, Sunni clerics urged Sunni to join the military (*WP,* April 2, 2005, A14.). Still others wanted the influence (*wasta*), power, and opportunities for corruption that came from being a security officer in a lawless land. Beyond question, many were anxious to serve their country. But what country? Kurdistan, a Shi'a theocracy, or a unified Iraq on the verge of dissolution? The U.S. had also counted on Iraqi oil to foot the bill for the occupation, but were soon disabused of this miscalculation. Since saboteurs had cut oil output to a fraction of capacity, it would be the U.S. that footed the bill.

The process of drafting a constitution thus became a four-way struggle between the U.S., the Shi'a, the Kurds, and the Sunni (Brown 2005). The Shi'a wanted an autonomous Islamic government in the south; the Kurds wanted a secular Kurdish government in the north and were biding their time waiting to see who would give them the best deal, the U.S. or the Shi'a. Both the Shi'a and the Kurds wanted their people in key positions at all levels, adding new complexities to U.S. efforts to rebuild Iraq's administrative and security systems. Both hinted at mass rebellions if they didn't get their way. Many Sunni were already in rebellion. Those who did participate in the Constitutional Assembly demanded a strong central government that could protect their interests, including jobs, security from Shi'a and Kurdish reprisals, and a generous share of Iraq's oil wealth. Both the Shi'a and the Sunni wanted the U.S. out of the country; the Kurds wanted U.S. protection against the Turks, but not U.S. interference in their efforts to broaden their control of northern Iraq.

How was a constitution to be forged by four groups with such opposing views? Four key points defied resolution: First, what was to be the role of Islam, and particularly Shi'a Islam? Was Iraq to be an Islamic republic on the pattern of Iran, or was it to be secular republic that embraced Islam as its moral foundation? The Shi'a leaders with ties to Iran inclined toward the former view and pushed for a Shi'a state within a state in southern Iraq. This was rejected by the Kurds and the Sunni as well as by Shi'a groups opposed to Iran's growing influence in their affairs. The second issue centered on the structure of the new Iraq. Would Iraq be a federal state with an autonomous Kurdish government in the north and an autonomous Shi'a religious government in the south, or would it be a unified state with a strong central government? The Kurds wanted autonomy in the north, but rejected a religious state in the south. The Shi'a clerics and the Sunni rejected expanded Kurdish autonomy in the north. The distribution of Iraq's oil wealth was also a thorny topic, as was the role of the U.S. in guiding Iraqi affairs. It was U.S. pressure, for example, that forced the addition of fifteen Sunni members to the committee drafting Iraq's new constitution (*NYT,* Aug. 25, 2005). The Shi'a prime minister pointedly asked for the "speedy withdrawal" of U.S. troops (*Guardian,* July 27, 2005). All of these issues will continue to be the fault lines of Iraqi politics for years to come.

There was also the practical matter of finding jobs for supporters. That, after all, is how political machines are built. If the leaders of Iraq's diverse groups don't find jobs for their supporters, they won't have supporters. This is all the more true in the chaotic economic environment of occupied Iraq. Iraqis are desperate for jobs and the government is the country's major employer.

So many problems and it was still round one. Once drafted, the constitution was scheduled a public referendum in October 2005, followed by new parliamentary elections a few months later. If two-thirds of the voters in three Iraqi provinces rejected the constitution, it would fail. The Sunni controlled four provinces. The Bush administration had a major stake in both elections. They were its last chance to salvage plans for transforming Iraq into the cornerstone of U.S. Middle East policy. In the meantime, the U.S. was debating its disengagement strategy (Terrill and Crane 2005).

Sunni threats to scuttle the constitution led to inordinate backroom bargaining that delayed parliamentary approval of the document until a few days prior to the plebiscite on its approval. A detailed discussion and the debate surrounding the constitution can be found in al-Marashi (2005). As a practical matter, most Iraqis knew little of its content and merely followed the advice of their political leaders (*Middle East Times,* Oct. 7, 2005).

Chaos, violence, and questionable election procedures made this the most improbable of elections, but the draft constitution managed to narrowly survive Sunni attempts to defeat it. The stage was set for equally improbable parliamentary elections in December 2005. The U.S. could claim that Iraq had been placed on the road to democracy. Realists warned that approval of the constitution had placed Iraq on the path to fragmentation and probable civil war (International Crisis Group 2005). The Shi'a religious leaders had consolidated their grip on southern Iraq much as the Kurds had taken a giant step toward autonomy in the north. The Sunni remained the odd group out despite vague promises by Iraq's Shi'a and Kurdish leaders in the Government to review all points of contention, including increased authority for Shi'a religious leaders (*Azzaman,* Oct. 28, 2005).

Much to the dismay of the U.S., the December 2005 parliamentary elections resulted in the continued dominance of a Shi'a religious alliance with strong ties to Iran. The Kurds finished second, and the Sunni cried foul. Sunni cooperation in the electoral process proved to be no more effective than boycotting it, and they rejected the results. The U.S.-backed candidate ran a poor last among the major contenders.

## THE ACTORS IN IRAQI POLITICS

Iraq's elite under Saddam Hussein consisted largely of family and Sunni Muslims from the Tikrit region. By 1986, Saddam's family occupied approximately 20 percent of the top positions in the Iraqi government, and virtually all senior positions in the security services upon which the regime depended for its survival (Baram 1989, 45). By the time of the U.S.-led invasion, several key family members had fallen by the wayside as the inner circle of Iraqi politics narrowed from Saddam Hussein's extended family to Saddam Hussein and his two sons, Uday and Qusai. With the promotion of his sons, other members of Hussein's more or less immediate family (such as half brothers, uncles, and sons-in-law) were either purged or moved outside the inner circle. Saddam Hussein and his sons made all the key decisions in Iraq.

Lesser elites included those security officers, bureaucrats, and party members who had access to Saddam Hussein and his entourage. It also included tribal and religious leaders who played ball with Saddam Hussein. None of these secondary elites had a voice in policy making, but most played a key role in distributing patronage to supporters of the regime. Each was also the patron of a large network of clients who did his bidding. Those in the lower levels of the elite structure had to make do with watches embossed with Saddam's image.

The struggle to determine who will replace Saddam Hussein and his entourage as the rulers of Iraq is now in full swing. The winners will be those who occupy the key positions in the Iraqi government and will certainly include the prime minister, his cabinet, and the heads of the various security services, the leadership of the parliament, and a largely symbolic president. It will also include kingmakers who operate from the shadows, not the least of whom are Iraq's senior religious leaders.

The dominant feature of the Iraqi elite structure is its fluidity. During the early years of the occupation it was the American-supported opposition leaders who headed the elite structure. They didn't have much popular support, but they had the United States. With the election of the Constitutional Assembly, power shifted to the Kurdish tribal leaders and the Shi'a clerics. The next round of elections saw the secular, pro-American politicians mounting a counterattack against the Kurds and the clerics. They failed miserably. Adding to the fluidity of the elite structure is the constant threat of assassination and rebellion.

Given the nature of Iraqi politics, it would be unrealistic to assume that family ties, ethnic and religious affiliations, and patron–client networks will cease to be vital elements in the political process. These are the ties that bind, but never more so than in the present environment of profound instability. Everything is up for grabs, including the country itself.

While the structure of the Iraqi elite will remain fluid for some time to come, one fact is clear: that structure will reflect the balance of power within this much-fragmented country. Our emphasis, accordingly, will be on examining the nature of Iraq's Shi'a, Kurdish, and Sunni communities. It is they who will determine the new elites, and it is they who decide whether Iraq will remain a united republic or dissolve into civil war. Each of these communities is divided into secular and religious factions, which are further fractured by regionalism, tribal affiliations, economic interests, foreign supporters, and personality conflicts. Added to the mix are a suddenly resurgent tribal leadership, not to mention the old political parties. The United States and Iraq's neighbors will also have a crucial voice in determining Iraq's future.

## The Shi'a

Iraq's Shi'a community constitutes approximately 60 percent of the Iraqi population and is concentrated largely in the southern provinces of the country. Migration from the south has made Baghdad a largely Shi'a city, with much of the Shi'a population crammed into massive slums such as Sadr City, which has more than two million residents. Southern Iraq is also the site of the Shi'a holy cities, the most important of which are Karbala and Najaf. The former is the burial site of Caliph Ali's son Husayn and the latter is home to the Shrine (tomb) of Ali.

Shi'a resentment of Sunni dominance is intense and reflects the substantial differences in doctrine that separate the two sects as well as decades of Sunni oppression (Cole 2002). Sectarian differences have also been reinforced by profound economic inequalities, with the average Iraqi Shi'a being far poorer than his Sunni counterpart.

Shi'a activism from the 1940s through the early 1960s was largely urban and organized by the Communist Party. With the crushing of the Communists in 1963, the political leadership of the Shi'a community shifted to the Shi'a clergy, a group that had been largely apolitical since the anti-British uprisings of the 1920s (Batatu 1981). The stimulus for political action among the Shi'a ulema appears to have been twofold. First, the Shi'a religious elite was becoming increasingly marginalized by the growing secularism of Iraqi society, a process introduced by the British occupation and reinforced by the radical regimes of the postrevolutionary era. For the younger generations of Shi'a, technology rather than religious science had become the order of the day. Wiley, for example, notes that the number of religious scholars in the holy city of Najaf declined from 12,000 prior to the British occupation to 600 in 1977 (Wiley 1992, 79).

Second, and more pressing, were Ba'athist efforts to bring the Shi'a clergy under party control (Batatu 1981). The summer of 1969 saw the closing of a major Shi'a university in Kufa, the city in which Ali was mortally wounded, as well as the expulsion of Iranian students in Karbala and Najaf. Iranians represented a sizable portion of the student population in the Iraqi seminaries and were viewed as a threat by the Iraqi regime. Iraqi seminary students were conscripted into the military, though the order was later rescinded in the name of national unity (F. Ibrahim 1996). As if that wasn't enough, the Shi'a religious establishments in the holy cities of Karbala and Najaf were placed under the supervision of the Sunni-controlled Ministry of Waqfs (religious endowments), a deep affront to the Shi'a clergy. Simultaneously, pressure was placed on *bazaaris* (merchants) to curtail their contributions to the Shi'a spiritual leaders. This was especially significant because the financial position of the Shi'a clergy had long been in decline. As if to underscore the regime's determination to destroy the financial base of the Shi'a clerics, some 3,245 merchants of Iranian nationality were deported to Iran. Many of those deported were actually of Iraqi origin, but their forefathers had claimed Iranian citizenship during the Ottoman years as a means of avoiding military service (F. Ibrahim 1996; Kelidar 1983). When economic pressures failed to achieve the desired results, prominent Shi'a clerics were assassinated, as were Shi'a merchants known for their generous contributions to the religious community. That process was intensified following the Shi'a uprisings of 1977.

Efforts to counter governmental repression were spearheaded by the Dawa Party. The Dawa, which had been founded about a decade earlier, was accused of inciting Shi'a demonstrations in both 1974 and 1977; the latter had posed a direct challenge to the authority of the Ba'athist regime. Khomeini's 1979 victory in Iran further radicalized the Shi'a clergy, with both the Dawa and the newly formed Mujahedin, a smaller but more radical group, urging open revolt against the regime. By 1980, the Ba'athist regime was under siege as Baghdad witnessed guerrilla warfare similar to that which had toppled the shah in Iran.

Saddam Hussein responded with maximum force. Key leaders of the Dawa Party were executed in response to the 1974 and 1977 disturbances, and 1980 would see the assassination of Sayyid Mohammed Baqir al-Sadr, the spiritual guide of the Dawa movement, whom opposition radio stations referred to as "the Khomeini of Iraq" (Batatu 1981, 590; *Victory News Magazine,* 2005). Indeed, the Iraqi opposition at the time claimed that some five hundred of their leaders and supporters were put to death between 1974 and 1980 (Batatu 1981). The same period also saw the continued expulsion of Iranian citizens from Iraq, many of whom had Iraqi roots that went back centuries.

Many observers, including the Ayatollah Khomeini, expected that the Shi'a would rise up en masse during the Iran–Iraq War. They did not. A Shi'a uprising did occur after the Gulf War of 1991, but it was easily suppressed. Why was Saddam Hussein able to impose his rule on a disadvantaged Shi'a majority that constitutes some 60 percent of the Iraqi population?

The answer to this question, while elusive and inconclusive, illustrates the complexity of Iraqi politics and particularly the politics of the Shi'a community. The first point is that the leadership of the Shi'a community was traditionally divided among three groups: members of secular parties such as the Communists and the Ba'athists, the Shi'a religious clergy, and the tribal sheikhs. In recent decades, the secular leadership of the Shi'a community was either coopted by the Ba'athist regime or crushed, as were the Shi'a tribal leaders (Baram 1997; F. Ibrahim 1996). Shi'a opposition within Iraq, accordingly, was largely expressed by the clergy. Secular Shi'a do not necessarily welcome the prospect of a religious state, and what remains of the secular Shi'a leadership cooperated with U.S. efforts to overthrow Saddam Hussein. If recent elections are any indication, it lacks a broad base of popular support.

To make matters worse, the Shi'a religious leadership is internally divided. Some religious leaders advocate political activism while others favor concentrating on prayer and good works. Salvation, according to the latter view, is more important in the grand scheme of things than the momentary gains of political activism. Equally divisive has been the bitter competition between the dominant ayatollahs for control of the Iraqi religious community and its holy cities. These tensions, in turn, are fueled by the struggle for dominance between the clergy of Iranian origin and those of Iraqi/Arab origin.

A brief summary of the ranks within the Shi'a ulema may serve to clarify the above points. By the nineteenth century, the practice had evolved of selecting a paramount ayatollah (which means "great sign of God") or *marja'-i-taglid-i-uzma,* literally translated as "highest source of imitation," to serve as the representative of the hidden imam. As a representative of the hidden imam, a paramount ayatollah possessed the power of interpreting religious texts (*ijtihad*) in a manner compatible with the wishes of the hidden imam, a powerful position that far transcended the realm of the profane. All paramount ayatollahs were regarded with awe by the masses. Paramount ayatollahs (*marji*) were selected by their peers on the basis of their writings and piety, and their views were usually binding with regard to religious issues. As a rule, there was one paramount ayatollah in each region of the Twelver world (Iran, Iraq, and Lebanon). The major branches of Shi'a Islam, including the Twelvers, are discussed in more detail in Chapter 7.

The paramount ayatollah or grand *marja* was followed in the hierarchy of religious elites by a variety of ayatollahs and they by less-established *hujjat al-Islam.*

All of these possessed the power to issue binding legal opinions on matters of religion (*ijtihad*), but they generally deferred to the views of their superiors within the religious hierarchy. All were selected by their peers on the basis of their scholarship and piety and each generally headed a circle of learning consisting of sheikhs or imitators. Of the latter, some were students while others managed mosques or schools. Sheikhs, in turn, were supported by the ordinary men of religion who taught children the Koran, led prayers, and performed similar religious duties. To a large extent, the influence of the ayatollahs was proportional to the size of their following among the sheikhs, the pious, and the population at large. This hierarchy was loose, with each layer "imitating" the layer above it on a more or less voluntary basis. It was also nonpolitical, with the ayatollahs devoting themselves to religious rather than secular issues (Batatu 1981).

This pattern would change with the ascendancy of the Ayatollah Khomeini, the leader of Iran's Islamic revolution. Under Khomeini, the power to interpret the wishes of the hidden imam became manifestly political and, as we will see in Chapter 7, provided Khomeini with a weapon of mass mobilization far more powerful than the guns of the shah.

With the passing of Iraq's reigning grand ayatollah in 1992, Saddam Hussein did his best to assure that he would be succeeded by an ascetic (nonpolitical) grand ayatollah of Iraqi Arab origin. The first condition would dampen the influence of Iraq's politicized clergy, while the second would establish an Arab alternative to Iranian leadership of the Shi'a community (Hidar 1999). By playing one religious leader against another, moreover, Hussein hoped to reduce the effectiveness of the clergy as a whole.

To further this end, Saddam Hussein identified Mohammed Sadiq as-Sadr, an ayatollah from a long line of Iraqi religious leaders, as the most suitable candidate for the leadership of Iraq's Shi'a community. In addition to being an Iraqi Arab, as-Sadr shared the ascetic, nonpolitical orientation of the deceased grand ayatollah. Rumors abounded of a deal between Hussein and as-Sadr, with as-Sadr's opponents referring to him as the "regime ayatollah" (*al-Katib,* March 1999). Whether or not this was the case, Saddam Hussein lost little time in paving the way for as-Sadr's ascendence. Only as-Sadr's sermons were broadcast over Iraqi radio and television, and he was allowed a freedom of movement denied to his competitors. As-Sadr was also given control of foreign students studying in Najaf and allowed to open offices in Iraq's predominantly Shi'a cities, a privilege also denied to his competitors (*al-Katib,* March 1999; Hidar 1999). Indeed, as-Sadr's competitors found themselves increasingly harassed by the regime, with still more rumors circulating that Saddam Hussein had ordered the assassination of non-Iraqi ayatollahs.

Once again, however, the regime's strategy backfired. As-Sadr's sermons struck a responsive chord among Iraqi Shi'a and, wittingly or unwittingly, he emerged as a potential competitor of Saddam Hussein. This danger would become manifest in the early months of 1998 as his sermons on peace and piety increasingly gave way to criticisms of the regime. He also urged his followers to attend the Friday prayers in person rather than watching them on television (*al-Katib,* March 1, 1999). Attendance at Friday prayers increased dramatically, with as-Sadr's Friday prayers reportedly attracting more than 100,000 worshipers crowded into the Grand Mosque of Najaf and its surrounding courtyards—a terrifying number for the embattled dictator (Hidar 1999). Saddam Hussein reportedly sent emissaries to as-Sadr urging that his sermons return to questions of faith and liturgy. This action was followed by the closing of as-Sadr's offices and the arrest of his lieutenants, but to no avail. As-Sadr responded by predicting that he would be assassinated, suggesting that "if Mohammed Sadr dies, [the matter] will be transferred to others" (Hidar 1999).

His prediction came true on February 18, 1999, when he and two of his sons were murdered by unknown assailants. Saddam Hussein was accused of the assassinations, but he was not the only party with a motive for eliminating as-Sadr. Elevation to the position of exalted *marja* is a function of support within the clergy, and as-Sadr's rise to preeminence posed a direct threat to the aspirations of other reigning ayatollahs. As-Sadr's competitors also blamed him for government harassment and were further incensed when as-Sadr issued a fatwa ordering Shi'a to pay their religious contributions directly to the poor and needy rather than going through the *marja* and their agents. Religious contributions (*zakat,* the *kums* [a 20 percent donation of income], and cash gifts) are normally administered by the clergy and are their main source of income. As-Sadr's fatwa thus threatened the economic viability of his competitors.

Iran's displeasure with as-Sadr was also intense. As-Sadr's implicit support of Saddam Hussein had dampened Iranian influence among Iraqi Shi'a and otherwise divided the Shi'a community. Iran also had little desire to see the emergence of a grand ayatollah among the Iraqi Arabs, nor was it anxious to see the resurgence of Najaf as a competitor to the Iranian city of Qum as the spiritual center of Shi'a faith. For Iran these were significant issues, for Iranian dominance of the Shi'a communities in Iraq and Lebanon had become a cardinal principle of Iranian foreign policy. To paraphrase *al-Qisi* in reference to the four *marja*s who were assassinated during 1998—it is possible to make two lists of the assassinated *marja*s: those assassinated by Saddam Hussein and those assassinated by Iran and its agents (*al-Qisi,* March 5, 1999, 20).

**Shi'a Politics in the Post-Saddam Era**     Such, then, was the scene with the collapse of Saddam Hussein and the destruction of his Ba'athist regime. The Shi'a were the majority group in Iraq and would inevitably dominate the elections. But which Shi'a? Would the secular Shi'a intellectuals courted by the U.S. return home to a hero's welcome and take charge of the government, or would power fall to the Shi'a clerics? If so, which clerics?

The U.S. strategy was twofold. First, Ayad Allawi, a secular Shi'a intellectual resident in London, was inserted as the head of a U.S.-sponsored transitional government designed to pave the way for the election of a constitutional assembly. At first glance, Allawi seemed to be an odds-on favorite. He was a respected secular Shi'ite who could appeal to the secular segment of Iraq's Shi'a majority, the exact size of which was a matter of speculation. He also controlled what passed for a government and had the full backing of the United States.

Just to hedge its bets, the U.S. took a lesson from Saddam Hussein and searched for a senior religious leader of Iraqi descent who showed little interest in political activism. They found him in the person of Sheikh al-Khoei, head of the al-Khoei Charitable Foundation in London and son of a former grand ayatollah. His role would be to focus Shi'a attentions on religion while Allawi ran the country. Al-Khoei was flown to Baghdad aboard a U.S. military aircraft and accompanied to the holy city of Najaf by U.S. special forces.

Alas, al-Khoei was assassinated within days of his arrival, with suspicion pointing to the as-Sadr movement headed by Muqtada as-Sadr, the son of Mohammed Sadiq as-Sadr, who had presumably been assassinated by Saddam Hussein in 1999. Ayatollah Sistani, another moderate, was placed under house arrest by as-Sadr's forces and threatened with assassination if he did not return to Iran. The U.S. came to his rescue, and despite his Iranian background, he became America's new man among the Iraqi Shi'a. He has survived, but some of his aides have been assassinated. In the American view, a moderate ayatollah, Iranian or not, was better than a radical as-Sadr attempting to compensate for his weak religious credentials by attacking the U.S. He headed a large militia, the Mehdi Army, and had broad support in the Baghdad slums. Sistani, if anyone, could keep him in check.

Things, however, did not go well for the Americans. Allawi was defeated in the elections and replaced by Ibrahim Jaafari, who favored an Islamic (Shi'a) government with strong ties to Iran. Sistani's moderation may have been more illusory than real. While keeping as-Sadr more or less in check, he had also used his profound influence as grand ayatollah to orchestrate the victory of the Shi'a clerics in the elections for the Constitutional Assembly. His hand was also evident in the establishment of strong ties between Iraq and Iran as well as in Shi'a demands for an autonomous Shi'a state in southern Iraq. In the meantime, SCIRI (the Supreme Council for Islamic Revolution in Iraq) and the Dawa Party, two Shi'a political organizations supported by Iran, were strengthening their positions in preparation for the next round of elections. If things went wrong, they, like as-Sadr, would be armed and ready. Was Sistani America's man in Iraq or Iran's? Ironically, it was as-Sadr who opposed the federation of Iraq into autonomous Shi'a and Kurdish regions. Perhaps he too feared a growth in Iranian influence. Armed clashes did occur between as-Sadr's militia and pro-Iranian groups in the run-up to the elections (*NYT,* Aug. 25, 2005).

## The Kurds

The Kurds constitute an ethnic community of about 20 million people occupying a contiguous region that includes portions of Turkey, Iraq, Iran, Syria, and the former Soviet Union. Turkey is home to the largest number of Kurds (10.8 million), followed in turn by Iran (5.5 million), former USSR (5 million), Iraq (4.1 million), and Syria (1 million) (Graham-Brown and Sackur 1995). These numbers vary markedly from source to source. The Kurds have pressed for an independent Kurdish state since the collapse of the Ottoman Empire, but to no avail (Khashan 1995; Khashan and Nehme 1996). Although most Kurds are Sunni Muslims, the Kurdish community also contains a significant Shi'a minority.

The Kurds share a common language, albeit a language fragmented into extremely different dialects. Most Kurds today speak one of two main dialects.

Sorani is the dominant Kurdish dialect in Iraq and Iran, while Kurmanji is spoken in Turkey and the Turkish border regions in Iraq. Kurmanji is also spoken in the Kurdish areas of the former Soviet Union. The Sorani and Kurmanji dialects are minimally compatible, making communication within the Kurdish community difficult. Linguistic and regional differences are overlaid by tribal and ideological conflicts, not to mention abiding personal rivalries within the Kurdish leadership.

As might be anticipated, the conflicted nature of Kurdish society made sustained opposition to Saddam Hussein's regime difficult (Barth 1953). This fact is well illustrated by the pervasive tension that exists between Iraq's two main Kurdish parties: the Kurdistan Democratic Party (KDP), headed by Massoud Barzani, and the Patriotic Union of Kurdistan (PUK), headed by Jalal Talabani. Barzani and Talabani have made no secret of their mutual antipathy. In addition to the mutual aversion of the two leaders, the KDP finds much of its support in the tribal countryside, while the PUK is favored by the urban intellectuals. The KDP also draws its support disproportionately from Kurmanji-speaking areas of Iraqi Kurdistan, while the PUK is stronger among the Sorani-speaking Kurds.

Saddam Hussein's brutal assault on the Kurds in 1987–1988 resulted in the formation of a United Front that included the PUK and the KDP as well as a number of minor political parties. Despite efforts to achieve greater unity, there was little that the United Front could accomplish in the face of Saddam's superior force. These circumstances changed with Iraq's defeat in the Gulf War of 1991. Fired by both American calls for revolt and the Shi'a uprising in the south, the Kurdish provinces of northern Iraq erupted in revolt. The long-sought goal of Kurdish independence was at hand, or so it seemed at the time.

The optimism was misplaced. Pressured by the Turks to prevent the emergence of a Kurdish state and fearful that the breakup of Iraq would find the Shi'a south aligned with Iran, the United States stood by as Saddam Hussein crushed both the Shi'a and the Kurdish revolts. The loss of life was devastating, and some sources suggested that as many as 1.5 million Kurds, approximately one-third of Iraq's Kurdish population, were forced to flee to either Turkey or Iran (Graham-Brown and Sackur 1995, 8).

Stunned by the magnitude of the calamity it had helped to create, the United States imposed a no-fly zone on northern Iraq. Inadvertently, and to the dismay of the Turks, the Kurdish region of northern Iraq was transformed into a quasi-independent state.

Elections for the establishment of a unified Kurdish government were held in 1992, but served largely to reveal the depth of the chasm dividing the two sides. The PUK and the KDP each won 50 seats in the 105-seat Kurdish National Assembly, making it impossible for either to rule effectively. To further complicate matters, each party dominated the regions of its traditional strength. Rather than having no government, Iraqi Kurdistan was now on the verge of having two, one dominated by the KDP, the other by the PUK. The struggle between the two groups was reflected in the staffing of government positions: each KDP employee was balanced by an equivalent employee of the same rank from the PUK. This applied to teachers, police, and all other positions in the government (Graham-Brown and Sackur 1995).

Fighting between the PUK and the KDP erupted again in 1994 and 1995, with the Kurdish quasi-state struggling to exist as best it could. Turkey, for its part, invaded northern Iraq in pursuit of Turkish Kurds who were rebelling against Ankara. The Kurdish quasi-government in Iraq offered little support to members of the PKK, the Kurdish group leading the rebellion against Turkey. Perhaps the fragile Kurdish government feared reprisals from Ankara. It may also have feared that a stronger PKK presence would further shatter the delicate balance in the region. Unsure of how to proceed, the United States did nothing.

In 2002 the two major Kurdish leaders in Iraq, Massoud Barzani (KDP) and Jalal Talabani (PUK), met with U.S. officials as part of U.S. efforts to work out an alliance with Kurds in its efforts to topple Saddam Hussein. Both leaders were cool to U.S. proposals, fearing that the U.S. would betray them much as it had in the 1991 Gulf War. Both stressed that Kurdish interests came before U.S. interests (*NYT,* July 6 and July 8, 2002).

Despite their unease over U.S. promises, both factions began to move toward closer cooperation and the eventual merging of their two governments. The Kurdish Parliament met in 2002 for the first time since the outbreak of armed conflict between the two main Kurdish groups in the mid-1990s (*Guardian,* Oct. 4, 2002). With Saddam deposed and the Constitutional Assembly elected, Barzani and Talabani worked out a gentlemen's agreement by which Talabani would accept the largely symbolic presidency of Iraq, offered by negotiations with the Shi'a, while Barzani controlled the reunified Kurdish government.

The two Kurdish governments were reunited in 2005, but tensions remained (*Economist,* May 25, 2005). The gentlemen's agreement served the purpose of presenting a unified front to the world, but it was short on details. Talabani had the glory, but worried that Barzani had too much power. Talabani wants the Kurdish presidency to be symbolic while real power resides with a prime minister selected by the Kurdish Parliament. Barzani wants a strong president supported by a long term in office (*Economist,* May 25, 2005).

Regardless of the tensions between their leaders, the Kurds will have a major voice in shaping the future of Iraq. Barzani has made it clear that independence is the ultimate Kurdish goal: "When the time comes, it will be a reality" (*Turkish Daily News,* Feb. 4, 2005). These are not empty words. The Kurds possess a battle-tested militia of 80,000 to 100,000 fighters, the Pesh Merga, that is more than a match for an Iraqi army still being cobbled together by the occupation authorities. It is not a match, however, for the Turkish military marshaled on its northern border. It is this reality that may induce Kurdish leaders to accept autonomy within a unified Iraq.

"Until the time is right," the Kurds are blocking any political arrangement that denies them full autonomy within the Iraq framework. They are also redrawing the "Green Line" that separates "Kurdistan" from the rest of Iraq to include oil-rich Kirkuk and the surrounding areas. The Arabs and Turkomen are being evicted from the region and have accused the Kurds of ethnic cleansing. The Kurds respond that they are merely reasserting their rightful control over areas from which they were expelled by Saddam Hussein (Lawrence 2005). As if to underscore the point, Kurdish has been declared the official language of Kirkuk.

## The Sunni

Sunni Arabs constitute some 20 percent of the Iraqi population and are largely concentrated in the "Sunni Triangle" that occupies much of central Iraq. It is not a particularly fertile area and possesses little in the way of mineral wealth. The Sunni made their mark in the military and parlayed military power into political power, a process well established by the Ottomans and reinforced by the British-imposed Sunni monarch. Sunni dominance under the monarch gave way to Sunni rule under the Arab nationalists and the Ba'ath, the only break in which was the Qasim interlude following the Iraqi Revolution during which the Communists were prominent. Retribution against the Sunni during the Qasim era was swift and brutal. It was also brief. The Sunni reasserted their control of the military, and it was Sunni Ba'athists who would rule Iraq until the U.S.-led invasion of 2003. Oppression would reach a new intensity under Saddam Hussein as Kurds were gassed and forcibly resettled in a effort to break their capacity for rebellion. Cooperative Shi'a were paid-off in positions and economic opportunities, but had little power. The Sunni controlled Iraq's oil wealth, most of which went to the Sunni. Not all Sunni were Ba'athists, but Sunni dominated the Ba'ath.

Now it is payback time as a Sunni minority stripped of its power ponders its prospects for survival. If they fear vengeance, it is not without cause. The vengeance has already begun with the dismantling of the Sunni-dominated security forces, the eviction of Sunnis from positions of power and patronage, and eviction of Arabs from Kurdish areas. The Shi'a, too, are extending the areas under their control. The Sunni decry the vengeance, the worst of which may be yet to come, but the Kurds and Shi'a say they are merely recovering their territories that were stolen by Saddam Hussein and his regime. They also note that Saddam Hussein could not have ruled for some twenty-five years without the complicity and active support of the Sunni community. His crimes were not his alone. It was the Sunni who dominated the dreaded security apparatus just as it was the Sunni who dominated the Republican Guards and other elite military units. In Middle Eastern cultures, responsibility is collective, not singular.

In facing an uncertain future, the Sunni had several options. One was to participate in the institution-building process in the hope of receiving security guarantees and their fair share of Iraq's resources. At the very least, they would be in a position of playing the Shi'a against the Kurds, whose alliance was shaky at best. Indeed, the Kurds have accused the Shi'a of hoarding power. Cooperation would also place the Sunni in the good graces of a U.S. administration anxious to gain Sunni support in stemming the rebellion against the U.S. occupation. The U.S. has also developed a new willingness to benefit from Sunni administrative skills, not to mention their expertise in security matters.

A second option was to sabotage the institution building by refusing to participate in the elections for a constitutional assembly that was designed to give the Shi'a and Kurds the dominant voice in shaping the future of Iraq. Why should the Sunni participate in a process that was going to relegate them to inferior status? Without Sunni participation, the draft constitution could not be considered a national constitution. If the Americans wanted a "national constitution" that would guarantee the unity of the country, they would have to devise a new electoral system that guaranteed the Sunni an equal voice in running the country. At the very least, the Shi'a and the Kurds should have to make concessions to the Sunni to go along with their proposed constitution.

Yet a third option was to plunge Iraq into civil war in which well-trained and well-armed Ba'athist units could seize control over key areas of the country. Added to the threat was the growing power of the Sunni jihadists. As the insurgency has indicated, Sunni groups that oppose the U.S. occupation have had little difficulty procuring weapons. Some were cached by Saddam Hussein before the war. Others have poured across Iraq's porous borders from neighboring countries that are either fearful of a Shi'a state or anxious to see the U.S. driven from the region. Once the Sunni had reestablished their military power, so the argument went, they could bargain with the Shi'a and the Kurds—and the United States—from a position of strength.

Which option was preferable? This depended on which of several Sunni groups you asked. Moderate Sunni gravitated toward the Iraqi Islamic Party and seemed to prefer the option of cooperating with the Constitutional Assembly. Iraq's Sunni religious leaders leaned toward the Sunni Association of Muslim Scholars (ulema) and advocated a boycott of the elections for the Constitutional Assembly. The remnants of the Ba'athist regime were intent on civil war. Complicating the mix were the Sunni jihadists, many of foreign origin, who had filtered into Iraq to join the jihad against U.S. occupation. In many ways, the jihadists were in a no-lose situation. The more they goaded the U.S. into retaliation, the more innocent Iraqis were killed and the more hostile they became to the occupation. Each American killed was a feather in their cap and promoted the jihadist cause. It didn't matter who killed the Americans: the jihadists took the credit. They were also positioning themselves to claim credit for driving the U.S. from Iraq when the U.S. actually left. In reality, the jihadists didn't seem to be in a hurry. The Americans were easy prey and killing Americans bolstered jihadist spirits. It also diverted American attention from the war on terror and prevented the U.S. from extending its grip on the region. Hundreds of jihadists were killed in action, but such was the will of God. Their reward was an eternity in heaven. In God we trust. Most Sunni did vote in the 2005 Parliamentary elections, but to what avail?

## THE CONTEXT OF IRAQI POLITICS

Iraqi politics, of course, is far more than a matter of actors and institutions. As we have seen in the tortuous efforts to forge Iraq's new political institutions, Iraqi politics are profoundly influenced by a broad variety of cultural, economic, and international factors.

### Political Culture

The dominant cultural influence on Iraqi politics, as we have seen throughout the chapter, is the supremacy of religious and ethnic identities over national identity.

For better or for worse, Iraq remains a collection of mutually hostile communities, loyalty to which is far stronger than loyalty to the state. Many Iraqis are very nationalistic, but for most religion and ethnic attachments come first. Ethnic and religious conflicts, in turn, have fostered intense distrust between both individuals and groups, as has Iraq's tribal past. Also reflective of Iraq's tribal past is the patriarchal style of rule that has characterized all of Iraq's leaders, not to mention their reliance on relatives to fill key positions within their regimes. Even within clans, interpersonal distrust remains intense. Blood is thicker than water, but it cannot guarantee loyalty. All of Iraq's leaders from the British to Saddam Hussein have played Iraq's ethnic and religious tensions to divide their opponents. As a result, these divisions have not healed with time.

Iraq, moreover, remains a society in transition. Secular ideologies such as liberal democracy compete with deeply held religious attachments. The latter, in turn, have found many of Iraq's Shi'a torn between loyalty to their Arabic roots and to a Shi'a faith championed by the Islamic Republic of Iran. Those advocating an autonomous religious state in southern Iraq believe that they can have both.

Iraqi efforts to forge a humane democracy must also contend with a pattern of historical evolution that suggests that Iraq's political culture is authoritarian. Iraqis have had little experience with democracy, and their patriarchal traditions do not incline in that direction. The depth of hostility between Iraq's ethnic and religious communities renders democracy that much more difficult.

Iraqi political culture is also characterized by profound alienation and apathy. Iraqis could not overthrow Saddam Hussein's regime by force, but they did little to support it. When the coercion stopped, so did the cooperation. Even the members of the Ba'ath Party were motivated more by opportunism and survival than dedication to the party's lofty goals. The same apathy and alienation now challenge Iraq's new leaders. Added to the mix are fear and a profound uncertainty about the future. Rather than getting involved, many Iraqis are waiting for the air to clear. Betting on the losing side is very dangerous in the murky world of Iraqi politics.

## The Political Economy of Iraqi Politics

Economic factors are equally important in explaining the pattern of Iraqi politics. As we have seen earlier, conflict over the distribution of Iraq's oil wealth is one of the major fault lines that threatens the unity of the new Iraq. The Sunni objection to a federal Iraq is, at least in part, motivated by the fear that the lion's share of Iraqi oil revenues will go to the Shi'a and Kurdish regions, both of which have generous oil reserves. Political economists might go further and suggest that the root of the conflict between Iraq's Shi'a, Sunni Arab, and Kurdish communities is essentially economic in nature: all have demanded a disproportionate share of Iraq's oil wealth and government jobs.

The Kurdish and Shi'a rebellions of the past were partially motivated by economic deprivation, as is the Sunni unrest today. The Sunni are clearly the economic losers in the political reshuffle, and they are doing their best to scuttle any arrangement that deprives them of what they consider a reasonable share of the nation's wealth. While most Sunni are not violent, the turmoil created by the jihadists and remnants of Saddam's forces does strengthen their bargaining position. As a practical matter, the resistance to the U.S. occupation is unlikely to be quelled without the support of the Sunni community. The Sunni price is economic equity.

An equitable distribution of Iraqi wealth will not bring religious tensions to an end, but it would be an important step in that direction. It would certainly provide the new Iraqi government with a basis for the legitimacy that it desperately needs. Indeed, given Iraq's history of conflict and violence, it is difficult to see how a democratic regime can survive without ensuring that all of Iraq's major groups have an economic stake in the system.

Finally, we might note that at least some of the opposition to the U.S. invasion is economic in nature. The U.S. promised a democratic and prosperous Iraq. To date, it has provided neither. The economy is in tatters. Some 35,000 private-sector firms remained closed almost three years after the invasion, and vital services, including drinking water and electric power, are far below pre-invasion levels. So is oil production, despite the end of the embargo (*Azzaman,* Aug. 10 and July 28, 2005). The Americans blame the rebellion against the occupation. The Iraqis increasingly blame the Americans. A Shi'ite cabinet minister recently expressed Iraqi frustrations by stating that "the presence of U.S.-led troops was as detrimental to the country's well-being as the devastation resulting from terror attacks." He went on to note that Iraq had become the most corrupt country in the world and that the U.S. occupation bears responsibility "for the chaos that has engulfed the country" (*Azzaman,* Aug. 18, 2005.)

Iraq's new leaders are doing their best to alleviate economic hardships by maintaining subsidies on basic goods and cutting taxes to the bone. Teachers' salaries have been doubled in an effort to keep them in the classroom (*Azzaman,* July 7, 2005). Unfortunately, all of this costs money that the Iraqis don't have. The budget for public services has been cut by 60 percent, with little hope of improvement in sight. Iraqi leaders are demanding billions of dollars in additional reconstruction aid despite an international decision to forgive some 80 percent of the country's $120 billion debt, much of it amassed by Saddam Hussein (*NYT,* Nov. 22, 2005, and July 19, 2005).

The above comments are not intended to suggest that all of Iraq's woes are economic in nature, merely that economics is a very vital element in Iraq's political equation.

### International Politics and the Future of Iraqi Politics

The influence of international factors on Iraqi politics has constituted such an integral part of this chapter that it requires little elaboration. Suffice it to say that Iraq is a country under occupation and that efforts to sustain its nascent political institutions are being influenced by a bewildering array of foreign pressures. The United States is attempting to build a stable and presumably democratic ally. Most Iraqis would subscribe to a stable democracy or some sort, but few have any interest in becoming a staging ground for U.S. control of the region. The Iranians are using their influence among Iraqi Shi'a to transform southern Iraq into an Islamic theocracy, a policy that the International Crisis Group refers to as "managed chaos" (2005, 22). In the process they are strengthening Shi'a political organizations and training Shi'a militias. Should the U.S. turn on the Shi'a, they will be ready. The Kurds don't want to remain part of Iraq, but are being forced to do so by U.S. pressure and the presence of Turkish forces massed on their border. The U.S. will leave; the Turks will not. The Sunni are engaged in a rebellion fueled by extremist groups in neighboring Sunni countries and the al-Qaeda terrorist network. Indeed, Iraq is rapidly being transformed into an international jihad supported by violent extremist groups throughout the world. The U.S. has accused Syria of direct complicity and, accused Jordan and Saudi Arabia of laxity in controlling extremist groups under their jurisdiction (*NYT,* Aug. 22, 2005).

One can only guess how all of this will play out. Many Iraqis are betting on a civil war and have largely ignored government demands that they turn in their heavy weapons. Others hold out hope that a federated Iraq buoyed by the equitable distribution of the country's oil wealth will lead to stability if not democracy. How well a federation of three mutually hostile religious–ethnic communities with differing systems of government could function remains to be seen. The absence of a federation, Iraq's national security adviser warns, will result in civil war (*Turkish Daily News,* Aug. 20, 2005).

# 7

# Iran

## Islamic Governance in Action

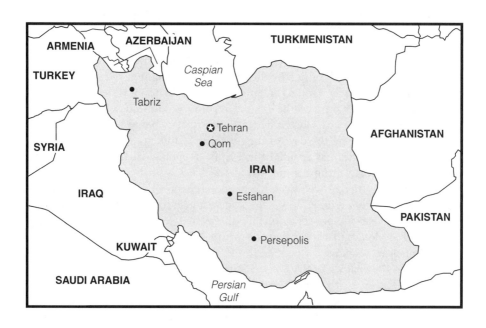

Iran is roughly the size of western Europe and possesses a population that has passed the 70 million mark. This figure is double that reported by the 1976 census, and Iran's rapid population growth has only recently begun to show signs of easing.

Geographically, Iran consists of a huge central plain ringed by mountains. The Farsis, or Persians, constitute approximately 55 percent of Iran's population and dominate the country's central plateau. The remaining 45 percent consists of a bewildering array of ethnic minorities, the largest of which are the Kurds, the

Azeris, the Arabs, and the Baluch. All retain a strong sense of ethnic identity, and many harbor separatist tendencies.

Persians rule the country and occupy most of the important positions in the government and economy. By and large, they either live in cities or farm the more fertile regions of the central plain. Iran's minorities resent Persian domination and would probably revolt if the opportunity presented itself. Revolt is all the more likely because Iran's largest minorities are part of larger ethnic communities that span two or more national borders. Iranian Azeris, for example, share a common border with Azerbaijan, an independent Azeri state created by the collapse of the Soviet Union in 1990. Iran's four million Kurds similarly view themselves as part of a larger Kurdish nation that encompasses a contiguous territory spanning northwestern Iran, northern Iraq, and southeastern Turkey (Koohi-Kamali 2003).

Iran has been a dominant force in the politics of the Middle East since the days of antiquity. It remains so today. Iran is more powerful than its Arab neighbors and the predominantly Muslim countries of Central Asia created by the breakup of the Soviet Union in 1990. It is less powerful than Turkey and Pakistan. This could change if Iran is successful in developing nuclear weapons, a process that the United States believes is well under way. Pakistan does have nuclear weapons. Turkey does not.

Also worrisome to the United States is Iran's role as the main exporter of the Islamic revolution. Iran did not create that revolution nor does Iran control it, but the overthrow of the shah of Iran by the Ayatollah Khomeini in 1979 signaled that no government, however strongly tied to the United States, was beyond the fundamentalists' reach. Export of the Islamic revolution continues to be a central theme of Iranian foreign policy, albeit a theme that is being pursued with less vigor than it was during the days of the Ayatollah Khomeini.

The United States has accused the Islamic Republic of Iran of supporting most Islamic terrorist groups in the world and has long maintained an embargo on key exports to Iran. As we saw in the previous chapter, the U.S. invasion of Iraq was at least partially designed to set the stage for a strike against Iran. Iran's rush to acquire nuclear weapons has further intensified tensions between the two countries. Iran denies that it supports terrorism, and it denies that it is attempting to build nuclear weapons.

Much to the chagrin of the United States, Iran's position as the world's largest Shi'a power has given it a major voice in shaping events in neighboring Iraq. Iraq is 60 percent Shi'a, and its Shi'a-dominated government has gone out of its way to develop strong ties with Tehran. Some fear that Iran is intent on developing a Shi'a crescent that would stretch from Iran to Lebanon and include the oil-rich provinces of Saudi Arabia. Again, Iran denies such accusations.

Finally, it should be noted Iran is a major oil producer and has much to say about the pricing of OPEC oil, although it exercises far less influence than Saudi Arabia. Oil revenues make Iran a major importer of products from more industrialized countries, a fact that has induced Japan, Russia, China, and the European Union to look kindly upon the Islamic republic. All have ignored the U.S. embargo. Indeed, Russia exports both weapons and nuclear power plants to the Islamic republic.

The Iranian government, as presently constituted, represents a fusion between traditional religious beliefs and modern (Western) political institutions (Clawson and Rubin 2005). This curious fusion, once viewed as an attempt to merge two contradictory forces, may prove to be a useful experiment in creating political institutions that are more in line with the culture of the Middle East than those imported from the West. That, however, remains to be seen.

## HISTORY AND CULTURE

Two facets of Iranian society distinguish Iran from its Arab neighbors. First, Iranians (Persians) are not Arabs. Rather, they represent a distinct ethnolinguistic configuration whose origins are lost in the far reaches of history. Iranians write in the Arabic script, but the Farsi language differs markedly from Arabic. In conjunction with Turkey and Israel, Iran constitutes part of the non-Arab periphery that forms a powerful vise around the region's much-divided Arab core. Much like other members of the periphery, Iran has found security in the disunity of the Arabs and would be very reluctant to see the emergence of a unified Arab state.

Second, the citizens of Iran are overwhelmingly members of the "Twelver" branch of Shi'a Islam. All Shi'a, as noted in the introductory chapter, believe that Ali, Mohammed's son-in-law and cousin, should have succeeded to the caliphate upon the Prophet's death. As such, they reject the orthodox line of succession accepted by the Sunni and believe that spiritual succession to the Prophet was vested in the sons of Ali and passed through them to their sons. Following the deaths of Ali's sons Hasan and Husayn, debates over succession would gradually fracture the Shi'a community into three branches based upon which of the historical imams entered occultation and became the hidden imam: the Zaidis (Fivers), the Isma'ilis (Seveners), and the Twelvers (Zakaria 1988, 306). The Twelvers are dominant in Iran, southern Iraq, and the Gulf, and are by far the largest of the Shi'a branches. Their beliefs are described by Henry Munson:

> Twelver Shi'is generally believe that all but the last of their twelve imams died as martyrs—the notion of martyrdom for the cause of God being more important in Shi'ism than in Sunnism. The twelfth imam is believed to have been in a state of "lesser occultation" (al-ghayba as-sughra) from about 874 through 940, during which period his wishes were transmitted to his followers by four deputies who were the only people who could see him. As of 940, he entered the state of the "greater occultation" (al-ghayba al-kubra) which will last until he returns shortly before the end of time to fill the earth "with justice and equity, just as it was filled with injustice and oppression." This last imam is variously known as "the imam of the age," "the hidden imam" and al-mahdi, "the rightly guided one" (Munson 1988, 26).

By the nineteenth century, the practice evolved of selecting a paramount ayatollah (marja'-i-taglid-i-uzma) to serve as the representative of the hidden imam.

In this capacity, paramount ayatollahs possessed the power to interpret religious texts (*ijtihad*) in a manner compatible with the wishes of the hidden imam, a powerful position that far transcended the realm of the profane. All were held in awe by the masses. Paramount ayatollahs were selected by their peers on the basis of their writings and piety, and their views were usually binding on religious issues. As a general rule, there was only one paramount ayatollah in each of the three main centers of the Twelver world: Iran, Iraq, and Lebanon.

The paramount ayatollah was followed in the religious hierarchy by a variety of lesser ayatollahs who also possessed the power of *ijtihad* but generally deferred to the views of the paramount ayatollah. They, too, were selected by their peers on the basis of their scholarship and piety, and each generally headed a circle of learning consisting of sheikhs. Some sheikhs were students, while others managed mosques or schools. Sheikhs, in turn, were supported by the ordinary men of religion who taught children the Koran, led prayers, and performed similar religious duties. To a large extent, the influence of the ayatollahs was proportional to the size of their following. The above hierarchy was loosely organized, with each layer "imitating" the layer above it on a more or less voluntary basis. It was also nonpolitical, with ayatollahs devoting themselves largely to religious issues.

This pattern would change with the ascendancy of the Ayatollah Khomeini, the leader of Iran's Islamic revolution. The Ayatollah Khomeini claimed the power to interpret the wishes of the hidden imam and used that power to transform Iran into the first Islamic theocracy of the modern era. He also used Iran's hierarchy of religious officials to hold the country together during the period of institutional collapse that followed the fall of the shah's regime. It was they who became Iran's new bureaucracy.

Sunni religious leaders possess neither the mystical powers of the ayatollahs nor the organizational apparatus of their Shi'a counterparts. This raises important questions concerning the ability of Sunni clerics to rule should they seize power in Saudi Arabia, Egypt, or any other predominantly Sunni country. It is one thing to overthrow unpopular leaders; it is quite another to govern a country without either the religious powers or the organizational networks that have been available to Iran's religious leaders.

In the remainder of the chapter we explore the blend of religion and politics that characterizes the Iranian political system today. As in the preceding chapters, we begin with a brief review of Iranian history and then move to a discussion of Iran's political institutions, the actors that guide those institutions, and the broader cultural, economic, and international factors that shape the context of Iranian politics.

## Tribal Origins

Iranian tribes entered the area that now bears their name about 900 BCE. They spoke an Indo-European language, but aside from that, little is known of their ethnic origins (Wilber 1963, 18). Cyrus seized power in 553 BCE, giving birth to a world empire that would eventually include Egypt and the ancient cities of Babylon and Athens. The Persian Empire reached its peak under Darius, who referred to himself as "the great king, king of kings, king of lands peopled by all races, for long king of this great earth, reaching even far away, son of Hystaspes, the Achaemenian, a Persian, son of a Persian, an Aryan, of Aryan descent." It was under Darius that Athens was captured in 480 BCE, but the city proved difficult to hold, and the forces of Darius retreated to what is now modern Turkey (Wilber 1963).

Arab armies conquered Iran in 640 CE, but it was the Iranians, far more civilized than the bedouin soldiers from the desert wastes of the Arabian Peninsula, who provided much of the administrative talent in the eastern regions of the Islamic empire.

It was in an Iraq dominated by Persian culture that Ali established the seat of his caliphate, and it was in Iraq that his son Husayn was assassinated en route to establishing a caliphate to rival that of the Syrian Umayyads, whom the followers of Ali viewed as usurpers. The venture collapsed, but the Iraqi cities of Karbala and Najaf, the burial places of Ali and Husayn respectively, have become profoundly important shrines for the Shi'a. Many Iranian Shi'a make pilgrimages to Karbala and Najaf rather than, or in addition to, the required pilgrimage to Mecca.

With the fall of the Umayyads in 749 CE, the caliphate shifted from Syria to Iraq where, under Abbasid rule, Persian influence in the Islamic world would reach its zenith. With the destruction of Baghdad by the Mongols in the middle of the thirteenth century, however, Iran was cut off from the mainstream of the Islamic world. Subsequently it fell prey to a series of invasions, most of them by Turkish tribes who eventually adopted Persian culture. Of these, the most notable was the Safavid invasion of the early sixteenth century. The Safavids eventually ruled an empire that extended from the Tigris River in Iraq to northern India.

The Safavids also converted Iran to Shi'a (Twelver) doctrine, thereby broadening the cultural divide that separated Iran from its Arab and Sunni neighbors (Melville 1996). Though less well known because of its minimal influence on the Arab world, the Safavid empire rivaled that of the Ottomans in Turkey. Indeed, Middle Eastern history between the sixteenth and eighteenth centuries is a pageant of conflict between two vast empires: the Ottomans in Istanbul and the Safavids in Tehran.

The Qajars, yet another confederation of Turkish tribes, seized power in 1794 and, much like the Safavids before them, adopted Persian culture. They would rule, at least in name, until 1924. While art and culture had flourished under the Safavids, Armajani describes the Qajar rule as "inept, unimaginative, superstitious, and selfish" (Armajani 1970, 220). The Qajars knew little of the dramatic transformation occurring in Europe and soon fell prey to the growing influence of the British and Russian empires (Bakhash 1978).

## The Colonial Era

Iran was not colonized per se by the European powers, but European influence had become so pervasive during the later years of the Qajar empire that each new shah was escorted to his coronation by the ambassadors of Britain and Russia. Both Britain and Russia, moreover, had extracted lucrative commercial concessions from weak and profligate shahs, the most notorious being the tobacco monopoly granted to the British in 1890 (Shuster 1912). The monopoly gave a British company control of the manufacture and distribution of tobacco in Iran, and initiated a dramatic rise in the price of this most necessary of products. Mass protests forced cancellation of the monopoly and laid the groundwork for the revolt of 1905. The revolt, in turn, resulted in the proclamation of Iran's first constitution. As in subsequent cases, mass opposition to the shah was brought about by an ungainly alliance of Islamic ulema (clergy), merchants, and an emerging class of Westernized intellectuals. The clergy resented the infusion of Western values in its religious preserve; the bazaaris (merchants) feared the competition of Western firms; and the intellectuals longed to rid Iran of the humiliation heaped upon it by the Western powers (Upton 1960, 25).

It was this era that saw the crystallization of Iranian nationalism. Like Arab nationalism, which was taking root during the same period, Iranian nationalism was a reaction to the growing involvement of the West in the affairs of the East. Iranians already possessed a strong sense of Iranian identity based upon their language, culture, and Shi'a Muslim faith, and the flames of nationalism spread rapidly.

Proclaimed in 1906, the new constitution provided for an elected parliament that was to share power with the shah. The parliament has survived in one form or another since that time but has done little to curb the authority of Iran's autocratic leaders.

Iran was occupied by the British and the Russians during the First World War amid fears that Iran's leaders would side with the Germans. Russia collapsed before the end of the war, tempting the British to transform Iran into a British protectorate. Failing in this, the British helped Reza Khan, the leader of Iran's Cossack brigade and the only organized military force in the country, to overthrow the remnants of the Qajar dynasty. The coup was successful, and Reza Khan changed his name to Reza Pahlavi and had himself crowned shah in 1925 (Cronin 1997).

Aside from his autocratic rule, Reza Shah had little in common with his predecessors. Rather, he chose to follow the lead of Atatürk and introduced draconian measures designed to transform Iran into a modern state. The power of the ulema was curbed and religious dress—veils for women and the fez for men—was prohibited. Western legal codes were substituted for Islamic law, and Iran's vast religious endowments were forcibly "borrowed" by the state. The former action undermined the spiritual authority of the ulema; the latter eliminated much of their income. A brief protest was curbed by force. The main voice against the regime was that of a young cleric named Ruhollah Khomeini.

Unlike Atatürk, Reza Shah was not a populist leader committed to bettering the lives of the masses (Zurcher 2004). To the contrary, he viewed modernization as a path for expanding his personal empire. By the end of his reign, the shah's personal landholdings included much of Iran's arable land.

The shah's regime, while essentially a military dictatorship, was supported by a parasitic aristocracy of large landowners, the members of which staffed the parliament (Upton 1960). Hunting, gambling, and palace intrigues were the order of the day.

Reza Shah's efforts to assert his independence from Britain led logically to closer relations with Germany and the Soviet Union. With the advent of World War II, the British occupied southern Iran and deposed Reza Shah in favor of his son, Mohammed Reza Pahlavi, then twenty-two years of age. The Soviets had simultaneously occupied northern Iran, while the United States occupied a central zone. All three forces withdrew from Iran at the end of the war, although the Soviets did so only under intense pressure from the United States and Britain.

Two decades of social reform and foreign occupation had produced profound changes in Iranian society. Of these, perhaps the most important was the emergence of a technical elite that embraced Western concepts of democracy, nationalism, and social equality. The more democratically oriented members of this Westernized elite formed the Nationalist Party while the leftists, with support from the Soviet Union, founded the Tudeh (Communist) Party. Particularly upsetting to both parties, the Nationalists and the Communists, was the Darcy oil concession granted to the British some thirty years earlier. This concession, like the tobacco monopoly of old, gave Britain the right to exploit Iran's oil reserves in exchange for a paltry royalty, most of which went to the shah (Elm 1992).

## The Era of Revolution and Optimism

Mohammed Reza Shah remained the symbolic leader of Iran during the Allied occupation of World War II, and he assumed full control of the Iranian government with the withdrawal of the Allied forces, albeit as a constitutional monarch. Just what that meant in the Iranian context remained to be seen.

Reasonable evidence suggests that the young shah was sincerely interested in pursuing a course of modernization that would improve the lot of the Iranian people (Zonis 1991). The shah was also aware that economic and social reforms were necessary to counter the growing popularity of the nationalists and the Communists (Zabih 1986). Reform would prove to be a daunting task. The shah was a weak, indecisive, and inexperienced leader and Iran was in turmoil (Mackey 1996).

No sooner had the last Allied troops withdrawn from Iran than Iranian nationalists, headed by Mohammed Mosaddeq, demanded that Iran nationalize the Anglo-Iranian Oil Company, the British operating company that managed Iran's oil production (Elm 1992; Bill and Louis 1988). The Anglo-Iranian Oil Company had become the premier symbol of foreign exploitation in Iran, and Mosaddeq's attacks on the company unleashed a wave of anti-Western emotions that propelled him into the premiership (Diba 1986; Gasiorowski and Byrne 2004). Indeed, so great had Mosaddeq's popularity become that the shah was forced to flee the country and Mosaddeq seized power supported by a coalition of nationalists and other parties of the left, including the Tudeh Party.

The moment was a glorious if chaotic one, but Mossadeq's government was soon subverted by a combination of clerical hostility and foreign (CIA) intervention. The Americans, still reeling from leftist revolutions in China and Egypt, could ill afford the loss of the shah and overthrew Mossadeq in 1953. The shah was duly returned to power.

In 1955, the shah joined the Baghdad Pact, a U.S.-sponsored alliance of Middle Eastern states designed to contain Soviet expansion in the region. Other members of the alliance were Turkey, Iraq, Pakistan, and Britain, the dominant foreign power in the Gulf region. In part, Iranian affiliation with the Baghdad Pact reflected the shah's subservience to the United States following his reinstatement by the CIA. The shah, however, also had his own motives for joining the alliance, not the least of which was a desire to counter Soviet pressure on Iran and to gain a steady supply of American arms. These were of key importance to the shah, who had developed an obsession with foreign policy and military power (Upton 1960; Zonis 1991). The Baghdad Pact also provided the U.S. with a convenient pretext for stabilizing the shah's regime should circumstances require—a matter of utmost concern to both parties following the Mosaddeq affair.

The toppling of Mosaddeq had depended more on luck than the reputed sagacity of the CIA, and both the shah and his American protectors well understood that business could not continue as it had before Mossadeq came to power (*CIA/NYT Index 2000*). For the monarchy to survive, the shah would have to confront the economic and political problems facing his country.

The reform process began in 1957 with the introduction of a forced two-party political system. One party would be the government party, while the other would be "His Majesty's loyal opposition." Both parties were controlled by close friends of the shah and offered little real choice to Iran's voters. Indeed, the new system enjoyed so little support that elections scheduled for 1960 had to be delayed because of popular unrest. When the elections were finally held in 1961, dissatisfaction with the results led to crippling strikes and mounting political violence, much of it organized by supporters of banned political movements such as the leftist National Front. His democratic initiative having proved fruitless, the shah proceeded to concentrate absolute power in his own hands (Saikal 1980).

Political reforms were followed during the early 1960s by sweeping economic reforms dubbed the "White Revolution," a term implying that a wise and caring monarch could do more to promote the welfare of his people than the bloody Communist (Red) revolutions that had devastated Russia and China. The White Revolution comprised a variety of economic and social initiatives including land reform, public ownership of industries, voting rights for women, profit sharing for workers, and a literacy corps to implement compulsory education in the rural areas (Hooglund 1982; Moghadam 1996).

The White Revolution was opposed by the landowners and the clergy, both of whom feared that its reforms would undermine their power: the landowners because it threatened to destroy the main source of their wealth, and the clergy because it promoted secular education and propagated anti-Islamic values (Moghadam 1996). Riots organized by the Ayatollah Khomeini erupted in 1963 and were brutally crushed by the shah. Khomeini was exiled to the holy city of Najaf in Iraq, from which he continued to attack the shah's policies via sermons and pamphlets smuggled into Iran via the bazaari (merchant) network. Khomeini resided in Najaf for thirteen years before he was forced to flee to Paris by Saddam Hussein, who was being pressured by the shah.

However forward-looking the shah's reforms may have been, the tensions produced by the White Revolution convinced both the shah and his American advisers that transforming the shah into a popular monarch would take time (Zonis 1991). Until that goal was accomplished, the security forces would be the ultimate guarantor of the shah's regime. Both the military and Savak, the shah's main intelligence organization, were strengthened and purged of suspected leftists. Iran had become a police state.

With the opposition suppressed, it was easy for the American leadership to conclude that Iran was well on its way to becoming an island of stability and development in an otherwise chaotic region (Bill 1988). Hopes of democracy had fallen by the wayside, but development theorists of the era largely agreed that such was the price of economic development (Palmer 1997). Democracy and human rights would come as soon as economic development had been achieved.

There were, of course, disquieting signs for those who chose to look beneath the surface. The brutality of Savak and other intelligence agencies generated alienation as well as fear (Bill 1988; Delannoy 1990). The bureaucracy was hopelessly corrupt, and popular hostility to the growing Western presence in Iran was mounting.

The shah now ruled Iran with an iron fist. With absolute power came delusions of grandeur and an obsession with transforming Iran into a world power. A vivid sign of the shah's new persona came in the fall of 1967 when he dispensed with the constitutional monarchy and had himself officially crowned shah-in-shah, a position that had been vacant since his father abdicated some twenty-six years earlier. Planes deluged Tehran with roses and the Tehran symphony "premiered the coronation hymn, 'You Are the Shadow of God' " (Mackey 1996, 230).

Increasingly confident of his power, in 1971 the shah dazzled the world with an extravagant celebration of the 2,500th anniversary of the Iranian monarchy. Held at Persepolis, the ancient capital of Iranian emperors, the fete was a staggering display of excess in the midst of poverty. Many world leaders were too embarrassed to attend.

The explosion in oil prices that accompanied the Arab–Israeli war of 1973 quadrupled Iran's oil revenues and pushed the shah's obsession with grandeur to new heights. Basking in his newfound wealth, the shah vowed to transform his agrarian nation into a major industrial power. As described by Zonis and Mokri, "Turning away from the emphasis on agricultural reform and rural development that had dominated economic policy since the White Revolution of 1962–63, the new oil-wealth-based goal of the shah was captured in the slogan 'Sweden by the year 2000.' Iran was to leave the Third World behind and become an industrially developed state providing a full range of welfare benefits to its citizens" (1991, 129).

Far from building a base of popular support for the shah, the White Revolution and the subsequent era of forced industrialization unleashed a backlash of mass hostility. The mid-1970s witnessed a dramatic increase in the activities of urban guerrilla groups, among the most active of which were the Fadaiyan-e Khalq, a group with links to the old National Front, and the Mujahedin-e Khalq, a group that blended Islamic morality with socialist economics. The supporters of the Ayatollah Khomeini had also become increasingly active and now posed a direct threat to the regime.

The shah responded to the escalating violence by announcing that henceforth Iran would be governed by a single political party, the Resurrection Party. All other political parties and movements were banned, and Iranians unwilling to work within the confines of the new party were urged to leave the country (Zonis and Mokri 1991).

The shah's quest for grandeur continued unabated throughout this period, and in 1976, approximately five years after Persepolis, he stunned the religious community by announcing that the traditional Islamic calendar based on the Prophet Mohammed's flight from Mecca to Medina would be replaced by an Iranian imperial calendar based upon the date of Cyrus the Great's ascension to the Iranian throne (Zonis and Mokri 1991). The shah seemed completely unaware of the Islamic revival that was swirling around him.

In 1977, the shah again changed tactics by declaring that constraints would be lifted on all popular expression other than that directed against the shah himself. As the shadow of God, he was to remain inviolable (Zonis 1991). Presumably this move was made in the hope that the masses would turn their hostility on Iran's politicians and bureaucrats rather than the shah himself. If so, the hope was in vain.

Seen in retrospect, the shah's desperate shifts of policy were an admission that he was losing control of the country (Green 1982). The beginning of the end came in January 1978 when students and teachers in the holy city of Qum staged a strike protesting publication of a government-sponsored article attacking the Ayatollah Khomeini, who was now orchestrating the Islamic revolution from his exile in Paris. Police fired on the crowd, unleashing a cycle of violence from which the regime could not recover. The final blow came that October when a strike by oil workers cut Iran's oil production by more than 80 percent. In January 1979, the shah departed for an extended vacation. His relatives and supporters had preceded him, taking much of Iran's wealth with them. A triumphant Ayatollah Khomeini returned to Iran the following month.

An era that began with delusions of grandeur collapsed without a murmur in the face of the Islamic revolution. With it collapsed the naïve assumption that the United States could control the affairs of its client states. The Saudis, in particular, began to question the efficacy of U.S. security guarantees. If the United States could not protect Iran, a vital ally in its struggle against the Soviet Union, could it protect anyone?

Why did a regime as powerful as the shah's, possessing the full backing of the United States, simply dissolve? A large part of the answer lies in the personality of the shah. Increasingly obsessed with dreams of empire that bordered on megalomania, the shah had simply lost touch with reality. The result was policies that squandered the country's oil wealth and ruptured the fabric of Iranian society (Zonis 1991).

Iran's senior political leaders must also accept their share of the blame. One of the main reasons that the shah's policies were out of touch with reality was the reluctance of his advisers to be the bearers of bad news. The shah didn't want to hear bad news and they found it more expedient to flatter than to criticize. Loyalty to the shah, unfortunately, did not include honesty or effective management. By and large, Iran lacked the institutional capacity to implement development at the staggering pace envisioned in the shah's modernization program. Instead, waste, bottlenecks, corruption, and mismanagement became the order of the day.

The fall of the shah can also be attributed to his inability to keep in touch with Iran's citizens. While the shah portrayed himself as the father of his country, his support among the masses was undermined by both a resurgent left and Khomeini's fundamentalists (Green 1982). The left found its base of support among Iran's students and intellectuals; the fundamentalists had become the champions of rural peasants and the urban poor. The shah's efforts to counter his opponents by creating a single party to facilitate direct contact with the people merely resulted in the establishment of yet another political bureaucracy staffed with opportunists seeking personal gain.

Popular discontent was fueled by a variety of factors, including the unrealistic expectations created by the shah's flamboyant promises of development and social welfare. Far more tangible was the lethal mix of unemployment and inflation brought about by the shah's forced industrialization of a largely agrarian country (Bayat 1987). Driven from the land by neglect of the agricultural sector, peasants swelled the slums of Tehran and other major cities. Some found work in the new factories, but most did not. Inflation led to escalating prices, with many doubling from month to month. Savings vanished, and a once prosperous middle class found itself struggling to make ends meet.

Cultural factors also contributed to popular discontent. Most Iranians remained wedded to their Shi'a traditions and viewed the shah's reforms as antireligious, a view reinforced by the sermons of Khomeini and others. At the same time, the Westernized intelligentsia were offended by the shah's subservience to the United States. Indeed, it would have been difficult to find a group that the shah had not offended in one way or another.

In theory, the power and resources of the United States should have been adequate to keep the shah in power during the difficult period of modernization. This, at least, was the belief of analysts who viewed the U.S. as a master chess player orchestrating the affairs of Iran and other client states to its own benefit. The shah was, after all, a vital element in the West's encirclement of the USSR, not to mention the fact that most of Iran's oil revenues were spent on American weapons. Alas, the United States turned out to be a novice in Middle Eastern affairs (Bill 1988). As the shah's regime crumbled, the U.S. dithered, unsure of how to shore up its ally. Far more damning, as Jim Bill recounts in great detail, the United States seemed to be as out of touch with Iranian realities as the shah (Bill 1988). The shah's advisers assured the U.S. that the mounting protests were the work of a small group of extremists and that the foundation of the shah's regime was sound. Wanting to believe that all was well, the United States allowed itself to be beguiled by conversations with the "official opponents" of the shah's regime who, while condemning the shah for human rights violations, saw little possibility that the monarchy would collapse.

In retrospect, then, it can be seen that the downfall of the shah's regime had several causes. Khomeini, although he demonstrated great skill in mobilizing his supporters, probably had less to do with the success of the Islamic revolution than did the erratic policies of the shah and the mystifying behavior of his U.S. advisers (Arjomand 1984).

## The Era of Islamic Resurgence

The victory of the Ayatollah Khomeini in 1979 served notice to the West that the Islamic revival had become a major force in world politics (Esposito 1990; Harris 2004). The shah's regime had been destroyed and the U.S., by implication, vanquished. The Ayatollah Khomeini returned to Iran riding a wave of popular emotion that swept all before it. His power would soon surpass that of the shah.

Khomeini's overriding goals were to consolidate his power domestically, to transform Iran into a religious state in spirit as well as form, and to export the Islamic revolution to Iran's immediate neighbors, and perhaps to the Middle East as a whole.

At a more personal level, the ayatollah had also vowed revenge against the United States and Saddam Hussein, the former for sustaining the shah's regime and the latter for evicting him from his sanctuary in Iraq's holy places.

None of these goals, however, were likely to be achieved unless the ayatollah could solve the massive domestic problems facing Iranian society. As the first Islamic revolution of the modern era, the new Islamic republic had to prove that it could govern and meet the needs of Iran's population. It was expected to fail on both counts, for the newly empowered ayatollahs had little experience in either area and were wedded to a religious philosophy that had more to do with life in early Arabia than with the challenges of the modern industrial world. The country's political institutions, moreover, were in a state of collapse as virtually everyone in positions of authority had either fled the country or been purged by the revolution. Bureaucratic services, such as they were, had ground to a halt, and most of Iran's much-vaunted military forces had simply vanished.

The same was true in the economic sphere, because Iran's technological and professional elite also had fled the country. The new government thus found itself without the engineers, doctors, and other professionals required to rebuild Iran's shattered infrastructure. Iran's neighbors and the major powers, moreover, were nervous about the new regime and eager to see it fall.

On the positive side, from the Iranian perspective, the Ayatollah Khomeini possessed a charisma that rivaled that of Gamal Abdel Nasser. In some ways the symbolic assets of the ayatollah may have been greater than those of Nasser, for they blended charisma born of revolution with a moral authority rooted in the Islamic faith. Many Iranians now referred to him as the Imam, or successor to Mohammed.

Nevertheless, the initial years of the revolution were chaotic as diverse groups vied for control of the "new Iran" (Zonis and Mokri 1991). The situation was clarified by a national referendum on the future of Iran that resulted in an overwhelming victory for Khomeini's vision of an Islamic republic. Elections for a Constitutional Assembly charged with drafting a constitution for the Islamic republic were also swept by Khomeini and consolidated the authority of the religious forces. The resultant constitution institutionalized the principle of rule by the *vilayat-i-faqih* (rule by a supreme religious leader), a topic that will be covered shortly. Both presidential and legislative elections were held early in 1980. They too resulted in sweeping victories for Khomeini's hand-picked candidates.

Now firmly in control, Khomeini banned his opponents, suspected and real, from all political activity. This included virtually all of the shah's supporters as well as members of the leftist groups who had supported the Islamic revolution in the naïve belief that they would soon be able to wrest authority from an antiquated clergy that lacked political experience. When the dust had settled, only two groups remained on the political stage: the Islamic Republican Party (IRP), a political organization composed largely of ulema, and the revolutionary committees (Daneshvar 1996). The IRP had been cobbled together by the clergy to manage the 1980 elections, while the revolutionary committees had emerged more or less spontaneously with the collapse of the shah's regime.

The revolutionary committees, most of which drew their membership from the radical Islamic groups that had spearheaded the revolution, seized control of most of Iran's local governments and ruled in the name of the revolution. The committees, although not of Khomeini's making, received his blessing and would become a major force in enforcing the ayatollah's dictates during the early years of the revolution (Zonis and Mokri 1991).

Despite Khomeini's power, the spontaneous nature of the revolutionary committees and other groups claiming to act in the name of the revolution made them difficult to control and often resulted in independent actions that caught the central government by surprise. Of these, perhaps the most dramatic was the 1979 seizure of the U.S. Embassy in Tehran by students demanding that the shah, now in the U.S. for medical treatment, be returned to Iran to stand trial for past crimes (Farber 2005). A large number of U.S. hostages had been detained, and now an untested Khomeini regime faced the threat of American retaliation. The Iranian government was divided on how best to handle the crisis. Abolhassan Bani Sadr, who had been elected to the presidency in 1980, urged that the hostages be released. Khomeini, however, sided with the students. Bani Sadr, whom Khomeini had said during the 1980 election campaign was like his son, was forced from office in 1982 (Zonis and Mokri 1991).

Crises also buffeted the Islamic republic from abroad. In December 1979, the Soviet Union invaded Afghanistan, a neighboring Islamic country, forcing the ayatollah to either support the Islamic resistance in Afghanistan or abdicate his self-proclaimed role as the leader of the Islamic world. He chose the former, earning the enmity of his powerful neighbor to the north.

A far more immediate threat to the survival of the Islamic revolution was Iraq's invasion of Iran in November 1980. With the army in disarray, the ayatollah

mobilized popular militias by drawing upon his religious authority and the organizational network provided by the revolutionary committees. As described by
Mackey:

> The Basij [popular militias] operated from nine thousand mosques, en-
> rolling boys below eighteen, men above forty-five, and women. Primarily
> the zealous products of poor, devout families from rural areas, they volun-
> teered for temporary duty in God's war between school terms or in the
> interim dividing one season's harvest and the next season's planting. At the
> front, a Basiji could be identified by his tattered leftover uniform and mis-
> matched boots (often picked up on the battlefield), the bright red or yellow
> headband stretched across his brow declaring God's or Khomeini's great-
> ness, and the large, imitation brass key, the key to paradise, that hung around
> his neck. The Basijis gained fame as human minesweepers in the massive
> assaults that characterized the 1982–1984 phase of the war. Boys as young
> as twelve, shaped by the fanaticism of the revolution, walked across mine-
> fields to clear the way for the advancing Pasdaran, followed by the army
> (Mackey 1996, 323).

The tenacity of the Iranian resistance stunned an Iraqi military that had overex-
tended its supply routes, and by 1982, the Iraqi forces were in full retreat. Saddam
Hussein signaled his willingness to make peace, but the Ayatollah Khomeini, sensing the opportunity to seize southern Iraq, refused. Seen in retrospect, this was
a mistake. Had the ayatollah accepted peace at this time, it is possible that Iran could
have won from Saudi Arabia and Kuwait the billions of dollars in war reparations
desperately needed to rebuild the country.

Meanwhile, Khomeini had initiated efforts to export the Islamic revolution:
the opening salvo had been a botched attempt to overthrow the government of
Bahrain in 1979. Saudi Arabia was also targeted as 100,000 Iranian participants in
the annual *hajj* raised pro-Khomeini posters and clashed with Saudi police. The
scene was repeated in 1983, and in December of the same year a series of bomb
attacks shook Kuwait, killing six people and injuring scores more (Mackey 1996).

In 1983, the ayatollah, still intent on precipitating a regional revolution,
inspired attacks on Western targets in Lebanon, a country that also possessed
a large Shi'a population. April of that year saw the U.S. Embassy in Beirut bombed
by the Islamic Jihad, a militia with strong ties to Iran. Two more bombings followed in October, one killing 241 U.S. Marines, the other 47 French soldiers.
Both the Americans and the French had been sent to Lebanon to stabilize the
war-torn country in the aftermath of the Israeli invasion of 1982. After the bombings, Westerners working in Lebanon were kidnapped by groups reputedly supported by Iran, including the Iranian-sponsored Hezbollah movement. Iran
claimed innocence, but a contingent of Revolutionary Guards from Iran had
played an key role in organizing the Hezbollah militia. The United States
remained frustrated but helpless, seeing little recourse but to increase its support
of Saddam Hussein.

The ayatollah was becoming increasingly aware of the dangers of isolation
(Ramazani 1989, 212). Syria and Libya had supported Iran from the beginning of

the Iran–Iraq War and played an important role in enabling Iran to avoid isolation in the region. Strong ties with Japan and Western Europe also helped, as did growing ties with China, which was becoming a major source of Iranian arms. Iran had previously favored U.S. goods, and both the European and the Asian states, as well as the Israelis, were anxious to pick up the slack caused by the American economic embargo. Indeed, Israel had been selling arms to Iran since the beginning of the war, in contravention of the U.S. boycott.

Although incomplete, the U.S. embargo was still taking its toll in the key defense and oil sectors, both of which depended heavily on the United States. The domestic pressures of the war, moreover, were mounting. Inflation had reached 35 percent, and Iran's "human wave" strategy of countering Iraq's technical superiority had left few Iranian families without a personal loss. Riots erupted in Tehran in April 1985 and were soon followed by uprisings in other major cities. The riots were crushed, but an undercurrent of resentment remained (Mackey 1996). The clerics themselves were unsure of the best means of coping with the domestic pressures and divided into moderate and hard-line factions.

In the late summer of 1985, the United States shipped weapons to Iran via Israel as part of an "arms for hostages" exchange. Lebanese militias released a few hostages at Tehran's request, paving the way for a secret visit to Iran in May 1986 by national security adviser Robert McFarlane and Lieutenant Colonel Oliver North of the National Security Council (Cavender, Jurik, and Cohen 1993). The Americans came bearing gifts, including a chocolate cake, matched sets of chrome-plated Magnum pistols, and spare parts for Iran's Hawk missiles. The United States had violated its own embargo. "Irangate," as the affair was dubbed by the U.S. press, was offset by continuing U.S. support of Iraq. This led to charges from both Iran and Iraq that the U.S. was encouraging them to destroy each other.

By now the Iran–Iraq War had disintegrated into a stalemate that pitted Iran's almost three-to-one superiority in manpower against Iraq's superiority in air power. In a stunning 1986 victory, Iran captured most of the Fao Peninsula and moved within fifty miles of Iraq's southern port city of Basra. Had Basra fallen, southern Iraq would have been under Iran's control and Iranian forces would have reached the borders of Saudi Arabia and Kuwait. Basra withstood Iran's "human wave" strategy, but not without the use of poison gas.

By 1987, the war had begun to tilt in Iraq's favor as Iraqi planes destroyed Iranian oil facilities and modified Soviet Scud missiles began to strike Tehran and other Iranian cities in what would later be termed the "war of the cities." Iraqi aircraft also bombed Iranian targets well beyond their normal range, leading to speculation that they had refueled in the Soviet Union (Segal 1988, 958).

Reverses in the war further increased the conflict among the clergy, and by 1987 the Ayatollah Khomeini was forced to take direct control of the government and abandon his preferred strategy of shifting his support between conservatives and reformers as the needs of the moment dictated. The Islamic Republican Party was disbanded as ineffectual, and the ayatollah enhanced his powers as *vilayat-i-faqih* by now claiming to rule in the name of the hidden imam. This new interpretation of the powers of the *vali-i-faqih*, according to Khomeini's opponents, "overrode even the Koran, a charge heatedly denied by the Ayatollah" (Mostyn 1991, 236).

The direct assertion of Khomeini's power stabilized the regime but could do little to stem Iran's losses in the war. With victory no longer in sight and the Islamic republic on the verge of collapse, Khomeini accepted Security Council Resolution 598, bringing the war to an end in 1988. He described the act as being more loathsome than drinking hemlock, and indeed he died the following year (Mackey 1996, 331). There were no victors in this war. Iran's military and non-military costs, including lost oil revenue, were estimated at $137 billion (Mackey 1996, 332). Casualty figures approached three-quarters of a million, and Iran's economic infrastructure had been decimated. Alnasrawi places Iran's total economic losses from the war at some $644.5 billion (Alnasrawi 1994). The Islamic revolution had not been destroyed, but it clearly had suffered a setback. Domestic problems also eroded the regime's popular support and left the clerics hopelessly divided among themselves.

The decade of Khomeini could claim a number of successes. The revolution had been consolidated, and Iran had a new set of political institutions, the nature of which will be discussed in the following section. The Islamic resurgence had spread throughout the region, and though the Iranian regime could not claim full credit for this, it was certainly part of the equation. Iran's foreign and regional enemies had also been kept at bay, although Iran remained relatively isolated both regionally and internationally. Saddam Hussein had not been destroyed, but his survival probably had more to do with U.S. and Saudi support than it did with Hussein's military prowess.

This said, the price of war and revolution had been devastating. Not only did little economic development take place during the Khomeini regime, but much of the economic infrastructure that had been developed under the shah was destroyed. The Iranian population had been exhausted by the war and was becoming increasingly weary of the regime's rigid moral codes. This disenchantment was particularly evident among the middle class that had embraced Westernization with a passion during the era of the shah. The ayatollah's exceptional charisma had enabled him to place his revolutionary goals above internal development. His successors would find this to be a far more difficult task.

## The Era of the New World Order

The death of the Ayatollah Khomeini on June 3, 1989, was followed the next year by the collapse of the USSR. What emerged was a new world order dominated by the United States and its allies. The advent of U.S. hegemony in the international arena coincided with an upsurge in the power of Islamic groups throughout the Middle East. The stage was thus set for a conflict between two seemingly irreconcilable forces, one whose power was based on its control of the world's economic and political systems and the other rooted in religious extremism. The policies pursued by Khomeini's successors would have much to say about the outcome of this clash of worldviews.

The Ayatollah Khomeini bequeathed Iran a political system that was a curious fusion of religious and secular institutions, an updated analysis of which will be provided in the concluding section of the chapter. For the moment, suffice it to say that power was divided between a supreme religious guide, a parliament or *majlis,* an elected president, and a variety of religious councils. No one was quite sure how this seemingly ungainly political arrangement would work, for all had been subservient to Khomeini's power. Many assumed that the new arrangement would not work at all.

The two figures who bore primary responsibility for guiding Iran into the era of the new world order were Ali Akbar Hashemi Rafsanjani, the reigning president of Iran, and Hojjat al-Islam Sayyed Ali Khamenei, the newly elected Supreme Guide. Both men were compromise candidates. Rafsanjani, the speaker of the *majlis,* had been tapped for the presidency after the ayatollah's initial choice lost favor and withdrew his candidacy. Khamenei, in turn, was the compromise choice to replace Khomeini when the Assembly of Experts found it difficult to agree on a more prominent theologian (Banuazizi and Weiner 1986; Gieling 1997). No one, of course, could replace Khomeini in terms of either his personal charisma or his stature as the earthly manifestation of the hidden imam. Nevertheless, the speed with which the Assembly of Experts moved to fill the position of Supreme Guide demonstrated the resilience of the Islamic regime, surprising many who had expected it to collapse with the ayatollah's death. Whatever their differences, the elite that succeeded Khomeini were all part of the religious establishment and possessed an overriding interest in preserving Iran's theocratic political system.

The elite also shared a common commitment to developing the economy and exporting the revolution, although little agreement existed on how best to achieve these two objectives. In this regard, the Iranian elite was now divided into hard-line and pragmatic factions, with the former committed to the export of the revolution and the latter arguing that the revolution was best served by internal development, even if it required building bridges with Iran's former enemies.

The ayatollah's death found each faction dominating a separate branch of the government. The pragmatists, headed by Rafsanjani, controlled the presidency, while the hard-liners, headed by Khamenei, controlled the parliament and much of the religious establishment. At least initially, the pragmatists appeared to have the upper hand, as Rafsanjani attempted to address Iran's spiraling budget deficit by reducing subsidies on food, housing, and other necessities. Restrictions on the private sector were also eased in the hope of stimulating greater economic growth than had been achieved by Iran's state-run industries. The public responded to the reduced subsidies with food riots in 1990, serving notice that the masses were growing restive with the revolution.

Iran was faring little better on the regional front than on the domestic front. The war with Iraq had ended in 1988, but relations between the two countries remained tense. Border flare-ups were common, and Iraq continued to occupy some 2,600 square miles of Iranian territory (Ramazani 1992, 396). Tensions were also heightened by Iraq's refusal to repatriate more than 100,000 Iranian prisoners of war as well as its continued claims to all of the Shatt-al-Arab (Ramazani 1992, 396).

It was against this background that Iranians went to the polls in 1989 to elect a new parliament. The pragmatists, led by President Rafsanjani, rallied under the banner of the Association of Combatant Clerics and advocated a revamping of Iran's economic and foreign policies. They were opposed by the Association of Combatant Clergy, a far more radical group advocating a continuation of Khomeini's policies on both the foreign and domestic fronts (Sarabi 1994). As indicated by their names, both groups were deeply rooted in Iran's religious establishment and were committed to theocratic rule. As the above discussion suggests, labels such as radical and moderate are confusing in the Iranian context (Fairbanks 1998).

The moderates emerged victorious, but were immediately faced with Iraq's invasion of Kuwait on August 2, 1990. This threatened to transform Iraq into the dominant state of the Gulf, a situation that, if allowed to stand, would have placed the Islamic republic in jeopardy (Ramazani 1992, 404). Iran condemned the attack and called for the immediate withdrawal of Iraqi forces. Equally problematic was Iran's fear that the United States would use the Iraqi attack as a pretext for strengthening its presence in the Gulf and thus posing a constant threat to Iran's security.

Iraq's invasion of Kuwait proved to be "manna from heaven" for Iran's Islamic leaders (Ramazani 1992, 397). Faced with a war that he could not win, Saddam Hussein made a frantic effort to gain Iranian support by evacuating the Iranian territory still under Iraqi control and releasing his Iranian prisoners. Iranian support, however, was not forthcoming. Iran declared its neutrality but formally adhered to all UN economic sanctions. With Saddam Hussein's war machine destroyed, Iran would again be the dominant power in the Gulf.

Dramatic as it seemed, the electoral victory of the moderates proved to be short-lived. Riots erupted in 1992 and 1993, and dissatisfaction with Rafsanjani's reforms was further signaled by the narrowness of his victory in the presidential elections of 1993.

With the moderates in disarray, the hard-liners seemed poised to seize power in the 1997 presidential elections. Their optimism was premature. Mohammed Khatami, the reform candidate, swept to a dazzling and totally unexpected victory with a resounding 69 percent of the vote. Equally impressive was the staggering 88 percent voter turnout, more than double that of the preceding presidential election. The voters had spoken, and they wanted change.

After a period of vacillation, the hard-liners accepted Khatami's victory, portraying it as an affirmation of popular support for Islamic rule (Fairbanks 1998). Missing from this bit of sophistry was the fact that only candidates approved by the clerics had been allowed to run for office. Nevertheless, Iran's religious theocracy was becoming the most democratic political system in the Islamic world.

Despite Khatami's dazzling victory, the presidency continued to be subordinate to the Supreme Guide and the hard-liners remained dominant in the *majlis*. Nevertheless, the size of Khatami's victory added new power to the presidency, pitting the religious authority of the Supreme Guide against the popular mandate of Khatami.

While stressing his total commitment to Islamic rule, Khatami minced few words in his efforts to reorient Iranian foreign policy. "In foreign relations we need an active and fresh presence based on our independence and national interests. It is important for us to defuse tensions and seek friendship and brotherhood in the international arena" (*IHT,* Aug. 20, 1997, 6). Words were supported by deeds with his appointment of the U.S.-educated Kamal Kharrazi as foreign minister and the Ayatollah Mohajerani as minister of culture. The latter had earlier been criticized for his advocacy of dialogue with the United States (*IHT,* Aug. 13, 1997, 2).

Khatami's resounding victory in the 1997 presidential elections was followed by an equally resounding victory for the reformists in the municipal elections of 1999. It was against this background that both sides prepared for the parliamentary elections scheduled for the spring of 2000. Yet another victory for the reformists would dispel any hard-line pretenses of mass support. The 2000 elections were not a matter of life or death for the hard-liners, but a serious setback could easily be interpreted as a mortal blow to their authority.

The hard-line strategy going into the 2000 election campaign blended intimidation with legalistic maneuvering designed to disqualify key reformist candidates. The campaign of intimidation began with the assassination of prominent reformist intellectuals but collapsed amid signs of a popular backlash. Officials in the intelligence services were duly blamed for the assassinations and removed from their positions. The assassinations gave way to legalistic attempts to curb the reformist press. The reformist newspaper *Salam* was closed in the summer of 1999 and its editors arrested on charges of "spreading falsifications, disturbing public opinion and publishing classified documents," the latter referring to the publication of the contents of a repressive press bill the day before its anticipated approval by the parliament (Samii 1999, 2). The editors in question were close to student leaders at the University of Tehran, and their arrest triggered student riots that soon engulfed Tehran and eighteen other cities. The student protests, in turn, led to confrontations between the students and hard-line vigilantes, with the security forces siding with the latter. Order was restored by mid-August and, as in the case of the earlier assassinations, key hard-line officials were forced to resign from their posts, not the least of whom was the minister of justice (*AP/Daily Star,* Aug. 16, 1999, 5). Khatami, for his part, responded to the challenge of the hard-liners by urging a massive turnout for the 2000 elections and by issuing press licenses to reformist groups. Every time a reformist paper was closed down, a new one would appear, or so it seemed.

The parliamentary elections were held in the spring of 2000, and the reformers swept to their third dazzling victory in as many years, receiving three-quarters of the seats in the *majlis* (Sick 2000). Turnout was around 80 percent, although estimates vary from source to source. The reformist victory was significant on several counts. First, the conservatives had lost control of the *majlis* for the first time since the revolution. The loss deprived them of a key pillar of political control and was all the more painful because both the judiciary and the security services had been compromised earlier by the violence of the election campaign. Second, the reformers were now in a position to pass legislation undermining conservative authority. Particularly important in this regard was the ability of the *majlis* to name half of the members of the all-powerful Council of Guardians, which will be discussed shortly. Also rumored to be on the agenda were plans to use the parliament's constitutional powers to investigate "the affairs of the country" as a weapon for probing the Republican Guards and the Basij, the military arm of the hard-liners. Third, the reformists were now in a position to vigorously pursue their reform agenda, a key element of which was rapprochement with the United States.

The threat to conservative dominance posed by the reformist victory spawned rumors of a planned coup by the Republican Guards. This did not materialize, but it did add yet another element of tension to Iranian politics (Namazi 2000). What did materialize were continued hard-liner efforts to muzzle the reformist press, as evidenced by a stern warning from the Supreme Guide on the dangers of opening the Iranian press to "American-style reformers" and "domestic hypocrites" (*Daily Star,* April 21, 2000). The conservatives also used their control of the Council of Guardians to strip the parliament of its ability to investigate agencies under the control of the Supreme Guide, including the Republican Guards, the Basij, the large benevolent associations that control much of Iran's wealth, and the state broadcasting system (Namazi 2000).

The stage was thus set for a confrontation between the reformers and the hard-liners on all fronts: the parliament, the press, and the street. The reformers possessed an overwhelming mandate for change, but faced the very real danger that efforts to press their advantage would cause the hard-liners to resort to violence. The hard-liners had also used their control of the legal and bureaucratic apparatus to block the reformers at every turn—so effectively that the end of 2000 would find Khatami publicly admitting: "I declare that after three and a half years as president, I don't have sufficient powers to implement the constitution, which is my biggest responsibility. . . . In practice, the president is unable to stop the violations . . . or force implementation of the constitution" (*IHT,* Nov. 27, 2000).

A showdown between the two sides appeared more and more inevitable as Iran moved toward the presidential elections scheduled for the summer of 2001. Another reformist victory seemed inevitable, but to what avail? Khatami himself seemed dubious about the utility of another term as president and refused to announce his candidacy for re-election until the closing days of the nomination process.

The elections were held in relative calm, and Khatami led the reformers to another stunning electoral victory, capturing 77.88 percent of the popular vote. The only discordant note was a sharp drop in voter turnout from 83 percent in 1997 to 67 percent in 2001 (*Tehran Times,* June 11, 2001).

Supreme Guide Khamenei again accepted the results with grace, citing Iran's eighth presidential election as a sterling example of Islamic democracy (*Tehran Times,* June 11, 2001). The Supreme Guide's generosity in congratulating Khatami on his victory disguised a counterrevolution that was now taking shape.

## Iran in the Era of Terror

The September 11, 2001, attacks on the United States were perpetrated by Osama bin Laden's al-Qaeda network, whose main base of support had been

Taliban-ruled Afghanistan. While not implicated in the attacks, the Islamic Republic of Iran was not above suspicion. Al-Qaeda and Iran appeared to have parted company, but their past links were outlined in Chapter 1 and are a matter of record. Both, moreover, shared a common goal of establishing Islamic governments throughout the Islamic world. Both believed that their goal of transforming the Middle East into an Islamic state could only be achieved by driving the United States from the region. The U.S., moreover, had supported Saddam Hussein in his long war with Iran, and remained a clear and present danger to the Islamic republic.

The challenge facing Iran, accordingly, was to avoid a U.S. attack while simultaneously preventing the U.S. from extending its position in the Gulf region. Tehran condemned the September 11 attacks and called for a global struggle against terrorism. However, Iran also demanded that the war against terror be directed by the United Nations rather than the United States, a position shared by the European Union and much of the world. The U.S. bombing of Afghanistan was also problematic. As the self-proclaimed guardian of Islam, Iran could not condone an attack on another Islamic country, not to mention a country on its own borders. Again, Iran chose the middle ground, condemning the U.S. bombing in the press, but privately warning Western diplomats that bin Laden and the Taliban were one and the same and that failure to destroy them would make them heroes (RFE/RL, 2001). Iran also went out of its way to arrest al-Qaeda supporters fleeing from Afghanistan, but it did not deliver them to the United States. None of these dilatory tactics pleased a U.S. administration intent of ridding the world of terrorism. More than ever, Washington viewed Iran as part of a global axis of evil.

Given Iran's record of supporting terrorism, one might assume that an attack on Iran would follow in short order. To the surprise of almost everyone, it was Iraq rather than Iran that bore the brunt of Washington's wrath. As we have seen in the preceding chapter, reasons for Washington's choice ranged from a fixation with Saddam Hussein's nuclear program and presumed links to terrorists to worry over Israeli security and a desire to control Iraq's vast oil reserves. High on the list was the suitability of Iraq as a staging ground for an attack on Iran. Iraq, so the logic went, could be toppled by air strikes. The Islamic regime in Iran was deeply entrenched and its overthrow would require a long and substantial buildup of U.S. facilities in the region.

Iraq thus became a proxy battleground in the simmering conflict between the U.S. and Iran. The U.S. occupied Iraq and attempted to forge a new Iraqi government beholden to Washington. Iran, while not challenging the U.S. directly, began to consolidate its substantial influence among Iraq's Shi'a majority. The leaders of the Shi'a opposition to Saddam Hussein had sought refuge in Iran, and it was they who seized control of Iraq's embryonic government.

Perhaps emboldened by the U.S. debacle in Iraq, Tehran accelerated its nuclear energy program. The U.S. had long accused Iran of developing nuclear weapons, a charge denied by Iran. It is known that Iran did acquire the blueprint for nuclear weapons from Pakistan (*Asia Times,* March 18, 2003). Iran's desire for nuclear weapons is easy to understand. Nuclear weapons would shore up its defense against

U.S. attacks and simultaneously make the Islamic republic the only nuclear power in the region other than Israel, a powerful position indeed. Not to be overlooked was the symbolic importance of nuclear weapons on the domestic front. The prospect of a nuclear program gave the regime a much-needed shot of nationalist adrenaline.

The nuclear issue intensified Washington's verbal war with Tehran and unleashed an international game of cat-and-mouse. Faced with Washington's demands for decisive international action against it, Iran parried by attempting to work out a compromise via the EU and the UN. The U.S. and the EU disagreed on the extent of the Iranian threat. They also disagreed on what should be done. The U.S. inclined toward force; the EU did not want another war. Thus far, the U.S. has allowed the EU to take the lead. By and large, it has had little choice in the matter. The grievous miscalculations of the Iraq war have come home to roost. In the meantime, Iran has bought time to maneuver. It has also gained the support of Russia and China; the former is intent on selling nuclear power stations to the Islamic republic.

The U.S., for its part, has retained the Israel card. With Saddam Hussein gone, Iran represents the main danger to Israel's survival. Israel has clearly announced that it would destroy Iranian nuclear facilities that were capable of producing nuclear weapons. Israel could not occupy Iran, but it could launch air strikes, a precedent for which was set by its earlier bombing of an Iraqi nuclear reactor. This alone would be sufficient to stall the Iranian nuclear program until the U.S. has time to regroup from its Iraqi adventure.

The surge in Iranian nationalism produced by U.S. rhetoric strengthened the hard-liners within Iran's ruling circles and dampened covert negotiations to ease tensions between the two countries. The masses were also losing patience with the reformers, who had proven inept at solving Iran's soaring economic and social problems. These pressures came to a head in the 2004 parliamentary elections and the 2005 presidential elections. The conservatives captured a two-thirds majority in the parliament, erasing a reformist majority of the same size. In the presidential election, the favored reformist candidate came in a distant fourth. As no candidate had managed to win a majority of the popular vote, a runoff election was held between the two leading candidates: Ali Akbar Hashemi Rafsanjani, a pragmatic moderate and former president, and Mahmud Ahmadinejad, the archconservative mayor of Tehran. Near-universal predictions of a Rafsanjani victory were thwarted by a last-minute rush of votes for Ahmadinejad. Despite the flawed nature of the elections, Iranian voters did have a choice (Bijan Khajehpour, Gulf/2000 communication, June 2005). Rafsanjani was a rich cleric who had been one of the founding fathers of the revolution. Ahmadinejad, by contrast, was a second-generation noncleric from a working-class background who continued to reside in a working-class neighborhood. While the former preached moderation, the latter preached social equality and revolution. Rafsanjani lost, and the hard-liners now control all of the main positions in the Iranian government: the Supreme Guide, the presidency, and the parliament. A reform movement that had promised democracy, human rights, and an opening to the West is in disarray.

Why did the reformists suddenly lose power after seven years of spectacular electoral success? The list of answers to this question is long and has much to say about Iranian politics and Iran's future. The most obvious answer is that the cards were stacked against the reformers. Before the 2004 parliamentary elections the Council of Guardians disqualified some 2,400 reformist candidates including several sitting members of parliament. A sit-in strike followed, but was eased after minor concessions were made. The Council of Guardians also sifted through the 1,014 candidates for the 2005 presidential elections, coming up with a final list of eight. All the reform candidates had been eliminated, but two were added to the list at the urging of an embarrassed Supreme Guide.

The key question, however, remains unanswered. There were two reform candidates on the presidential ballot. Why did they fare so poorly? The most persuasive answer is that the reformists didn't reform. The reformist members of the parliament compromised with the conservative hard-liners who dominated other branches of the government and hopes for true reform went for naught (Saghafi 2004). Much the same was true at the presidential level. Khatami chose to work within the established framework rather than use his overpowering popular majorities to change it. Intellectuals, the hard core of his organization, became disillusioned with tepid reforms and lost their zeal. This was even more the case among the urban poor. Promises of reform brought only more hardship to a population that was already hurting. Resentment of the rich increased proportionally. One way or another, the reformists cut themselves off from their support base. Ahmadinejad was from a working-class background and promised to focus on the needs of the poor and bring an end to corruption and the glaring inequalities of Iranian society. Added to the mix were charges of vote rigging and the inability of the reformists to present their message on state-controlled television. They used the Internet and a press vulnerable to censorship, but these media had a minimal audience among the peasants and urban poor. Perhaps the reformers were too closely identified with efforts to work out a reconciliation with the United States. Washington's threats were not helpful.

With the reformists in eclipse, several new questions come to the fore. First, can the hard-liners do better at solving Iran's social and economic problems than the mixed power structure of the past two decades? Second, whither Iranian foreign policy? Will Iran work out a reconciliation with the United States, or will it reemphasize the export of the Islamic revolution and press its quest for nuclear weapons? Is reform dead in Iran?

## IRANIAN POLITICS TODAY AND BEYOND

Answers to these questions require a closer examination of Iran's political institutions, the actors that guide Iranian politics, and the broader cultural, economic, and international contexts that shape the broader contours of Iranian politics. It is to this task that we turn next.

## Elites and Institutions

Iran entered the twenty-first century with a dual political system that divided power between its spiritual authorities and its popularly elected leaders. Spiritual authority resides in a *vali-i-faqih,* or Supreme Guide, elected by the eighty members of the Assembly of Experts, a council composed of Iran's leading religious authorities (Banuazizi 1994, 5).

The powers of the Supreme Guide are subject to a variety of interpretations, but he is generally viewed as a divinely inspired religious scholar (jurist) entrusted to speak in the name of the hidden imam in matters regarding the interpretation and application of religious law (Moussavi 1992). As Iran is governed by religious law, the Supreme Guide has the final say on almost everything. At the same time, Khamenei lacks either the religious or popular stature of the Ayatollah Khomeini, and the Supreme Guide is now viewed by some scholars as being the first among equals (Mozaffari 1993). He is clearly the most powerful man in Iran, but his powers are not absolute.

Also falling in the realm of religious authority are the Assembly of Experts, the Council of Guardians, and the Expediency Council. The Assembly of Experts plays a vital role in ensuring continuity by choosing the Supreme Guide, but is less involved in day-to-day politics. The Council of Guardians, by contrast, screens legislation to assure that it is in conformity with the Sharia (religious law) as interpreted by Shi'a theologians. Draft legislation deemed offensive is returned to the *majlis* for modification. The Council of Guardians also screens candidates for elected office, all of whom must be acceptable to the religious establishment. As noted earlier, the Council of Guardians disqualified 2,400 reformist candidates in the 2004 parliamentary elections. By performing these roles, the Council of Guardians serves as the interface between the two halves of the Iranian political system, the religious and the secular. The council, a bastion of Islamic conservatism, had frequent conflicts with reform parliaments of the past decade. A bill could not become law without its assent, so the Council of Guardians had a near veto over the legislative process. In many instances, the reformers caved in rather than create a crisis, a policy that earned them the scorn of their supporters. Contentious bills were sent to the Expediency Council for resolution, but the result was largely the same.

The role of the Expediency Council, as its name suggests, is to expedite the performance of the Iranian government by ensuring that conflict between its diverse branches do not impede the effective operation of the state. If a deadlock occurs between the *majlis* and the Council of Guardians, the issue is resolved by the Expediency Council, the members of which represent the branches of the political system, including the Supreme Guide, the presidency, and the judiciary. The arbitration of the Expediency Council is not binding, but the only other option is for the Supreme Guide to call a referendum, something that he has been reluctant to do (*Ketabehafteh*/NetIran, Feb. 5, 2005). The *majlis* can take it or leave it.

In addition to arbitrating between the Council of Guardians and the *majlis,* the Expediency Council also advises the Supreme Guide on policy issues and investigates malfeasance wherever it finds it. It does not make laws, but its power is awesome. In 2000, for instance, the Expediency Council denied the *majlis* the right to investigate all state agencies directly under the control of the Supreme Guide (*Asr-e Ma*/NetIran, April 12, 2000). The most powerful institutions in the country were thus placed beyond the control of the only elected body in Iran. These included the Republican Guards, the Council of Guardians, the Ministry of Justice, and the intelligence (security) services. Membership on the Expediency Council is determined by the Supreme Guide, who also selects its president.

Secular authority, if that is the proper word, is exercised by a president and a *majlis* (parliament) elected directly by the people in a quasi-democratic environment. Political campaigns in Iran reflect the duality of its political system and feature everything from the Internet and TV commercials to Friday prayer sermons. Public debates and mass rallies are not allowed (Sarabi 1994).

The power of the president, in contrast to that of the Supreme Guide, rests upon a popular mandate. The great divide between the Supreme Guide and the presidency, then, is the fundamental divide between power based upon divine law and power based upon human law (Abdo 1999; Fairbanks 1998). President Khatami's victories in the 1997 and 2001 presidential elections gave him an overwhelming mandate to extend Iranian democracy, ease religious restrictions, curb corruption, address Iran's pressing economic problems, and normalize relations with the West. Progress toward achieving these reforms was slight and the voters deserted the reformers in the 2005 elections. Now the political system can speak with a single voice. Many find this frightening.

The president and his cabinet manage the affairs of state, direct the bureaucracy, and propose legislation to the *majlis*. Control of the administrative apparatus adds to the power of the president but is not his prerogative alone. The Supreme Guide also controls part of the administrative hierarchy, including the state security apparatus, the Ministry of Justice, and the state-controlled television network.

The Iranian *majlis* resembles other parliamentary bodies, with the differences noted above. While lacking the power of either the Supreme Guide or the president, the parliament has played a vigorous role in shaping economic and social policy. Its influence in the areas of security and foreign policy has been less pronounced. Its role as a reformer was disappointing. After the parliament passes a bill, it is screened by the Council of Guardians before being submitted to the Supreme Guide for his assent. Upon approval by both the president and the Supreme Guide, legislation is sent to the appropriate administrative department for execution.

In addition to passing legislation, the *majlis* ratifies presidential nominations for cabinet positions; on several occasions it has failed to do so (Baktiari 1996a; BBC, Oct. 3, 2004). It was assumed that the conservative parliament elected in 2004 would find little cause for alarm in Ahmadinejad's nominees, but this has not proven to be the case. Debate over proposed ministers was bitter, and key Ahmadinejad nominees were rejected (*Tehran Times,* Aug. 25, 2005). The *majlis* has a reputation for intrigue among Iran's diverse factions and its policies are not always easy to predict.

The composition of Iran's elite reflects the complexity of its political system. The elite hierarchy is headed by the Supreme Guide, followed in turn by the president, the chairmen of the Council of Guardians and the Expediency Council, and the speaker of the *majlis*. With Ahmadinejad's 2005 presidential victory, the circle of power in Iran has narrowed to a reasonably tight group of senior clerics and conservative religious officials who effectively make all of the key decisions, the *majlis* notwithstanding. Many are linked by family and marriage alliances. In addition to their formal authority, the power of the senior members of the elite depends upon their broader support within the clergy and other critical elements of Iranian society, including the masses. Much of Khatami's power, for example, rested upon his landslide victories in the 1997 and 2001 presidential elections and the victory of the reformists in the 2000 parliamentary elections. That power waned with the defeat of the reformers in the 2004 parliamentary and 2005 presidential elections. Ahmadinejad, by contrast, enjoys a strong base of support among the Revolutionary Guards, one of Iran's two standing armies, and the Basij. He has played an active role in both. His populist, Robin Hood promises to take from the rich and give to the poor are also well calculated to give him a strong personal following among Iran's poor. The second tier of the elite structure includes senior members of parliament, governors, mayors of Iran's largest cities, key military and security officers, senior members of the cabinet, the higher rungs of the clergy, members of the Council of Guardians and the Expediency Council, editors of major newspapers, and key economic leaders, including the heads of the large religious charities that control about one-fourth of the Iranian economy. Although it does not share the decision-making powers of the core elite, this vast secondary elite is overwhelmingly dominated by the clergy and has much to say about how the policies of the regime will be executed. Indeed, the struggle to control these key positions provides the most visible dynamic of the Iranian political system, and experts attempting to predict the course of Iranian politics devote much of their attention to keeping score of who controls what.

In this regard, four main tendencies now compete for power in Iran: the radical right, the conservative right, the pragmatists, and the liberals (Rajaee 1999; Seifzadeh 2003; Siavoshi 1997). Conflicts between the four factions, each of which is outlined below, center on three basic issues: economic policy, social (religious) policy, and foreign policy (Banuazizi 1994, 4). The radical right and the conservative right are often referred to as the conservatives or hard-liners; the liberals and the pragmatists as the reformers.

**The Radicals**    The radical right favors a strict application of Islamic religious law, including its moral codes and restrictions on female dress. It also favors a quasi-socialist economic system in which land ownership is restricted, the economy regulated, major enterprises placed under state control, labor legislation strengthened to improve the rights of workers, and increased financial assistance provided to the poor and destitute (Banuazizi 1994). The quasi-socialism of the radicals is based not on Marxism but on Koranic statements about equality and social justice. In the foreign policy sphere, the radicals have been strong advocates of exporting the Islamic revolution and have taken a hard line in opposing cooperation with the United States.

The radicals were particularly strong during the early years of the Islamic revolution, but their power ebbed during the post-Khomeini era as the emphasis of Iranian politics shifted from ideological fervor to finding practical solutions to Iran's pressing domestic problems. Nevertheless, the strong support that the radicals enjoy among the workers, peasants, members of the lower middle class, the Revolutionary Guards, the Basij, and the bazaaris ensures that they will remain a significant force in Iranian politics.

Ironically, it was the challenge posed by Khatami and the reformists that forced the radicals to reinvent themselves as "neoconservatives" capable of appealing to Iranian youth (Jamshidi 2004; Khosrokhavar 2004). Middle-aged and well-educated, they blend deeply conservative religious views with nationalism and promises of development and economic equality. Their statements on democracy and privatization remain ambivalent, but they appear willing to accept some of each as long as they promote their vision of a deeply Islamic state.

Ahmadinejad, the newly elected president of Iran, clearly belongs to this group. He doesn't speak of socialism, but he spends a great deal of time bashing privatization and talking about economic equality and closing the gap between the rich and the poor. His anti-American views are pronounced and he appears to have a deep suspicion of capitalists and foreigners (Pirouz and Reed 2005). Within a few months of his election, he precipitated an international crisis for suggesting that Israel should be wiped off the map. He further placed his stamp on the Iranian government by purging moderates in the diplomatic corps and other key bureaucratic agencies. The "neo-cons" also control a majority of the 2004 (seventh) *majlis* and dominate the cabinet.

**The Conservatives**    The conservatives also demand a strict application of Islamic religious law, including its moral codes and restrictions on female conduct. Unlike the radicals, however, they are staunch advocates of private property and resist government intervention in economic affairs. Chambers of commerce and other commercial or bazaari associations are closely aligned with the conservatives and have established a strong position in the bureaucracy and the judiciary. The conservatives also find support in the theological schools as well as many of Iran's numerous religious associations. The Supreme Guide and the Council of Guardians are in their camp, making them the most powerful force in Iranian politics. They base their authority on their religious credentials and have not spent inordinate time worrying about elections and popular opinion. They have suffered accordingly, as first the reformists and then the neoconservatives have captured the parliament and presidency. Of the two, they clearly prefer the neoconservatives; indeed, the lines between the two groups are fluid.

**The Pragmatists**    The pragmatists came to the fore during the Rafsanjani presidency and generally view government as a harmonious alliance between the presidency and the clergy. While the clergy focuses on moral considerations, the presidency pursues pragmatic solutions to the problems of government and the economy, with the exact direction of policy reflecting the needs of the moment. If current conditions require greater economic liberalization or coop-eration with the West, so be it. The important thing is to preserve the religious character of the revolution while strengthening its political and economic foun-dation. Rafsanjani was precluded by law from seeking a third consecutive term as president but was subsequently named the president of the Expediency Council, thereby ensuring that the pragmatists retained a strong voice in the politics of the Islamic republic. It was widely predicted that he would win the 2005 presidential elections, but he was upset by Ahmadinejad.

**The Liberals**    The liberals represent the most moderate segment of the Islamic establishment and place a strong emphasis on democracy and human rights within the framework of Iran's Islamic constitution. The liberals also call for a softer and more flexible application of religious rule than the fire and brimstone preached by the factions of the right, and they have become outspoken advocates of rapproche-ment with the United States. The liberals were avid supporters of President Khatami, but Khatami was not as liberal as his supporters might have wished.

**Elite Fragmentation**    When the Western popular press refers to the hard-liners, they generally have in mind the radicals and the conservatives, both of whom favor the strict application of religious law in Iranian society. In much the same manner, the popular press refers to the pragmatists and liberals as reformers. However, one should not lose sight of the fact that both the hard-liners and the reformers are fragmented into multiple factions, and in distinguishing among them personality is often as important as doctrine (Seifzadeh 2003). Indeed, some eighteen reformist factions were represented in the sixth *majlis* (AP, Gulf/2000, Feb. 24, 2000). The more extreme among these would prefer a return to a secu-lar state. Advocates of this point of view generally find themselves in prison.

The more the elite has allowed itself to become embroiled in factional con-flict over priorities and strategies, the more policy making has become a matter of bargaining between factions. When bargaining fails, policy becomes immobi-lized or each faction pursues its goals independent of the others. The radicals pur-sue the export of the revolution while the reformers send signals of moderation and cooperation to the West. Perhaps the total conservative control established by the 2004 and 2005 elections will bring an end to the political immobilization of the past decade. Or perhaps it won't. Ahmadinejad may prove too extreme for Iran's mainline power structure. Indeed, his campaign attacks on corruption, incompetence, and Iran's glaring disparities between rich and poor were point-edly said to have occurred after the passing of Ayatollah Khomeini. It would have been improper to impugn a saint, but Ahmadinejad did point the finger at the failings of Iran's religious leadership during the post-Khomeini years.

## The Implementation of Policy: The Bureaucracy
## and Security Apparatus

The effectiveness of the decision-making institutions surveyed above is inti-mately linked to a massive bureaucracy and an equally pervasive network of secu-rity organizations. The role of the bureaucracy is to implement the decisions of the elite. The decisions that it cannot or will not execute don't get implemented. It is the security services that keep the regime in power. Problems abound in both institutions.

**The Bureaucracy**    The adjectives that come to mind when describing the Iranian bureaucracy are bloated, corrupt, lethargic, wedded to red tape, self-serving, and risk-averse. Reflecting this reality, a sarcastic President Khatami proclaimed: "We're not getting results in proportion to the hard work our employees put in. Our enthusiastic and hard working administrators are locked in a sedate, inert, sluggish and overlapping bureaucratic system" (Reuters/*Daily Star,* Aug. 27, 1999, 5).

As the pace of development stagnated, the elite squabbled over solutions for the bureaucratic morass. While some argued for stricter penalties for corruption and mismanagement, others pressed for greater reliance on capitalism and the private sector to get things done. Progress, however, has been halting. Corruption is rampant at all levels of the political system and efforts to liberalize the economy are strangled by bureaucratic regulations. A comparable bureaucratic nightmare also chokes public services, all of which remain under government control (BBC, Feb. 13, 2004). Bureaucrats, by and large, are poorly paid and demand bribes for even routine services. One has to get along. Bureaucratic aversion to risk taking has much to do with the fluid nature of Iranian politics. The creativity of today could well become the treason of tomorrow. For those who supported reformist policies, that tomorrow has now arrived. By and large, however, everybody is protected by one group or another in Iran's seamless network of patron–client relationships. One serves the patron rather than the country.

Iran's bureaucratic problems, however, are not merely the result of venal officials. They also reflect a fragmented elite that has been unable to formulate clear policy objectives. How does one serve two governments, one religious and the other secular? Invariably, unclear and confused decisions lead to flawed policy implementation. Public services are dismal and Iran's state-owned industries, which account for about 60 percent of the economy's output, are unproductive.

This is not news to Iranians. Corruption and Iran's bureaucratic malaise were key issues in Ahmadinejad's 2005 campaign platform, much as they were in the platforms of the competing candidates. In one of his first speeches as president-elect, Ahmadinejad vowed "to invite a group of competent and efficient individuals to help administer the country" (*Tehran Times,* July 28, 2005). If only it were that easy.

**The Security Services**    The security apparatus of the Islamic republic consists of three distinct military organizations and a variety of intelligence and internal security services. The primary military organizations are the regular army and the Revolutionary Guards, each of which contains army, air, and naval components. The third military organization is the Basij, a large volunteer militia (Cordesman 1999). It may have as many as 9 million members. The intelligence and covert activities agencies include the Ministry for Intelligence and Security (VEVAK), the secret intelligence services, and Khamenei's special bureau. Needless to say, Iran's leaders are mindful of security issues. Most are designed to protect the regime; others are charged with foreign operations.

The regular military had been the pride of the shah, but was decimated by the revolution. More than 250 of the shah's top officers were executed, while many more fled into exile. All in all, the regular military lost approximately half of its officers (Cann and Danopoulos 1997). The regular army has now been rebuilt under the watchful eye of the clergy, but it is counterbalanced by the Revolutionary Guards. The Revolutionary Guards were cobbled together from religious loyalists in 1979 in order to sustain the Islamic revolution during its early days. Almost immediately they were thrown into battle against the Iraqis, an experience that, over the next eight years, transformed them into a credible and disciplined force. The process of professionalization has continued in post-Khomeini years, with the Revolutionary Guards "now being closer to a regular military force" (Cordesman 1999, 37).

At the same time, the Revolutionary Guards are charged with protecting the Islamic revolution and have not been reluctant to make their ultraconservative political views known. In 1999, they accused Khatami's policies of creating the riots of that year, and the following year they accused the reformist press of aiding the enemies of Iran (Samii 2005). They have also been linked with the Islamic Iran Development Coalition and the Islamic Revolution Devotee's Society, groups that played a crucial role in wresting power from the reformers in the 2003 local elections, the 2004 parliamentary elections, and the 2005 presidential elections. Four of the eight candidates approved by the Council of Guardians occupied leadership positions in the Revolutionary Guards, including Ahmadinejad. This, combined with the strong ties between the Revolutionary Guards and the Supreme Guide, suggests that their power is increasing.

In contrast, the Basij is still known more for its zeal than its discipline. Supporting the latter are the "gangs of street thugs" known as the Ansar-e Hezbollah (Helpers of the Party of God), who are often aligned with specific conservative members of the clergy and act as vigilantes (Cordesman 1999, 39). Others describe the Basij and associated groups as a mafia. Ahmadinejad was closely linked with the Basij and received their strong support in both the 2003 local elections and the 2005 presidential elections. The former made him the mayor of Tehran; the latter the president of the country (*Guardian,* June 25, 2005). Powerful support indeed.

The internal security forces consist of the police, the gendarmerie, and the Islamic Revolutionary Committees. In 1991, these three units were merged into the Law Enforcement Forces of the Islamic Republic (Cordesman 1999). Little is known about the various intelligence organizations other than the fact that they are both pervasive and powerful.

The security apparatus poses a serious dilemma for Iran's religious elite. By creating a security apparatus strong enough to sustain the revolution, the clergy has created a counterweight to its own domination. While few anticipate a coup, there have been persistent charges that the Revolutionary Guards, a group under the control of the Supreme Guide, have become his master.

Efforts to keep the security services subservient to the political leadership have taken at least five forms. First, each of the diverse elements in the security apparatus possesses a separate command structure. Coordination committees and the centralized control of the Supreme Guide offer some coordination, but competition between the various organizations is substantial (Cordesman 1999). Second, virtually all senior command positions are held by the clergy (Cordesman 1999). Third, the members of the security units are recruited largely from the middle and lower classes, which have traditionally supported the revolution (Cann and Danopoulos 1997). Fourth, members of the various security units are subjected to intense indoctrination. Fifth, communication between security organizations is carefully monitored by the Ideological–Political Directorate (IPD), which has penetrated all levels of the military (Cann and Danopoulos 1997).

The ramifications of this system of control are profound. First, performance and coordination have been sacrificed to concerns of loyalty. Competence is important, but loyalty comes first. Second, factionalism exists within the security apparatus in spite of its generally conservative orientation. The regular army, in particular, inclines toward the moderate camp, with letters from senior generals openly supporting democracy (Cann and Danopoulos 1997).

## THE GROUP BASIS OF IRANIAN POLITICS

While the contradictions within the Iranian political system are a function of elite and institutional conflict, they are also a function of the growing complexity of Iran's group mosaic (Amirahmadi 1996). Indeed, conflicts within the elite have facilitated, if not encouraged, the proliferation of political groups as each faction seeks to bolster its base of support (Bakhash 1998; Gheissari and Nasr 2004).

### Political Parties

Although the emergence of full-fledged political parties has been discouraged, a variety of groups linked to Iran's four main ideological tendencies have taken on most of the functions of political parties, including the endorsement of candidates. The situation, however, remains fluid as most of these associations lack a broad membership base and are usually little more than a coalition of like-minded factions, each headed by a dominant personality jealous of his power (Sick 2000). They emerge to meet the needs of the moment, only to disappear and perhaps reemerge under a new format. Many overlap with student, economic, and military groups such as the Republican Guards and the Basij. At the same time, there is a clear line between the conservative currents on one hand and reformist currents on the other. An effort to list all of Iran's diverse parties and groups is beyond the scope of the chapter and probably defies the imagination. A few are briefly described here to provide a glimpse of the whole picture.

Iran's clerics long organized much of Iran's political activity via the Association of Combatant Clergy. The diversity of views within the association was too great to be contained within a single organization, and in 1987, the reformist wing of the clergy broke away and formed the Association of Combatant Clerics (Fairbanks 1998; Javad-Rouh 2004). Each, obviously, wanted to retain its image as devotees of the Ayatollah Khomeini and rightful heirs of the revolution.

A clear line was thus established between the right (clergy) and the left (clerics). Other lay political groups then began to cluster around the two core organizations. The political left drew heavily upon student organizations such as the Students Loyal to Imam Khomeini and broader-based organizations such as the Office for Fostering Unity. These gave way to a bewildering list of other groups including the Servants of Construction and the Coordination Council of Groups Loyal to Imam Khomeini. Both supported Khatami in the 1997 presidential elections. Perhaps the closest equivalent to a true political party at the moment is the Islamic Iran Participation Party (IIPP) headed by President Khatami's brother. The IIPP was formed prior to the municipal elections of 1999 and was the dominant group in the sixth *majlis*. It was active in the 2004 parliamentary elections and the 2005 presidential election, as was the Revolutionary Mujahideen Organization. All of the parties of the left drew much of their support from students, intellectuals, technicians, and other middle-class groups.

The political right, in turn, was long represented by the Islamic Coalition Association (Party), a group that traces its origins to an alliance of religious groups formed in 1963 to promote a more religious Iran; it played a key role in fomenting the revolution. It is probably the most powerful conservative party in Iran. The pronouncements of their leaders remain vague but have much in common with the doctrine of the neoconservatives discussed earlier. The incoming party leader responded to a question on modernity and tradition by saying, "I don't know what you mean by modern criteria. Our party relies on the people. Our infrastructure are the mosques and the pulpits. All members announce their views and we make up our minds collectively" (Habibi 2004, 2). The Islamic Coalition Association is now linked with the Islamic Iran Developers Alliance and the Islamist Engineers Association, groups that played a key role in Ahmadinejad's presidential election. More directly aligned with the conservative policies of the Supreme Guide are the Coordination Council for the Islamic Revolutionary Forces and the Association of Combatant Clergy.

Both the left and right were fragmented among the diverse candidates for the 2005 presidential election, but conservative groups generally united behind Ahmadinejad in the second round of the presidential elections. The left seemed less enthusiastic about Rafsanjani, a pragmatist-cum-reformer with strong links to the more moderate conservatives.

## Pressure Groups

Many of the parties listed above are extensions of key groups within Iranian society. Particularly strong in this regard have been the bonyads, the bazaaris, and the technocrats.

**Bonyads**     The bonyads are religious charities that were established after the revolution with funds confiscated from the shah and his relatives (Mozaffari 1991).

Among the largest of the funds is the Foundation of the Oppressed, which possesses billions of dollars in assets and controls an estimated 1,200 companies including five-star hotels, shipping lines, and a massive amusement park in Tehran. Much the same is true of the Foundation for the Dispossessed and War Disabled. Some sources say the bonyads control from 10 to 20 percent of the Iranian economy (*Economist,* A Survey of Iran, Jan. 19, 2003). The figure could be as high as 60 percent if the oil sector is deleted from the equation.

The bonyads fall somewhere between the public and private sectors, depending upon the advantages to be gained, and their leaders report directly to the Ayatollah Khamenei. The profits of the bonyads are designed to help the poor, but they also provide an invisible source of income for the Supreme Guide, the Revolutionary Guards, and other pillars of the conservative establishment. It is also probable that bonyad profits find their way into support of fundamentalist militias in Lebanon and elsewhere (*CSM,* Feb. 1, 1995). And profits there are. The bonyads are tax-exempt, ignore government regulations, and import foreign goods duty-free (Khosrokhavar 2004). Other importers rightly claim that this is unfair competition, but they lack the power to alter the situation. The conservative power structure is too dependent on bonyad funds to level the economic playing field.

This does not mean that the bonyads are efficient. Most have also become huge bureaucracies and have been plagued with the same corruption and mismanagement as the government bureaucracy. It is easy to make profits when there are no taxes or import duties. Even with this advantage, not all bonyad companies are profitable and some are threatened with closure (*Economist,* A Survey of Iran, Jan. 19, 2003).

**Bazaaris**    The term *bazaaris,* as described by Mozaffari, refers primarily to the middle and lower sectors of the Iranian business community and is applied only to those socio-occupational strata such as guilds (*asnaf*), craftsmen (*pishehvaran*) small shopkeepers (*kasabah*), wholesalers (*bunak-daran*), exchange agents (*sarrafan*), brokers (*dallalan*), and retail merchants (*furushandehgan*), as well as a certain number of large businessmen (*tujjar*) who have remained part of the traditional bazaari system. The bazaaris are an essentially urban and petit-bourgeois phenomenon (Mozaffari 1991, 378).

Mozaffari goes on to note that the bazaaris are far more than an economic middle class (Mozaffari 1991). The bazaaris adhere to a code of commercial, ethical, and religious conduct that has enabled them to act as a coherent group and thereby to dominate most of the commercial activity in the country (Denoeux 1990).

The bazaaris have long enjoyed a close relationship with the ulema, with bazaari contributions formerly providing one of the ulema's main sources of income. The two groups also share a common suspicion of Westernization, and intermarriage between the two groups has been frequent.

The link between the bazaaris and the ulema is both cultural and economic. The more the Westernization of Iran proceeded, the more dominance of commercial activity in Iran shifted from the bazaaris to a class of large merchants with close ties to the palace. Quite logically, this resulted in conflict between the bazaaris and the monarchy and led to an alliance with a clergy equally challenged by the monarch's pursuit of Westernization.

Cooperation between the bazaaris and the ulema was intensified by the modernization programs of Reza Shah and his son, Mohammed Reza (Kurzman 2004; Smith 2004). Adding insult to injury was the emerging "oil bourgeoisie" that acquired fabulous wealth under the shah's tutelage while the bazaaris were being subjected to regulation and increased taxation (Mozaffari 1991). The bazaaris had supported earlier revolutions against royal authority, and the Islamic revolution would be no exception.

The bazaaris constituted one of the main pillars of Iran's Islamic regime, and benefited accordingly. Most domestic trade and distribution activity was in the hands of the bazaaris, as was a large share of the import–export trade. They also played a major role in the "parallel economy," as Mozaffari describes black-market activities tacitly accepted by the government to allow for the circulation of goods that would otherwise be in short supply (Mozaffari 1991, 387).

The strength of the bazaaris today has been cramped by seven years of economic reform; it is estimated that they now only control about 8 percent of the economy. Gone are the days when they could bring a government to its knees. They are still tied to the conservatives, but not necessarily the neoconservatives who vow to redistribute wealth to the poor. It is also not clear that the bazaaris speak with a single voice. Some inclined toward Rafsanjani in the 2005 presidential elections; other favored more extremist candidates including Ahmadinejad (*Daily Star,* June 16, 2005).

**Clergy**    The clergy consists of about 180,000 "men of religion" ranging from the Supreme Guide, the most powerful man in Iran, to the lowest of the village mullahs (*NYT,* Jan. 30, 2000). Iran is a theocracy, and the clergy dominate most positions of influence surveyed in our discussion of political elites, the main exception being President Ahmadinejad. The clerical hierarchy substitutes for a political party in the sense that it provides the organizational network that links the elites to the masses. Elite goals are explained to the masses, and mass concerns are communicated to the elite. When demonstrations of mass support are required, it is the clergy who mobilize the faithful. The clergy are also the main agents of socialization, teaching, preaching, and ensuring that Islamic values permeate the educational system and the press. The eyes of the clergy are also ever-vigilant in spotting infractions of Islamic morality and threats to the regime. Many would say that they are overzealous and that their zeal is undermining support for the regime.

The effectiveness of the clergy in sustaining the regime is based upon a common commitment to the survival of the revolution as well as the organizational structure that links the Supreme Guide to the lowest of the mullahs. All, however, is not well. The clergy, like most other groups in Iran, is finding it difficult to keep its factional conflicts from interfering with its effectiveness. The 1997 election of Khatami to the presidency laid the foundation for a secular challenge to the priestly powers of Khamenei, that challenge was reinforced by the 2000 parliamentary elections and Khatami's reelection in 2001. The clergy gained a respite with the collapse of the reformists in the 2004 parliamentary and 2005 presidential elections. Whether the clergy can hold back the secular threat will depend to a large degree on the success of Mahmud Ahmadinejad. Indeed, Supreme Guide Khamenei warned the new leadership that the "people were thirsting for justice and up in arms over corruption" (*Intiqad,* June 28, 2005). The imam of the Mosque of Tehran similarly warned the new president that it was his responsibility to prove to the world that Islam was capable of solving Iran's problems (*Intiqad,* June 17, 2005).

**Students**  Iranian students played a key role in challenging the rule of the shah, and Iran's universities were routinely closed down during periods of crisis, often for several months at a time. Ironically, a new generation of students, few of whom have recollections of the shah, are now challenging the reign of the ayatollahs (Radio Free Europe, Jan. 21, 2000, v. 3, n. 3; *Daily Star,* May 23, 2000, 5). It was students who precipitated the riots of 1999 and lesser demonstrations throughout Khatami's presidency. Most demonstrations demanded greater democracy, and sometimes even called openly for secularism. In 2002, for example, students protested the death sentence imposed on a history professor for suggesting that the clerics did not have a divine right to rule. The sentence was commuted. Nevertheless, arrests have been frequent and harsh, as have clashes between students and hard-line vigilantes.

The declining zeal of the students was manifest in the 2004 parliamentary and 2005 presidential elections, and probably had less to do with the harshness of the hard-liners' repressive measures than it did with the failure of reformists to live up to their promises. Hope gave way to disillusionment and Khatami was booed in a 2004 speech at the University of Tehran. When asked why he had retreated rather than change the system, he responded that he had never intended to change the system, merely improve it (*Asia Times,* Dec. 10, 2004).

Youth, students and otherwise, will remain a problem for Iran's conservative leaders. Some, especially the upscale youth of North Tehran, mock the clergy by transforming conservative dress into Islamic chic. Many also drink and dance at private parties. The majority of Iran's youth are preoccupied with finding a stable future in a declining economy and don't drink or dance. Symptomatic of their concerns were rumors that their requests for admission to Iran's universities would be turned down in they voted for the reform candidates. Others worried about a loss of job opportunities (Saghafi 2004). The clerics must meet the needs of Iran's youth if they are to avoid future explosions of student unrest.

**Women**  Iranian women have become increasingly well organized in recent years and have forced the government to restore some of the rights that Khomeini earlier abrogated as contradicting Islamic practice (Paidar 1995). A wife can now sue her husband for support if the "court decides that the wife has performed her wifely duty towards her husband" (Kar 1996, 37). Winning such legal battles, as Kar notes, continues to be an uphill struggle, for all the judges are men. Banuazizi finds that Iranian women have "continued to make substantial gains in literacy and educational attainment, sustained their participation in the work force, and thereby kept a significant presence in public life as teachers, journalists, managers, and factory workers" (Banuazizi 1994, 7). This topic continues to be the subject of heated debate on Internet chat sites (see Gulf/2000, Jan.–Feb. 2001; Moallem 2005).

Much, however, remains to be done if Iranian women are to regain the rights that they achieved under the monarchy. With the advent of Islamic rule in Iran, Homa Hoodfar writes, "arbitrary divorce, polygamy, and temporary marriage, all of which had been outlawed or restricted by the shah's regime, have made a triumphant return, turning the lives of many women upside down" (Ashtiani 2003; Kar 1996). Mehranguiz Kar notes that "a woman is not permitted to legally choose her first husband! Regardless of her age, a woman must have her marriage endorsed by her father or paternal kin for it to be legal" (Kar 1996, 37). The struggle continues, however, and progress is being made. In 2002, the *majlis* voted to make women equal in divorce, and in 2005 women legislators proposed a comprehensive change in Iran's legal system as it related to "marriage settlement, blood money, alimony, retribution, the Qoranic determined boundaries" ( Jazini 2005, 1). Alas, this was in the last year of the reformist parliament. If the legislation is to become law, it will have to be approved by the radical conservative parliament. The outlook is not bright.

Other groups have experienced even more difficulty in finding their voice under the rules of the Islamic republic. Iran's workers, for example, now belong to Islamic associations in their workplaces rather than to independent labor unions (Banuazizi 1994, 6). The voice of ethnic minorities in the affairs of the Islamic republic has also been limited, despite the fact that they represent 45 percent of the population. Both Kurds and Arabs rioted in 2005, the former stirred by Kurdish nationalism in Iraq. Religious tensions are also running high in Sunni Baluchistan, and the Afghan border has been inundated with refugees and drug smugglers.

**Opposition Groups**   Formal opposition groups are banned in the Islamic republic, with the most visible opposition to the Islamic regime coming from the Mujahedin-e Khalq, an Iraqi-based revolutionary organization. The Mujahedin-e Khalq became increasingly bold during the final years of Saddam Hussein, targeting offices in the center of Tehran. With Saddam Hussein's fall, the U.S. embraced the Mujahedin-e Khalq in its covert war against Iran despite the fact that it was on Washington's list of terrorist organizations. Washington retreated, but hasn't given up the project completely. (E. Rubin 2003).

Aside from the Mujahedin-e Khalq, opposition currents include remnants of the old Iranian left, much of which is now coalescing around the reformist faction of the clergy. This was a matter of some concern to Khatami, whose liberal tendencies were far more constrained than those of his supporters. Indeed, it is probable that many in the reformist camp were merely using Khatami as a wedge to achieve their secular goals. Where they will turn next is a matter of conjecture.

## THE CONTEXT OF IRANIAN POLITICS

In addition to its institutions and actors, Iranian politics is also a function of the cultural, economic, and international environments in which it occurs. Each of these factors will have much to say about the course of the Islamic revolution during the coming decade.

## Political Culture and Mass Behavior

As Iran's dominant religion, Shi'a Islam is a core component of the country's political culture (Kamrava 2003). The vast majority of Iranians are Shi'a Muslims and have been acculturated in a Shi'a environment that influences their value structure and view of the world. This does not mean that all Iranians are religious fanatics or even that most Iranians are deeply religious. It does mean, however, that a very large number of Iranians support Shi'a values. This was made obvious by the Ayatollah Khomeini's ability to mobilize the Iranian population against the shah as well as his subsequent ability to prosecute the war against Iraq (Dorraj 1997; Wells 2003). Although the zeal of the masses has abated in recent years, Shi'a Islam continues to be the main source of legitimacy for the Iranian regime. This fact is not lost on the ayatollahs, and the regime's efforts to strengthen Islamic values border on the obsessive (Ram 1993).

In addition to its Shi'a base, Iranian political culture includes an abiding concern for social justice, Iranian nationalism, and a belief that Western exploitation in Iran must be resisted by force (Farsoun and Meshayekhi 1992). Social justice and anti-Westernism were the dominant themes of the Islamic revolution (Bakhash 1998; Bayat 1997; Zonis and Mokri 1991). They have also become the dominant themes of Iran's neoconservatives.

Iranian political culture has other elements as well. Many Iranians were exposed to the West during the prerevolutionary era and embraced the Western values of democracy and human rights. They also developed a desire for economic development and the material advantages of Western society. Resisting the exploitation of Western colonialism was not incompatible with a desire for democracy and prosperity, and it is this desire that found expression in the stunning electoral victories of Khatami and the reformers.

Other facets of Iranian political culture have also created problems for the country's Islamic leaders. Particularly detrimental to the clerics' efforts to mobilize mass support for their programs is a pervasive sense of alienation, psychological withdrawal, insecurity, and interpersonal distrust. Alienation, originally a product of the shah's rule, has been extended by the severity of the religious rule and economic hardships (Bayat 1997; Zonis and Mokri 1991). Interpersonal distrust and insecurity find their origins in kinship rivalries and centuries of arbitrary rule (Zonis 1991). The secret police and groups of vigilantes such as the Basij only make things worse.

While these characteristics of Iranian political culture are sufficiently widespread to influence the politics of the Islamic republic, it is important to stress that Iranian political culture is far from monolithic. The culture of the middle classes differs from that of the masses; urban culture from that of the countryside; youth culture from that of the parents and grandparents; and the nationalism of the Farsi majority from that of the ethnic minorities who constitute some 45 percent of the Iranian population. The various clerical factions also have widely differing views of how much non-Islamic content should be allowed in the political dialogue (Siavoshi 1997).

Iran's population has also increased from approximately 31 million at the beginning of the Islamic revolution to some 70 million today. This is not a minor consideration, for it indicates that well over one-half of today's population was born after the revolution. These children of the revolution are now beginning to reach adulthood and the future of the regime could well hinge on its ability to socialize them into an Islamic way of life. This may not be an easy job, for although the regime claims that some 96 percent of its children attend schools of one form or another, the effectiveness of the regime's indoctrination program remains suspect. Iranian youth voted disproportionately for Khatami in the 1997 and 2000 elections, indicating a clear break with the ultraconservative doctrines of the Khomeini era. The growing urbanization of Iranian society—over 50 percent of the population now lives in cities—also suggests that the newer generations will be exposed to a broader range of ideological and material temptations than their rural counterparts (Sharbatoghlie 1991).

The influence of mass behavior on Iranian politics in the post-Khomeini era extends far beyond the realm of voting. Cynicism and psychological withdrawal have been particularly evident among the middle class, a segment of the Iranian population that must play an active role in governance and the economy if the revolution is to develop effective political institutions and break the cycle of economic lethargy. This is all the more true given the disillusionment that followed the collapse of the reform movement in 2004 and 2005. People perform according to the regime's script, but they do so without enthusiasm. While the form of a theocratic society has been established—women wear Islamic dress, and displays of Islamic piety have become ubiquitous—it is not clear that the Iranian population has embraced its spirit. TV satellite dishes abound although they are prohibited. Bureaucratic corruption is rampant, and middle-class women, while conforming to the letter of Islamic dress requirements, taunt the authorities by "using the head cover as a means of personal adornment rather than concealment, thus 'turning an object of control into one of protest'" (Banuazizi 1994, 7; Friedl and Afkhami 1994; Paidar 1995). Some dating has also returned among college students, albeit in a subdued format (*IHT,* Nov. 28, 2000). Also present are increasing signs of a survivaloriented culture that views the political system as an object of fear to be avoided whenever possible and exploited for personal gain when the opportunity presents itself.

The above trends are well illustrated by the dismal record of Iran's recently introduced local councils. According to the architect of the project, people with no experience were elected to the councils on the basis of family and ethnic connections. Once there, they became obsessed with cars, cell phones, and other perks of office. Civic ethics were noticeable by their absence. Lavish promises before the elections gave way to distain for the public once they were over. Fraud, opportunism, and corruption became the norm. The project's designer even went so far as to suggest that Iran's long history of dictatorship, going back before the Islamic revolution, had produced a dictatorial mentality that was intolerant of others. Everyone, in his view, attempts to get ahead by tearing down others (Piran 2003). Unfortunately, the same problems are all too prevalent at the national level.

## Political Economy

The vacillation of Iran's post-Khomeini leadership is also a function of a declining economy, as is the growing restiveness of the Iranian population (Karshenas and Pesaran 1995). In many ways, Iran's economy is still attempting to recover from the turmoil of the early revolutionary era and eight years of war with Iraq (Bayat 1997).

The regime is now focusing on domestic development, but the process has not been easy. As much as 80–85 percent of economic activity in Iran is linked to government-controlled enterprises, including the bonyads. All are more responsive to political rather than market forces. Small- and medium-size firms provide the core of a vigorous private sector, but often find it difficult to compete with public-sector firms that don't pay taxes and have little need to make a profit. Foreign investors could provide a much-needed stimulus to the Iranian economy, but are deterred by bureaucratic and legal obstacles (Luxford 2005). Those who have penetrated the Iranian markets often find that agreements signed with the elected half of Iran's government are sabotaged by its religious branches. The economic reforms proposed by Khatami and the reformers addressed many of these problems, but internal opposition made implementation difficult. The opponents of sweeping privatization seized power in 2004 and 2005, dampening hopes for a radical change in Iran's economic policies. Ahmadinejad has promised a vigorous role for the private sector. He has also promised that it will be closely regulated by the government.

The regime's erratic economic policies, in turn, have led to high unemployment, high prices, and serious inflation: unemployment is currently more than 15 percent, and the rate of inflation is more than 15 percent a year (*Economist*, Survey of Iran, 2003; Luxford 2005). Average salaries in Iran are in the range of $200 per month; the middle class makes two or three times that much (*NYT*, July 3, 2005). Prices are increasing faster than incomes, and a majority of Iranians are falling deeper into the hole. Making matters worse, from the psychological perspective, is the growing gap between the winners and the losers. While 10 percent of the population enjoys extreme wealth, some 30 percent live below the poverty line.

To ease the plight of the poor, the government provides subsidies on a wide range of necessities, including utilities, basic foods, and fuel. The inclusion of fuel is ironic, for Iran, a major oil producer, finds itself in the position of having to import refined oil—about 10 percent of total imports—which it then resells below cost. The subsidies absorb money that could be used for investment in a sounder economic infrastructure, but Iran's leaders fear the political repercussions of reducing them (Bayat 1997). Plans are also afoot to give shares in Iran's state-owned companies to the poorest of Iran's citizens (*Middle East Times*, Nov. 4, 2005). The neoconservative victories in 2004 and 2005 were based in part on promises that they would not reduce subsidies on basic items. Paired with these promises were scare tactics warning that a reformist victory would end subsidies and throw the poor deeper into despair. Curiously, the neoconservative campaigns concentrated more on economic deprivation than they did on Islamic society.

Also in the economic realm is Iran's continued dependence on oil for some 80 percent of export earnings and about 40–50 percent of government revenue (*Economist,* Survey of Iran, 2003). This oil dependence makes the Iranian economy vulnerable to swings in the world price of oil and to punitive pressures from the United States. Iran is attempting to break its dependence on oil by shifting to natural gas and nuclear energy. For the moment, the surge in oil prices has brought Iran massive economic surpluses. This bodes well for the neoconservative leadership, which may now be able to both subsidize the poor and restructure the Iranian economy. That, however, remains to be seen. Iranian politics has a long record of ignoring economic logic.

## International Interdependence

The influence of foreign powers on the politics of Iran has been the most dominant single theme in the preceding discussion, and it defies easy summary. Suffice it to say that the Pahlavi dynasty was founded and sustained by the Western powers. In the process, Iran was transformed into a rentier state whose economy was dominated by the export of oil, the proceeds from which were used to buy arms and luxury products from the West. Although it spent billions of dollars on arms, the monarchy did not fight a single sustained war.

The Islamic revolution was, in large part, a popular rejection of a repressive monarchy that placed the interests of the West above those of its own citizens. The Islamic revolution, in turn, posed a direct threat to Western interests in the Middle East and was challenged by crippling boycotts and a devastating war with Iraq. The West did not start the Iran–Iraq War, but Saudi Arabia and Kuwait, both staunch allies of the United States, were deeply involved in the process.

This is not to suggest that all of Iran's problems are of external origin, for this is not the case. Foreign intervention, however, exacerbated domestic problems and made the tortuous process of development even more difficult.

Foreign influence continues to shape the politics of Iran. Perhaps the most urgent challenge to the Islamic republic concerns its future relations with the United States. Khatami and the reformers attempted to open a dialogue with the United States, but were stymied by conservative forces in both countries (Beeman 2005). The situation deteriorated further in the aftermath of the September 11, 2001, attacks, and the subsequent U.S.-led attack on Iraq. Iranian efforts to develop nuclear energy raised the specter of a nuclear Iran and brought more threats from Washington. Indeed, Washington's accusations of terrorism and nuclear weapons are eerily reminiscent of the threats that preceded the U.S.-led attacks on Iraq. Power in Iran has now shifted to radical conservatives who are hostile to the U.S. and, if one is to believe their speeches, who are dedicated to the export of the Islamic revolution, the elimination of U.S. influence in the region, and the destruction of Israel.

The United States and Iran, then, are on a collision course. For the moment, Iraq is the U.S.'s primary battleground in the Middle East, which gives Iran a clear advantage. The U.S. is bogged down in a disastrous occupation and searching for exit strategies that will allow it to save face. These are not easy to come by. In the meantime, Iranian ties with the Shi'a-controlled Iraqi government are multiplying. The international environment, moreover, appears to be evolving in Iran's favor. While the U.S. continues to impose economic sanctions, largely to its own detriment, the Europeans and Japanese are anxious to do business with an Iranian regime willing to sign lucrative arms and construction contracts. The Russians are providing nuclear power stations. Even many of the U.S.'s Arab allies are reluctant to support a policy toward Iran that is increasingly interpreted by their citizens as being imperialist and anti-Islamic (Ramazani 1998).

This said, it is doubtful that either the United States or Israel will accept a nuclear Iran. Iran denies that it intends to build nuclear weapons, but it has acquired the capacity to do so from Pakistan (*NYT,* March 9 and 11, 2005; Venter 2005). Information on Iran's progress in constructing nuclear weapons remains vague (*NYT,* March 9, 2005). Israeli intelligence predicts that Iran will have nuclear weapons in five years (*Ha'aretz,* Jan. 25, 2005). Other estimates suggest that eight to ten years is more likely (*NYT,* Aug. 3, 2005). Similar predictions for Iraq proved inaccurate. Iran already possesses missiles with a range of over a thousand miles, well within striking distance of Israel (BBC, Oct. 5, 2004). In the meantime, reports abound of U.S. jets overflying potential Iranian targets (*Guardian,* Jan. 29, 2005). The U.S. denies the allegations, but acknowledges that it is updating its war plan for Iran (*WP,* Feb. 10, 2005). Britain, America's staunchest ally in the Iraq war, has proclaimed war on Iran to be inconceivable (*Guardian,* Nov. 4, 2004). The European Union and the United Nations are attempting to diffuse the situation. The U.S. wants assurances—read inspections— that Iran is not producing nuclear weapons. Iran's conservative leaders are unlikely to give them. Iran boasts that 25,000 Iranians have volunteered for suicide duty in order to stop a U.S. invasion (Afrasiabi 2004).

## LOOKING TOWARD THE FUTURE

To the extent that present trends offer a guide to the future, the preceding assessment suggests that Iran will continue to lumber along during the next decade much as it has in the past. Strong policy initiatives are likely to be dampened by the fragmentation of the Iranian elite, foreign pressures, the weakness of the Iranian economy, and the growing apathy of the Iranian masses. The strengthening of the military and other coercive agencies, however, should assure that the clerics will continue to dominate the country for the remainder of the decade, probably longer.

The most immediate threat to the Islamic republic is an attack by the United States. Escalations in global terrorism and the fear of a nuclear Iran make that threat very possible. For the moment, however, the U.S. is still licking its Iraq wounds. An Israeli attack is far more likely. Would an Israeli attack cause the Middle East to erupt in anger? Probably, but would that matter? Middle Eastern leaders are too fragmented and self-serving to take concerted action against Israel. If they were otherwise, they would have acted long ago. Would global terrorism increase? Absolutely. For those who think outside of the box, there remains the possibility of a U.S. nuclear attack on Iran. This possibility seems extremely remote, but who knows what would happen in the wake of another September 11?

# 8

# Turkey

## Middle Eastern or European?

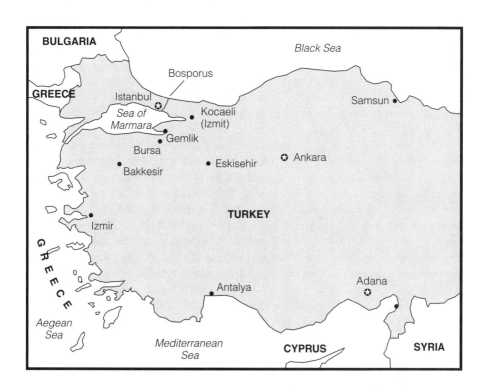

Turkey stands at the crossroads of Europe and the Middle East. Indeed, Istanbul's Atatürk Bridge long served as the only land link between the two regions. For some five hundred years before World War I, Turkey ruled large areas of both. The Ottoman capture of Constantinople in 1453 spelled the end of the Byzantine

Empire and forced the Eastern Church into retreat. At its height in 1683, the Ottoman Empire extended from Algeria in North Africa to the gates of Vienna. All of the Middle East with the exception of Iran had fallen under its sway, as had all of eastern Europe with the exception of Russia. The vast empire included Greece as well as strongholds in Italy. The Ottomans were the superpower of the sixteenth and seventeenth centuries.

Ottoman power peaked at the end of the seventeenth century and then began a slow decline. By the mid eighteenth century, that decline had become a rush. The once dominant power of the region had become the "sick man of Europe." The empire survived until the end of World War I, largely because the European powers were unable to decide on a suitable burial. Britain, France, and Russia all coveted parts of the empire; each feared that the empire's demise would tip the fragile balance of European power in favor of its adversaries.

The Turkey that emerged from the ashes of World War I consisted of the Turkish heartland. Even that would not have survived if Mustafa Kemal had not rallied what remained of the Ottoman forces and resisted the dismemberment of his country. Kemal was a Turkish nationalist, but his vision of the new Turkey had little in common with the Ottoman Empire of old. Turkey, in his view, could only regain its power by becoming part of the West. This meant industrialization. It also meant secularization. If the Ottoman Empire had led the charge of Islam against the Christian West, the new Turkey would lead the charge for the Westernization of the Middle East. That process has now reached its apex with Turkish application for membership in the European Union.

And yet, the process of Westernization in Turkey has had mixed results. The Turkish constitution states that Turkey is a secular state, but its current prime minister is the head of a moderate Islamic party that advocates greater Islamic influence in the affairs of government. The wearing of religious dress (head scarves) is forbidden in public schools and government buildings, but is very much in evidence among the more religious segment of the Turkish population. A plebiscite on the issue is being discussed. In a curious irony, it is now the moderate wing of the Islamic movement that is negotiating Turkey's entrance into the EU. This prospect alarms many citizens of the EU, as does Turkey's record on democracy and human rights. Turkey is a democracy, but it is a democracy in which civilian politicians pay close attention to the views of the generals. Indeed, the military views itself as the guardian of Turkish secularism.

In reality, Turkey continues to be a mélange of East and West, each part struggling for the country's soul. To understand this struggle it is necessary to begin at the beginning. We start with a brief examination of the Ottoman Empire, and then move to the recasting of the Turkish state in the aftermath of World War I, and from there to the evolution of Turkish politics in the post–World War II era.

# HISTORY AND CULTURE

## The Ottoman Empire

The Ottomans began as border raiders on the fringe of the Byzantine Empire during the early fourteenth century. The Byzantine Empire had long been in decay and the Ottoman raiders prospered. Christian areas were the primary target of their raids because Islamic prohibitions against killing Muslims depressed the zeal of their men. It is also probable that the Christian areas had greater wealth than the surrounding Muslim areas. Be that as it may, Christians were as welcome to join their raiding parties as Muslims, and many did so with zeal. Indeed, as the empire expanded, many of its generals and admirals were Christians. As new territories were conquered, successful warriors were rewarded with fiefdoms in proportion to their deeds. Much as in feudal Europe, the new landed aristocracy kept the peace and provided a cavalry for the sultan's campaigns. The sultan received his share of the spoils from battles won, presumably about 20 percent, and the warrior aristocracy kept the rest. Both prospered. Again, little distinction was made between Christians and Muslims. The goal was wealth, empire, and the spread of Islam.

As the spoils of the era consisted of humans as well as gold and jewels, the Ottomans soon found themselves awash in slaves. Always practical, the Ottomans nominally converted young Christian boys to Islam and trained them as elite soldiers loyal only to the sultan. This was easily done, for the young slaves, called *janissaries,* were not encumbered with local or family loyalties. The janissaries provided a powerful counterweight to a feudal aristocracy whose loyalty to the sultan was questionable. By the middle of the sixteenth century the number of janissaries exceeded 10,000 and they formed the core of the sultan's army. When conquests failed to provide enough Christian youth to staff the janissaries, a draft of the empire's European provinces was instituted to fill the void. Eventually, the janissaries attended palace schools and assumed major administrative positions in the empire. When the ruling sultan was weak, it was often they who became the power behind the throne. The sultans had become dependent upon janissary support. Indeed, it was not unusual for new sultans to begin their reign by lavishing gifts upon the janissaries. Muslim youth could not be janissaries because Islam forbade the taking of Muslims as slaves. Those inclined toward a military career joined the infantry or became part of the feudal cavalry.

This combination of feudal cavalry, janissaries, and infantry drove the dazzling expansion of the Ottoman Empire. As the empire expanded, so did its administrative apparatus. While the sultan busied himself with matters of grand strategy, a grand vizier and diwan (cabinet) of lesser viziers administered affairs of state. All viziers were appointed by the sultan and served at his pleasure. Weak sultans depended on the viziers as well as on the janissaries. Many sultans were corrupted by the harem and had little interest in the affairs of empire. The power of the grand vizier increased apace.

In the middle of the sixteenth century the reigning caliph, the successor to the Prophet Mohammed and head of Islam, died while in Turkish custody. The sultan proclaimed himself the new caliph, and Ottoman sultans retained the title until it was abolished by Atatürk in 1924. Religious authority had been added to dynastic authority. This was an important consideration, for it gave the sultan an aura of legitimacy among his Muslim subjects long before the advent of nationalism.

As caliph, the sultan had the final word on Islamic affairs and maintained a large "Islamic institution" to parallel the palace bureaucracy. This included a vast array of judges, teachers, and religious leaders, collectively referred to as the ulema. The ulema were headed by the grand mufti, referred to as the *sheikh al-Islam,* who was the supreme interpreter of Islamic law, albeit in consultation with the caliph–sultan. Mosques flourished, most with affiliated schools that taught Arabic, the language of the Koran and much of the literature of the era. Larger mosques maintained secondary schools or even universities. This is not to suggest that the sultan–caliph was unduly religious. At the empire's peak, the palace entertained thoughts of a grand religion that would incorporate Islam, Christianity, and Judaism. The power of the sheikh al-Islam grew as that of the sultan waned, and during the declining years of the empire the sheikh al-Islam became the sultan's rival.

The Ottomans made little effort to forcibly convert Christians and Jews to Islam. They remained under the authority of their own religious leaders but lived in peace as long as they paid tribute to the Sublime Porte, as the Ottoman government was referred to in Europe. This arrangement was formalized as the *millet* system with each religious community, Jewish, Catholic, and Orthodox, having its own set of religious laws and courts administered by its own senior religious leader. *Millets* for Protestants and other groups were eventually added to the mix. There were clear economic advantages to this arrangement. Christians and Jews paid heavy taxes for the right to live in peace among Muslims. Muslims did not. Christians and Jews also played a key role in the commerce of the Ottoman Empire.

Why did so powerful an empire slip into the long and irreversible decline that would find it dubbed the "sick man of Europe"? Explanations are many. Some focus on a series of weak leaders corrupted by the pleasures of the harem and dominated by their mothers. Many of the sultans were under sixteen years old upon taking office and were easily beguiled by strong viziers and clever janissaries. Others were incompetent or had little interest in politics. Whatever the case, corruption and palace intrigues flourished. An empire that had dazzled the world under gifted leaders found itself adrift. Conquests ceased and rebellions in the provinces became commonplace. The tribute that had provided much of the empire's wealth declined accordingly. Tax farmers and corrupt officials attempted to squeeze ever more money from the peasants, but succeeded only in alienating the subjects from their sultan.

In the meantime, the industrial revolution that had transformed England, France, and Germany into military superpowers bypassed Turkey. Once a leader in military technology, Turkey remained an agrarian backwater unable to compete with the modern armies of the West. Unable to resist the power of modern military powers, large swathes of the empire were colonized by the West. Others, mainly in eastern Europe, declared their independence.

Particularly humiliating were the capitulations. Under the old *millet* system, the non-Islamic groups were allowed to live according to their own religious laws and had their own courts. Foreigners were similarly expected to be kept in line by their respective embassies. These were administrative conveniences initiated by the sultan to better control his vast empire. As the empire declined, a series of unequal treaties called the *capitulations* granted similar powers to France, Russia, and other European powers. France became the protector of Catholics in the empire, Russia the protector of the Orthodox. Ottoman efforts to control the activities of Catholic or Orthodox subjects threatened an international crisis. The major powers also demanded the right to try their nationals in separate courts. Thus they were immune from Ottoman law. Tax privileges followed suit. Jews, Greeks, and anyone else with sufficient money managed to acquire a foreign passport and passed from under the control of Ottoman law.

Efforts to reform the empire were frequent but unsuccessful (Lewis 2002). Of these the most notable were the Tanzimat of 1839, and the Young Turk movement that followed some fifty years later. The Tanzimat was a reform program put into place by the reigning grand vizier in an effort to stem the total collapse of the empire. The government was to be reorganized along the lines of "old, pure, and tolerant Muslim practices," a concept embodied in the Turkish word *tanzimat* (Fisher 1964, 316). The harshness of government oppression was eased by providing governors with elected councils to guide their activities. In 1876 a constitution was proclaimed and a parliament elected. Neither was particularly successful. Local notables dominated the local councils and had little interest in reforming a system that worked to their advantage. The Parliament met but was soon disbanded by Sultan Abdul Hamid, often dubbed the "Red Sultan" because of his bloody massacre of Armenians between 1894 and 1897. More than 100,000 Armenians were slaughtered in an attempt to stem growing separatist tendencies in Turkey's Armenian provinces (Fisher 1964, 331). Turkish historians suggest the number of deaths was far fewer and attribute the massacre to a flare-up of tensions between the Kurdish and Armenian communities. In any case, the Tanzimat era saw a vast expansion in Turkish education and a growing number of Turks began studying in the West. Abdul Hamid II, however, had little interest in either democracy or liberal education.

The Committee for Progress and Union, the core of the Young Turk movement, emerged in 1889 as a secret military society opposed to the oppressive policies of Abdul Hamid II. Its primary goals were Turkish nationalism, a more liberal political system, and an end to foreign influence in Turkish affairs. Other opposition groups emerged to join the battle. All were referred to as "Young Turks," as were various reform groups that preceded the Committee for Progress and Union. In 1908, Abdul Hamid II was forced to restore the constitution and schedule elections for the Chamber of Deputies. When he attempted to backtrack the following year, he was deposed in favor of his brother, Mehmed V. For all of his paranoia and oppression, Abdul Hamid II had ignored the common practice of consolidating his power by murdering his brothers. Mehmed V, who claimed not to have read a newspaper in twenty years, paved the way for the collapse of the Ottoman Empire in World War I.

**Consequences of the Ottoman System of Rule**    Turkey sided with Germany in World War I and suffered accordingly. The Allied powers, with the exception of the United States, wanted vengeance. Adding to Western demands for vengeance was the slaughter and mass deportation of Armenians in 1915 and 1916 following a premature proclamation of an Armenian state. Estimates of the deaths range from somewhere around 800,000 to 200,000. Armenians cite the former figure; Turks, the latter. Most Western historians suggest something in between. Whatever the exact death toll, a horrendous number of Armenians perished at the hands of the Turks (Fisher 1964, 366). Demands for vengeance masked a long-standing European desire to dismember the "sick man of Europe" and annex its Asian territories to the empires of Britain and France. Political cartoons of the era portrayed European leaders stalking a large turkey, their knives at the ready (Cox 1887). Britain had the largest appetite, envisioning control of Egypt, Iraq (Mesopotamia), Palestine, Arabia, and even Iran and parts of the Caucasus. France eyed Greater Syria and parts of Asian Turkey itself, including the Straits of Marmara separating Asian and European Turkey. Italy wanted the Dodecanese Islands and parts of southwestern Asia Minor. Greeks dreamed of a greater Greece that extended to the Bosporus if not Istanbul—the renamed Constantinople—and the territories beyond. The Armenians demanded an independent Armenia; the Kurds an independent Kurdistan. The Arabs demanded an Arab kingdom that encompassed Palestine, Arabia, and Greater Syria. Britain had earlier made promises to that effect to encourage an Arab rebellion against the Turks during the early years of the war, though Palestine was exempted from consideration. The Russians had traditionally demanded control of the Orthodox areas of the empire and the straits that separated European Turkey from Asian Turkey. Russia, however, had dissolved in revolution and was well on its way to becoming the Union of Soviet Socialist Republics (USSR), the world's first communist power. The lone holdout was President Woodrow Wilson of the United States. Wilson had recently proclaimed his Fourteen Points for a sane and peaceful world, the key elements of which were an end to colonialism and a prohibition against the acquisition of territory by force. According to Wilson, the diverse "nationalities" of the empire should receive a secure independence. The Arabs, Greeks, Kurds, and Armenians applauded. The British and French did not. Wilson was also the author of the League of Nations, but his proposals for a powerful league capable of enforcing world peace were rejected by all, including the U.S. Congress.

Despite several international conferences called to carry out the dismemberment of Turkey, American opposition to colonialism and intense jealousy between Britain and France delayed a final settlement until the Lausanne Conference of 1922–1923. By that time the realities on the ground had changed. Mustafa Kemal had mobilized what remained of the Ottoman military and driven the Greeks from most occupied Turkish territory. Britain and France could have intervened, but the occupation of Turkey had proven difficult and the citizens of both countries had lost their taste for war. In the final settlement, France added Greater Syria to its existing colonies in North Africa (Morocco and Algeria) and the British claimed the mandates for Palestine and Iraq. They were already in control of Aden (South Yemen), Egypt, and the Gulf sheikhdoms. The Jews were promised a "national home" in Palestine, but the Arabs, Kurds, and Armenians came away empty-handed, previous promises notwithstanding.[1]

The Greeks were also disappointed in their dreams of a greater Greece, and in the summer of 1923 a forced exchange of populations between the two hostile countries was supervised by the League of Nations. Some 1.5 million Greeks were transferred from Turkey to Greece and approximately 500,000 Turks were removed from Greece and resettled in Turkey. The Ottoman Empire was gone, but Turkey remained.

Curiously, the Ottoman Empire left few traces in eastern Europe. The *millet* system had left Christian religious communities largely intact, and nationalism had gradually taken root in the Balkans. Yugoslavia was cobbled together from Croatia, Bosnia, Serbia, and a few smaller regions. Large Muslim enclaves remained throughout eastern Europe and were predominant in Albania, Bosnia, and the Kosovo region of Serbia. All have been the site of intense conflict in recent years. The eastern European Muslims were not Turks but local residents who had converted to Islam to avoid the taxation imposed on Christians and to otherwise gain the prerogatives enjoyed by Muslims under Ottoman rule. Some may also have converted to protect their sons from being conscripted as janissaries (Fisher 1964). This, however, is a matter of conjecture.

Ottoman rule in the Arab world also left few traces other than the Ottoman legal code, vestiges of which remain throughout the region. The Arabs were predominantly Muslim and did not view the Turks as colonialists. Arab nationalism didn't take root until the 1930s, and then it was limited to intellectual circles. Mohammed Ali, the pasha (a blend of governor and general) of Egypt, had rebelled against the Sublime Porte in the early nineteenth century, but this had little to do with Arabism or Arab nationalism. Mohammed Ali was an Albanian.

In Turkey itself, the Young Turks and other intellectuals of the late nineteenth and early twentieth centuries searched for ways to shore up a decaying empire. Some advocated pan-Islam as a means of better mobilizing the Arabs and other Muslim communities to the empire's cause: the "sick man" would be saved by transforming it from a predominantly Turkish affair into an Islamic empire. Others sought salvation of the empire through pan-Turkism, a view that focused on the mobilization of the large Turkish communities resident in the Caucasus, Syria, and Iraq (Mesopotamia). Only a minority focused on a narrow Turkish nationalism centered on the Turkish heartland. Mustafa Kemal was part of this minority.

---

1 The present country of Armenia had earlier been ceded to Russia and would become part of the Soviet Union. It emerged as an independent country with the dissolution of the Soviet Union in 1991.

The issue was largely theoretical, for the Turkish defeat in World War I left few options. Mustafa Kemal rallied the remnants of the Ottoman army to salvage the Turkish heartland, but he had inherited an agrarian country surrounded by enemies and wracked by poverty, superstition, fatalism, corruption, and alienation. The forced transfer of the Greek population had also destroyed much of Turkey's commercial class.

## Turkey under Atatürk: The First Republic

Mustafa Kemal blamed Turkey's woes on Islam and a decaying monarchy. Turkey had been humiliated by the West because it remained mired in the past and had failed to keep pace with the West's intellectual enlightenment and industrial development. The only way for Turkey to regain its rightful place in the world community, in his view, was to Westernize. This meant secularism, enlightenment, and industrialization. It also means an end to the Ottoman monarchy and the transformation of Islam into a personal religion divorced from politics.

Abolishing the monarchy was relatively simple. Kemal convened the Grand National Assembly that had been established during the later years of the Ottoman Empire and had it proclaim Turkey a republic. He was proclaimed its president. These were not difficult tasks, for Kemal had become an immensely popular figure and his hastily created Republican People's Party (RPP) totally dominated the Assembly. The RPP was his personal tool, and it carried out his orders without a murmur.

Kemal's formula for transforming Turkey into a modern state was based on six points, often referred to as Kemalism or, later, Atatürkism: republicanism, secularism, populism, nationalism, statism, and reformism (Parla 2004). Kemalism was a vague ideology that evolved over time; distinctions between its six principles were blurred. To focus on its theoretical shortcomings, however, is to miss the point. Kemalism was designed to cut Turkey's ties with the past and to provide Turks with a guiding ideology other than Islam.

Of the six principles, republicanism was the least ambiguous. The Grand National Assembly abolished the monarchy in 1924 and Turkey was proclaimed a republic. But republicanism did not imply democracy. Kemal ruled by his control of the military and the RPP. He also used the state's propaganda agencies to transform himself into a charismatic figure of mythic proportions. All in all, Kemal wielded as much power as the most powerful of sultans, perhaps even more. It also seems that Kemal was impressed by Mussolini's forced mobilization of Italy and was a close observer of Hitler's rise in Germany. Unlike Mussolini and Hitler, Kemal had no aspiration for empire or colonial aggrandizement (Mango 2002; Zurcher 2004). Nevertheless, the Grand National Assembly continued to serve as a symbol of democracy and 1930 would see an abortive experiment with two-party democracy. Kemal asked one of his close associates to form an opposition party and selected members of the RPP were told to join it. The formation of an opposition party had less to do with democracy than with a desire to provide a safety valve for growing hostility to Kemal's reforms. Unexpected support for the new party—just how much remains a matter of debate—led to its cancellation. Turkey remained a dictatorship until the end of the Second World War.

The concept of secularism also brooked little ambiguity. Kemal blamed Islam for Turkey's backwardness and launched a vicious attack on Islamic institutions and traditions. Turkey, according to Kemal, would be secular in both form and attitude. The attack on Islam began in earnest in 1925 with the forbidding of dervish (Sufi) orders and the closing of their schools, shrines, and mausoleums. Symbols of Islam such as the fez were outlawed. Veils were discouraged, but not outlawed at this point. In 1926, the Swiss legal code replaced the Ottoman legal code, depriving Islamic law of its preeminent role. The Gregorian calendar also replaced the Islamic calendar. In later years polygamy would be abolished (not many men could afford it) and the constitution amended to delete the clause that Turkey was an Islamic state. Religious instruction was also removed from both public and private schools, and Sunday replaced Friday, the Muslim holy day, as the official day of rest (Fisher 1964; Zurcher 2004). From 1928 onward, Turkish was written in the Latin alphabet rather than the Arabic, a reform that had been discussed under the Ottomans. This was a practical reform inasmuch as the Arabic alphabet did not lend itself to the expression of Turkish, but it also represented another break with the past.

Turkish nationalism, in turn, was designed to instill pride and self-volition in a Turkish population still in the grip of Islamic fatalism. Kemal wanted a "can-do" culture, and the myths developed to achieve this end often took on extraordinary proportions. A Turkish historical thesis claimed that Turks were white Aryans of Central Asian origins who had been "forced by drought and hunger to migrate to other areas such as China, Europe and the Near East. In so doing they created the world's great civilizations" (Zurcher 2004, 191). Attila the Hun and Genghis Khan became national heroes and were portrayed as great civilizers. This myth was taught in public schools until the 1940s.

Populism was a particularly vague concept, but it generally focused on welding the Turkish population into a modern nation whose government cared for the needs of its people. Tax burdens were eased, people were made equal before the law (in sharp contrast to the capitulations of the Ottoman era), and illiteracy, then around 80 percent, was attacked with a vengeance. All villages were required to have at least elementary schools, and high schools, teachers' colleges, and universities proliferated in the major cities. People were also required to have a family name. The Grand National Assembly conferred the name of Atatürk, "father of the Turks," on Kemal.

Statism was a new economic strategy adopted to transform Turkey from an overwhelmingly agrarian country into an industrial power. Capitalists and private entrepreneurs were encouraged to stimulate an industrial revolution in Turkey, but they were few in number. Capitalists also seemed reluctant to invest in long-range projects with unsure returns. Atatürk was also in a hurry, and was wary of foreign investment. The state, accordingly, had little choice but to play the role of investment banker and entrepreneur. The government (state) planned and financed new industries. When the going got tough, it was the state that provided the money to keep them afloat. Some industries were sold to the private sector, but most remained under state control.

Reformism was something of a catch-all category that embodied Atatürk's rejection of the conservatism of the Ottoman Empire. Little of the past, in his view, was worth retaining. Government, economy, society, and culture all had to be reformed to bring Turkey on a par with the West. Women were emancipated and encouraged to become everything from doctors to airplane pilots. They were also given the right to vote. Sporting clubs were encouraged and opened to both men and women. Soccer became the national sport and was played by both sexes. Corruption, the scourge of the Ottoman Empire, was curbed by draconian penalties. Education curricula were reshaped to curb fatalism and preach the doctrines of self-volition and personal responsibility.

**How Well Did It All Work?**   Mustafa Kemal (Atatürk) died in 1938, probably as a result of high living, long nights, and excessive drinking. He was succeeded in office by Ismet Pasha Inönü, his prime minister and revolutionary colleague. Kemalism remained in place until the end of World War II. How well did it succeed? This remains something of a debate. The face of Turkey was changed. This is beyond question. Islam was separated from the affairs of government, industrial development took root, railroads spanned the country, a rudimentary electricity grid was established, education flourished, women were emancipated, and Turkish independence was secured. Outside observers were impressed and Western scholars recommended Kemalism as a formula for modernizing less developed countries.

Nevertheless, clouds loomed on the horizon. The first was the backsliding that occurred with the passing of the iron hands of Atatürk and Inönü. As Turkey became more democratic, politicians began to soften Turkey's secular face in an effort to gain votes of a population still wedded to Islam and particularly to its more mystical elements. Turkey was on the path to modernity, but it remained an Islamic country. This process is continuing and Turkey is now governed by a moderate Islamic party. Corruption has also made a comeback.

A second cloud was the result of excessive state intervention in the economy. As in most socialist or partially socialist countries, state enterprises were used to ease rising unemployment and were soon overstaffed and inefficient. The government kept them afloat and inflation soared. Agriculture, the cornerstone of the Turkish economy, also suffered. These and related economic policies continue to haunt the Turkish economy. Finally, Atatürk's authoritarian, paternalistic style of rule provided little preparation for Turkey's eventual transition to democracy and emphasis on human rights. As we shall see in the remainder of the chapter, the results have been painful.

## World War II and the Era of Optimism (1946–1960)

Turkey's foreign policy in the years leading up to World War II was one of studied neutrality between the Allied and Axis powers. Sympathy was with the former, but the reality of German military strength could not be ignored. The Allies pressed Turkey to enter the war, but the Turks stalled until February 1945, when war was declared on an all-but-defeated Germany. This symbolic gesture earned Turkey membership in the United Nations.

The years that followed were ones of great optimism. Turkey joined the North Atlantic Treaty Organization (NATO), the U.S.-led alliance forged to prevent further Soviet inroads into Europe, including Turkey. Foreign military and economic aid poured into Turkey as the United States rushed to strengthen a key frontline ally in its battle against Communism. Turkey reciprocated, sending troops to Korea and joining the Baghdad Pact, America's Middle East counterpart to NATO. When Iraq dropped out of the alliance in 1958, Turkey and Iran became the key elements in America's plan to keep the Arab world and its oil free of Communism. Turkey prospered accordingly.

There was also cause for optimism on the domestic front. The Democratic Party (DP) was allowed to register in 1946, ushering in a new experiment in democracy. Labor unions were also allowed to form, albeit without the right to strike or participate in political activities. The RPP scored a fraudulent victory in the 1946 elections for the Grand National Assembly, but it would be its last victory for some time. The Turkish public had tired of the excesses of Kemalism, and in the 1950 elections the Democratic Party captured 408 seats in the Grand National Assembly as opposed to 69 for the RPP, a crushing defeat indeed (Zurcher 2004, 217). The DP scored an even more impressive victory in the 1954 elections.

All, however, was not well. The DP controlled the Grand National Assembly, but it did not control the military or the bureaucracy. Its relations with both were tense. To make matters worse, the economy declined, which led to mass grumbling. The International Monetary Fund (IMF) provided emergency loans, but only on the condition that Turkey cut back on social programs and liberalize (privatize) its economy. Massive student protests were the result. The DP might have been defeated in the 1957 elections, but it used its massive majority in the Grand National Assembly to outlaw any effective opposition to its rule. Turkey had returned to authoritarian rule. The DP also played the religious card by relaxing Turkey's secular rules, an election ploy pioneered by the RPP during the earlier elections of the era. The call to prayer in Arabic was reinstated, new mosques and schools for preachers were built, religious electives returned to the school curricula, and religious literature was allowed to proliferate. The military, the protector of Kemalism, could take no more and staged a coup d'état in October 1960. The era of optimism had come to an end.

### The Era of Reassessment: The Second Republic (1960–1980)

It would be the military that assessed the problems that led to the coup of 1960. First and foremost were efforts to prevent a return to authoritarian rule. The Senate was added to the parliament to counterbalance the power of the Grand National Assembly. Another addition was the Supreme Court, which was empowered to declare laws of the parliament unconstitutional. Turkish universities were given autonomy to protect their freedom of expression. Now the police could only enter campuses at the invitation of the rector. Just in case the new organizational arrangements didn't cure the country's ills, the military was provided with the constitutional authority to protect the interests of the country.

The new constitution was duly ratified by a popular vote and new elections were held in 1961. The greater freedom had resulted in the emergence of some eleven political parties; the RPP, now reconstituted as a party of the center left, came out on top. The Justice Party, the heir to the disbanded Democratic Party, ran a close second. They would alternate as the dominant power in the parliament over the next several elections. Optimists suggested that Turkey might be moving toward a two-party democracy.

This optimism was misplaced. In its effort to stem authoritarianism, Turkey's new constitution had erred on the side of flexibility. Governments (prime minister and cabinet) were weak and found it difficult to act decisively. The dominant parties were loose coalitions and defections were frequent. While the RPP moved to the left and became the advocate of social welfare, the Justice Party gradually transformed itself into the party of Islam and traditional values. At the same time, the search for votes had led both parties to accept the reality that Turkey remained an Islamic country. Both inclined toward accommodation rather than confrontation. Even some elements in the military were willing to acknowledge that attempts to suppress Islam had merely spawned extremism. Mosques were built, shrines restored, and schools provided with curricula designed to foster responsible Islam. Similar programs were implemented in the training schools for preachers. Better the moderates than the fundamentalists (Zurcher 2004, 247). These efforts strengthened the position of an official Islam acceptable to the military but did little to alter the mystical or popular Islam of the villages.

Turkish politics were also being reshaped by a phenomenal wave of social change. Education mushroomed and peasants poured into the cities in search of a better way of life. Many found little but unemployment and flocked to shantytowns that became an extension of their villages. Population experts of the time began to speak of the "ruralification" of the urban areas. Rather than being modernized by the urban environment, conservative rural values were transforming the cities. With time, the residents of the shantytowns became an important pressure group, demanding electricity and other utilities. Politicians complied, compounding Turkey's budget difficulties. The process continues today, with approximately one million people a year migrating to Turkey's already crowded cities (*Turkish Daily News,* April 20, 2005). During the same period, the migration of Turkish workers to Germany and other European countries became a rush. In 1962 there were some 13,000 Turkish workers in Europe. By the end of the 1970s the figure had reached 2.5 million. Remittances poured into Turkey, as did demands for a higher quality of life. Political groups of all varieties flourished in both Turkey and Europe, many advocating extremist views ranging from communism to Islamic rule.

Turkey's political leaders were immobilized by the dazzling pace of change. The country's massive, self-serving bureaucracy was unresponsive to the demands of the politicians and the mammoth state industries remained lethargic. Rather than providing revenues for the cash-strapped nation, they consumed them. The oil shock produced by the 1973 Arab–Israeli war threatened economic chaos.

The generals could wait no longer: in 1971 they exercised their constitutional right to protect the country. The prime minister was presented with an ultimatum demanding a credible government and an end to the anarchy. Reforms were drawn up, but a wave of terrorist attacks spurred the army to proclaim martial law in large sections of the country. Leftists were blamed for the terror, and a witch hunt was carried out against anyone suspected of leftist tendencies, reportedly with the cooperation of the ultranationalists and the covert support of the United States (Zurcher 2004, 259). The United States viewed the Islamic extremists throughout the region as a useful ally in the struggle against Communism.

**Cyprus**    Having made its point, the military returned to the barracks. Politics continued as usual. The Justice Party ruled until 1973, then it gave way to a succession of RPP governments buoyed by Bülent Ecevit's swift handling of the Cyprus crisis. The island of Cyprus had long been ruled by the Ottoman Empire, but its population was about 80 percent Greek. Britain had taken control of the island following World War I, but granted Cyprus its independence in the years following World War II. Tensions between the Greek and Turkish communities flared, but were contained by international pressure. In 1974, however, Greek officers in the Cypriot national guard seized power and proclaimed *enosis* (unity) with the Greek mainland. Many Turks were killed, and Ecevit ordered the Turkish army to invade Cyprus and secure the Turkish areas. The Turkish army occupied about 40 percent of the island nation and Ecevit became a national hero. The United Nations condemned Turkey and the U.S. threatened economic reprisals, but Turkey refused to budge. Turkish–American relations deteriorated, but soon normalized. The U.S. could ill afford to alienate a key ally in its encirclement of the USSR. Nor was it interested in a war between Turkey and Greece, both of whom were members of NATO. A forced exchange of populations, some by fear and others at gunpoint, followed the Turkish occupation and in 1983 the Turkish-controlled area of Cyprus was proclaimed the Turkish Republic of Northern Cyprus. Relations between Greece and Turkey have remained tense amid continuing international pressure to reunify the divided island. The issue has become one of several sticking points in Turkey's negotiations for membership in the European Union—of which Greece is already a member.

Despite popular acclaim for its handling of the Cyprus question, the RPP was unable to achieve a majority in the Grand National Assembly. Weak coalition governments became the norm and the economy suffered accordingly. Economic crises coincided with rises in violence. Extremist groups of the left clashed with extremist groups of the right. Some right-wing groups were fundamentalists; others were extreme nationalists called Grey Wolves. The Grey Wolves enjoyed the covert support of the police and security forces. Radical groups of all varieties profited from Turkey's growing pool of alienated youth.

Their alienation was not difficult to understand. Turkish universities could accommodate only 20 percent of the applicants, and even many of the graduates faced a future of menial positions or unemployment. Battles raged for control of both the universities and the street. Casualties from the violence rose from 230 in

1977 to more than 1,200 in 1979 (Zurcher 2004, 263). Extremist groups claimed control of squatter areas, and one leftist group transformed a Black Sea village into a soviet like those that followed the Russian Revolution. Gang warfare gave way to attacks on public figures.

On September 12, 1980, the military again seized power. The parliament was dissolved and political parties and the larger trade unions were disbanded. Their leaders were also arrested. All in all, some 30,000 people were arrested by the end of the year; by the end of 1981, that figure had soared to 122,600. Some 80,000 remained in prison a year later, but violence had decreased by 90 percent (Zurcher 2004, 279). The Second Republic had come to an end. So had public dissent.

## The Era of Islamic and Kurdish Resurgence

A new constitution was drafted in 1982 and presented to the public for ratification. The reigning general was guaranteed a seven-year term as president, normal freedoms and rights were restricted, and the power of the military to interfere in civilian affairs was increased. The constitution was overwhelmingly adopted—by 91 percent of the vote—in all but the Kurdish areas (Zurcher 2004, 281). People who refused to vote were fined. The Third Republic had been born.

Buoyed by their new powers, the generals banned politicians who had guided the Second Republic from political activity for a period of ten years. Academics, students, and bureaucrats were banned from participating in political parties. Petitions for new parties were vetted by the military. Most, including the obvious successors to the Justice Party and the RPP, were rejected. Only three parties participated in the 1983 elections. The Motherland Party, the one least favored by the generals, emerged victorious. A majority of its supporters were people who had voted for the old Justice Party. Despite intense factionalization and the close supervision of the military, it remained in power until 1991.

The problems confronting Turgut Özal, the prime minister and leader of the Motherland Party, were threefold: inflation, an Islamic resurgence, and a Kurdish revolt. The core of Turkey's economic crisis during the 1980s was an inflation rate of some 80 percent. In practical terms, this meant that Turkish wage earners lost about half of their purchasing power. Özal initiated a series of reforms to free the Turkish economy from government controls. This policy had long been urged by the International Monetary Fund, but it was executed in a flawed manner that resulted in a wave of economic scandals including some linked to Özal's family. As so often happens during the early stages of economic liberalization, the rich and influential got richer at the expense of the average citizen.

Of far more concern to the generals, at least some of whom had presumably benefited from Özal's liberalization policies, was the resurgence of Islamic fervor. No country in the Middle East had been immune from the emotional wave produced by the victory of the Ayatollah Khomeini's Islamic revolution in Iran, and Turkey was no exception. As in the past, the politicians of the era attempted to maximize their vote by appealing to moderate Islamic sentiments. Unlike their counterparts in the Arab world, a majority of Turkish voters were not ready for an Islamic state. They were ready for greater morality in government.

One of the more interesting intellectual currents of this period was an attempt to fuse Islam and Turkish nationalism. According to the Turkish–Islamic Synthesis, as it was called, Turkish culture was a blend of 2,500 years of Turkish history and 1,000 years of Islamic history. Intellectual Islam, as opposed to the mystical Islam of the villages, was also pro-business and appealed to the broad section of the business community that was more interested in economic growth than in the purity of Turkey's secular traditions. Even many in the military found the Turkish–Islamic Synthesis appealing. Islam, in their view, would be controlled by making it part of the national ideology. Others in the military remained wary, the overthrow of the shah's regime in Iran being fresh in their minds. The circumstances in the shah's Iran and Turkey were different, but not that different. Both were dominated by the military and both were tied to the United States, the world's most powerful nation. That had not been enough to stem the Islamic tide.

The generals were also aware that the popular Islam as practiced in the villages and shantytowns was far more emotional and inclined to violence than the intellectual Islam of the urban middle class. The violence of the late 1970s had demonstrated just how rapidly the situation could deteriorate if not kept in check. Violent groups in the Islamic movement had played a key role in fomenting that violence and could do it again at a moment's notice. The harangues and probable financial support of the Ayatollah Khomeini encouraged them to do so.

**The Kurdish Rebellion**   Of more immediate concern was the Kurdish rebellion sparked by the formation of the Workers' Party of Kurdistan (PKK) in 1978 by Abdullah Öcalan. Other Kurdish organizations had long been in existence, but these were largely intellectual affairs designed to advocate the rights of Kurds and keep the dream of a united Kurdistan alive. Öcalan's PKK, by contrast, stressed Marxism and armed conflict. Rather than targeting intellectuals, it aimed its message at the poor and less educated youth of the Kurdish towns and villages, most of which were concentrated in the areas adjoining the Kurdish regions of Iraq. Öcalan's appeal struck a responsive chord and young Kurds flocked to his ranks. Many received military training in Lebanon's Beqaa valley, and then filtered back into Turkey. The training was provided by Syrian and Palestinian officers. Turkish–Syrian relations deteriorated while Turkish cooperation with the Iraqi government of Saddam Hussein improved. Both had a vested interest in crushing the Kurds. Not all Kurds supported the rebellion, but many did, and Turkey's leaders found themselves confronted with a long and deadly conflict. The PKK also formed alliances with urban extremist groups and was able to bring the war to Turkey's main cities. Things might have been far worse if the main Kurdish groups in Turkey and Iraq had not been fragmented by tribal, personality, and ideological conflicts. All Kurdish groups longed for the independent Kurdistan promised at the end of World War I, but each was also intent on keeping rival groups from seizing control of the independence movement. They fought the governments of whatever country they were in, and they fought each other.

By the end of the era of Islamic and Kurdish revival, then, Turkey was faced with a dual threat: Islamic rule and Kurdish separatism. While Turks dreamed of union with Europe, they were being drawn ever deeper into the conflicts of the Middle East.

## Turkey in the Era of the New World Order

The era of the new world order ushered in by the collapse of the Soviet Union had minimal impact on Turkey. Turkey was a longtime ally of the United States and, unlike Iran and Syria, had little to fear from American dominance of the region. To the contrary, the end of the Cold War enabled Turkey to normalize relations with Russia and gave it a free hand in dealing with Syria, the prime supporter of the PKK. A strong show of Turkish military force was sufficient to cut Syrian links to the PKK and Öcalan was eventually captured. The rebellion declined accordingly. The collapse of the USSR also offered vast opportunities for the spread of Turkish influence in the newly emergent countries of Central Asia, most of whom were predominantly Islamic and Turkish in culture. Whether these ties are enough to bind is a matter of debate (Pope 2005). The U.S. feared that Central Asia would fall prey to Iranian influence, and encouraged the extension of Turkish influence in the region. The U.S. no longer needed Turkey to contain the USSR, but Ankara remained a key element in U.S. plans to secure the Middle East and its oil.

However, the U.S.–Turkish alliance was not without its strains. The collapse of the USSR was followed in short order by Saddam Hussein's occupation of Kuwait and the resulting Gulf War. In the heat of the crisis, the United States encouraged revolts among Iraqi Shi'a in the south of Iraq and Iraqi Kurds in the northern provinces that bordered on Turkey. Both revolted, only to find at the war's end that the allied powers, having driven Saddam Hussein from Kuwait, had decided to leave him in power as a counterweight to Iran. Wiser heads had also convinced the U.S. president that a U.S. occupation of Iraq would be suicidal. Saddam Hussein's response, as we have seen in Chapter 6, was swift and brutal. Both Shi'a and Kurds were attacked with a vengeance. Reports of the ensuing slaughter left the United States little option but to impose no-fly zones in the predominantly Shi'a and Kurdish areas. For all intents and purposes, the Turkish areas of northern Iraq became an autonomous, self-governing region. Ankara did not protest Saddam Hussein's attacks on the Kurds, but it was bitterly opposed to the establishment of an embryonic Kurdish republic on its southern borders. In the Turkish view, a Kurdish republic in Iraq would invariably fuel secessionist passions among Turkish Kurds.

But it was not America that would have the greatest influence on Turkish politics during the era of the new world order. Rather it was dreams of membership in the European Union. Membership in the EU would bring secularism, democracy, and sustained economic growth. Ironically, Turkey could only be admitted to the EU if it demonstrated that it was already a secular and humane democracy dedicated to the principles of market economics.

Pressure to bring Turkey into compliance with EU standards and a continuing economic crisis—inflation was reaching record highs—forced a return to democracy and economic reform. The results were mixed. Governments proved unstable and efforts to liberalize the economy, including the sell-off of some government firms, resulted in corruption scandals. The period, however, was marked by two firsts: the election of Turkey's first female prime minister, Tansu Çiller, and, subsequently, the emergence of an openly Islamic political party as Turkey's largest vote-getter.

Çiller symbolized the new, young, and European Turkey. The Islamic Welfare Party symbolized a resurgent Islam, albeit a moderate Islam that spoke of honesty and tolerance rather than of an Islamic state. Both had a broad popular appeal. In the flush of victory, some overly zealous members of the Islamic Welfare Party questioned the wisdom of joining the EU and spoke openly of closer Turkish relations with the Palestinians. Two key elements of Turkish policy were under attack: secularism and Turkey's traditional alliance with Israel.

In 1997, the military again intervened and the Islamic Welfare Party was removed from office. It was the fourth military intervention in the post–World War II era. Indeed, it seemed as if military interventions were occurring at ten-year intervals. A weak coalition of minor-parties formed a caretaker government that ruled until the 1999 elections. Another weak coalition government took office following the 1999 elections, but found it difficult to solve Turkey's deepening economic crisis. Once again Turkey begged loans from the International Monetary Fund in exchange for written pledges to privatize its economy and met other IMF demands. It was the seventeenth such promise since World War II. Corruption scandals abounded and the government totally lost credibility with its handling of the massive earthquake that devastated Istanbul a few months later. Little if anything was done during the critical first twenty-four hours, and the death total would eventually be estimated at 15,000. Material losses reached the $25 billion mark. The army also received its share of the criticism. In the meantime, the Islamists split into moderate and radical factions, with the moderates emerging dominant.

### The Era of Global Terrorism (2001 and Beyond)

Turkey embraced America's war on terror, as well it should have: Turkey was a longtime ally of the United States and it had suffered more than its share of terrorist violence. The majority of that terrorism was attributed to the PKK and radical leftist groups, but a Turkish Hezbollah group (unrelated to Hezbollah movements in other Middle Eastern countries) had been active in the 1990s (Nugent 2004). Whatever its cause, terror was terror. Turkey willingly agreed to play a major role in Afghanistan and continues to do so. This by itself eased the image that Western powers alone were involved in the war against the Taliban. The war on terror also legitimized the military's efforts to keep an eye on all radical groups, Islamic and otherwise.

The two countries, however, parted company over President George W. Bush's planned attack on Iraq. The Bush administration had taken Turkish cooperation in its war against Iraq for granted. It was stunned and angry when Turkey refused to go along. Turkey saw little danger from Saddam Hussein, its ally in the struggle against Kurdish independence. On more than one occasion Saddam Hussein had turned a blind eye as Turkish troops crossed the border in search of their prey. A brisk black market had also emerged between Turkey and Iraq as the Iraqis paid top dollar to bypass American sanctions. What Turkey most feared was that the fall of Saddam Hussein would lead to the emergence of a Kurdish state on its southern border. The U.S. offered a lucrative package of some $26 billion in aid (between $4 billion and $6 billion in grants and about $20 billion in loans) to sway the Turkish parliament, not to mention trade concessions that would allow Turkish textiles easy access to the American market. This package gave the Turks pause, but the negotiations broke down over the Turkish desire to command its own troops in northern Iraq, the obvious goal of which would be to prevent an independent Iraqi Kurdistan (Park 2003). This was not a minor threat, for Turkey had already marshaled 20,000 troops, supported by tanks and artillery, on the Turkish–Iraqi border (*Guardian,* Jan. 30, 2003). Iraqi Kurds, for their part, threatened to shoot Turkish soldiers on sight (*NYT,* March 20, 2003). A strong Turkish presence in northern Iraq would spell finis for the Kurdish support upon which the U.S. was dearly counting. The Turks eventually granted the U.S. the use of its air space and a few other minor concessions, but the bitterness remained. U.S. Secretary of State Donald Rumsfeld chose the second anniversary of the war to blame U.S. problems in Iraq on Turkey's refusal to allow the U.S. Fourth Infantry to cross its territory at the onset of the war. Everyone, it seemed, was responsible for the Iraq fiasco except the Bush administration.

Differences over the future of Kurdistan, however, were not the only issues dampening Turkish support for the war. Like much of the Middle East, an overwhelming majority of the Turkish population was hostile to the war, 94 percent by some estimates (*NYT,* Feb. 19, 2003). Islamic sensitivities were clearly part of the picture. Turkish leaders have not always been sensitive to public opinion, but its prime minister, the head of the newly elected Justice and Development Party, most certainly was. He had been swept to power in 2002 with 34 percent of the vote and was clearly basking in the popularity that resulted from his willingness to stand up to the Americans. The RPP had come in a distant second with 19 percent of the vote. They were the only two parties to meet the 10 percent minimum vote required for representation in the Assembly and, according to the Turkish voting system, split the Assembly seats in proportion to their vote totals. This gave the Justice and Development Party an overwhelming majority. The core issues in the victory of the Justice and Development Party appear to have been a rejection of the instability, corruption, financial chaos, and military meddling of the preceding years. Tayyip Erdogan, the party's leader, was also a charismatic individual from a working-class background who had promised to end poverty. Islam was obviously a factor, but a competing Islamic party of more extreme views fared poorly in the elections. This suggests that the Turkish appetite for Muslim extremism was muted.

While Turkey and the U.S. have gone to exaggerated lengths to patch up their faltering alliance, the reality of an independent Kurdistan in Iraq draws ever closer and is a constant topic of discussion in the Turkish press. Turkish pressures on both the Iraqi government and the U.S. have increased apace. Turkish commandos have been arrested in northern Iraq and Turkish troops remain poised on the Iraqi border. The Turkish military has warned Iraqi Kurds not to form an army, a clear reference to the growing power of Kurdish militias (*Kurdistan Observer,* June 29, 2005). A Turkish attack on Kurdish strongholds is not out of the question. Turkey insists that it has the right to make raids into Iraq and is already laying the political groundwork for such an attack by claiming to be the protector of Iraq's some

1 million Turkomans (ethnic Turks), who are concentrated on the fringes of Iraqi Kurdistan (*Daily Star,* July 15, 2005). Turkey has been particularly critical of the Kurdish eviction of Turkomans from Kirkuk, a policy Turkey claims is tantamount to ethnic cleansing (*Turkish Daily News,* Jan. 20, 2005). A Turkish attack on Iraq could throw the region into chaos. If the U.S. is nervous, it is not without cause. U.S. bombing of Turkoman areas in its antiterror campaign also brought a sharp rebuke from the Turks (Singh 2004).

In the meantime, Turkey is betting on membership in the European Union. The Turkish constitution has been further amended to meet EU standards, the most profound changes being a curtailment of the military's budgetary autonomy. The Grand National Assembly now has the right to demand the details of military spending, something formerly denied on the grounds of national security. The military has also been removed from government committees that oversee broadcasting and higher education (World Tribune.com, May 13, 2004). Both were deemed necessary to protect the secular nature of the Turkish state. Rather than remain a separate branch of government, the military is ceding its authority to civilian rule. Other amendments revised the Turkish penal code to bring it in line with EU human rights legislation. The free hand of the police and security forces will presumably be curbed accordingly. Such is the price of membership in the EU.

One is thus faced with a curious situation in which an Islamic prime minister is leading the charge for Turkey's membership in a union that will bind Turkey to Europe. This is not as incongruous as it may seem. Preparing Turkey for membership in the EU may have been precisely the excuse that the pro-Islamic Justice and Development Party needed to clip the wings of the military and pave the way for a democratic Islamic state in Turkey. This prospect is very much on the mind of the military.

It is also a primary concern of Europeans. Muslim populations in Europe are already blamed for drugs, crime, high welfare costs, and soaring unemployment that now hovers around 10–12 percent in France and Germany. The EU expanded to an unwieldy twenty-five members in 2004, with Romania and Bulgaria poised to join in 2007. Turkey would follow at a date yet to be determined provided that it meets the criteria for membership as determined by a series of European evaluation commissions. That, at least, was the plan before France and the Netherlands rejected a proposed European Constitution in 2005. For the moment, immediate plans for expansion are on hold as the EU struggles to regain its focus. Both the EU and Turkey maintain that Turkish membership is on track, but the situation remains iffy. During the summer of 2005 a bitter debate took place in the European Commission, the executive agency of the EU, over the viability of the Turkish application for membership. Opponents of Turkish membership suggested that Turkey be granted some sort of secondary status in which Turkey's workers would be denied free access to Europe. Efforts to kill Turkey's application failed, but even optimists on the commission suggest that extended negotiations for full membership could take ten or fifteen years. The leaders of Europe's member states will have the final say, but they, too, have become increasingly pessimistic (*Guardian,* June 30, 2005). The Turkish question also became a key issue in the German elections of 2005. The ruling Democratic Socialist Party supported Turkish membership in the EU; the favored Christian Democratic Party vowed to kill it. The Turks, for their part, demand full status in the EU. If it happens, the impact of a European rejection of Turkey could be profound.

Other issues shaping Turkish policy in the era of terror include Iranian attempts to develop nuclear weapons and a resurgence of the PKK. Both are being watched very carefully.

## POLITICS IN TURKEY

The historical evolution of Turkey has produced a very complex society that is struggling to balance secularism with its Islamic faith, democracy with the desire for security, and statism with economic liberalization. All of these choices are linked to the most basic of questions: is Turkey European or is it Middle Eastern? In the remainder of the chapter we will examine the components of a Turkish political system that must reconcile these choices. As in earlier chapters this includes Turkey's political institutions, the actors that drive those institutions, and the broader cultural, economic, and international factors that shape both.

### The Political Institutions of Turkey

On the surface, Turkey resembles most other parliamentary democracies. Turks vote for members of parliament, the Grand National Assembly, at least once every five years. The election system is based on proportional representation with parties receiving seats in the Assembly in proportion to the popular vote. The only joker in this system is the requirement that a party receive 10 percent of the vote. If it doesn't, its share of seats in the Assembly will be divided among those that do make the grade. As noted above, only two parties passed the 10 percent bar in the 2002 elections: the Justice and Development Party (JDP) and the Republican People's Party. The JDP received 34.2 percent of the vote and gained a staggering 363 of the 550 seats in the Assembly. The RPP won the remainder.

Once the election is over, the members of parliament elect the prime minister. The prime minister is usually the head of the dominant party in the Assembly, but the choice is made by the president. As a practical matter, little is to be gained by not selecting the leader of the dominant party: without his or her support, the Assembly would become immobilized and nothing would get done. The prime minister then selects the members of the Council of Ministers. Collectively they are generally referred to as the Government, with a capital G. If the Government loses a vote of confidence in the Assembly, it resigns. The president may ask a leading member of the Assembly to form a new Government, but more often than not, the Assembly is dissolved and new elections are held. The prime minister also has the right to dissolve parliament and call new elections at the time of his or her choosing.

Following this script, the leader of the Justice and Development Party was elected prime minister following the 2002 elections, and his normal term will run until 2007. Rumors are rife, however, that he will call early elections to capitalize on a wave of popularity based on an improving economy and his strong stand against the U.S. The JDP denies this intent, but the prospect of extending its power until 2010 or 2011 is tempting (*Turkish Daily News,* June 19, 2005). A renewed popular mandate would clearly strengthen its position vis-à-vis the military. It would also enable the party to elect the next president of Turkey and give it complete control of the Turkish political system. This is a concern for both the military and the EU.

This scenario is very possible. The members of the Assembly elect the president of the republic for a seven-year term; an absolute two-thirds majority is required. The president is the head of state and "shall ensure the implementation of the Constitution, and the regular and harmonious functioning of the organs of the state" (Constitution, Article 104). Thinly veiled in this bland phrase is the ability to intervene if the Assembly becomes immobilized or strays too far from the secular path enshrined in the constitution. This is all the more significant because, as the constitution unabashedly declares, the president represents "the Supreme Military Command of the Turkish Armed Forces on behalf of the Turkish Grand National Assembly, [and has the power] to decide on the mobilization of the Turkish Armed Forces, to appoint the Chief of the General Staff, to call the National Security Council to meet and to preside over the National Security Council" (Constitution, Article 104). In sum, the military intervention in the political system has to come by way of the president. How different things could be if the JDP elects the next president of Turkey.

Presidents also play a substantial legislative role because they are required to sign legislation passed by the Assembly within fifteen days. If they do so, the legislation becomes law. They also have the option of sending the legislation back to the Assembly for further consideration. If the Assembly passes the legislation again, the president may allow it to become law unsigned, thereby expressing his or her displeasure. If the president vetoes the legislation, the legislation may be submitted to a national referendum. If the public approves the legislation, it becomes law. The president also appoints the justices of the Constitutional Court and other state agencies and may, if he so desires, chair the meetings of the cabinet.

Turkey's constitutional framework is rounded out by a Constitutional (Supreme) Court empowered to declare laws passed by the Grand National Assembly unconstitutional. It has not been reluctant to use this power in order to protect the secular nature of the Turkish state. When the Assembly legalized the wearing of head scarves in 2005, for example, the Constitutional Court promptly declared the new law unconstitutional and it was rejected by the president. Not only is the court an important branch of the Turkish government, it is also a bastion of secularism. This was to be expected, for its eleven members and four substitute members are appointed by the president from among senior judges on lower courts. These including the Council of State (head administrative court), the High Court of Appeals, the Military High Court of Appeals, the High Military Administrative Court, and the Audit Court. Judges serve until the mandatory retirement age of sixty-five. If the presidency slips from the hands of the secularists, the secular bias of the Constitutional Court could follow suit. Indeed, after the court rejected the head scarf law, the speaker of the Assembly rebuked it, suggesting that the Assembly had the power to abolish the Constitutional Court (*Turkish Daily News,* May 3, 2005). Lower levels of the justice system are less dramatic and are overtaxed, underfunded, and, according the Justice Ministry inspectors, lax in their implementation of long-standing legislation designed to reform the legal system (*Turkish Daily News,* May 20, 2005).

In addition to outlining the framework of the government, the constitution, a lengthy document of some seventy pages, outlines the rights of Turkey's citizens. By and large, these are the political rights listed in most constitutions; the numerous restrictive clauses have been eliminated to appease the European Union. The constitutional provision for State Security Courts, the major violator of human rights, was also annulled to please the EU. Amendments to the constitution are similar to other legislation, but require an absolute majority of the total membership of the Assembly. They become effective if signed by the president. If they aren't, they may be presented to the voters as a referendum.

How well does Turkey's parliamentary system work? Not well at all, according to the head of the Assembly's Constitutional Commission (*Turkish Daily News,* March 11, 2005). Coalition Governments (prime minister and Cabinet), the norm until recently, are weak and fragmented; they seldom stay the course for a full parliamentary term. Some last only a few months. Little gets done unless all ministers, who usually hold widely divergent views, can agree on everything (Ciftci, Forrest, and Tekin 2003). What one Government does, the next undoes.

The overwhelming majority currently enjoyed by the Justice and Development Party, by contrast, concentrates too much power in the hands of a single party and, in practice, a small handful of party leaders. The Turkish prime minister, in the view of the head of the Constitutional Commission, "has twice as much power than his British, German or Italian counterparts" (*Turkish Daily News,* March 11, 2005). The head of the commission urges a change to a presidential system similar to that of the United States in which power would be divided between the president and a legislature. Neither would be able to dominate the other. As if to underscore his point, he notes that the JDP holds a nearly two-thirds majority (66 percent) and thus could, if it so chose, rewrite the Turkish constitution and create a presidential system of government. He urges it to do so while it has the chance. The counterargument is that Turkey's earlier experiment with a bicameral parliament produced confusion and led to chaos. The debate goes on.

Be that as it may, Turkey's main divergence from the normal parliamentary pattern has been the shadowy presence of the military as an independent branch of government. The 1982 constitution formalized the power of the military to intervene in politics; as we have seen, it has done so on four occasions in the post–World War II era, most recently in 1997. It was the military's role in politics that made Turkey something less than a democracy. That has now been rectified, perhaps.

Also problematic is the scourge of corruption. High-ranking officials of past regimes are now fighting corruption charges. Eight were former ministers, one of whom was a prime minister (*Turkish Daily News,* March 6, 2005). Things are still being sorted out, but somewhere along the line $46 billion disappeared. The Republican People's Party, though not among the accused, chipped in by accusing the ruling Justice and Development Party of being "swamped" by corruption and using illegal means to stack the police and bureaucracy with its members. The JDP sharply denied these accusations, including some leveled at its members of parliament, and has vowed to uproot corruption of all varieties and at all levels (*Turkish Daily News,* Feb. 14, 2005). It is also clear that corruption exists at all levels of society, including the business community and the bureaucracy. In some cases, it has even been captured on TV (*Guardian,* Dec. 7, 2001). Charges against the police and military have been more timid.

All in all, the changing nature of Turkey's political institutions has made them more democratic and more humane. It is not clear that they have addressed the problem of corruption that is widely recognized as one of the major contributors to the growing disaffection of Turkey's citizens (Aliriza 2001). Much also remains to be done in the area of human rights. Laws have been passed, but it is not clear that they are being implemented. These and related problems may have more to do with the human factor in Turkish politics and are not easily addressed by simply passing laws.

**Elites**    The Turkish republic was crafted by Atatürk and his supporters in the military and the RPP. They were the elite. Atatürk's wishes had the force of law, and the closer one was to Atatürk and his circle of advisers, the more power one had. They created Turkey's political institutions to implement their vision of a modern, secular Turkey, and they changed those institutions at will. This has now changed. The last eighty years have seen Turkey evolve from a nation largely controlled by one man into a nation guided by laws and institutions. Elites still have the major voice in deciding who gets what, when, and how, but now they are subservient to Turkey's political institutions rather than standing above them. In the process, Turkey's elites have become increasingly pluralistic. An Islamic prime minister now shares power with military leaders committed to a secular Turkey. More and more, each checks the power of the other. In much the same manner, bureaucrats who long had a free hand in managing Turkey's economy now find their power balanced by the growing influence of the capitalist business elites. There also appears to be greater mobility both among and within the Turkish elites. The once dominant Republican People's Party, the bastion of the old Kemalist ideology, has been relegated to the position of an opposition party. Powerful leaders, as the trials of several ministers suggests, do fall from grace. In their wake, new political leaders from outside the "old school" are making their way into power, not the least of whom is Prime Minister Tayyip Erdogan, an individual from a working-class background. The situation is still evolving, but the changes seem to bode well for the future of Turkish democracy. The more elites differ, the more likely it is that they will provide the electorate with a meaningful choice of candidates and the more likely they are to listen to the views of the public.

Judging by their impact on policy making, today's key elites would be the prime minister, the president, and the chief justice of the Constitutional Court. In addition, cabinet ministers have extraordinary power in their respective areas.

The influence of the chief of staff and other key generals clearly gives them elite status. Their power may be less than it was in the days of yore, but their views are weighed carefully. Senior bureaucrats play a key role in shaping legislation, and an even greater role in determining the pace and success of its implementation. Footdragging by the bureaucracy ensures that the policies that they oppose will be implemented slowly, if at all. Bureaucratic elites, in the final analysis, can out-wait most political elites, most of whom have little specialized knowledge of how to get things done. Wishing does not make it so. Business elites have increased their power with privatization. Labor leaders have seen their influence decrease, but they remain key actors in the political system. Religious leaders in Turkey are less influential that in neighboring Islamic countries, but are watched with care by the military. This by itself testifies to their potential influence. The leaders of the main opposition parties also enjoy a modicum of influence, for who knows what the next elections will bring.

**Political Parties**   During the early years of the republic there was but one polit-ical party, the Republican People's Party. The 2002 elections, by contrast, were contested by more than eleven political parties, only two of which, the JDP and the RPP, managed to achieve the 10 percent required for representation in the Assembly. This was a dramatic change from the 1999 elections, the first following Turkey's most recent military intervention, in which five parties gained represen-tation in the Assembly. Does this mean that Turkey is evolving into a two-party political system, one religious and the other secular? The weaker parties have expressed this concern. For the present, it is just as likely that Turkey will slip back into a system of multiparty coalitions, none of which is capable of providing firm leadership.

To put the situation in perspective, it should be noted that Turkey's party system from the 1980s onward was characterized by exceptional fluidity. Parties formed, merged, fragmented, and re-formed with a different name or face. In-dividuals were often more important than ideology. A few claimed to be national parties, but many were linked to ethnic groups or regions of the country (Carkoglu 2002). Parties in power fared well in eras of economic prosperity but often saw their vote collapse when the economy faltered—which was often. The electorate was particularly volatile, with approximately one-fourth of Turkey's voters changing parties from one election to the next. In part, this was because the parties themselves had changed names. It also reflected deepening frustration with endemic corruption and the inability of the government to meet the needs of a large segment of the Turkish population. In some cases, popular parties were dissolved by the military.

The stunning victory of the JDP came as a shock to political observers. A full 50 percent of Turkish voters changed parties, considerably more than the earlier norm. Accordingly, any speculation on the future of the JDP requires a few words about the party and its constituency. The JDP claims to be a moderate Islamic party that combines concern for the poor with commitments to honest government, the EU, and economic reform (capitalism). All of this suggests that it is a slightly right-of-center party with a program not radically different from that of the Christian Democratic parties of Germany and Italy. Appearances, however, can be deceiving. Not all members of the party are as moderate as its leader and, like the Islamic Welfare Party of the 1990s, may push a vigorous Islamic agenda. Indeed, the JDP is already being accused of promoting its Islamic goals through its education policy and by appointing its supporters to the judiciary and the police. Its overriding of a presidential rejection of the bill lifting the ban on head scarves added to the fray (*Turkish Daily News,* July 3, 2005). Also problematic are the inherent contradictions within its program. Adopting the IMF's capitalist reforms almost always creates hardships for the poorer classes, which is where the JDP finds much of its support (Carkoglu 2002). The party also finds support among farmers accustomed to price supports for their produce and small firms accustomed to protection from foreign imports. Implementation of the IMF reform package would seriously affect both groups. Corruption in Turkey, moreover, is deeply entrenched. It is unrealistic to expect the JDP or any other party to eradicate corruption in the short run, especially during the new era of human rights. Unlike Atatürk, Turkey's new leaders must pursue the struggle against corruption via a sluggish court system. Even membership in the EU, which the JDP has pursued with apparent vigor, finds minimal support among JDP voters (Carkoglu 2002).

All of this suggests that the JDP may be cutting itself off from its support base. It also suggests that the future dominance of the JDP is far from being a foregone conclusion. This is all the more the case because the JDP's 34 percent of the vote in the 2002 elections was hardly a mandate. Its electoral victory also took place during an economic crisis, not to mention the turmoil surrounding the constitutional modifications required to bring Turkey in line with EU regulations. Circumstances during the next election may not be so favorable, and Turkey's large pool of floating voters could well shift to a new party with even grander promises of prosperity and honest government.

Be this as it may, the JDP won an even larger percentage of the vote in the 2003 local elections, 42 percent, a figure that it has maintained in 2005 opinion polls. There appear to be several explanations for the JDP's support. In general, the center of gravity of Turkey's voters is moving to the right (Carkoglu 2002). This benefits the JDP, the strongest party of the right. The JDP has also ridden the wave of anti-Americanism by frequent criticism of the U.S. administration and its pro-Kurdish policies. Much the same is true of Turkey's increasingly pro-Islamic stand on the enduring conflict between Israel and the Palestinians. Once a strong ally of Israel, Erdogan has referred to Ariel Sharon as a terrorist. This plays well among his traditional supporters, as do efforts to allow students from Turkey's Islamic high schools to enter Turkish universities without meeting the necessary requirements for secular course work. He backed away from these and similar policies when the military expressed its concern, but he had made his point with the Islamic constituency. At the more practical level, the JDP has managed to deliver on most of its promises. The economy has been stabilized and the poor have received free textbooks, with rumored cuts on consumer goods and cigarette taxes to follow (Rubin 2005). This is not a minor concern, for at least 50 percent of Turks smoke—more, if a casual stroll through the streets of Istanbul and Ankara is any indication. The JDP's ability to stabilize the economy while cutting taxes and increasing aid to the poor has some economists puzzled. Where is the money coming from? One answer is that it is coming from rich Gulf investors who want to promote Islam in Turkey (Rubin 2005).

The RPP, in contrast to the JDP, continues to represent Turkey's nationalistic and secular traditions. It has strong support in the military and bureaucracy as well as among much of the urban middle class and Turkey's substantial Shi'a minority estimated to constitute between 10 and 30 percent of the population. This should be sufficient to guarantee that it exceeds the 10 percent requirement for seats in the Assembly, but it is unlikely to return the RPP to its former status as Turkey's dominant party. The RPP has been beset by internal divisions over religious, economic, and personality issues, and like the JDP, a few of its members of parliament have resigned in protest and eventually joined one of the smaller parties. While the RPP and the JDP disagree on most things, both were annoyed by the symbolic defections and jointly passed a law depriving the smaller parties of state funding. Discussion of Turkey's remaining parties is beyond the scope of this chapter; new elections could easily bring a new champion. Much depends on the economy, as well as on Turkey's progress in gaining membership to the EU.

**Military and Civil-Military Relations**  Of Turkey's diverse interests, none is more powerful than the military. Recent constitutional amendments have softened its power, but a recent headline in the *Turkish Daily News* asked "Who wields the power?" (*Turkish Daily News,* March 27, 2005). The import of the short article was that the constitutional changes now make it possible to reduce the military's influence, but that Turkey has some way to go before that goal becomes a reality. As noted earlier, the military's constitutional right to intervene in Turkish politics has been modified to read that the president is the military's link to the Government. This is not standard fare in Western constitutions, and it is not clear that the opponents of Turkey's membership in the European Union are impressed.

Two main factors shape the influence of the military of Turkish politics. First is its vast size. In 2001, military personnel numbered 609,700 excluding the *jandarma* (rural police under partial military control), who add 528,000 to that figure. Land forces constitute the vast majority of the military: 495,000. The air force and the navy account for between 50,000 and 60,000 each, as do the commandos, with the Special Warfare Commandos adding another 20,000 (Turkish Government 2001a). The latter specialize in fighting the Kurds. All in all, Turkey possesses the second largest military in NATO; only that of the United States is larger. The U.S. is one of the world's wealthiest countries; Turkey is not. With a military budget of some $12 billion, little is left to go around. The military is opposed to any reduction in its budgetary allocation, claiming that it needs even more money to confront the political instability in Iraq. The Government is unwilling to challenge this assertion. It wasn't until recently, it will be recalled, that the Government had the right to know how the military was spending its vast budget.

Size alone does not explain the political influence of the military (Altinay 2004). It is also the most cohesive and disciplined organization in Turkey. The military shares a common commitment to Atatürk's vision of a secular and Westernized Turkey and it views itself as the guardian of Turkey's secularism. The cohesion of the military and its zealous pursuit of secularism is explained by the fact that the Turkish officer corps is a self-perpetuating elite that derives most of its members from the military and bureaucratic establishments (Library of Congress 1995; Momayezi, n.d.). Indoctrination is intense and continuous. If some Turkish officers differ from the official view, they don't say so publicly. Ground troops are mostly peasants.

In addition to shaping Turkish politics from behind the scenes, senior military leaders have also been vocal in discussing public issues. The chief of the General Staff, for example, recently declared, among other things, that Turkey is not an Islamic state and that the nation will resist any attempts to make it one. Strong support was given to the Turkish government on Cyprus, the U.S. was criticized for being soft on Kurds, and Armenia was chastised for attempting to blemish Turkey's reputation internationally by talking about the massacres (*Turkish Daily News,* April 23, 2005). Strong stuff indeed. The police are distinct from the military, and subject to greater influence by the ruling party (Ozcan and Gultekin 2000).

**Bureaucracy and Politics in Turkey**  The Turkish bureaucracy is a massive affair officially charged with implementing the laws of the land in an honest, efficient, and impartial manner. Unfortunately, the bureaucracy is none of the above. By and large, its political views reflect the Kemalist vision of a secular and Western Turkey. Policies that support those views are facilitated; others are delayed, often until a new Government is in office. This is particularly true of the bureaucracy's role as guardian of Kemal's statist tradition of government interference in the economy, a role that provides it with both power and growing opportunities for corruption. Turkey's shift to capitalism threatens the bureaucracy's power and is being resisted. Finally, it should be noted that the Turkish bureaucracy is a bloated apparatus that absorbs much of the budget left behind by the military. The IMF has demanded that it be severely trimmed, but that would be politically unpopular. The Turkish bureaucracy is also a very effective pressure group that knows how to protect its interests.

## Pressures and Interests: The Core of Civil Society

While most of the headlines focus on elections and political parties, many of the key actors in the Turkish political arena are barred from participation in partisan politics or are technically banned from the political process all together. All have a profound influence on Turkish politics.

**Islamic Interests and the Re-Islamization of Turkey**  Turkey's Islamic revival has been discussed throughout this chapter and needs little elaboration other than to note that Islamic sentiments are far from homogeneous. While some groups incline toward extremism, the vast majority are moderate. Nevertheless, Turkey is now ruled by an avowedly Islamic party for the second time in a decade. Mosques and religious schools flourish as do Sufi (dervish) groups and student organizations. Indeed, many were encouraged during the 1970s by Turkey's secular government as a counterweight to communist and other leftist groups. Once the left was crushed, Islamic groups represented the only broad-based opposition to a Kemalist tradition tarnished by corruption, oppression, and economic crises. This does not mean that Turkey is on the verge of becoming an Islamic state, but it does mean that religion has taken root among the populace and will become an increasingly potent force in elections to come. This is all the more the case because rural migration has brought popular Islam to the cities.

The Justice and Development Party is nudging the process along, but not at a pace likely to provoke a military reaction. The wife and daughter of the prime minister wear head scarves to official functions, and the Assembly has recently passed a law providing imams (clergy) for the some 23,532 mosques that lack them. This, the Government argued, was essential to prevent unqualified and potentially inflammatory imams from filling these positions. Perhaps the greatest threat to the Islamic revival comes from the Islamic movement itself. If violent jihadist groups such as the Turkish Hezbollah gain a following, the military will intervene. This, however, has yet to happen.

The Turkish government attempts to keep an eye on Islamic groups and institutions by requiring them to register with Religious Affairs Directorate. Sermons in Turkish mosques are prepared by the Supreme Board of Religious Affairs, a supposedly impartial board affiliated with the Religious Affairs Directorate (*Turkish Daily News,* March 26, 2005). The official sermons stress Turkey's democratic and secular traditions, but it is not clear how these themes are presented by more traditional imams. Monitoring tens of thousands of preachers, as we saw in the discussion of Egyptian politics, is a difficult task. It would be unrealistic to assume that Turkey's imams and religious teachers are as moderate as its ruling party.

**Minorities**    Aside from Christians, Turkey doesn't recognize religious or ethnic minorities. The last census to acknowledge their existence was conducted in 1965. All subsequent estimates of population size are based upon these estimates and rates of presumed population growth. As a result, claims of population size vary widely. Ethnic minorities probably constitute at least 15 percent of the Turkish population, probably more. Of these, the Kurds are by far the largest. Their efforts to assert ethnic uniqueness have been met with force. The Alevi, according to the Turkish press, constitute about one-fifth of Turkey's 70 million citizens. Their efforts to assert their uniqueness have been met with indifference.

The Alevi are Turkish Shi'a and share some similarities with the Alawi sect discussed at length in the discussion of Syrian politics (Chapter 4). Turkey is also home to other Shi'a sects, but it has become common practice among Sunni Turks to refer to all Shi'a as Alevi. The Alevi have traditionally been strong supporters of Turkish secularism, presumably because secularism provides their best guarantee against oppression by Turkey's Sunni majority. Outbreaks of Sunni–Alawi violence in 1993 and 1995 led to growing unease among Turkish

Alevi as well as heightened cultural awareness. Alevi community organizations have strengthened apace. The Alevi also have their own political parties and have petitioned the government to acknowledge Alevi Islam in school books, to train Alevi prayer leaders, and to provide funding for the Federation of Alevi Foundations. The Alevi do not pose the threat of violence, but they have threatened to take their complaints to the European Court of Human Rights (*Turkish Daily News,* June 22, 2005). Other Turkish minorities include Arabs, Jews, Christians of various denominations, and a variety of small ethnic groups, including Armenians. Their political relevance is minimal.

**The Kurds**    The Kurdish struggle for independence has been a dominant theme in Turkish politics since the outbreak of PKK violence in 1984, some six years after the organization was founded. The Kurds, as discussed in Chapter 6, are a large ethnic group of some 20 million members that occupies a broad area of southern Turkey, northern Iraq, and adjacent areas in Syria, Iran, and the former Soviet Union. The early negotiations following World War I promised an independent Kurdistan, but that provision was dropped from the final peace treaty. Atatürk refused to recognize Turkey's Kurds as a separate ethnic group and launched a program of forced Turkification (assimilation). Kurds were referred to as Mountain Turks or Eastern Turks and the speaking of Kurdish in public was cause for arrest.

Restrictions on the Kurds eased during Turkey's transition to democracy, and a variety of Kurdish groups emerged to assert the Kurdish claim for recognition as a distinct ethnic group. Most would flourish, only to be banned by the government during periods of crisis. Speaking Kurdish in public is no longer against the law, but as late as the mid-1990s, Kurdish prison inmates were required to speak to their lawyers in Turkish (Library of Congress 1995).

PKK violence has abated for the moment, but fears of renewed Kurdish demands for independence surged with the U.S. invasion of Iraq and the prospect of an independent Kurdish state. Kurdish parties were again banned. The Turkish government claims that the vast majority of its Kurdish citizens do not support separation, but acknowledge that the influence of Kurdish "fanatics" is increasing (*Turkish Daily News,* April 7, 2005).

The political impact of the persistent tension between Turks and Kurds is profound. The Kurdish drive for independence is the major source of political violence in Turkey and a major justification for increases in the military budget. It also confronts Turkey with the very real prospect that the emergence of a Kurdish state in Iraq will fuel new Kurdish rebellions in Turkey. Stringent military measures to prevent this have brought ringing condemnations from human rights groups and soured relations between Turkey and the United States. The EU, too, has been critical of Turkish handling of its Kurdish problem. The military, for its part, is determined to prevent the dismemberment of the Turkish state.

**Business and Labor**    After the end of World War II, the Istanbul business community convinced the government to broaden the scope of the private sector in Turkey's development plans. The move was supported by the dominant parties of the era, and the influence of business groups would increase over time. It has become a rush with the liberalization of the Turkish economy demanded by the EU and the International Monetary Fund. Turkey possesses the same array of business groups as most countries. At the top are the Union of Chambers of Commerce and Industry and the Society of Turkish Industrialists. The latter represents larger firms that are better able to compete with the increasing competition from foreign firms and has been a strong supporter of economic liberalization. The former inclines toward smaller companies that are less able to compete globally and are less anxious to see the liberalization of protective tariffs (*Turkish Daily News,* Jan. 11, 2005).

Turkish workers were granted the right to form unions in 1947, albeit without the right to strike or become involved in politics. With the growth in Turkey's industrial base, the unions become increasingly relevant and the dominant parties actively courted their support. The Confederation of Turkish Labor Unions (Türk-Is) was formed in the early 1950s with support from the International Confederation of Trade Unions, but remained weak. The right to strike was promised, but not enacted for another decade.

Türk-Is was later joined by a rival, the Confederation of Revolutionary Trade Unions (DISK), a leftist organization that played a prominent role in the political turmoil of the late 1970s. Strikes escalated, and in 1980 DISK members occupied factories and engaged in pitched battles with the security forces. DISK was banned after the military coup of the same year.

Business groups have strengthened with the transition to privatization. The labor unions have suffered accordingly. Government firms were overstaffed and demanded little of workers. The management of the privatized firms demands fewer workers and greater productivity. The resulting tension provoked strikes and some violence throughout Turkey, but to no avail. International pressure for greater privatization remains inexorable (*Turkish Daily News,* Feb. 17, 20, and 26, 2005).

**Students and Politics**    Students throughout the Middle East are the most volatile segment of society and are invariably the first to protest what they perceive to be the injustices of the government. If their uprisings aren't crushed, political, labor, ethnic, and religious radicals soon join the fray. Turkey is no exception. Student protests and violence during the 1950s precipitated the military coup of 1960. The crisis passed, and to alleviate further tensions the students were granted more rights including the designation of universities as autonomous entities. Conciliation opened the door to ideological conflicts of all varieties, including the birth of the PKK. Armed clashes among student groups were common, and precipitated the coup of 1980. Conciliation gave way to repression. The government reasserted its control over the universities and purged radical professors and anyone else who opposed the Kemalist vision of a secular Turkey. Student activism revived during the 1990s, but was dampened again by the 1997 military intervention. A bill offering amnesty to some 675,000 students expelled from Turkish universities since 2000 has passed the Assembly and is currently tied up in the Constitutional Court (*Turkish Daily News,* March 4, 2005). The head of the Higher Education Board, the agency responsible for regulating Turkey's higher education system, has lamented the distrust between the government and the universities (*Turkish Daily News,* May, 21, 2005). In the meantime, some 1.7 million high school students are sitting for national exams that will determine their future.

**Women and Social Groups**   The situation of Turkish women provides a graphic illustration of the tension between tradition and modernity that permeates most areas of Turkish life. The Turkish Constitution guarantees women full political and social rights and a 2001 amendment to the Turkish legal code established their total equality with men. Women abound in Turkish universities, and represent a key component of the Turkish labor force. As in most countries, professional women in Turkey are expected to have better qualifications than males and to work harder for less (*Flying Broom,* Jan. 4, 2005). Turkish women are less active in politics, but their participation is increasing. On average, women constitute about 5 to 7 percent of party election lists and are valued for their ability to get out the female vote. They play a lesser role in decision making and are often controlled by male party leaders (Keskin 1997). This said, Turkey has had a female prime minister who took a back seat to no one.

In sharp contrast to "modern" Turkey, some 40 percent of the marriages in the south and southeast of the country are arranged, a figure that drops to 22 percent in Ankara, the capital. Amnesty International claims that one-third of Turkish women are subjected to domestic violence by family members, and accused the Turkish government of severe laxity in enforcing laws designed to protect women (*Guardian,* June 2, 2004). Honor killings remain common among rural populations including rural migrants to Turkey's major cities, although statistics are vague on such matters. The Turkish government has responded to these charges by noting that it had made great progress in addressing the problem. It also acknowledged that "much more needed to be done" (*Guardian,* June 2, 2004). The president of the Turkish Women's Union claims that 90 percent of Turkish women are abused at least psychologically and economically, and accused the government of consciously discouraging the education of women (*Turkish Daily News,* May 22, 2005). She also had strong words for Turkish television serials, which she said portrayed traditional roles for women. Members of the EU Parliament announced that they intend to monitor the situation very closely (*Turkish Daily News,* July 7, 2005). No doubt, their reports will offer yet more ammunition for the opponents of Turkish admission to the EU.

Turkey possessed some 211 women's organizations during the mid-1990s. Some are loose affiliates of Turkey's diverse political parties. Others include charities and mutual assistance groups designed to address the problems of abused women. The problem, however, is not easily solved. A large poll of some 8,000 women conducted by Hacettepe University (Ankara) found that 39 percent of the women surveyed believed that husbands may have a legitimate right for violence against their wives. Obviously, such attitudes can only be changed with education. Reasonable cause for violence, according to the respondents, included "refusal to have sex, neglecting the children, thriftless behavior, contradicting their husbands, and burning the dinner" (BBC, Oct. 22, 2004).

The resurgence of Islam has also clouded the issue, a dilemma that came to the fore with the head scarf issue. Many well-educated women view religion as an essential component of a just and moral society. If women want to wear head scarves, a legitimate expression of their piety, so be it. Ironically, secular female activists now find themselves defending the head scarf as a women's rights issue. Women, in their view, must have the right to make that choice. To complicate the issue even further, religious schools banned the wearing of head scarves in order to preclude a backlash from a military establishment antagonistic to religious schools. Islamic education was more important than the right to wear head scarves.

**Guest Workers**    Another social group of interest is the large body of Turkish workers who migrated to Germany and other countries of Western Europe during the economic boom of the 1960s. Germany needed workers and the Turks were welcomed. Initially, most were males who stayed for a relatively short period of time and then returned to Turkey. As the years passed, they stayed longer and brought their families. Many became permanent residents in Germany. Either way, remittances from the guest workers became an important component of the Turkish economy. Rural Turks invested in tractors and other agricultural equipment that played a crucial role in transforming and modernizing Turkish agriculture. Other funds sent from abroad were invested in small businesses and otherwise represented an economic boom for the guest workers' extended families.

Despite the Turkish workers' efforts to acquire German citizenship, their integration into German society remained tenuous (Kastoryano 2002). The welcome of the 1960s and 1970s faded with the downturn of the German economy and the reunification of East and West Germany in 1990. Suddenly Germany was awash in unemployed East German workers, and guest workers were blamed for unemployment rates well above the 10 percent mark. Neo-Nazi violence against Turks mounted, and even the moderate press associated the guest workers with crime, drugs, and terrorism.

For their part, the Turkish guest workers tended to associate with other Turks and to remain more attuned to the politics of Turkey than the politics of Germany. As within Turkey itself, their attitudes seem to polarize along secular and religious lines. Many saw German democracy and industrial power as a model of what Turkey should be. Others reverted to their Islamic traditions. Still others prefer a synthesis of Islam and modernity (Schiffauer 2002). The appearance of head scarves increased tensions between Germans and the Turkish community and several German states (*länder*) have banned the wearing of head scarves in schools. All three trends have found expression in Turkish politics with fundamentalist currents in Germany being accused of fueling the Islamic revival in Turkey (Rubin 2005).

**Public Opinion**    In addition to voting in elections at both the local level, Turkish citizens are also polled regularly about a variety of topics. A recent international poll that included both Europe and select countries in the Islamic world addressed a variety of questions that have been discussed in this chapter. They are summarized in Table 8.1. Other polls found strong support for membership in the

**T A B L E   8.1   Common Concerns of Turkish Citizens**

| Question | Yes% | No% | NR% |
|---|---|---|---|
| Is Islamic extremism a threat to Turkey? | 47 | 34 | 19 |
| Violence against civilian targets is justified? | 14 | 6 | 66 |
| Democracy can work here? | 48 | | |
| Islam plays a large role in political life? | 62 | | |
| Favorable views toward Christians? | 21 | 63 | |
| Favorable views toward Jews? | 18 | 60 | |
| Favorable views toward Muslims? | 83 | 11 | |
| Should head scarves be banned? | 29 | 64 | |

SOURCE: Pew Global Attitudes Project, 2005

European Union, but expressed substantial anti-Americanism. About half of the respondents believed that Turkey was surrounded by enemy countries (*Turkish Daily News,* March 28, 2005.)

## Is Turkey a Civil Society?

Is Turkey a democratic civil society? The answer is a qualified yes ( Jacoby 2004; White 2002). Political parties and political interest groups abound and the press is free, though reluctant to criticize the military. As the citations throughout this chapter suggest, bad news is presented with the good. Elections since 1997 have been free and fair. Those elected, including the pro-Islamic Justice and Development Party, have been allowed to take office, and they do rule. All of this bodes well for the future of Turkish democracy. Clouds, however, remain on the horizon. The most obvious of these is Turkey's long history of military intervention and the military's continuing influence on the political process. Also problematic is the nature of the groups that constitute the base of Turkey's civil society. While many are democratic, others incline to violence or favor an Islamic state. To date, however, the dominance of a moderate pro-Islamic party has not harmed Turkish democracy. Indeed, it may have softened latent tensions that have been simmering for decades. The Islamic resurgence is not going away and the existence of a viable Islamic party of moderate social views is probably the best way to isolate the religious extremists (Palmer and Palmer 2004).

## THE CONTEXT OF TURKISH POLITICS

While elites, parties, and groups dominate Turkey's decision-making process, much of the impetus for these decisions comes from a broad range of cultural, economic, and international factors. Not the least of these are the Islamic revival, a never-ending series of economic crises, and the pervasive influence of the EU.

## Political Culture and Political Behavior: Kemalism versus Islam

Cultural influences are never far below the surface of Turkish politics. The low levels of political participation among females, for example, is generally attributed to a traditional political culture that stresses the subservience of women and discourages political involvement (Keskin 1997). Cultural traditions also condone violence against women, and laws to the contrary are not seriously enforced by local authorities. As noted above, many women accept male dominance as the natural order of things. Attitudes toward women have clearly changed, but not as rapidly as one might expect in a country that has an eighty-year history of secularism and legal equality.

This, however, is not the case with attitudes toward female participation in the workplace. Two family incomes are becoming an economic necessity, and education now enhances a woman's marriageability in many areas of Turkey. Governments have jumped on the bandwagon by paying girls to go to school. The laws of economics are succeeding where the laws of the government have failed.

Atatürk's efforts to replace Turkey's Islamic traditions with those of the West have similarly encountered considerable opposition and backsliding. This is not to say that they have failed. Rather, they have polarized Turkish political culture into Islamic and Western camps. Most Turks probably fall between the two extremes, preferring a political environment that blends democracy and prosperity with Islamic moral values. The RPP and the Justice and Development Party currently symbolize the two poles of Turkish political culture, the Islamic and the secular. The moderation of both parties has been dictated by a desire to capture the large number of Turkish voters who are looking for a middle ground. The EU's worries aside, moderate Islam, at least as practiced in Turkey, has demonstrated that it is compatible with democracy. Whether or not the Islamic–secular dichotomy can provide the basis for a stable two-party political system remains to be seen.

Turkish nationalism, another of the key elements in Atatürk's efforts to modernize Turkish society, has taken root (Keyman and Icduygu 2005). Turks are very nationalistic. Some, especially the military, adhere to the secular nationalism envisioned by Atatürk, as do a spate of right-wing extremist groups (Akgun 2002). For most Turks, however, Turkish nationalism is colored by the glories of Turkey's Islamic past and a protective concern for their faith. Few see the need to distinguish between the two. A pervasive anti-Americanism has been fueled by both. U.S. efforts to intimidate Turkey into supporting the U.S.-led attack on Iraq were widely resented, as is the unfortunate appearance that the U.S. has declared war on Islam. The prospect of a U.S.-condoned Kurdistan in northern Iraq has added more fuel to the fire.

Finally, we should note that Atatürk's vision of a statist economy produced cultural repercussions that continue to pose problems for his heirs. Part of the legacy was the creation of a massive government sector that suffers from the lethargy of most socialist organizations. Wages are low, security high, and incentives for innovation and hard work minimal—hardly a prescription for solving Turkey's economic crises.

A second aspect of the problem is a dependence on the government. Atatürk, father of the Turks, established an intensely centralized political system that blended patriarchal and military authority. The leader was a wise and caring father responsible for guiding his flock along the path of modernity. The state provided and the military ensured that Turkey's citizens followed orders. Just as Turks learned nationalism, so they learned to be dependent on the state for their basic needs. That formula no longer works in an era of global competition.

Dependence on the government, moreover, does not necessarily translate into support for the government. According to government reports, some 74 percent of Turks evade their taxes (Rubin 2005). They have also evaded most of the regulations designed to regulate corruption and otherwise transform Turkey into a secular state. The Assembly is debating ways to transform the "Turkish psyche" in order to make it more European; not the least of the measures being considered are fines on behavior that endangers public health and safety (*Turkish Daily News,* March 20, 2005).

## Political Economy

Economics influences Turkish politics in the same way that it influences politics throughout the world. Leaders are praised when the economy is strong and condemned when it is weak. Low wages and unemployment breed frustration and are blamed for alienation, political violence, crime, and drugs. In the case of Turkey, an endless series of economic crises have also been blamed for the volatility of its political system and the resurgence of Islamic sentiments (Öni,s and Rubin 2003). If secular leaders can't solve Turkey's problems, so the logic goes, perhaps a religious party can. At least they are compassionate and will fight corruption. This logic seems to be supported by a large floating block of voters who shift from party to party in the hope that someone can find a solution for Turkey's economic problems.

Turkey has survived its economic crises by borrowing money from the International Monetary Fund, but that, too, comes at a cost. The IMF has been increasing its pressure on Turkey to cure the causes of its malaise, most of which the IMF attributes to the unproductive nature of Turkey' numerous state-owned industries, excessive tariffs, overregulation by a predatory bureaucracy that consumes exorbitant resources, and mounting welfare costs including subsidies of basic necessities (*Economist,* A Survey of Turkey, March 19, 2005). All, according to the IMF, must be trimmed; only in this way will Turkey's citizens increase their productivity and break their dependency on the state.

Such stark measures pose the threat of increased unemployment and escalating political tensions. They also portend an increase in Islamic religious sentiments. As things currently stand, 82 percent of the poor, about 25 percent of the Turkish population, are not covered by social security (*Turkish Daily News,* May 20, 2005). Recent governments have attempted to walk a fine line between alleviating poverty and pleasing the IMF. Progress on enacting the IMF reforms has been steady, but not as rapid as the IMF, or the EU, would like. The rich have prospered; the poor have not.

The pace of reform has picked up under the pro-Islamic JDP, and the economy appears to have stabilized, despite growing military expenditures and the willingness of the Islamic government to lower taxes and provide more services to the poor. The popularity of the Islamic government has increased accordingly. The business community is pleased. The Prophet Mohammed was a merchant and Islam is not opposed to capitalism. As in the United States, the religious right and the economic right have worked out a harmonious relationship that benefits both. The military remains nervous.

The ability of Turkey's Islamic government to stabilize the economy while simultaneously lowering taxes and increasing welfare spending has provoked a serious question. Where is the money coming from? Part of it is coming from the remittances of Turkish workers in Germany and other western European countries, much of which is carried by hand and not recorded in government statistics. Other funds are reportedly provided by large business conglomerates linked to various Islamic organizations. Still other funds are provided by rich Gulf Arabs who want to promote Islam in Turkey. This so-called "green money"—green is the symbolic color of Islam—helps the Justice and Development Party stabilize the Turkish economy, provide welfare, reduce taxes, and simultaneously expand the reach of its political apparatus (Rubin 2005). This is murky stuff, and Turkish colleagues view these claims with skepticism. Nevertheless, they are a source of worry to the military. They also worry Israelis who fear that the price of "green money" is a reduction in Turkish support for the Jewish state.

## International Interdependence

In economics as well as politics, then, Turkey is hostage to a bewildering array of foreign pressures. Most have been discussed at length throughout the chapter and will simply be listed at this point to illustrate just how intimately Turkish politics is tied to its foreign environment (Ismael and Aydin 2003).

Heading the list is Turkish desire for membership in the European Union. EU membership would make Turkey European and is widely perceived as the ultimate solution to Turkey's economic and political problems. So great is the allure of EU membership that Turkey has gone to extraordinary lengths to bring its political and economic system into conformity with EU guidelines. It has also subjected itself to the humiliation of endless EU commissions sent to evaluate its progress in everything from banking policy to human rights. Whatever the Turks do, the EU seems to want more. Membership in the EU would be the fulfillment of Atatürk's dream. Rejection by the EU, on the other hand, could have a profoundly destabilizing impact on Turkey. This is a very real possibility. For the moment, however, both sides are keeping the dream alive.

Pulling in the opposite direction is the war in Iraq and Turkish fears that a Kurdish republic will be established in northern Iraq (Uslu, Toprak, Dalmis, and Aydin 2005). Turkey has accused the U.S. of promoting Kurdish autonomy, a charge denied by a U.S. administration that insists that Iraq will remain a unified country governed from Baghdad. What Turkey fears and the U.S. refuses to admit is the possibility that the Kurds will seize power in the north once the U.S. leaves. This would raise the very real prospect of a Turkish invasion, possibly with the support of an Iraqi government intent of preserving its control of Iraq's massive oil revenues. Turkish troops are already on the border, and the precedent for such cooperation was well established by Saddam Hussein. Such an invasion would probably scuttle Turkey's aspirations for EU membership and draw Turkey ever deeper into the morass of Middle Eastern politics.

The unstable situation in Iraq also offers the very real prospect of an Iraqi government guided by Shi'a religious leaders with close ties to Iran, a subject discussed in Chapters 6 and 7. Whether a pro-Islamic government in Iraq would stimulate Islamic currents in Turkey remains to be seen. Iran has supported Islamic movements in Sunni countries in the past. Turkey's military is far more concerned about this possibility than is the ruling JDP. Iran's rush to develop nuclear weapons is a concern to both. A nuclear Iran would tip the region's balance of power in favor of Iran.

Tensions between Turkey and the United States are very real, but neither side seems inclined to jeopardize a long history of mutual cooperation (Robins 2003). The U.S. no longer needs Turkey as a counterweight to the Soviet Union, but it does look to Turkey as an important stabilizing force in a region beset by fundamentalism and terrorism (Ismael and Aydin 2003). Crucial to this endeavor is the three-way alliance between Turkey, Israel, and the U.S. that has endured for several decades (Altunisik 2000; Bengio 2004; Olson 2001). Turkey may be critical of Israel's treatment of the Palestinians, but it does conduct joint military maneuvers with Israel and is a major purchaser of Israeli weapons. Turkey, for its part, sees little to gain by being at odds with the world's leading economic and military power. Well over fifty military and economic agreements bind the two countries, and that situation is unlikely to change as long as Turkey's efforts to join the EU remain in limbo.

Lesser regional concerns include Syria and Cyprus. Syria poses no military threat to Turkey, and relations between the two countries improved dramatically once Syria stopped supporting the PKK. Indeed, Turkey has flaunted its new friendship with Syria as a signal to Washington that it is irritated with America's policies in Iraq. While the U.S. is attempting to overthrow the Ba'athist regime, Turkey is standing at Syria's side. Some tensions remain between Syria and Turkey, mainly because of Syria's long-standing claim to the Alexandretta region of Turkey and because Turkey is intent on damming river networks critical to Syria's water supply. The same tensions over water exist between Turkey and Iraq.

Cyprus is more a matter of national pride than anything else. Turkey intervened to protect the interests of Cyprus's Turkish population and cannot back down without losing face. Greece supports the Greek Cypriots, but is too weak to challenge Turkey militarily. The main cost of the Cyprus situation is its negative impact on Turkey's application for membership in the EU.

## LOOKING TOWARD THE FUTURE

Turkey's future will be shaped by the fate of its application for full membership in the European Union more than by any other single factor. Turkey is attempting to bring itself in line with European expectations, but the picture remains clouded. Europe remains concerned about issues of human rights, the pace of economic liberalization, the fear of Turkish workers inundating Europe, Islamic fundamentalism, terrorism, and the issues of Cyprus and Kurdistan. Adding to the confusion is a clear European bias against Muslims and the shock to the EU posed by the defeat of its proposed constitution. Many Europeans believe that the EU is already too large and too diverse to operate as an effective unit. Whatever the case, it will be the EU that decides whether Turkey will be European or will remain torn between its European and Middle Eastern heritages. In the meantime, Turkey is likely to continue on its course of fusing its religious and secular traditions in a democratic framework that blends moderate Islam with economic liberalization.

# References

Aarts, Paul, and Gerd Nonneman, eds. 2005. *Saudi Arabia in the Balance: Political Economy, Society, Foreign Affairs.* New York: New York University Press.

Abboushi, W. F. 1985. *The Unmaking of Palestine.* Wisbech, Cambridgeshire, England: Middle East & North African Studies Press.

Abdulhamid, Anmar. 2005 (June 22). "For Syrian Optimists, Now Is the Time to Reconsider." *Daily Star* (Lebanon; www.dailystar.com.lb).

Abdel-Latif, Omayma. 2000 (Nov.). "Dreaming of Better Times." *Al-Ahram Weekly Online*, Issue 509.

Abdo, Geneive. 1999. "Electoral Politics in Iran." *Middle East Policy* 6(4): 128.

Abdou, Johnny. 1999. *Al Assad: Strategy, Independence* (in Arabic). Paris: S. Abdou.

Abdullah, Ali. 2004 (June 27). "Forbidding Kurdish Parties a Step Away from Inclusion" (in Arabic). Al-Jazeera: www.aljazeera.net. Accessed Aug. 14, 2004.

Abedin, Mahan. 2005. "The Dangers of Silencing Saudi Dissent." *Asia Times Online*: www.atimes.com.

Abir, Mordechai. 1993. *Saudi Arabia: Government, Society, and the Gulf Crises.* London: Routledge.

Aburish, Said. 1994. *The Rise, Corruption, and Coming Fall of the House of Saud.* London: Bloomsbury.

Aflaq, Michel. 1963. *The Struggle of the Common Destiny* (in Arabic). Damascus: Dar el-Adaab.

Afrasiabi, Kaveh L. 2004 (Dec. 16). "How Iran Will Fight Back." *Asia Times Online*: www.atimes.com.

Agence France Presse. 2005 (Oct. 29). "Israeli Aircraft Kills Palestinian Militant in Gaza." *Daily Star* (Lebanon; www.dailystar.com.lb).

Ahmad, Ahmad Yousef. 1984. "The Dialectics of Domestic Environment and Role Performance: The Foreign Policy of Iraq." In *The Foreign Policies of Arab States* (147–174), ed. Bahgat Korany and Ali E. Hillal Dessouki. Boulder, CO: Westview Press.

Ajami, F. 1992. *The Arab Predicament.* 2nd ed. Cambridge: Cambridge University Press.

Akgun, Birol. 2002 (March). "Twins or Enemies: Comparing Nationalist and Islamist Traditions in Turkish Politics." *Middle East Review of International Affairs Journal* 6(1): http://meria.idc.ac.il.

Al-Anaani, Khalil. 2004 (Dec. 30). "The Sunni and Shia and the Iraqi Elections: To Where?" (in Arabic). Al-Jazeera: www.aljazeera.net. Accessed on Jan. 7, 2005.

Al-Ahram Survey. 1998 (June). *Public Opinion Survey: Preliminary Results* (in Arabic). Cairo: Al-Ahram Center for Political and Strategic Studies.

Al-Angari, Haifa. 1997. *The Struggle for Power in Arabia*. Reading, UK: Ithaca Press.

Al-Baiya'nooni, Ali Sadr Eddin. 2001 (Nov. 29). "The Political Future of the Making of the Brotherhood in Syria" (in Arabic). Al-Jazeera Broadcast on July 7, 1998: www.aljazeera.net. Ahmed Mansour, moderator.

Al-Bana, Akram. 2003 (Jan. 23). "Reading the Reality and Results of the Syrian Elections" (in Arabic). Al-Jazeera Online: www.aljazeera.net.

Al-Fatah, Sadeq Abdo. 1990. *Nights and Caprices of Farouk* (in Arabic). Cairo: Library Madbouli.

Al-Freih, Mohammed. 1995. *The Historical Background of the Emergence of Muhammad Ibn 'Abd al-Wahhab and His Movement*. Ann Arbor, MI: UMI Dissertation Information Service.

Al-Gosaibi, Abdul Rahman. 1998. *My Life in Administration* (in Arabic). Beirut: Arab Organization for Studies and Publishing.

Al-Hadidi, Salah Addin. 1984. *Witness to the Yemen War* (in Arabic). Cairo: Library Madbouli.

Al-Haroub, Khalid, moderator. 2003 (July 15). "Secularism in the Arab World" (in Arabic). Al-Jazeera Broadcast. Published at www.aljazeera.net on Jan. 10. 2005. Accessed Feb. 21, 2005.

Al-Haroub, Khalid. 2005 (Jan. 10). "The Democratic Choice in Syria" (in Arabic). Al-Jazeera Online: www.aljazeera.net.

Al-Hashimi, Tarig, and Ahmed Barak. 2005 (Jan. 2). "Diverse Positions on Iraq's Elections" (in Arabic). Mohammed Abd Al-Azim, moderator. Al-Jazeera Online: www.aljazeera.net.

*Al-Hawadith*. 1998 (Nov. 27). "Syria on the Door of the 7th Legislative Session" (in Arabic), 30–34.

Aliriza, Bulent. 2001 (March 5). "Turkey Crisis: Corruption at the Core." Washington, DC: Turkey Update, Turkey Project, Center for Strategic and International Studies (www.csis.org).

Al-Iyash, Esam. 1998a (Nov. 20). "Desert Thunder in the Fridge and the Alternative Is Assassinations and a Military Coup" (in Arabic). *Al-Hawadith*, 18–25.

Al-Iyash, Esam. 1998b (Nov. 27). "Qusai Guardian of the Regime and Uday Contractor of the Dollars" (in Arabic). *Al-Hawadith*, 18–22.

Allam, Abeer. 2000. "Less Work, More Play for State Bureaucrats." *Middle East Times*, 2: www.metimes.com/2K/issue2000–2/eg/less_work.htm.

Allan, J. A. 1997. "'Virtual Water': A Long-Term Solution for Water-Short Middle Eastern Economies?" *An Occasional Paper*. London: SOAS (www.soas.ac.uk/waterissues/occasionalpapers/OCC03.PDF).

Allan, J. A. 1999. "Water in International Systems: A Risk/Society Analysis of Regional Problems." *An Occasional Paper*. London: SOAS (www.soas.ac.uk/waterissues/occasionalpapers/OCC22.PDF).

Allan, Tony (J. A.). 2001. *The Middle East Water Question.* London: I. B. Tauris.

Allport, Gordon W. 1954. *The Nature of Prejudice.* Cambridge, MA: Addison-Wesley.

Al-Manoufi. 1979. *The Changing Political Culture of the Egyptian Village* (in Arabic). Cairo: Al-Ahram Center for Political and Strategic Studies.

Al-Marashi, Ibrahim. 2005 (Sept.). "Iraq's Constitutional Debate." *Middle East Review of International Affairs 9*(3). Article 8: http://meria.idc.ac.il.

Al-Miraazi, Hafiz. 2003 (Nov. 11). "The Opposition Abroad (Syria) and Political Blackmail" (in Arabic). Al-Jazeera Online Broadcast. Accessed Feb. 21, 2005.

Alnasrawi, Abbas. 1991. *Arab Nationalism, Oil, and the Political Economy of Dependency.* New York: Greenwood.

Alnasrawi, Abbas. 1994. *The Economy of Iraq.* Westport, CT: Government Press.

Al-Nimir, Saud, and Monte Palmer. 1982. "Bureaucracy and Development in Saudi Arabia: A Behavioural Analysis." *Public Administration and Development 2*: 93–104.

Alpher, Joseph. 1995. "Israel: The Challenges of Peace." *Foreign Policy 101*: 130–45.

Altinay, Ayse. 2004. *The Myth of the Military-Nation: Militarism, Gender, and Education in Turkey.* New York: Palgrave.

Al-Qaisi. 1999 (Aug. 13). "Has the Hour of Liquidation Come?" (in Arabic). *Al-Waton al-Arabi,* 20–21.

Al-Rasheed, Madawi. 1996a (Jan.). "Saudi Arabia's Islamic Opposition." *Current History 95*(597): 16.

Al-Rasheed, Madawi. 1996b (July–Aug.). "Mirage in the Desert." *Index on Censorship 25*(4): 73.

Al-Rasheed, Madawi. 1996c (Summer). "God, the King and the Nation: Political Rhetoric in Saudi Arabia in the 1990s." *Middle East Journal 50*(3): 359.

Al-Shaibi, Kamil. 1991. *Sufism and Shi'ism.* England: LAAM, Ltd.

Al-Sharbasi, Al Sayeed Al Sharbini. No Date. *Principles of Socialism in Islam* (in Arabic). Cairo: Selections from Radio and Television.

Altunisik, Meliha. 2000. "Turkish-Israeli Rapproachment in the Post–Cold War Era." Pre-publication version. Middle East Technical University, Department of International Relations, Ankara, Turkey.

Al-Turabi, Hassan. 1997. "Islamic Fundamentalism in the Sunna and Shi'a Worlds." Sudan Foundation Religious File Number 6, www.sufo.demon.co.uk/reli006.htm. Accessed June 26, 2002.

Al-Zaatar, Yasir. 2004a (Nov. 21). "Fatah after Arafat: Liberation Movement or Ruling Party" (in Arabic). Al-Jazeera: www.aljazeera.net. Accessed Dec. 15, 2004.

Al-Zaatar, Yasir. 2004b (Dec. 26). "The Iraqi Islamic Party: The Occupation at a Time When the Islamists Regret Their Error" (in Arabic). Al-Jazeera: www.aljazeera.net. Accessed January 7, 2005.

Al-Zaiyat, Mansour. 2002 (Aug. 11). "Sharia and Life Series: Islamic Groups and Violence." Al-Jazeera interview by Mahir Abdullah (in Arabic) at http://www.aljazeera.net/programs/shareea/articles/2002/8/8–11–1.htm.

Al-Zayyat, Muntasir. 2004. *The Road to al-Qaeda: The Story of Bin Laden's Right-hand Man.* London: Pluto Press.

Amiel, Barbara. 2000 (Nov. 27). "While the World Condemns Israel, This Tragedy Will Never End." *Jerusalem Post,* Internet Edition, 1–15.

Amin, Galal. 1995. *Egypt's Economic Predicament*. Leiden, Netherlands: E. J. Brill.

Amin, Galal. 2000. *Whatever Happened to the Egyptians? Change in Egyptian Society from 1950–Present*. Cairo: American University in Cairo Press.

Amin, Galal. 2004. *Whatever Else Happened to the Egyptians? From the Revolution to the Age of Globalization*. Cairo: American University in Cairo Press.

Amirahmadi, Hooshang. 1996. "Emerging Civil Society in Iran." *SAIS Review 16*(2): 87–107.

An-Nafisi, Abdullah Fand. 1982. *The Gulf Cooperation Council: The Political and Strategic Framework*. London: Ta-Ha Publishers Ltd.

Ansari, Harried. 1985. "Mubarak's Egypt." *A World Affairs Journal: The Middle East 84*: 498.

Ansari, Harried. 1986. Egypt: *The Stalled Society*. Cairo: American University in Cairo Press.

Anscombe, Frederick Fallowfield. 1997. *The Ottoman Gulf*. New York: Columbia University Press.

Anthony, John Duke. 2004 (Feb. 20). "The Gulf Cooperation Council: Strengths." *GulfWire Perspectives*.

Antonius, George. 1965. *The Arab Awakening*. New York: Capricorn Books.

Aoude, Ibrahim G. 1994. "From National Bourgeois Development to Infitah: Egypt 1952–1992." *Arab Studies Quarterly 16*(1): 1–23.

Apiku, Simon. 1999. "Interior Minister Ruffles the Feathers of Top Brass." *Middle East Times,* 38.

Arab, Mohammed K. 1988. "The Effect of the Leader's Belief System on Foreign Policy: The Case of Libya." Unpublished dissertation, Florida State University.

Arab Political Documents. 1963. "Minutes of the Tripartite Union: Talks Held in Cairo between the Delegations of the UAR and the Syrian and Iraqi Republics (Excerpts)." Lebanon: PSPA Department of the American University of Beirut, 75–217.

Arian, Asher. 1997. *Politics in the Israeli Second Republic*. London: Chatham House.

Arjomand, Said Amir. 1984. *The Shadow of God and the Hidden Iman*. Chicago: University of Chicago Press.

Armajani, Yahya. 1970. *Middle East: Past and Present*. Englewood Cliffs, NJ: Prentice-Hall.

Aronoff, Myron J. 1989. *Israeli Visions and Divisions: Cultural Change and Political Conflict*. New Brunswick, NJ: Transaction Publishers.

Ashtiani, Zohreh. 2003 (Nov. 18). "Women's Rights in an Interview with Nasser Katoozian: Traditional Institutions Need Revision." *Yas-e-no, Daily Newspaper*, 1(208): 11 (www.netiran.com).

Atabaki, Touraj, and Eric J. Zurcher, eds. 2004. *Men of Order: Authoritarian Modernization under Ataturk and Reza Shah*. London: I. B. Tauris.

Ayrout, Henry Habib. 1962. *The Egyptian Peasant*. Translated by John Williams. Boston: Beacon Press.

Ayubi, Nazih. 1980. "The Political Revival of Islam: The Case of Egypt." *International Journal of Middle East Studies 12*: 481–99.

Ayubi, Nazih. 1982 (July). "Bureaucratic Inflation and Administrative Inefficiency: The Deadlock in Egyptian Administration." *Middle Eastern Studies 18*: 242.

Azimi, Hussein. 2000. "Acute Social and Political Tussles in Iran, Reflection of Fundamental Conflicts in the Country's Economic Structure." *Payame Emrouz* (cultural, social, and economic magazine) *42*: 41–44 (www.netiran.com).

Baer, Robert. 2004. *Sleeping with the Devil: How Washington Sold Our Soul for Saudi Crude.* New York: Random House (Three Rivers).

Bahgat, Gawdat. 1991. *The Impact of External and Internal Forces on Economic Orientation: The Case of Egypt.* Ph.D. dissertation, Florida State University.

Baker, Raymond W. 1978. *Egypt's Uncertain Revolution under Nasser and Sadat.* Cambridge, MA: Harvard University Press.

Bakhash, Shaul. 1978. *Iran: Monarchy, Bureaucracy and Reform under the Qajars, 1858–1896.* London: St. Anthony's Middle East Monographs.

Bakhash, Shaul. 1998. "Iran's Remarkable Election." *Journal of Democracy 9*(1): 80–94.

Baktiari, Bahman. 1996a. *Parliamentary Politics in Revolutionary Iran. The Institutionalization of Factional Politics.* Gainesville: University Press of Florida.

Baktiari, Bahman. 1996b. "The Governing Institutions of the Islamic Republic of Iran: The Supreme Leader, the Presidency, and the Majlis." In *Iran and the Gulf: A Search for Stability,* ed. Jamal al-Suwaidi. Abu Dhabi, UAE: Emirates Center for Strategic Studies and Research.

Banuazizi, Ali. 1994 (Nov./Dec.). "Iran's Revolutionary Impasse: Political Factionalism and Societal Resistance." *Middle East Report 191*: 2–8.

Banuazizi, Ali, and Myron Weiner, eds. 1986. *The State, Religion and Ethnic Politics.* New York: Syracuse University Press.

Barakat, Halim. 1993. *The Arab World: Society, Culture, and State.* Berkeley: University of California Press.

Barakat, Mohammed, and Mahmood Sadiq. 1998 (Nov. 17). "Has the Thought of Religious Violence in Egypt Receded?" (in Arabic). *Al-Waton al-Arabi,* 4–8.

Baram, Amatzia. 1989. "The Ruling Political Elite in Ba'thi Iraq, 1968–1986: The Changing Features of a Collective Profile." *International Journal of Middle East Studies 21*(4): 447–93.

Baram, Amatzia. 1997. "Neo-Tribalism in Iraq: Saddam Hussein's Tribal Policies, 1991–96." *International Journal of Middle East Studies 29*: 1–31.

Baram, Amatzia. 2000a (Spring). "The Effect of Iraqi Sanctions: Statistical Pitfalls and Responsibility." *Middle East Journal 54*(2): 1–31.

Baram, Amatzia. 2000b (Dec.). "Saddam Husayn between His Power Base and the International Community." *Middle East Review of International Affairs Journal 4*(4): 1–14: http://meria.idc.ac.il.

Baram, Amatzia, and Barry M. Rubin. 1993. *Iraq's Road to War.* New York: St. Martin's Press.

Barnett, Michael N. 1992. *Confronting the Costs of War: Military Power, State, and Society in Egypt and Israel.* Princeton, NJ: Princeton University Press.

Barth, Fredrik. 1953. *Principles of Social Organization in Southern Kurdistan.* Oslo: Brodrene Jorgensen A/A Boktrykkeri.

Bartov, Hanoch. 1981. 48 Shanah Veod 20 Yom (48 Years and 20 More Days). Tel Aviv: Maariv Book Guild, 482–89. Reprinted as "The Turning Point in the October 1973 War," 247–51, in *Israel in the Middle East: Documents and Readings on Society, Politics and Foreign Relations, 1948–Present,* ed. Itamar Rabinovich and Jehuda Reinharz. Oxford: Oxford University Press, 1984.

Barzilai, Gad. 1999. "War, Democracy, and Internal Conflict: Israel in a Comparative Perspective." *Comparative Politics 31*(3): 317–18.

Batatu, Hanna. 1978. *The Old Social Classes and the Revolutionary Movements of Iraq.* Princeton, NJ: Princeton University Press.

Batatu, Hanna. 1981. "Iraqi Underground Shi'a Movements: Characteristics, Causes and Prospects." *Middle East Journal 35*(4): 578–94.

Batatu, Hanna. 1999. *Syria's Peasantry, the Descendants of Its Lesser Rural Notables, and Their Politics.* Princeton, NJ: Princeton University Press.

Bauer, Yehuda. 1970. *From Diplomacy to Resistance: A History of Jewish Palestine, 1939–1945.* Philadelphia: Jewish Publication Society.

Bayat, Assef. 1987. *Workers and Revolution in Iran: A Third-World Experience of Workers' Control.* London: Zed Books.

Bayat, Assef. 1997a (Winter). "Cairo's Poor: Dilemmas of Survival and Solidarity." *Middle East Report*: www.merip.org/mer/mer202/poor.htm.

Bayat, Assef. 1997b. *Street Politics: Poor People's Movements in Iran.* New York: Columbia University Press.

BBC Monitoring International Reports. 2004 (Jan. 6). "Saudi Opposition Site Details of Prince Sultan's Kidnap in June." *Financial Times Information.*

Beattie, Kirk J. 1994. *Egypt during the Nasser Years.* Boulder, CO: Westview Press.

Beeman, William. 2005. *"The Great Satan" vs. "The Mad Mullahs": How the United States and Iran Demonize Each Other.* Westport, CT: Greenwood.

Begin, Menachem. 1951. *The Revolt: Story of the Irgun.* New York: Henry Schuman.

Behrens-Abouseif. 1990. *Islamic Architecture in Cairo: An Introduction.* Cairo: American University in Cairo Press.

Beinin, Joel. 1998. *The Dispersion of Egyptian Jewry.* Berkeley: University of California Press.

Belqaziz, Abd Allah, ed. 2004. *The PLO and the Intifada: Yield and Future* (in Arabic). Beirut: Center for Arab Unity Studies.

Bengio, Ofra. 2004. *The Turkish-Israeli Relationship: Changing Ties of Middle Eastern Outsiders.* New York: Palgrave Macmillan.

Ben-Gurion, David. 1971. *Israel: A Personal History.* New York and Tel Aviv: Funk and Wagnalls, and Sabra Books, 561–63. Reprinted as "Social and Ethnic Tensions in the Late 1950s," 141–43, in *Israel in the Middle East: Documents and Readings on Society, Politics and Foreign Relations, 1948–Present,* ed. Itamar Rabinovich and Jehuda Reinharz. Oxford: Oxford University Press, 1984.

Ben-Meir, Alon. 1996. "The Dual Containment Strategy Is No Longer Viable." *Middle East Policy 4*(3): 58–71.

Bennis, Phyllis, et al. 2004 (Sept. 30). "A Failed 'Transition': The Mounting Costs of the Iraq War." Washington, DC: Institute for Policy Studies and Foreign Policy in Focus.

Berque, Jacques. 1967. *Egypt: Imperialism and Revolution.* New York: Praeger.

Bianchi, Robert. 1989. *Unruly Corporatism: Associational Life in Twentieth-Century Egypt.* New York: Oxford University Press.

Bichler, Shimson. 1994. "Political Power Shifts in Israel, 1977 and 1992: Unsuccessful Electoral Economics or Long-Range Realignment?" *Science and Society 58*(4): 415–39.

Biger, Gideon. 1989. "The Shatt-Al-Arab River Boundary: A Note." *Middle Eastern Studies 25*(2): 248–51.

Bill, James A. 1984 (Fall). "Resurgent Islam in the Persian Gulf." *Foreign Affairs 63*: 108–27.

Bill, James A. 1988. *The Eagle and the Lion: The Tragedy of American-Iranian Relations.* New Haven, CT: Yale University Press.

Bill, James A., and William Roger Louis, eds. 1988. *Musaddiq, Iranian Nationalism, and Oil.* Austin: University of Texas Press.

Bill, James, and Robert Springborg. 1997. *Politics in the Middle East.* New York: HarperCollins.

Bin Jadw, Ghasan. 2004 (Dec. 11). "The Hamas Movement and the Future of the Resistance" (in Arabic). Al-Jazeera Broadcast: www.aljazeera.net.

Blanch, Ed. 2003 (Dec.). "Hammering Hamas: The Gloves Are Well and Truly Off as Israeli Security Forces Continue with Operation Fine Tuning 1, Intended to Incapacitate and Ultimately Eliminate Hamas." *The Middle East, 340*(28): InfoTrac #A111574492.

Bodansky, Yossef. 2001. *Bin Laden: The Man Who Declared War on America.* New York: Random House.

Bonne, Alfred. 1955. *State and Economics in the Middle East.* London: Routledge & Kegan Paul.

Boukra, Leiss. 2002. *Algerie la terreur sacrée.* SA Lausanne: FAVRE.

Brands, H. W. 1993. *Into the Labyrinth: The United States and the Middle East, 1945–1993.* New York: McGraw-Hill.

Brecher, Michael. 1974. *Decisions in Israel's Foreign Policy.* London: Oxford University Press.

Brichta, Avraham. 1998. "The New Premier–Parliamentary System in Israel (Israel in Transition)." *Annals of the American Academy of Political and Social Science 555*: 180–92.

Brockelmann, Carl. 1960. *History of the Islamic People.* New York: Capricorn Books.

Brown, Nathan J. 2003. *Palestinian Politics after the Oslo Accords: Resuming Arab Palestine.* Berkeley: University of California Press.

Brown, Nathan J. 2005 (July). "Iraq's Constitutional Process Plunges Ahead." *Policy Outlook: Democracy and Rule of Law.* Washington, DC: Carnegie Endowment for International Peace.

Busse, Herbert. 1997. *Islam, Judaism and Christianity: Theological and Historical Affiliations.* Princeton, NJ: Markus Wiener Pub.

Butler, Richard. 2000a. *The Greatest Threat: Iraq, Weapons of Mass Destruction, and the Crisis of Global Security.* New York: Public Affairs.

Butler, Richard. 2000b. *Saddam Defiant: The Threat of Weapons of Mass Destruction, and the Crisis of Global Security.* London: Weidenfeld & Nicolson.

Campagna, Joel. 1996 (Summer). "From Accommodation to Confrontation: The Muslim Brotherhood in the Mubarak Years." *Journal of International Affairs 50*(1): 278–304.

Cagaptay, Soner. 2002 (Dec.). "The November 2002 Elections and Turkey's New Political Era." *Middle East Review of International Affairs Journal 6*(4): http://meria.idc.ac.il.

Cahen, Judith. 2002 (Nov.). "Les deboires du 'printemps de Damas.'" *Le Monde Diplomatique*: www.monde-diplomatique.fr/2002/11/CAHEN/17032.

Cann, Rebecca, and Constantine Danopoulos. 1997. "The Military and Politics in a Theocratic State: Iran as a Case Study." *Armed Forces and Society 24*(2): 269–88.

Carkoglu, Ali. 2002 (Dec.). "Turkey's November 2002 Elections: A New Beginning?" *Middle East Review of International Affairs Journal, 6*(4): http://meria.idc.ac.il.

Carleton, Alford. 1950 (Jan.). "The Syrian Coups d'Etat of 1949." *Middle East Journal 4*(1): 1.

Carter, B. L. 1986. *The Copts in Egyptian Politics*. London: Croom Helm.

Cavender, Gay, Nancy C. Jurik, and Albert K. Cohen. 1993. "The Baffling Case of the Smoking Gun: The Social Ecology of the Political Accounts in the Iran-Contra Affair." *Social Problems 40*(2): 152–65.

Cause, F. Gregory, III. 1994. *Oil Monarchies: Domestic and Security Challenges in the Arab Gulf States*. New York: Council on Foreign Relations Press.

Cause, F. Gregory, III. 1999 (May). "Getting It Backward on Iraq." *Foreign Affairs 78*(3): 54.

Chabry, Laurent, and Annie Chabry. 1987. *Politique et Minorites au Proche-Orient: Les Raisons d'une Explosion*. Paris: Editions Maisonneuve and Larose.

Champion, David. 1999. "The Kingdom of Saudi Arabia: Elements of Instability within Stability." *Middle East Review of International Affairs Journal 3*(4): http://meria.idc.ac.il.

Ciftci, Sabri, Walter Forrest, and Yusuf Tekin. 2003. "Parliamentary Committees in a Nascent Party System: Committee Assignments in the Turkish General Assembly." Paper presented at Midwest Political Science Association (MPSA) meeting, Chicago.

Clarke, Richard A. 2004. *Against All Enemies: Inside America's War on Terror*. New York: Free Press.

Clawson, Patrick, and Michael Rubin. 2005. *Eternal Iran: Continuity and Chaos*. New York: Palgrave Macmillan.

Cleveland, William. 2004. *A History of the Modern Middle East*. Boulder, CO: Westview Press.

Cockburn, Andrew, and Patrick Cockburn. 1999. *Out of the Ashes*. New York: HarperCollins.

Cohen, Aryeh Dean. 1999 (Sept. 14). "Sand Defends Authors of Controversial History Book." *Jerusalem Post*.

Cohen, Raymond. 1990. *Culture and Conflict in Egyptian-Israeli Relations*. Bloomington: Indiana University Press.

Cohen, Raymond. 1994a (June). "Israel's Starry-Eyed Foreign Policy." *Middle East Quarterly 1*(2): 28–41.

Cohen, Raymond. 1994b (Sept.). "Culture Gets in the Way." *Middle East Quarterly 1*(3): 45–54.

Cole, Juan Ricardo. 1993. *Colonialism and Revolution in the Middle East*. Princeton, NJ: Princeton University Press.

Cole, Juan [Ricardo]. 2002. *Sacred Space and Holy War: The Politics Culture and History of Shiite Islam*. London: I. B. Tauris.

Coon, Carleton S. 1961. *Caravan: The Story of the Middle East*. Rev. Ed. New York: Holt, Rinehart and Winston.

Cordesman, Anthony H. 1999. *Iraq and the War of Sanctions: Conventional Threats and Weapons of Mass Destruction*. London: Praeger.

Cordesman, Anthony. 2004. "The Prospects for Stability in Saudi Arabia in 2004." A three-part report shared with Saudi-US Relations Information Service.

Cordesman, Anthony H., and Nawaf Obaid. 2005. *National Security in Saudi Arabia: Threats, Responses, and Challenges.* Washington, DC: CSIS Press.

Cox, Samuel S. 1887. *Diversions of a Diplomat in Turkey.* New York: Charles L. Webster & Co.

Cressey, George B. 1960. *Crossroads: Land and Life in Southwest Asia.* Chicago: Lippincott.

Cronin, Stephanie. 1997. *The Army and the Creation of the Pahlavi State in Iran, 1910–1926.* London: I. B. Tauris.

Cuno, Kenneth M. 1992. *The Pasha's Peasants.* Cambridge: Cambridge University Press.

Dabrowska, Karen. 1994. "Opposition in Disarray." *The Middle East 240*: 9–10.

Dahy, Talal. 1988. *The Military Organization as an Agent for Modernization in the Third World Countries: Case Study—National Guard in Saudi Arabia.* Ph.D. dissertation, Florida State University.

Danesh-Jaafari, Davoud. 2001 (Nov.). "State Expediency Council and the Economy." *Eqtesad-e Iran, Monthly Magazine 33*: 32–33.

Daneshvar, Parviz. 1996. *Revolution in Iran.* New York: St. Martin's Press.

Dann, Uriel. 1969. *Iraq under Qassem: A Political History, 1958–1963.* New York: Praeger.

Darwish, Adel. 1994 (June). "Water Wars." Lecture given at the Geneva Conference on Environment and Quality of Life.

Darwisha, Adeed. 2003 (Winter). "Arab Nationalism in the Twentieth Century: From Triumph to Despair. *Middle East Policy 10*(4): InfoTrac #A111857058.

Davis, Eric. 1987. "The Concept of Revival and the Study of Islam and Politics." In *The Islamic Impulse* (37–58), ed. Barbara F. Stowasser. London: Croom Helm.

Dawn, C. Ernest. 1962 (Spring). "The Rise of Arabism in Syria." *Middle East Journal 16*(2): 145.

De Corancez, Louis A. 1995. *The History of the Wahabis: From Their Origin until the End of 1809.* Translated by Eric Tabet. Reading, UK: Garnet Publishing.

Dekmejian, R. Hrair. 1975. *Egypt under Nasser: A Study in Political Dynamics.* Albany: State University of New York Press.

Dekmejian, R. Hrair. 1985. *Fundamentalism in the Arab World.* Syracuse, NY: Syracuse University Press.

Dekmejian, R. Hrair. 1991. "The Arab Republic of Syria." In *Politics and Government in the Middle East and North Africa* (188–208), ed. Tareq Y. Ismael and Jacqueline S. Ismael. Miami: Florida International University Press.

Dekmejian, R. Hrair. 1994. "The Rise of Political Islamism in Saudi Arabia." *Middle East Journal 48*(4): 627–43.

Dekmejian, R. Hrair. 1995. *Islam in Revolution: Fundamentalism in the Arab World.* Syracuse, NY: Syracuse University Press.

Dekmejian, R. Hrair. 1998. "Saudi Arabia's Consultative Council." *Middle East Journal 52*(2): 204–18.

Delannoy, Christian. 1990. *Savak.* Paris: Stock.

de la Gorce, Paul-Marie. 2004 (July). "La Syrie sous Pression." *Le Monde Diplomatique*: www.monde-diplomatique.fr.

de Planhol, Xavier. 1959. *The World of Islam.* Ithaca, NY: Cornell University Press.

Denoeux, Guilain Pierre. 1990. *Informal Networks, Urbanization, and Political Unrest in the Middle East: The Cases of Egypt, Iran, and Lebanon.* Ph.D. thesis.

Denoeux, Guilain. 2005 (Fall). "The Politics of Corruption in Palestine: Evidence from Recent Public-Opinion Polls." *Middle East Policy 12*(3): Middle East Policy Council, www.mepc.org.

Derhally, Massoud. 2005 (November). "Piling On the Pressure." Arabian Business: www.itp.net/business/features/details.php?id=3390

Dia, Mamadou. 1996. *Africa's Management in the 1990s and Beyond: Reconciling Indigenous and Transplanted Institutions.* Washington, DC: World Bank.

Diamond, Larry. 2005. *Squandered Victory: The American Occupation and the Bungled Effort to Bring Democracy to Iraq.* New York: Times Books.

Diba, Farhad. 1986. *Mossadegh: A Political Biography.* London: Croom Helm.

Diwan, Ishac, and Michael Walton. 1994 (Sept.). "The Economy of the West Bank and Gaza: From Dependent to Autonomous Growth." *Finance and Development 31*(3): InfoTrac #A16063125.

Djalili, Mohammad-Reza. 2005. *Geopolitique de l'Iran.* Bruxelles: SA Diffusion Promotion Information.

do Ceu Pinto, Maria. 1999. *Political Islam and the United States: A Study of US Policy Towards Islamic Movements in the Middle East.* Reading, UK: Garnet Publishing (also Ithaca Press).

Doran, Michael Scott. 1999. *Pan-Arabism before Nasser.* New York: Oxford University Press.

Doran, Michael Scott. 2004 (Jan./Feb.). "The Saudi Paradox." *Foreign Affairs:* www.foreignaffairs.org.

Dorraj, Manocheht. 1997. "Symbolic and Utilitarian Political Value of a Tradition: Martyrdom in the Iranian Political Culture." *The Review of Politics 59*(3): 489–521.

Dodwell, Henry. 1931. *The Founder of Modern Egypt: A Study of Muhammad Ali.* Cambridge: Cambridge University Press.

Drysdale, Alasdair, and Raymond A. Hinnebusch. 1991. *Syria and the Middle East Peace Process.* New York: Council on Foreign Relations Press.

Duffield, John S. 2005 (June). "Oil and the Iraq War: How the United States Could Have Expected to Benefit, and Might Still." *Middle East Review of International Affairs Journal 9*(2). Article 7: http://meria.idc.ac.il.

Dumas, Marie-Lucy, ed. 1995. *Repertoire des Paris Integristes Musulmans. Tombe 1: La Méditerranée.* Paris: CHEAM.

*Economist.* 2005 (Jan.). "Saudi Arabia Risk: Political Stability Risk." *Economist* Intelligence Unit RiskWire, Part 32.

Eddy, William Alfred. 1954. *FDR Meets Ibn Sa'ud.* Kohinur Series (no. 1). New York: American Friends of the Middle East.

Eickelman, Dale F., and James Piscatori. 1996. *Muslim Politics.* Princeton, NJ: Princeton University Press.

Eisenhower, Dwight David. 1965. *Waging Peace, 1956–1961: The White House Years.* London: Heinemann.

El-Aref, Aref. 1944. *Bedouin Love, Law and Legend.* Jerusalem: Cosmos Publishing Co.

El-Din, Khaled Mohi. 1992. *Memories of a Revolution: Egypt 1952.* Cairo: American University of Cairo Press.

El Ebraash, Wa'eil, and Kemal El Shathli. 2000 (July 8–14). "The Cleansing of the National Democratic Party" (in Arabic). *Rose el Youssef,* 12–14.

El-Gamassy, Mohammed Abdel Ghani. 1993. *The October War: Memoirs of Field Marshal El-Gamassy of Egypt.* English translation by Gillian Potter, Nadra Marcus, and Roselta Frances. Cairo: American University of Cairo Press.

El-Gawhary, Karim. 1997 (July–Sept.). "Nothing More to Lose: Landowners, Tenants, and Economic Liberalization in Egypt." *Middle East Report Online:* www.merip.org.

El-Ghobashy, Mona. 2005 (Feb. 2). "Egypt Looks Ahead to Portentous Year." *Middle East Report Online:* www.merip.org.

El Khazen, Farid. 2000. *The Breakdown of the State in Lebanon, 1967–1976.* London: I. B. Tauris.

Elliot, Matthew. 1996. *Independent Iraq: The Monarchy and British Influence, 1941–58.* London: I. B. Tauris.

Elm, Mostafa. 1992. *Oil, Power, and Principle: Iran's Oil Nationalization and Its Aftermath.* Syracuse, NY: Syracuse University Press.

Emerson, Rupert. 1960. *From Empire to Nation.* Cambridge, MA: Harvard University Press.

Erdogdu, Erkan. 2002 (June). "Turkey and Europe: Undivided but Not United." *Middle East Review of International Affairs Journal* 6(2): http://meria.idc.ac.il.

Esposito, John L., ed. 1990. *The Iranian Revolution: Its Global Impact.* Miami: Florida International University Press.

Etzioni-Halevy, Eva. 1977. *Political Culture in Israel: Cleavage and Integration among Israeli Jews.* New York: Praeger.

Ezrahi, Yaron. 1998. *Rubber Bullets: Power and Conscience in Modern Israel.* Berkeley: University of California Press.

Fahmy, Khaled. 1997. *All the Pasha's Men.* Cambridge: Cambridge University Press.

Fairbanks, Stephen C. 1998. "Theocracy versus Democracy: Iran Considers Political Parties." *Middle East Journal* 52(1): 17–31.

Fandy, Mamoun. 2004. *Saudi Arabia and the Politics of Dissent.* New York: Palgrave.

Fandy, Mamoun. 1999. *Saudi Arabia and the Politics of Dissent.* New York: St. Martin's Press.

Farah, Tawfic, ed. 1987. *Pan-Arabism and Arab Nationalism: The Continuing Debate.* Boulder, CO: Westview Press.

Farber, David R. 2005. *Taken Hostage: The Iran Hostage Crisis and America's First Encounter with Radical Islam.* Princeton, NJ: Princeton University Press.

Farid, Abdel Majid. 1994. *Nasser: The Final Years.* Reading, UK: Ithaca Press.

Farsoun, Samih K., and Mehrdad Meshayekhi, eds. 1992. *Iran: Political Culture in the Islamic Republic.* London: Routledge.

Fars News Agency. 2004. (July 17). "Interview with New ICS Leader Mohammad Nabi Habibi." *Resalat* (daily newspaper), no. 5349. Online: www.netiran.com/php/artp.php?id=1743.

"Fatwa: What Is Jihad in Islam?" 2002. *Islam Online,* April 10. http://www.islamonline.net/fatwa/english/FatwaDisplay.asp?FatwaID=18243.

Fernea, Robert A., and William Roger Louis. 1991. *The Iraqi Revolution of 1958.* London: I. B. Tauris.

Fisher, Sydney N. 1964. *The Middle East: A History.* New York: Alfred A. Knopf.

Flory, Maurice, and Pierre-Satheh Agate, eds. 1989. *Le système regional Arabe*. Paris: Editions du Centre National de la Recherche Scientific.

Fraser, T.G. 1980. *The Middle East, 1914–1979*. London: Edward Arnold.

Freedman, Robert O. 2005 (March). "The Bush Administration and the Arab–Israeli Conflict: The Record of the First Four Years." *Middle East Review of International Affairs 9*(1). Article 7: http://meria.idc.ac.il.

Friedl, Erika, and Mahnaz Afkhami, eds. 1994. *In the Eye of the Storm: Women in Post-Revolutionary Iran*. Syracuse, NY: Syracuse University Press.

Fulanain. 1928. *The Marsh Arab*. Philadelphia: Lippincott.

Gallman, Waldemar J. 1964. *Iraq under General Nuri: My Recollections of Nuri Al-Said, 1954–1958*. Baltimore, MD: Johns Hopkins University Press.

Galnoor, Itzahak, David H. Rosenbloom, and Allon Yaroni. 1998. "Creating New Public Management Reforms: Lessons from Israel." *Administration and Society 30*(4): 393–418.

Gansler, Jacques S., and Hans Binnendijk, eds. 2004. *Information Assurance: Trends in Vulnerabilities, Threats, and Technologies*. Washington, DC: National Defense University.

Gara'yaba, Ibrahim. 2004 (June 9). "The Violence of Islamic Groups in Iraq: Will This Be the Last?" (in Arabic). Al-Jazeera: www.aljazeera.net. Accessed July 25, 2004.

Garg, Prem C., and Samir El-Khouri. 1994 (Sept.). "Aiding the Development Effort for the West Bank and Gaza." *Finance & Development 31*(3): InfoTrac #A16063127.

Gasiorowski, Mark J., and Malcolm Byrne, eds. 2004. *Mohammad Mosaddeq and the 1953 Coup in Iran*. Syracuse, NY: Syracuse University Press.

Gause, Gregory. 1994. *Oil Monarchies: Domestic and Security Challenges in the Arab Gulf States*. New York: Council on Foreign Relations Press.

Gellner, Ernest. 1987. *The Concept of Kinship (and Other Essays on Anthropological Method and Explanation)*. Oxford: Basil Blackwell.

Gellner, Ernest, and Charles Micaud, eds. 1972. *Arabs and Berbers: From Tribe to Nation in North Africa*. Lexington, MA: D.C. Heath and Co.

Gelvin, James L. 1998. *Divided Loyalties: Nationalism and Mass Politics in Syria at the Close of the Empire*. Berkeley: University of California Press.

George, Alan. 2003. *Syria: Neither Bread nor Freedom*. New York: Zed Books.

Gershoni, I., and James Jankowski. 1995. *Redefining the Egyptian Nation, 1935–1945*. Cambridge: Cambridge University Press.

Gheissari, Ali, and Vali Nasr. 2004 (Summer). "Iran's Democracy Debate." *Middle East Policy 11*(2): 94–107. InfoTrac #A118417353.

Gieling, Saskia. 1997. "The Marja'iya in Iran and the Nomination of Khamanei in December 1994." *Middle Eastern Studies 33*(4): 777–87.

Gilbert, Martin. 1979. *The Arab-Israeli Conflict: Its History in Maps*. 3rd ed. London: Weidenfeld and Nicolson.

Gilboa, Eytan, and Yaron Katz. 1999. "The Media Campaign: The Shift to Alternative Media." *Middle East Review of International Affairs Journal, 3*(4): http://meria.idc.ac.il.

Gillespie, Kate. 1984. *The Tripartite Relationship: Government, Foreign Investors and Local Investors during Egypt's Economic Opening*. New York: Praeger.

Gillespie, Kate, and Clement Henry. 1995. *Oil in the New World Order*. Gainesville: University Press of Florida.

Gilsenan, Michael. 1978. *Saint and Sufi in Modern Egypt: An Essay in the Sociology of Religion*. Oxford: Oxford University Press.

Ginat, Rami. 1997. *Egypt's Incomplete Revolution*. London: Frank Cass.

Gluckman, Max. 1965. *Politics, Law and Ritual in Tribal Society*. New York: New American Library.

Goldschmidt, Arthur. 1988. *Modern Egypt: The Formation of a Nation-State*. Boulder, CO: Westview Press.

Gomaa, Salwa S. 1991. "Leadership and Elections in Local Government." Perspectives in the Center—Local Relations: *Political Dynamics of the Middle East*. M.E.S. Series No. 28, 34–63.

Gomaa, Salwa S. 1998. *Environmental Policy Making in Egypt*. Gainesville: University Press of Florida.

Gordon, Joel. 1992. *Nasser's Blessed Movement*. New York: Oxford University Press.

Gordon, Michael, and Bernard E. Trainor. 1994. *The Generals' War: The Inside Story of Conflict in the Gulf*. Boston: Little, Brown.

Gorst, Anthony, and Lewis Johnman. 1997. *The Suez Crisis*. London: Routledge.

Graham-Brown, Sarah. 1999. *Sanctioning Saddam*. London: I. B. Tauris.

Graham-Brown, Sarah, and Zina Sackur. 1995. "The Middle East: The Kurds— A Regional Issue." *Writenet country papers*: www.unhcr.ch/refworld/country/writenet/wrikurd.htm.

Grant, Audra, and Mark Tessler. 2002 (Fall). "Palestinian Attitudes toward Democracy and Its Compatibility with Islam: Evidence from Public Opinion Research in the West Bank and Gaza." *Arab Studies Quarterly* 24(4): InfoTrac #A101531216.

Green, Jerrold D. 1982. *Revolution in Iran: The Politics of Countermobilization*. New York: Praeger.

Gresh, Alain. 2000 (Nov.). "Oil for Food: The True Story." *Le Monde Diplomatique*, 1–7.

Gresh, Alain. 2003 (June). "Les Grands Écarts de l'Arabie Saoudite." *Le Monde Diplomatique*: www.monde-diplomatique.fr/2003/06/GRESH10233.

Gunaratna, Rohan. 2002. *Inside Al Qaeda: Global Network of Terror*. New York: Columbia University Press.

Gunter, Michael M. 1992. *The Kurds of Iraq: Tragedy and Hope*. New York: St. Martin's Press.

Habib, Kamal. No Date. "Jihadist Currents in Saudi Arabia: Roots and Transformations" (in Arabic). Al-Jazeera Broadcast: www.aljazeera.net. Accessed on July 11, 2004.

Habib, Rafiq. 1989. *Religious Protest and Class Conflict in Egypt* (in Arabic). Cairo: Sinai for Publishing.

Habibi, Mohammad Nabi. 2004 (July 17). Interview. *Resalat* (daily newspaper), no. 5349. Online: www.netiran.com/?fn=artd(1743). Accessed Nov. 23, 2005.

Hadar, Leon T. 1999. "Israel in the Post-Zionist Age: Being Normal and Loving It." *World Policy Journal* 16(1). (Internet version; no page numbers.)

Ha'fiz, Yassin. 1963. *Concerning the Experience of the Baath Party in Political Thought, Vol. I* (in Arabic). Damascus: House of Damascus for Printing and Publishing.

Haj, Samira. 1997. *The Making of Iraq, 1900–1963*. Albany: State University of New York Press.

Halm, Heinz. 1997. *Shi'a Islam: From Religion to Revolution*. Translated from German by Allison Brown. Princeton, NJ: Markus Wiener Pub.

Hamad, Majdi, et.al. 1999. *Democratic Islamic Movements* (in Arabic). Beirut: Center for Arab Unity Studies.

Hamid, Berlinti Abdel. 1992. *The Marshal and I* (in Arabic). Cairo: Library Madbouli.

Hamidi, Ibrahim. 1998 (Dec. 14). "Syria: Weekly Review." *Al-Wasat,* 20–21.

Hamidi, Ibrahim. 2001 (Jan. 8). "Syria: Intellectuals Organize Clubs, Civil Society and Human Rights" (in Arabic). *Al-Wasat,* 18–19.

Hamidi, Ibrahim. 2005 (Jan. 12). "Can Syria Keep Its Islamist Genie in the Bottle?" *Daily Star* (Lebanon; www.dailystar.com.lb).

Hammond, Andrew. 2000. "Personal Status Law Not a Personal Choice." *Middle East Times,* 3.

Hamouda, Adel. 1990. *How the Egyptians Mock Their Leaders* (in Arabic). Cairo: House of Sphinx Publishers.

Hamza, Khidir, and David Albright. 1998. "Inside Saddam's Secret Nuclear Program." *Bulletin of the Atomic Scientists 54*(5): 26–33.

Hamzeh, Nizar. 2000. "Lebanon's Islamists and Local Politics: A New Reality." *Third World Quarterly 21*(5): 739–59.

Hamzeh, Nizar, and Hrair Dekmejian. 1996. "A Sufi Response to Political Islamism: Al-Ahbash of Lebanon." *International Journal of Middle East Studies 28*: 217–29.

Harel, Amos. 2004 (Jan. 9). "Shin Bet: 50% Drop in the Number of Israelis Killed by Terror in 2003." *Ha'aretz.* Online: www.haaretz.com/hasen/spages/38116.html.

Harik, Iliya. 1997. *Economic Policy Reform in Egypt.* Gainesville: University Press of Florida.

Harris, David. 2004. *The Crisis: The President, the Prophet, and the Shah—1979 and the Coming of Militant Islam.* New York: Little, Brown.

Harris, William. 2005 (Summer). "Bashar al-Assad's Lebanon Gamble." *Middle East Quarterly 12*(3): www.meforum.org/article/730.

Hart, Parker T. 1998. *Saudi Arabia and the United States: Birth of a Security Partnership.* Bloomington: Indiana University Press.

Hasba'ni, Ahmed. 2000 (Oct. 30). "Bashar Takes Hold of Syria's Destiny and Its Development" (in Arabic). *Al-Ousbou al-Arabi,* 20–21.

Hass, Amira. 2005 (Oct. 24). "Quartet Envoy: Israel Acting As If Disengagement Never Happened." *Ha'aretz Online*: www.haaretz.com/hasen/spages/643616.html.

Hassan-Gordon, Tariq. 2000. "State Regrets Election 'Inconvenience' to Journalists." *Middle East Times.*

Hatina, Meir. 2001. *Islam and Salvation in Palestine: The Islamic Jihad Movement.* Tel Aviv: Moshe Dayan Center for Middle Eastern and African Studies.

Hazelton, Fran, ed. 1994. *Iraq since the Gulf War: Prospects for Democracy.* London: Zed Books.

Heikal, Mohammed H. 1962. *What Happened in Syria* (in Arabic). Cairo: National Publishing House.

Heikal, Mohammed H. 1983. *Autumn of Fury: The Assassination of Sadat.* London: Andre Deutsch.

Henry, Clement M. 1996. *The Mediterranean Debt Crescent: Money and Power in Algeria, Egypt, Morocco, Tunisia, and Turkey.* Gainesville: University Press of Florida.

Hermann, Margaret G., Charles F. Hermann, and Richard D. Anderson. 1992. "Explaining Self-Defeating Foreign Policy Decisions: Interpreting Soviet Arms for

Egypt in 1973 through Process or Domestic Bargaining Models?" *American Political Science Review 86*(3): 759–67.

Hersh, Seymour M. 1999 (April 5). "Annals of Espionage: Saddam's Best Friend." *The New Yorker,* 32–42.

Herzig, Edmund. 1995. *Iran and the Former Soviet South.* Washington, DC: Brookings Institution.

Herzl, Theodor. 1896. *A Jewish State.* New York: American Zionist Emergency Council, 1946.

Herzog, Ze'ev. 1999 (Oct. 29). "Deconstructing the Walls of Jericho." *Ha'aretz Magazine.*

Heydemann, Steven, ed. 2004. *Networks of Privilege in the Middle East: The Politics of Economic Reform Revisted.* New York: Palgrave Macmillan.

Hibra, Karem. 2000 (July 29). "Rapid-Fire Judicial Decisions." *Rose El Youssef,* 20–21.

Hidar, Asaad. 1999 (March 7). "As-Sadr in the Week Before" (in Arabic). *Al-Wasat,* 13–14.

Hinnebusch, Raymond A. 1980. "Political Recruitment and Socialization in Syria: The Case of the Revolutionary Youth Federation." *International Journal of Middle East Studies 2*: 143–74.

Hinnebusch, Raymond A. 1985. *Egyptian Politics under Sadat: The Post-Populist Development of an Authoritarian Modernizing State.* Cambridge: Cambridge University Press.

Hinnebusch, Raymond A. 1988. *Egyptian Politics under Sadat: The Post-Populist Development of an Authoritarian Modernizing State.* Boulder, CO: Lynne Rienner Publishers.

Hinnebusch, Raymond A. 1990. *Authoritarian Power and State Formation in Ba'athist Syria.* Boulder, CO: Westview Press.

Hinnebusch, Raymond A. 1993. "State and Civil Society in Syria." *Middle East Journal 42*(2): 247–49.

Hitti, Philip K. 1956. *History of the Arabs from the Earliest Times to the Present.* 6th ed. London: Macmillan.

Hitti, Philip K. 1959. *Syria: A Short History.* New York: Macmillan.

Hobbes, Thomas. 1651. *Leviathan.* Chicago: Henry Regnery, 1965.

Holden, David, and Richard Johns. 1981. *The House of Saud.* London: Pan Books.

Holland, Matthew F. 1996. *America and Egypt: From Roosevelt to Eisenhower.* Westport, CT: Praeger.

Hooglund, Eric J. 1982. *Land and Revolution in Iran, 1960–1980.* Austin: University of Texas Press.

Hope, Hugh. 2005. *Sons of the Conquerors: The Rise of the Turkic World.* New York: Overlook Duckworth.

Hosseinzedeh, Esmail. 1989. *Soviet Non-Capitalist Development: The Case of Nasser's Egypt.* New York: Praeger.

Hourani, Albert. 1997. *History of the Arab Peoples.* New York: Fine Communications.

Hubbel, Steve. 1992 (Sept.). "Fundamentalist Gains." *Middle East International,* 25.

Husaini, Ishak Musa. 1956. *The Moslem Brethren: The Greatest of Modern Islamic Movements.* Beirut: Khayat.

Ibrahim, Farhad. 1996. *Confessionalism and Politics in the Arab World: The Shi'a Program in Iraq* (in Arabic). Translated from German by the Center for Cultural Studies and Translations. Cairo: Library Madbouli.

Ibrahim, Saad Eddin. 1980. "Anatomy of Egypt's Militant Islamic Groups: Methodological Note and Preliminary Findings." *International Journal of Middle East Studies 12*(4): 423–53.

Ibrahim, Saad Eddin. 1996. *Egypt, Islam, and Democracy*. Cairo: American University of Cairo Press.

Imam, Sarnia. 1987. *Who Rules Egypt?* (in Arabic). Cairo: Arab Futures Publishing House.

International Crisis Group. 2004 (July 14). "Can Saudi Arabia Reform Itself?" A Report by the International Crisis Group.

International Crisis Group. 2005a (March 21). "Iran in Iraq: How Much Influence?" *Middle East Report* No. 38. Brussels.

International Crisis Group. 2005b (Sept. 26). "Unmaking Iraq: A Constitutional Process Gone Awry." *Middle East Briefing* No. 19. Brussels.

Iraq Review Watch. 2004 (Sept.). "Disorder, Negligence and Mismanagement: How the CPA Handled Iraq Reconstruction Funds." Report No. 7. New York: Open Society Institute.

Ismael, Tareq, and Mustafa Aydin, eds. 2003. *Turkey's Foreign Policy in the 21st Century: A Changing Role in World Politics*. Burlington, VT: Ashgate.

Ismael, Tareq, and Jacqueline Ismael. 1991. "The Republic of Iraq." In *Politics and Government in the Middle East and North Africa*, ed. Tareq Y. Ismael and Jacqueline S. Ismael. Miami: Florida International University Press, 151–87.

Jabar, Kamal S. 1966. *The Arab Baath Socialist Party*. Syracuse, NY: Syracuse University Press.

Jabar, Karam. 2000a (Nov. 10). "Election File: Statements of Jamal Mubarak" (in Arabic). *Rose El Youssef,* 14–16.

Jabar, Karam. 2000b (Nov. 17). "Election File: False Tears Succeed in Deceiving Some of the Voters." *Rose El Youssef,* 16–17.

Javad-Rouh, Mohammad. 2004 (June 24). "Islamist Engineers Pass Two Eras Alike." *Sharq* (daily newspaper), No. 223, 7; www.netiran.com/php/artp.php?id=1590.

Jazini, Mahsa. 2005 (Jan. 26). "Motion on Women's Comprehensive Legal and Judicial System Amends 70% of Laws Related to Women." *Iran* (daily newspaper), 3042: 6; www.netiran.com/php/artp.php?id=3378.

Johansen, Julian. 1996. *Sufism and Islamic Reform in Egypt: The Battle for Islamic Tradition*. Oxford: Clarendon Press.

Jacoby, Tim. 2004. *Social Power and the Turkish State*. London: Frank Cass.

Jamshidi, Iraj. 2004 (April 13). "Conservatives vs. Conservatives." *Sharq* (daily newspaper); www.netiran.com/php/artp.php?id=881.

Jennings, Ray S. 2003 (April). "The Road Ahead: Lesson in Nation Building from Japan, Germany, and Afghanistan for Postwar Iraq." *Peaceworks*. Washington, DC: U.S. Institute of Peace.

Joseph, Nevo. 1998 (July). "Religion and National Identity in Saudi Arabia." *Middle Eastern Studies 34*.

Joseph, Suad, ed. 1999. *Intimate Selving in Arab Families: Gender, Self, and Identity*. Syracuse, NY: Syracuse University Press.

Joyner, Christopher C. 1990. *The Persian Gulf War*. New York: Greenwood.

Kamil, Omar. 2000 (Dec.). "Rabbi Ovadia Yosef and His 'Culture War' in Israel." *Middle East Review of International Affairs Journal 4*(4): 1–18, http://meria.idc.ac.il.

Kamrava, Mehran. 2003 (Summer). "Iranian Shi'ism under Debate." *Middle East Policy 10*(2): 102–13. InfoTrac #A103799911.

Kar, Mehranguiz. 1996 (Jan.). "Women and Personal Status Law in Iran: An Interview with Mehranguiz Kar." *Middle East Report,* 36–38.

Karsh, Efrain. 1991. *Soviet Policy towards Syria since 1970.* Houndmills, Basingstoke Hampshire, UK: Macmillan.

Karsh, Efrain, and Inari Rautsi. 1991. *Saddam Hussein.* New York: Faith Press.

Karshenas, Massoud, and M. Hashem Pesaran. 1995. "Economic Reform and the Reconstruction of the Iranian Economy." *Middle East Journal 49*(1): 89–111.

Kassem, May. 2000. *In the Guise of Democracy: Governance in Contemporary Egypt.* New York: Ithaca Press.

Kastoryano, Riva. 2002. *Negotiating Identities: States and Immigrants in France and Germany.* Princeton, NJ: Princeton University Press.

Kelidar, Abbas. 1983. "The Shi'i Imami Community and Politics in the Arab East." *Middle Eastern Studies 19*(1): 3–16.

Kemp, Geoffrey, and Jeremy Pressman. 1997. *Point of No Return: The Deadly Struggle for Middle East Peace.* Washington, DC: Carnegie Endowment for International Peace.

Kepel, Gilles. 2004. *The War for Muslim Minds: Islam and the West.* Translated by Pascale Ghazaleh. Cambridge, MA: Belknap Press of Harvard University Press.

Kerr, Malcolm H. 1971. *The Arab Cold War: Gamal Abd Al-Nasir and His Rivals, 1958–1979.* London: Oxford University Press.

Kerr, Malcolm H., and El Sayed Yassin. 1982. *Rich and Poor States in the Middle East: Egypt and the New Arab Order.* Boulder, CO: Westview Press.

Keskin, Burcak. 1997 (Dec.). "Political Participation Patterns of Turkish Women. *Middle East Review of International Affairs Journal,* http://meria.idc.ac.il.

Kessler, Martha Neff. 1987. *Syria: Fragile Mosaic of Power.* Washington, DC: National Defense University Press.

Keyman, E. Fuat, and Ahmet Icduygu, eds. 2005. *Citizenship in a Global World: European Questions and Turkish Experiences.* New York: Routledge.

Khadduri, Majid. 1955. *War and Peace in the Law of Islam.* Baltimore: Johns Hopkins University Press.

Khadduri, Majid. 1960. *Independent Iraq, 1932–1958.* London: Oxford University Press.

Khalife, Osama F. 2001. "Arab Political Mobilization and Israeli Responses." *Arab Studies Quarterly.*

Khalil, Ashraf. 2000 (Oct. 22). "The Empire Strikes Back." *Cairo Times.*

Khalil, Samir. 1989. *Republic of Fear.* Berkeley: University of California Press.

Khan, Amil. 2000. "British Lord Weighs In on Elections." *Middle East Times.*

Khashan, Hilal. 1995. "The Labyrinth of Kurdish Self-Determination." *International Journal of Kurdish Studies 8*(1–2): 5–31.

Khashan, Hilal. 2000a (Aug.). *Policy Focus: Arab Attitudes toward Israel and Peace.* Washington, DC: Washington Institute for Near East Policy.

Khashan, Hilal. 2000b. *Arabs at the Crossroads: Political Identity and Nationalism.* Gainesville: University Press of Florida.

Khashan, Hilal, and Simon Haddad. 2000 (June). "The Coupling of the Syrian-Lebanese Peace Tracks: Beirut's Options." *Security Dialogue 31*(2): 201–14.

Khashan, Hilal, and Michel Nehme. 1996. "The Making of Stalled National Movements: Evidence from Southern Sudan and Northern Iraq." *Nationalism and Ethnic Politics* 2(1): 111–38.

Khashan, Hilal, and Monte Palmer. 1998 (Dec.). "The Social and Economic Correlates of Islamic Religiosity." A paper presented at the Middle East Studies Association for North America, Chicago.

Khosrokhavar, Farhad. 2004 (Winter). "The New Conservatives Take a Turn." *Middle East Report;* www.merip.org/mer/mer233/khosrokhavar.html.

Khoury, Dina R. 1997. *State and Provincial Society in the Ottoman Empire: Mosul, 1540–1834.* Cambridge: Cambridge University Press.

Khoury, Philip S., and Joseph Kostiner. 1990. *Tribes and State Formation in the Middle East.* Berkeley: University of California Press.

Kienle, Eberhard. 1990. *Ba'ath v. Ba'ath.* London: I. B. Tauris.

Kienle, Eberhard, ed. 2003. *Politics from Above, Politics from Below: The Middle East in the Age of Economic Reform.* London: Saqi.

Kingseed, Christian Cole. 1995. *Eisenhower and the Suez Crisis of 1956.* Baton Rouge: Louisiana State University Press.

Koohi-Kamali, Farideh. 2003. *The Political Development of the Kurds in Iran: Pastoral Nationalism.* New York: Palgrave Macmillan.

Kornhauser, William. 1959. *The Politics of Mass Society.* New York: Free Press.

Kostiner, Joseph. 1993. *The Making of Saudi Arabia, 1916–1936.* New York: Oxford University Press.

Krimly, Rayed. 1999. "The Political Economy of Adjusted Priorities: Declining Oil Revenues and Saudi Fiscal Policies." *Middle East Journal* 53(2): 256.

Kunz, Diane B. 1991. *The Economic Diplomacy of the Suez Crisis.* Chapel Hill: University of North Carolina Press.

Kurzman, Charles. 2004. *The Unthinkable Revolution in Iran.* Cambridge, MA: Harvard University Press.

Lacy, Robert. 1981. *The Kingdom: Arabia and the House of Sa'ud.* New York: Harcourt Brace and Jovanovich.

Lane, E. W. 1954. *Manners and Customs of the Modern Egyptians.* London: J. M. Dent & Sons.

Laqueur, Walter, and Barry Rubin, eds. 1984. *The Israel-Arab Reader: A Documentary History to the Middle East Conflict.* Canada: Penguin Books.

Laqueur, Walter, and Barry Rubin, eds. 1990. *The Human Rights Reader.* New York: New American Library.

Laswell, Harold D. 1958. *Politics: Who Gets What, When, How.* New York: World Publishing Co.

Lawrence, Quil. 2005 (March 11). "Kurdish Green Line, Turkish Red Line." *Middle East Report;* online: www.merip.org.

Lawson, Fred Haley. 1992. *The Social Origins of Egyptian Expansionism during the Muhammad Ali Period.* New York: Columbia University Press.

Lawson, Fred Haley. 1996. *Why Syria Goes to War.* Ithaca, NY: Cornell University Press.

Lazaroff, Tovah. 2002 (Jan.). "Reservists Refuse to Serve in 'War for Peace Settlements.'" *Jerusalem Post.* Online: http://jpost.com/editions/2002/01/28/news/news.42407.html.

Le Gac, Daniel. 1991. *La Syrie du General Assad*. Bruxelles: Editions Complètes.

Lerner, Daniel. 1958. *The Passing of Traditional Society*. Glencoe, IL: Free Press.

Lesch, Ann M., and Mark Tessler. 1989. *Israel, Egypt and the Palestinians*. Bloomington: Indiana University Press.

Leverett, Flynt. 2005. *Inheriting Syria: Bashar's Trial by Fire*. Washington, DC: Brookings Institution Press.

Levy, Reuben. 1957. *The Social Structure of Islam*. Cambridge: Cambridge University Press.

Lewis, Bernard. 1958. *The Arabs in History*. New York: Harper and Brothers.

Lewis, Bernard. 2002. *The Emergence of Modern Turkey*. New York: Oxford University Press.

Library of Congress Reference Service. http://lcweb2.loc.gov/frd/cd/trtoc.html.

Liebman, Charles, and Bernard Susser. 1998. "Judaism and Jewishness in the Jewish State." *The Annals of the American Academy of Political and Social Science 555*: 15–25.

Lippman, Thomas. 2004. *Inside the Mirage: America's Fragile Partnership with Saudi Arabia*. Boulder, CO: Westview Press.

Lofgren, Hans. 1993. "Economic Policy in Egypt: A Breakdown in Reform Resistance?" *International Journal of Middle East Studies 25*(3): 407–21.

Long, David E. 1997. *The Kingdom of Saudi Arabia*. Gainesville: University Press of Florida.

Long, David. 2005. *The Culture and Customs of Saudi Arabia*. Westport, CT: Greenwood Press.

Longgood, William F. 1957. *Suez Story: Key to the Middle East*. New York: Greenberg.

Longrigg, Stephen H. 1953. *Iraq, 1900–1950: A Political, Social and Economic History*. London: Oxford University Press.

Lukitz, Liora. 1995. *Iraq*. London: F. Cass.

Lustik, Ian S. 1988. *For the Land and the Lord: Jewish Fundamentalism in Israel*. New York: Council on Foreign Relations Press.

Luxford, Kate. 2005 (June). "Euromoney.com." *Euromoney 36*(434). InfoTrac #133684158.

MacAskill, Ewen, and Duncan Campbell. 2005 (Feb. 17). "Iran and Syria Confront US with Defence Pact." *Guardian Unlimited*: www.guardian.co.uk.

Mackey, Sandra. 1996. *The Iranians: Persia, Islam and the Soul of a Nation*. New York: Dutton.

Maisa, Jamal. 1993. *The Political Elite in Egypt* (in Arabic). Beirut: Center for Arab Unity Studies.

Makram-Ebeid, Mona. 1996 (March). "Egypt's 1995 Elections: One Step Forward, Two Steps Back?" *Middle East Policy 4*(3):119–36.

Mango, Andrew. 2002. *Ataturk: The Biography of the Founder of Modern Turkey*. New York: Overlook Press.

Mansingh, Surit. 1986. *Foreign Relations in India: A Country Study*, ed. Richard Nyrop. Washington, DC: U.S. Government Printing Office, 459–502.

Marriott, J. A. R. 1956. *The Eastern Question: An Historical Study in European Diplomacy*. 4th ed. London: Oxford University Press.

Marsot, Afaf Lufti Al-Sayyid. 1984. *Egypt in the Reign of Muhammad Ali*. Cambridge: Cambridge University Press.

Matthee, Rudi. 2005. *The Pursuit of Pleasure: Drugs and Stimulants in Iranian History: 1500–1900*. Princeton, NJ: Princeton University Press.

Mauran, Hussein, and Riyadh Elm Eddin. 1999 (Aug. 30). "Details of the Attempted Coup against al-Mad" (in Arabic). *Al-Waton al-Arabi*, 4–7.

McCausland, Jeffrey. 1993. *The Gulf Conflict*. London: International Institute for Strategic Studies.

McDermott, Anthony. 1988. *Egypt from Nasser to Mubarak: A Flawed Revolution*. London: Croom Helm.

McNamara, Robert. 2003. *Britain, Nasser and the Balance of Power in the Middle East, 1952–1967: From the Egyptian Revolution to the Six-Day War*. London: Frank Cass.

Melhem, Hisham. 1997 (Spring). "Syria between Two Transitions." *Middle East Report*, 2–7.

Melville, Charles. 1996. *Safavid Persia: The History and Politics of an Islamic Society*. London: I. B. Tauris.

Meyer, Thomas. 1988. *The Changing Past: Egyptian Historiography of the Urabi Revolt, 1882–1883*. Gainesville: University Press of Florida.

*Middle East Contemporary Survey*. 1978–1979. Shiloah Center for Middle Eastern and African Studies, Tel Aviv University. New York: Holmes & Meier.

Miller, Judith. 1994 (Nov.–Dec.). "Faces of Fundamentalism: Hassan al-Turabi and Muhammed Fadlallah (Sudanese and Lebanese Islamic Fundamentalist Leaders)." *Foreign Affairs* 73(6): 123–43.

Miller, Judith, and Laurie Mylroie. 1990. *Saddam Hussein*. Paris: Presses de la Cité.

Mitchell, George. 2001. The Mitchell Report. Provided by BBC News: http://news.bbc.co.uk/2/hi/in_depth/middle_east/2001/israel_and_the_palestinians/key_documents/1632064.stm.

Mitchell, Richard. 1969. *The Society of Muslim Brothers*. London: Oxford University Press.

Moallem, Minoo. 2005. *Between Warrior Brother and Veiled Sister: Islamic Fundamentalism and the Politics of Patriarchy in Iran*. Berkeley: University of California Press.

Moghadam, Fatemeh E. 1996. *From Land Reform to Revolution: The Political Economy of Agricultural Development in Iran, 1962–1979*. London: I. B. Tauris.

Momayezi, Nasser. No Date. *Civil-Military Relations in Turkey*. Unpublished paper for the Center for Middle Eastern Studies, University of Texas at Austin.

Mostyn, Trevor. 1991. *Major Political Events in Iran, Iraq and the Arabian Peninsula, 1945–1990*. New York: Facts on File.

Moubayed, Sami. 2001 (Jan. 18). "Bashar Brings Unexpected Political Freedom." *Daily Star*, 6.

Moubayed, Sami. 2005a (April 9). "US Designs on Syria's Kurds." *Asia Times* Online: www.atimes.com.

Moubayed, Sami. 2005b (May 10). "No Room for Political Islam in Syria." *Asia Times* Online: www.atimes.com.

Moubayed, Sami. 2005c (June 22). "A Hint of Glasnost for Syria." *Asia Times* Online: www.atimes.com.

Moubayed, Sami. 2005d (July 19). "Bashar Assad Ensured the Baath Was Here to Stay." *Daily Star*, Lebanon: www.dailystar.com.lb.

Moussalli, Ahmad. 1999. *Moderate and Radical Islamic Fundamentalism: The Quest for Modernity, Legitimacy, and the Islamic State*. Gainesville: University Press of Florida.

Moussavi, Ahmad Kazami. 1992. "A New Interpretation of the Theory of Vilayat-i Faqih." *Middle Eastern Studies* 8(1): 101–107.

Mozaffari, Mehdi. 1991. "Why the Bazaar Rebels." *Journal of Peace Research* 28(4): 377–91.

Mozaffari, Mehdi. 1993. "Changes in the Iranian Political System after Khomeini's Death." *Political Studies* 41(4): 611–17.

Mubarak, Hosni. 1985 (Nov. 14). "Address to the Egyptian Parliament." *Al-Ahram*.

Mubarak, Hosni. 1987 (Nov. 6). "This Is My Word to the Arab Summit in Amman" (in Arabic). *Al-Waton al-Arabi*, 28–33.

Mubarak, Hosni. 1999. Interview (in Arabic). *Al-Hawadith*, 19–24.

Mufti, Malik. 1996. *Sovereign Creations*. Ithaca, NY: Cornell University Press.

Mullaney, Francis Cabrini. 1995. *The Role of Islam in the Hegemonic Strategy of Egypt's Military Rulers (1952–1990)*. Ann Arbor, MI: UMI Dissertation Information Service.

Munson, Henry, Jr. 1988. *Islam and Revolution in the Middle East*. New Haven, CT: Yale University Press.

Musallam, Ali Musallam. 1996. *The Iraqi Invasion of Kuwait*. London: British Academic Press.

Muslih, Muhammad. 1999. *The Foreign Policy of Hamas*. New York: Council on Foreign Relations.

Mustafa, Hala. 1992. "Les Forces Islamiques et l'Experience Democratique en Egypte." In *Democratie et Democratizations Dans le Monde Arabe*. Cairo: Dossiers de CEDEJ, 379–97.

Mustafa, Hala. 1995. *The Political System and the Islamic Opposition in Egypt* (in Arabic). Cairo: Markaz al-Mahrusa. Translated title: *The State and the Opposition Islamic Movements between Truce and Confrontation in the Eras of Sadat and Mubarak*.

Myre, Greg. 2003 (Sept. 25). "27 Israeli Reserve Pilots Say They Refuse to Bomb Civilians." *New York Times*. Online: http://www.nytimes.com/2003/09/25/international/middleeast/25MIDE.html.

Nada, Joseph. 2002a. "Interview with Joseph Nada, Commissioner of International Political Affairs for the Muslim Brotherhood." Part 2 of six interviews by Ahmed Mansour (in Arabic). *Al-Jazeera* (Aug. 13, 2002). Online: www.aljazeera.net/programs/century_witness/articles/2002/8/8/13–1.htm.

Nada, Joseph. 2002b. "Interview with Joseph Nada, Commissioner of International Political Affairs for the Muslim Brotherhood." Part 3 of six interviews by Ahmed Mansour (in Arabic). *Al-Jazeera* (Aug. 18, 2002). Online: www.aljazeera.net/programs/century_witness/articles/2002/8/8/18–1.htm

Nakash, Yitzhak. 1994. *The Shi'is of Iraq*. Princeton, NJ: Princeton University Press.

Namazi, Siamak. 2000 (April 23). "The IRGC, Khamenei, and Fate of Iran's Reform Movement." Gulf 2000 List.

Nash, Manning. 1966. *Primitive and Peasant Economic Systems*. San Francisco, CA: Chandler Publishing Co.

Nasser, Gamal Abdul. 1955. *Egypt's Liberation: The Philosophy of the Revolution*. Washington, DC: Public Affairs Press.

Nasser, Gamal Abdul. No Date. *Speeches and Press Interviews for the Years 1954–65*. Cairo: Information Department.

Neguib, Mohammed. 1955. *Egypt's Destiny*. Garden City, NY: Doubleday and Co.

Nehme, Michel. 1994. "Saudi Arabia, 1950–80: Between Nationalism and Religion." *Middle Eastern Studies 30*(4): 930–43.

Nehme, Michel. 1995. "The Shifting Sands of Political Participation in Saudi Arabia." *Orient,* 45–60.

Nehme, Michel. 2003. *Fear and Anxiety in the Arab World.* Gainesville: University Press of Florida.

Nonneman, Gerd. 1986. *Iraq, the Gulf States, and the War.* London: Ithaca Press.

Norton, Augustus Richard, ed. 1994. *Civil Society in the Middle East.* Leiden, Netherlands: E. J. Brill.

Noueihed, Lin. 2005 (May 16). "Syria's Stateless Kurds Hope for New Rights." *Yahoo News,* http://story.news.yahoo.com.

Noyes, James H. 1997. "Does Washington Really Support Israel?" *Foreign Policy 106*: 144–60.

Nugent, John T. 2004 (March). "The Defeat of Turkish Hizballah as a Model for Counter-Terrorism Strategy." *Middle East Review of International Affairs Journal.* 8(1): http://meria.idc.ac.il.

Nyrop, Richard. 1983. *Egypt: A Country Study. Area Handbook.* Washington, DC: U.S. Government Printing Office.

Ofteringer, Ronald, and Ralf Backer. 1994 (March–June). "A Republic of Statelessness: Three Years of Humanitarian Intervention in Iraqi Kurdistan." *Middle East Report*: 40–45.

Olson, Robert. 2001. *Turkey's Relations with Iran, Syria, Israel, and Russia, 1991–2000: The Kurdish and Islamic Questions.* Costa Mesa, CA: Mazda Pub.

Öni, s, Ziya, and Barry Rubin, eds. 2003. *The Turkish Economy in Crisis.* London: Frank Cass.

Open Society Institute and the UN Foundation. No Date. "Iraq in Transition: Post-Conflict Challenges and Opportunities." N.p: Open Society Institute and the UN Foundation.

Orlinsky, Harry M. 1961. *Ancient Israel.* 2nd ed. Ithaca, NY: Cornell University Press.

Orr, Akiva. 1994. *Israel: Politics, Myths, and Identity Crises.* London: Pluto Press.

Owen, R. 1992. *State, Power and Politics in the Making of the Modern Middle East.* London: Routledge.

Oz, Amos. 1995. *Under This Blazing Light.* Cambridge: Press Syndicate of Cambridge University Press.

Ozcan, Yusuf Ziya, and Recep Gultekin. 2000 (June). "Police and Politics in Turkey." In George Mair and Roger Tarling, eds. *The British Criminology Conference: Selected Proceedings, Vol. 3.* Papers from the British Society of Criminology Conference, Liverpool, July 1999.

Paidar, Parvin. 1995. *Women and the Political Process in Twentieth-Century Iran.* (Cambridge Middle East Studies, No. 1.) Cambridge: Cambridge University Press.

Palmer, Monte. 1960. "Iraq and Arab Unity." Unpublished master's thesis, University of Wisconsin.

Palmer, Monte. 1992 (March). "Will a Decade of Foreign Aid Be Lost?" *Al-Ahram Weekly* (Cairo), 12.

Palmer, Monte. 1997. *Political Development: Dilemmas and Challenges.* Itasca, IL: F. E. Peacock.

Palmer, Monte. 2006. *Comparative Politics: Political Economy, Political Culture, and Political Interdependence.* 3rd ed. Belmont, CA: Thomson/Wadsworth.

Palmer, Monte, Ali Leila, and El Sayeed Yassin. 1988. *The Egyptian Bureaucracy.* Syracuse, NY: Syracuse University Press.

Palmer, Monte, and Princess Palmer. 2004. *At the Heart of Terror: Islam, Jihadists, and America's War on Terrorism.* Lanham, MD.: Rowman and Littlefield.

Palmer, Monte, Earl Sullivan, and Madhia Safty. 1996. "The Relationship between Economic and Religious Attitudes in Egypt." Paper presented at the 1996 meeting of the Middle East Studies Association of North America, Providence, RI.

Pappe, Ilan. 2004. *A History of Modern Palestine.* Cambridge: Cambridge University Press.

Park, Bill. 2003 (June). "Strategic Location, Political Dislocation: Turkey, the United States, and Northern Iraq." *Middle East Review of International Affairs Journal,* 7(2): http://meria.idc.ac.il.

Parla, Taha. 2004. *Corporatist Ideology in Kemalist Turkey: Progress or Order?* Syracuse, NY: Syracuse University Press.

Parsa, Misagh. 2000. *States, Ideologies, and Social Revolution.* New York: Cambridge University Press.

Perthes, Volker. 1997. *The Political Economy of Syria under Asad.* London: I. B. Tauris.

Perthes, Volker, ed. 2004. *Arab Elites: Negotiating the Politics of Change.* Boulder, CO: Lynne Rienner Publishers.

Peters, F. E. 1994. *Muhammad and the Origins of Islam.* Albany: State University of New York Press.

Pew Global Attitudes Project. 2005 (July). "Islamic Extremism: Common Concerns for Muslim and Western Publics." Washington, DC: Pew Research Center; www. pewglobal.org.

Phillips, David. 2005. *Losing Iraq: Inside the Postwar Reconstruction Fiasco.* Boulder, CO: Westview Press.

Pipes, Daniel. 1990. *Greater Syria: The History of an Ambition.* New York: Oxford University Press.

Piran, Parviz. 2003 (March). "Performance of Councils." *Nameh* (monthly newspaper) 21:12–16. Online: www.netiran.com.

Pirouz, Babak, and Stanley Reed. 2005 (June 28). "A Watershed in Iranian Politics." *Business Week Online.* InfoTrac Article #A133639073.

Polk, William R. 2005. *Understanding Iraq.* New York: HarperCollins.

Polk, William R., David M. Stamler, and Edmund Asfour. 1957. *Backdrop to Tragedy: The Struggle for Palestine.* Boston: Beacon Press.

Pope, Hugh. 2005. *Sons of the Conquerors: The Rise of the Turkish World.* New York: Overlook Press.

Posusney, Marsha P. 1997. *Labor and the State in Egypt, 1952–1994.* New York: Columbia University Press.

Quandt, William. 1990. *The United States and Egypt.* Washington, DC: Brookings Institution.

Quilliam, Neil. 1999. *Syria and the New World Order.* Reading, UK: Ithaca Press.

Qusti, Raid. 2004 (Oct. 20). "Arab News: Fatwas According to Tribal Norms." http://gulf2000.columbia.edu.

Rabbani, Mouin, and Chris Toensing. 2005 (June 1). "Mahmoud Abbas' Mission Improbable." *Middle East Report Online*: www.merip.org

Rabil, Robert G. 2003. *Embattled Neighbors: Syria, Israel, and Lebanon*. Boulder, CO: Lynne Rienner Publishers.

Rabinovich, Itamar, and Jehuda Reinharz, eds. 1984. *Israel in the Middle East: Documents and Readings on Society, Politics and Foreign Relations, 1948–Present*. Oxford: Oxford University Press.

Radio Free Europe/Radio Liberty. 2001 (Oct. 8). *RFE/RL Iran Report 4*(38): www.rferl.org.

Radwan, Zeina Abdul Majid. 1982. *First Report: The Religious Dimension in the Appearance of Veiling* (in Arabic). Cairo: National Center for Social and Criminal Research.

Rajaee, Farhang. 1999. "A Thermidor of 'Islamic Yuppies'?: Conflict and Compromise in Iran's Politics." *Middle East Journal 53*(2): 217.

Ram, Haggay. 1993. "Islamic 'Newspeak': Language and Change in Revolutionary Iran." *Middle Eastern Studies 29*(2): 198–220.

Ramachandran, Sudha. 2005 (March 18). "'Brothers' in Arms." *Asian Times Online*: www.atimes.com/atimes/South_Asia/GC18Df06.html.

Ramazani, R. K. 1989. "Iran's Foreign Policy: Contending Orientations." *Middle East Journal 43*(2): 202–17.

Ramazani, R. K. 1992. "Iran's Foreign Policy: Both North and South." *Middle East Journal 46*(3): 393–412.

Ramazani, R. K. 1998. "The Shifting Premise of Iran's Foreign Policy: Towards a Democratic Peace?" *Middle East Journal 52*(2): 177–87.

Ramet, Sabrina Petra. 1990. *The Soviet–Syrian Relationship since 1955*. Boulder, CO: Westview Press.

Rashid, Ahmed. 2000. *Taliban: Militant Islam, Oil and Fundamentalism in Central Asia*. New Haven, CT: Yale University Press.

Ribak, Rivka. 1997. "Socialization through Conversation: Political Discourse in Israeli Families." *Comparative Education Review 41*(1): 71–96.

Richards, Alan. 1991. "The Political Economy of Dilatory Reform: Egypt in the 1980s." *World Development 19*(12): 1721–30.

Richards, Alan, and John Waterbury. 1990. *A Political Economy of the Middle East: State, Class, and Economic Development*. Boulder, CO: Westview Press.

Rizk, Hamdi. 1999a (Oct. 30). "Egyptian Muslim Brotherhood" (in Arabic). *Al-Wasat*, 31.

Rizk, Hamdi. 1999b (Aug. 16). "Egyptian Parliamentary Deputies in the Dock" (in Arabic). *Al-Wasat*, 20–25.

Robins, Philip. 2003. *Suits and Uniforms, Turkish Foreign Policy since the Cold War*. Seattle: University of Washington Press.

Robinson, Glenn E. 1998. "Elite Cohesion, Regime Succession and Political Instability in Syria." *Middle East Policy 5*: 159–79.

Rodinson, Maxime. 1969. *Israel and the Arabs*. Middlesex, England, UK: Penguin.

Rodinson, Maxime. 1973. *Israel: A Colonial–Settler State?* New York: Monad Press.

Roth, Cecil. 1963. *History of the Jews*. New York: Schocken Books.

Rubin, Barry. 1999. "External Factors in Israel's 1999 Elections." *Middle East Review of International Affairs Journal 3*(4): http://meria.idc.ac.il.

Rubin, Elizabeth. 2003 (July 13). "The Cult of Rajavi." *New York Times Magazine,* 5.

Rubin, Michael. 2005 (Winter). "Green Money, Islamist Politics in Turkey." *Middle East Quarterly, 12*(1); online: www.meforum.org/article/684.

Rubin, Uri. 1995. *The Eye of the Beholder: The Life of Muhammad as Viewed by the Early Muslims.* Princeton, NJ: Darwin Press.

Rugh, Andrea B. 1986. *Reveal and Conceal: Dress in Contemporary Egypt.* Cairo: American University in Cairo Press.

Saadeq, Mahmoud. 1999a (April 2). "For the First Time: Thoughts of a Social Islamic Party in Egypt" (in Arabic). *Al-Waton al-Arabi,* 4–8.

Saadeq, Mahmoud. 1999b (May 28). "Wanted Dead or Alive" (in Arabic). *Al-Waton al-Arabi,* 4–7.

Sachar, Howard M. 2005. *A History of Jews in the Modern World.* New York: Alfred A. Knopf.

Sachs, Susan. 2000 (Jan. 28). "Egypt Makes It Easier for Women to Divorce Husbands." *New York Times.*

Safran, Nadav. 1988. *Saudi Arabia: The Ceaseless Quest for Security.* Ithaca, NY: Cornell University Press.

Saghafi, Moran. 2004 (Winter). "The New Landscape of Iranian Politics." *Middle East Report* 233. Online: www.merip.org/mer/mer233/saghafi.html.

Sahliyeh, Emile. 1988. *In Search of Leadership.* Washington, DC: Brookings Institution.

Saikal, Amin. 1980. *The Rise and Fall of the Shah.* Princeton, NJ: Princeton University Press.

Saleh, Heba. 1990 (Feb.). "Undercover: Why Are More Egyptian Women Wearing Veils? Social Scientists Suggest a Variety of Reasons." *Cairo Today,* 67–69.

Sal'eh, Mohammed. 2000 (Oct. 30). "Egypt: The Elections Revive the Soul of the Brotherhood" (in Arabic). *Al-Wasat,* 22–23.

Salih, Roshan Muhammed. 2004 (July 13). "Unemployment Threatens Saudi Stability." Al-Jazeera: English.aljazeera.net.

Salmanzadeh, Cyrus. 1980. *Agricultural Change and Rural Society in Southern Iran.* Cambridge, England, UK: MENAS Press.

Samii, Abbas W. 2005 (June 17). "The Reverberating Impact of the Revolutionary Guards." *Daily Star* (Lebanon); www.dailystar.com.lb.

Samii, Abbas W. 1999. "The Contemporary Iranian News Media." *Middle East Review of International Affairs 3*(4): http://meria.idc.ac.il.

Sarabi, Farzin. 1994. "The Post-Khomeini Era in Iran: The Elections of the Fourth Islamic Majlis." *Middle East Journal 48*(1): 89–107.

Saudi Arabian Government. 1998. Statement before the Preparatory Committee for the World Summit for Social Development.

Schacht, Joseph. 1964. *An Introduction to Islamic Law.* Oxford, UK: Clarendon Press.

Schemm, Paul. 1999. "Islamist Students Arrested before Vote." *Middle East Times,* no. 39.

Schiffauer, Werner. 2002 (Oct. 16.) "Democratic Culture and Extremist Islam." *Open Democracy* website: www.opendemocracy.net/democracy-turkey/article_679.jsp.

Scholch, Alexander. 1981. *Egypt for the Egyptians!* London: Published by Ithaca Press for the Middle East Center, St. Anthony's College.

Schulz, Helena L. 2002 (Fall). "The 'al-Aqsa Intifada' as a Result of Politics of Transition." *Arab Studies Quarterly, 24*(4): InfoTrac #A101531217.

Schulz, Helena. 2003. *The Palestinian Diaspora: Formation of Identities and Politics of Homeland*. London: Routledge.

Schwartz, Michael. 2005 (Aug. 11). "The Iranian Nightmare." *Asian Times Online*: www.atimes.com.

Schwartz, Nancy L. 1994. "Representation and Territory: The Israeli Experience." *Political Science Quarterly 109*(4): 615–45.

Seale, Patrick. 1988. *Asad of Syria*. London: I. B. Tauris.

Segal, David. 1988. "The Iran–Iraq War: A Military Analysis." *Foreign Affairs 66*(5): 946–63.

Seifzadeh, Hossein S. 2003 (Winter). "The Landscape of Factional Politics and Its Future in Iran." *Middle East Journal, 57*(1): 57–76. InfoTrac Article #A104680769.

Shaeebi, Emad F. 2005 ( Jan. 9). "A Confused Syrian Society and Anticipated Reform" (in Arabic). Al-Jazeera, www.aljazeera.com. Accessed Feb. 21, 2005.

Sha'ib, Muktar. 1999 (Sept. 27). "Egypt: Four Scenarios for Political Change in the 4th Term of President Mubarak" (in Arabic). *Al-Wasat*, 24–25.

Shanker, Thom. 2005 ( July 28). "2 Panels Cite U.S. Problems in Stabilizing After Combat." *New York Times* Online: www.nytimes.com.

Sharabi, Hisham. 1988. *Neopatriarchy: A Theory of Distorted Change in Arab Society*. New York: Oxford University Press.

Sharbatoghlie, Ahmad. 1991. *Urbanization and Regional Disparities in Post-Revolutionary Iran*. Boulder, CO: Westview Press.

Sharett, Moshe. 1978. *Yoman Ishi* (Personal Diary). Tel Aviv: Maariv, 1024–25. Reprinted as "Israel's Foreign and Middle Eastern Policy," 95–98, in *Israel in the Middle East: Documents and Readings on Society, Politics and Foreign Relations, 1948–Present*, ed. Itamar Rabinovich and Jehuda Reinharz. Oxford: Oxford University Press, 1984.

Sharkansky, Ira. 1991. *Ancient and Modern Israel: An Exploration of Political Parallels*. Albany: State University of New York Press.

Sharkansky, Ira. 1997a. "Religion and Politics in Israel and Utah." *Journal of Church and State 39*: 523–41.

Sharkansky, Ira. 1997b. *Policy Making in Israel: Routines for Simple Problems and Coping with the Complex*. Pittsburgh: University of Pittsburgh Press, 523–41.

Sheffer, Gabriel. 1996. *Moshe Sharett: Biography of a Political Moderate*. Oxford, UK: Clarendon Press.

Shemesh, Haim. 1992. *Soviet–Iraqi Relations, 1968–1988*. Boulder, CO: Lynne Rienner Publishers.

Shemesh, Moshe. 2004 (Spring). "The Palestinian Society in the Wake of the 1948 War: From Social Fragmentation to Consolidation." Israel Studies: InfoTrac #A118689075.

Shepard, William. 1987. "Islam and Ideology: Towards a Typology." *International Journal of Middle East Studies 19*: 307–36.

Shihab, Zaki. 1999 (March 21). "Iraq" (in Arabic). *Al-Wasat*, 18–19.

Shlaim, Avi. 1995. "Israeli Politics and Middle East Peacemaking." *Journal of Palestine Studies 24*(4): 20–31.

Shlaim, Avi, and Avner Yaniv. 1980. "Domestic Politics and Foreign Policy in Israel." *International Affairs 56*: 242–62.

Shlaim, Avi, and Raymond Tanter. 1978. "Decision Process, Choice, and Consequences: Israel's Deep-Penetration Bombing in Egypt, 1970." *World Politics*: 483–516.

Shoreh, Berween. 1998 (Dec. 7). "Another AUC Book Slashed by the Censor." *Middle East Times 49.*

Shukri, Ghali. 1990. *Masks of Terror: Research on the New Secularism* (in Arabic). Cairo: Dar al-Fikr.

Shuster, W. Morgan. 1912. *The Strangling of Persia.* New York: The Century Company.

Siavoshi, Sussan. 1997. "Cultural Policies and the Islamic Republic: Cinema and Book Publication." *International Journal of Middle East Studies 29*(4): 509–30.

Sick, Gary. 2000 (Feb. 26). "Iran's Election: Out of Chaos, Change." Gulf/2000 List.

Silverfarb, Daniel. 1994. *The Twilight of British Ascendancy in the Middle East: A Case Study of Iraq, 1941–1950.* London: Macmillan.

Singh, K. Gajendra. 2004. "Turkey Snaps over U.S. Bombing of Its Brethren." *Asia Times Online*: www.atimes.com.

Simons, Geoff. 1998. *Saudi Arabia: The Shape of a Client Feudalism.* Chippenham, Wiltshire, UK: Anthony Rowe, Ltd.

Singerman, Diane. 1995. *Avenue of Participation: Family, Politics, and Networks in Urban Quarters of Cairo.* Princeton, NJ: Princeton University Press.

Sirageldin, Ismail A., Naiem Sherbiny, and M. Ismail Serageldin. 1984. *Saudis in Transition: The Challenges of a Changing Labor Market.* New York: Oxford University Press.

Smith, Benjamin. 2004. "The Islah Party in Yemen: Political Opportunities and Coalition Building in a Transitional Polity." In *Islamic Activism: A Social Movement Theory Approach,* ed. Quintan Wiktorowica. Bloomington: Indiana University Press.

Smith, Charles D. 1992. *Palestine and the Arab–Israeli Conflict.* 2nd ed. New York: St. Martin's Press.

Smith, Robertson. 1903. *Kinship and Marriage in Early Arabia.* Boston: Beacon Press.

Smith, Wilfred Cantwell. 1957. *Islam in Modern History.* New York: New American Library of World Literature.

Smolansky, Oles, and Bettie Smolansky. 1991. *The USSR and Iraq: The Soviet Quest for Influence.* Durham, NC: Duke University Press.

Smooha, Sammy. 1998. "The Implications of the Transition to Peace for Israeli Society." *The Annals of the American Academy of Political and Social Science 555*: 26–45.

Spiegel, Steven L. 1985. *The Other Arab-Israeli Conflict: Making America's Middle East Policy, from Truman to Reagan.* Chicago: University of Chicago Press.

Springborg, Robert. 1989. *Mubarak's Egypt: Fragmentation of the Political Order.* Boulder, CO: Westview Press.

Sprinzak, Ehud. 1991. *The Ascendance of Israel's Radical Right.* New York: Oxford University Press.

Sprinzak, Ehud, and Larry Diamond, eds. 1993. *Israeli Democracy under Stress.* Boulder, CO: Lynne Rienner Publishers.

State of Israel. 1999. *Budget Policy: Israeli Draft Budget for Fiscal Year 1999.*

Sullivan, Dennis J. 1990. "The Political Economy of Reform in Egypt." *International Journal of Middle East Studies 22*: 317–34.

Sullivan, Dennis Joseph. 1994. *Private Voluntary Organizations in Egypt.* Gainesville: University Press of Florida.

Sullivan, Tim. 1986. *Women in Egyptian Public Life*. Syracuse, NY: Syracuse University Press.

Sumaida, Hussein. 1991. *Circle of Fear: A Renegade's Journey from the Mossad to the Iraqi Secret Service*. Canada: Stoddart.

Szyliowicz, Joseph S. 1991. *Politics, Technology and Development*. New York: St. Martin's Press.

Tabatabai, Muhammad Husayn. No Date. *Shi'a*. Qum, Iran: Ansariyan Publications.

Teitelbaum, Joshua. 2005 (Sept.). "Terrorist Challenges to Saudi Arabian Internal Security." *Middle East Review of International Affairs, 9*(3): http://meria.idc.ac.il.

Ternisien, Xavier. 2005. *Les Frères Musulamans*. Paris: Fayard.

Terrill, W. Andrew, and Conrad C. Crane. 2005 (Oct.). *Precedents, Variables, and Options in Planning a U.S. Military Disengagement Strategy from Iraq*. Carlisle, PA: Strategic Studies Institute.

Tessler, Mark. 1994. *A History of the Israeli–Palestinian Conflict*. Bloomington: Indiana University Press.

Tessler, Mark, Monte Palmer, Tawfic Farah, and Barbara Ibrahim. 1987. *The Evaluation and Application of Survey Research in the Arab World*. Boulder, CO: Westview Press.

Thomas, Gordon. 1999. *Gideon's Spies: The Secret History of the Mossad*. New York: St Martin's Press.

Thompson, Paul. 2004. *The Terror Timeline: Year by Year, Day by Day, Minute by Minute, A Comprehensive Chronicle of the Road to 9/11—and America's Response*. New York: HarperCollins.

Tibi, Bassam. 1997. *The Challenge of Fundamentalism: Political Islam and the New World Disorder*. Berkeley: University of California Press.

Toledano, Ehud. 1990. *State and Society in Mid-Nineteenth-Century Egypt*. Cambridge: Cambridge University Press.

Trapp, Frank J. 1994. *Does a Repressive Counter-Terrorist Strategy Reduce Terrorism?: An Empirical Study of Israel's Iron Fist Policy for the Period 1968 to 1987*. Unpublished Ph.D. dissertation: Florida State University.

Turkish Government. 2001a (July). Turkey/Military Service. Situation Report. Directorate for Movements of Persons, Migration and Consular Affairs, Asylum and Migration Division.

Turkish Government. 2001b (Oct. 17). *Constitution of the Republic of Turkey*. Office of the Prime Minister, Directorate General of Press and Information. http://www.byegm.gov.tr/mevzuat/anayasa/anayasa-ing.htm.

Twitchell, Karl S. 1958. *Saudi Arabia*. Princeton, NJ: Princeton University Press.

United Arab Republic. 1963. Minutes of the Sessions of the Unity Discussions (in Arabic). Cairo: Kutub Quameya.

United Nations Development Programme, 2005. *Arab Human Development Report 2004*. New York: UNDP.

United States Department of State. 1999. *Patterns of Global Terrorism, 1999*.

United States Department of State. 2004 (Aug.). "Background Note: Syria." Bureau of Near Eastern Affairs: www.state.gov/r/pa/ei/bgn/3580.htm.

United States Embassy. 1994. "Foreign Economic Trends and Their Implications for the United States." Report for the Arab Republic of Egypt. Cairo: U.S. Embassy.

United States Government. 1998. Country Report on Economic Policy and Trade Practices: Egypt.

United States Government. 2003 (May 26). "A Performance-Based Roadmap to a Permanent Two-State Solution to the Israeli-Palestinian Conflict." *Jerusalem Post* Internet Edition: www.jpost.com.

Upton, Joseph M. 1960. *The Modern History of Iran: An Interpretation.* Cambridge, MA: Harvard University Press.

Uslu, Nasuh, Metin Toprak, Ibrahim Dalmis, and Ertan Aydin. 2005 (Sept.). "Turkish Public Opinion toward the United States in the Context of the Iraq Question." *Middle East Review of International Affairs 9*(3). Article 5: http://meria.idc.ac.il.

Vakili-Zad, Cyrus. 1994. "Conflict among the Ruling Revolutionary Elite in Iran." *Middle Eastern Studies 30*(3): 618–31.

Valibeigi, Mehrdad. 1993. "Islamic Economics and Economic Policy Formation in Post-Revolutionary Iran: A Critique." *Journal of Economic Issues 27*(1): 793–812.

Van Dam, Nikolaos. 1996. *The Struggle for Power in Syria: Politics and Society under Asad and the Ba'ath Party.* London: I. B. Tauris.

Van der Mulen, F. A. 1957. *The Wells of Ibn Saud.* New York: Praeger.

Vassiliev, Aleksei Mikhailovich. 1998. *The History of Saudi Arabia.* London: Saqi Books.

Venner, Fiammetta. 2005. *OPA: l'Islam sur de France. Les ambitions de l'UOIF.* Paris: Calmann-Levy.

Venter, Al J. 2005. *Iran's Nuclear Option: Tehran's Quest for the Atom Bomb.* Havertown, PA: Casemate Pub.

*Victory News Magazine.* No Date. "The Role of Muhammad Baqir Al-Sadr in Shi'a Political Activism in Iraq from 1958 to 1980." www.victorynewsmagazine.com/Shahid Baqir1.

Viorst, Milton. 1995. "Changing Iran: The Limits of the Revolution." *Foreign Affairs 74*(6): 63–76.

Viorst, Milton. 1996. "The Storm and the Citadel." *Foreign Affairs 74*(1): 93–107.

Volker, Perthes. 2004. *Syria Under Bashar al-Asad: Modernisation and the Limits of Change.* Oxford: Oxford University Press for the International Institute for Strategic Studies.

Wahba, Mourad Magdi. 1994. *The Role of the State in the Egyptian Economy, 1945–1981.* Reading, UK: Ithaca Press.

Warriner, Doreen. 1957. *Land Reform and Development in the Middle East: A Study of Egypt, Syria and Iraq.* London: Royal Institute of International Affairs.

Waterbury, John. 1978. *Egypt: Burdens of the Past/Options for the Future.* Bloomington: Indiana University Press.

Waterbury, John. 1983. *The Egypt of Nasser and Sadat: The Political Economy of Two Regimes.* Princeton, NJ: Princeton University Press.

Weber, Max. 1947. *The Theory of Social and Economic Organization.* New York: Macmillan.

Weede, Erich. 1986. "Rent-Seeking or Dependency as Explanations of Why Poor People Stay Poor." *International Sociology 1*(4): 421–41.

Weeden, Lisa. 1998. "Acting 'As If': Symbolic Politics and Social Control in Syria." *Comparative Studies in Society and History 40*(3): 503–23.

Wells, Matthew C. 2003 (Fall). "The Freud/Weber Connection: The Case of Islamic Iran." *Journal for the Psychoanalysis of Culture and Society 8*(2): 214–23. InfoTrac #A109568050.

White, Jenny B. 2002. *Islamist Mobilization in Turkey: A Study in Vernacular Politics. Studies in Modernity and National Identity Series.* Seattle: University of Washington Press.

Wilber, Donald N. 1963. *Iran: Past and Present.* Princeton, NJ: Princeton University Press.

Wiley, Joyce N. 1992. *The Islamic Movement of Iraqi Shi'as.* Boulder, CO: Lynne Rienner Publishers.

Winrow, Gareth. 1995. *Turkey in Post-Soviet Central Asia.* Washington, DC: Brookings Institution.

Wittes, Tamara Cofman, ed. 2005. *How Israelis and Palestinians Negotiate: A Cross-cultural Analysis of the Oslo Peace Process.* Washington, DC: U.S. Institute of Peace.

Wittfogel, Karl A. 1957. *Oriental Despotism: A Comparative Study of Total Power.* New Haven, CT: Yale University Press.

Wolfowitz, Paul. 2003 (Oct. 31). "Mideast Conflict Huge Obstacle to US Goals." *Jerusalem Post*: www.jpost.com (accessed Dec. 3, 2003).

Woodward, Bob. 2002. *Bush at War.* New York: Simon & Schuster.

Woodward, Bob. 2004. *Plan of Attack.* New York: Simon & Schuster.

Woodward, Peter. 1992. *Nasser.* London: Longman.

World Bank. 1955. *The Economic Development of Syria.* Baltimore: Johns Hopkins Press.

World Bank. 1992. *World Bank Report, 1992: Development and the Environment.* New York: Oxford University Press.

World Bank 1996. *World Bank Report, 1996: From Scarcity to Security: Averting a Water Crisis in the Middle East and North Africa.* New York: Oxford University Press.

Yamani, Hani A. Z. 1998. *To Be a Saudi.* London: Janus Publishing Co.

Yazdi, Majid. 1990. "Patterns of Clerical Political Behavior in Post-War Iran, 1941–1953." *Middle Eastern Studies* 26(3): 281–308.

Yishai, Yael. 1998a. "Civil Society in Transition: Interest Politics in Israel." *The Annals of the American Academy of Political and Social Science 555*: 147–62.

Yishai, Yael. 1998b. "Regulation of Interest Groups in Israel." *Parliamentary Affairs 51*(4): 568.

Youssef, Hassan Pasha, Head of Royal Diwan. 1983. Interviews with author in Cairo.

Zabih, Sepehr. 1986. *The Left in Contemporary Iran: Ideology, Organization and the Soviet Connection.* London: Croom Helm.

Zahran, Gamal All. 1987. *Egyptian Foreign Policy, 1970–1981* (in Arabic). Cairo: Library Madbouli.

Zakaria, Rafiq. 1988. *The Struggle within Islam: The Conflict between Religion and Politics.* London: Penguin Books.

Zalmanovitch, Yair. 1998. "Transitions in Israel's Policy Network." *The Annals of the American Academy of Political and Social Science 555*: 193–208.

Zaqzuq, Hamdi D. 1999 (Jan. 4). "Interview with the Minister of Wafqs" (in Arabic). *Al-Wasat,* 23–25.

Zeghal, Malika. 2005. *Les Islamistes Marocains: Le Defi à la Monarchie.* Paris: Editions la Decouverte.

Zein, Rania. 1996 (March 6). "Old Theory Rekindles New Debate. Kissing Cousins: Marriage among Relatives Sets New Records in the Middle East. Social Benefit or Medical Danger?" *Al-Jadid,* 9.

Zeine, Zeine N. 1958. *Arab-Turkish Relations and the Emergence of Arab Nationalism.* Beirut: Khayat.

Zeine, Zeine N. 1960. *The Struggle for Arab Independence.* Beirut: Khayat.

Ziadeh, N. A. 1957. *Syria and Lebanon.* New York: Praeger.

Zietoun, Mark. 2005 (May 21–22). "Hydro-Hegemony." Selected Papers and Presentations at workshops held at Kings College, London.

Zisser, Eyal. 2005 (Sept.). "Syria, the United States, and Iraq: Two Years after the Downfall of Saddam Hussein." *Middle East Review of International Affairs 9*(3). Article 2: http://meria.idc.ac.il.

Zonis, Marvin. 1991. *Majestic Failure: The Fall of the Shah.* Chicago: University of Chicago Press.

Zonis, Marvin, and Cyrus Amir Mokri. 1991. "The Islamic Republic of Iran." In *Politics and Government in the Middle East and North Africa,* ed. Tareq Y. Ismael and Jacqueline S. Ismael. Miami: Florida International University Press, 114–50.

Zurcher, Erik J. 2004. *Turkey: A Modern History.* London: I. B. Tauris.

Abbreviations Frequently Used in Text Citations:

AP: Associated Press

BBC: British Broadcasting Corporation

*CSM: Christian Science Monitor*

*IHT*: International Herald Tribune

*JP: Jerusalem Post*

*NYT: New York Times*

UP: United Press

*WP: Washington Post*

# Index